Discovering Christ

In

The Gospel Of Luke

Volume 1

Discovering Christ

In

The Gospel Of Luke

Donald S. Fortner

Volume 1

Go *publications*

Go Publications
The Cairn, Hill Top, Eggleston, Co. Durham, DL12 0AU, ENGLAND

© Go Publications 2012
First Published 2012

British Library Cataloguing in Publication Data available

ISBN 978-1-908475-00-8

Printed and bound in Great Britain
By Lightning Source UK Ltd.

Publisher's Dedication

This book is dedicated to David J. Burrows.

"When thou art converted, strengthen thy brethren."
Luke 22:32

Contents

Foreword
(Part 1)

The purpose of Luke's Gospel is supplied in the first verse of the first chapter of the book. Luke tells his friend, Theophilus, of his plan to "set forth in order a declaration of those things which are most surely believed among us". Pause for a moment and reflect on this. Luke is telling Theophilus that if he wants to know what Christians believe he can read it in this book. Furthermore, he is telling us, too, that all who call themselves followers of Jesus Christ must also believe these things. For these things of Jesus Christ "are most surely believed amongst us".

We live in days when many people claim to be Christians. They say they are followers of Jesus yet they definitely do not believe the things which Luke says were once "most surely believed" by the apostles and disciples of the Lord Jesus Christ. This should not be the case. Christian teaching is not a hotchpotch of ideas or a jumbled bag of doctrines where followers pick and mix what they choose to believe.

On the contrary, Luke clearly states these are the things "most surely believed", and in twenty four chapters of holy scripture Luke sets out the beliefs of the Apostolic church concerning the life and ministry of the Lord Jesus. He gives no quarter to doubts, disbelief or duplicity. Luke will not allow us to identify with the Lord Jesus and claim to be his followers while denying what he did and taught.

We also encounter others who tell us it is not helpful to be dogmatic about what we believe. They tell us it is not possible to clearly establish what one has to believe to be a Christian. They say things such as "God knows the heart" or "There are different views upon this matter" or "It is not necessary to be overly emphatic on these points." Well, to such we repeat what Luke says. Here, in his gospel, are "those things which are most surely believed among us".

Let us take some examples: Luke tells us

1. The grace of God is sovereign: in chapter 4:25-27 Luke shows that God's goodness is directed only to certain individuals and it is discriminating. It had been so in the past in the times of Elijah and Elisha, it was now, in the time of Christ. The people of Nazareth wanted a miracle but

would receive none. Those in the synagogue to whom Christ spoke understood precisely what the Master was saying. God is not at the beck and call of man. The favours of God, and the grace of God, are dispensed sovereignly according to the will of God and not the will of man. This simple fact of God's sovereignty so angered the people of Nazareth that they tried to kill the Son of God almost before his ministry was begun. Yet sovereign grace was one of the things most surely believed.

2. Salvation is to be found in Christ alone: speaking of Simeon's testimony of Christ in chapter 2:30 Luke tells us how this old saint of the Lord looked for the "consolation of Israel". He was waiting for the Messiah to be revealed. Then one day he held in his arms the child Jesus. Full of the Holy Spirit he blessed God and declared, "Mine eyes have seen thy salvation." Our Lord tells Zacchaeus, "This day is salvation come to this house". Christ is Salvation. This was another of those things most surely believed.

3. Eternal election: when the Lord sent out seventy preachers in Luke 10:1 they appear to have stormed Satan's citadel with the gospel message. They saw amazing things "and returned again with joy, saying, Lord, even the devils are subject unto us through thy name." However, the Lord's reply directed them to rejoice in their election; God's choice of them from everlasting. This shows that God's election to eternal life is of particular persons, known by name; that it is sure, and certain, and irreversible. It was one of those things most surely believed.

4. Salvation is God's work alone: when a rich young ruler met Jesus in Luke 18 it became clear that obtaining salvation was eluding, naturally speaking, this most eligible of men. The disciples were astonished and asked if not this man "Who then can be saved?" The Lord Jesus answered, "The things which are impossible with men are possible with God." Salvation in the life of any sinner requires an act of divine proportions to change the heart, focus the desire of the soul upon Christ overthrow all human self-righteousness. That only a spiritual work of God will bring a man to deny himself, take up the cross and follow Christ was another of those things most surely believed.

Continued in Volume 2

Chapter 1

Christ The Son Of Man

Each of the four gospels was written by divine inspiration, each revealing the person and work of our Lord Jesus Christ, but each one was intended by the Holy Spirit to set forth a particular, distinct aspect of our Saviour's person and work. None of the gospel narratives taken alone gives us a complete view of Christ; but all four taken together tell us plainly and fully who the Lord Jesus Christ is, what he did, why he did it and where he is now. Matthew was written to show us that our Lord Jesus Christ is the divine Messiah, the Redeemer-King promised in the Old Testament scriptures. Mark was inspired to present the Lord Jesus as Jehovah's righteous Servant. John's gospel sets forth the glorious divinity of the Lord Jesus Christ as God the Son, the second person in the Holy Trinity. Luke's gospel was designed and written to show us the perfect and glorious humanity of our Saviour. Just as John shows us that our Redeemer is the Son of God, Luke shows us that he is the Son of man.

Son Of Man
Luke was inspired of God to present our Saviour distinctly as "the Son of man". That is the title our Lord used to describe himself more than any other. As we read the Gospel of Luke, the One we meet here is the Redeemer-King Matthew described, the Righteous Servant Mark portrayed, and the incarnate God John declares. He is the same Person; but Luke presents him primarily as the Man who is God, while John presents him as the God who is also man.

Luke gives us more details than either Matthew or Mark about our Saviour's birth. Luke alone tells us a little bit about our Lord's childhood. He stresses more than the other gospel writers our Redeemer's dependence upon his Father in prayer, his poverty, and his sympathy with men. He does this because it is his purpose to show us that our Saviour's perfect humanity is just as essential to his saving work as his divinity. He could not accomplish his mission were he not both God and man in one glorious person. Luke's message is essentially contained in the words of our Lord in chapter 19. "For the Son of man is come to seek and to save that which was lost" (19:10).

Luke And Acts
Luke specifically wrote his gospel to a man named "Theophilus". This is the same man to whom he addressed the Book of Acts. Both Luke and Acts were written specifically for this man Theophilus (Acts 1:1, 2). We know nothing about him, except what Luke himself tells us. This Theophilus was a man of rank and honour. Luke calls him "most excellent Theophilus". Not many noble are called (1 Corinthians 1:26), but some are. God has chosen some of all ranks. The name Theophilus means either "lover of God", or "loved of God". The Book of Acts is really a continuation of Luke's Gospel, as he indicates in the opening verses of Acts 1. The Gospel of Luke describes the works of Christ while he was on the earth. In the Book of Acts Luke picks up right where he left off in his gospel narrative; only in Acts he describes the works of the ascended Christ through his church.

In Acts 1, Luke describes his gospel as "a treatise of all that Jesus began both to do and teach, until the day in which he was taken up." Though they did not record every word and deed of Christ (John 21:25), Luke and the other gospel writers did record all that the Holy Spirit inspired, all that we need to know, particularly all that Christ did and said relating to the salvation of his people; his obedience to the Father, his conformity to the law, and his death as our Substitute, by which he brought in everlasting righteousness and obtained eternal redemption for us.

Things Most Surely Believed
Then Luke tells us that the Lord Jesus Christ gave his commandments by the Holy Spirit to chosen apostles, and by them to his church. All the doctrines and ordinances, faith and practice of the church are by the commandment of Christ, laid down in the Word of God (2 Timothy 3:16). Both in Acts and here, at the very outset of his gospel, Luke tells us that his intention in writing this gospel narrative was "to set forth in order a declaration of those things which are most surely believed among us" (1:1).

14

Contrary to popular opinion, believers are people who believe some things, some specific things, and all believers believe them. All Christians do, most assuredly, believe some specific things. We believe those things revealed in the Book of God. Anyone who does not believe that which God reveals in the inspired volume of holy scripture is not a Christian, is not a believer, and does not know God, no matter what he may profess. Roger Ellsworth wrote, "The church is a community of faith, a community that tenaciously holds with overpowering conviction to a distinct body of truths."

Yes, there are some things all true Christians believe. Luke makes no bones about this. Neither should we. Let men accuse us of being narrow-minded dogmatists, out of step with the rest of the religious world, and heap upon us whatever ugly names they choose, the Word of God plainly declares that some things are vital. Some things must be known and believed. Those who do not believe these things are not saved.

Luke tells us that he wrote his gospel "to set forth in order those things which are most surely believed among us." All who are, like Theophilus, lovers of God love those things most surely believed among us. What are those things? Luke does not leave us to decide for ourselves what they are. He tells us plainly some of those things most assuredly believed by all who know and love, trust and worship the God of Glory.

Luke shows us that all men are sinners in need of God's salvation; lost, ruined, dead in trespasses and sins, under the curse of God's holy law, and totally incapable of changing their condition. He tells us that the Lord Jesus Christ came to seek and to save that which was lost, like the lost coin, the lost sheep, and the lost Son (chapter 15).

Luke also shows us that the Man, Jesus, is the Christ and that he is the incarnate God. All who are taught of God believe that the Son of God came into this world in the flesh (1:35; 9:20).

Every believer gladly confesses, with Zacharias, that the Lord Jesus Christ has effectually accomplished and obtained salvation for sinners by his obedience and death as the sinners' Substitute (1:68). Remember, that which Zacharias spoke concerning the accomplishments of Christ, he spoke being filled with the Holy Ghost. He tells us that Christ accomplished redemption and explains exactly what that means (1:67-79).

This salvation which Christ obtained for his elect by his blood atonement, by effectual, accomplished redemption, comes to sinners by the gift of God, according to his own sovereign, eternal purpose of grace in Christ, as a matter of pure grace (4:25-27).

And Luke shows us that God's grace in Christ is so abundantly free that every sinner in this world who needs it has it (9:11). It is still true today, the

Lord Jesus Christ heals all who have need of healing. That is to say, he saves all who need salvation.

Luke's Distinctives

As we read the Gospel of Luke, we cannot help noticing that Luke tells us many precious things that are not even mentioned by any of the other inspired writers. Luke alone gives us historic information about Zacharias and Elizabeth, the parents of John the Baptist, and tells us about John's birth. Only Luke tells us about the angel's announcement to Mary of our Saviour's birth. It is only in Luke's Gospel that we read of Simeon, Anna, and Mary's song. Luke alone gives us information about our Redeemer's childhood. None of the other gospel narratives tell us about the conversions of Zacchaeus and the dying thief. Only Luke gives us the parables of The Good Samaritan, The Pharisee and the Publican, The Prodigal Son, and The Rich Man and Lazarus. Only Luke tells us about the Lord's walk with two of his disciples along the Emmaus road after his resurrection. How thankful we are for these things! For these things, we are indebted to Luke, "the beloved physician".

Luke Himself

Who was this man, Luke? As we have seen, both this gospel narrative and the book of Acts were written by Luke. But who was Luke? He was a man of such modesty that he never mentions his own name, even when he wrote about events in which he played a prominent role. Yet, he was, obviously, a man of remarkable usefulness in the early church.

Paul calls him, "Luke the beloved physician" (Colossians 4:14). As I observed concerning Theophilus, not many of the wise and noble of this world are called, but some are; and Luke was one of them. He was Paul's constant, faithful companion. He accompanied Paul on his second missionary journey as far as Philippi. There, after the Lord raised up a gospel church, Luke stayed behind, probably to take care of and further instruct the young saints at Philippi in the things of God.

Seven years later, while Paul was on his third missionary journey, he and Luke joined up again at Philippi. As Paul went on his way to Jerusalem, Luke went with him. When Paul was arrested at Caesarea, Luke was with him. Luke was still by Paul's side when they sailed for Rome. He went with his friend through the perils of the sea and stayed by his side when he was arrested at Rome. Luke alone stayed with Paul to the end. When Paul was about to lay down his life as a martyr for Christ, he wrote, "Only Luke is with me" (2 Timothy 4:11).

Luke was a Gentile, as his name indicates, the only Gentile who was chosen of God to write a portion of the inspired volume of holy scripture.

The Son Of Man

Luke gives us a portrait of the Son of man, the Man Christ Jesus. All the gospel writers show us both the divinity and the humanity of Christ; but John was distinctly written to set forth our Lord's eternal deity; and Luke was distinctly written to show us his perfect humanity. Let us never forget that our Lord Jesus Christ lived upon this earth the life of a perfect man, completely obedient to the will of God, as our Surety, Representative, Mediator, and Substitute, without sin in nature, thought, word, or deed. Had he not been a perfect man, he could not have been our Saviour. Therefore, Luke was inspired of God to show us the perfection of our Saviour as a real man.

The Lord Jesus Christ was a Man of great courage. He was not a hard, abrasive man; but he was a courageous man. This boldness and courage is seen most distinctly in our Lord's preaching. He knew that he was his Father's Servant. Therefore, he spoke the Word of God with unflinching courage (chapter 4). When he was advised to flee from Herod, he said, "Go tell that old fox that I am doing what I came here to do, and that he can't stop me" (Luke 13:32).

When the time came for him to lay down his life as our sin-atoning Substitute, our Saviour set his face like a flint to go up to Jerusalem that he might accomplish the will of him that sent him (9:51). Fearlessly and unfalteringly, our Saviour steadily walked, step by step, with determinate resolution, up to Mount Calvary to lay down his life for us, according to the will of God, not in defeat, but in victory, not to be pitied, but worshipped.

Our Lord Jesus Christ was also a Man of great tenderness, compassion, and sympathy. He declared in his very first sermon, that he came here to preach the gospel to the poor, to set the captive free, and to give sight to the blind (4:18, 19). Luke constantly portrays the Lord Jesus as a man full of compassion, drying tears of sorrow, pitying the outcast, entertaining despised publicans, receiving sinners, healing all who had need of healing. Let every man learn from the Master. Manhood, real manhood, involves both courage and compassion.

Moreover, and this is very, very important, as the perfect Man, our Lord Jesus Christ was a man of implicit faith. He believed God perfectly. He lived in constant fellowship with God as a man. What an example of consecration and faith he gave us! His very first recorded words were, "I must be about my Father's business" (2:40). His last words before his final breath of mortality were, "Father, into thy hands I commend my spirit" (23:46).

On at least eight other occasions, Luke describes our Lord Jesus as a man of faith, calling upon God his Father, our Father, in prayer: at his baptism (3:21); after healing the leper (5:16); before choosing his disciples (6:12); before Peter's great confession (9:18); at his transfiguration (9:29); before teaching his disciples how to pray (11:1); in Gethsemane (22:42); and, as he hung upon the cross (23:34).

As God's servants in this world, we all must confess, with shame and sorrow, that we are often weak, hard hearted, and unbelieving. But, blessed be God, that Man who is our divine Saviour lived before God in the perfection of manhood for us: perfect in courage, perfect in tenderness, mercy and compassion, perfect in faith! But he is more than an exemplary man.

Luke presents this holy man, the Lord Jesus Christ, to us as God's Salvation. He brought salvation to sinners. He won it by his obedience. He bought it with his blood. He secured it by his ascension into heaven. He gives it by his grace. But Luke tells us more. He tells us that the Lord Jesus Christ himself is Salvation (2:25-32). Salvation is not a creed, a confession, a church, or an experience. Salvation is a Person, the Lord Jesus Christ. We rejoice in the blood and righteousness of Christ and adore his doctrine; but it is the Lord Jesus Christ himself that we trust, love and worship. "Unto you that believe, he is precious."

The gospel we preach is the good news of salvation accomplished and secured by the obedience and death of the God-man, Christ Jesus. Luke, speaking in perfect harmony with all the prophets and apostles, tells us that this salvation is God's Salvation — his work, his property, his gift. It is a finished work. It is a work accomplished for sinners of every race, Jew and Gentile, everywhere. This salvation demands faith in Christ, a faith that only God himself can give, a faith that willingly bows to Christ as Lord, a salvation to be preached to all the world.

Luke's object is to show us the humanity of our Saviour; but his humanity would be of no value to us, all that he was and did as a man would be totally without benefit to us, if he is not God. So Luke shows us that this great man is much more than that. He shows us that this great man is the almighty God.

He has all power over all things, and exercises it all the time. The God-man, our Mediator, has complete authority over all evil (Luke 4:12, 35; 9:38; 11:14). He controls all of what men call "the elements of nature" (Luke 8:22-25; 9:12-17; 5:4-11). He has total dominion over life and death (Luke 8:41, 42; 7:11-15). He has total dominion over sickness, disease, and trouble (Luke 5:12, 13; 7:1-10; 4:38-40; 5:18-25; 6:6-10; 18:35-43). He has power in heaven and in earth to forgive sins (Luke 5:24; 7:48). He has the power and authority to bless people (Luke 6:20-22), and to give people eternal life in heaven (Luke 23:43; 24:50). All things are in his hands (John 17:2).

Gospel For Sinners

The gospel of God is a gospel for sinners; the good news of redemption obtained and salvation finished for poor, needy, lost sinners. And Luke's Gospel is just that. It is good news for needy sinners. Luke shows us the compassionate love of Christ in becoming man to save us. He traces our Lord's descent back to Adam, and shows him as the Son of man and the Son of God, the Saviour of men. He is both the "Son of the Highest" and the Son of the lowest.

Like Matthew, Luke gives us our Lord's genealogy (3:23-38); but it is not the same. Matthew's account of the genealogy begins with Abraham and traces the Saviour's lineage up to Joseph. Luke begins with the Saviour and traces his lineage back to Adam, and then to God himself. Matthew shows us our Saviour's lineage through Joseph, him "being (as was supposed) the son of Joseph" (3:23). Luke traces his lineage through Mary.

The Shepherds

Instead of the visit of the Magi, Luke tells us of the common shepherds, to whom the Saviour's birth was announced as glad-tidings of peace to all people, "To you is born a Saviour, which is Christ the Lord."

Simeon And Anna

Aged Simeon said, "Mine eyes have seen thy salvation", as he took the holy child in his arms. And Anna "spake of him to all that looked for redemption in Israel." Luke records his compassion to the Widow of Nain (7:11-18), and of his tenderness and mercy toward the woman that was a sinner (7:36-50). Luke tells us the story of Zacchaeus and of the consequent murmuring of the Pharisees because he had gone to be a guest with a man which was a sinner (19:1-10).

The Parables

The parables recorded in Luke's Gospel are intended to display both our Redeemer's compassion, and his saving power and efficacy. The parable of The Good Samaritan shows us how condescending Christ is in the exercise of his saving mercy. The parable of The Pharisee and the Publican show the contempt of our Saviour for self-righteous religionists and his great mercy, love, and grace to needy sinners. The parable of The Importunate Widow shows us how that all who need and seek his grace find it at the throne of grace. The parable of The Lost Sheep, The Lost Coin, and The Lost Son shows us the great joy there is in the very heart of God over the lost one that is found. In the parable of the Great Supper (14:16-24; Matthew 22:1-14), it

19

is Luke who tells us of the Lord's command to go out into the highways and hedges and compel them to come in. And the words, "Yet there is room", seem to echo throughout these 24 chapters.

Luke alone tells us when our Lord beheld the city, he wept over it (19:41-44). It is Luke who describes the Saviour's bloody sweat in Gethsemane (22:39-46). Luke tells us of the saving power possessed by our Saviour, as he hung upon the cursed tree, displayed in saving the dying thief, gathering as it were, even in his agony, the first-fruits of his atonement (23:39-43).

Luke alone tells of our Lord's walk on the Emmaus road with two of his troubled disciples after his resurrection (chapter 24). It may be, as some have suggested, that Luke was one of those two disciples. He tells of our Lord eating a piece of broiled fish and honey to show us his perfect humanity, even after his resurrection. Yes, blessed be his name, that Man, who is risen and exalted, is still a man touched with the feeling of our infirmities, full of sympathy, and is the omnipotent God, able to help in time of need!

The Last Scene
The last scene in the Gospel of Luke is one Luke alone gives us (chapter 24). In verses 44-47 the Lord condescends to confirm the shaken faith of his fearful disciples and opens their mind to understand the scriptures.

"And he said unto them, These are the words which I spake unto you, while I was yet with you, that all things must be fulfilled, which were written in the law of Moses, and in the prophets, and in the psalms, concerning me. Then opened he their understanding, that they might understand the scriptures, And said unto them, Thus it is written, and thus it behoved Christ to suffer, and to rise from the dead the third day: And that repentance and remission of sins should be preached in his name among all nations, beginning at Jerusalem."

Then, he issues his commission to his church, assuring us of the power of his Spirit to do his work (vv. 48, 49). "And ye are witnesses of these things. And, behold, I send the promise of my Father upon you: but tarry ye in the city of Jerusalem, until ye be endued with power from on high." And in verses 50-53 the crucified, risen Son of man ascends to Glory to take his place on his throne as the God-man, and blesses his people as he ascends his throne. As he did, we read, "And he led them out as far as to Bethany, and he lifted up his hands", those nail pierced hands into which the Lord God has placed the reins of the universe as our Mediator, "and blessed them", as the High Priest whose sacrifice God had accepted. "And it came to pass, while he blessed them, he was parted from them, and carried up into heaven." There he sits, King forever, our almighty and all-prevailing Advocate, God over all, full of mercy, love and grace. "And they worshipped him, and returned to

Jerusalem with great joy: And were continually in the temple, praising and blessing God." Let us worship him, obey him with great joy, and ever be found praising and blessing our God because of this Man who is our Saviour.

Forasmuch as many have taken in hand to set forth in order a declaration of those things which are most surely believed among us, Even as they delivered them unto us, which from the beginning were eyewitnesses, and ministers of the word; It seemed good to me also, having had perfect understanding of all things from the very first, to write unto thee in order, most excellent Theophilus, That thou mightest know the certainty of those things, wherein thou hast been instructed (Luke 1:1-4).

Chapter 2

Things Most Surely Believed Among Us

There are four things to be learned from these opening words of Luke's gospel. I must give them to you with great brevity; but I pray that God the Holy Spirit, whose words they are, will burn them into our hearts.

Some Things All Christians Believe

The first thing to be learned from the opening words of Luke's gospel is the fact that there are some things all true Christians believe. Luke does not mince words about this. Neither should we. Let men accuse us of being narrow-minded dogmatists, out of step with the rest of the religious world, and heap upon us whatever ugly names they choose, the Word of God plainly declares that some things are vital. Some things must be known and believed. Those who do not believe these things are not saved.

Luke tells us that he wrote his gospel, "to set forth in order those things which are most surely believed among us." All who are, like Theophilus, lovers of God, love those things most surely believed among us. What are those things? I will give them to you in five, unmistakable statements.

(1.) All men and women are sinners in need of God's salvation, lost, ruined, dead in trespasses and sins, under the curse of God's holy law, and totally incapable of changing their condition. Like the lost coin, the lost sheep, and the lost son, described in the parable (Luke 15), none could ever be saved except the triune God seek us out, find us and bring us home to himself by redeeming blood and omnipotent grace. (2.) Jesus Christ is the incarnate God. The Son of God came in the flesh (9:20). (3.) The Lord Jesus Christ has effectually accomplished and obtained salvation for sinners by his obedience and death as the sinners' Substitute (1:68). (4.) This salvation comes to sinners by the gift of God, according to his own sovereign, eternal purpose of grace in Christ, as a matter of pure, free, sovereign grace (4:25-27). (5.) God's grace in Christ is so abundantly free that every sinner in this world who needs it has it (9:11).

Eyewitnesses And Ministers

The second thing revealed here is the fact that God's servants tell only what they know from firsthand experience, by direct experience, by divine revelation, as those who are taught of God. Luke describes the apostles as those men who were "eyewitnesses and ministers of the word". I am aware that these words, in their strict interpretation, apply only to the apostles, those who saw the Lord Jesus in the flesh and learned the gospel directly from his lips. But there are no apostles, in the official sense of that word today. Does that mean the text has no meaning for us? Of course not! All true gospel preachers, like the original apostles, are "eyewitnesses and ministers of the word".

"That which was from the beginning, which we have heard, which we have seen with our eyes, which we have looked upon, and our hands have handled, of the Word of life; (For the life was manifested, and we have seen it, and bear witness, and show unto you that eternal life, which was with the Father, and was manifested unto us;) That which we have seen and heard declare we unto you, that ye also may have fellowship with us: and truly our fellowship is with the Father, and with his Son Jesus Christ" (1 John 1:1-3).

Faithful men do not deal in second hand goods, or debate about matters of doubtful disputation. They tell what they know, report what they have seen, and teach what they have been taught of God. I take no license with the scriptures when I tell you that all that Luke says in verses two and three is applicable to all true gospel preachers.

"Even as they delivered them unto us, which from the beginning were eyewitnesses, and ministers of the word; It seemed good to me also, having had perfect understanding of all things from the very first, to write unto thee in order, most excellent Theophilus."

We preach that which we have experienced by the grace of God, as eyewitnesses. We are ministers, servants of the Word of God (2 Corinthians 2:17; 4:7). God's servants are men who have a God-given, complete, comprehensive understanding of all things spiritual.

When Luke says that he had "perfect understanding of all things", he was not suggesting infallible knowledge, but complete knowledge. And every servant of God, every man called and gifted of God to preach the gospel has that same knowledge of holy scripture. That man who has not yet learned the message of the scriptures is not yet called and gifted of God to be a preacher. Such a man is not apt to teach and is not fit to teach, because he has nothing worth teaching.

The words, "from the very first" (v. 3), should be and most commonly are translated "from above" (John 3:31, 19:11; James 1:17, 3:15, 17). God's servants are men who get their knowledge, their understanding, and their message from above. By the preaching of the gospel they set forth the things of God in order, in an orderly fashion, before men.

The Word Of God

Third, Luke here teaches us that the Bible is the Book of God's writing, the inspired Word of God. In their strict sense, these words must be understood as a claim to divine inspiration. Most commentators, especially the modern men who love to appear intellectual, try to prove that Luke used this source or that as the historic basis for his gospel narrative. Such speculations tend to undermine our sense of the Bible's divine inspiration and authority as the Word of God. This Book is The Book of God, given to us by supernatural, divine inspiration. Let us always reverence it, not as the word of men, but as the very Word of God himself (1 Thessalonians 2:13; 2 Timothy 3:16; 2 Peter 1:21).

Because the Bible is the Word of God, let us always bow to it, submitting our reason, learning and experience, our emotions, traditions and prejudices to the scriptures. If we see something in the Bible that we cannot understand or reconcile with some other passage of scripture, the fault is not with the Word of God, but with our puny brains.

To Make Us Wise Unto Salvation

Fourth, we are here taught that the purpose of God in giving us his Word is to make us wise unto salvation. Blessed are they who, like Timothy, have grace bestowed upon them by which they know "the holy scriptures, which are able to make them wise unto salvation through faith which is in Christ Jesus" (2 Timothy 3:15).

"But these are written, that ye might believe that Jesus is the Christ, the Son of God; and that believing ye might have life through his name" (John 20:31).

"He that believeth on the Son of God hath the witness in himself: he that believeth not God hath made him a liar; because he believeth not the record that God gave of his Son. And this is the record, that God hath given to us eternal life, and this life is in his Son. He that hath the Son hath life; and he that hath not the Son of God hath not life. These things have I written unto you that believe on the name of the Son of God; that ye may know that ye have eternal life, and that ye may believe on the name of the Son of God" (1 John 5:10-13).

Jesus Christ is God's Salvation. This great salvation is the gift of God's grace. God gives it to every sinner who believes the record he gave concerning his Son. Will you believe God; or will you die in your sins? God help you to believe on the Lord Jesus Christ.

"There was in the days of Herod, the king of Judaea, a certain priest named Zacharias, of the course of Abia: and his wife was of the daughters of Aaron, and her name was Elisabeth. And they were both righteous before God, walking in all the commandments and ordinances of the Lord blameless. And they had no child, because that Elisabeth was barren, and they both were now well stricken in years. And it came to pass, that while he executed the priest's office before God in the order of his course, According to the custom of the priest's office, his lot was to burn incense when he went into the temple of the Lord. And the whole multitude of the people were praying without at the time of incense. And there appeared unto him an angel of the Lord standing on the right side of the altar of incense. And when Zacharias saw him, he was troubled, and fear fell upon him" (Luke 1:5-12).

Chapter 3

When God Broke His Long Silence

For four hundred years no one on earth had received any word from God. For four hundred years no prophet had been inspired to write a word of inspiration. For four hundred years no angel had been sent from heaven to earth with a message from God to man. No revelation had been given, no vision had been granted. No word had come from God in four hundred years. Then, God spoke again! God chose one man and sent his angel to him with glad tidings from the throne of God. No one had heard from God since the days of the prophet Malachi. Then God spoke.

Can you imagine what it must have been like to have been a man, faithful, devout, serving God in his appointed place, knowing that no one had heard from heaven in four hundred years, then, suddenly, to have an angel of the Lord appear to you alone with a word of divine revelation? That is what we have before us in this passage.

The first thing recorded in Luke's gospel is the appearance of an angel to one of the ordinary priests in Israel, named Zacharias. The angel announced to this old man that his wife, who was an old woman, well past the age of child-bearing, was, by direct, divine intervention, going to have a son, and that his son would be the forerunner of the long-awaited Messiah.

What a word of grace! It was too good for this old man to believe. Being a faithful man, Zacharias knew that God had promised four hundred years before that when Messiah came some man in the spirit and power of Elijah would go before him to prepare his way before the people (Malachi 3:1).

It is, I am sure, impossible for us 2,000 years later to grasp what an astounding thing this was. God made the promise four hundred years earlier. Then the heavens were silent. Not another word was given. Then, suddenly, without any preparatory work, God sent his angel to a certain old man to tell him that Daniel's prophetic weeks were about to be fulfilled. "Messiah, the Prince" was about to be revealed (Daniel 9:25). That "seed" of Abraham, in whom all the nations of the earth would be blessed, was about to come

(Genesis 22:18). "The Desire of all nations", who would fill the house of God with glory, would soon be revealed from heaven (Haggai 2:7). We cannot grasp the extent of this revelation given to such a man in such circumstances, yet, there are several things in the verses before us to instruct our souls.

Divine Election

First, we have before us an example of divine election. God the Holy Spirit tells us that God sent his angel to "a certain priest named Zacharias, of the order of Abia." God did not send his angel to the High Priest. God did not send his angel to all the priests. But God sent his angel to "a certain priest named Zacharias." Let men and women fuss and squirm as they may, the Book of God teaches the doctrine of God's sovereign electing grace. God Almighty, in all his works of grace, chooses some and passes by others, according to the good pleasure of his will.

God has, from eternity, chosen some certain sinners, as the objects of his love and grace, to be the heirs of eternal life; and at the appointed time of love, he sends his angel (a gospel preacher) to announce to them the good news of his salvation in Christ. He not only sends a preacher with the message of grace, he sends his Spirit to bring the word of grace home to the heart of his elect by the omnipotent power of his irresistible grace (1 Thessalonians 1:4, 5; 2 Timothy 1:9, 10).

When God has a special work to do, he has certain men especially and specifically chosen to do the work. Usually, those men who are chosen of God for very special things are the men who we would consider the least likely. Zacharias was one of the common, everyday priests, from the course of Abia.[1] He was probably unknown by name to anyone, except a small circle of friends, family, and acquaintances.

God knows where his chosen servants are. He knows what he will do with them. And when the time comes for them to perform his work, he calls them to it and equips them for it.

"Righteous Before God"

Second, Zacharias and Elizabeth set before us the character of the righteous. We are told that "they were both righteous before God." They were not naturally righteous. The Word of God tells us plainly that "There is none righteous, no, not one. There is none that understandeth. There is none that seeketh after God. We are all gone out of the way. We are together become unprofitable. There is none that doeth good, no, not one" (Romans 3:10-12).

---

[1] When the temple was built there were twenty-four courses (classes) of priests. The course of Abia was the eighth of the twenty-four (1 Chronicles 24:10).

Zacharias and Elizabeth were made righteous by the grace of God, by the righteousness of Christ being imputed to them in justification and imparted to them in sanctification, in the new birth. These two things go hand in hand. None are sanctified but those who have been justified by Christ. And all who were justified at Calvary are, at God's appointed time of grace, sanctified by the Holy Spirit in regeneration.

Both Zacharias and his wife Elizabeth were "righteous before God". Theirs was not merely the outward righteousness of the Pharisees before men, but that righteousness which stands before God and is accepted of him. They were righteous in God's sight. And they were "both righteous before God." What a blessed home that is in which both a man and his wife are the recipients of God's grace in Christ, when both walk together before God in the paths of righteousness!

"They were both righteous before God, walking in all the commandments and ordinances of the Lord blameless." This believing couple, this old man and woman here show us the character of true faith. True faith walks in obedience to the Word of God. It is written, "he that doeth righteousness is righteous" (1 John 3:7). Believers are men and women who, in the habit of their lives, in the tenor of their lives, live in submission and obedience to the revealed will of God. God's saints are not rebels.

Not only is it true that God's saints live righteously in the tenor of their lives; the Spirit of God tells us plainly that that new man, "created in righteousness and true holiness", that new nature in us that "is born of God doth not commit sin" and "cannot sin, because it is born of God" (Ephesians 4:24; 1 John 3:9).

Here is another trait found in God's saints. They submit to and keep the ordinances of divine worship. These two old saints kept the ordinances of divine worship in a day when few in Israel did. To most, the ordinances of divine worship were a burden they did not care to bear. But Zacharias and Elizabeth delighted in them. God's people still do. Believing men and women confess Christ in believer's baptism, assemble with God's saints in public worship and remember the Redeemer together in the sweet communion of God's family at the Lord's Table.

Moreover, they were blameless in their behaviour before men. John Gill correctly gives this meaning to that word "blameless". "They were so strict in their lives and conduct that none of their acquaintances had any just reason to reproach them."

A Crook In The Lot

Third, in verse seven we see that there is a crook in the lot of every believer. The lot of the believer is a blessed lot. The life of faith in Christ is a life of joy and gladness. We are the people blessed of the Lord. In this doomed, damned, sin-cursed world we have a good hope through grace of eternal life in Christ. But there is a crook in the lot of us all. In this world it has pleased our God to lay trials upon his people, sometimes heavy trials, by which he is resolved to try and prove our faith, trials by which he will ultimately make our faith to shine.

For Zacharias and Elizabeth the trial was the barrenness of Elizabeth's womb. We read in verse 7 "And they had no child, because that Elisabeth was barren, and they both were now well stricken in years." This was the crook in their lot. We can hardly fathom how heavy a trial that was in ancient times. In those days to be childless was a shameful thing to a man and one of the most bitter sorrows a woman could endure (1 Samuel 1:10).

The grace of God does not exempt us from trials and troubles, heartaches and sorrows in this world. Not even exemplary faithfulness, to the point of blamelessness, will keep us from the trials of faith. If we follow Christ, we must never consider it some strange thing when God tries our faith. This is the portion of our cup, given to us by the infinite wisdom and goodness of our heavenly Father, by which he chastens us, "that we may be partakers of his holiness" (Hebrews 12:5-11). We may not think so at the time; but our trials are great blessings of grace, by which our ever-gracious God drives us into the arms of Christ, drives us to our knees in prayer, and drives us to the scriptures. In the world to come we will see them in better light than we do now (James 1:12; 1 Peter 1:7).

Place Of Blessing

Fourth, we see in verses 8-11 that the place of divine blessing is the house of our God, the house of prayer.

"And it came to pass, that while he executed the priest's office before God in the order of his course, According to the custom of the priest's office, his lot was to burn incense when he went into the temple of the Lord. And the whole multitude of the people were praying without at the time of incense. And there appeared unto him an angel of the Lord standing on the right side of the altar of incense."

Let me be crystal clear here. There is nothing we can do which will automatically secure God's blessings. Sacramental religion is utter idolatry. You will not automatically be blessed of God by church attendance, Bible reading, or even prayer. Yet, the Word of God does specifically tell us that God has ordained a place of worship, and that he commonly meets his people in the place of worship which he has established.

In the typical, ceremonial days of the Old Testament the Lord God established his worship first in the tabernacle in the wilderness, then in the temple. He promised to meet sinners upon the mercy-seat in the holy of holies on the Day of Atonement (Exodus 25:22). He did, from time to time, visit and meet with sinners in other places; but he never promised to meet a man anywhere else; and no one could expect to meet him anywhere else.

It was Zacharias' privilege and responsibility to burn incense in the house of God in the holy place every morning and every evening (Exodus 30:1, 7, 8). That might not seem like much of a job in the eyes of men; but it was the job God gave him, and he did it faithfully, even when he was an old man. Others may have looked upon it as a meaningless religious ritual; but Zacharias considered it his highest honour. He went about his duty, serving and worshipping the Lord God, purely for his glory.

And what a privilege his work was! That altar of incense which he kept burning day and night was typical of the unceasing intercession of Christ for us as our great High Priest, who lives forever to make intercession for us (Hebrews 7:25).

The Lord God sent his angel to Zacharias with the good news of Messiah's coming, the good news that he who would be the forerunner of our Redeemer, Saviour and King was about to be born to his own wife Elizabeth. Where was this old man when God met him? What was he doing when the Lord sent his angel to him and so greatly blessed him? He was in the house of God. He was worshipping God. He was doing that which God had given him the privilege of doing for the glory of his name and the good of his people.

You and I cannot expect God's blessings upon us, upon our own souls, or upon our families; we cannot expect God to meet us, speak to us, or honour us, if we wilfully despise his will and his worship (1 Samuel 2:30; Hebrews 10:23-29).

There is only one place where the Son of God promises he will meet with, speak to, and reveal himself to his people, and that place is the assembly of his saints, gathered in his name (Matthew 18:20). This place, the church of the living God, the assembly of sinners saved by the grace of God, is called "the house of God" and "the temple of God", because that is where God meets with his people. To neglect his house, his worship, his Word, and the assembly of his saints is to despise him

Angelic Interest
Fifth, we are once more shown that which is the single great interest and concern of the holy angels. Countless books have been written about angels. Most of them reveal the utter ignorance and superstition of the authors and tell us nothing about the angels of God. The simple fact is we do not know much about them. But the one thing that is clearly revealed about them is completely missed by most who write about them.

The scriptures plainly and repeatedly show us that the angels of God have only one great, singular interest and concern. They seem to care about only one thing. These holy creatures, who cry continually before the throne of God, "Holy, holy, holy, is the Lord of hosts", do not seem to care about anything except that one great work of God by which his glory is revealed and made known.

These holy creatures have a deep, abiding, all-consuming interest in the redemptive work of Christ and the salvation of God's elect in him. The angels always stand before the throne of grace, looking upon the mercy-seat (Isaiah 6). An angel announced the birth of John the Baptist, our Lord's forerunner. An angel announced the birth of Christ, and a chorus of angels sang when he came into this world to save us. When our Saviour was tempted, the angels of God ministered to him. The angels of God are ministering spirits sent forth to minister to those who shall be the heirs of God's salvation (Hebrews 1:14). The angels of heaven gather with God's saints to learn from redeemed sinners "the manifold wisdom of God" displayed in our redemption by Christ (Ephesians 3:10). The angels rejoice in the presence of our God every time God saves a sinner by his grace. The angels of God will come with Christ at the last day to gather his elect from the four corners of the earth into everlasting glory.

J. C. Ryle wrote, "Let us strive to be like them, while we are upon earth, to be of their mind and to share their joys. This is the way to be in tune for heaven. It is written of those who enter in there that they shall be 'as the angels.'"

May God the Holy Spirit give us grace to imitate the angels of God in this. Let us make the redeeming work of Christ and the salvation of sinners in him the all-consuming interest of our hearts and lives.

Perfect Holiness And Sinful Man

Sixth, as we read verse 12 we see the effect perfect holiness has upon a sinful man. "When Zacharias saw him, he was troubled, and fear fell upon him." Zacharias was a righteous man in Christ; but he was a sinful man by nature, and he knew it. When he stood before a perfectly holy angel, his soul quaked within him. We have seen this scene repeated many times in scripture. Moses trembled before the burning bush. Manoah and his wife were fearful because the Angel of the Lord appeared to them. Daniel quaked as he stood before the Lord at the great river Hiddekel. The women who saw the angel at the empty tomb were fearful. John fell before the face of the angel that spoke to him on Patmos. They all, like Zacharias, when they saw holy angels and visions of things belonging to the world of eternal things, trembled with fear.

If these, who were made holy by the grace of God, trembled in the presence of holy angels, how do you hope to stand before the presence of God's infinite holiness (Nahum 1:5, 6) in the Day of Judgment? The only hope there is for our poor souls is Christ, the only Mediator between God and men. All who take refuge in him, all who trust him shall stand without sin and without fear before the august majesty of God's perfect holiness, with clean hands and pure hearts.

"But the angel said unto him, Fear not, Zacharias: for thy prayer is heard; and thy wife Elisabeth shall bear thee a son, and thou shalt call his name John. And thou shalt have joy and gladness; and many shall rejoice at his birth. For he shall be great in the sight of the Lord, and shall drink neither wine nor strong drink; and he shall be filled with the Holy Ghost, even from his mother's womb. And many of the children of Israel shall he turn to the Lord their God. And he shall go before him in the spirit and power of Elias, to turn the hearts of the fathers to the children, and the disobedient to the wisdom of the just; to make ready a people prepared for the Lord" (Luke 1:13-17).

Chapter 4

Filled With The Holy Ghost From His Mother's Womb

John the Baptist was a remarkable man, a man separated and distinguished from other men by the hand of God even before he was born. In Luke 1:13-17 we are allowed to hear the message the angel Gabriel delivered to his father Zacharias in the temple before he was born, before he was even conceived in his mother's womb. It is a message full of spiritual instruction. May God the Holy Spirit seal it to our hearts.

That which stands out most prominently in these verses and the lessons they are intended to convey is the fact that God's ways are not our ways. That fact should never surprise us. The Lord has shown us in his Word and by experience that "as the heavens are higher than the earth, so are his ways higher than our ways, and his thoughts than our thoughts" (Isaiah 55:9). William Cowper wrote,

> God moves in a mysterious way
> His wonders to perform.
> He plants his footsteps in the sea,
> And rides upon the storm.

Our Prayers And God's Answers
The first lesson in this passage is a lesson about prayer. I hope we will all lay it to heart. God's answers to our prayers are often delayed for a long, long time. Sometimes, perhaps most often, the Lord graciously and wisely delays answering our prayers for many, many years. That certainly was the case with Zacharias and Elizabeth. No doubt, they had often prayed for the Lord to give them a child. It looked as though they had prayed in vain. Now, they were old people. The thought of having children had completely vanished from their minds. They had ceased long ago mentioning this matter to the Lord. Yet, the very first words that fell from the lips of the angel to this old

man were, "Fear not, Zacharias: for thy prayer is heard; and thy wife Elisabeth shall bear thee a son, and thou shalt call his name John."

We must never attempt to prescribe to our God how or when to do anything. He knows and does what is best, in the best way, and at the best time. He knows the best time for his people to be born; and he knows the best time for them to be born again.

And we should never conclude that our prayers are not answered because they are not answered in the way or at the time we desire. Do not conclude that the Lord ignores your supplications because he does not immediately gratify your desires. Prayer has something to do with believing God; and the Lord often tries our faith in him by delaying our requests.

Prayer also has something to do with seeking and submitting to the will of God. Prayer is not simply bombarding God with our desires, be they ever so sincere. Prayer is seeking the will and glory of God, bowing our will to his will. It may be that the Lord sometimes delays our requests, not because he does not intend to answer them, but because he is determined to make us willing for him not to answer them.

The fact is none of us know what to pray for as we ought. The experience of the Apostle Paul recorded in 2 Corinthians 12:8-10 certainly teaches this. Because we do not know what is best, we do not know how to pray for anything as we ought. It is written, "We know not what we should pray for as we ought" (Romans 8:26).

Prayer is not for the gratification of our carnal lusts. It is not the means by which we obtain what we want from the Lord. Prayer, true prayer, involves submission to the will of God. It is the cry of the believer's heart to his heavenly Father to do what is right and best. If I am God's child, if truly I know him and trust him, I want what he has purposed. I bow to him, surrendering my will to his will, my desires to his purpose, my pleasure to his glory, knowing that his will is best. Therefore, when we pray (in our ignorance), the Holy Spirit cleans up our prayers and presents to the Father the true groanings of our hearts (Romans 8:26).

Paul tells us plainly that though the Lord graciously refused to give him what he asked for, he graciously granted him what he really wanted and needed. John Gill wrote ...

"The Lord always hears and answers his people sooner or later, in one form or another, though not always in the way and manner they desire; but yet in such a way as is most for his glory and their good. The apostle had not his request granted, that Satan might immediately depart from him, only he is assured of a sufficiency of grace to support him under the exercise, so long as it should last."

Our Lord Jesus taught us ever to surrender our will to the Father's will. When the will of God appears to contradict that which might appear to be most pleasing to our flesh, we ought always to follow our Master's example, saying, "Not my will, but thine, be done" (Luke 22:42; cf. John 12:27, 28). I repeat, we do not know what is best for us, best for the glory of God, best for his kingdom, or best for the accomplishment of his purpose. Let us, therefore, wisely bow to his will in all things (Romans 8:26).

Grace For Our Children

Look at verses 14 and 15, and learn a second thing. Here is a lesson all parents should always bear in mind. Grace must be the principle thing we seek for our sons and daughters.

"And thou shalt have joy and gladness; and many shall rejoice at his birth. For he shall be great in the sight of the Lord, and shall drink neither wine nor strong drink; and he shall be filled with the Holy Ghost, even from his mother's womb."

What a blessed word this is from God! Zacharias was assured, before his son was born, that his only son would be numbered among the sons of God![2]

What more could any parent desire? Nothing can give a believing father and mother greater joy than to see their sons and daughters experience, possess and walk in the grace of God. Just before promising this old man that his son would be filled with the Holy Ghost, the angel of the Lord said to Zacharias, not only are you going to have a son, you are going to have a son who is chosen of God, "And thou shalt have joy and gladness; and many shall rejoice at his birth"!

Above all things, seek grace for your children. Beauty, brilliance, wealth and honour, even health and happiness are utterly insignificant when compared to this. Our sons and daughters need Christ. They need the grace of God in Christ. Let us seek, earnestly seek, the grace of God in Christ for our children. Happy is that father who is assured upon good grounds that his son or daughter is chosen of God, redeemed by Christ and born of the Spirit!

True Greatness

The third lesson is a lesson about true greatness. It is found in verse 15. True greatness is greatness in the sight of the Lord. "For he shall be great in the sight of the Lord."

---

[2] Let all those who are blessed of God with the burden of caring for children with limited mental capacity, or who have lost children in infancy, be cheered with this fact. God has granted you the rare privilege of being assured that you have a child who will be numbered among the redeemed in Glory.

Men always measure greatness by a very short stick. That which men call greatness is nothing. Politicians and presidents, doctors and lawyers, philosophers and statesmen, artists and authors, athletes and movie stars all who are called and admired as great by little fools are utterly insignificant to the angels of God. Those who are great before men, they count nothing. Those who are great in the sight of God, they count great. We will be wise to learn to measure greatness the way they measure it. The angels of God measure greatness by God's measuring stick.

Let us seek for ourselves and our children this true greatness, greatness before God, greatness in the world to come, greatness forever. What is this greatness in the sight of God? It is, the greatness of grace, the greatness of divine approval, the greatness of faith, the greatness of all who believe, the greatness of Christ. Our Saviour said, "Verily I say unto you, Among them that are born of women there hath not risen a greater than John the Baptist: notwithstanding he that is least in the kingdom of heaven is greater than he" (Matthew 11:11).

Divine Sovereignty

Look at verse 15 again, and learn something about the operations of God. God always acts in total sovereignty; and his sovereignty defies explanation. Here we are told that John the Baptist was filled with the Holy Spirit from his mother's womb. "For he shall be great in the sight of the Lord, and shall drink neither wine nor strong drink; and he shall be filled with the Holy Ghost, even from his mother's womb."

Almost everyone presumes that to mean that John the Baptist was regenerated in his mother's womb. But that is not what the text says. Some use this as a basis for baptizing babies. Some use it as a proof text to show that God does not necessarily use the preaching of the gospel to save his elect.

Let us be honest with the scriptures. Do not grab a verse or a statement, rip it out of its context, and make it mean whatever you want it to mean. We build our doctrine on the plain statements of scripture, not on the whims of our wild imaginations.

To be filled with the Holy Spirit is to be controlled by the Holy Spirit, no more and no less (Ephesians 5:18). When the scriptures tell us that John the Baptist was filled with the Holy Spirit from his mother's womb, it asserts that John, like Jeremiah, was sanctified, set apart, and ordained to be the prophet of the Highest, before he came out of his mother's womb (Jeremiah 1:5). The same thing was true of the apostle Paul (Galatians 1:15, 16).

While still in his mother's womb, John, under such an influence of the Spirit of God, leaped for joy at the salutation of Mary to his mother Elizabeth

(Luke 1:41, 44). Like David, he was under the constant protection and care of God's mercy, love, and grace, from his mother's womb (Psalm 22:9, 10).

Even before he was born, God began preparing him for the work he had for him to do. God the Holy Spirit gave him special gifts and grace, qualifying him for the work for which he was chosen.

God's Messengers

In verses 16 and 17 we are taught something about those men who are sent of God as his messengers to men. They are God's blessings upon men. No man is a greater blessing to men than those men who are sent from God as his messengers.

"And many of the children of Israel shall he turn to the Lord their God. And he shall go before him in the spirit and power of Elias, to turn the hearts of the fathers to the children, and the disobedient to the wisdom of the just; to make ready a people prepared for the Lord."

That is an accurate, angelic, biblical description of the character, conduct, work, and usefulness of a gospel preacher. He, as an instrument in the hands of God, turns the hearts of men. He turns the hearts of Israel, God's elect. He turns them from ignorance to knowledge, from darkness to light, from superstition to revelation, from unbelief to faith, and from sin to righteousness.

Obviously, the work of turning sinners to Christ is the work of God our Creator, not the work of a man; but the Spirit of God here describes it as the work of a man, because it is a work God performs by human instrumentality, by the instrumentality of gospel preaching (Romans 10:17; 1 Peter 1:23-25; James 1:18).

The messenger of grace goes before the Lord, walks before God in the Spirit and power of Elijah, seeking God's message, God's grace and God's will for his people, seeking God's glory, and serving to build God's kingdom. By the preaching of the gospel, he makes ready a people for the Lord, prepares chosen, redeemed sinners to meet the Lord at his appearing.

The gospel preacher is a man sent from God, filled with the Holy Ghost, proclaiming God's salvation. "How beautiful upon the mountains are the feet of him that bringeth good tidings, that publisheth peace; that bringeth good tidings of good, that publisheth salvation; that saith unto Zion, Thy God reigneth"!

These are the men we need. These are the men God uses. Blessed are those people to whom God sends such men! By them, God calls out his elect. By them, Christ is uplifted and glorified. By them, God leads his people.

"And Zacharias said unto the angel, Whereby shall I know this? for I am an old man, and my wife well stricken in years. And the angel answering said unto him, I am Gabriel, that stand in the presence of God; and am sent to speak unto thee, and to shew thee these glad tidings. And, behold, thou shalt be dumb, and not able to speak, until the day that these things shall be performed, because thou believest not my words, which shall be fulfilled in their season. And the people waited for Zacharias, and marvelled that he tarried so long in the temple. And when he came out, he could not speak unto them: and they perceived that he had seen a vision in the temple: for he beckoned unto them, and remained speechless. And it came to pass, that, as soon as the days of his ministration were accomplished, he departed to his own house. And after those days his wife Elisabeth conceived, and hid herself five months, saying, Thus hath the Lord dealt with me in the days wherein he looked on me, to take away my reproach among men" (Luke 1:18-25).

Chapter 5

Unbelief

Here is Zacharias, a man of great faith and faithfulness, stricken dumb by the angel of God because of his unbelief. One of the first corruptions of the human race was the horrible sin of unbelief. It is recorded in Genesis chapter three that our mother, Eve, being beguiled by the serpent, was persuaded to unbelief. She believed the devil's lie without reason and did not believe God, whom she had every reason to believe. Such is the natural wickedness of the human heart. We are all naturally inclined to believe the devil's lie regarding all things, without the slightest justification for doing so, and naturally inclined not to believe God, when we have every reason for doing so.

Unbelief is an original and universal corruption of all men. It is the deepest seated of all corruption. And it is at once the worst of all corruptions and the father of all other corruptions. If pride is the mother of all sin, unbelief is the father.

Yes, I did say unbelief is the worst of all the corruptions of fallen humanity. Nothing so highly honours God as believing him; and nothing so vilely dishonours God as unbelief. Yet, horrible as this offence is, it is the sin we most readily excuse in rebels and most easily justify in ourselves. May God the Holy Spirit unmask this devil who yet resides in us all, expose his ugly face, and inspire our hearts to oppose him with vengeance. Unbelief is found in the hearts of the strongest believers.

Zacharias was a truly remarkable man. He believed God when very few did. He worshipped God in Spirit when almost all around him were entirely given over to ceremonialism. Yet, when Gabriel told him that his wife would soon bear him a son, this faithful old man said, "Oh, no. You must be mistaken. Not my wife. I'm too old and she is too" (v. 18).

Why did Zacharias not believe the angel's message? It was because the angel's message was totally contrary to human reason, experience and science. The basis of faith is divine revelation; but the basis of unbelief is human reason. As J. C. Ryle put it, "Where reason begins, faith ends."

This well instructed priest in Israel had read in the Book of God about Abraham, Sarah and Isaac. He knew about God's wonders with Manoah and his wife, and the birth of Samson. He was aware of what God did for Hannah. Zacharias knew all those historic facts better that we do. He knew very well that the Lord our God is the sovereign, omnipotent Monarch of the universe.

He knew that with God nothing is impossible. He knew that the God who could cause the sun to go backwards ten degrees could easily reverse the aging process of an old woman's womb.

There was nothing wrong with Zacharias' doctrine. The problem was with his heart. When it came to the personal, practical application of divine truth to his own life and his own experience, Zacharias, this man of great faith, was overcome with unbelief! But we must not censure old Zacharias alone. His fault is the common fault of us all. All God's people on this earth are plagued with unbelief. It is a fault, a sin, a horrible evil in us all. The histories of Abraham, Lot, Moses and Peter stand as glaring beacons to warn us, to make us aware of this monstrous devil which resides in us all. Let us pray, honestly and earnestly, like the poor, distraught father in Mark 9, "Lord, I believe; help thou mine unbelief"!

How our unbelief must shock the angels of God. It was this same angel, Gabriel, who 490 years earlier brought a message from the throne of God to Daniel, assuring him of the coming and redemptive accomplishments of the Lord Jesus Christ, who would be cut off as the sinners' Substitute, not for his own sins, but for ours (Daniel 9:26). Daniel believed God's word. Daniel, a prisoner at Babylon, without one shred of external evidence, believed God! But Zacharias, who virtually lived in the temple, who had the entire Old Testament, with all the recorded miracles wrought by God, when that same angel spoke to him, turned his heart not toward God and his Word, but toward his own life experiences and learned reason. Therefore, he was filled with unbelief.

God no longer speaks to men by angels (Hebrews 1:1-3), though they were frequently messengers of mercy in days gone by. Still, the Lord God does have angels today (pastors, Revelation 1-3), by whom he speaks to men upon the earth, by whom he shows fallen men his wonders (Psalms 96:3, 4; 105:3-7). But our unbelief puts a heavy, dark, thick veil over the Word of God. Unbelief hides the glory of God from us (John 11:40). Unbelief holds back the blessings of God from us (Isaiah 48:16-19). And unbelief keeps the Lord from performing his mighty works among us (Mark 6:3-6). Obviously, God's will and God's work is not thwarted or even slightly impeded by our unbelief. Yet, the scriptures make it plain that a man's unbelief is an evil for which he is responsible. Faith is God's gift and operation. Unbelief is our sin.

No sin is more vile, reprehensible and dishonouring to God than unbelief. As nothing dishonours God like unbelief, so nothing provokes him to wrath and judgment like unbelief.

"While it is said, today if ye will hear his voice, harden not your hearts, as in the provocation. For some, when they had heard, did provoke: howbeit not all that came out of Egypt by Moses. But with whom was he grieved forty years? Was it not with them that had sinned, whose carcases fell in the wilderness? And to whom sware he that they should not enter into his rest, but to them that believed not? So we see that they could not enter in because of unbelief. Let us therefore fear, lest, a promise being left us of entering into his rest, any of you should seem to come short of it. For unto us was the gospel preached, as well as unto them: but the word preached did not profit them, not being mixed with faith in them that heard it. For we which have believed do enter into rest, as he said, As I have sworn in my wrath, if they shall enter into my rest: although the works were finished from the foundation of the world" (Hebrews 3:15-4:1-3).

What is it that makes unbelief such a base, vile thing? Unbelief is a denial of God's power, a denial of his Word, and a denial of his veracity (1 John 5:9-11). By unbelief, man asserts that God is a liar!

Unbelief, perhaps more than anything else, compels our heavenly Father to use his rod of correction upon his children.

God never punishes his people for sin. He punished our sins in his dear Son at Calvary. But he is a truly loving Father. As such, he chastens his children with the rod of correction (Hebrews 12:5-11). Zacharias' unbelief brought the Father's rod down heavily upon him. He was stricken deaf[3] and dumb by the hand of God for at least nine long months. Divine chastisement is sometimes lengthy; but always suitable. The ears that refused to hear God's Word were stricken deaf, until Zacharias learned to hearken to the Word of God. The tongue that refused to speak God's praise was tied, until it learned to speak forth Jehovah's praise.

Unbelief Will Bring Sinners To Eternal Ruin
"The Father loveth the Son, and hath given all things into his hand. He that believeth on the Son hath everlasting life: and he that believeth not the Son shall not see life; but the wrath of God abideth on him" (John 3:35, 36).

Yes, faith is the gift of God. No one can believe, except God give him faith. Yet, unbelief is the deliberate, wilful choice of rebels. And God will not hold any guiltless for their rebellion against him and his Son.

All Unbelief Will Soon Come To An End
The Lord God will soon cause all men to see all truth with absolute clarity. In that day, those who perish in unbelief will be convinced of all truth, but brought into everlasting contempt. And, blessed be his name, in that day, when the Lord visits us again as he did Elizabeth of old (vv. 24, 25), he will

---

[3] The fact that others communicated to him with signs (v. 62) implies that he was deaf as well as dumb.

take away our reproach forever. Thanks be unto our God, we will not forever struggle with these evil hearts of unbelief!

Until that day, let us watch and pray against this terrible sin, by which our God is so greatly dishonoured. Unbelief robs us of peace. Unbelief makes our knees weak and our hands heavy. Unbelief takes the joy out of our salvation. Unbelief destroys patience. Unbelief makes contentment impossible. It is written, "If ye will not believe, surely ye shall not be established" (Isaiah 7:9). Let us seek grace from our God to trust him implicitly, for the glory of his name. Unbelief trembles before a maid. Faith slays Goliath. Unbelief trembles in a thunderstorm. Faith sleeps in a lions' den. Unbelief paces the floor. Faith believes God. Unbelief dishonours our God. Faith honours him.

Unbelief

"And in the sixth month the angel Gabriel was sent from God unto a city of Galilee, named Nazareth, to a virgin espoused to a man whose name was Joseph, of the house of David; and the virgin's name was Mary. And the angel came in unto her, and said, Hail, thou that art highly favoured, the Lord is with thee: blessed art thou among women. And when she saw him, she was troubled at his saying, and cast in her mind what manner of salutation this should be. And the angel said unto her, Fear not, Mary: for thou hast found favour with God. And, behold, thou shalt conceive in thy womb, and bring forth a son, and shalt call his name JESUS. He shall be great, and shall be called the Son of the Highest: and the Lord God shall give unto him the throne of his father David: And he shall reign over the house of Jacob for ever; and of his kingdom there shall be no end" (Luke 1:26-33).

Chapter 6

The Greatness Of Our Saviour

The verses before us contain the most sublime things ever revealed to men. May God the Holy Spirit fill our hearts with wonder, faith, love, and praise as we now behold the wonders of God's grace here set before us.

Christ's Humiliation

Everything connected with our Saviour's incarnation displays his great humiliation as our Mediator. Gabriel was sent to an obscure town in Galilee called Nazareth. All of Galilee was looked upon by the Jews with contempt; and the most contemptible village in the region was Nazareth. It was a common thought among them that nothing good could come out of Nazareth (John 1:46). Mary, the woman chosen to be the mother of our Lord's human body and nature, was a very poor woman from a very poor area. There was nothing about her that the world would consider enviable or great.

Everything involved in the incarnation of our Saviour was arranged and brought to pass by God's wise and good providence. He who orders all things in heaven, earth and hell according to his own sovereign will chose a poor, despised woman in a poor despised village to be the vessel by which he would send our Saviour into this world.

What a great stoop the God of glory made when he stooped to save us from our sins! "For ye know the grace of our Lord Jesus Christ, that, though he was rich, yet for your sakes he became poor, that ye through his poverty might be rich" (2 Corinthians 8:9). Our Saviour's great love for us, that love that constrained him to take our nature into union with himself that he might live and die as our Substitute, ought to constrain us to love him and live not for ourselves, but for him who loved us and gave himself for us. Let us in all things have the mind of Christ and follow his example. "Seekest thou great things for thyself? Seek them not"!

"Let this mind be in you, which was also in Christ Jesus: Who, being in the form of God, thought it not robbery to be equal with God: But made himself of no reputation, and took upon him the form of a servant, and was made in the likeness of men: And being found in fashion as a man, he humbled himself, and became obedient unto death, even the death of the cross" (Philippians 2:5-8). "For I have given you an example, that ye should do as I have done to you" (John 13:15).

"Be of the same mind one toward another. Mind not high things, but condescend to men of low estate. Be not wise in your own conceits" (Romans 12:16).

Let us seek grace from our God to live continually in the spirit of Christ, with the mind of Christ, for the benefit of God's elect. As our Lord Jesus identified himself with our poverty, both spiritually and materially, let us never despise poverty in others, or be ashamed of it in ourselves, if the Lord brings us into such a condition. Riches make no one honourable; and poverty makes no one dishonourable. Men grovelling for riches and honour remind me of a dog digging for moles. The filthy rodent just isn't worth the dig.

Saving Grace

God's choice of Mary stands in holy scripture as a beautiful picture of his sovereign, saving grace to needy sinners.

"To a virgin espoused to a man whose name was Joseph, of the house of David; and the virgin's name was Mary. And the angel came in unto her, and said, Hail, thou that art highly favoured, the Lord is with thee: blessed art thou among women. And when she saw him, she was troubled at his saying, and cast in her mind what manner of salutation this should be. And the angel said unto her, Fear not, Mary: for thou hast found favour with God" (vv. 27-30).

Romanism places Mary on the highest pedestal imaginable, making her a mediatrix, or a co-mediator with Christ, ascribing to her an immaculate nature and divine power. When a previous pope was shot, he ascribed his recovery from the assassin's bullet not to God the Father, God the Son, or God the Holy Spirit, but to Mary. Such veneration of Mary is utterly contemptible idolatry. It must never be honoured as an acceptable thing. Such idolatry is not Christian, but pagan.

Mary is never presented as an immaculate, sinless woman, but as a sinner saved by grace, just like you and me. This she gladly acknowledged. We read in Luke 1:46, 47, "And Mary said, My soul doth magnify the Lord, And my spirit hath rejoiced in God my Saviour."

It is true, she is called "a virgin" but she is never referred to as "the virgin". Her virginity is mentioned repeatedly in the scriptures, not so much to honour her[4] as it is to declare the fact that the Lord Jesus Christ came into this world as the woman's seed, by miraculous, divine intervention. The body

---

[4] Virginity is truly an honourable thing among women. Chastity ought always to be cherished and protected; but it does not make one honourable before God.

of our Saviour, that holy thing prepared in Mary's virgin womb, was specifically prepared by God the Holy Spirit to be a suitable body for our Saviour to make him a sacrifice for our souls. "Wherefore when he cometh into the world, he saith, Sacrifice and offering thou wouldest not, but a body hast thou prepared me" (Hebrews 10:5).

Mary's name indicates what she was and what we all are by nature. "Mary" means "bitter rebel". It is the same as the name of Moses' sister, Miriam, and the name Naomi applied to herself, Mara. Yet, Mary was the object of God's sovereign, distinguishing grace.

The Lord God chose Mary for salvation and chose her for the high honour of being the mother of our Saviour's humanity. Mary was not the mother of God! The words, "highly favoured" (v. 28), could also be translated, "graciously accepted". Mary was graciously accepted of God in Christ by an act of sovereign grace, just like we are (Ephesians 1:6).[5] The Lord was with her, just as he is with us: to protect her, provide for her, save her and to bless her.

Mary was a woman blessed of God. "Blessed art thou among women"! The word "blessed" is exactly the same word used to describe the blessedness of all God's elect in Christ, the distinguishing blessedness of grace. Mary was, like all who are saved by God's free grace in Christ, blessed of God in and with Christ. Like us, she was blessed of God from eternity with all spiritual blessings in heavenly places, according as she was chosen in eternal, electing love. She was blessed with redemption and the free forgiveness of all her sins, as the object of God's covenant grace, in Christ her Mediator.

In a word, Mary found favour with God! "Thou hast found favour with God"! Mary did not bless God. God blessed her. God did not find favour in Mary's eyes. Mary found favour in God's eyes. The phrase in verse 30 is exactly the same as that in verse 28. It simply means that Mary was a sinner chosen from among women as the object of God's mercy, love and grace, and blessed by him with all grace.

We must never exalt Mary above this level to a position of idolatrous envy, because believers, all believers, have a far nearer relationship to Christ than Mary enjoyed as his earthly mother. Her relationship, the relationship given to her in providence, was a purely carnal, physical, temporary relationship. Ours is a permanent, spiritual relationship. We are truly the Saviour's family (Mark 3:15). Mary's great blessedness was not in her physical relationship to Christ, but in her spiritual relationship. Our Master himself tells us that it is more blessed to believe on him than to have carried him in the womb (Luke 11:27, 28).

---

[5] Mary was full of grace in exactly the same way every saved sinner is, by the bounty of God's grace in Christ. She was the object of grace; but she was not made the giver of grace!

Christ's Greatness

The primary thing revealed in this passage of scripture is the glorious greatness of our Saviour, the Lord Jesus Christ. Gabriel's announcement was no ordinary birth announcement. It was not the announcement of the birth of a mere man, but the announcement of the incarnation of God! Gabriel was sent to proclaim that God the Son was about to take humanity into union with himself, and enter into this sin cursed world to save his people from their sins. Look at what we are told in verses 31-33.

"And, behold, thou shalt conceive in thy womb, and bring forth a son, and shalt call his name JESUS. He shall be great, and shall be called the Son of the Highest: and the Lord God shall give unto him the throne of his father David: And he shall reign over the house of Jacob for ever; and of his kingdom there shall be no end."

The child born from Mary's virgin womb was and is God the Son given in human flesh (Isaiah 9:6). "God was manifest in the flesh" (1 Timothy 3:16). Our Saviour is Immanuel, God with us, God in our nature. None but the incarnate God could save us. And this great, incarnate God came into this world as our Mediator and covenant Surety on a specific mission: to save his people from their sins. His name was called, "Jesus", because he was sent here to "save his people from their sins" (Matthew 1:21). And that which he was sent to do, that which he came to do, he has done.

As Joshua did for Israel what Moses never could, so the Lord Jesus Christ, our Joshua, did what the law could never do. He brought us to God!

"There is therefore now no condemnation to them which are in Christ Jesus, who walk not after the flesh, but after the Spirit. For the law of the Spirit of life in Christ Jesus hath made me free from the law of sin and death. For what the law could not do, in that it was weak through the flesh, God sending his own Son in the likeness of sinful flesh, and for sin, condemned sin in the flesh: That the righteousness of the law might be fulfilled in us, who walk not after the flesh, but after the Spirit" (Romans 8:1-4).

A Fivefold Declaration Of Our Saviour's Greatness

"He shall be great." Christ is great in all his offices. Greater than all who went before him. And greater than all who come after him.

He "shall be called the Son of the Highest." Our Lord Jesus Christ is God the Son.

"The Lord God shall give unto him the throne of his father David." Our Saviour has won the right to rule the universe as our God-man Mediator (Psalm 2:8; John 17:2; Romans 14:9).

"And he shall reign over the house of Jacob forever." He is the Head of his body, the Church and her King as well.

"And of his kingdom there shall be no end." The Lord Jesus did not come here to rule as a King over that little piece of land called "Israel" for a few hundred years. He rules as King in Zion forever!

All the kingdoms of this world have been and are designed of God only for the building of the kingdom of our God and his Christ. The kingdoms of this world are only the scaffolding by which our God builds his kingdom. Like Nineveh, Babylon, Egypt, Tyre, Carthage, Rome, the British Empire and the Soviet Union, all the nations and empires of this world shall perish and all men shall be made to bow before this great and glorious King, who alone shall reign forever (Philippians 2:9-11; Daniel 7:14, 27).

"Then said Mary unto the angel, How shall this be, seeing I know not a man? And the angel answered and said unto her, The Holy Ghost shall come upon thee, and the power of the Highest shall overshadow thee: therefore also that holy thing which shall be born of thee shall be called the Son of God. And, behold, thy cousin Elisabeth, she hath also conceived a son in her old age: and this is the sixth month with her, who was called barren. For with God nothing shall be impossible. And Mary said, Behold the handmaid of the Lord; be it unto me according to thy word. And the angel departed from her" (Luke 1:34-38).

Chapter 7

"How Can These Things Be?"

The angel Gabriel appeared to Mary and announced God's grace and mercy to her. He told her that she had been chosen of God to be that virgin through whom the Messiah would come into the world, by whom the Seed of woman would come, through whom God the Father would send his Son, the Lord Jesus Christ, to save his people from their sins.

God the Spirit has recorded all that is needful for our soul's edification regarding the mystery of the incarnation of our blessed Saviour in the few verses before us. I call your attention to six things in these verses.

The Wonder Of Faith

Earlier in this chapter (vv. 18-20), we saw that when Zacharias asked, "Whereby shall I know this?", his question was an expression of unbelief. Yet, when Mary asked virtually the same thing, her question was an expression of faith (v. 45). Zacharias asked what he did because he looked upon the promise of God as a thing impossible. Mary asked what she did because she looked upon the promise of God as astonishing.

Mary's words are an expression of admiration. She knew that the Son of God was coming into the world in human flesh, that Messiah must come into the world as a woman's seed, untainted by Adam's transgression, that God was going to send his Son into the world through the womb of a virgin; and now she knew that she was that virgin!

Mary's words expressed her desire to know how the Lord would do this great, wondrous thing. She did not question the fact that God would do as he said. She simply desired to know how he would do it.

Mary could not imagine how such an amazing work could be accomplished, since she was indeed a virgin, as she put it, "Seeing I know not a man." True faith often expresses itself in words of amazement and astonishment. David was astonished at God's promise to him and his house; but he believed the promise (2 Samuel 7). Mephibosheth was astonished that David would look on such a dead dog as he thought himself to be before such a magnificent king; but he believed David's word. So it is with God's people. We often ask, "Why would the Lord love me?" "Why would he choose me?" "Why would Christ die for me?" "How can God use me?" Yet, we believe that which the Lord God has revealed in his Word.

The Mystery Of The Incarnation

In response to Mary's question, Gabriel explained the mystery of the incarnation with absolute reverence, using the simplest words possible to declare the most profound mystery in the universe.

"And the angel answered and said unto her, The Holy Ghost shall come upon thee, and the power of the Highest shall overshadow thee: therefore also that holy thing which shall be born of thee shall be called the Son of God" (v. 35).

We ought always to follow this angelic example of total reverence regarding the things of God. Vain questions, carnal debate, idle speculations about holy things are utterly out of place. Divine things are divine. They are to be treated as divine. Here is the great mystery of godliness. "God was manifest in the flesh"! "The Word was made flesh, and dwelt among us." Robert Hawker rightly observed ...

"The Word of God teacheth, that all the persons of the Godhead were engaged in the formation of the human nature of Christ. Concerning God the Father, it was said by Christ, under the spirit of prophecy, ages before his incarnation: a body hast thou prepared me. Compare Psalm 40:6 with Hebrews 10:5. And that God the Son had a hand in it is evident, for the Holy Ghost by Paul saith; that he took not on him the nature of angels, but the seed of Abraham. And again, he took of flesh and blood (Hebrews 2:14, 16). And in this chapter we have the wonderful relation of the part which God the Holy Ghost had in the work, in his overshadowing power."

When God sent his Son into this world, he prepared a body for him called, "that holy thing", in which our redemption could be accomplished (Hebrews 10:5). He took part of our flesh and blood (Hebrews 2:14). He became what we are. When he came into this world, he took hold of the seed of Abraham (Hebrews 2:15), took hold on his covenant people to save them.

This great Saviour was "made of a woman" (Galatians 4:4-6). Yet, our great Saviour is himself God (Colossians 2:9). What more should be said? What more can be said? To go beyond these simple statements of divine Revelation would be to foolishly rush in where angels fear to tread and darken counsel by words without knowledge.

The Work Of The Triune God

"And the angel answered and said unto her, The Holy Ghost shall come upon thee, and the power of the Highest shall overshadow thee: therefore also that holy thing which shall be born of thee shall be called the Son of God" (v. 35).

As the incarnation was a work involving all three persons in the Triune God, the salvation of our souls is the work of the Triune God, Father, Son and Holy Spirit. We were chosen by God the Father in eternal election, purchased by God the Son in effectual redemption, and sanctified by God the Spirit in sovereign regeneration.

Yet, we must not fail to notice the unique work of God the Spirit, with regard to the Lord Jesus Christ. As God the Father always points to and glorifies Christ, so God the Spirit always points us to and glorifies the Lord Jesus Christ.

Did God the Son come into this world in human flesh? It was God the Spirit who prepared a body for him in the womb of a virgin. Did the Lord Jesus die to make atonement for our sins? It is written that he "through the eternal Spirit offered himself without spot to God" (Hebrews 9:14). Did the crucified Christ rise from the dead for our justification? It is written, "he was justified in the Spirit" (1 Timothy 3:16). Our Redeemer was "quickened by the Spirit" (1 Peter 3:18). Does the Prince of Peace give comfort to his people? It is by the Holy Spirit who is our Comforter. Does Christ our Prophet teach us? It is by the Spirit of Truth. In all things, especially in the affair of our salvation, the Triune God is one.

The Condescension Of Grace

Our God is so gracious, so good, so merciful that he condescends to help our weaknesses. Grace anticipates our weakness and inability. We see this beautifully set forth in verse 36. Though Mary believed God's promise, though she asked for no sign, the Lord condescended to encourage her faith, by telling her of another miraculous birth, by which God would fulfil his prophetic Word. "And, behold, thy cousin Elisabeth, she hath also conceived a son in her old age: and this is the sixth month with her, who was called barren."

As soon as Mary found herself with child, she took off to see her cousin, Elizabeth. How they must have helped one another. Both were in embarrassing, difficult situations. While they were together, they ministered to one another and encouraged one another in the worship of God, celebrating his goodness and his grace.

The Omnipotence Of Our God

Here is the pillar of our confidence, the strength of our faith, and the solace of our souls in all things! "With God nothing shall be impossible" (v. 37). Our peace in this world, our confidence regarding the purposes, promises and grace of our God stand and fall with our firm persuasion of our heavenly Father's absolute omnipotence.

With our God, nothing is impossible! He who called the universe into being by the mere exercise of his will, he who created all things out of nothing by the bidding of his power, he who upholds all things by the word of his power can perform all his purposes, all his promises and all that we need, at all times!

That which is impossible with us is a piece of cake for our God. Nothing is too hard for the Lord! "With God all things are possible" (Mark 10:27). I cannot express the message of verse 37 any better than J. C. Ryle did in his *Expository Thoughts on the Gospel of Luke*. Ryle wrote ...

"There is no sin too black and bad to be pardoned. The blood of Christ cleanseth from all sin. There is no heart too hard and wicked to be changed. The heart of stone can be made a heart of flesh. There is no work too hard for a believer to do. We may do all things through Christ strengthening us. There is no trial too hard to be borne. The grace of God is sufficient for us. There is no promise too great to be fulfilled. Christ's words shall never pass away, and what he has promised he is able to perform. There is no difficulty too great for a believer to overcome. When God is for us, who shall be against us? The mountains shall become as a plain. Faith never rests so calmly and peacefully as when it lays its head on the pillow of God's omnipotence."

Our great and glorious God is the omnipotent God, the God of omnipotent ability to do exceeding abundantly above all that we ask or think. Child of God, be assured, "With God nothing shall be impossible"! He is able to complete the work of his grace in you. He is able to keep you. He is able to save you to the uttermost (Philippians 1:6; 2 Timothy 1:12; Hebrews 7:25).

> The Lord is King! Who then shall dare
> Resist his will, distrust his care,
> Or murmur at his wise decrees,
> Or doubt his royal promises?
>
> 'Til God all-wise can make mistakes,
> His pow'r abate, his love forsake,
> His children must not cease to sing
> The Lord Omnipotent is King!
>
> Josiah Conder

If indeed we believe God, if indeed our God is omnipotent, surrendering ourselves to him in all things should be in our minds the simplest, most reasonable thing in this world. Oh, may God give us grace to follow Mary's example in this matter. In verse 38, she shows us by humble example ...

The Surrender Of Faith

"And Mary said, Behold the handmaid of the Lord; be it unto me according to thy word. And the angel departed from her." The great privilege granted to Mary, like all truly great privileges, involved (at least for the present) great and costly difficulty. Though it would ultimately be her everlasting honour, for the present, Mary knew her honourable name and reputation, her marriage to a good and honourable man, and her respect from family and friend alike would very possibly be in jeopardy. These things presented no small trial to her faith. But, believing God, for the honour of God, to do the will of God, Mary was willing to risk everything. She raised no objections. She asked no questions. She asked no favours. She simply bowed to the will of God, with ready and willing heart.

May God be pleased to give me such grace, that I may be willing to go anywhere, endure anything, and do anything, whatever the cost, in obedience to his will, for the glory of Christ. Faith is most noble when it yields blind obedience to the will of God.

"And Mary arose in those days, and went into the hill country with haste, into a city of Juda; And entered into the house of Zacharias, and saluted Elisabeth. And it came to pass, that, when Elisabeth heard the salutation of Mary, the babe leaped in her womb; and Elisabeth was filled with the Holy Ghost: And she spake out with a loud voice, and said, Blessed art thou among women, and blessed is the fruit of thy womb. And whence is this to me, that the mother of my Lord should come to me? For, lo, as soon as the voice of thy salutation sounded in mine ears, the babe leaped in my womb for joy. And blessed is she that believed: for there shall be a performance of those things which were told her from the Lord" (Luke 1:39-45).

Chapter 8

A Visit To The Hill Country

When I was a boy, there was one delightful ray of sunshine in my dark life, one thing which was always sure to give me a season of pure pleasure and happiness. At least once a year, I would get to go for a week or more to the mountains to visit my dad's family. My grandmother, great aunt, and my aunts and uncles were always a pleasure to be around. I remember dreaming, with delightful anticipation, about going to the hills of Spruce Pine, North Carolina. The happiest days of my childhood were spent in the hills.

In these verses the Spirit of God takes us with Mary to the hill country of Judah. She went there to visit her aging cousin Elisabeth. What a pleasurable, instructive and spiritually beneficial visit it was.

A Beneficial Communion

"And Mary arose in those days, and went into the hill country with haste, into a city of Juda; And entered into the house of Zacharias, and saluted Elisabeth. And it came to pass, that, when Elisabeth heard the salutation of Mary, the babe leaped in her womb; and Elisabeth was filled with the Holy Ghost: And she spake out with a loud voice, and said, Blessed art thou among women, and blessed is the fruit of thy womb" (vv. 39-42).

Here we see Mary and Elisabeth, a young virgin and an elderly mother in Israel, walking together in delightful, blessed fellowship and communion. They were cousins, but their fellowship was much more and much, much sweeter and beneficial than the companionship of family. Their fellowship with one another was the fellowship of faith. Their communion was the communion of grace.

When I talk about fellowship and communion, I am talking about the fellowship of believers, the communion of grace in Christ. We who believe "have all things common". We have a common salvation, a common election, a common atonement, a common hope, a common family, a common warfare and a common inheritance. Luke tells us that these dear saints, when they visited with one another, were mutually benefited, spiritually benefited by each other. Their hearts were cheered. Their minds were uplifted. Their souls were refreshed. Their spirits were edified.

As they visited and communed with one another, discussing the grace of God, the wonders of his providence, and the excellence of his mercy, his covenant, his promises and his faithfulness, Elisabeth was filled with the Holy Ghost; and Mary was inspired to sing a new song of praise to the Lord.

We should always regard the fellowship of God's saints as one of our greatest privileges in this world. Sadly, J. C. Ryle rightly observed, "There are many who fear the Lord and think upon his name, and yet forget to speak often one to another." That ought not be the case. "As iron sharpeneth iron, so doth the countenance of a man his friend ... As in water face answereth to face, so the heart of man to man" (Proverbs 27:17, 19).

"They that feared the LORD spake often one to another: and the LORD hearkened, and heard it, and a book of remembrance was written before him for them that feared the LORD, and that thought upon his name" (Malachi 3:16). What a refreshing break in our pilgrimage, what an oasis in this desert, what a resting place in this troubled world a season of fellowship with God's saints is! Let us never take this privilege lightly. "Let brotherly love continue. Be not forgetful to entertain strangers (especially fellow strangers!): for thereby some have entertained angels unawares" (Hebrews 13:1, 2).

Fellowship with God's saints is as near as we come to heaven on earth. We will be wise to seize every opportunity to enjoy the company of God's elect in the assembly of public worship and in private company. When we have the privilege, let us take care that our company is helpful, not harmful, edifying, not a hindrance, to our brothers and sisters in Christ. We should speak to one another, as Mary and Elisabeth did, about the things of God. And in the house of God, when God's messenger has delivered God's message to your soul, speak to one another about the message.

Our chosen companions in this world should always be companions in the grace of God. I do not suggest that we live as hermits in this world, that we isolate ourselves from society. That would be irresponsible. I do not suggest that we treat other people contemptuously. That would be horribly wicked. Yet, believers should never choose unbelievers for their companions in any sphere of life. I am always concerned when I see anyone who professes to be a child of God choosing to spend his or her leisure time with unbelievers. Such a choice is like choosing to take fire into your bosom. It is like inviting a traitor into your camp. It is bringing a thief into your home. No good can come from it (1 Corinthians 5:6; 15:33, 34; 2 Corinthians 6:14, 15).

A Believer's Confession

"And whence is this to me, that the mother of my Lord should come to me? For, lo, as soon as the voice of thy salutation sounded in mine ears, the babe leaped in my womb for joy" (vv. 43, 44).

Often, we think that God's saints in days gone by were very terribly ignorant concerning the person and work of Christ. Like us, many of them were weak and ignorant of many things. They often expressed themselves poorly. They often behaved in a way that was contrary to the gospel, and contrary to their God given faith. They were, after all, men and women like us!

Yet, those men and women in days of old who knew God were also given the mind of Christ (1 Corinthians 2:16). Elisabeth's language in verse forty-three, where she called Mary "the mother of my Lord", is the language of remarkable faith. It is a confession of faith every bit as remarkable as that of Peter, who confessed, "Thou art the Christ, the Son of the living God."

We must not put words in her mouth, but when she made this confession concerning the baby in Mary's womb, Elisabeth acknowledged that the child conceived in Mary's womb was the long expected Messiah, the son of David, the Son of God, the Saviour of the world. She understood what Mary sang in verses 46-55.

"And Mary said, My soul doth magnify the Lord, And my spirit hath rejoiced in God my Saviour. For he hath regarded the low estate of his handmaiden: for, behold, from henceforth all generations shall call me blessed. For he that is mighty hath done to me great things; and holy is his name. And his mercy is on them that fear him from generation to generation. He hath showed strength with his arm; he hath scattered the proud in the imagination of their hearts. He hath put down the mighty from their seats, and exalted them of low degree. He hath filled the hungry with good things; and the rich he hath sent empty away. He hath holpen his servant Israel, in remembrance of his mercy; As he spake to our fathers, to Abraham, and to his seed for ever."

Elisabeth's confession was an acknowledgement of voluntary surrender to, and faith in, Christ as her Lord (1 Corinthians 12:3). This dear old saint had learned and gladly acknowledged what all must soon acknowledge: Jesus Christ is Lord (Philippians 2:9-11).

A Blessed Confidence

"And blessed is she that believed: for there shall be a performance of those things which were told her from the Lord" (v. 45). Here, we see an old, old woman, a woman who had learned the folly of both vanity and flattery, speaking in glowing terms about the blessedness of faith in Christ, the blessedness of believing God.

It is indeed a blessed thing to believe God. Faith has always been a grace by which God's saints in this world have obtained a good report (Hebrews 11:1-16). The story of God's saints is a story of faith, the narrative of chosen, redeemed sinners who, believing God, were and are blessed of God. By faith, they embrace God's promises, walk with God, endure hardships, look to Christ, endure temptations, triumph over the world, the flesh and the devil, live, die and enter into glory!

There is a great volume of instruction contained in these words "Blessed is she that believed." Faith is nothing less than confidence in God. Read Elisabeth's words again. "And blessed is she that believed: for there shall be a performance of those things which were told her from the Lord." Faith is confidence that God will accomplish all his Word, that he will perform all his promises, that he will fulfil his every decree (Philippians 1:6).This faith is the gift of God (Ephesians 1:19; 2:8; Colossians 1:12). Blessed is that sinner to whom it is given in the behalf of Christ to believe on his name (Philippians 1:29). Do we know anything about this precious gift of faith? "Blessed are they that have believed" (John 20:29).

> Oh, gift of gifts! Oh, grace of faith!
> My God, how can it be
> That Thou, who hast discerning love,
> Shouldst give that gift to me?
>
> Ah, Grace! Into unlikeliest hearts
> It is Thy boast to come;
> The glory of Thy light to find
> In darkest spots a home.
>
> Thy choice, (O God of goodness!) then
> I lovingly adore;
> Oh, give me grace to keep Thy grace,
> And grace to long for more!
>
> Fredrick W. Faber

A Visit To The Hill Country

"And Mary said, My soul doth magnify the Lord, And my spirit hath rejoiced in God my Saviour. For he hath regarded the low estate of his handmaiden: for, behold, from henceforth all generations shall call me blessed. For he that is mighty hath done to me great things; and holy is his name. And his mercy is on them that fear him from generation to generation. He hath shewed strength with his arm; he hath scattered the proud in the imagination of their hearts. He hath put down the mighty from their seats, and exalted them of low degree. He hath filled the hungry with good things; and the rich he hath sent empty away. He hath holpen his servant Israel, in remembrance of his mercy; As he spake to our fathers, to Abraham, and to his seed for ever. And Mary abode with her about three months, and returned to her own house" (Luke 1:46-56).

Chapter 9

Mary's Song

After Mary heard the good news of Christ's incarnation she went to visit her older, beloved cousin Elizabeth, who was six months pregnant with John the Baptist. When the two women met together, they talked of the marvellous things God had done for them and taught them. Both were full of faith and joy. They were mutually inspirational to one another.

What a blessing good companions are! They help each other in the way. Happy are those family meetings where Christ is the theme of thought and conversation! When we meet with our families and friends, let us pray that our time together may be both pleasant and profitable. We ought to always try to be spiritually helpful to those around us, to those who come under our influence.

Mary

Mary, the mother of our Lord, is held before us in the Book of God as a great example of God's saving grace. Being taught of God, she was a woman of remarkable faith. She believed God's revelation concerning a totally unprecedented matter, scientifically impossible, and believed it without any evidence to support her. The angel of the Lord said to her, "The Holy Ghost shall come upon thee, and the power of the Highest shall overshadow thee: therefore also that holy thing which shall be born of thee shall be called the Son of God" (Luke 1:35). In verse 45, after the baby in Elisabeth's womb leaped for joy, because of the incarnate God in Mary's womb, Elisabeth said of Mary, "Blessed is she that hath believed: for there shall be a performance of those things which were told her from the Lord." Let every child of God pray that the Holy Spirit might grant us the kind of faith he gave Mary.

Mary was a woman of remarkable knowledge, too. She had a clear, firm knowledge and understanding of holy scripture. As we read Mary's hymn, though she was but a young woman, we see she had a ready grasp of the Old

Testament. She quotes the Psalms, refers to God's works of old, refers to his goodness to Leah and repeats many of the words of Hannah's prayer in 2 Samuel 2. All who have been made the recipients of God's saving mercy should seek to become more and more fully and more and more experimentally acquainted with holy scripture. "Let the word of Christ dwell in you richly in all wisdom; teaching and admonishing one another in psalms and hymns and spiritual songs, singing with grace in your hearts to the Lord" (Colossians 3:16).

Such a knowledge of holy scripture can never be attained without regular, daily study; but the benefits of such study will prove priceless. When she needed them most, Mary had a firm grasp of the promises of God in the Bible; and these strengthened her faith.

That which Mary knew and believed caused her to be a truly humbled soul before God. True faith and spiritual knowledge never swell the heart with pride. Rather these are the things by which the Lord breaks his own and makes them humble and contrite before him. J. C. Ryle rightly observed ...

"She who was chosen of God to the high honour of being Messiah's mother, speaks of her own 'low estate', and acknowledges her need of a Saviour. She does not let fall a word to show that she regarded herself as a sinless, 'immaculate' person. On the contrary, she uses the language of one who has been taught by the grace of God to feel her own sins, and so far from being able to save others, requires a Saviour for her own soul."

As humility is the daughter of saving faith, gratitude is the daughter of humility. All who experience God's free favour and saving grace in Christ are filled with thanksgiving to God; and Mary certainly demonstrates such thanksgiving. That which stands out in this hymn, perhaps above everything else, is the fact that Mary considered herself a debtor to mercy alone. She sought to magnify the Lord her God, from whom all mercy and grace springs.

Her knowledge of Christ as God her Saviour filled Mary with contentment. She was a poor woman. We have no evidence that she ever ceased to be afflicted with poverty. When the Saviour died, he committed his poor mother to the care of one of his disciples. Yet, Mary appears to have been perfectly content. In all that is written about her in holy scripture, the Holy Spirit never gives even a hint of dissatisfaction in her. Having Christ to be her Saviour, she wanted no more. She says, "My spirit hath rejoiced in God my Saviour" (v. 47). In verse 56 we read that "Mary returned to her own house." Though she was blessed in the most extraordinary manner, she was content to go back to her modest home and become the wife of a simple carpenter. May God give us that blessed spirit of contentment, so that we can say with Paul, "I have learned, in whatsoever state I am, therewith to be content. I know both how to be abased, and I know how to abound: every where and in all things I am instructed both to be full and to be hungry, both to abound and to suffer need" (Philippians 4:11, 12).

Mary's Song

In Luke 1:46-56, God the Holy Spirit has preserved for our learning the song Mary composed and sang when she and Elizabeth met one another. It is a song of praise to God, arising from a heart of faith, humility, gratitude and love. Robert Hawker writes:

"The song of Mary is full of the breathings of a soul under the influence of the Holy Ghost. How blessedly she speaks of God her Saviour; evidently showing, that she had a perfect apprehension of what the Prophets had taught, concerning the miraculous conception; and therefore knew, that the child then in her womb was, in one and the same moment, her Son and her Saviour! And how blessedly she speaks of the low estate, both in the temporal poverty of her father's house, and the spiritual reduced estate, by reason of sin, to the whole race of Adam. And the personal dignity to which she, a poor, young, and humble Virgin, was exalted. He that is mighty (said she) hath done to me great things. Great indeed, and, until that period, never heard of before; and never to be again wrought in the earth. And how beautifully she ends her hymn of praise, in singing the sure deliverance of the Church, by this stupendous event. He hath holpen (said she) his servant Israel: meaning, he hath redeemed the Church of God, in the Israel of God, his chosen; thus confirming the Covenant made with Abraham, that in his seed should all the families of the earth be blessed (Genesis 12:3. with Galatians 3:16)."

Notice, as you read this sweet song of praise, that everything spoken of in it is spoken of as though it had already been accomplished, though, as yet, Christ had not even been born. Why is that? The answer should be obvious: That which God has purposed was finished when he purposed it. Here are seven truths to learn from Mary's song.

First, Mary gives praise to the Lord God, who was in her womb, for being her Saviour. "And Mary said, My soul doth magnify the Lord, And my spirit hath rejoiced in God my Saviour" (vv. 46, 47). If Christ is our Saviour, we have reason to sing! As she sang his praise, unlike most who pretend to sing his praise today, Mary spoke of her God with great reverence. Yet, trusting Christ, she claimed a personal interest in Christ. Thus, she magnified her Lord by acknowledging him as her Lord and ascribing greatness to him as God her Saviour. The word "magnify" here means to enlarge and make room for. Mary flung open the gates of her soul for the King of glory to come in! She rejoiced in her Lord. That word means "danced". Like her great grandfather David, Mary danced before the Lord.

Second, Mary's song of praise was inspired by the wondrous mystery of Christ's incarnation (2 Corinthians 9:15). Mary sang this song because she believed the report of the angel Gabriel. "And the angel said unto her, Fear not, Mary: for thou hast found favour with God. And, behold, thou shalt conceive in thy womb, and bring forth a son, and shalt call his name JESUS. He shall be great, and shall be called the Son of the Highest: and the Lord God shall give unto him the throne of his father David: And he shall reign over the house of Jacob for ever; and of his kingdom there shall be no end. Then said Mary unto the angel, How shall this be, seeing I know not a man? And the angel answered and said unto her, The Holy Ghost shall come upon thee, and the power of the Highest shall overshadow thee: therefore also that holy thing which shall be born of thee shall be called the Son of God" (Luke 1:30-35). Let sinners sing praise to God: Immanuel is come! (Matthew 1:21).

Third, Mary particularly gives praise to God for his particular, distinguishing grace. "For he hath regarded the low estate of his handmaiden: for, behold, from henceforth all generations shall call me blessed" (Luke 1:48). God chose her to be the mother of our Redeemer. She was blessed of God in Christ. She was blessed because Christ was in her by a supernatural work of grace and power by God the Holy Spirit. She is called blessed because of God's goodness to her as the object of his grace. We who are the objects of God's special love and distinguishing grace have reason to sing his praise!

Fourth, Mary gives praise to the Lord God because of his glorious holiness. She declares, "Holy is his name" (v. 49). That which caused Moses, Isaiah and Daniel to tremble caused Mary to rejoice, because she saw clearly that God in his holiness had provided a holy Sacrifice. Holiness seen through the blood shed at Calvary is the most comforting and delightful thing in the world. Let this heart sing God's praise. I have seen mercy and truth meet together. I have seen righteousness and peace kiss each other.

Then, fifth, Mary offers praise to the Lord for the great things he has done. "For he that is mighty hath done to me great things; and holy is his name. And his mercy is on them that fear him from generation to generation. He hath showed strength with his arm; he hath scattered the proud in the imagination of their hearts. He hath put down the mighty from their seats, and exalted them of low degree. He hath filled the hungry with good things; and the rich he hath sent empty away" (Luke 1:49-53).

God has done great things in providence, in the incarnation, in redemption, in the experience of grace. He puts down the mighty, exalts them of low degree, fills the hungry with good things and the rich he sends away empty. "Oh that men would praise the LORD for his goodness, and for his wonderful works to the children of men" (Psalm 107:31). "The righteous shall see it, and rejoice: and all iniquity shall stop her mouth. Whoso is wise, and will observe these things, even they shall understand the lovingkindness of the LORD" (Psalm 107:42, 43).

Sixth, Mary gives praise to the Lord God for his unfailing help. "He hath holpen his servant Israel, in remembrance of his mercy" (Luke 1:54). The word "holpen" means to place one's hand under the fallen, prostrate one, and lift him to his feet.

God helps his elect. He always remembers mercy to his own. "I will sing of the mercies of the LORD for ever: with my mouth will I make known thy faithfulness to all generations" (Psalm 89:1).

Last, in verse 55, Mary gives praise to the Lord her God for his covenant faithfulness. "As he spake to our fathers, to Abraham, and to his seed for ever" (Luke 1:55). In Christ God has fulfilled his promises to the fathers, and particularly his promise to Abraham; the woman's seed (Genesis 3:15), the lamb provided (Genesis 22), the blessings of grace (Galatians 3:13-16).

An Example
While God abideth faithful, I have reason to sing his praise. Let us each, from the depths of our hearts, join Mary in this song of praise to our great God and Saviour, the Lord Jesus Christ.

Let us honour him for who he is, worship him for all that he has done, praise him for his distinguishing grace (1 Corinthians 1:26; 2 Corinthians 4:7) and magnify his great faithfulness!

"Now Elisabeth's full time came that she should be delivered; and she brought forth a son. And her neighbours and her cousins heard how the Lord had shewed great mercy upon her; and they rejoiced with her. And it came to pass, that on the eighth day they came to circumcise the child; and they called him Zacharias, after the name of his father. And his mother answered and said, Not so; but he shall be called John. And they said unto her, There is none of thy kindred that is called by this name. And they made signs to his father, how he would have him called. And he asked for a writing table, and wrote, saying, his name is John. And they marvelled all. And his mouth was opened immediately, and his tongue loosed, and he spake, and praised God. And fear came on all that dwelt round about them: and all these sayings were noised abroad throughout all the hill country of Judaea. And all they that heard them laid them up in their hearts, saying, What manner of child shall this be! And the hand of the Lord was with him" (Luke 1:57-66).

Chapter 10

"The Hand Of The Lord Was With Him"

The very last word spoken by God in the Old Testament was a word of promise and prophecy, a promise of mercy and a prophecy of the coming of another Elijah to prepare the way for Christ, the Messiah, our Saviour.

"Behold, I will send you Elijah the prophet before the coming of the great and dreadful day of the LORD: And he shall turn the heart of the fathers to the children, and the heart of the children to their fathers, lest I come and smite the earth with a curse" (Malachi 4:5, 6).

Four hundred years had passed; but now Malachi's prophecy was fulfilled. Six months prior to the birth of our Saviour, John the Baptist was born by the special intervention of God.

How easily we ought to believe God! He who gave life to Elizabeth's dead womb can do "whatsoever seemeth him good"! "With God nothing shall be impossible"! We ought to believe him implicitly and trust him confidently, without the slightest doubt, even when (especially when) all things appear to contradict his Word. The decree of God is absolute, and cannot be altered. The Word of God is inerrant and must be fulfilled. The promises of God in Christ are yea and amen and can never become nay. God Almighty will do; indeed, he who is God must do all that he has said. If one word from God shall fall to the ground, the whole Book of God crumbles to nothing but a religious myth!

Notice that the birth of John the Baptist was looked upon as a singular, special act of God's great mercy upon Elizabeth. "Her neighbours and her cousins heard how the Lord had shewed great mercy upon her; and they rejoiced with her" (v. 58). It was an act of divine mercy that caused her to conceive, an act of special mercy that carried an old woman through a full term pregnancy, an act of mercy that gave her strength to deliver, and an act of great mercy that gave birth to the child. The birth of a child is a remarkable instance of God's great mercy; and with the mercy comes a tremendous responsibility. Happy are those homes where these things are known.

The Blessedness Of Affection
In all the circumstances surrounding John's birth, the Lord has graciously scattered nuggets of grace for the edification of our souls. We have before us in the conduct of Elizabeth's family and friends an example of that milk of human kindness, love, affection and care, which ought to flow from our breasts to one another. "They rejoiced with her" (v. 58).

Let all who name the name of Christ follow their example. How much more happiness there would be in this evil world, if such conduct were not so rare. Sympathy in time of sorrow costs little, but is of great value. Oil in your car's engine may appear to be an insignificant thing; but it is vital to the engine's movement; and expressions of care and sympathy may seem insignificant, but they are not. A kind word on a dark day is seldom forgotten. A consoling hand on heavy shoulders is a sweet succour. A thoughtful card at the appropriate time is invaluable. A word of congratulation to one who imagines he is unnoticed is a great boon. A word of appreciation, kindness, encouragement, or thoughtfulness is never out of order.

Pastors, elders, preachers, teachers, and deacons must never forget that thoughtfulness, kindness, and compassion are the very essence of ministering to the souls of men. "Pure religion and undefiled before God and the Father is this, To visit the fatherless and widows in their affliction, and to keep himself unspotted from the world" (James 1:27). In all the strife about words and battles over doctrine, in all the controversies raging about "great" theological issues, we must never overlook or fail to give affection and sympathy to one another (Romans 12:15; Galatians 6:1, 2).

The gospel of Christ, while it sets forth the righteousness, justice and truth of God, is also a great revelation of the love of God and the kindness of our Saviour. The Lord Jesus Christ saw our need and supplied it by the sacrifice of himself (John 3:14-16; Romans 5:8; 1 John 3:16, 17; 4:9-11).

Our Saviour's name is Jehovah-Jireh. He still sees our need and runs to our relief. What an example of kindness he left us. He went to the marriage feast in Cana to celebrate a wedding with some friends in John 2. He went to Bethany in John 11 to weep by the grave of a friend with his broken-hearted sisters. Words are inadequate to describe the blessedness of affection in the eyes of those who need it and receive it.

"And be ye kind one to another, tenderhearted, forgiving one another, even as God for Christ's sake hath forgiven you. Be ye therefore followers of

God, as dear children; And walk in love, as Christ also hath loved us, and hath given himself for us an offering and a sacrifice to God for a sweetsmelling savour" (Ephesians 4:32-5:2).

The Benefit Of Afflictions

As long as we are in this world, we will be children in need of instruction, protection, provision, and discipline, children under the care of our heavenly Father. In verses 59-64 we see in Zacharias' conduct an example of a corrected child.

This old, old man was still a child of God, a child of God who required his Father's rod, even in his old age. Because of his unbelief, Zacharias had been deaf and dumb for nine long months. But those months of affliction had not been useless. He who was so slow to believe now believed every word that proceeded from the mouth of God.

No doubt, the nine months of his adversity had been spent wisely by Zacharias. In all likelihood he learned more about himself and about God, more about the character of his own heart and more about the goodness, grace and glory of God in those nine months than he had learned in all his life previously. Correction had given him instruction. He was now ashamed of his unbelief.

Like Job, he could say, "I have heard of thee by the hearing of the ear, but now mine eye seeth thee" (Job 42:5). Like Hezekiah, when the Lord left him, he found out what was in his heart (2 Chronicles 32:31).

We will never escape trouble in this world of woe. Man is born to trouble as the sparks fly upward (Job 5:7). But in the time of trouble we ought to seek grace that we may learn by the rod of discipline. Any and every sorrow that humbles us, drives us to our knees, and brings us to our God is a great blessing of his grace and evidence of his love. Someone once said, "Sanctified afflictions are spiritual promotions." Trials do not change anything; but they reveal everything.

William Cowper wrote:

> 'Tis my happiness below
> Not to live without the cross,
> But the Saviour's power to know,
> Sanctifying every loss;
> Trials must and will befall;
> But with humble faith to see
> Love inscribed upon them all,
> This is happiness to me.

God in Israel sows the seeds
Of affliction, pain, and toil;
These spring up and choke the weeds
Which would else o'erspread the soil:
Trials make the promise sweet,
Trials give new life to prayer;
Trials bring me to his feet,
Lay me low, and keep me there.

Did I meet no trials here,
No chastisement by the way,
Might I not with reason fear
I should prove a castaway?
Bastards may escape the rod,
Sunk in earthly vain delight;
But the true-born child of God
Must not, would not, if he might."

The Best Of Ambitions

We all have great ambitions for ourselves; but we have especially great ambitions for our children. We want and seek so many things for them; and we make great plans for them. But when I read the last sentence of verse 66, I thought to myself, "This is the best of all ambitions, indeed, the only ambition that is truly worth pursuing with all our hearts." "And the hand of the Lord was with him"!

This great blessing which was upon John the Baptist is the thing we ought to seek, desire, and pray for on behalf of our sons and daughters. "The hand of the Lord was with him." This is "the one thing needful", the one thing that will benefit their souls, the one thing that can never be lost, the one thing that will go with them beyond the grave!

"The hand of the Lord was with him" to protect him, to convert him, to prepare him for his work, to strengthen him in his work, to comfort him in his trials, to sustain him in his dying hours, and to carry him into glory. What the hand of the Lord did for John the Baptist it can do for our sons and daughters as well. Let us seek it for them.

"The Hand Of The Lord Was With Him"

"And his father Zacharias was filled with the Holy Ghost, and prophesied, saying, Blessed be the Lord God of Israel; for he hath visited and redeemed his people, And hath raised up an horn of salvation for us in the house of his servant David; As he spake by the mouth of his holy prophets, which have been since the world began: That we should be saved from our enemies, and from the hand of all that hate us; To perform the mercy promised to our fathers, and to remember his holy covenant; The oath which he sware to our father Abraham, That he would grant unto us, that we being delivered out of the hand of our enemies might serve him without fear, In holiness and righteousness before him, all the days of our life. And thou, child, shalt be called the prophet of the Highest: for thou shalt go before the face of the Lord to prepare his ways; To give knowledge of salvation unto his people by the remission of their sins, Through the tender mercy of our God; whereby the dayspring from on high hath visited us, To give light to them that sit in darkness and in the shadow of death, to guide our feet into the way of peace. And the child grew, and waxed strong in spirit, and was in the deserts till the day of his shewing unto Israel" (Luke 1:67-80).

Chapter 11

Three Great Reasons For Praise

The Prophecy
Zacharias was not a prophet; but his song was a prophecy. It stands before us as one of the most instructive prophesies ever given. He was not a musician; but his prophecy was a song, one of the greatest hymns ever written. What qualified him to write this song and give this prophecy? Luke tells us in verse 67. "Zacharias was filled with the Holy Ghost, and prophesied."

God not only forgave the old man for his unbelief, he poured out his grace upon him in an extraordinary manner by filling him with the Holy Ghost. To be filled with the Holy Ghost is to be controlled by the Spirit. Every believer ought to seek, always, to be filled with the Holy Spirit, ruled by the Holy Spirit in every aspect of our lives (Ephesians 5:18). The Spirit filled life is not an emotional frenzy of senseless religion. The Spirit filled life is a life of wisdom, "understanding what the will of the Lord is" (Ephesians 5:17). It is a life of thanksgiving and praise, "giving thanks always for all things unto God the Father in the name of our Lord Jesus Christ" (Ephesians 5:20). And it is a life of voluntary submission, submitting my will and my life to Christ and his people, "submitting yourselves one to another in the fear of God" (Ephesians 5:21).

But there is another sense in which a man is filled with the Holy Ghost. Zacharias was filled with the Holy Ghost in the sense that he was given a special unction, a special anointing to deliver the Word of God. He was divinely inspired. That is what every God-called preacher wants and seeks. He wants, more than words can express, to preach to those who hear him as a man filled with the Holy Ghost, to deliver a message directly from God to eternity bound sinners, for the praise, honour and glory of God alone! It will be your mercy to pray that God will grant that to his servant every time you go to the house of God for worship. In these last words of Luke 1 we have a message directly from God to his people, for our good and his glory.

The grace of God toward Zacharias in this passage is as instructive as it is remarkable. The Lord graciously removed the affliction he had brought upon himself by unbelief, though he had done nothing to merit such mercy, or even to seek it. Let us never fail to remember that God's grace does not wait upon us. Grace comes before we seek it; and we can never deserve it. It flows to chosen sinners from God's free, sovereign love for us in Christ.

Because of his unbelief, the Lord had made the old priest a deaf-mute for nine months. Now, the Lord graciously took away his reproach, opened his mouth, loosed his tongue, and unstopped his ears. What will this old man say? What will he talk about? Miracles? No. His experiences? No. The angelic visit? No. Zacharias spoke not as a man, but as a prophet. He spoke for God. So he passed by all those things which tickle men's ears and spoke about God, his grace, his Son, his redemption, his salvation and his praise!

The passage before us contains the very first words spoken by Zacharias after the Lord loosed his tongue. He had been a deaf mute for nine long months. But now, after the birth of his son, John the Baptist, the old servant of God speaks to God in a song of praise; and his song of praise to God was, to his newborn son and to all future generations, a song of instruction. Moreover, his song of praise and instruction was a prophecy concerning both the person and work of Christ and the ministry of John the Baptist. Hawker again writes:

"No sooner is his tongue untied, but the Lord loosens both heart and tongue to speak the Lord's praise; and to proclaim the Lord's mercy. And how doth he praise the Lord? Do not fail to observe, it is, as the God of Israel: Israel's God in covenant. All, and every part of redemption is, to perform the mercy, promised. Yes! For the Lord's Christ is the mercy promised: the first born in the womb of mercy; the whole of mercy; yea, mercy itself in the full; for there is no mercy, but in Christ. Everything which can be called mercy must have Christ in it, or it is no mercy, be it what it may. It must have its very nature from Christ; its sweetness from Christ, its value from Christ, and its everlasting continuance from Christ. And hence Zacharias harps upon this sweet string; that it was to perform the mercy promised, and to fulfil Jehovah's covenant and oath, in all the blessings of Christ, for evermore."

God Our Saviour

This old man, filled with the Holy Ghost, gave praise to God for three specific reasons; and every believer has great reason to give praise to God for these three things: God our Saviour (v. 68), God's great salvation (vv. 69-75), and God's chosen servant (vv. 76-80).

Zacharias' first word of thanksgiving and praise is about God our Saviour. "Blessed be the Lord God of Israel; for he hath visited and redeemed his people" (v. 67). Let us ever be quick with praise and thanksgiving to the great God, our Saviour. "Blessed be the Lord God of Israel"! We must never forget to thank God for his blessings; but we ought to thank and praise him first and foremost for his Being! "Blessed be the Lord God of Israel"! The entire first chapter of Ephesians is taken up with blessing God our Saviour, the great, glorious, triune God. There the Apostle Paul was inspired to write out words of praise, ascribing blessedness and glory to God the Father who planned salvation for us, to God the Son who purchased salvation for us, and to God the Holy Spirit who performs salvation in us. "Not unto us, O LORD, not unto us, but unto thy name give glory, for thy mercy, and for thy truth's sake" (Psalm 115:1). Let us ever give praise to our God because he is God. "Bless the Lord, O my soul. All that is within me, bless his holy name" (Psalm 103:1).

God's Great Salvation
After ascribing all praise, honour and glory to God, Zacharias offers thanksgiving and praise for God's great salvation. That which fills a man's mouth when he is filled with the Spirit is God's salvation (vv. 69-75).

What a description we have here of God's salvation! In verse 69 we are told that God has "raised up an horn of salvation". Those words tell us four things about salvation: (1.) It is God's work. God raised up this horn of salvation. (2.) It is an exalted salvation for it is "raised up". (3.) It is a powerful, omnipotent salvation. The horn is a symbol of power. (4.) It is a bountiful salvation "a horn", a cornucopia, "of salvation".

God's salvation is for a specific people. It was never God's intention or purpose to save all men. He did not send his Son to save all men. God's salvation is for his elect, the house of David, the Israel of God.

In verse 70 we see that this great salvation of which we speak is a Bible salvation, spoken of by all the prophets, "As he spake by the mouth of his holy prophets, which have been since the world began."

God's salvation is a very old salvation. This was not some new thing, which Christ came to do, and John came to preach. God's salvation was spoken of, ordained and accomplished by the triune God in eternity (Romans 8:29, 30; Ephesians 1:3-6; 2 Timothy 1:9). And faithful men have spoken about God's great salvation since the beginning of time. Adam told his sons about it. Enoch proclaimed it. Noah preached it. Job declared it. And it was spoken of by all the prophets of God. God's prophets have always spoken about just one thing; God's salvation. And they still do.

Salvation is the complete deliverance of our souls from all our enemies into the glorious liberty of the sons of God. "That we should be saved from our enemies, and from the hand of all that hate us" (v. 71).

"Who shall lay any thing to the charge of God's elect? It is God that justifieth. Who is he that condemneth? It is Christ that died, yea rather, that is risen again, who is even at the right hand of God, who also maketh intercession for us. Who shall separate us from the love of Christ? shall tribulation, or distress, or persecution, or famine, or nakedness, or peril, or sword? As it is written, For thy sake we are killed all the day long; we are accounted as sheep for the slaughter. Nay, in all these things we are more than conquerors through him that loved us. For I am persuaded, that neither death, nor life, nor angels, nor principalities, nor powers, nor things present, nor things to come, Nor height, nor depth, nor any other creature, shall be able to separate us from the love of God, which is in Christ Jesus our Lord" (Romans 8:33-39).

Salvation is an act and work of God's covenant mercy. It is the performance of "the mercy promised to our fathers, and to remember his holy covenant; The oath which he sware to our father Abraham" (vv. 72, 73). Salvation is the performance of God's mercy, God's covenant and God's oath (Hebrews 6:16-20).

God wrought salvation causes sinners to become the willing servants of God forever. "That he would grant unto us, that we being delivered out of the hand of our enemies might serve him without fear, In holiness and righteousness before him, all the days of our life" (vv. 74, 75). The Lord our God has saved us that we might serve him. Do you see that? Those who are saved by God serve God without fear, in true holiness and righteousness, the holiness and righteousness of Christ that he has made ours by his grace, walking before him in his immediate presence all the days of our lives. What a blessed privilege that is!

God's Chosen Servant
Zacharias offered praise and thanksgiving to God for God himself. Then he gave thanks to God for his great salvation. In verses 76-80 Zacharias expresses praise and thanksgiving for the gift of his chosen servant.

"And thou, child, shalt be called the prophet of the Highest: for thou shalt go before the face of the Lord to prepare his ways; To give knowledge of salvation unto his people by the remission of their sins, Through the tender mercy of our God; whereby the dayspring from on high hath visited us, To give light to them that sit in darkness and in the shadow of death, to guide our

80

feet into the way of peace. And the child grew, and waxed strong in spirit, and was in the deserts till the day of his shewing unto Israel."

Faithful, gospel preachers are the gifts of Christ to his church in this world. It is by these chosen men, specifically called and gifted for the work of the gospel, that God speaks to, ministers to, calls, converts, edifies, comforts, corrects, feeds and cares for chosen sinners in this world (Ephesians 4:11-16).

Gospel preachers do not seek, or want praise from men. Faithful men seek and crave the praise of God alone. We must never make idols out of God's servants, treating them as priests, mediators, or lords over our souls. Yet, God's servants are not to be despised and treated as useless things. Both the welfare of your own soul and the happiness and peace of God's church is greatly determined by the love and respect God's people show for and to those who preach the gospel to them (1 Thessalonians 5:12, 13).

Here, in Luke 1:76-80 we see an old, old man talking about his own son; but talking about his son not as his son, but as God's messenger to men. What Zacharias said here concerning John the Baptist is specifically a prophecy concerning that great man and his extraordinary ministry. However, it is also a declaration of every faithful gospel preacher's work in this world.

The gospel preacher is the servant of God, whose business it is to prepare the way of the Lord (v. 76; Isaiah 40:3, 4). Men who are God's servants are sent with a specific message to declare, by which they prepare the way of the Lord (vv. 77-79). It is every preacher's business and responsibility, his only business and responsibility, "To give knowledge of salvation". He cannot give salvation; but he must give the knowledge of it. And there is no knowledge of salvation apart from the preaching of the gospel.

The salvation we proclaim is not a general salvation hoped for, but the salvation of "his people" accomplished. The only way salvation can come to sinners is "by the remission of their sins". The source and cause of this salvation by the remission of sins is "the tender mercy of our God"! The only way this salvation could ever be accomplished is by the incarnation, life, and death of Christ as our Substitute, "Whereby the dayspring from on high hath visited us". It is the preacher's business "to give light to them that sit in darkness". By the preaching of the gospel, God's servants "guide our feet into the way of peace".

For every chosen preacher, God has appointed "the day of his showing to Israel" (v. 80). If a man is chosen of God for this great and glorious work, he will not need to wave his own flag and toot his own horn. God knows where he is. At the time appointed, God will show his people who he is. "And when this cometh to pass, (lo, it will come,) then shall they know that a prophet hath been among them" (Ezekiel 33:33).

"And it came to pass in those days, that there went out a decree from Caesar Augustus, that all the world should be taxed. (And this taxing was first made when Cyrenius was governor of Syria.) And all went to be taxed, every one into his own city. And Joseph also went up from Galilee, out of the city of Nazareth, into Judaea, unto the city of David, which is called Bethlehem; (because he was of the house and lineage of David:) To be taxed with Mary his espoused wife, being great with child. And so it was, that, while they were there, the days were accomplished that she should be delivered. And she brought forth her firstborn son, and wrapped him in swaddling clothes, and laid him in a manger; because there was no room for them in the inn" (Luke 2:1-7).

Chapter 12

The Birth Of Our Saviour

Here the Holy Spirit tells us about the birth of the incarnate Son of God (not the birth of the Son of God; but the birth of the incarnate Son of God), the Lord Jesus Christ, our Saviour and Redeemer. Never, since the world began, was there such a birth. This was the birth of him for whom and by whom the worlds were made. Here we see God manifest in the flesh (1 Timothy 3:16). What we have before us in these verses is the birth of him of whom all the law and the prophets of the Old Testament spoke. The Lord Jesus Christ was born as a man at Bethlehem that he might die as a man at Calvary to redeem his people from the curse of the law. This is exactly what our Lord Jesus himself tells us in Matthew 20:28, and what the Holy Spirit tells us in Galatians 4:4, 5.

The Purpose Of Our Saviour's Birth
Luke does not record the purpose of Christ's birth in our text. But the Holy Spirit has recorded it for us in many places in holy scripture. And it would be pointless for me to write about Christ's birth, if I did not tell you why he came into this world in human flesh. We are told the purpose of our Saviour's birth in the angel's message to Joseph some nine months before this. "And she shall bring forth a son, and thou shalt call his name JESUS: for he shall save his people from their sins" (Matthew 1:21).

The Lord Jesus Christ was God the eternal Son before he came into this world in human flesh. The Son of God had a people in this world, called "his people", before he came here to save them. These people are God's elect, sinners chosen to salvation from eternity (2 Thessalonians 2:13, 14). The Lord Jesus Christ came into this world on an errand of mercy, as our

Substitute, Representative and Covenant Surety, to save his people from their sins. And, blessed be his name, he did what he came here to do. He saved his people, all of them, from their sins (Hebrews 10:5-14).

The Lord Jesus Christ saves his people from their sins by three mighty acts of grace, which he alone could perform: first, the Lord Jesus saved all his people by blood redemption, by effectual atonement, by the satisfaction of divine justice, when he laid down his life for us at Calvary (Galatians 3:13, 14; Hebrews 9:12); second, the Lord Jesus saves his people, each one redeemed by his blood, by the irresistible power and grace of his Holy Spirit in regeneration (Ephesians 2:1-5); and, third, the Lord Jesus will save his people by the resurrection of our bodies in the last day.

The Time Of Our Saviour's Birth

We have in this passage a marvellous display of God's wisdom and of his sovereignty. We are specifically informed that our Saviour was born into this world in those days when Caesar Augustus, the first Roman emperor, made a "decree that all the world should be taxed".

This is an important fact in the whole scheme of things. The Lord God promised, through his servant Jacob, that Israel would not cease to be a civil state until Christ came to redeem and save his people (Genesis 49:10). Luke here tells us of the precise fulfilment of Jacob's prophecy. The Jews were under the dominion of Rome. They had lost all legal, civil power as a nation. Strangers ruled over them and demanded taxes from them. The nation of Israel was without a government of its own for the first time in their history. No sooner did Augustus tax the world than Messiah came! It was the "due time" and "the fulness of time".

Divine providence had now arranged the best time possible for Christ to come into the world. When he had fully proved that the world by wisdom knew not God (1 Corinthians 1:21), God stepped into the world to make himself known. Religious ritualism had left men and women utterly ignorant of God and morally bankrupt. The philosophers, poets, historians, architects and rulers of all the Gentile world left the human race in spiritual darkness, moral corruption and political violence that only grew worse with time.

Yet, at this precise time required, for the first time since the tower of Babel, all the civilized world was under one government. By the time he sent his Son into the world, God had arranged the whole world in such a way as to make a path for the gospel into all the world. Let us ever find solace for our souls in this fact. All the events of this world, all history, all governments, all times are in the hands of our great God.

"My times are in thy hand" (Psalm 31:15). He always knows and always does what is best. We ought never worry and fret about the course and condition of this world, even in such dark days as these. We act like we know better than God what is best. What foolishness! I once read that Martin Luther used to frequently say to his worrying, fretting friend, Philip Melanchthon, "Philip, stop trying to govern the world." We would be wise to heed those words. Let us ever live in this world as the loyal subjects of the all-wise King of kings and Lord of lords. He who is our God is God indeed, God over all! He is too wise to err, too good to do wrong, and too strong to fail.

The Place Of Our Saviour's Birth
Our Saviour was not born in Nazareth of Galilee, where Mary and Joseph resided. Instead, he was born at Bethlehem. The prophet Micah had prophesied hundreds of years before it came to pass that the Lord Jesus must be born at Bethlehem (Micah 5:2); and so it came to pass.

Once more, we have before us a marvellous display of God's sovereign, absolute rule of all things in providence to accomplish the good purpose of his grace toward chosen sinners. He, who orders all things in heaven, earth, and hell, turns the hearts of kings whithersoever he will. "The king's heart is in the hand of the LORD, as the rivers of water: he turneth it whithersoever he will" (Proverbs 21:1). It was the Lord God who caused Augustus to make this decree and begin enforcing it at precisely the time when Mary's pregnancy had come to full term.

Neither Augustus nor Cyrenius had any idea what they were doing, or why. I have no doubt at all, being typical politicians, they acted only upon the unprincipled principle of expediency. What they were actually doing was carrying forth the eternal designs of our God for the salvation of his people and the glory of his own great name. Like the king of Assyria, they meant it not so, neither did their hearts think so, but they were performing the work of the Lord (Isaiah 10:5-12).

This act of the first Roman emperor was an act which laid the foundation for the kingdom of God, before which all the kingdoms of this world must soon bow and crumble. Observe this and rejoice to know that our God graciously and wisely rules and overrules all things, the good and the evil, for the accomplishment of his will. "Surely the wrath of man shall praise thee: the remainder of wrath shalt thou restrain" (Psalm 76:10).

Our heavenly Father's providential rule of the universe ought to quieten our hearts while we sail through the troubled waters of this world. If we believe God, we should never be greatly disturbed by the affairs of this world, or the conduct of earthly rulers. We ought to regard all things as the will of God. We should look upon every action of every political ruler as the oracle of God. It mattered not whither Shimei cursed David or praised David,

God blessed him! Let us learn to regard all men and all devils, too, as creatures of God Almighty, created to serve his purpose, without the ability to think, wriggle, or move, except by the will of God (Ecclesiastes 5:8).

The Manner Of Our Saviour's Birth

"And she brought forth her firstborn son, and wrapped him in swaddling clothes, and laid him in a manger; because there was no room for them in the inn." Let us never forget that it was through his own great humiliation that the Son of God obtained eternal glory for us. It was through his life of holy suffering as well as his death that he obtained eternal redemption for us (2 Corinthians 8:9).

Learn this, too, and learn it well. God is no respecter of persons; and we must not be. We must never allow ourselves to form opinions of people's character and worth based upon their poverty or wealth, their face or place, or their race or rank. May God the Holy Spirit give us grace to follow our Saviour's example in dealing with one another (Philippians 2:1-11). O Holy Spirit, give us the mind of Christ!

The Birth Of Our Saviour

"And there were in the same country shepherds abiding in the field, keeping watch over their flock by night. And, lo, the angel of the Lord came upon them, and the glory of the Lord shone round about them: and they were sore afraid. And the angel said unto them, Fear not: for, behold, I bring you good tidings of great joy, which shall be to all people. For unto you is born this day in the city of David a Saviour, which is Christ the Lord. And this shall be a sign unto you; Ye shall find the babe wrapped in swaddling clothes, lying in a manger. And suddenly there was with the angel a multitude of the heavenly host praising God, and saying, Glory to God in the highest, and on earth peace, good will toward men. And it came to pass, as the angels were gone away from them into heaven, the shepherds said one to another, Let us now go even unto Bethlehem, and see this thing which is come to pass, which the Lord hath made known unto us. And they came with haste, and found Mary, and Joseph, and the babe lying in a manger. And when they had seen it, they made known abroad the saying which was told them concerning this child. And all they that heard it wondered at those things which were told them by the shepherds. But Mary kept all these things, and pondered them in her heart. And the shepherds returned, glorifying and praising God for all the things that they had heard and seen, as it was told unto them" (Luke 2:8-20).

Chapter 13

The Message Of The Incarnation

The incarnation and birth of our Lord Jesus Christ is an undeniable fact of history. Let carping scoffers say and do what they will, it is a fact that cannot be denied. Yet, it is a fact the meaning of which very, very few understand. The meaning of the incarnation can be understood only by those who are taught of God. All spiritual knowledge comes by divine revelation. Those who are taught of God are well taught. But until a person is taught of God, he cannot know, discern, or understand anything spiritual (1 Corinthians 2:12-14). With that fact in mind, let us ever pray, as we open the Book of God, that God the Holy Spirit will teach us the wondrous things revealed in the Book. Here are four plain truths.

The Men Chosen
First, in verse 8 we see the men chosen by God to whom the glad tidings of Christ's birth first came and by whom the message of his birth was first proclaimed. "And there were in the same country shepherds abiding in the field, keeping watch over their flock by night." The first announcement of Christ's birth did not come to the princes, priests and educated men at Jerusalem. God passed by the scribes, Pharisees and Sadducees, and made himself and his word known to a few weak, uneducated, insignificant, poor, despised shepherds.

Here we see something of God's method of grace. God is no respecter of persons. It is his common method of operation to pass by the high and mighty, and choose the poor and lowly. He normally passes by the wise and prudent, leaving them in the confusion of their imaginary brilliance, and reveals his grace and glory in Christ unto babes.

This is God's common method of operation in all things. He chooses the most unlikely vessels to be vessels of mercy, and the most unlikely instruments to be the tools with which he performs his wondrous works in this world. Poverty is no barrier against grace. Lack of education, or even natural ability, is no barrier against usefulness. God has mercy on whom he will; and he uses whom he will (James 2:5; 1 Corinthians 1:26-29).

These men were shepherds, hardworking, labouring men, and worshippers of God. Honest labour is no barrier to divine worship. Really, there should be no need for that statement; but there are some who seem to think that piety is sitting at home, reading their Bibles, studying theology and letting other people assume their responsibilities. Nothing could be further from the truth. Our Lord teaches us plainly that men and women who neglect their families and responsibilities in the name of worshipping and serving God are liars and hypocrites who have denied the faith.

He who worships God best does so as he serves him in this world. Honest labour is no barrier to holiness. Diligent work is no hindrance to divine instruction. Moses was keeping sheep when God appeared to him in the bush, and called him to be a prophet. Gideon was threshing wheat when the Lord called him to deliver Israel. And Elisha was ploughing the field when the Lord God made him a prophet. In fact, I cannot find any place in the Book of God where any man ever volunteered to be a prophet, except a false prophet.

The Angelic Messengers
Second, in verses 9-14 Luke tells us that the angel of the Lord was sent of God to announce our Saviour's birth. Then, suddenly, a great multitude of angels appeared, praising God. The language used by the Spirit of God in this passage seems to suggest that all the host of heaven, all the angels of God, suddenly flew like a bolt of lightning to join in the praise of the incarnate God. It is written, "When he bringeth in the firstbegotten into the world, he saith, And let all the angels of God worship him" (Hebrews 1:6).

The first worshippers of the incarnate God were not the sinners he had come to save, but the angels of God who had never sinned. No doubt, there is much more here than I am able to grasp; but when I think of the entire host of heaven rushing to the earth to worship our Saviour, as he came into the world, two things are obvious: first, what great interest the angels of God have in the person and work of Christ! And, second, how greatly the angels of heaven must love God's elect! They protect God's chosen, preserving the elect unto salvation (Hebrews 1:14). They rejoice in the conversion of redeemed sinners (Luke 15:10). The angels meet with the assemblies of God's saints, that they might learn from us the wonders of redemption

(Ephesians 3:10). And they shall be gathered with us in the general assembly of elect men and elect angels in heaven (Hebrews 12:22-24).

The Message

Third, I want us to see and understand the message of the incarnation set before us in verses 10-14. In verse 10 we read, "And the angel said unto them, Fear not: for, behold, I bring you good tidings of great joy, which shall be to all people". The message of the incarnation is a message of "good tidings". The gospel of the grace of God is not good advice. It is good news, "good tidings". The coming of Christ to save his people reveals the good will and amazing love of God to his elect. The good tidings of grace declare that all the law and prophets are fulfilled in Christ. These are "good tidings of great joy", of joy unspeakable and full of glory, the everlasting joy and peace of God's salvation.

The good tidings of grace proclaimed in the gospel are "to all the people". The words, "which shall be to all the people", do not suggest that the gospel brings joy to all without exception. The gospel does not bring joy to all men. It brought no joy to Herod, the Scribes, the Pharisees, or the Sadducees. To some it brings greater condemnation. To the reprobate and unbelieving, it is a savour of death unto death. But it does bring this great joy to all nations, to all God's elect, scattered among the nations, and to all needy sinners everywhere.

The message of the incarnation is the proclamation of the sovereign Lord who has come to save his people from their sins. "For unto you is born this day in the city of David a Saviour, which is Christ the Lord" (v. 11). The "you" unto whom Christ was born, whom he came to save, is God's elect, his people, the seed of Abraham (Isaiah 9:6; Hebrews 2:14-16). This One of whom the angel spoke is "a Saviour". A Saviour is one who saves, not one who merely tries to save, or merely offers salvation. Our Lord Jesus Christ is the Lord Jesus Christ, our Saviour!

He is the Christ, God's anointed. The man who is our Saviour, anointed of God, is himself the Lord. He is the Lord our God, the Lord our Righteousness, and the Lord of all. He is the Lord and the Saviour of whom Isaiah spoke. Luke, writing by divine inspiration in verse 12, tells us pointedly that the virgin and her child, of whom Isaiah spoke (Isaiah 7:14), is Mary and the Lord Jesus, her virgin born child. "And this shall be a sign unto you; Ye shall find the babe wrapped in swaddling clothes, lying in a manger."

The message of the incarnation, the message of the gospel is the revelation and declaration of the glory of God in Christ. "And suddenly there was with the angel a multitude of the heavenly host praising God, and saying,

Glory to God in the highest, and on earth peace, good will toward men" (vv. 13, 14). The psalmist declared that his glory would be great in God's salvation (Psalm 21:5); and it is! The gospel is called "the gospel of the glory of God". We see the wisdom and power of God in creation. We see the justice and truth of God in the law. We know something about the holiness and righteousness of God by nature. But the glory of God is nowhere seen so clearly as it is revealed in the coming, obedience and death of the Lord Jesus Christ as the sinner's Substitute.

Only in Christ crucified do we see how God can be both a just God and a Saviour (Isaiah 45:20; Romans 3:24-26). Only at Calvary do we see all the infinite perfections of God's glorious, holy Being in complete and perfect harmony. We see his wisdom and prudence in the scheme of redemption. His mercy, love and grace are made manifest in giving his Son to be our sin-atoning sacrifice. We behold his justice and truth in the execution of our blessed Redeemer, when he was made sin for us. And we see and know his immutable faithfulness in forgiving sin for Christ's sake. The Lord God has saved us for his name's sake (Psalm 106:8; Ephesians 1:3-14); and he shall show forth the greatness of his glory in us in the last day (Ephesians 2:7).

The gospel, the message of the incarnation, is the proclamation on earth of peace "on earth peace". The gospel nowhere promises political peace, civil peace, domestic peace, or carnal peace of any kind. Just the opposite. Our Lord said, "I came not to send peace, but a sword." The peace which has come to the earth is Christ himself, who is our Peace (Ephesians 2:14). Jesus Christ our Lord, our Daysman, our Mediator, our Substitute has made peace between the holy Lord God and fallen, guilty sinners, by the blood of his cross. He has made a legal and a lasting peace for us; and Christ, who is our peace, gives us peace, "peace which passeth all understanding" (Philippians 4:7). He gives us the peace of his pardon, the peace of his providence and the peace of his presence. And our blessed Saviour establishes and maintains peace between men (Colossians 3:10, 11).

The message of the incarnation is God's "good will towards man". The Holy Spirit does not leave us to guess what that good will of God toward man is. This is not a book in which we must fill in the blanks. God the Holy Spirit tells us exactly what the good will of God is. God's good will is the salvation of his elect by Christ Jesus, for the everlasting praise and glory of his own great name (John 6:37-40; Ephesians 1:3-12).

Obedient Faith

Fourth, we must not overlook the obedience of faith exemplified in these shepherds in verses 15-19.

92

"And it came to pass, as the angels were gone away from them into heaven, the shepherds said one to another, Let us now go even unto Bethlehem, and see this thing which is come to pass, which the Lord hath made known unto us. And they came with haste, and found Mary, and Joseph, and the babe lying in a manger. And when they had seen it, they made known abroad the saying which was told them concerning this child. And all they that heard it wondered at those things which were told them by the shepherds. But Mary kept all these things, and pondered them in her heart."

They had God's Word. Their duty was plain. No doubt the messengers were unusual. The message of God was given in an unusual way. Yet, without a moment's hesitation, without the least hint of doubt or question, they did exactly what God told them to do.

When our path of duty is clear, when we know what the will of the Lord is, when we know what he would have us to do, we must not confer with flesh and blood. Obedience is always right.

These shepherds did not stop and say to themselves or one another, "Who will take care of our sheep? Someone must keep them from the wolves." They left their sheep in the care of him who told them to go to Bethlehem. Let us do the same.

God has called me to preach the gospel. That is my responsibility. I am his servant. If I would serve him faithfully, I must leave the care of my family in his hands. Anything less on my part would be disobedience. In fact, the Lord God has specifically promised that none shall ever suffer loss by obeying him (Exodus 34:23, 24).

As with these shepherds, our journey's end will be glorious. Our pilgrimage through this world, begun in faith, will end in praise. "And the shepherds returned, glorifying and praising God for all the things that they had heard and seen, as it was told unto them" (v. 20). So it shall be with us (Revelation 19:1-6).

"And when eight days were accomplished for the circumcising of the child, his name was called JESUS, which was so named of the angel before he was conceived in the womb. And when the days of her purification according to the law of Moses were accomplished, they brought him to Jerusalem, to present him to the Lord; (As it is written in the law of the Lord, Every male that openeth the womb shall be called holy to the Lord;) And to offer a sacrifice according to that which is said in the law of the Lord, A pair of turtledoves, or two young pigeons" (Luke 2:21-24).

Chapter 14

"According To The Law"

Everything our Saviour did as a man he did "according to the law". When the Lord Jesus Christ came into the world to save his people from their sins, he willingly put himself under the law and became voluntarily subject to the law in all things as a man. He did so because God cannot justify the guilty except upon the grounds of strict justice. Righteousness must be maintained and justice must be satisfied in the exercise of mercy, love and grace. He who is our God and Saviour is "a just God and a Saviour" (Isaiah 45:20). "By mercy and truth iniquity is purged" (Proverbs 16:6). Our blessed Saviour magnified the law and made it honourable as our Substitute, "that we might receive the adoption of sons" in the sweet experience of his saving grace (Isaiah 42:21; Galatians 4:4, 5).

Though the yoke of the law was a heavy yoke, and only a shadow of good things to come, if we would have those good things, Christ must bear the law's heavy yoke for us. And he did it as our willing Substitute and Surety. Though the carnal ordinances of the law were what the Holy Spirit calls "weak and beggarly elements" (Galatians 4:9), and but the "rudiments of the world" (Colossians 2:8, 20), our Lord Jesus Christ submitted to all the ordinances and institutions of the law as a man, that he might fulfil the law for us and bring it to an honourable end. He fulfilled all the law for us, from the beginning to the end of his manhood, that he might by his obedience unto death bring in everlasting righteousness for us and put away our sins forever, and that he might do so in a way that honours God.

Here in Luke 2:21-24 the Spirit of God shows us how the Lord Jesus, as our Saviour, Mediator, Surety and Substitute, from the very beginning of his holy manhood, fulfilled the law of God in the room and stead of his people.

Circumcised Surety
When he was just a baby, eight days old, the Lord Jesus Christ was circumcised as our covenant Surety. Circumcision was instituted under the

law as a symbol of the new birth. The cutting away the filth of the flesh showed the necessity of God's elect being purified by his grace (Titus 3:5, 6). But Christ had no sin. Why was he circumcised? The answer is obvious. He was circumcised as our Surety.

Circumcision identified him as one with Abraham's seed whom he came to save (Hebrews 2:16, 17). Circumcision required the shedding of blood. Here he shed a few drops of blood, by a painful act done to him, by order of God's law, as a foreshadowing of the pouring out of his life's blood unto death, by the order of God's law, in the most painful, ignominious manner possible. By submitting to this ordinance of the law, our blessed Saviour voluntarily made himself a debtor to do the whole law for us (Galatians 5:3).

Circumcision was the legally required pledge of every Israelite, that he was a debtor to keep the whole law. Our Lord Jesus Christ, "by being circumcised", wrote Thomas Goodwin, "did as it were set his hand to it, being made sin for us." The ceremonial law consisted much in sacrifices. Christ hereby obliged himself to offer, not the blood of bulls and goats, but his own blood as our Substitute.

It is a blessed thing to see the Christ of God standing before the law in our place, at the very beginning of his humanity, as he entered this world to redeem and save his people, making himself a debtor to the law, that we might never be debtors to the law (Romans 6:14, 15; 7:4; 8:1-4; 10:4).

Named Saviour
When he was circumcised, the incarnate God was named as our Saviour. "His name was called JESUS, which was so named of the angel before he was conceived in the womb." This name, "JESUS", or Joshua, was given to our Lord by the express command of God by the angel, both to Joseph and to Mary, before he was conceived in the womb (Matthew 1:21; Luke 1:31).

"Jesus" was a common name in ancient times (Colossians 4:11); and many are called "Jesus" who are not Saviours at all. Our Lord was given this name because it was the name of two very eminent types of him in the Old Testament: Joshua who led Israel into the land of promised rest, and Joshua the priest upon his throne, who represented the removal of sin by Christ (Zechariah 3:1-5), and also represented our Lord Jesus Christ upon his throne as our Intercessor King (Zechariah 6:11-13). Our Lord Jesus Christ was named Jesus because he was sent into this world to save his people from their sins (Matthew 1:21); and save them he shall. "His name shall endure for ever: his name shall be continued as long as the sun: and men shall be blessed in him: all nations shall call him blessed" (Psalm 72:17).

How sweet the name of Jesus sounds
In a believer's ear!
It soothes his sorrows, heals his wounds,
And drives away his fear.

It makes the wounded spirit whole,
And calms the troubled breast,
'Tis manna to the hungry soul,
And to the weary, rest.

Dear name! The rock on which I build,
My shield and hiding place:
My never failing treasury filled,
With boundless stores of grace!

John Newton

The Firstborn

Our Lord Jesus Christ was presented in the temple at Jerusalem as the Firstborn, "according to the law".

"And when the days of her purification according to the law of Moses were accomplished, they brought him to Jerusalem, to present him to the Lord; (As it is written in the law of the Lord, Every male that openeth the womb shall be called holy to the Lord)" (Luke 2:22, 23).

Mary came to the temple to offer her sacrifices for ceremonial purification forty days after the Lord Jesus was born, "according to the law" (Leviticus 12:4-6). Certainly, we have before us a reminder of the fact that there is no cleansing from uncleanness of any kind, except by the blood of a sacrifice. If we would be clean before God, it must be by blood.

The Lord Jesus came into his temple to fulfil the prophecy given by Malachi (Malachi 3:1). And our Saviour, the God-man, came into the temple, according to the law of God, as the firstborn, as God's firstborn, that one who is sanctified and holy before God (Exodus 13:2; Numbers 3:13).

Christ is the Firstborn among many brethren (Romans 8:29), the Firstborn of every creature (Colossians 1:15), and the Firstborn from the dead (Colossians 1:18). Throughout the Old Testament, the preeminence of our Lord Jesus Christ as our Saviour was typified as the first, firstborn, firstfruits and the firstlings of the flock and of the herd. Indeed, everything recorded in the Old Testament foreshadows him who is the Alpha and the Omega, the First and the Last, and the Sum and the Substance of all things in the salvation of his people (Luke 24:25-27, 44). There is nothing in the Book of God that does not speak of our all-glorious Christ, nothing that does not, in one way or another, set forth his supremacy, excellence and glory as God our Saviour. Nowhere is this fact more evident than in those passages dealing with the firstborn.

The firstborn symbolized a father's might and strength, "the excellency of dignity and the excellency of power" (Genesis 49:3). In that awesome night, when the Lord God slew the firstborn of both man and beast among the Egyptians (Exodus 12:29), he claimed the firstborn of both man and beast in Israel as his own, requiring that they be sanctified unto him (Exodus 13:2).

It was God himself, and God alone, who put a difference between the firstborn in Egypt and the firstborn in Israel on that night. We are expressly taught by the Spirit of God that everything on that passover night was typical of Christ, who as "our Passover was sacrificed for us" (1 Corinthians 5:7). The sprinkling of the blood of the lamb of the first year, without blemish, and without spot, on the houses of the Israelites, was the one thing that put a difference between the firstborn of Israel and the firstborn of Egypt. The blood of the lamb alone saved them from destruction. This we are plainly told in Exodus 11:7.

As it was on that great night of judgment and mercy, so the year of Christ's redeemed is both the day of vengeance and the day of salvation (Isaiah 63:3-5). When the Son of God died as our Substitute upon the cursed tree, he both bore all the vengeance of God's holy wrath for us, to the full satisfaction of divine justice; and obtained eternal redemption and salvation for us (Hebrews 9:12). At the same time, he declares, "the day of vengeance is in my heart". Yes, there is a day appointed and fixed by him, when our God will execute judgment in the firstlings of his enemies, as well as of mercy in the firstlings of his people.

The birthright of the firstborn among the children of Israel gave him primacy in the family. To him belonged the right of priesthood (Numbers 3:12, 13; 3:40-45; 8:15-18). The firstborn was given a double portion among his brethren (Deuteronomy 21:17). And to the firstborn it was promised, "thou art he whom thy brethren shall praise: thy hand shall be in the neck of thine enemies; thy father's children shall bow down before thee" (Genesis 49:8). All these Old Testament declarations were intended to show forth the majesty of Christ as "the firstborn among many brethren". All the offering required of God for every male that opened the womb pointed to our Lord Jesus (Exodus 13:2; 34:19, 20; Leviticus 12:6; Luke 2:21-24).

Robert Hawker suggested that the scriptures, when speaking of "the firstborn that openeth the womb", must have been prophetic of the virgin birth of our Saviour. He wrote, "For strictly and properly speaking, none but the Lord Jesus ever did open the womb ... In every other instance, from the creation of the world, as anatomists well know, it is accomplished at the time of conception." Our blessed Saviour, "the firstborn", was conceived in Mary's virgin womb by the overshadowing power of God the Holy Spirit. He opened Mary's virgin womb when he came forth from it to accomplish our redemption. Thus, throughout the Levitical dispensation, the firstborn of man and beast directed the eye of faith to him whom the triune God appointed to have everlasting preeminence as "the firstborn". In all things it is, was and forever shall be the will of the eternal God, that Christ have preeminence in all things as the God-man, our Mediator and Redeemer.

Poorest Of Men
Though he is God the Son, when he came into this world to redeem and save his elect, our blessed Lord Jesus, the Firstborn, became the poorest of men, that he might bring us into the unsearchable riches of his grace and his kingdom. We see this in Mary's sacrifice (v. 24). The law required worshippers to bring a lamb of the first year for a burnt offering and a young pigeon or turtledove for a sin offering, except if they were very poor. If they were very poor, they were allowed to bring two young pigeons or two turtledoves (Leviticus 12:6-8), the one for a burnt offering and the other for a sin offering. Mary was a poor woman.

Mary offered, "A pair of turtledoves, or two young pigeons." "For ye know the grace of our Lord Jesus Christ, that, though he was rich, yet for your sakes he became poor, that ye through his poverty might be rich" (2 Corinthians 8:9).

"And, behold, there was a man in Jerusalem, whose name was Simeon; and the same man was just and devout, waiting for the consolation of Israel: and the Holy Ghost was upon him. And it was revealed unto him by the Holy Ghost, that he should not see death, before he had seen the Lord's Christ. And he came by the Spirit into the temple: and when the parents brought in the child Jesus, to do for him after the custom of the law, Then took he him up in his arms, and blessed God, and said, Lord, now lettest thou thy servant depart in peace, according to thy word: For mine eyes have seen thy salvation, Which thou hast prepared before the face of all people; A light to lighten the Gentiles, and the glory of thy people Israel. And Joseph and his mother marvelled at those things which were spoken of him. And Simeon blessed them, and said unto Mary his mother, Behold, this child is set for the fall and rising again of many in Israel; and for a sign which shall be spoken against; (Yea, a sword shall pierce through thy own soul also,) that the thoughts of many hearts may be revealed" (Luke 2:25-35).

Chapter 15

Christ Our Light, Our Glory And Our Salvation

Here is an accurate description of every saved sinner. "And, behold, there was a man in Jerusalem, whose name was Simeon; and the same man was just and devout, waiting for the consolation of Israel: and the Holy Ghost was upon him" (v. 25). This is the only place in the Bible where Simeon's name is mentioned. We know nothing about him, except what is revealed in these eleven verses. But this man is set before us in words which identify his character as one who had been saved by the free and sovereign grace of God. He was a just man, upright and honest in his dealings with men. He was devout, devoted to the worship, service, will and glory of God. He was waiting for the Christ, the consolation of Israel. "And the Holy Ghost was upon him." All believers are people who live in and walk in the Spirit.

Here is a revealed fact. "And it was revealed unto him by the Holy Ghost, that he should not see death, before he had seen the Lord's Christ" (v. 26). Without question, this refers to the fact that the Lord God had specifically and supernaturally revealed to Simeon that he would not die until he had seen Christ with his own eyes. Here is a revealed fact. Not one of God's elect shall die until they have seen Christ with the eye of faith (2 Peter 3:9).

Here is a blessed Guide. "And he came by the Spirit into the temple: and when the parents brought in the child Jesus, to do for him after the custom of the law" (v. 27). When we come to the house of God, by the Spirit of God, we are sure to meet the Son of God there!

Here is a glorious Salvation. "Then took he him up in his arms (by personal faith), and blessed (praised) God, and said, (in confident hope) Lord, now lettest thou thy servant depart in peace, according to thy word: For mine eyes have seen thy salvation, Which thou hast prepared before the face of all people; A light to lighten the Gentiles, and the glory of thy people Israel. And

Joseph and his mother marvelled at those things which were spoken of him" (vv. 28-33).

Here is a Saviour and a gospel despised by all men in every age, except those to whom he is revealed. "And Simeon blessed them, and said unto Mary his mother, Behold, this child is set for the fall and rising again of many in Israel; and for a sign which shall be spoken against; (Yea, a sword shall pierce through thy own soul also,) that the thoughts of many hearts may be revealed"(vv. 34, 35).

These verses of inspiration reveal four simple, but blessed, spiritual truths, gospel truths, which we ought to lay to heart.

1. God Never Leaves Himself Without A Witness

In the worst of places, in the darkest of times, the Lord God still has his seven thousand who have not and will not bow the knee to Baal. Most in every age wear the mark of the beast; but God's elect will not and cannot, because their names were written in the Lamb's book of life, by the pen of immutable grace, before the world began (Revelation 13:8).

The Church of God may be small in the midst of Babylon, the great whore; but the gates of hell shall never prevail against it. God's little flock may be driven into the wilderness; but the Good Shepherd still carries his lambs in his bosom and feeds them by his grace. The woman is persecuted by the dragon of hell; but God providentially causes all the world to be her helper (Revelation 12). God never leaves himself without a witness. He always has a Lot in Sodom, an Obadiah in Ahab's household, a Daniel in Babylon, a Jeremiah in Zedekiah's court, a Simeon in Jerusalem and an elect remnant in an apostate age.

2. Those Who Have Seen Christ Have No Reason To Fear Death

Yes, it is possible to die without fear. The Lord Jesus Christ came here to deliver his own from the fear of death (Hebrews 2:14, 15). Many die in frustrated resignation, with a helpless, baseless hope of peace and release from misery. There appear to be "no bands in their death". There are very few who die in confident peace; but every believer ought to die in peace (Roman 8:31-39; 2 Corinthians 5:1-9; Exodus 15:16-19). There is no deliverance from the fear of death except by looking to him whose death is the death of death; but those who trust Christ have no reason to be afraid of death. Our Lord Jesus has done many things to deliver us from this fear of death and the bondage that accompanies it.

He has destroyed the power of death by dying in our place and rising again. Since all of God's elect were partakers of flesh and blood, under the dominion of death, Christ became a man to suffer and die for us. It was not possible for our Representative to satisfy the claims of Divine justice against us unless he lived and died in our nature. By his substitutionary death on the cursed tree and his triumphant resurrection, the Son of God destroyed the power of Satan and the power of the grave over us. We are now more than conquerors in him. Why then should we fear death?

The Lord Jesus delivers us from the fear of death by removing our sin. "The sting of death is sin." It is sin which causes men torment in death; but in Christ we have no sin. In him we are fully forgiven. By his blood our sins are washed away. If we are born of God, we are in Christ; "and in him is no sin" (1 John 3:1-5). Be sure you have the forgiveness of sin by faith in Christ, and fear death no more. To die forgiven, "accepted in the Beloved", is not really to die at all. It is simply the departure out of this world into the Father's house.

The law of God held us in bondage to the sentence of death and condemnation; but "Christ hath redeemed us from the curse of the law" (Galatians 3:13). "Christ is the end of the law for righteousness to everyone that believeth" (Romans 10:4). He is the end of the law's power to condemn. In the book of God's holy law there is no legal claim of condemnation upon any believer. Christ satisfied that claim for us. Why then should we fear? If I am in Christ, I am dead to the law (Romans 7:4; 8:1-4).

The Lord Jesus Christ delivers us from the fear of death by changing the character of death. For the unbeliever, death is a horrible thing. For the unbeliever, anything short of death is mercy. But, for the believer, death is a great blessing. John Trapp wrote ...

"To those that are in Christ death is but the day-break of eternal brightness; not the punishment of sin, but the period of sin. It is but a sturdy porter opening the door of eternity, a rough passage to eternal pleasure."

Why should Israel be afraid to cross the swelling Jordan into the land of promise with the ark of God before them? The fact is believers do not die in the sense that others do. Our Lord said, "Whosoever liveth and believeth on me shall never die." To the ungodly, death is the penalty of sin; but to the believer, it is just a change of location. Death to the wicked is the execution of justice, but to the believer, it is a deliverance from sin. To the worldling, death is the beginning of sorrows, but to the believer, it is admission into glory. To the rebel, death is imprisonment, but to the believer, it is freedom.

3. Wherever True Faith Is Found, There Is Gospel Knowledge And Spiritual Understanding

This man, Simeon, had a clear knowledge of the person and work of our Lord Jesus Christ. This is important. Blessed are those who are thus taught of God (Isaiah 54:11-14; John 6:45). Faith in Christ is not a leap in the dark. It is confidence based upon the revelation of God. It is the result of being taught of God. It is obvious Simeon knew that God has an elect people in every race, Jew and Gentile, who are the true Israel of God. He understood that all men and women by nature are engulfed in great spiritual darkness. But he also knew that the Lord Jesus Christ, the very baby he held in his arms, is the Light of the world and the glory of God, the glory of the Triune God, the revelation of the glory of God and the glory of his people (Jeremiah 9:23, 24; 1 Corinthians 1:30, 31). Simeon knew that the Lord Jesus Christ is himself God's salvation. Salvation is not a system of doctrine, a religious creed, or a reformation of life. Salvation is a Person; and that Person is the Lord Jesus Christ.

4. Certain Things Always Follow Christ And His Gospel

We are told in verses 34 and 35 that many will fall by him and many will be resurrected by him. To some, he is a stumbling stone and a rock of offence. To others, he is the sure Foundation, upon which we are built. "Unto you therefore which believe, he is precious." And this is according to the will, purpose and design of God (Isaiah 8:14; Romans 9:33; 1 Peter 2:8; Jude 4). Yet, pain and persecution will be the lot of all who trust him and follow him. And this, too, is by the will of our God and heavenly Father (Philippians 1:29).

"And there was one Anna, a prophetess, the daughter of Phanuel, of the tribe of Aser: she was of a great age, and had lived with an husband seven years from her virginity; And she was a widow of about fourscore and four years, which departed not from the temple, but served God with fastings and prayers night and day. And she coming in that instant gave thanks likewise unto the Lord, and spake of him to all them that looked for redemption in Jerusalem. And when they had performed all things according to the law of the Lord, they returned into Galilee, to their own city Nazareth. And the child grew, and waxed strong in spirit, filled with wisdom: and the grace of God was upon him" (Luke 2:36-40).

Chapter 16

To Them That Look For Redemption

At the very moment Simeon held Christ in his arms and called him God's Salvation, Anna came into the temple, observed the things spoken by Simeon, worshipped the child Christ Jesus as her Saviour, and testified of him as such "to them that looked for redemption". Are you, like those in Jerusalem to whom Anna spoke, looking for redemption? I pray that the Lord God has caused your eyes to fall upon this page because he has caused you to be looking for redemption, deliverance and salvation. If you are looking for redemption, look to Christ, look away to Christ. He alone is the Redeemer of sinners, in whom alone we have redemption through his blood, even the forgiveness of sins.

In these verses we read about a godly woman, whose name is mentioned nowhere else in the Bible. Anna, like Simeon, is one of those people mentioned only by Luke. In verses 25-35 Luke tells us about a godly old man who worshipped and testified of the Lord Jesus Christ in his earliest infancy. Here, he tells us of the worship and testimony given by an old woman as she beheld the Lord's Christ.

Anna The Prophetess
The name "Anna" here is the same as "Hannah", the mother of Samuel in the Old Testament. The name means "grace", or "gracious". Anna was the kind of woman her name signifies. She was a gracious woman. She had experienced the grace of God. She was saved by grace, walked in grace and told others about that grace.

This woman was "a prophetess". Though prophecy had ceased among the Jews for four hundred years, it now revived as a signal of Christ's, the Messiah, coming into the world.

In this day of utter disregard for God's Word, in which women are being ordained and sent out by almost all religious denominations as deacons, preachers, missionaries, evangelists, pastors and theologians, I must say something about the fact that Anna was a prophetess. Were it not for the universal confusion in the religious world about female preachers, I would pass over these words with little comment. But the fact that such confusion prevails compels me to speak.

There are a few instances of female prophets, prophetesses, in the scriptures, both before and after the coming of Christ: Miriam, the sister of Moses and Aaron, Deborah, the wife of Lapidoth, Huldah, the wife of Shallum; and this woman, Anna, at the time of Christ's birth. Later, in the Book of Acts, we read about four daughters of Philip the Evangelist, who were prophetesses.

Does this mean that it is proper for God's church to ordain women as deacons, missionaries, preachers, evangelists and pastors today? No! The Word of God absolutely and clearly forbids such nonsense. The teachings of holy scripture in this regard are so plain that error here is without excuse (1 Corinthians 14:34, 35; 1 Timothy 2:11, 12). These are offices which, by God's order, are for men only. This is not a matter of sexism, male chauvinism, or anything of the kind. It is a matter of reverence for God and obedience to his Word.

In all things godly women are modest, gladly living in subjection to their husbands. Believing women are not rebels to God, his order or his Word. Just as men are to be in subjection to Christ and to all who are put in authority over them; just as deacons, elders and churches are to be in subjection to their pastors; just as children are to be in subjection to their parents; women are to be in subjection to their husbands. In the house of God, women serve in subjection to men. They are never to be placed in a position of dominance over men.

What about these who are called "prophetesses" in the scriptures? Do we just ignore them? No. But we do not build our doctrine on obscure statements. We build our doctrine on the plain instructions of holy scripture, given in the place or places where the subject under consideration is taught. The fact that there were prophetesses in the Old Testament and through the Acts of the Apostles does not nullify the prohibitions given in the Epistles to female preachers. However, when the Word of God speaks of female prophets, and of women prophesying, that does not imply that they were preachers.

The word "prophetess" may simply refer to a woman who is a worshipper of God, as appears to be the case where it first appears (Exodus 15:20), referring to Aaron's sister, Miriam. It is also used to describe the wife of a prophet (Isaiah 8:3). So it does not necessarily refer to a female who stood forth in public to preach. The word "prophesy" does not necessarily mean, "instruct", "foretell" or "preach" in a public way. The word is used commonly to speak simply of worship, praise and witnessing (1 Corinthians 11:5, and throughout chapters 14 and 15).

A prophetess was a woman who worshipped God, praised him and bore witness to him. As stated regarding Miriam, the word "prophetess" was used in ancient times much like we use the word "worshipper" today. We might say of such women, "they worship God". That would be the same thing as saying, "they prophesy".

The only female preacher ever spoken of in a church in the New Testament was that wicked woman at Thyatira, who called herself a prophetess, but whom our Lord calls "Jezebel" (Revelation 2:20). When God sets women up as rulers over men, it is an act of judgment, not an act of grace (Isaiah 3:12).

Character And Conduct

This woman, Anna, was "the daughter of Phanuel". Her father's name is the same as that which Jacob gave to the place where he saw God face to face (Genesis 32:30, 31). "Phanuel" means "the face of God". How appropriate! Anna, Phanuel's daughter, saw the face of God in Jesus Christ!

Next, Luke tells us that Anna was "of the tribe of Aser" or Asher. Asher was one of the ten tribes carried away into captivity. Yet, even in Asher, there was a remnant according to the election of grace. God has his elect everywhere. He preserves his elect, even when he judges their nation. And at the appointed time, he calls them by his grace, and brings them out of bondage, darkness, condemnation and death into the glorious liberty of the sons of God.

"She was of great age." Anna was an old, old woman. She had lived in widowhood for 84 years! That means, if she had gotten married, as Jewish girls of the time often did, at the age of twelve, and lived with her husband for seven years before he died, she was at least 103 years old. Yet, she was constantly in the house of God, worshipping him, and doing what she could in the service of his kingdom and glory.

The things which Anna did and the things she spoke are here recorded by divine inspiration to teach us, encourage us, and strengthen us in the faith of Christ. And the first thing set before us in verses 35-37 is a picture of the believer's character and conduct. Anna was a woman of irreproachable character. She was what the Holy Spirit describes as "a widow indeed" (1 Timothy 4:5). This old woman is held before us as an example of true godliness.

"And there was one Anna, a prophetess, the daughter of Phanuel, of the tribe of Aser: she was of a great age, and had lived with an husband seven years from her virginity; And she was a widow of about fourscore and four years, which departed not from the temple, but served God with fastings and prayers night and day."

She was not a godly woman by nature, but a sinner. She did not make herself godly by austere discipline. She was converted and made godly by the grace of God that was upon her. Grace experienced makes the ungodly godly (2 Corinthians 5:17; Titus 2:11, 12; Ephesians 2:8-10). Anna's character and conduct are described in simple, but powerful words. She "served God with fastings and prayers night and day."

Many, who do not know the gospel, who have never experienced the saving grace of God in Christ and the transforming power of that grace, look upon these things as remarkable, exceptional qualities in a believer. They consider them ideal, but not essential to the believer's character. Nothing could be further from the truth. The character described in these two verses, the character of this old saint is not the target at which we must shoot, but the genuine character of all true believers. This is the character of those who are born of God, of those who walk in the Spirit (Galatians 5:16-25). "Ye are not in the flesh, but in the Spirit" (Romans 8:9).

Anna was also a woman of moral chastity. She was a virgin when she married. Her husband died after only seven years. And she remained chaste throughout her years, chaste and virtuous in an age of horrible profligacy and immorality.

This old woman was, throughout her years, faithful in the worship of God. She "departed not from the temple". Obviously, that does not mean that she never left the temple. She could not have come in at that moment, if she had not been outside. This is simply a declaration that she did not, as so many do, forsake the assembly of God's saints (Hebrews 10:25). When the doors of the temple were open, Anna made it her business to be there.

You will notice that Anna's commitment to the worship of God publicly is placed before her private devotion. Why? Because, when public worship is despised, there is no private worship. To depart from the assembly of God's saints, to depart from the worship of God is to forsake the Lord altogether. The first step to apostasy is the neglect of public worship (Hebrews 10:23-29).

Anna was a woman who loved the house of God. She looked upon it as that place where God promised to meet with, reveal himself and speak to his people. Therefore, she "departed not from the temple". She was devoted and consecrated to her God. "She served God with fastings and prayers night and day."

The Jews had reduced fasting and prayer to empty religious rituals, rituals by which they endeavoured to show their piety and devotion to one another. They considered the outward husk to be the meat. So they threw the grain away and kept the husk. That is exactly the way it is with most religious people. Their religion is all outward. It is all show. They substitute the saying of prayers for praying. They replace devotion of heart with regular fastings.

Most people think of prayer as the means by which we get God to do what he otherwise would not do. They imagine that if prayer does not work, and we really want to get God's attention and put the squeeze on him, fasting will do the job. That is not the case.

Fasting and prayer always go together. The two are never separated. In the sixth chapter of Matthew's Gospel our Lord Jesus tells us plainly that we are not to make an outward show of them before men. Though fasting may involve an abstinence from food for a period of time, and prayer is, in public worship and in family worship, very properly audible, primarily, fasting and prayer are matters of the heart.

Fasting is a synonym for voluntary, deliberate self-denial, consecration, and devotion (1 Corinthians 6:19, 20). Prayer is the believer's communion with, faith in, worship of and submission to the will and glory of God as we walk before him in this world.

Looking For Redemption

"And she coming in that instant gave thanks likewise unto the Lord, and spake of him to all them that looked for redemption in Jerusalem" (v. 38). Anna loved Christ, her God and Saviour. When she heard Simeon's prophecy, she also gave thanks to God for his Son, her Saviour. "Thanks be unto God for his unspeakable gift"! She "spake of him to all them that looked for redemption in Israel". She loved him whom she trusted, because she had been made to experience his love for her. It is written, "We love him, because he first loved us" (1 John 4:19).

Believers in every age are a people who look for redemption, who look for Christ. God's people, from the days of Adam and Eve, through all the days and years of Old Testament history, in the days of Simeon and Anna, in the days of the apostles and in this day, are a people looking for the redemption of Israel, the redemption of God's true Jerusalem, his true Israel. Believers are a people looking for and waiting for Christ the Redeemer, that One who is our Redemption (1 Thessalonians 1:10; Titus 2:14; Romans 13:11). Our "redemption draweth nigh".

Christ is our Redemption (1 Corinthians 1:30). We look to him alone and look to him always for redemption. The Lord God always has a people in this world, even as he did in Anna's day and in that wicked city, who look for the

111

redemption of Israel, who believe and confidently hope, in the teeth of all that they see, that Christ will redeem, that he will completely deliver all his people from all the consequences of sin, by his sovereign power and effectual grace.

Christ's Humanity

"And when they had performed all things according to the law of the Lord, they returned into Galilee, to their own city Nazareth. And the child grew, and waxed strong in spirit, filled with wisdom: and the grace of God was upon him" (vv. 39, 40). What a declaration these words are of the glorious humanity of our Lord Jesus Christ!

"The child grew" in body, and in physical strength and stature. "And waxed strong in spirit". As a man with a real human soul as well as a real human body, the Lord Jesus grew strong in his soul. He grew into a man of strong constitution, strong character, strong will and strong affection.

"Filled with wisdom" he was filled with wisdom as our Surety in whom are hid all the treasures of wisdom and knowledge. But these words describe the natural wisdom and the spiritual wisdom into which our Saviour grew as a man.

"And the grace of God was upon him." The love and favour of God was upon him as his beloved Son, in whom he is well-pleased. The gifts and graces of God's Spirit, the fruit of the Spirit, was upon him. Ryle wrote ...

"Our Lord partook of everything that belongs to man's nature, sin only excepted. As a man he was born an infant. As a man he grew from infancy to boyhood. As a man he yearly increased in bodily strength and mental power, during his passage from boyhood to full age. Of all the sinless conditions of man's body, its first feebleness, its after growth, its regular progress to maturity, he was in the fullest sense partaker. We must rest satisfied with knowing this. To pry beyond is useless."

Why did the Lord of glory stoop so low? Why did he condescend to such utter servitude? The answer is found in John 3: 16, 17. "For God so loved the world, that he gave his only begotten Son, that whosoever believeth in him should not perish, but have everlasting life for God sent not his Son into the world to condemn the world; but that the world through him might be saved."

To Them That Look For Redemption

"Now his parents went to Jerusalem every year at the feast of the passover. And when he was twelve years old, they went up to Jerusalem after the custom of the feast. And when they had fulfilled the days, as they returned, the child Jesus tarried behind in Jerusalem; and Joseph and his mother knew not of it. But they, supposing him to have been in the company, went a day's journey; and they sought him among their kinsfolk and acquaintance. And when they found him not, they turned back again to Jerusalem, seeking him. And it came to pass, that after three days they found him in the temple, sitting in the midst of the doctors, both hearing them, and asking them questions. And all that heard him were astonished at his understanding and answers. And when they saw him, they were amazed: and his mother said unto him, Son, why hast thou thus dealt with us? behold, thy father and I have sought thee sorrowing. And he said unto them, How is it that ye sought me? wist ye not that I must be about my Father's business? And they understood not the saying which he spake unto them. And he went down with them, and came to Nazareth, and was subject unto them: but his mother kept all these sayings in her heart. And Jesus increased in wisdom and stature, and in favour with God and man" (Luke 2:41-52).

Chapter 17

Lessons From The Master's Boyhood

What was life like for our Saviour, as he grew up in the home of Joseph and Mary? What occupied his time? How did he and his family live day by day? Those might be interesting questions; but they are questions for which no answers are given in the Word of God.

All that we know about our Master's boyhood, youth and early manhood we have given to us in these twelve, short verses of inspired history. We know absolutely nothing else about the earthly life of our Saviour from his infancy until he was thirty years old, except that which is written in these twelve verses.

That is as it should be. God the Holy Spirit has given us everything that is needful and profitable for our souls. We would be wise to recognize this fact. It is both the depth of folly and the height of arrogance for men to speculate about things God has chosen not to reveal. It is an act of wisdom, faith and humility to simply believe and heed that which is revealed. Here, the Holy Spirit gives us the history of our Master's boyhood. May he graciously teach us the lessons it is intended to convey.

Our Only Hope
As the believer's only hope of life before God is the death of Christ, our only rule of life is the example of Christ. Do you understand these two things? Our hope of salvation, eternal life, the forgiveness of sins and everlasting acceptance with the holy Lord God is the expiatory sacrifice and sin-atoning death of our Lord Jesus Christ. We live by his death. Christ's payment cancelled our debt. His obedience was our obedience. His judgment was our judgment. His death was our death. All the obedience he performed, all the agony he suffered, all the hell he endured, all the debt he paid was as our Surety! Our life is in his blood!

We are justified by his blood (Romans 5:9). We have forgiveness through his blood (Ephesians 1:7). We are reconciled to God by the blood of his cross (Colossians 1:20). We drink his blood for the quenching of our souls' thirst

(John 6:55). It is his blood that purges our consciences from dead works and satisfies the demands of the conscience (Hebrews 9:14). It is his blood by which we are brought nigh (Ephesians 2:13), who were by nature far off from God. It is his blood that gives us peace (Colossians 1:20). His blood gives us free access to the holiest and emboldens us to come to God upon the blood sprinkled mercy-seat (Hebrews 10:19-22). We are sanctified by his blood (Hebrews 13:12). His blood is the purchase money and ransom price paid for the redemption of our souls (Acts 20:28). His blood is the seal of the everlasting covenant (Hebrews 13:20). His blood cleanses us from all sin (1 John 1:7, 9). His blood speaks for us in heaven (Hebrews 12:24). His blood will give us the victory at last (Revelation 12:11).

> Dear, dying Lamb, Thy precious blood
> Shall never lose its power
> Till all the ransomed church of God
> Be saved to sin no more.
>
> E'er since by faith I saw the stream
> Thy flowing wounds supply,
> Redeeming love has been my theme
> And shall be till I die.
>
> When this poor, lisping, stammering tongue
> Lies silent in the grave,
> Then in a nobler, sweeter song,
> I'll sing Thy power to save!
>
> William Cowper

Our obedience has nothing to do with our salvation. We are saved by Christ's obedience unto death as our Substitute. If you would be saved, you must look away from yourself to Christ. You must trust Christ alone. Oh, may God give you grace to trust him now!

Our Only Rule
Our only hope of life is Christ. That is the first thing, and the most difficult thing to be learned. The second thing is this: The believer's rule of life, the pattern by which we must mould our lives in all things is the example of Christ. Our blessed Saviour was much, much more than an example for us to follow; but he was and is the example by which our lives must be moulded. Is this not what he taught us (John 13:13-15; 1 Peter 2:21)? In the passage

before us God the Holy Spirit gives us a very brief, but very instructive picture of the family life of our blessed Saviour when he was a boy.

Marriage

The first thing that strikes me in this passage is that it gives us a lesson about marriage (vv. 41-43).

"Now his parents went to Jerusalem every year at the feast of the passover. And when he was twelve years old, they went up to Jerusalem after the custom of the feast. And when they had fulfilled the days, as they returned, the child Jesus tarried behind in Jerusalem; and Joseph and his mother knew not of it."

Husbands and wives ought to help one another in the worship and service of Christ. Joseph and Mary worshipped God together. Every year, at the appointed time, they went together to Jerusalem to keep the Feast of the Passover. It was their custom to observe all the ordinances of divine worship, in the appointed place, at the appointed time, in the appointed way. Joseph and Mary honoured God, and honoured him together.

The trip from Nazareth to Jerusalem was long, dangerous, difficult and costly. They did not have much; but all that they had in Nazareth, they left for at least two weeks, three times a year, to go up to Jerusalem to worship God.

Some would say this was a matter of great irresponsibility on their part. How could they, especially such a poor couple, be so irresponsible as to neglect their property for two weeks at a time? It was not irresponsibility at all, but faith. They believed the God they worshipped. He has promised to prevent us from suffering any loss by devotion to him. Has he not?

"Thrice in the year shall all your men children appear before the Lord GOD, the God of Israel. For I will cast out the nations before thee, and enlarge thy borders: neither shall any man desire thy land, when thou shalt go up to appear before the LORD thy God thrice in the year" (Exodus 34:23, 24).

They knew God's will; and they obeyed it. They knew that the worship of God was the one thing they had to do and had to have. And they worshipped their God together. Side by side, they walked into the house of God. Side by side, they prayed. Side by side, they sang Jehovah's praise. Side by side, they heard his Word.

Let every married man and woman observe and learn from this couple. Let every man and woman contemplating marriage lay these things to heart. You will never make a decision so important as the decision you make about who you marry. Nothing will have a greater effect upon your soul for good or

117

evil. The person you marry will either help you upward or drag you downward. Your marriage partner will either lead you to heaven or to hell.

Will you hear the counsel of God's Word? Let me say what I have to say about this briefly, but with great plainness of speech. Seek your life long companion by divine guidance. Marriage is forever. Marry only in the Lord. Worship God as a family. I have never known anyone who gave heed to the counsel of these few sentences who regretted doing so. I know many who ignored this counsel who daily lament their rebellion.

Nothing is as important to you and your family as the public worship of our God and Saviour. These days, men and women treat church attendance as a matter of convenience. I warn you, you do so only to the ruin of your own soul, and to the ruin of your family (Hebrews 10:23-25).

Presumption

In verse 44 we see a second lesson. "They, supposing him to have been in the company"[6]. We should never presume upon the goodness of God, or presume the Lord's presence with us in our most solemn services or our most diligent labours. I know the Lord's promises (Matthew 18:20; 28:20), and rejoice in them. But I know this too, if we would have the Lord's presence with us in his house, we must want it and seek it. If we would have his power and blessing upon our labours, we must need it and depend upon it. And if we would have Christ in our company, we must stay in his company.

Obedience

Third, in the example of our blessed Saviour, we are given a lesson about obedience (vv. 45-47).

"And when they found him not, they turned back again to Jerusalem, seeking him. And it came to pass, that after three days they found him in the temple, sitting in the midst of the doctors, both hearing them, and asking them questions. And all that heard him were astonished at his understanding and answers."

Parents ought to see to it that their children obey them. Unruly, disobedient, ill-mannered children are produced by self-centred, selfish, irresponsible parents. And children will be wise to learn obedience. The surest path to happiness and well-being in this world is for children to honour and obey their parents (Ephesians 6:1-3). Our Saviour left us an example to follow, even as a child. He subjected himself to his parents (v. 51). And that

---

[6] It was customary with the Jews, when traveling to the appointed feasts, for the men to walk together in one group and the women in another, in large caravans. It is, therefore, perfectly understandable that Joseph presumed that the child was with Mary and the women, and that Mary presumed he was with Joseph and the men.

reverent subjection to his parents formed a part of the obedience he performed as our Surety, gaining him favour with God as a man (v. 52).

Christianity

Fourth, in verse 49, we are given a lesson about Christianity. "And he said unto them, How is it that ye sought me? Wist ye not that I must be about my Father's business?" What a solemn question! Let every child of God apply it to himself personally. It is our business in life to be about our Father's business. Christianity is living for God. May God the Holy Spirit give us grace to do so.

"Now in the fifteenth year of the reign of Tiberius Caesar, Pontius Pilate being governor of Judaea, and Herod being tetrarch of Galilee, and his brother Philip tetrarch of Ituraea and of the region of Trachonitis, and Lysanias the tetrarch of Abilene, Annas and Caiaphas being the high priests, the word of God came unto John the son of Zacharias in the wilderness. And he came into all the country about Jordan, preaching the baptism of repentance for the remission of sins; As it is written in the book of the words of Esaias the prophet, saying, The voice of one crying in the wilderness, Prepare ye the way of the Lord, make his paths straight. Every valley shall be filled, and every mountain and hill shall be brought low; and the crooked shall be made straight, and the rough ways shall be made smooth; And all flesh shall see the salvation of God" (Luke 3:1-6).

Chapter 18

The Making Of A Prophet

These words describe the beginning of this gospel age. After four hundred years of silence, God spoke again. And the voice by which he spoke was John the Baptist, that mighty Elijah, specifically raised up by God to prepare the way of the Lord, by whom God shook the heavens and the earth.

In Ephesians 4:11 the Holy Spirit tells us that Christ's ascension gifts to his church include apostles, pastors, teachers, evangelists and prophets. In that fourth chapter of Ephesians the Apostle was inspired of God to quote a portion of Psalm 68, which is a prophetic declaration of the accomplishments of Christ as our Mediator. Redemption has been accomplished by the blood of Christ. His resurrection declares that the sins of God's elect, which were made his and imputed to him, have been put away by his sacrifice. The Man who died for us at Calvary is now enthroned in glory and has received gifts of grace, gifts which he daily bestows upon his church for the salvation of his people.

"The chariots of God are twenty thousand, even thousands of angels: the Lord is among them, as in Sinai, in the holy place. Thou hast ascended on high, thou hast led captivity captive: thou hast received gifts for men; yea, for the rebellious also, that the LORD God might dwell among them. Blessed be the Lord, who daily loadeth us with benefits, even the God of our salvation. Selah. He that is our God is the God of salvation; and unto GOD the Lord belong the issues from death" (Psalm 68:17-20).

These ascension gifts of Christ, as I said, include apostles, pastors, teachers, evangelists and prophets. It is obvious that there is no continuing apostolic or prophetic office in a strict sense. The last apostle was Paul, and the last prophet was John the Baptist. Evangelists, as the Word is used in the

Word of God, are not itinerant preachers, but what we now call missionaries, church planters. Pastors and teachers are those men called and gifted of God for the work of the ministry, preaching the gospel in a local church, building up the saints in the faith, edifying the body of Christ. The words "pastors and teachers" might be read more accurately "pastors/teachers". They do not refer to two separate offices, but to the work of the pastor.

A Prophet
Because the term "prophet" is given as an ascension gift of Christ to his church, it is obvious that the word does not apply in this context to an office that was terminated before the Lord's ascension.

It is very difficult to find anything useful being said or written in our day on the ministry of these men. What is a prophet? The word, as it is used regarding the New Testament era, seems to refer to men with extraordinary gifts, men who have a remarkable understanding of the scriptures, men who have a keen awareness of the times in which they live and the message required to meet the need of the hour.

The work of the New Testament prophet is shrouded in indefiniteness and lost in a fog of haziness. We know the old definition, "A forthteller rather than a foreteller." We apply the term generally to preachers as spokesmen for God. But here is a distinctive calling separate from that of evangelist or pastor. Yet, the prophet may be an evangelist or a pastor.

A prophet, in this distinct sense of the word, appears to be a man distinctly gifted of God to lead his people in crucial times, with boldness and authority, which only God can give. Clearly, there were such men in the early church (Acts 11:27, 28; 13:1). At least six are named in Acts 11 and 13: Agabus, Barnabas, Simeon, Lucius, Manaen and Saul.

There have never been many prophets, at least not many true prophets. But are there none? Our times cry for such men. Is there not a prophet? Are there none today to stand in the gap and dare speak for God? Never was the need greater and the supply smaller than today.

The prophet is a voice in the wilderness. It is his business to sound the trumpet, proclaim the Word of God, and press the claims of the sovereign God upon the hearts and lives of men. He does not work on details or set up programs. He does not devise schemes to raise funds or plan stage productions. A prophet does not belong on boards and committees. He is a solitary soul and does his best work alone. He is not a parrot, a puppet or a promoter. A prophet is never a team player. He is not a religious politician. He is a voice, a lone, dogmatic voice.

He is nothing but a prophet. If he tries to be or do anything else, he is an embarrassment to himself and to everyone around him. He is not a politician;

and he is never popular with politicians either in state or church. He is not cowed by dignitaries. When necessary, he will call Herod a fox, even when he knows it may cost him his life.

A prophet is an unreconstructed rebel, an odd number in a day of regimentation. He has no more patience with mere religion than Isaiah had when he thundered against it, or Amos when he called on Israel to come to Bethel. It is his business to say what others cannot, will not, or at least do not say.

The politician has his eye on the next election, instead of the nation's welfare. And I fear most preachers are more politician than prophet. They are more interested in your approval than your soul. They have their eyes on denominational promotion, the next rung of the ladder, a higher seat in the synagogue, and being called a rabbi.

The prophet has no axe to grind, but lays the axe of holy scripture to the root of every tree in the groves of the world's idolatry. He does not know the meaning of the word "compromise". His subject never varies. He relentlessly calls rebels to surrender, demanding utter surrender to the claims of Christ, the crucified, risen, exalted Lord. "Repent, for the kingdom of heaven is at hand"! "All flesh is grass"! "Behold, your God"! "Behold, the Lamb of God, which taketh away the sin of the world"!

As far as God's prophet is concerned, the grass is no greener in the next pasture. He seeks no man's office, position or honour. His concern is for the will, and glory, and truth, and kingdom of God.

Churches today are looking for scholars, specialists, socialisers and showmen. We need some seers, some prophets who, like Isaiah, have seen God in his holiness, themselves in their sinfulness, and the crucified Lamb of God in the midst of his throne.

The prophet does not pack the house, or produce impressive statistics. He may get but poor response; but whether they hear or not, those who hear him know that a prophet has been among them. People do not crowd churches to hear prophets. In an age of ear-itch religionists, most everyone calls God's prophets "troublers of Israel". And wherever a prophet's voice is heard, trouble, of one kind or another, is sure to follow. Whenever John the Baptist or the Apostle Paul came to town, whether they preached in the church-house, the jail-house, or the open fields, either a revival or a riot broke out. No one ignores a prophet!

The prophet is never popular with the Pharisees, and has no desire to be. Organized religion is never more organized than when it attempts to silence a prophet. "Which of the prophets have not your fathers persecuted?" "Ye are the children of them that killed the prophets." So said the greatest of prophets to the Pharisees of his day. From Abel to Zacharias, our Master said, prophets have been stoned while living and honoured when dead. Let no one be misled by the monuments men build to dead prophets. They are only the gestures and attempts of one generation to cover up the crimes of their fathers in preceding generations.

The prophet is not popular at home. In all four gospels we read our Lord's declaration, "A prophet is not without honour save in his own country and in his own house." But prophets do have their reward, and so do those who befriend them, even with a cup of cool water. God will not overlook the "prophet's chamber", where his unpopular servant has been made to feel at home.

There are not many candidates for Elijah's mantle. His path is not an easy path to follow. There are many ways of getting rid of prophets. John the Baptist's head is not brought in on a charger these days. There are smoother and more skilful ways of silencing lone dissenters like Micaiah in these days of refined malice against God. Some can even be promoted into silence. Success has stopped some mouths when persecution failed.

Like John the Baptist, the prophet is out to pull down the high places, build up low places, and make a way for the Lord. His theological interpretation of holy scripture is not a matter of learned speculation, but of passionate conviction. His preaching is not intended to make sinners feel good about themselves, but to bring them down in the dust before God by the burning, penetrating application of his Word to their hearts. Others may comfort when afflicted; but the prophet afflicts the comfortable. We are trying to accomplish now by pep, publicity, propaganda and promotion what once was done by preaching. The woods are full of trained religious personnel, (they are called preachers!); but we need prophets, men in whom the Word of the Lord burns like fire, men who carry and are weighed down with "the burden of the Word of the Lord"!

Any young Elisha in line for Elijah's mantle will need the mind of a scholar, the heart of a child and the hide of a rhinoceros. He may irk those who like to preserve the status quo, for he is a disturber of Israel, but no one else can take his place. Oh, may God raise up some prophets in our midst in this dark, dark day!

Perhaps he will cause some Samuel to read these lines long after my name is forgotten among men, who will hear what the Lord says and who will speak what he hears. There is not much prospect as to pay, promotion or prestige. But there has always been "yet one man" who will scorn the hatred of Ahab and seek the honour of God.

Luke 3:1-6 describes the making of such a man, the making of a prophet. Prophets are made, called, gifted, raised up and sent forth by God, at the time and in the place where they are needed, to "prepare the way of the Lord"!

Desperately Needed

God raises up a prophet when a prophet is desperately needed. I cannot think of a time in scripture when God raised up a prophet to twiddle his thumbs, sipping tea with old ladies, coaching little league ball teams, or running businesses. God's prophets are raised up to meet the crying need of his people in the hour of desperate need, with evil abounding on all sides. He raised up Moses to deliver Israel from Egyptian bondage. He sent Samuel to find his chosen king for Israel and establish him as God's King. The Lord God called Elijah to lead Israel, while Ahab and Jezebel sought to establish idolatry. He sent Isaiah to proclaim his salvation, when all hope seemed to be gone. And he raised up Jeremiah to prepare the people for judgment.

In a time of desperate need the God of Glory raised up John the Baptist, as a mighty Elijah, to prepare the way of the Lord. Verses 1 and 2 tell us that John the Baptist was sent into the world at a time of abounding social, political and spiritual wickedness.

Who can imagine a time more infamously evil than the days of Tiberius Caesar, Pontius Pilate, Herod and his brother, Philip? These men made our modern Washington crowd look like a bunch of Augustinian monks! When John the Baptist came preaching the gospel, the world seemed to be given over completely into the hands of the wicked. As Job put it, "The earth is given into the hand of the wicked" (Job 9:24). If these men were the rulers of the world, what must the people have been like?

The religious world was in just as sad a condition as the political world. In fact, religion was so degenerate, even among the Jews, that it was just a reflection of the world. Instead of converting the world, the world had converted the church. Annas and Caiaphas were the high priests.

The Word of God specifically stated that there was to be but one high priest; but the Word of God was no longer in vogue. It was irrelevant as far as the religion of the age was concerned. The church, the priests, the preachers, the religious leaders of the age did everything, gauged everything, made every judgment, and formed every doctrinal statement by opinion polls, by the opinions of a godless, reprobate people!

We must never be in despair regarding the truth of God and the cause of God in this world, no matter how bleak things may appear. Let us never allow the wickedness of the age in which we live deter us from the work God has given us. "He that observeth the wind shall not sow; and he that regardeth the clouds shall not reap" (Ecclesiastes 11:4). What God has done in the past, he can do again. When darkness abounds, it is only a good background upon which God may be pleased to show forth his blazing glory in Christ!

Distinctly Called

A prophet is a man distinctly called of God. "The word of God came to John, the son of Zacharias in the wilderness" (v. 2). A message from heaven came upon his heart, seized his soul, captivated his mind and took over his life. I do not know how to put my finger on it, but I know this: No man has any business engaging in the work of the ministry who has not been called of God to the work. He who runs without being sent, has no message to deliver, no work to do, no mandate to accomplish. But when a man is called of God, he knows exactly what he must do. He knows exactly what his message is. And he goes about his work with the tenacity of a mule and the courage of a lion.

If a man is called of God to this great and glorious, heart-rending work, he knows the Word of the Lord, the message of the gospel. He is gifted of God to preach the gospel, "apt to teach". Such a man does not have to look for a place to preach, or promote himself in any way. God puts him in the work. John was in the wilderness when the word of the Lord came to him. If a man is called of God, God gives him a hearing; and he is engaged in the work. This call of God separates the man called and gifted of God unto the work of the gospel (Romans 1:1-4). No man is called of God to preach the gospel who is not preaching the gospel.

Clear Message

God's prophet is a man with a message, a clear, distinct message from God, demanding the surrender of rebels to the throne of the great King! "And he came into all the country about Jordan, preaching the baptism of repentance for the remission of sins" (v. 3). The "baptism of repentance" (believer's immersion) is the gospel ordinance by which believing sinners are commanded and delight to confess their faith in Christ (Acts 2:38; 8:36; 10:48; 22:16). In the ordinance of baptism we symbolize the finished work of our Lord Jesus, our death, burial and resurrection with him as our Substitute.

The words, "for the remission of sins", should be read, "because of the remission of sins." We are not baptized to have our sins remitted. We are baptized because Christ has put away our sins by the sacrifice of himself. Baptism is the believer's declaration that he has been turned to God by Christ Jesus. John came preaching repentance, the turning of sinners to God by the Saviour; the very same message gospel preachers in every age are sent to proclaim, redemption accomplished by the crucified Saviour (2 Corinthians 5:17-21).

God's prophet is a man who knows who he is and what he must do. He is just a voice. It is his business to prepare the way of the Lord, and make his paths straight.

"As it is written in the book of the words of Esaias the prophet, saying, The voice of one crying in the wilderness, Prepare ye the way of the Lord, make his paths straight. Every valley shall be filled, and every mountain and hill shall be brought low; and the crooked shall be made straight, and the rough ways shall be made smooth" (vv. 4, 5).

Every gospel preacher is sent of God to tell eternity bound sinners that they must prepare to meet God, to tell them by what path God comes to them and by what path they must come to him, and to declare it plainly. It is the business of God's ambassador to your soul, as the voice of one crying in the wilderness, to fill up every valley, pull down every barrier, make every crooked thing straight and every rough thing smooth, which stands between your soul and your God.

God's prophet is a man who goes about his work with the confidence of absolute success. We know that our work is not in vain in the Lord. We know that God's Word will not return to him void. It will accomplish that which he pleased. It will prosper in the thing to which he sends it. And when our work is done "All flesh shall see the salvation of God" (v. 6). You will see God's salvation, either as a believer or as a rebel; but see it you will, either to the saving of your soul or to the damning of your soul (2 Corinthians 2:14-16). You will acknowledge and confess the salvation of God, either in the blessed experience of repentance, or in the horrifying experience of everlasting torment.

Prepare to meet thy God. Are you, or are you not prepared to meet God? Are you washed in the blood of his dear Son? Are you robed in his righteousness? Do you have on the wedding garment of his grace? Are you prepared to meet God?

127

"Then said he to the multitude that came forth to be baptized of him, O generation of vipers, who hath warned you to flee from the wrath to come? Bring forth therefore fruits worthy of repentance, and begin not to say within yourselves, We have Abraham to our father: for I say unto you, That God is able of these stones to raise up children unto Abraham. And now also the axe is laid unto the root of the trees: every tree therefore which bringeth not forth good fruit is hewn down, and cast into the fire. And the people asked him, saying, What shall we do then? He answereth and saith unto them, he that hath two coats, let him impart to him that hath none; and he that hath meat, let him do likewise. Then came also publicans to be baptized, and said unto him, Master, what shall we do? And he said unto them, Exact no more than that which is appointed you. And the soldiers likewise demanded of him, saying, And what shall we do? And he said unto them, Do violence to no man, neither accuse any falsely; and be content with your wages" (Luke 3:7-14).

Chapter 19

Baptist Preaching

John the Baptist was no ordinary man in any sense of the word "ordinary". He was a remarkable man, a remarkable believer and a remarkable preacher. It was impossible to ignore him, or pretend he was not around. Though few who heard him believed his message, everyone who heard him was affected by what they heard.

In the eleventh chapter of Matthew our Lord gave his own opinion about John the Baptist. Read what he says there about this remarkable man.

"And as they departed, Jesus began to say unto the multitudes concerning John, What went ye out into the wilderness to see? A reed shaken with the wind? But what went ye out for to see? A man clothed in soft raiment? behold, they that wear soft clothing are in kings' houses. But what went ye out for to see? A prophet? yea, I say unto you, and more than a prophet. For this is he, of whom it is written, Behold, I send my messenger before thy face, which shall prepare thy way before thee. Verily I say unto you, Among them that are born of women there hath not risen a greater than John the Baptist: notwithstanding he that is least in the kingdom of heaven is greater than he" (Matthew 11:7-11).

A preacher of such character and influence is a preacher whose example all preachers ought to follow. He sets the pattern for what preaching is and how it is to be done. What were the leading features of the Baptist's ministry? What were the primary characteristics of his preaching? These things are clearly set out in the inspired record given by Luke in the passage before us.

John the Baptist's work as God's prophet, as a preacher, is to be measured, like every preacher's work is to be measured, not by his traits of personality, oratorical ability, social graces, and theological acumen, but by his message, by what he preached. In the inspired record of John's life and ministry five things stick out as distinct characteristics of the Baptist's preaching.

Redemption By The Blood

First, and foremost, the first Baptist preacher preached redemption and remission of sins by the blood of Christ. John came preparing the way of the Lord, preaching the baptism of repentance, because of the remission of sins (v. 3). He incessantly pointed sinners to Christ, calling upon all who heard him to trust, love and follow Christ. Even when he was in prison, about to be sacrificed for his faithfulness, he sent his disciples to the Lord Jesus to have the Saviour's person and work confirmed to them by the Saviour himself (Matthew 11:2-6). In the first chapter of John's Gospel, John the apostle speaks in glowing terms about John the Baptist and his preaching (John 1:15-30, 34-37).

Blessed is that man whose preaching is full of Christ, who spends his time and uses his opportunities to talk to eternity bound sinners about the precious blood of the Lamb of God. Blessed are they who hear him (Isaiah 52:7). All who know Christ esteem his blood precious; and all who preach Christ preach his blood precious (1 Peter 1:18-20). His blood is precious blood because it is his blood, the blood of God incarnate (Acts 20:28). It is sin-atoning blood (Romans 3:24; 5:11). Our Saviour's blood is eternally efficacious blood (Hebrews 9:12; Ephesians 1:7). It is divinely ordained blood, blood shed by the purpose of God (Acts 2:23). And the blood of Christ is precious because it is redeeming blood (Galatians 3:13, 14).

The Baptist's preaching was the preaching of blood atonement by the crucified Lamb of God. Paul's motto was his motto. Indeed, this is the motto of every preacher called and sent of God. "I determined not to know any thing among you, save Jesus Christ, and him crucified" (1 Corinthians 2:2). "God forbid that I should glory, save in the cross of our Lord Jesus Christ" (Galatians 6:14).

Holy Boldness

Second, John the Baptist knew that he spoke for God, with God's power and authority, and, therefore, preached with a confidence that gave him holy boldness and courage before men. John the Baptist was a man, not a sissy, or a wimp, but a man. He was not a reed shaken in the wind, bending with the breeze of popular opinion. This was not a pampered pastor who dared not offend those who pampered him. John the Baptist was God's servant. You could tell it when he preached

"Then said he to the multitude that came forth to be baptized of him, O generation of vipers, who hath warned you to flee from the wrath to come? Bring forth therefore fruits worthy of repentance, and begin not to say within yourselves, We have Abraham to our father: for I say unto you, That God is able of these stones to raise up children unto Abraham" (vv. 7, 8).

130

John saw the rottenness and hypocrisy of the religious world around him, and denounced it with pointed sharpness. His head was not turned by popularity. He courted no man's favour and feared no man's frown. He cared not who might be offended by his message. The spiritual disease of those standing before him was desperate. He knew desperate disease required desperate measures. John the Baptist lived in desperate times, much like our own. He knew the day demanded desperate plainness of speech.

How sad it is that there are so few like this first Baptist preacher today! These days, the first, primary rule of preaching is "Do not offend"! Preachers have a castrating fear of giving offence by direct, forthright, plain preaching.

If a man would be faithful to your souls, he cannot flatter you. If he would do you good, he dare not flinch from exposing your inmost corruption and sin by the Word of God, demanding and pressing upon you the claims of Christ, forcing you, if he can, to repentance toward God and faith in Christ. If a man's object in preaching is to please you, rather than serve your soul's eternal good, he is not the servant of God (Luke 6:26; Galatians 1:10).

Because he was God's servant, John told these people three things, which are true of and ought to be declared to all men: (1.) They were a generation of vipers, as deceitful as they were vile. (2.) They were under and fully deserving of the wrath of God. And (3.) God did not need them to fulfil himself or make himself happy. John told these proud sons of Abraham, "God is able of these stones to raise up children unto Abraham."

When John the Baptist demanded that those he baptized "bring forth fruits worthy of repentance", the word translated "bring forth" is the very same word used by the apostle in 1 John 3:4 and 7, when he tells us that people "committing sin" are yet without Christ, and that those "doing righteousness" have been made righteous. The word has the idea of practice, not of acts. Fruits "worthy of repentance", fruits that show repentance to be genuine are "the fruit of the Spirit" produced and formed in the believer, fruits reflected in the believer's practice of life (Galatians 5:22, 23). A person's true character is seen, not in isolated acts, but in the habit of his life.

Everlasting Hell

John the Baptist spoke plainly and forcibly about the wrath of God and everlasting damnation in hell. He did not hold back the fact that there is "wrath to come". He faithfully warned all who heard him that God cut down every unprofitable tree and "cast it into the fire".

The subjects of divine justice, judgment, wrath and the everlasting torments of the damned in the fires of hell are always offensive to human nature. Men do not like to hear that they are going to hell. It is the nature of all men to love to hear smooth things; not peril, danger and punishment.

People are willing to pay false prophets good money to tell them what they want to hear (Isaiah 30:10). But that man who is faithful to God, faithful to the Book and faithful to your soul will, like John the Baptist, like Christ himself, like all the prophets of old, and like all the apostles, warn you, with passion in his soul, to "flee from the wrath to come".

Fear of hell is not the primary motive for repentance and faith in Christ; but you will never seek heaven until you fear going to hell. You will never seek God's salvation until you fear God's wrath. You will not flee to Christ, the sinner's only City of Refuge, until the avenger of justice is on your trail.

Hell is real. God Almighty must and will punish sin. It is that God who swears, "the soul that sinneth, it shall die", who drove Adam and Eve out of the garden, destroyed the world in the flood of his wrath, rained fire and brimstone upon Sodom and Gomorrah, nailed his own Son upon the cursed tree and poured out on him all the fires of hell for his people, when he was made sin for us.

Axe To Root

In his preaching the Baptist laid the axe to the root of every fruitless tree. With earnestness and conviction, he endeavoured to destroy every refuge of lies in which sinners seek to hide from God.

"And now also the axe is laid unto the root of the trees: every tree therefore which bringeth not forth good fruit is hewn down, and cast into the fire" (v. 9).

When the multitudes of religious people, whose lives were manifestly wicked, stood before him, he plainly declared to their faces in public that they were hypocrites. It is vain to say with our lips, "I believe God", if by our works we deny him. It is worse than vain. Such hypocrisy will gradually harden the heart and sear the conscience. A confession of faith without the consecration of faith is hypocrisy. Baptism without death and resurrection life in Christ is a sham. Eating the bread and wine of the Lord's Supper, if I do not feed upon the Redeemer's flesh and blood, is eating and drinking damnation to myself. To use the words of Inspiration, "Faith without works is dead"! Such faith is nothing but the faith of devils (James 2:14-26).

John boldly and plainly denounced the commonly held notion of covenant family salvation. The Jews, like multitudes today, thought they were certainly saved people, children of God, because they were Abraham's descendants. John told them that their pedigree was no claim to grace (v. 8). Saving faith is a personal thing. It is not a family heirloom (John 1:12, 13). When Paul said to the Philippian jailer, "Believe on the Lord Jesus Christ, and thou shalt be saved, and thy house", he was not saying, "If you believe, God will save everyone (or anyone) in your house." He was saying, "If you believe, you will be saved, and if your family believes, they will be saved as well."

Doing Right

John faithfully brought the gospel home to the hearts and lives of his hearers in the most practical way possible (Luke 3:10-14). When the people asked him, "What shall we do then?" he told each one who professed faith in Christ by believer's baptism to live according to his profession, for the glory of God. He said to them all, live no longer in selfish, self-centred gratification, but in love, kindness, charity and generosity. Is that not the obvious meaning of verse 11? "He answereth and saith unto them, he that hath two coats, let him impart to him that hath none; and he that hath meat, let him do likewise."

The Baptist told the converted publicans to be fair and honest with all men, especially because the publicans were known for both dishonesty and severity. "Then came also publicans to be baptized, and said unto him, Master, what shall we do? And he said unto them, Exact no more than that which is appointed you" (vv. 12, 13).

John told those soldiers who were converted by the grace of God to take care not to be violent and abusive with people under their power, and to be content with God's provision. "And the soldiers likewise demanded of him, saying, And what shall we do? And he said unto them, Do violence to no man, neither accuse any falsely; and be content with your wages" (v. 14).

It should also be noted that John said nothing to indicate anything unlawful about either paying taxes or collecting them, or about serving as a soldier. Remember, these publicans and soldiers were employees of the Roman Empire, one of the most morally corrupt, idolatrous systems of government the world has ever known. Our business is not with the kings of this world, but with the King of the world. Our concern is not the governing of kingdoms and nations, but with the kingdom of God.

Five Distinctive Themes

These five things characterized the Baptist's preaching:
The preaching of blood redemption by Christ.
Courage and boldness for the glory of God.
Plain warnings about the wrath of God.
Plainness of speech in destroying the refuges in which sinners would hide from God.
Godly behaviour.

May God be pleased to revive such preaching in these dark, dark days, for the glory of Christ and the everlasting good of his elect!

"And as the people were in expectation, and all men mused in their hearts of John, whether he were the Christ, or not; John answered, saying unto them all, I indeed baptize you with water; but one mightier than I cometh, the latchet of whose shoes I am not worthy to unloose: he shall baptize you with the Holy Ghost and with fire: Whose fan is in his hand, and he will throughly purge his floor, and will gather the wheat into his garner; but the chaff he will burn with fire unquenchable. And many other things in his exhortation preached he unto the people. But Herod the tetrarch, being reproved by him for Herodias his brother Philip's wife, and for all the evils which Herod had done, Added yet this above all, that he shut up John in prison" (Luke 3:15-20).

Chapter 20

John The Baptist: A Faithful Preacher

The greatest blessing God bestows upon men and women this side of eternity is the gift of a faithful gospel preacher in their midst (Isaiah 52:7, 8). What a blessing it is for God to plant a gospel church with a faithful pastor in your backyard! The most severe judgment God sends upon men this side of eternity is the judgment of taking from them the ministry of the gospel, the faithful preaching of the Word of God, God's ordained means of grace to chosen, redeemed sinners (Romans 10:17).

In these verses of scripture Luke gives us his final word about the life and ministry of John the Baptist. In the first twenty verses of this chapter the Holy Spirit directed Luke's pen in showing us the faithfulness of John the Baptist as a preacher of the gospel, holding him before us as an example to be followed by all who are called and sent of God into the glorious work of the gospel ministry.

In the verses now before us Luke uses John's example to show us five distinct characteristics of a faithful preacher. But Luke is not here addressing preachers. He is addressing God's saints. This is God's Word to you and me. You see, that which the scriptures require of faithful, gospel preachers is also required of all faithful men and women. All believers are God's servants; and the one thing God requires of us all is faithfulness (1 Corinthians 4:1, 2).

One of my unceasing, daily prayers is that God would be pleased to make me faithful in all things, as his servant. Knowing something of the fickleness of my own heart, I know that if faithfulness is found in me, it will be God's doing. The Lord has made this a matter of constant prayer with me for more than forty years. The older I get, and the more I know of the things of God and of my own nature, the more I see the power and deceitfulness of the cares of this world, the more earnest I am in asking this one thing of my God. Oh, for grace to be faithful to my God, his Son, his Word, his will, his glory, and his people! What does this faithfulness involve? At least these five things.

A Faithful Ministry Disturbs Men

True preaching is disturbing, heart-piercing, thought provoking. It disturbs men, especially religious men. Luke tells us that when men and women (religious men and women, men and women who presumed that they knew God) heard the Baptist preach, they were "in expectation, and all men mused in their hearts of John, whether he were the Christ."

The word "mused" means reasoned, considered, weighed. When people heard John preach, they were provoked to thoughtful consideration of his message. When a man comes from the throne of God with a message from God, preaching with a God-given knowledge and understanding, he simply cannot be ignored. Those who hear his message are compelled to weigh his words.

That is always a hopeful sign. I am always delighted to see people evidently considering the things of God. When men and women begin to think, I rejoice. Thinking is not faith. Consideration is not conversion. But it is a hopeful sign.

The gospel of the grace of God, the Word of God, the truth of God is always verified by honest examination. Truth never fears examination. The problem with most people is that God is not in their thoughts. They never consider divine truth (Psalm 10:4; Isaiah 1:3). If you are not in too big a hurry to go to hell, you would be wise to get alone with God and this Book, and consider just three things.

Pause for a while and first consider who and what you are. Then take a little time to consider who the Lord Jesus Christ is, why he came into this world and what he has done. "Consider how great this man was"! "Consider him that endured such contradiction of sinners against himself"! Finally, will you stop for a while and consider your end?

"But unto the wicked God saith, What hast thou to do to declare my statutes, or that thou shouldest take my covenant in thy mouth? Seeing thou hatest instruction, and castest my words behind thee. When thou sawest a thief, then thou consentedst with him, and hast been partaker with adulterers. Thou givest thy mouth to evil, and thy tongue frameth deceit. Thou sittest and speakest against thy brother; thou slanderest thine own mother's son. These things hast thou done, and I kept silence; thou thoughtest that I was altogether such an one as thyself: but I will reprove thee, and set them in order before thine eyes. Now consider this, ye that forget God, lest I tear you in pieces, and there be none to deliver. Whoso offereth praise glorifieth me:

and to him that ordereth his conversation aright will I shew the salvation of God" (Psalm 50:16-23).

God's servants make no effort to avoid examination. We court it. I know, beyond a shadow of doubt, that the gospel I preach is the truth of God. I know that it will answer every need of your heart and every demand of your conscience.

A Faithful Preacher Always Exalts Christ

When men came seeking to confer great and high honours upon John, he turned their thoughts away from himself to Christ. As the friend of the bridegroom rejoices in the glory of the bridegroom, so the servant of God rejoices in the glory of Christ, and seeks none for himself (John 3:29, 30). Faithful men serve Christ, exalt Christ, point sinners to Christ, and preach Christ. They do not serve their own interests (1 Corinthians 4:1-5; 2 Corinthians 4:1-5).

"Let a man so account of us, as of the ministers of Christ, and stewards of the mysteries of God. Moreover it is required in stewards, that a man be found faithful. But with me it is a very small thing that I should be judged of you, or of man's judgment: yea, I judge not mine own self. For I know nothing by myself; yet am I not hereby justified: but he that judgeth me is the Lord. Therefore judge nothing before the time, until the Lord come, who both will bring to light the hidden things of darkness, and will make manifest the counsels of the hearts: and then shall every man have praise of God" (1 Corinthians 4:1-5).

"Therefore seeing we have this ministry, as we have received mercy, we faint not; But have renounced the hidden things of dishonesty, not walking in craftiness, nor handling the word of God deceitfully; but by manifestation of the truth commending ourselves to every man's conscience in the sight of God. But if our gospel be hid, it is hid to them that are lost: In whom the god of this world hath blinded the minds of them which believe not, lest the light of the glorious gospel of Christ, who is the image of God, should shine unto them. For we preach not ourselves, but Christ Jesus the Lord; and ourselves your servants for Jesus' sake" (2 Corinthians 4:1-5).

By this standard every man's ministry must be judged. Does he preach Christ? Does he point sinners to Christ? Does he exalt, magnify, extol and honour Christ? As the Son of God? As the Lord our Righteousness? As the effectual Redeemer? As the sovereign Saviour? As the Monarch of the Universe? It matters not how learned he is, how many degrees he wears, how well he dresses, or even how well he speaks. The thing that matters is what he speaks. Does he preach Christ?

By this same standard judge all doctrine, all religious activity and all religious instruction. Does it point you to Christ, make you think more of Christ, cause you to lean on Christ, or does it point you to yourself, cause you to think of yourself and cause you to lean on yourself, on the church and on the pastor?

A Faithful Preacher Knows And Acknowledges His Own Inabilities
When the people presumed that John was himself the Christ, he quickly pointed out that he not only was not the Christ, but that he was utterly incapable of doing anything for their souls. "John answered, saying unto them all, I indeed baptize you with water; but one mightier than I cometh, the latchet of whose shoes I am not worthy to unloose: he shall baptize you with the Holy Ghost and with fire" (v. 16).

That is exactly what Paul had to deal with in 1 Corinthians 1-3. The power and efficacy of the gospel does not depend upon the preacher, but upon Christ. "Our sufficiency is of God." A man can preach the gospel to you; but a man cannot make you believe it. A man can see the expressions on your face; but a man cannot read your heart. A man can baptize you in water; but a man cannot put you in Christ. A man can give you the bread and wine of the Lord's Supper; but a man cannot cause you to eat Christ's flesh and drink his blood. A man can show you the way; but a man cannot put you in the way. That is God's work!

"John answered, saying unto them all, I indeed baptize you with water; but one mightier than I cometh, the latchet of whose shoes I am not worthy to unloose: he shall baptize you with the Holy Ghost and with fire:" Essentially, John is saying three things here. These three things every gospel preacher is keenly and acutely aware of, all the time.

1. I cannot save you or damn you. I am neither your Saviour nor your judge. You should not expect anything from me, or confess anything to me.

2. I am not worthy of your slightest esteem, reverence, or praise. I'm not fit to untie my Master's shoes. I am honoured beyond imagination, if he allows me to just take off his shoes.

3. The Lord Jesus Christ is both the Saviour of the world and the Judge of the world. He will baptize you with the Holy Ghost and with fire. That is to say, he will baptize you with the Holy Spirit in his almighty saving grace. Or, if you do not bow to him, if you are not saved by his grace, he will baptize you with fire in the Day of Judgment.

Be wise. Do not rest with anything less than the operation of Christ himself in your soul. You may have been immersed in water; but has Christ immersed you in grace? Your name is written on this church roll; but is your name written in heaven? You eat the bread and wine at the Lord's Table; but are you feasting on Christ? Do not settle for the outward husks of religion. Make certain that Christ is yours. Soon, you will stand before his bar. How will it be for your soul that great and terrible day?

Faithful Men Point Sinners To Death, Judgment And Eternity

John spoke of the Lord Jesus as that One "Whose fan is in his hand, and he will throughly purge his floor, and will gather the wheat into his garner; but the chaff he will burn with fire unquenchable" (v. 17).

There is a day of reckoning. One day soon we will all stand before the judgment seat of Christ, the great white throne. In that great day all things will be made manifest. In this world the kingdom of God is a field full of mixed seed, wheat and tares. The church is a fold of sheep and goats. Every gospel church is a mixed assembly of believers and unbelievers, saints and hypocrites, possessors of grace and professors of grace.

No man, no group of men is able to distinguish one from the other. None of us can distinguish sheep from goats, wheat from tares, and saints from hypocrites. We are too easily deceived. Therefore our Lord tells us to let them grow together. But there is a day coming, when he who knows all things will separate the precious from the vile. Give diligence to make your calling and election sure.

Faithful Men Are Faithful Unto Death

"And many other things in his exhortation preached he unto the people. But Herod the tetrarch, being reproved by him for Herodias his brother Philip's wife, and for all the evils which Herod had done, Added yet this above all, that he shut up John in prison" (vv. 18-20).

Time is the great revealer. In time you and I will all show our cards. We will eventually make ourselves known. We may not make ourselves known to ourselves; but we will be obvious to everyone else. Believers continue in faith. Faithful men and women are faithful to the end, no matter what it costs.

I did not say faithful people do not sin. I said they continue in faithfulness. They continue in the way. They continue to follow Christ, until they are with him in glory. And faithful preachers are faithful unto death, just like John the Baptist. May God make us faithful. Let us be found faithful unto the end.

"Now when all the people were baptized, it came to pass, that Jesus also being baptized, and praying, the heaven was opened, And the Holy Ghost descended in a bodily shape like a dove upon him, and a voice came from heaven, which said, Thou art my beloved Son; in thee I am well pleased. And Jesus himself began to be about thirty years of age, being (as was supposed) the son of Joseph, which was the son of Heli, Which was the son of Matthat, which was the son of Levi, which was the son of Melchi, which was the son of Janna, which was the son of Joseph, Which was the son of Mattathias, which was the son of Amos, which was the son of Naum, which was the son of Esli, which was the son of Nagge, Which was the son of Maath, which was the son of Mattathias, which was the son of Semei, which was the son of Joseph, which was the son of Juda, Which was the son of Joanna, which was the son of Rhesa, which was the son of Zorobabel, which was the son of Salathiel, which was the son of Neri, Which was the son of Melchi, which was the son of Addi, which was the son of Cosam, which was the son of Elmodam, which was the son of Er, Which was the son of Jose, which was the son of Eliezer, which was the son of Jorim, which was the son of Matthat, which was the son of Levi, Which was the son of Simeon, which was the son of Juda, which was the son of Joseph, which was the son of Jonan, which was the son of Eliakim, Which was the son of Melea, which was the son of Menan, which was the son of Mattatha, which was the son of Nathan, which was the son of David, Which was the son of Jesse, which was the son of Obed, which was the son of Booz, which was the son of Salmon, which was the son of Naasson, Which was the son of Aminadab, which was the son of Aram, which was the son of Esrom, which was the son of Phares, which was the son of Juda, Which was the son of Jacob, which was the son of Isaac, which was the son of Abraham, which was the son of Thara, which was the son of Nachor, Which was the son of Saruch, which was the son of Ragau, which was the son of Phalec, which was the son of Heber, which was the son of Sala, Which was the son of Cainan, which was the son of Arphaxad, which was the son of Sem, which was the son of Noe, which was the son of Lamech, Which was the son of Mathusala, which was the son of Enoch, which was the son of Jared, which was the son of Maleleel, which was the son of Cainan, Which was the son of Enos, which was the son of Seth, which was the son of Adam, which was the son of God" (Luke 3:21-38).

Chapter 21

Lessons From The Master's Baptism And Genealogy

We know virtually nothing about the childhood, youth, teenage years and early adulthood of our Saviour. We know he was born at Bethlehem, that Joseph and Mary fled with him to Egypt when he was about two years old and that he was found in the temple conversing with the religious leaders of the temple when he was twelve. We know nothing else about our Lord's earthly existence until he was thirty years old. All three of the synoptic gospels (Matthew, Mark and Luke) begin to describe our Lord's life and ministry as a man in exactly the same way at his baptism. That fact alone makes his baptism and ours matters of tremendous importance.

Baptism And Faith
In the Word of God baptism and faith always go together (Acts 8:36-38). Baptism is distinctly an ordinance of the New Testament. It is a distinctly gospel ordinance. There was nothing like it in the Old Testament, and nothing pointing to it.

Many have the notion that John's baptism was somehow different from the baptism practised by our Lord, his disciples and us; but there is not a shred of evidence for that notion. There is no evidence that any of our Lord's disciples were baptized by anyone, except John. John's baptism, like ours, was the baptism of repentance because of the remission of sins (v. 3). And John's baptism, like ours, was the symbolic fulfilment of righteousness (Matthew 3:13-17). It was a picture of redemption, a picture of the gospel. It was a picture not of cleansing by the gift of life, but of ransom by the death of Christ, not of regeneration by the Holy Spirit, but of redemption by the obedience of Christ unto death as our Substitute.

"Then cometh Jesus from Galilee to Jordan unto John, to be baptized of him. But John forbad him, saying, I have need to be baptized of thee, and comest thou to me? And Jesus answering said unto him, Suffer it to be so now: for thus it becometh us to fulfil all righteousness. Then he suffered him. And Jesus, when he was baptized, went up straightway out of the water: and, lo, the heavens were opened unto him, and he saw the Spirit of God descending like a dove, and lighting upon him: And lo a voice from heaven, saying, This is my beloved Son, in whom I am well pleased" (Matthew 3:13-17).

John's baptism, like ours, was an act by which men and women publicly renounced their former religion and publicly identified themselves with Christ and his people.

Our Lord Jesus treated this blessed ordinance of the gospel as a matter of highest esteem, giving it great honour, and placing great importance upon it. He walked all the way from Galilee to the Jordan River in order to be immersed by John the Baptist.

Baptism must never be regarded by us as a point of indifference, or a matter of slight importance. This is the ordinance of Christ, an ordinance of divine worship, which our Master commands us to keep.

I will say no more in this study about this blessed ordinance of the gospel than is here specifically stated by God the Holy Spirit. I have no creed to defend, no denomination to uphold, no tradition to maintain. I make no effort to mould the scriptures to a confession of faith. Believers mould their faith, their doctrine and their practices to the Word of God.

Here are five things taught throughout the New Testament and clearly set before us in our Saviour's example. These five things are so obvious, so plainly set before us, that none can misunderstand them or fail to see them, except those who are wilfully blinded by religious tradition.

Baptism is an ordinance of worship, not a sacrament. That distinction is important. An ordinance is a rule or command. A sacrament is an outward sign of an inward grace, or a means by which grace is conferred. Our Lord's baptism conferred no grace upon him. It washed away no sin from him. And it was not a sign of anything inward. It was that which he was behoved to do as Jehovah's Servant, because it symbolized the fulfilment of all righteousness by his obedience unto death.

Baptism is immersion. Immersion is not a mode, or even the mode of baptism. Immersion is baptism. That is what the word means. Without immersion, there is no baptism. Sprinkling is not immersion. It is sprinkling. Pouring is not immersion. It is pouring. Baptism is immersion.

Baptism is for adults only. Our Lord Jesus was thirty years old when he came to be baptized by John.

Baptism is for believers only. The prerequisite to baptism is faith (Acts 8:36-38). We are specifically told that our Saviour was praying when he was baptized. The practice of sprinkling and/or pouring water on infants, and calling the ritual, "baptism", is as foreign to the scriptures as rosary beads! If we would worship God, we must not add to his Word, or alter his ordinance.

Our baptism as believers, as followers of Christ, is a reflection of our Lord's baptism (Romans 6:3-6). In this blessed ordinance of worship believers are buried with Christ in the watery grave and rise with him from the grave, because that is exactly what has happened to every regenerate person. When Christ died, we died with him When he arose, we arose with him. In our baptism we confess to the world that we trust Christ and his obedience unto death as our Substitute for the whole of our salvation, and that we have been raised from death to life by his Spirit.

The Trinity And Redemption

When our Lord Jesus was baptized, all three Persons in the Godhead displayed a manifest concern in the affair of our redemption. God the Son was baptized. God the Spirit descended upon him in an openly revealed physical form, as a dove. And God the Father spoke from heaven.

We worship the Triune God, the Three-in-One Jehovah. "For there are three that bear record in heaven, the Father, the Word, and the Holy Ghost: and these three are one" (1 John 5:7). Throughout the New Testament, we see the fact of the Holy Trinity and the involvement of all three of the divine Persons in the work of grace. Both in the baptismal requirement that believer's be baptized "in the name of the Father, and of the Son, and of the Holy Ghost" (Matthew 28:19), and in the benedictions of grace from the Triune God upon the churches (2 Corinthians 13:14), we are taught that the three of the Godhead are engaged to save chosen sinners. This fact is asserted with clarity in Ephesians 1:3-14, 2 Thessalonians 2:13, 14 and 1 Peter 1:2).

> No man can comprehend
> The mighty Three-in-One,
> Or fathom what to rescue man,
> The Triune God has done.
> With confidence we boast
> What nature never learned,
> That Father, Son, and Holy Ghost
> To save are all concerned.

The Father's love, so grand,
His Son did sacrifice!
The Son for us his life resigned.
The Spirit grace applies.
The Trinity we praise,
Through Jesus Christ, our King.
With gratitude and love we raise
Our voice his praise to sing.

To God the Father be,
Who sent his Son to die,
Glory, and to the Son for He
Most willingly complied!
Praise God the Holy Ghost,
Who in Jesus reveals
God's love and grace for sinners lost,
And his salvation seals!

Grace And Mediation

We have before us a marvellous display of our Lord's covenant office as our God-man Mediator. The voice which spoke from heaven said, "Thou art my beloved Son. In thee I am well pleased."

The only way God Almighty can or will save fallen, guilty sinners is through a Mediator. And the Lord Jesus Christ is the Mediator, the only Mediator there is, between God and men (1 Timothy 2:5). Everything God has for sinners, everything God requires of sinners and everything God gives to sinners is "in him", in Christ. He who is Mediator between God and men must be both God and man. And he who is our Mediator must be one in whom God is well pleased. The Lord God is well pleased with our Redeemer's holy and infinitely meritorious nature as our God-man Mediator. He is well pleased with our Representative's holy life of perfect obedience for us. He is well pleased with our Substitute's death, by which he made complete satisfaction to divine justice, by the sacrifice of himself in the room and place of his people.

The Lord God is well pleased with the merit, the infinite merit of Christ's obedience unto death as our Substitute, but there is more stated here than that. When the Lord God said, "Thou art my beloved Son. In thee I am well pleased", he declared that he is well please not just with his Son, but well pleased in his Son. God Almighty is well pleased with his people in his Son!

Read the scriptures and rejoice. If you are in Christ, God is well pleased with you in him (Ephesians 1:3-6; Numbers 23:21; Psalm 32:1, 2; Romans 4:8; Jeremiah 50:20; Ecclesiastes 9:7).

> Bold shall I stand in that great day,
> For who aught to my charge shall lay,
> While through Christ's blood absolved I am,
> From sin's tremendous curse and blame!
>
> Nikolaus Ludwig von Zinzendorf

Humanity And Death

In verses 23-38 we have a long list of names. Here we are given the names of 75 people. Were it not for the fact that their names are in this genealogical record[7], most of the names would have long ago gone into oblivion. Who remembers them? Who cares who they were, where they lived, what they did or what they had? No one!

What frail, dying creatures we are! Like us, these men all once lived upon the earth. They had the same joys we have, the same sorrows, the same griefs and the same troubles. As we all soon must, all these men died and are buried in the earth. Each one has now gone to his own place, as soon we must.

Yes, we too are passing away and soon must be gone. Let us forever bless God and give thanks to him that in this dying world we have a living Saviour! Let us make it our one great concern to be joined to him, who is the Resurrection and the Life. May God give us grace to live day by day in this world of time and trouble as dying men and women who live for eternity.

---

[7] All who read the Scriptures with care know that there is some difficulty reconciling the records of our Lord's genealogy. If we compare Matthew's account with Luke's account, there appears to be an obvious conflict in the recorded names given between David and Joseph. Between David and Abraham, Matthew's record and Luke's agree. But between David and Joseph, they appear to be two different family trees. In all likelihood there are. It appears that Luke was inspired to give us our Lord's maternal genealogy, while Matthew and Mark give us his paternal genealogy. Heli, being Mary's father, would have been Joseph's father-in-law, his father by marriage. He would have been listed as such in the maternal genealogy of the family.

145

"And Jesus being full of the Holy Ghost returned from Jordan, and was led by the Spirit into the wilderness, Being forty days tempted of the devil. And in those days he did eat nothing: and when they were ended, he afterward hungered. And the devil said unto him, If thou be the Son of God, command this stone that it be made bread. And Jesus answered him, saying, It is written, That man shall not live by bread alone, but by every word of God. And the devil, taking him up into an high mountain, shewed unto him all the kingdoms of the world in a moment of time. And the devil said unto him, All this power will I give thee, and the glory of them: for that is delivered unto me; and to whomsoever I will I give it. If thou therefore wilt worship me, all shall be thine. And Jesus answered and said unto him, Get thee behind me, Satan: for it is written, Thou shalt worship the Lord thy God, and him only shalt thou serve. And he brought him to Jerusalem, and set him on a pinnacle of the temple, and said unto him, If thou be the Son of God, cast thyself down from hence: For it is written, he shall give his angels charge over thee, to keep thee: And in their hands they shall bear thee up, lest at any time thou dash thy foot against a stone. And Jesus answering said unto him, It is said, Thou shalt not tempt the Lord thy God. And when the devil had ended all the temptation, he departed from him for a season" (Luke 4:1-13).

Chapter 22

The Temptation Of Christ

In order to save us from our sins the Lord Jesus Christ, the Son of God, not only became a man so that he could die for us as our Substitute; but he humbled himself as a man. I am certain that we cannot fathom the depths of his humiliation. And I am equally certain that we should not try. In fact, everything I have heard or read by men attempting to explain the various aspects of our Lord's humiliation, though done with the desire to honour him, has appeared to me to be a desecration of that which is most sacred.

Instead of trying to fathom the unfathomable, let us rather simply bow before the revelation of God in holy scripture and worship that One who, though he was rich, yet for our sake, became poor, that we through his poverty might be made rich.

In order to redeem and save his people, the Lord Jesus Christ had to live in perfect obedience to God while enduring all the consequences of sin. He must triumph over Satan yet suffer the wrath of God to the full satisfaction of justice. He must bring in everlasting righteousness as a man.

One great part of our Master's obedience was his temptation in all points as a man and his overcoming temptation, his triumphing over Satan in temptation, that he might be for us a merciful and faithful High Priest in things pertaining to God. This is what we have before us in Luke 4:1-13.

Real Temptation
Immediately after his baptism, Christ was harassed with the temptations of Satan. "He suffered being tempted;" and he "was tempted in all points like as we are, yet without sin" (Hebrews 2:18, 4:15). He was tried and tested with all sorts of temptations, just like we are. Yet, he had no sin and did no sin.

Satan tempted him, but not by stirring up some corruption, or provoking some lust in him, as he does when he tempts us to evil. David is an example of the way we are tempted. He was tempted, like we are, when Satan stirred up the lust of pride and vanity that was in him to number the people. But there was no sin, no corruption in Christ to be stirred. The old serpent found nothing in him with which to work.

Our Lord was not tempted by Satan putting any evil into him, as he put it into the heart of Judas Iscariot to betray his Lord, and put it into the hearts of Ananias and Sapphira to lie unto the Holy Ghost.

And Satan got no advantage over the Lord Jesus by any of his temptations, as he so often does us. Oh, no! Our Saviour triumphed over his adversary and ours in all things. The devil was forced to leave our Lord after these temptations in the wilderness, just as he was in the garden of Gethsemane. And, at last, our great Redeemer crushed the serpent's head in complete victory at Calvary, and bound the dragon of hell in the chain of his omnipotence, that he should deceive the nations no more.

Thank God, he who is our tempter, our adversary, our accuser, he who is far too cunning and powerful a foe for us, has been bound by our Saviour. Our adversary the devil still goes about, walking up and down in the earth as a roaring lion, seeking whom he may devour. But he is a bound lion. His fangs and claws have been removed. Insofar as God's elect are concerned, all he can do is roar (John 12:31-33; Revelation 12:10; 20:1-3).

Yet, we must never fail to remember that these temptations of Christ were real. Our Lord Jesus was tempted in all points, just like we are. The lust of the eye, the lust of the flesh and the pride of life (1 John 2:16), by which he got advantage over Adam and Eve in the Garden of Eden, and by which he still deceives and overthrows many, are the very weapons Satan used against our Master.

Obedient, Yet Tempted

The Lord Jesus was tempted "when he was full of the Holy Ghost" (v. 1). Luke tells us that our Lord was filled with the Holy Spirit when he was tempted. Matthew, Mark and Luke tell us that he was led of the Spirit into the wilderness of temptation. These things are not written to fill up space. They are written for our learning. They tell us plainly that nothing shields a believer from Satan's temptations. Nothing will prevent us from temptation, but the will of God. Nothing we do can keep the tempter away. No matter how fervent we are in prayer, no matter how completely we may walk in the Spirit, no matter how sensitive and submissive we are to the Spirit's leading, we will still be tempted of the devil to do evil.

In fact, Matthew specifically informs us that "Jesus was led up of the Spirit into the wilderness to be tempted of the devil." In other words, the temptations to which we are subjected are, like all other aspects of the believer's life, according to the will of God and designed by him for our good. Like our Master, God's people learn obedience by the things we suffer, even from the hands of our adversary the devil.

Our Lord's temptations came in the wilderness. Matthew, Mark, and Luke tell us that the temptations took place in the wilderness, where there was no one and nothing to support him. Mark tells us that he was there exposed to the wild beasts. Matthew and Luke tell us that his temptations came after he had been miraculously sustained by God through a period of forty days and nights of fasting. This, too, is important. Our Master's temptations came at a time when he was physically weak and hungry. Satan is a cunning, crafty adversary. He suits his temptations to the constitution of our nature, the circumstances we are in and the situations in which we are found.

Our Saviour was tempted just after his baptism. He had just come from a time of solemn worship and deliberate, consecrated obedience. He had just been baptized, in order to fulfil all righteousness (symbolically), as a pledge of his determination to obey his Father's will unto death as our Substitute. Our Lord had just been highly, publicly honoured as the Son of God, in whom the Father is well pleased. He had just experienced the miraculous power of God in sustaining him in life without any natural means. He was sustained not by bread, but by the word (the decree) of God.

There is often only a step from great privileges and blessings to great trials and troubles. We must never forget this. Even in our most solemn frames and at the times of our greatest usefulness, we must "watch and pray".

John Gill writes upon this, "So it often is with his members; that as he was tempted, after his baptism, after the Spirit of God had descended upon him, and filled him with his gifts and graces without measure; and after he had had such a testimony from heaven of his divine Sonship: so his people, after they have had communion with God in ordinances, and have had some sealing testimonies of his love, fall into temptations, and fall by them; as the disciples of Christ after the supper, who, when tempted, all forsook him and fled, and one denied him."

Three Great Evils
All that is in the world, all our troubles, all our trials, all our temptations, all our rebellions, all the misery we bring to others, and all the woe we bring upon ourselves are the result of three great evils, as John describes them: "the lust of the flesh, the lust of the eyes, and the pride of life." These were, as I have already said, the ruin of Adam and Eve, and of our race in the Garden of Eden. And these are the areas wherein our Master was tempted of Satan. They have to do with unbelief, worldliness and presumption.

Three times we see our Saviour tempted of the devil, assaulted by the fiend of hell, as he cunningly attempted, with feigned politeness, to draw the holy One of God into sin. Each assault was the work of one who is a master in deceit. We will be wise to carefully observe both the subtlety of the serpent and the wisdom of our Saviour in each of these temptations.

Lust Of The Eye

First, Satan tempted the Lord Jesus to unbelief, to the lust of the eye.

"And the devil said unto him, If thou be the Son of God, command this stone that it be made bread. And Jesus answered him, saying, It is written, That man shall not live by bread alone, but by every word of God" (vv. 3, 4).

Here Satan tried to get the Lord Jesus to distrust his Father's care, the care of him who had sustained him for forty days and nights without food. Our Saviour was hungry and weak. But he had just received a public declaration, by which his Father owned him as the Son of God. So the hissing serpent offers him a very "kind, sensible" suggestion. The sense of it is this: The devil picked up, or pointed to a rock and said, "Since you're the Son of God, and you are hungry, why don't you just turn this rock into a loaf of bread and have a bite to eat?"

Why should he wait? Why should the Creator of all things sit still and starve? Why not command the stone to become bread? What possible evil could there be in that? The answer is found in our Lord's rely. Being familiar with the Old Testament scriptures, the Master resisted Satan and escaped his snare by quoting from Deuteronomy 8:3. "And he humbled thee, and suffered thee to hunger, and fed thee with manna, which thou knewest not, neither did thy fathers know; that he might make thee know that man doth not live by bread only, but by every word that proceedeth out of the mouth of the LORD doth man live."

Our Lord refused to turn the stone to bread, because he refused to live by carnal reason. He refused to walk by sight. He was determined to live by faith, trusting the word[8] of God. He would not turn the stone into bread, because it was not his Father's will that the stone be turned into bread.

Though our Lord performed countless miracles for the benefit of others, he never performed even one for his own benefit. He preferred to remain hungry than to violate his Father's will. With the hunger pangs and physical weakness of going forty days and nights without food, the Lord Jesus in effect said to Satan, like Job of old, "Though he slay me, yet will I trust him."

If we would honour God, we must follow Christ's example. Let us ever choose trusting him, believing him, walking by faith, rather than leaning on the arm of the flesh. Our Father's will is always best; and he will provide everything we need as we walk in his will, in his way, trusting him.

---

[8] The "word" of God, here and in the context of Deuteronomy, refers not to the scriptures, but to the oracle, purpose and decree of God.

There is another, obvious reason why he refused to turn the stone into bread. He was living on this earth as a man, as our Representative and Substitute, and you and I are not able to turn a rock into a loaf of bread. If he would live and die for us, as our Redeemer, he had to live and die as we must, as a man. If he would be touched with the feeling of our infirmities, he had to feel what we feel in the same circumstances.

I cannot help thinking that he may have had a third reason for refusing the devil, though he was terribly hungry. He refused to make sport for and entertain the fiend of hell. He had nothing to prove to himself or to the devil. He was and is the Son of God. He knew it. His Father had just declared it. And, though pride would jump at the chance to prove it by displaying it before the prince of darkness, our Master refused to gratify him. But the heart of the matter is this. Satan tried to get Christ not to trust his Father's wise and good providence. When Apollyon persuades us to walk by sight, by the lust of the eye, rather than trust God's providence, we have fallen victim to his devices.

Lust Of The Flesh

Second, Satan tried to entice the Holy One into sin by the lust of the flesh, by worldliness.[9] he tried to get the Lord Jesus to grasp worldly power by compromise.

"And the devil, taking him up into an high mountain, showed unto him all the kingdoms of the world in a moment of time. And the devil said unto him, All this power will I give thee, and the glory of them: for that is delivered unto me; and to whomsoever I will I give it. If thou therefore wilt worship me, all shall be thine. And Jesus answered and said unto him, Get thee behind me, Satan: for it is written, Thou shalt worship the Lord thy God, and him only shalt thou serve" (vv. 5-8).

The devil took the Lord Jesus by his permission up on top of one of those high mountains surrounding Jerusalem, and offered him all the kingdoms of the world, if he would just fall down and worship him.

Try to get a sense of the brazenness of the wicked one. He waved his hands, with a confident smile and, by a diabolical and false representation of things to the sight, he showed the Lord Jesus "all the kingdoms of the world, and the glory of them", alluring him with a promise that the whole world would "fall down and worship him". Imagine that!

For Satan to promise these to Christ was hellishly impertinent. The whole world was his already! The earth is his, and the fullness thereof, the world,

---

[9] This was actually the third temptation in the successive order given in Matthew 4; but for some reason not revealed to us the Holy Spirit inspired Luke to place this temptation second. Perhaps it was done just to give the goats a can to chew. Obviously, there is no significance to the fact.

and they that dwell therein. He made it all. He owns it all. Besides that, all power in heaven and earth is given our Lord as the God-man Mediator, to rule them, use them and dispose of them as he will. For Satan to pretend that these were his to give, that they were in his power to dispose of to whomsoever he pleased, was intolerable arrogance.

Understand this. There is nothing in this world, nothing in the universe which belongs to Satan, nothing over which he has power, except as Christ our God gives it to him. This is the same devil who, we are told in the Book of Job, cowers before God's throne to give account of his doings, who could not wiggle his finger against Job without God's permission. Why he could not even go into a herd of hogs, without the Lord Jesus giving him permission to do so. For him to propose to Christ that he should fall down and worship him was the height of insolence and impudence! But that is his nature. Never expect less from him or from those who dance by his lead.

Again, John Gill comments, "This shows what the original sin of the devil was, affectation of Deity, and to be worshipped as God; hence he has usurped the title of the God of this world; and has prevailed upon the ignorant part of it, in some places, to give him worship: and, indeed, to sacrifice to idols, is to sacrifice to devils: but, not content with this, he sought to be worshipped by the Son of God himself; than which nothing could be more audacious and impious; wherefore Christ rejected his temptation with indignation and abhorrence; saying, 'Get thee behind me, Satan; for it is written, Thou shalt worship the Lord thy God, and him only shalt thou serve.'"

The devil here appeals to the Master to by-pass the misery and agony of the cross. He was promised the world as the reward for his obedience unto death, the throne of universal monarchy, upon his finishing the Father's will as our sin-atoning Sacrifice. Satan was just offering him an easier way to get it all. All he required was what appears to be a small concession. He does not require that the Master cease to worship God, or to worship him above God, or even worship him permanently. He only demanded that he fall down and worship him, adore him, acknowledge him once, and that in private.

The concession seemed to be small. The promise was great. The way was easy. Why should he not take the easy way out? Why should he not grab such an enormous prize? Why shouldn't we? The answer is found in our Master's quotation of Deuteronomy 6:13. We are to worship God alone and serve him alone. The glory of God must be our dominant concern. For that, for the glory of God, we ought to gladly sacrifice anything.

Let us ever beware of worldliness, the love of the world (1 John 2:15-17; Matthew 6:31-33). Beware of covetousness, which is idolatry (Luke 12:15). May God the Holy Spirit give us grace ever to set our affection on our Saviour, not on this perishing world (Colossians 3:1-5).

Pride Of Life

Third, Satan tempted the Son of God with the pride of life, urging him to act in daring presumption.

"And he brought him to Jerusalem, and set him on a pinnacle of the temple, and said unto him, If thou be the Son of God, cast thyself down from hence: For it is written, he shall give his angels charge over thee, to keep thee: And in their hands they shall bear thee up, lest at any time thou dash thy foot against a stone. And Jesus answering said unto him, It is said, Thou shalt not tempt the Lord thy God. And when the devil had ended all the temptation, he departed from him for a season" (vv. 9-13).

This time the devil quotes scripture (Psalm 91:11). In fact, one of Satan's favourite weapons is the Bible. He takes the Holy Book of Inspiration and twists it, perverts it, misuses it and abuses it for his own devices. Again, the Lord Jesus referred the devil to Deuteronomy 6. This time he quoted verse 16. "Ye shall not tempt the LORD your God, as ye tempted him in Massah."

What a wonderful, public, undeniable proof it would be that he is indeed the Son of God and the Messiah, and a clear fulfilment of Psalm 91, if the Lord Jesus would dive off that high, high wall of the temple, with all the scribes, and Pharisees, and people watching, as the angels of God swept down from heaven and gave him a gentle landing. After all, this was the promise of the psalms. Surely, since God had not predestined his death at this time, he could not die by diving off the wall. Could he? For him to have heeded Satan's allurement would have been an act of self-exaltation and pride, as well as an act of complete irresponsibility, tempting God by presuming upon his goodness. Our Saviour did not yield. The glory of his Father was more important to him than the fickle approval and applause of men. May the same ever be true of us!

The Lord Jesus Christ is just the Saviour and Great High Priest we need. "For in that he himself hath suffered being tempted, he is able to succour them that are tempted" (Hebrews 2:18).

"Seeing then that we have a great high priest, that is passed into the heavens, Jesus the Son of God, let us hold fast our profession. For we have not an high priest which cannot be touched with the feeling of our infirmities; but was in all points tempted like as we are, yet without sin. Let us therefore come boldly unto the throne of grace, that we may obtain mercy, and find grace to help in time of need" (Hebrews 4:14-16).

As he foiled Satan in the wilderness and crushed his head at Calvary, so he knows how to deliver you and me out of our temptations; and blessed be his name, he will! "And the God of peace shall bruise Satan under your feet shortly. The grace of our Lord Jesus Christ be with you. Amen."

"And Jesus returned in the power of the Spirit into Galilee: and there went out a fame of him through all the region round about. And he taught in their synagogues, being glorified of all. And he came to Nazareth, where he had been brought up: and, as his custom was, he went into the synagogue on the sabbath day, and stood up for to read. And there was delivered unto him the book of the prophet Esaias. And when he had opened the book, he found the place where it was written, The Spirit of the Lord is upon me, because he hath anointed me to preach the gospel to the poor; he hath sent me to heal the brokenhearted, to preach deliverance to the captives, and recovering of sight to the blind, to set at liberty them that are bruised, To preach the acceptable year of the Lord. And he closed the book, and he gave it again to the minister, and sat down. And the eyes of all them that were in the synagogue were fastened on him. And he began to say unto them, This day is this scripture fulfilled in your ears. And all bare him witness, and wondered at the gracious words which proceeded out of his mouth. And they said, Is not this Joseph's son? And he said unto them, Ye will surely say unto me this proverb, Physician, heal thyself: whatsoever we have heard done in Capernaum, do also here in thy country. And he said, Verily I say unto you, No prophet is accepted in his own country. But I tell you of a truth, many widows were in Israel in the days of Elias, when the heaven was shut up three years and six months, when great famine was throughout all the land; But unto none of them was Elias sent, save unto Sarepta, a city of Sidon, unto a woman that was a widow. And many lepers were in Israel in the time of Eliseus the prophet; and none of them was cleansed, saving Naaman the Syrian. And all they in the synagogue, when they heard these things, were filled with wrath, And rose up, and thrust him out of the city, and led him unto the brow of the hill whereon their city was built, that they might cast him down headlong. But he passing through the midst of them went his way, And came down to Capernaum, a city of Galilee, and taught them on the sabbath days. And they were astonished at his doctrine: for his word was with power" (Luke 4:14-32).

Chapter 23

A Riot In The Synagogue

When a small town boy grows up, goes out and makes a name for himself, and comes back home, all the old men extol him, the women admire him, and the children idolize him. He becomes the talk of the town. The local weekly newspaper runs a front page story about him, with huge pictures. The boy no one knew or gave much attention to has become the town hero, and the town looks for a stage, so that they can show him off to the world. The poorer and more despised the town, the greater the hero.

That is just the picture we have before us in Luke 4:14. The Lord Jesus grew up in Nazareth. The common saying was, "Can anything good come out of Nazareth?" But here was a home town boy, a native son who had proved everybody wrong, insofar as Nazareth was concerned. "Jesus returned in the power of the Spirit into Galilee: and there went out a fame of him through all the region round about. And he taught in their synagogues, being glorified of all" (vv. 14, 15).

In a very brief time the Master's doctrine and preaching had made him a very famous man. His miracles were talked about everywhere. Now he had come home.

Public Worship

Though the Lord Jesus Christ was and is the Object of all true worship, while he lived in this world as a man, as a child of God, our Master faithfully worshipped God in public and in private. Our Saviour set before us an example to follow. In all things he is the pattern we are to copy.

"And he came to Nazareth, where he had been brought up: and, as his custom was, he went into the synagogue on the sabbath day, and stood up for to read. And there was delivered unto him the book of the prophet Esaias. And when he had opened the book, he found the place where it was written" (vv. 16, 17).

Our Lord needed none of the blessings we gain from divine worship. Yet, he was always faithful in public worship. He came to the house of God for the glory of God and for the benefit of others, not for himself. He forsook not the assembly of the saints. At all appointed times the Lord Jesus was found in the house of God, worshipping with the people of God. Luke tells us it was, "his custom". May God the Holy Spirit teach us to follow his example (Matthew 18:20; Hebrews 10:23-26).

Reading Scripture

One of the most blessed aspects of public worship is the reading of holy scripture. Even in their most degenerate times, the Jews retained and showed great reverence for the Word of God. Great emphasis was given to the reading of holy scripture.

It is a sad fact that most churches of our day place very little, if any, emphasis upon the public reading of the Word of God. That should not be. No part of the worship service is more important than the reading of the Word of God. When the scriptures are read, we receive direct, verbally inspired instruction from God himself.

I have never conducted a public worship service without giving a special place to the reading of God's Word, and I never intend to do so. I consider it to be as important as prayer, praise and preaching.

In the synagogue worship of the Jews a prominent place was given to the reading of holy scripture every sabbath day (Luke 4:16; Acts 13:15). The apostle Paul told the young pastor, Timothy, to give attendance to reading the scriptures, exhorting the saints and teaching the doctrine of the gospel (1 Timothy 4:13). That is the way preachers are supposed to conduct the services of public worship. The epistles of the New Testament were written to be read in the churches, and our Lord's letters to the churches of Asia (Revelation 2, 3) were to be read to the churches.

The importance of this practice cannot be overstressed. In every local church there are some who either cannot or do not read the Word of God for themselves, and some who read so poorly that they do not read correctly. Reason and common sense should teach us the usefulness of publicly reading the scriptures to them. If men and women are to worship God, they must know what God says in his Word. God's Word alone, not the preacher's comments about it, is inspired and authoritative (2 Timothy 3:16, 17). Therefore, prominence should be given to the reading of holy scripture in every assembly of the church. Hezekiah Harvey wrote ...

"The omission of this would imply that the words of man are of higher moment than the words of God. The scriptures should have a large and reverent use in the pulpit, as the fountain of all instruction and the sole standard of faith and practice."

Primarily, it is the pastor's responsibility to read the scriptures to the congregation. When he does, he may choose a passage relating to his message for the hour and give a brief exposition as he reads. But such expositions should always be carefully prepared, so that he does no violence to the text. Spontaneous, unprepared comments are seldom either accurate or helpful and display a terrible lack of reverence for the Word of God.

The pastor may ask one of the men of the church to read the scriptures. If anyone is asked to do so, he must not take the work lightly, for he has the responsibility of reading God's Word to his people. The portion he chooses to read and the way he reads it will set the tone for the entire worship service. He must seek the direction of God's Spirit with care. I make the following recommendations to anyone entrusted with this task.

Select a devotional passage, a portion of scripture that will lead the hearts of God's people to Christ. Select a brief passage. Generally, it is best to select just one passage. And always select a passage by which God has spoken to your own heart.

Familiarize yourself with the passage you plan to read. Read it carefully, prayerfully and studiously at home. Read it several times, noting the punctuation of the text. Be certain that you understand the portion of scripture you read to the church. If you do not understand it, select another portion to read.

Read the passage carefully and distinctly. Remember you are not reading for yourself alone. You are reading to the congregation. Read loudly enough that everyone present can hear you distinctly! If you are not accustomed to reading in public, read the passage aloud at home. It is frustrating to try to follow a reading that cannot be heard.

Read the Word of God without comment. Leave it to the preacher to do the preaching. When the scriptures are read, it is so that God's people may hear God speak to their hearts by his Word.

Isaiah's Prophecy
"The Spirit of the Lord is upon me, because he hath anointed me to preach the gospel to the poor; he hath sent me to heal the brokenhearted, to preach deliverance to the captives, and recovering of sight to the blind, to set at liberty them that are bruised, To preach the acceptable year of the Lord" (vv. 18, 19).

157

The portion of scripture our Saviour read on this occasion was Isaiah 61, one of the many passages describing the work of the Messiah and the salvation he would accomplish. Our Lord probably read the entire passage; but Luke simply refers to verses 1 and 2. This is what God declared the work of his Son would be, when he came to save his people from their sins. This is what Christ came to do. And this is what he has done and is doing.

"The spirit of the Lord GOD is upon me; because the LORD hath anointed me to preach good tidings unto the meek; he hath sent me to bind up the brokenhearted, to proclaim liberty to the captives, and the opening of the prison to them that are bound; To proclaim the acceptable year of the LORD, and the day of vengeance of our God; to comfort all that mourn" (Isaiah 61:1, 2).

Our Master was, as a man, a preacher anointed for the work by his Father and prepared for the work by the special gift of his Spirit. Preaching, true preaching requires these three things: (1.) the Spirit of God, (2.) the anointing of God and (3.) the message of God. But our Master was more than a preacher. He is our Saviour. We preach what he did. He preached what he himself performed! He preached the gospel, glad tidings and good news, not good advice. Modern preaching is nothing but advice given to sinners, telling dead sinners what they must do. The gospel of Christ is the proclamation of good news, telling poor sinners what Christ has done.

Our Saviour preached the gospel to the poor. Without question, he preached to multitudes who were materially poor; but the word here translated "poor" refers to "the meek", those poor sinners who are broken before God, meek, knowing that they have nothing to offer the holy Lord God, and have no ability to produce anything he might accept from them. They are poor, meek, humbled and broken by the weight of sin and guilt before God's glorious holiness.

The Lord Jesus Christ heals, binds up, the brokenhearted. He makes blind eyes to see, and gives comfort and liberty to bruised souls. The Son of God opens prison doors and sets the captive free. All this grace he pours out to sinners upon the basis of justice satisfied by blood atonement, proclaiming the acceptable year of the LORD, the day God's righteous vengeance and justice was satisfied at Calvary.

Scripture Fulfilled
"And he closed the book, and he gave it again to the minister, and sat down. And the eyes of all them that were in the synagogue were fastened on him. And he began to say unto them, This day is this scripture fulfilled in your ears" (vv. 20, 21).

Christ is the message of holy scripture! He was the fulfilment of this passage (Isaiah 61); and he was and is the fulfilment of all the Old Testament scriptures. All the law, all the prophets, all the types, all the psalms, all the proverbs and all the history of the Old Testament speak about the Lord Jesus Christ and find their fulfilment in him.

"And beginning at Moses and all the prophets, he expounded unto them in all the scriptures the things concerning himself" (Luke 24:27).

"And he said unto them, These are the words which I spake unto you, while I was yet with you, that all things must be fulfilled, which were written in the law of Moses, and in the prophets, and in the psalms, concerning me. Then opened he their understanding, that they might understand the scriptures" (Luke 24:44, 45).

This is not an invention or conclusion drawn from current theological understanding. The saints of God in ancient times knew that the scriptures spoke of their coming Redeemer. It is a great mistake to underestimate the faith and knowledge of God's saints in the Old Testament. God's elect were saved in the Old Testament in exactly the same way we are saved today. God has only one way of saving sinners. That way, as you know, is Christ alone, by grace alone, through faith alone. Christ was the Object of all true faith in the Old Testament, just as he is today.

What amount of knowledge those Old Testament believers had, I cannot tell. It is not clearly revealed. But those earliest saints were not morons, either mentally or spiritually. We know that they understood and believed the gospel.

Eve understood the promise that the Redeemer would be a man of the woman's seed (Genesis 3:15). Abel knew about blood atonement (Genesis 4). Abraham knew that the Redeemer would be God incarnate (Genesis 22:8). David clearly understood that forgiveness is sure through the blood atonement of a crucified Substitute (Psalm 22; 32, 51). Enoch even spoke plainly about the Lord's second advent (Jude 14). Even Job, in that which is probably the first book written in the Inspired Volume, describes Christ as our Redeemer and speaks of the resurrection at the last day (Job 19:25-27).

Isaiah understood that the sinner's Substitute is both God and man in one person, whose work of redemption and grace must be effectual to the salvation of chosen sinners (Isaiah 7:14; 9:6-9; 52:13-53:12).

Numerous other references could be given. These are truly only a few; and they were randomly selected. Yet, they will suffice to make my point irrefutable. Old Testament saints knew and trusted the Lord Jesus Christ as their effectual, almighty, crucified, risen, reigning Saviour. It is also clear, to even a casual reader of holy scripture, that the saints of the Mosaic era clearly understood and rejoiced in the doctrines of God's free and sovereign grace in

Christ. Divine Sovereignty (Psalms 115:3; 135:6; Daniel 4:35-37; Isaiah 46:9-11). Total Depravity (Psalm 14). Unconditional Election (Psalm 65:4; 2 Samuel 23:5). Limited Atonement (Isaiah 53:8-11). Irresistible Grace (Psalms 65:4; 110:3). Perseverance of the Saints (Psalm 23:6).

In a word, God gave faith to his chosen in the Old Testament, just as he gives us faith, by supernatural revelation, by revealing Christ to and in chosen sinners. Obviously, the Revelation of God in scripture was not as full in Job's day as it was in Moses', or in Moses' day as it was in Malachi's, or in Malachi's day as it was in John the Baptist's, or in John the Baptist's day as it was in Paul's. But the Revelation was clear; and the faith of God's saints was exemplary (Hebrews 11).

I must personally acknowledge that I have never begun to experience the quality of faith that Noah exhibited in building the ark, Abraham exhibited on Mount Moriah, or Moses exhibited in dealing with Pharaoh and Israel. Those men believed God. They knew, worshipped and trusted the Lord Jesus Christ, of whom the Old Testament speaks (John 5:39). The Book of God is all about the Son of God and the redemption he accomplished by his blood.

Everyone who heard the Lord Jesus preach was greatly impressed by his preaching. As we shall see, they were not impressed with what he preached, but with the way he preached it. What a danger! "And all bare him witness, and wondered at the gracious words which proceeded out of his mouth. And they said, Is not this Joseph's son?" (v. 22) "Take heed therefore how ye hear" (Luke 8:18). They heard with pleasure, but not with profit. They nodded their heads, but did not bow their hearts.

These fine, church going, Bible thumping, hymn singing folks were expecting the Son of God to entertain them with his wonders. Read verses 23 and 24. "And he said unto them, Ye will surely say unto me this proverb, Physician, heal thyself: whatsoever we have heard done in Capernaum, do also here in thy country. And he said, Verily I say unto you, No prophet is accepted in his own country."

In verses 25-27 the Lord Jesus declared to these proud Jews that God Almighty is always sovereign in the exercise of his mercy, love and grace. In other words, he said, "I will be gracious to whom I will be gracious. I will have mercy on whom I will have mercy."

"But I tell you of a truth, many widows were in Israel in the days of Elias, when the heaven was shut up three years and six months, when great famine was throughout all the land; But unto none of them was Elias sent, save unto Sarepta, a city of Sidon, unto a woman that was a widow. And many lepers were in Israel in the time of Eliseus the prophet; and none of them was cleansed, saving Naaman the Syrian."

Synagogue Riot

This message of divine sovereignty was too much for proud, self-righteous men and women to endure!

"And all they in the synagogue, when they heard these things, were filled with wrath, And rose up, and thrust him out of the city, and led him unto the brow of the hill whereon their city was built, that they might cast him down headlong" (vv. 28, 29).

What did our Master say to enrage these people so? He used no obscenities. He did not ridicule them, belittle them or call them names. All he did was assert that salvation is of the Lord, God is totally sovereign in the affair of salvation, God Almighty is no man's debtor and no one deserves God's grace! And how did our Master react to the enraged mob? He just went right on about his business as the servant of God. He was not their servant, but God's. What an example!

"But he passing through the midst of them went his way, and came down to Capernaum, a city of Galilee, and taught them on the sabbath days. And they were astonished at his doctrine: for his word was with power" (vv. 30-32).

What was the cause of this rage? We must never forget that the gospel we preach is a savour of life to some and of death to others. The Lord Jesus preached that doctrine which always has, always must and always will enrage carnal men, though the Son of God himself be the preacher. The sweet gospel doctrine of divine sovereignty (Matthew 11:25, 26; John 17:2, 3, 9; Romans 9:6-33) is odious and offensive to lost religionists, to men and women whose hearts are enmity against God. The sovereign God, particularly his sovereignty in the exercise of his saving mercy, stands in glaring opposition to the pride of will-worshipping man and his idolatrous freewill, works religion. The preaching of the gospel always raises bitter resentment instantly among such rebels.

We must not look for or labour for the approval of men. Labour with your eye toward eternity. There is a time to dig and a time to reap, a time to sow the seed and a time to gather the harvest, a time to tear down and a time to build. God alone determines the time! Our business is to serve him, with persevering faithfulness. He requires nothing more and nothing less than faithfulness from his servants. Oh, may he graciously give us that faithfulness, for Christ's sake!

"And came down to Capernaum, a city of Galilee, and taught them on the sabbath days. And they were astonished at his doctrine: for his word was with power. And in the synagogue there was a man, which had a spirit of an unclean devil, and cried out with a loud voice, Saying, Let us alone; what have we to do with thee, thou Jesus of Nazareth? art thou come to destroy us? I know thee who thou art; the Holy One of God. And Jesus rebuked him, saying, Hold thy peace, and come out of him. And when the devil had thrown him in the midst, he came out of him, and hurt him not. And they were all amazed, and spake among themselves, saying, What a word is this! for with authority and power he commandeth the unclean spirits, and they come out. And the fame of him went out into every place of the country round about. And he arose out of the synagogue, and entered into Simon's house. And Simon's wife's mother was taken with a great fever; and they besought him for her. And he stood over her, and rebuked the fever; and it left her: and immediately she arose and ministered unto them. Now when the sun was setting, all they that had any sick with divers diseases brought them unto him; and he laid his hands on every one of them, and healed them. And devils also came out of many, crying out, and saying, Thou art Christ the Son of God. And he rebuking them suffered them not to speak: for they knew that he was Christ. And when it was day, he departed and went into a desert place: and the people sought him, and came unto him, and stayed him, that he should not depart from them. And he said unto them, I must preach the kingdom of God to other cities also: for therefore am I sent. And he preached in the synagogues of Galilee" (Luke 4:31-44).

Chapter 24

Lessons From Capernaum

When the Jews at Nazareth threw him out of their synagogue and tried to murder him for preaching the gospel, our Lord came down to Capernaum, another Galilean city.

Ordained Means
The first thing that stands out in this passage is the fact that gospel preaching is God's ordained means of grace. This portion of scripture begins and ends with statements about our Lord Jesus preaching the gospel.

"And (the Lord Jesus) came down to Capernaum, a city of Galilee, and taught them on the sabbath days. And they were astonished at his doctrine: for his word was with power" (vv. 31, 32).

"And he said unto them, I must preach the kingdom of God to other cities also: for therefore am I sent. And he preached in the synagogues of Galilee" (vv. 43, 44).

Our Saviour placed great importance upon the preaching of the gospel. In fact, he said, "I must preach the kingdom of God ... for therefore am I sent." Preaching was his business.

I stress this fact because we live in a day in which preaching is belittled, set aside and considered out of date by the religious world. While I readily acknowledge that most preaching is irrelevant, gospel preaching is not. Rather, the preaching of the gospel is the most important aspect of the church's life and ministry in every age.

Ever beware of those who make little of preaching, and of any tendency to set aside the ministry of the Word. The church is never stronger than her pulpit. The church is strong when the pulpit is strong. The church is irrelevant when the pulpit is irrelevant. The preaching of the gospel is God's ordained means of grace to his people, the means by which he saves, edifies, comforts and directs his people in this world.

"Wherefore he saith, When he ascended up on high, he led captivity captive, and gave gifts unto men ... And he gave some, apostles; and some, prophets; and some, evangelists; and some, pastors and teachers; For the perfecting of the saints, for the work of the ministry, for the edifying of the body of Christ: Till we all come in the unity of the faith, and of the knowledge of the Son of God, unto a perfect man, unto the measure of the stature of the fulness of Christ: That we henceforth be no more children, tossed to and fro, and carried about with every wind of doctrine, by the sleight of men, and cunning craftiness, whereby they lie in wait to deceive; But speaking the truth in love, may grow up into him in all things, which is the head, even Christ: From whom the whole body fitly joined together and compacted by that which every joint supplieth, according to the effectual working in the measure of every part, maketh increase of the body unto the edifying of itself in love" (Ephesians 4:9, 11-16).

Look at what Luke tells us about our Lord's preaching, in Luke 4:31, 32, 43, 44. Our Saviour was a preacher of doctrine. His doctrine was astonishing. He preached "the kingdom of God". His word fell upon the hearts of men with power. His every word was intentional, weighty, powerful. His gospel came "in demonstration of the Spirit and power". Let every preacher seek wisdom and grace from God the Holy Spirit to imitate the Master.

Demons

Another thing that stands out in this passage and needs to be understood is the fact that Satan, and hell, and demons are real.

"And in the synagogue there was a man, which had a spirit of an unclean devil, and cried out with a loud voice, Saying, Let us alone; what have we to do with thee, thou Jesus of Nazareth? art thou come to destroy us? I know thee who thou art; the Holy One of God. And Jesus rebuked him, saying, Hold thy peace, and come out of him. And when the devil had thrown him in the midst, he came out of him, and hurt him not. And they were all amazed, and spake among themselves, saying, What a word is this! for with authority and power he commandeth the unclean spirits, and they come out. And the fame of him went out into every place of the country round about" (vv. 33-37).

I cannot say much about this, because I know little about it; but I want to be understood. Demonology is not something to play with or ignore. Hell is not a nightmare. It is real. Satan is not imaginary, but the prince of darkness. Demons are not mythical monsters, but fallen angels. Satan, and hell, and the demons of hell are bent upon the destruction of our souls and the dishonour of our God.

I do not mean to suggest that these things are now, or ever can be, out of control. That is not the case. "For this purpose", the Book tells us, "Christ was manifested, that he might destroy the works of the devil." And he demonstrates his power over hell in this fourth chapter of Luke's gospel. What does this passage tell us about the devil? The devil is an unclean spirit. This unclean spirit works evil in the souls of men, just as he did in their bodies during the days of our Lord's earthly ministry. Those who are under Satan's strongest influence are often found in the house of God. The devils, the demons of hell have nothing to do with Christ (v. 34). "For, verily, he took not on him the nature of angels; but he took on him the seed of Abraham."

The Lord Jesus Christ always has the devil under his control (vv. 35, 36). When he says to hell, "Hold thy peace", all hell holds its peace! With authority and power, he commands the unclean spirits.

Knowledge And Salvation

Even the demons of hell have faith, doctrinally accurate faith, better faith than most Baptists (they believe and tremble!); but not saving faith. Beware of unsanctified knowledge. It is a dangerous snare by which many are destroyed. Knowledge is not salvation. Head knowledge, without heart experience, is a positive curse.

Spiritual knowledge, gospel knowledge, a saving knowledge of Christ is knowledge accompanied by faith, inspiring hope and producing love.

We must never be content with knowing Bible facts, Bible history, Bible "trivia", or even Bible doctrine. Salvation is knowing God as he has revealed himself in the person and work of his Son, the Lord Jesus Christ (John 17:3).

Here are some questions worth considering: Does my knowledge of sin make me hate it? Does my knowledge of Christ cause me to trust him, love him and honour him? Does my knowledge of God's will cause me to seek, in all things, to obey it? Does my knowledge of doctrine make me useful to others? Does my knowledge of grace make me gracious? If the knowledge I have does not move my heart heavenward and does not make Christ precious to me, my knowledge is useless knowledge that will only add to my condemnation in hell.

A Mighty Saviour

Learn this and rejoice The Lord Jesus Christ is a mighty Saviour.

"And he arose out of the synagogue, and entered into Simon's house. And Simon's wife's mother was taken with a great fever; and they besought him for her. And he stood over her, and rebuked the fever; and it left her: and immediately she arose and ministered unto them. Now when the sun was setting, all they that had any sick with divers diseases brought them unto him; and he laid his hands on every one of them, and healed them. And devils also came out of many, crying out, and saying, Thou art Christ the Son of God. And he rebuking them suffered them not to speak: for they knew that he was Christ. And when it was day, he departed and went into a desert place: and the people sought him, and came unto him, and stayed him, that he should not depart from them" (vv. 38-42).

Demons and disease alike flee before the word of his power. By the touch of his hand the fever is removed and the fainting body is made strong. J. C. Ryle rightly observed …

"We see sicknesses and devils alike yielding to his command. He rebukes unclean spirits, and they come forth from the unhappy people whom they had possessed. He rebukes a fever, and lays his hands on sick people, and at once their diseases depart, and the sick are healed."

"We cannot fail to observe many similar cases in the four gospels. They occur so frequently that we are apt to read them with a thoughtless eye, and forget the mighty lesson which each one conveys. They are all intended to fasten in our minds the great truth that Christ is the appointed Healer of every evil which sin has brought into the world. Christ is the true antidote and remedy for all the soul-ruining mischief which Satan has wrought on mankind. Christ is the universal physician to whom all the children of Adam must repair, if they would be made whole. In him is life, and health, and liberty. This is the grand doctrine which every miracle of mercy in the gospel is ordained and appointed to teach. Each is a plain witness to that mighty fact, which lies at the very foundation of the gospel. The ability of Christ to supply to the uttermost every need of human nature is the very cornerstone of Christianity. Christ, in one word, is 'all'."

Our Lord Jesus Christ is the Antidote for the old serpent's poison. He is the remedy for our ruin. He is the Physician for our sin-sick souls. He is our Life, our Health and our Liberty. Our Lord Jesus Christ is an able, almighty, omnipotent Saviour. "He is able also to save them to the uttermost that come unto God by him, seeing he ever liveth to make intercession for them" (Hebrews 7:25).

Our blessed Saviour still enters the strong man's house, binds him, casts him out, and takes possession of the house. It is still true that all upon whom he lays his hands, all to whom he speaks in saving power, are healed by him, immediately. And all who are healed by Christ gladly serve him and his people (v. 39).

When the day of grace dawns upon redeemed sinners, all who have known his saving power, tasted his grace and experienced his mercy, still lay hold of him, stay him, and plead with him ever to abide with them (v. 42). Spirit of God, cause us to "stay" him, that he may not depart from us!

"And it came to pass, that, as the people pressed upon him to hear the word of God, he stood by the lake of Gennesaret, And saw two ships standing by the lake: but the fishermen were gone out of them, and were washing their nets. And he entered into one of the ships, which was Simon's, and prayed him that he would thrust out a little from the land. And he sat down, and taught the people out of the ship. Now when he had left speaking, he said unto Simon, Launch out into the deep, and let down your nets for a draught. And Simon answering said unto him, Master, we have toiled all the night, and have taken nothing: nevertheless at thy word I will let down the net. And when they had this done, they inclosed a great multitude of fishes: and their net brake. And they beckoned unto their partners, which were in the other ship, that they should come and help them. And they came, and filled both the ships, so that they began to sink. When Simon Peter saw it, he fell down at Jesus' knees, saying, Depart from me; for I am a sinful man, O Lord. For he was astonished, and all that were with him, at the draught of the fishes which they had taken: And so was also James, and John, the sons of Zebedee, which were partners with Simon. And Jesus said unto Simon, Fear not; from henceforth thou shalt catch men. And when they had brought their ships to land, they forsook all, and followed him" (Luke 5:1-11).

Chapter 25

"Nevertheless, At Thy Word"

In this portion of holy scripture the Holy Spirit gives us his record of the call of our Lord's first three disciples. This is a more detailed account of their call to the work of the ministry than we have had before. May he by whom these words were inspired teach us the lessons they are intended to convey to us.

It is obvious that these eleven verses are intended to show us something of what is involved in believing and obeying the Lord Jesus Christ. We must both trust and obey the Son of God. Obedience does not save us or sanctify us; nevertheless, where there is no obedience there is no salvation and no sanctification. Where faith comes, obedience follows.

Pressed To Hear
Luke tells us that "the people pressed upon" the Lord Jesus "to hear the Word of God." When they did, the Lord Jesus gave them their desire. Learn then that those who seek to hear the Word of God shall be taught of God.

"And it came to pass, that, as the people pressed upon him to hear the word of God, he stood by the lake of Gennesaret, And saw two ships standing by the lake: but the fishermen were gone out of them, and were washing their nets. And he entered into one of the ships, which was Simon's, and prayed him that he would thrust out a little from the land. And he sat down, and taught the people out of the ship" (vv. 1-3).

Here is a multitude of eternity bound men and women pressing upon the Saviour "to hear the Word of God". What a blessed press! Like Mary, these men and women chose that one thing needful. They sat at Christ's feet to hear his word.

What Peter saw here, he later experienced in Caesarea, at the house of Cornelius (Acts 10:33). Cornelius said to Peter, as he arrived to preach, "Now therefore are we all here present before God, to hear all things that are commanded thee of God."

Blessed are they who come to the house of God to hear the Word of God. They who come to be fed shall be fed. They who come to be taught shall be taught. They who come seeking comfort shall find comfort. They who come seeking grace shall find grace. They who come seeking Christ shall find Christ. Hear what God himself says about this. "I have not spoken in secret, in a dark place of the earth: I said not unto the seed of Jacob, Seek ye me in vain: I the LORD speak righteousness, I declare things that are right" (Isaiah 45:19).

Human Instruments

In verse 4, we see how that our great and glorious Lord God condescends to use human instruments to perform his great and wondrous works. "Now when he had left speaking, he said unto Simon, Launch out into the deep, and let down your nets for a draught."

The catching of this great draught of fish was miraculous; but the fishermen were just fishermen. The boats were just boats. The nets were just nets. But they were fishermen, boats and nets God was pleased to use.

There are many who object to this plain revelation of Scripture, fearing that it limits God and gives men a hand in God's operations of grace. Moses did not part the Red Sea. God parted the sea using Moses' rod. The disciples did not multiply the loaves and fish. The Lord Jesus did that; but he let those blessed men distribute food to the hungry. He who raised Lazarus from the dead could have easily moved the stone from the mouth of the tomb; but he chose to use men like you and me to roll away the stone from the mouth of the tomb. So, too, in the salvation of chosen, redeemed sinners, God condescends to work by means of human instruments. It is written, "It pleased God by the foolishness of preaching to save them that believe."

The instruments God uses are themselves utterly useless and insufficient for their work; and they acknowledge that fact. "Master, we have toiled all night and have taken nothing." Why was this the case? Was it because there were no fish in the sea? No. Were they unskilled in their work? Certainly not. These were master seamen. Were they lacking in diligence? No. They had toiled all night. Why, then, had they caught nothing? Because we must ever be reminded that the instruments themselves are worthless and useless. Our Saviour said, "Without me, ye can do nothing." But with him, we can do all things.

When the Son of God is at the helm of the boat, by some mysterious power, hordes of fish are drawn into the net.

The Lord usually performs his work in the most unlikely places. Our Master always chooses the most unlikely people as the objects of his grace, the most unlikely men to be his servants, and the most unlikely places to perform his works. He commanded the disciples to launch out into the deep. But, if you fish in lakes, you know that you are not likely to catch many fish in the deep waters.

Faith And Obedience

Faith is obedient to Christ. "And Simon answering said unto him, Master, we have toiled all the night, and have taken nothing: nevertheless at thy word I will let down the net" (v. 5). Let men say what they will, God says, "Faith without works is dead;" and it is. Men may attempt, if they dare, to justify disobedience, but faith is obedient to the will and Word of God. Believers are not rebels, but willing servants.

The Master said, "Launch out into the deep, and let down your nets for a great draught." This was a command which was manifestly contrary to reason and contrary to experience. These men had been fishing all night. But it was Christ the Lord who gave the command. And obedience to the Word and will of God requires immediate, unquestioning, selfless, self-denying compliance. "Whatsoever he saith unto you, do it."

> Trust and obey, trust and obey,
> For there's no other way
> To be happy in Jesus,
> But to trust and obey.
> John B. Sammis

Christ Our God

"And when they had this done, they inclosed a great multitude of fishes: and their net brake. And they beckoned unto their partners, which were in the other ship, that they should come and help them. And they came, and filled both the ships, so that they began to sink. When Simon Peter saw it, he fell down at Jesus' knees, saying, Depart from me; for I am a sinful man, O Lord. For he was astonished, and all that were with him, at the draught of the fishes which they had taken" (vv. 6-9).

There may be some things involved in Peter's prayer which are not commendable. But I know this. What Peter here expressed is exactly what sinners feel when they see the glory of God in Christ. When sinners are made to see the goodness, grace, power, and glory of God in Christ, they are overwhelmed at their unworthiness to stand before his presence.

This miracle performed by our Saviour caused Peter to be overwhelmed with a sense of the Saviour's Godhead. This is evident from the fact that he fell down at the Master's feet, crying out, "Depart from me, for I am a sinful man, O Lord." Peter seems to have remembered, suddenly, what the Lord had said to Moses in the Mount. "Thou canst not see my face, for there shall no man see me and live" (Exodus 33:20). Thinking, as holy men did in ancient times, he concluded that the sight of God meant immediate death. That is clearly what Manoah thought, when the angel of the Lord (the pre-incarnate Christ) appeared to him and his wife and did wondrously. He said to his wife, "We shall surely die, because we have seen God" (Judges 13:22).

Suddenly remembering these things, Peter was overwhelmed with a conscious sense of sin and begged the Lord to depart from him. He was convinced that nothing short of omnipotent power could have produced such a miracle as he had seen. He was suddenly seized with a sense of the fact that he was in the immediate presence of God, the Almighty!

Honour For Honour
God honours those who honour him. In his word of judgment to Eli concerning his sons the Lord God said, "Wherefore the LORD God of Israel saith, I said indeed that thy house, and the house of thy father, should walk before me for ever: but now the LORD saith, Be it far from me; for them that honour me I will honour, and they that despise me shall be lightly esteemed" (1 Samuel 2:30).

Nothing honours God like obedient faith. "Behold, to obey is better than sacrifice" (1 Samuel 15:22). When Peter launched out and let down his nets, he caught the fish; and faithfulness in small things always leads to greater things. So, we read in verse 10 that "Jesus said unto Simon, Fear not; from henceforth thou shalt catch men." Peter, James, and John, who were faithful to Christ as fishermen, were made by Christ to be fishers (catchers) of men!

Three Demands
Read Matthew 4:19 and Luke 5:11 together and you will see that the call of Christ demands and produces three things. "And he saith unto them, Follow me, and I will make you fishers of men" (Matthew 4:19) "And when they had brought their ships to land, they forsook all, and followed him" (Luke 5:11).

When the Master calls sinners by his grace, and when he calls men saved by his grace into the work of the ministry, he requires three things from them, three things which only he can produce, but three things we must give.

Faith: If we would be the servants of God, if we would be men-fishers, we must believe him!

Forsaking: If we would follow Christ, we must forsake all to do so.

Following: If we would be used of God, we must obey him: his will, his Word and his Spirit.

An Allegory

This historic event, like all historic events recorded in holy scripture, has an allegorical meaning. The whole event is a remarkable picture and type of the history of God's church and its work in this world. The ships carrying Christ and his people across the sea with the Word of God represent gospel churches. The fishermen are representatives of gospel preachers and their work. The net cast is the gospel of the grace of God, which we preach to all men. The sea represents the world. The shore represents eternity. The miraculous draft of fish caught and brought to shore represents the success of our labours in compliance with the Master's Word, the salvation of God's elect.

"And it came to pass, when he was in a certain city, behold a man full of leprosy: who seeing Jesus fell on his face, and besought him, saying, Lord, if thou wilt, thou canst make me clean. And he put forth his hand, and touched him, saying, I will: be thou clean. And immediately the leprosy departed from him. And he charged him to tell no man: but go, and shew thyself to the priest, and offer for thy cleansing, according as Moses commanded, for a testimony unto them. But so much the more went there a fame abroad of him: and great multitudes came together to hear, and to be healed by him of their infirmities. And he withdrew himself into the wilderness, and prayed" (Luke 5:12-16).

Chapter 26

How Does A Sinner Approach
The Lord To Obtain Mercy?

Piecing together the accounts of Matthew, Mark and Luke, it appears that this event took place just after our Lord had finished his Sermon on the Mount. "The people were astonished at his doctrine: For he taught them as one having authority, and not as the scribes." When he came down from the mountain, great multitudes followed after him. And this one man full of leprosy made his way through the crowd. He came through the great mass of men, crying, "Unclean, unclean." When he got to the Saviour, he fell down at his feet and worshipped him, saying, "Lord, if thou wilt, thou canst make me clean." "And Jesus put forth his hand, and touched him, saying, I will; be thou clean."

Here is an unclean leper seeking mercy from the hands of Christ; and he obtained the mercy he sought. The Lord made him whole.

When I read about this leper and the mercy he obtained from the Lord Jesus, I think to myself, "If one has been made whole, why not another? Does God forgive sin, then why not my sin? Does God justify the ungodly, then why not me? Does Christ receive sinners, then why not me? Is there mercy with the Lord for the guilty, then why not for me? Did Christ die for sinners, then why not for me? Does God save the unrighteous, then why not me?"

If we would obtain mercy, we must seek mercy like this poor leper, from the hands of the Lord Jesus Christ. Let every saved sinner, as he reads again of God's free, saving grace in Christ, remember and rejoice in what the Lord has done for him by his matchless, free and sovereign grace in Christ Jesus.

Let every poor, lost soul, whose uncleanness before God causes him to crave the cleansing Christ alone can give, look to the Son of God by faith.

Deep Sense Of Need

This poor wretch came to the Lord Jesus with a deep sense of his need. We do not read anything else in the Bible about the history of this man. We do not know who his parents were, where he was from, how old he was, or what became of him. He seems to be set before us for one reason only, and that is to show us how a sinner must come to the Lord Jesus if he would obtain mercy. And the first thing is this: If we would obtain mercy from Christ, we must come to him because we need him. No sinner will ever come to Christ in faith until God the Holy Spirit creates in him a sense of his need. No one seeks mercy until he needs mercy.

You are familiar with what leprosy is and what it represents. Leprosy was a loathsome disease, common during the days of our Lord's earthly ministry. It was a disease so peculiar that it was always considered a mark of divine displeasure on those who were afflicted with it (Numbers 12:10; 2 Kings 5:27; 2 Chronicles 26:19). Because they were ceremonially unclean, lepers were not allowed to walk in the company of others, or come into the house of God.

Leprosy fitly represents the plague of sin with which sons of Adam are diseased. It is to the body what sin is to the soul. W. M. Thomson, in his famous work, "The Land and the Book", describes lepers in Israel as follows.

"The hair falls from the head and eyebrows. The nails loosen, decay and drop off. Joint after joint of the fingers and toes shrink up and slowly fall away. The gums are absorbed and the teeth disappear. The nose, the eyes, the tongue, and the palate are slowly consumed."

The leper was a miserable, outcast creature. He was walking death. Leprosy, like sin, was a loathsome, unclean disease. Leprosy, like sin, was (by human means) an incurable disease. Leprosy, like sin, was a consuming disease. Leprosy, like sin, was the sure forerunner of death.

The man here held before us by the Spirit of God had a keen sense of his desperate need. Here is a man whose body was covered from head to toe with leprosy. His disease was always before him. There was no hiding it. His body was covered with ulcers oozing with a liquid of sickening smell. His body was racked with pain. Luke tells us that he was "full of leprosy". He knew that he needed help. He needed supernatural, merciful, divine help. He needed the help of God. Without it, he would surely die.

This is the very reason men and women do not come to Christ. They do not have any sense of need. They do not know their need of Christ. But when the plague of sin in a man's heart causes his very soul to burn with fever; when the sinners knows he is lost, helpless, unclean and doomed, that without Christ he must surely die, then he seeks him.

Christ The Healer

Christ alone has power to heal our souls. The cleansing from leprosy was portrayed in the ceremonial law (Leviticus 14); but it is the gospel that reveals the cure. The cleansing of grace is found only in Christ (Ezekiel 36:25; 1 John 1:7-9). His blood alone can cleanse the leprous soul. His mercy alone can save. Christ alone can make the unclean clean and righteous before God. Those who know their need of mercy will soon obtain mercy.

> All the fitness he requireth
> Is to feel your need of him.

And it is the work of God the Holy Spirit that makes us know our need of Christ. Robert Hawker wrote, "This poor creature, which came to Jesus, is the representative of every poor sinner, when convinced of the leprosy of sin, from the teaching of God the Holy Ghost. Such an one is convinced of Christ's ability, because God the Spirit hath taught him who Christ is, and what Christ is able to perform." Joseph Hart gives us the same thing in one of his great hymns ...

> What comfort can a Saviour bring
> To those who never felt their woe?
> A sinner is a sacred thing;
> The Holy Ghost hath made him so.
> New life from him we must receive,
> Before for sin we rightly grieve.

> This faithful saying let us own,
> Well worthy 'tis to be believed,
> That Christ into the world came down,
> That sinners might by him be saved.
> Sinners are high in his esteem.
> And sinners highly value him.

Utter Humiliation

This leper came to the Lord Jesus in utter humiliation. Matthew tells us he came "worshipping". Luke says that, "Seeing Jesus, he fell on his face". Mark tells us that he came "kneeling". That is just the way sinners must come to the Saviour, kneeling and falling on their face at his feet, worshipping! The sinner must come down, down from his pride, down from his self-righteousness, down from his self-sufficiency! He must come down in his own eyes, down, down, down, all the way down to the feet of Christ (Luke 18:9-14).

If ever we see who and what we are, we will come down. You and I are poor sons and daughters of Adam, full of uncleanness, cursed, condemned and ready to die. We are utterly helpless and completely unworthy of God's slightest notice.

If ever we see who Christ is and what he is, we will come down. He is holy, righteous and true. He is a God full of mercy, love and grace. He is a God able and willing to save. He is a Fountain opened for cleansing. He is God, whose glory it is to forgive sin.

God knows how to bring sinners down to the feet of his Son. Psalm 107 is a song of praise to God for his wondrous work of providence by which he brings chosen sinners down. But providence alone will not cause sinners to seek the Lord. God brings sinners down by causing his holy law to enter their hearts, exposing their sin, pronouncing their uncleanness and declaring their guilt (Romans 7:9). And God brings sinners down by the gospel, by revealing Christ to them and in them (Zechariah 12:10; Galatians 1:15, 16).

Do you feel your desperate need of Christ? Has your heart been broken and humbled at the feet of Christ? Are you sweetly compelled, like Job, to cry, "I have heard of thee by the hearing of the ear: but now mine eye seeth thee. Wherefore I abhor myself, and repent in dust and ashes" (Job 42:5, 6)?

Great And Weak Faith

This poor leper came to the Lord Jesus in very weak faith, but faith that obtained great grace; and that makes the weakest faith great faith (Hebrews 11:6). I do not know how he came to have faith in Christ. Perhaps he had heard our Lord preach. Perhaps he was familiar with the Old Testament prophets. Perhaps he had heard the fame of our Lord from others. But this much is certain: he knew who Christ was. He believed his claims. And he came to the Saviour in faith, because God the Holy Spirit had given him faith in Christ (Ephesians 2:8; Colossians 1:12).

The leper came to the Lord by himself. Others had been led to Christ by one of his disciples, but not this man. Others were picked up and brought to the Lord, but not the leper. Others, who could not come and were not brought, were blessed by a visit from the Lord himself, but not this leper. Everyone had given this poor man up as a hopeless case. He was a lonely, isolated man. No man cared for his soul. No one could or would take him to the Saviour. But it is our Lord's delight to save the hopeless, the helpless and the friendless.

This leper came to the Lord Jesus against many obstacles. He had no precedent to follow. No leper had come to the Saviour before him. He had no promise of cure. He was not invited to come. And he had no legal right to come. Yet, the leper came to Christ confessing faith in him. He worshipped the Lord Jesus Christ as God. It appears that he believed him to be the very God by whom others like him were healed in days of old. He bowed to and worshipped Christ as his Lord. He knew Christ had it in his power to make him clean and whole. And he confessed his faith in Christ in his own words. He did not merely repeat a prayer someone else told him to say!

In all those things this man's faith appears to be great and remarkable. Truly, it was. Yet, he displayed a great weakness of faith. Though he had no doubt that the Lord Jesus was able to heal him, he doubted whether he would heal him. He said, to the Lord Jesus, "If thou wilt, thou canst make me clean."

All God's children in this world know by experience what it is to come to the Lord Jesus with such weakness of faith. Where is the saved sinner who has not come to the throne of grace, seeking mercy and grace in time of need, while very greatly in doubt that God would give the mercy and grace needed? God forgive our unbelief!

It was in just such weakness of faith that this poor leper came to the Saviour. But such is the greatness of our Saviour's grace, such is the character of our God "who delighteth in mercy", that the weakness of our faith does not restrain his arm of grace! The Lord Jesus was moved with compassion toward this poor soul (Mark 1:41). "And he put forth his hand, and touched him, saying, I will; be thou clean" (v. 13).

Total Submission

This leper came to the Lord Jesus Christ, knowing his need of him, in great humiliation and in faith. And he came to the Saviour in total submission. He recognized that the whole issue was in the hands of Christ. He cried, "Lord, if thou wilt, thou canst make me clean."

He understood what few understand. Grace is God's prerogative alone. Salvation depends entirely upon the will of the Lord our God, who has mercy on whom he will have mercy. Christ alone has the right to save and the power to save; and the whole matter of salvation is according to his own sovereign will (Romans 9:16, 18). Recognizing the sovereignty of Christ's power and the sovereignty of his will, the leper submitted to the Lord with joyful hope. He simply threw himself upon Christ. And we must do the same. "Lord, if you will, you can save me."

Yet, he had hope. The Lord had never refused such a request before. And there is hope for us. God never has yet turned away one seeking, believing, submissive sinner. It seems likely, therefore, that he will not turn any away now.

> Perhaps he will admit my plea,
> Perhaps will hear my prayer;
> But if I perish, I will pray,
> And perish only there.
>
> I can but perish if I go,
> I am resolved to try;
> For if I stay away I know,
> I must forever die.
>
> But if I die with mercy sought,
> When I the King have tried;
> This were to die (delightful thought!)
> As sinner never died.
>
> Edmund Jones

The leper could not be worse off, even if he had been rejected. And if it were to happen that you sued for mercy and obtained it not, what would be your loss?

Mercy Obtained

But that was not the case. This poor leper obtained the mercy he desperately needed. "He put forth his hand, and touched him, saying, I will; be thou clean." The Lord Jesus was moved with compassion toward him. And being moved with compassion toward him, he healed him immediately and completely.

Yet, there is more. The Lord Jesus healed this poor leper by touching him. Imagine that! Infinite, spotless purity reached down and touched utter corruption! The spotless Lamb of God took into union with himself our nature. He became one of us that he might save us poor, leprous sinners from our sin and make us clean by the sacrifice of himself. Upon the cursed tree, our Lord Jesus Christ was made sin for us (2 Corinthians 5:21). He who is altogether holy and pure, clean and righteous was made unclean before his own holy law, just as the priest who burned the red heifer with her dung was made unclean by the sacrifice required in Numbers 19:7. The Lord Jesus was made sin for us, that we might be made the righteousness of God in him. He died for his elect, the just for the unjust, because there was no other way he could make us just!

An Important Lesson
When we read verses 14 and 15, we will find a very important lesson taught by our Master.

"And he charged him to tell no man: but go, and shew thyself to the priest, and offer for thy cleansing, according as Moses commanded, for a testimony unto them. But so much the more went there a fame abroad of him: and great multitudes came together to hear, and to be healed by him of their infirmities" (vv. 14, 15).

This cured leper's disobedience to the Saviour's express command is here recorded by divine inspiration for a reason. The Holy Spirit is here showing us that there is a time to be silent about the things of God, as well as a time to speak (Ecclesiastes 3:7). Our Saviour says, "Give not that which is holy unto the dogs, neither cast ye your pearls before swine, lest they trample them under their feet, and turn again and rend you" (Matthew 7:6).

I realize that this is a matter to be dealt with carefully; but sometimes we serve the cause of Christ better by silence than by speech. It is best for us to be silent when the cause of Christ cannot be served by us speaking. We do not serve the cause of Christ by trying to cram our doctrine down the throats of those who oppose it. It is best to leave such people alone, until God opens the door to minister to them. It is best for us to be silent when those around us have no interest in hearing the good news of God's grace. It is best for us to be silent when those around us only quibble and scoff at the things of God. And it is certainly best for us to be silent when we are supposed to be doing something else. It is a rare thing for an employer to pay a man wages to teach others the things of God.

No doubt, this man was sincere and blazed the matter abroad because he wanted all around him to know what great grace he had experienced. But the result was "that Jesus could no more openly enter into the city." There is a zeal which is "not according to knowledge". Such zeal causes much harm. I would not attempt to prescribe to any when he should be silent and when he should "blaze abroad" the things of God. Yet, I do know that there are times when we serve our Saviour and the interests of his kingdom far more effectively in silence than in other ways. Commenting on this passage, J. C. Ryle cautions ...

"The subject is a delicate and difficult one, without doubt. Unquestionably the majority of Christians are far more inclined to be silent about their glorious Master than to confess him before men and do not need the bridle so much as the spur. But still it is undeniable that there is a time for all things; and to know the time should be one great aim of a Christian. There are good men who have more zeal than discretion, and even help the enemy of truth by unseasonable acts and words."

May God give us the Spirit of wisdom, that we may serve and not hinder his cause in this world, that we may serve our Saviour with good sense. We must never be fearful to confess Christ before Pharaoh, as Moses did, or before Herod, as John the Baptist did. Yet, we must not cast the pearls of his grace before swine to be trampled beneath their feet with contempt.

Still, there is more. Not only did the Saviour command this healed leper to "tell no man", he also said, "but go, and shew thyself to the priest, and offer for thy cleansing, according as Moses commanded, for a testimony unto them." He told him to go and show himself to the priest, specifically "for a testimony unto them." He was told to go to the priest, so that the priest would pronounce him clean, as a testimony to the priests, either a convincing testimony to them that the Lord Jesus was the Son of God and true Messiah, or a standing testimony against them forever.

Certainly there is still more in this command. For all grace and mercy we should, first and foremost, show ourselves to the Lord Jesus Christ, our great High Priest and Almighty Saviour, the Author and Giver of all. He is to be eyed and acknowledged first in all things. In all things let us live before him and unto him, not before men and unto men. As Paul puts it, "Do I seek to please men? for if I yet pleased men, I should not be the servant of Christ" (Galatians 1:10).

How Does A Sinner Approach The Lord To Obtain Mercy?

"And it came to pass on a certain day, as he was teaching, that there were Pharisees and doctors of the law sitting by, which were come out of every town of Galilee, and Judaea, and Jerusalem: and the power of the Lord was present to heal them. And, behold, men brought in a bed a man which was taken with a palsy: and they sought means to bring him in, and to lay him before him. And when they could not find by what way they might bring him in because of the multitude, they went upon the housetop, and let him down through the tiling with his couch into the midst before Jesus. And when he saw their faith, he said unto him, Man, thy sins are forgiven thee. And the scribes and the Pharisees began to reason, saying, Who is this which speaketh blasphemies? Who can forgive sins, but God alone? But when Jesus perceived their thoughts, he answering said unto them, What reason ye in your hearts? Whether is easier, to say, Thy sins be forgiven thee; or to say, Rise up and walk? But that ye may know that the Son of man hath power upon earth to forgive sins, (he said unto the sick of the palsy,) I say unto thee, Arise, and take up thy couch, and go into thine house. And immediately he rose up before them, and took up that whereon he lay, and departed to his own house, glorifying God. And they were all amazed, and they glorified God, and were filled with fear, saying, We have seen strange things to day" (Luke 5:17-26).

Chapter 27

Four Of The Most Important Men In The Bible

We have before us four of the most important men in the Bible. So far as I know, not one of them was a preacher. None of them wrote a word of inspiration. These four men were not prophets or apostles. They appear to have been insignificant, if not totally unknown among their peers. The names, ages and birth places of these four men are not mentioned anywhere in the Word of God. Yet, these four men rank among the most important men in the Bible, because these four, unknown nobodies were instruments by which God brought one of his elect sheep to Christ. These four men had a friend who was paralyzed, both physically and spiritually; and they brought their friend to Christ; and the Lord Jesus both healed their friend and forgave his sin. The story of their remarkable faith and zeal is recorded in Matthew, Mark and Luke. Never in all the world did any mortals perform a more important work than these four men. Because of their labours, a sinner was saved and God was glorified.

Try to get a picture in your mind of the scene before us in Luke 5:17-26. It is a very remarkable story. These four men knew who Christ is and they knew the power of his grace. They knew a man who needed their Saviour. They knew where the Lord Jesus was to be found. They resolved together to bring their friend to the Saviour. And by thoughtful planning, labour and perseverance, these four men succeeded in getting their friend to Christ.

The work required much time and effort; but they were in dead earnest. They knew that Christ had the power to save their friend; and they knew that their friend needed his grace. They were determined to let nothing stand in their way. They were determined to get their friend to Christ. They could not heal his disease. They could not save his soul. They could not forgive his sin.

Nor did they know whether or not the Lord would do these things for him. But they could get their friend to Christ. What they could do they were determined to do. And as a direct result of their diligent labours, a sinner was saved and God was glorified. Nothing in all the world could be more important. When the Lord Jesus saw their faith, he forgave that man's sin.

God the Holy Spirit holds these four men up before our eyes as examples for us to follow. They show us the importance and the necessity of personal evangelism.

Five Facts

We know that "salvation is of the Lord." No man can save himself; and we cannot save other men. It is not possible for us to create a new heart in another person. We cannot give them repentance and faith in Christ. We cannot reveal Christ to a man's heart. But there are some things that we can do. And what we can do, we must do. Here are five facts plainly revealed in the Word of God.

All men by nature are totally depraved, helplessly lost and spiritually dead. No man will ever, of his own accord, by his own free-will, seek the Lord and come to Christ (Romans 3:10-12).

God has an elect people in this world whom he has chosen for himself in eternal love and determined to save (Romans 8:29, 30).

The Lord Jesus Christ has redeemed those chosen of God by his own precious blood; and, by the merit and efficacy of his blood, he shall bring them into the bliss and glory of eternal life in heaven (Isaiah 53:9-11).

God the Holy Spirit shall effectually quicken, regenerate and preserve all of those who were chosen by God the Father and redeemed by God the Son, calling them to faith in Christ by irresistible grace (Psalms 65:4; 110:3).

And God uses men to reach the hearts of men with the gospel (1 Corinthians 1:21).

As he used the Hebrew maid to convince Naaman, used Andrew to find Peter, used the Samaritan woman to call his elect in Samaria, and used Philip to call the Ethiopian Eunuch, so the Lord God still uses saved sinners in his mighty operations of grace by which he saves chosen sinners.

It is God's good pleasure to use sinful men to proclaim the gospel to sinful men. He could use angels. He could speak to men directly. But he has chosen to speak to men through us. What a privilege he has given us (2 Corinthians 4:7). This is no limitation to God's sovereignty. It is the marvel of his sovereign grace that he is pleased to use us (1 Corinthians 1:26-29).

Five Questions

I pray that God the Holy Spirit will kindle a fire in our hearts and inspire us to zealously give ourselves to the business of bringing sinners to Christ.[10]

Do you know the Lord Jesus Christ and the gospel of his grace? I am not asking whether or not you are a religious person. I am not asking about your doctrinal beliefs, your denominational affiliation, or your works of morality. I am asking this one thing: do you know the Lord Jesus Christ? Has he been revealed in your heart? Have you seen his face, heard his voice and followed him? If you are truly united to Christ by faith, if you do love him, surely you want others to know him (Romans 10:1).

Do you know the gospel of the grace of God? Do you know how it is that God saves sinners by the substitutionary sacrifice of his own dear Son? (John 3:14-16; Romans 3:24-26).

The universal testimony of holy scripture is, "By grace ye are saved"! Salvation is by grace, because sinners need grace (Ephesians 2:1-5). Totally depraved, spiritually dead sinners must be saved by grace, because they are totally incapable of saving themselves, or of assisting in the salvation of their souls. Salvation by grace excludes all boasting on the part of man (Ephesians 2:8, 9; 1 Corinthians 4:7). "It is not of him that willeth, nor of him that runneth, but of God that showeth mercy." Salvation by grace gives all the praise, honour and glory to the triune God for what he has done (Ephesians 1:6, 12, 14). Praise, honour and glory to God the Father for election and predestination, to God the Son for redemption and forgiveness, to God the Holy Spirit for regeneration and preservation. Salvation by grace is a door of hope for helpless, guilty sinners. If God required us to do something to be saved, none would ever be saved. But, since the whole of salvation is by grace, there is hope for sinners who are incapable of doing anything to please God. Salvation by grace is salvation from sin (Matthew 1:21). Grace saves us from both the penalty of sin and the dominion of sin. Grace is not a license to sin. Grace never justifies a life of sin. Grace makes sinners the servants of righteousness. But how does grace save?

Grace does not save us by overlooking our sins and pretending that they do not exist (Ezekiel 18:20), or by enabling us to keep the law of God (Galatians 3:21), or by giving us religious ceremonies to observe (Galatians 5:2) and good works to perform (2 Timothy 1:9).

Grace saves by substitution, by transferring the sins of God's elect to Christ and punishing him for them as our Substitute (Romans 3:24; 2 Corinthians 5:21; Galatians 3:13; Ephesians 1:7; 1 Peter 2:24). The Lord Jesus Christ's substitutionary redemption upholds and satisfies the justice of

---

[10] The reader will find detailed studies on this event in my expositions of Matthew 9 and Mark 2.

God. Our Lord Jesus Christ was made sin for his people so that our sins might be justly imputed and charged to him. When he was made sin for us, the Lord God poured out on him all the fury of his holy law and offended justice. Because he exhausted his wrath on our Substitute, the Lord Jesus, the Lord God declares, to all for whom Christ died, "Fury is not in me" (Isaiah 27:4). He is to every believing sinner both "a just God and a Saviour" (Isaiah 45:20-22).

Grace saves us by making us the righteousness of God in Christ (2 Corinthians 5:21), by imputing Christ's righteousness to us and by making us "partakers of the divine nature" (2 Peter 1:4) in regeneration, giving us life and faith in Christ (Colossians 2:12). Grace saves by making Christ and his sin-atoning death precious to our hearts. The death of Christ is of absolutely no benefit to any sinner until he believes the gospel. "Christ in you (is) the hope of glory" (Colossians 1:27). "He that believeth on him is not condemned: but he that believeth not is condemned" (John 3:18).

Grace saves us by keeping and preserving us unto eternal glory (1 Peter 1:5). "The gifts and callings of God are without repentance" (Romans 11:29). That which grace begins, grace will complete (Philippians 1:6). Grace will not be frustrated. Grace can never fail!

If you know Christ, you ought to confess him. If you know the gospel, you ought to tell it. The Saviour says, "Ye are witnesses of these things" (Luke 24:48; Acts 5:32; 10:39; 2 Timothy 2:2).

Do you know any place where sinners are sure to hear the gospel, any place where Christ is preached?

Do you know of a place where the power of God is present to heal the souls of men? Every gospel church is such a place. The church of Christ is to be a sounding board for the gospel. Our one purpose for existence in this world, our one business in life is to preach the gospel of Christ.

Every pastor, every gospel preacher is responsible to make it his business, every time he speaks to eternity bound sinners in God's name, to preach the gospel to them (1 Corinthians 2:2; 9:16). The preacher must have but one real ambition in life; and that one ambition must be to hold Christ up and point men and women to him, saying, "Behold the Lamb of God." He alone is the Substitute for sinners. He alone is the Saviour of men. There is hope for sinners in him. There is redemption in him. There is righteousness in him. There is life in him. There is salvation in him. There is safety in him.

The preaching of the gospel is the power of God unto salvation (Romans 1:16; 1 Corinthians 1:18, 24; 2:2-5). Bring sinners with you to the place where "the power of the Lord is present to heal them." In that place where God speaks to your heart and reveals Christ to you, he may do the same for others.

Do you have any real love and concern for the glory of God and the souls of men?

Do you know anyone who needs healing? I know this: That about which we are truly concerned, that which is really important to us is that about which we will be diligent and earnest. J.C. Ryle wrote …

"Why is it that so many people take no pains in religion? How is it that they can never find time for praying, Bible reading, and hearing the gospel? What is the secret of their continual string of excuses for neglecting the means of grace? How is it that the very same men who are full of zeal about money, business, pleasure or politics, will take no trouble about their souls? The answer to these questions is short and simple. These men are not in earnest about salvation."

If the glory of Christ is important to you, the worship of Christ will be important to you. If the souls of your children are important to you, you will see to it that they hear the gospel. If the souls of men are important to you, you will do what you can to see to it that they hear the gospel.

Do you not know that this world is passing away? Do you not know that men are perishing? Do you not know that hell is real, heaven is real, eternal death is real, eternal life is real?

What Can We Do To Bring Sinners To Christ?
We cannot all become preachers and missionaries. We cannot all be Bible teachers. And I do not suggest that we all should be preachers, missionaries and teachers. But there are some things that you and I can and should do for the glory of God and the salvation of his elect.

We can adorn the gospel of the grace of God by our daily lives (Titus 2:10). Let us seek grace to live in accordance with what we profess, or it will be of no value to anyone for us to try to be witnesses of the gospel. See to it that your profession and your practice are in agreement.

We can all tell what we know. We do not have to be theologians to be faithful witnesses. A faithful witness is one who simply tells what he knows to be true. Do you know that Christ is precious? Tell it. Do you know that God forgives sin? Tell it. Do you know that salvation is by grace through faith? Tell it. Make it your business to talk to people about Christ and the gospel.

We can all distribute gospel literature to our friends and neighbours. We can all bring people with us to hear the gospel. We can give of our means for the furtherance of the gospel. We can all greet people who attend the house of worship with warmth and friendliness. We can all earnestly pray for the conversion of sinners.

Why Should We All Diligently Give Ourselves To This Work?
I have been very plain and pointed in stating things we can and should do for the furtherance of the gospel and the conversion of sinners. May God the Holy Spirit give us grace to take these things to heart. We all have a terrible tendency to become slothful and negligent in the matter of witnessing to men. Let me make one last effort to stir our hearts and inspire our souls with zeal in this matter.

We should be faithful witnesses of the gospel, because men and women are perishing in unbelief and sin. Our Lord has commanded us to be his witnesses. The love of Christ constrains us to proclaim the good news of salvation and grace to others. This is the means which God has ordained for the conversion of sinners. And the work of evangelism is a glorious, soul-cheering work (James 5:20). Above all, let us give ourselves to this work for the glory of God. Nothing more glorifies God than the salvation of his elect.

So, let us dedicate ourselves to the glory of God. Let us be faithful in all that concerns the gospel of Christ. Let us give ourselves to the work of evangelism. Make it your business to be a faithful witness for Christ. Become Christ's ambassador to your family. Be the Lord's missionary in your community.

"And after these things he went forth, and saw a publican, named Levi, sitting at the receipt of custom: and he said unto him, Follow me. And he left all, rose up, and followed him. And Levi made him a great feast in his own house: and there was a great company of publicans and of others that sat down with them. But their scribes and Pharisees murmured against his disciples, saying, Why do ye eat and drink with publicans and sinners? And Jesus answering said unto them, They that are whole need not a physician; but they that are sick. I came not to call the righteous, but sinners to repentance" (Luke 5:27-32).

Chapter 28

"A Publican Named Levi"

We have before us the story of an immortal soul, a man who had managed to amass a considerable measure of wealth, wealth gained, very likely, by oppression, but wealth nonetheless. Yet, this man was empty inside. He was troubled in his soul. His wealth could not buy him peace, or silence his conscience. Though he did not know it, this man was a chosen object of grace, an appointed vessel of mercy, for whom the time of love had come. Here we see him visited by the Son of God and called by his irresistible power and grace.

This is a story which ought to be of great interest to all who know the value of their immortal souls and desire God's salvation. These verses describe the conversion of Levi (Matthew), one of Christ's first disciples.

Like Levi, you and I were born in sin. Like him, we lived according to the course of this world, walked after the lusts of our flesh, and were by nature the children of wrath. "But God, who is rich in mercy, for his great loved wherewith he loved us, even when we were dead in sins, hath quickened us together with Christ" (Ephesians 2:4, 5).

Had he not come to us, we would never have come to him. Had he not called us, we would never have called upon him. Had he not turned us, we would never have been turned. Had he not converted us by his almighty grace, we would never have been converted.

Our Lord Jesus Christ tells us that we must be converted, or we must perish forever in hell. This conversion is God's work. It is the turning of our souls to God. Conversion is accomplished by God the Holy Spirit turning sinners to the Saviour. He turns chosen, redeemed sinners from unbelief to faith, from rebellion to surrender, from enmity to love, from sin to righteousness, from self-righteousness to Christ. Have you been converted? Are we being converted? Is God working in us, turning us to himself? If we have been converted, we are being converted. This work of grace is not over until it is finished. Believing sinners continually cry unto the Lord for converting grace (Psalm 85:10; Jeremiah 31:18, 19; Lamentations 5:21).

Let us see what God the Holy Spirit teaches us about conversion in the story of Levi's conversion, as it is preserved for us by divine inspiration here in Luke's Gospel. May he give us grace to honestly compare our own experience to Levi's. If we are converted, the changes which were wrought in him by the grace and power of God have also been wrought in us.

Levi's Conversion

"And after these things he went forth, and saw a publican, named Levi, sitting at the receipt of custom: and he said unto him, Follow me. And he left all, rose up, and followed him" (vv. 27, 28). Here we see the power of Christ's grace in effectual calling. Here was a publican called by the Son of God. As soon as he was called, he willingly left all and followed Christ.

Levi is called Matthew, meaning "gift of God", throughout the New Testament because he was given by God the Father to the Son. He was given to Christ in the covenant of grace before the world began. He is now given to Christ in saving grace (John 6:37-45). Here the Holy Spirit tells us how he received that salvation, which is the gift of God.

Levi was a publican, a tax-collector. He was thoroughly absorbed with his good career. He thought of nothing but money, how to get it, how to spend it, and how to get more. He was not seeking the Lord. He appears not even to have any consciousness of need in his soul. There were no preparations that preceded the Saviour's call. Levi did not first experience deep feelings of guilt, experience a great time of mourning and repentance, or even acquire great knowledge. The Saviour called; and, as the result of the Saviour's call, Levi followed him. What grace there is here, surprising, omnipotent, free grace! He who said, "I am found of them that sought me not" (Isaiah 65:1), found Levi, and graciously caused Levi to find him by the effectual, distinguishing call of his omnipotent mercy.

Can you imagine how utterly surprised Levi must have been on that day when grace overtook and conquered him? The fact is, God's saving grace is always surprising in the experience of it. Here is the blessed, sovereign intervention of grace. The Lord Jesus passed by. He saw Levi; and he called him. That is the way he works yet today.

194

Here is the blessed choice and decision of faith. "He left all, rose up, and followed him." Because he followed Christ, this worthless, useless, hated man became a useful man of indescribable benefit to the souls of men. Effectual grace always produces effects in the lives of saved sinners. Levi (Matthew) wrote one of the four inspired gospel narratives known the world over. He became a blessing to millions. He left a name never to be forgotten. He was a man used of God for much good to many. As soon as the Saviour called, he obeyed. No sooner did the Lord Jesus open his heart to receive him than Levi opened his house to the Saviour; and this publican, who obtained mercy from the Lord, invited other publicans to come and find mercy also. Christ is all; and there is enough in Christ for all.

We should never despair of any. Had we seen this man in this situation, I do not doubt that most, if not all, who read these lines would have said, "There is a man consumed with the world" and passed on, presuming that he would never come to Christ. May God the Holy Spirit keep us from such arrogant folly. None are too wicked, too hardened, too worldly, too lost to be saved by Christ. No sins are too bad, too vile, too many to be forgiven. No heart is so dead, so corrupt, so consumed with the world that it cannot be conquered by the Lion of the tribe of Judah. None are beyond the reach of God's saving arm. "With God nothing is impossible"!

Are you converted? Has the Lord snatched you from destruction, lifted you from the pit of corruption, raised you from the dead? Have you "left all and followed" Christ? I urge you now to come to Christ. He who called Levi is still calling sinners. There is atonement still in Christ's precious blood. There is righteousness still in the Son of God. There is yet forgiveness with God. The Son of God still clothes naked, needy sinners with the garments of salvation.

Levi's Celebration
"And Levi made him a great feast in his own house: and there was a great company of publicans and of others that sat down with them" (v. 29). This was a feast for laughter and celebration (Ecclesiastes 10:19). Levi regarded his conversion as a matter of great joy. He wanted others to rejoice with him in what he had experienced; and he wanted others to know the grace he knew, the Christ he knew, the God he knew. No doubt, many of his friends looked upon his conversion as a thing to be pitied; but Levi knew he had reason to celebrate!

There is not a higher day, a day more to be celebrated, a day more to be remembered than the day of grace. Graduation, marriage, the birth of a child, all pale compared to this. When God saves a sinner, when a lost soul is converted to Christ, it is the birth of a soul, the rescue of a sinner, the pardon of a condemned prisoner, the opening of the prison doors, the coronation of a king, the making of a priest, the adoption of a son, the forgiveness of all sin, the bestowing of righteousness and the acceptance of a sinner.

Levi's Concern

This sinner, converted and saved by the grace of God, was concerned for the souls of others. He wanted others to be converted and saved by grace. So when he made his party, he invited a great company of publicans and sinners to come. He knew what their souls needed and did what he could to meet the need. J. C. Ryle rightly observed ...

"It may be safely asserted that there is no grace in the man who cares nothing about the salvation of his fellow men. The heart which is really taught by the Holy Spirit will always be full of love, charity, and compassion. The soul which has been truly called of God will earnestly desire that others may experience the same calling."

He went to great expense and trouble to get his lost friends into the company and presence of Christ the Saviour. Saved sinners are never content to go to heaven alone. The expense of providing such a large, lavish feast for a huge number of guests (as the word "feast" implies) was great. It appears that Levi considered no cost too great to get sinners in the company of the Saviour. May God give us each the grace to use our place, our property and our possessions for the everlasting benefit of immortal souls. Having received mercy, we ought to make it our business to show others the mercy, love and grace of God in Christ.

Perhaps, you think, "What can I do?" Do what you can to bring Christ to sinners and sinners to Christ. As Moses said to Hobab, you can say to others, "Come thou with us, and we will do thee good" (Numbers 10:29). As the Samaritan woman said to the men of the city, you can say to those around you, "Come see a man who told me all things that ever I did. Is not this the Christ?" You can say to your family what Andrew said to his brother, Peter, "We have found the Christ."

Levi's Critics

"But their scribes and Pharisees murmured against his disciples, saying, Why do ye eat and drink with publicans and sinners?" (v. 30). They are hardly worth mentioning, but since they are barely mentioned by Luke, I will barely mention them, too. If you seek to walk with God and serve the souls of men, you will have plenty of people around to find fault with what you do. I recommend that you handle critics the way Levi did. Do not handle them. Leave it to the Lord Jesus to handle them as he will.

Levi's Christ

"And Jesus answering said unto them, They that are whole need not a physician; but they that are sick. I came not to call the righteous, but sinners to repentance" (vv. 31, 32).

"What a lovely view," says Robert Hawker, "to behold the Great Redeemer, encircled at Matthew's table, with Publicans and Sinners! The murmuring of the Pharisees is just as might be expected, and such as hath marked Pharisees in all ages. But what a lovely answer the Lord gave to the charge. The very character of Christ, as the Physician of the Soul, naturally led him to haunts of sickness, for the exercise of his profession. And by referring them to that memorable passage in the prophet (Hosea 6:6). Jesus took the words as applicable to himself in confirmation of his office Jehovah-Rophe, I am the Lord that healeth thee (Exodus 15:26)."

The Lord Jesus Christ came to call sinners to repentance. None but sinners will come to Christ. And every sinner who comes to Christ is received by him. The only way we can come to Christ (walk with him in faith) is as sinners in need of mercy (Colossians 2:6).

"And they said unto him, Why do the disciples of John fast often, and make prayers, and likewise the disciples of the Pharisees; but thine eat and drink? And he said unto them, Can ye make the children of the bridechamber fast, while the bridegroom is with them? But the days will come, when the bridegroom shall be taken away from them, and then shall they fast in those days. And he spake also a parable unto them; No man putteth a piece of a new garment upon an old; if otherwise, then both the new maketh a rent, and the piece that was taken out of the new agreeth not with the old. And no man putteth new wine into old bottles; else the new wine will burst the bottles, and be spilled, and the bottles shall perish. But new wine must be put into new bottles; and both are preserved. No man also having drunk old wine straightway desireth new: for he saith, The old is better" (Luke 5:33-39).

Chapter 29

"The Old Is Better"

The Lord Jesus had just saved an elect sinner by his almighty grace, an old publican named Levi (Matthew). Having experienced the saving goodness of God's grace, having been forgiven of all sin, having seen the glory of God in the face of Christ, this sinner gladly forsook all and followed Christ.

Not only did he follow Christ, he wanted others to know him and follow him. He wanted other sinners to know the grace he now knew. He wanted other sin-sick souls to know the healing of the Master's hand. So he threw a lavish dinner party in honour of the Son of God. Hoards of people came: tax collectors; Romans; Jewish scribes; Pharisees; disciples of John the Baptist; the Lord's own disciples; the Son of God himself; and numerous sinners.

When the scribes and Pharisees saw the Lord Jesus and his followers mingling with such riffraff, they raised their eyebrows and said, "Why do you eat with publicans and sinners?" The Master responded by saying, "They that are whole need not a physician, but they that are sick. I came not to call the righteous, but sinners to repentance."

Being totally ignorant of what he said, knowing that they were neither sick nor sinners (at least in their own opinion), they seem to have totally ignored the Saviour's words. But observing that John's disciples kept the same outward religious customs and ceremonies (saying public prayers, fastings, etc.) that they kept, and the Lord's disciples did not, the scribes and Pharisees perceived an opportunity to create trouble. They thought they could divide Christ's kingdom. They thought they could drive a wedge between John the Baptist and the Lamb of God, by pointing out these glaring differences.

Often Swayed

True believers are sometimes weak believers; and weak believers are often swayed and easily sidetracked, especially by the religious practices and customs of men. "And they said unto him, Why do the disciples of John fast often, and make prayers, and likewise the disciples of the Pharisees; but thine eat and drink?" (v. 33) In Matthew 9:14 the Holy Spirit shows us that John's disciples were influenced strongly by these customs of the Pharisees.

John's disciples, though true disciples, were greatly impressed by the Pharisees' outward show of religion in public prayers, displays of fasting and the ostentatious washing of hands before eating. Christ's sheep will not follow a stranger. God's saints have an unction from the Holy One and cannot be deceived with regard to the gospel. But God's saints in this world are only frail, fickle, sinful men and women of flesh and blood. Sometimes they fall under the influence of wicked men, thinking that they are doing good. Sometimes, by bad influence from people they think are sincere, they get sidetracked by meaningless issues.

That is exactly what happened here with John's disciples. They got to listening to the Pharisees, with whom they had in common the practice of religious, ceremonial fasting. Ignoring the indescribably far greater issues of redemption, grace, and forgiveness, they joined the Pharisees (of all people!), carping and criticizing the Lord Jesus and his disciples because they did not join in public displays of fasting.

If you will look at Matthew's account (Matthew 9:14), you will see clearly that it was not just the Pharisees who raised this issue, but John the Baptist's disciples with the Pharisees.

May God the Holy Spirit keep us from being moved away from the simplicity that is in Christ. We must not be side-tracked by the issues of carnal religion, from the gospel of Christ. If he can do so, Satan will use such things to divide the church of God (Ephesians 4:1-6).

Bride And Bridegroom

In verses 34 and 35 our Saviour teaches us a glorious fact about our relationship with him and with one another. All true believers are the bride of Christ and he is our bridegroom.

"And he said unto them, Can ye make the children of the bridechamber fast, while the bridegroom is with them? But the days will come, when the bridegroom shall be taken away from them, and then shall they fast in those days."

This gospel age, is the time of our marriage feast. It is a time for feasting at the banqueting table of grace, a time for celebration and joy, not a time for mourning and fasting.

Fasting in the Old Testament was a symbol of repentance and mourning. Certain fasts were prescribed under the law as times of personal and national public humiliation. But the Pharisees ignored the spiritual thing symbolized and capitalized on the outward ceremony. They not only insisted on keeping the fast days prescribed by the law, they added many, many more. In conjunction with their show of humility, these proud hypocrites added specified times of prayer, public shows of devotion, by which they could prove to the world around them and to one another how very holy and humble, devoted and diligent, good and godly they were! Our Lord and his disciples had nothing to do with such nonsense. Neither should we!

With regard to fasting, our Lord's doctrine is clear. His presence and grace removes all need for sorrow and mourning (that which fasting symbolized) among his people. He said, "When the Bridegroom is taken away, then the bride will be sorrowful and mourn." And there was a time of weeping for the bride, when the Lord of Glory was crucified and buried. But with the resurrection of our Lord, his exaltation and enthronement, and the out-pouring of the Spirit of grace upon us, we now rejoice with joy unmingled. The bride's fasting days are over! Our sins are gone! Grace, righteousness and eternal life are ours! Christ, our faithful Saviour, our divine Bridegroom, is with us to provide for us, protect us and comfort us. Why should we fast? These things rejoice our hearts!

The Lord Jesus here identifies himself as our Bridegroom and all chosen, redeemed sinners as his bride (Ephesians 5:25-30). The Son of God espoused himself to us in eternity. He bought us and washed us in his own blood. We are wed to him by faith, wearing the wedding garments of his provision. We are his bride and he is our Husband.

What does that mean? We are the objects of his tender love. We are privileged to enjoy a mystical union with the Son of God. We are forever his. "What God hath joined together, let no man put asunder"! "He hateth putting away"! We shall forever participate in and possess all that is his (Romans 8:17). He who is the Bridegroom of our souls will one day present us before his Father and all the universe as his chaste virgin, spotless, holy, blameless!

No Mixing
In verses 36-38 the Lord Jesus tells us that in spiritual matters we must never attempt to mix things that differ.

"And he spake also a parable unto them; No man putteth a piece of a new garment upon an old; if otherwise, then both the new maketh a rent, and the piece that was taken out of the new agreeth not with the old. And no man putteth new wine into old bottles; else the new wine will burst the bottles, and be spilled, and the bottles shall perish. But new wine must be put into new bottles; and both are preserved."

Our Saviour delivered this parable in response to the question raised by John's disciples and the Pharisees about fasting. With the Pharisees, fasting had become a common, publicly advertised ceremony. It was an outward show of holiness, piety and devotion. John's disciples seem to have placed great emphasis upon this religious custom as well. But our Lord always dealt with it as an insignificant thing and insisted that in fasting, in prayer and in giving (Matthew 6:16-18), in fact in anything and everything, we must never make a show of religion!

It may have been proper, our Lord says to John's disciples, for the friend of the bridegroom and his disciples to fast. But to require the bridegroom and his disciples to fast was as ludicrous as sewing a piece of new cloth in an old garment, or putting new wine into old bottles, or wineskins.

Actually the parables here given were simply proverbial sayings that may be applied to many things. Essentially, their meaning is simply this: never try to mix things that do not mix. Many great evils that have arisen in the church could have been avoided if the lesson of these parables had simply been heeded. And many of the evils exiting in the church today could be corrected if this lesson was followed.

In spiritual matters, we must never attempt to mix things that differ. Just as under the Mosaic law the mixture of linen and wool and the ploughing of an ox and an ass together were prohibited, so in this age, we cannot mix and must never try to mix, law and grace, flesh and spirit, Christ and the world, or carnal ordinances with spiritual worship.

The problem at Galatia was that the Judaisers tried to put the old wine of Mosaic laws and ceremonies into the new bottle of grace. They tried, like many today, to mix Judaism and Christianity. They tried to hold both to the law and the gospel. They wanted both Moses and Christ. They tried to mix physical circumcision with spiritual circumcision. Such a mixture can never take place. Either we are under the law, or we are free from the law. It cannot be both (Galatians 5:1-4).

In the early church many tried to mix the philosophies and religious customs of a pagan world with the gospel of Christ, just as they do today. Nothing is new under the sun. In the earliest days, after the apostles, and even while the apostles were living, there were those who attempted to make the gospel palatable to the world by mixing the religious customs, traditions and opinions of paganism with the gospel of Christ. The result was disastrous then, and shall be now. In those days compromise paved the road to Romanism. Today, many are paving a road back to Romanism as fast as possible.

We must never try to mix flesh and spirit or works and grace in the worship and service of our God (Philippians 3:3). There is absolutely no place in the worship of God for crosses, pictures representing the Lord Jesus Christ, our God, images or pictures of angels, religious relics or symbols, law rule, sabbath keeping, ceremonialism, crossings, kneelings, or anything not prescribed by our Lord and practised by his disciples in the New Testament.

Many professing Christians today constantly attempt to stitch Christ and the world together. How many there are who seem determined to prove our Lord wrong, who try to serve both God and mammon. They wear the name of Christ in profession, but serve the world. They want to enjoy the new wine of Christ; but they want to drink it from the old bottle of the world. They will not utterly despise the new garment of discipleship, but they want it without cost or cross. They try to sew it to the old garment of pleasure, covetousness and love of the world. They will find one day soon that they have attempted what cannot be done.

We must not attempt to put new wine into old bottles. Law and grace, flesh and spirit, the world and Christ simply cannot be mixed. We must choose one and hate the other.

In verse 39 our Lord shows us that in spiritual things "the old is better", always better. "No man also having drunk old wine straightway desireth new: for he saith, The old is better."

The gospel of Christ is often compared to wine in scripture. Wine is representative of the Saviour's blood in the Lord's Supper. The gospel is comparable to wine because of its sweetness, its reviving quality and its calming effect. If ever you taste the old wine of the gospel, the old wine of free grace, you will not want the new wine of this apostate age (Jeremiah 6:16).

"And it came to pass on the second sabbath after the first, that he went through the corn fields; and his disciples plucked the ears of corn, and did eat, rubbing them in their hands. And certain of the Pharisees said unto them, Why do ye that which is not lawful to do on the sabbath days? And Jesus answering them said, Have ye not read so much as this, what David did, when himself was an hungred, and they which were with him; How he went into the house of God, and did take and eat the shewbread, and gave also to them that were with him; which it is not lawful to eat but for the priests alone? And he said unto them, That the Son of man is Lord also of the sabbath" (Luke 6:1-5).

Chapter 30

"The Second Sabbath After The First"

There is a phrase used in the opening verse of this sixth chapter of Luke that is found nowhere else in the Bible. It is a phrase which has been the subject of much debate for hundreds of years. The phrase is "The second sabbath after the first."

Some of the great theologians of the past tell us that this phrase refers to the sabbath following the cutting of the first sheaf of harvest during the Jews' passover week. Others say the phrase refers to the three great sabbaths kept by the Jews every year (The Feast of Passover, The Feast of Pentecost, The Feast of Tabernacles), and that this sabbath was the sabbath kept during the Feast of Pentecost.

Certainly, this phrase refers to a sabbath day commonly known to the Jews living at the time as "the second sabbath after the first", or (more literally) "the second first sabbath." But who cares which one it was?

What is more important is this: why did God the Holy Spirit inspire and direct Luke to these particular words here? That I am interested in knowing; and the answer is very simple. The Lord of the sabbath had come to fulfil and forever abolish the first, carnal, ceremonial sabbath of the law, that he might establish that blessed, second sabbath of the gospel, that he might forever be the Sabbath Rest of his people. Christ is our Sabbath.

A Deadly Sin

First, the Spirit of God here sets before us a glaring example of a deadly sin. We are told that on a certain sabbath day our Lord Jesus and his disciples walked through the corn fields. As they did, the disciples, being hungry, picked some ears of the grain, rubbed it in their hands, and had a snack.

Immediately, the Pharisees charged the Lord's disciples with what they thought was a very serious crime. These men had broken the fourth commandment of the law. They had done work on the sabbath day! However, the deadly sin revealed here is not seen in the action of the disciples, but in the action of the Pharisees.

The most deadly sin of all is the sin of self-righteousness. Our Lord warns us in many ways and repeatedly to beware of the leaven of the Pharisees. That leaven which corrupts and destroys everything it touches is self-righteousness and hypocrisy. Self-righteousness and hypocrisy attach great importance to outward things in religion, things other people see, applaud and reward; but it neglects inward, spiritual heart worship.

These Pharisees were sticklers for sabbath keeping, but notorious for covetousness (Luke 16:14). They strained the tiniest gnat from their ceremonial religious cup regarding some things, and swallowed the camel in other matters. They were quick to censor, criticize, and condemn others.

God hates the spirit of the Pharisee! God Almighty hates self-righteousness. Nothing is more abhorrent to him than the stench of self-righteousness (Isaiah 65:1-5; Luke 18:9-14; Micah 6:6-8; Matthew 23:23).

And nothing is more likely to keep a sinner from Christ than self-righteousness (Romans 9:30-10:4). Religion without Christ is the most damning thing in this world. Every act, practice, profession and pretence of religion without Christ is eating and drinking damnation to your soul, not discerning the Lord's body, not understanding the gospel.

A Defending Saviour

Second, the Lord Jesus Christ is set before us in this passage as a defending Saviour. No sooner did the Pharisees accuse the disciples of evil than the Lord Jesus took up their cause and defended them against their accusers. He answered the cavils of their enemies. He did not leave his followers to answer for and defend themselves. He answered for them and defended them.

What a blessed, encouraging, delightful picture this is of our Saviour's unceasing work on our behalf! We read in the Book of God of one who is called "the accuser of the brethren, who accuses them day and night" (Revelation 12:10). He is Satan, the prince of darkness. How often we accommodate our accuser, giving him many grounds for his accusations! How many charges he might justly lay against us! But he, who is our Saviour, ever pleads our cause, both in heaven and on earth, and defends us. Christ is our Rock, our Salvation, our Refuge, our Defence and our Defender (1 John 2:1, 2; Romans 8:28-35).

When my adversary, the devil, accuses me of some evil by the lips of a man on earth, I respond, "Let Christ answer for me." When the fiend of hell accuses me of horrid evils in my own mind and conscience, as he often does, I respond, "Let Christ answer for me." In the day of judgment should that wicked one be allowed to appear, point his accusing finger, and attempt to have my crimes charged against me, I will yet respond, "Let Christ answer for me."

A Delightful Sabbath

Third, the Spirit of God points us to a delightful sabbath. I read one commentator's explanation of this passage, and could hardly believe what he put on paper. I knew he was inclined toward legality; but I was still surprised by what he wrote. As he attempted to protect sabbath observance, he said, "We must not interpret the Lord's words in this passage as an indication that the fourth commandment is no longer to bind Christians."

The Lord Jesus Christ did not come here to bind his people with the rigours of legal bondage. He came here to set his people free. He who is our Saviour is both the Lord of the sabbath and our Sabbath (Luke 6:5). The Word of God speaks clearly.

"Christ is the end of the law for righteousness to every one that believeth" (Romans 10:4).

"Let no man therefore judge you in meat, or in drink, or in respect of an holy day, or of the new moon, or of the sabbath days: Which are a shadow of things to come; but the body is of Christ" (Colossians 2:16, 17).

Christ, as the Lord of the sabbath, is the one who established it. He is the one for whom it was established. He is the one to whom it pointed, the one typified by it. Christ is the one who fulfilled it. Having fulfilled it, he abolished it forever (Romans 10:4; Colossians 2:16, 17).

We rejoice to keep the gospel sabbath of faith; but the pretentious practice of observing a carnal, legal sabbath day is specifically prohibited in Colossians 2:16. We keep that which is here called, "the second Sabbath after the first", the blessed sabbath of rest in Christ. Coming to him, we cease from our own works and rest in him (Matthew 11:28-30; Hebrews 4:9-11). The penalty of not keeping this sabbath is death, eternal death. That is the penalty God places upon all the works men do for salvation (John 3:36).

I heard the voice of Jesus say,
"Come unto me and rest;
Lay down, thou weary one lay down,
Thy head upon my breast."

I came to Jesus as I was,
Weary, and worn, and sad;
I found in him a resting place,
And he has made me glad!

Horatius Bonar

207

"And it came to pass also on another sabbath, that he entered into the synagogue and taught: and there was a man whose right hand was withered. And the scribes and Pharisees watched him, whether he would heal on the sabbath day; that they might find an accusation against him. But he knew their thoughts, and said to the man which had the withered hand, Rise up, and stand forth in the midst. And he arose and stood forth. Then said Jesus unto them, I will ask you one thing; Is it lawful on the sabbath days to do good, or to do evil? to save life, or to destroy it? And looking round about upon them all, he said unto the man, Stretch forth thy hand. And he did so: and his hand was restored whole as the other. And they were filled with madness; and communed one with another what they might do to Jesus" (Luke 6:6-11).

Chapter 31

"On Another Sabbath"

Why did the Lord Jesus do so many of his miraculous works of healing on the sabbath day? Why did he so often go out of his way to say and do things he knew would be most offensive to the Pharisees? How does the Son of God meet rebel sinners? What was the nature and purpose of the sabbath? Who is Jesus Christ? Was he just a man, as many blasphemously assert; or is he both God and man in one glorious, inseparable person? Does it really matter what we think about who Christ is? What is involved in the Lord's call? How does God call sinners to life and faith in Christ? What affect does the gospel of Christ and the power of his grace have upon men?

These are all questions which are clearly and decisively answered by the Holy Spirit in Luke 6:6-11. Here, Luke gives us a very brief, but very instructive narrative of the healing of a man with a withered arm on the sabbath day. Like all of our Lord's miracles, this miraculous healing is a picture of the saving operations of his grace in and upon chosen sinners. The miracle was performed specifically to give us an instructive picture of God's salvation.

A Deliberate Confrontation
The first thing we see in this passage is our Lord's deliberate confrontation of the Pharisees (vv. 6, 7, and 9).

"And it came to pass also on another sabbath, that he entered into the synagogue and taught: and there was a man whose right hand was withered. And the scribes and Pharisees watched him, whether he would heal on the sabbath day; that they might find an accusation against him ... Then said Jesus unto them, I will ask you one thing; Is it lawful on the sabbath days to do good, or to do evil? to save life, or to destroy it?"

The preaching of the gospel is always confrontational. God's servants are sent to his enemies and sent to confront them, not to coddle them, pamper them and bargain with them, but, as the ambassadors of God himself, to confront them with the claims of the sovereign Lord. There is no such thing as faith in Christ apart from surrender to Christ as Lord (Luke 14:25-33).

We see this confrontation clearly exemplified by our Saviour in this passage. Our Lord Jesus Christ deliberately confronted the Pharisees, both by his words and his works. He always does. The Son of God always confronts sinners at their point of rebellion and demands that they surrender to him as their Lord. That is the way he dealt with both the rich young ruler (Luke 18) and the Samaritan woman (John 4). This is exactly what we see in this passage, too. Here is just one of many examples of our Lord confronting these self-righteous, religious hypocrites on the sabbath.

Did you ever notice how often our Saviour performed his miraculous works on the sabbath day? Did you ever wonder why he chose the sabbath for so many of these displays of his omnipotent mercy? It was on the sabbath day that he healed this man's withered arm. It was on the sabbath day that he cured the demoniac in the synagogue (Mark 1:21-28). The woman who was afflicted with an infirmity for eighteen years was cured by his mercy on the sabbath day (Luke 13:10-18). It was the sabbath day when our Lord Jesus healed the man with the dropsy (Luke 14:1-6). It was on the sabbath day that he healed the lame man by the pool of Bethesda (John 5:16). And it was on the sabbath day that he healed the man born blind (John 9:1-12).

These things were not done on the sabbath day accidentally. They were performed on the sabbath day for the calculated purpose of our Lord to assert his claim of dominion over all things as Lord, even of the sabbath (v. 5). It was Christ himself who kept the first sabbath. It was Christ himself who gave the law of the sabbath. As a man, he became subject to the law in all things. Yet, he is Lord of the law. As such, because he is God as well as man, he cannot be put under the yoke and bondage of the law. The law does not rule the King. The King rules the law. And Christ is the King.

The Lord Jesus chose to perform his work of mercy upon this poor, needy soul on the sabbath day in order to expose and condemn the hypocrisy and mean-spirited traditions of religious legalists. As it was in our Lord's day, so it is in ours. There is no point at which religious legalists are more hypocritical, more bound by the religious customs and traditions of men, and more mean-spirited than in their efforts to impose and enforce sabbath laws upon men.

The Pharisees could not answer our Lord's question about whether it was right to do good on the Sabbath because they would not answer it, lest they expose themselves. Their intention was to accuse the Master. If he refused to heal this man, they wanted to accuse him, either of weakness and inability to heal him, or of cruelty for not healing him. Any answer they might give would have exposed them. These religious hypocrites would have preferred the man be left with an impotent arm, rather than see him healed. They were far more interested in maintaining the rigours of the law (or at least their interpretation of the law), than in relieving the needs of men. And they excused their meanness in the name of honouring God!

Our Lord Jesus chose to perform this miracle of mercy on the sabbath to show us plainly what the true nature and purpose of the sabbath was. The sabbath day, like all other ordinances of the legal, Mosaic age, was designed and instituted to portray the gospel of Christ. It was never intended merely to be a day of religious bondage, but a day portraying the rest of faith in Christ. The sabbath was designed to show sinners how God does men good, eternal good, who deserve evil, by causing sinners to rest in Christ (Matthew 11:28-30). The sabbath was ordained to show us how God has purposed from eternity to save life by the obedience of Christ. It was a picture of Christ's finished work and of our resting in him, ceasing from our works by faith in him.

The Son of God chose to perform this miracle on the sabbath to display the fact that he had come to fulfil and forever put an end to the law of the sabbath (v. 9). Yes, Christ is the end of the law (Romans 10:4). He finished it, fulfilled it, and put an end to it.

"Let no man therefore judge you in meat, or in drink, or in respect of an holyday, or of the new moon, or of the sabbath days: Which are a shadow of things to come; but the body is of Christ" (Colossians 2:16, 17).

A Divine Attribute

The second thing we see in this narrative is the display of a divine attribute. "But he knew their thoughts, and said to the man which had the withered hand, Rise up, and stand forth in the midst. And he arose and stood forth" (v. 8). The Lord Jesus "knew their thoughts". This is another of those many, many almost casual, nonchalant references given in the New Testament, by which the Holy Spirit declares the fact of our Saviour's eternal Godhead. This man, Jesus of Nazareth, is a man; but he is more than a man. This man is the omniscient, all-knowing God (Hebrews 4:13).

He who is our Saviour is and must be God in human flesh. It cannot be stated too emphatically or too often that Christ is, indeed, "over all God blessed forever". Every attempt of men to compromise his absolute, eternal deity is both a denial of the gospel and blasphemy. Those who tell us that Christ is not God, absolutely God, omniscient, omnipotent, omnipresent, immutable, eternal, just and holy, are not Christians, but pagans

211

masquerading as Christians. Only one who is himself God knows, sees, and hears the thoughts of men.

Nothing is more humbling and, at the same time, comforting and encouraging to believing hearts than our blessed Saviour's omniscience. To the religious hypocrite, this is a terrifying thing. To the believer, it is delightful. Let us be humbled by the fact that our dear Saviour knows us inside out. Nothing is hidden from him. Yet, we ought to rejoice in this, too, our blessed Saviour knows what we really are. This was the thing that gave Peter consolation after his horrible sin. He said to the Lord Jesus, "Thou knowest that I love thee." Our great Redeemer's name is Jehovah-Jireh, "The Lord will see." "The Lord will provide." "The Lord will be seen."

An Effectual Command
The third thing we see in this passage is an effectual command. The Lord Jesus, we read, "said to the man which had the withered hand, Rise up, and stand forth in the midst. And he arose and stood forth ... And looking round about upon them all, he said unto the man, Stretch forth thy hand. And he did so: and his hand was restored whole as the other" (vv. 8, 10).

Unlike the pretended miracles of Papists and Pentecostals, our Lord's miraculous works were performed in broad daylight, performed upon people everyone present knew were impotent, and performed in the most public manner possible. He was not a pretend healer. He is the Healer. But the message of our text is not about the healing of a man's withered hand. The healing of this man's withered hand was a miracle performed by our Lord to portray the far greater miracle of grace he performs upon chosen sinners, when he saves us by his omnipotent mercy! The healing of this man is a most instructive picture of the almighty, effectual call and irresistible grace of God, by which we are brought from death to life in Christ. Look at it ...

"He said to the man with the withered hand". Here is a particular, personal call. It is written, "He calleth his own sheep by name." This was also a discriminating, distinguishing call. We have no idea how many others were present, or with what needs they had come. But Luke tells us plainly that on this occasion the Master called none but this man alone. How we ought to thank God for his special, discriminating grace (Psalm 65:4; Matthew 22:14; 1 Corinthians 4:7). Josiah Conder said it well,

> 'Tis not that I did choose Thee,
> For Lord that could not be.
> This heart would still refuse Thee,
> Hadst Thou not chosen me!

Next, the Lord Jesus called this man to do what he had absolutely no ability to do. The Master issued an impossible command. He said to the man with a dried up, withered, paralyzed arm, "Stretch forth thy hand." If he could stretch forth his hand, he would not have been there.

I stress this point, because men often tell us, "If the sinner has no ability to repent and believe the gospel, he cannot be called to do so." Such attempts to deny the gospel of Christ simply will not hold water. The Lord Jesus commanded this man to stretch forth his withered hand.

"And he did so: and his hand was restored whole as the other." How can this be? Find out the answer and you will find out how spiritually dead sinners arise from the dead and flee to Christ. This man did not stretch forth his hand by the mere exercise of his will. He did not just decide to stretch forth his hand. He did not just muster the power from within himself to stretch forth his hand. But he did stretch forth his hand. How? The answer is found in Luke 18:26, 27. God who issued the command gave power to obey the command; and he stretched forth his hand.

By preaching the gospel, spiritually dead sinners are called to arise from the dead, to stretch forth their withered hands, and lay hold of Christ by faith. Any sinner who obeys the gospel, any sinner who believes on Christ, any sinner who rises from his spiritual grave and comes to Christ is immediately made whole and has eternal life.

But there is a problem. No sinner can do it. Remember, the sinner is dead! He has no ability to stretch forth his hand. He has no ability to come to Christ. However, when the Lord God Almighty, by the life-giving power of his omnipotent, irresistible grace, calls the dead sinner, the sinner rises from death, stretches forth his withered hand, lays hold of Christ and is made whole.

There is no power in preachers. When all a person hears is the voice of a preacher, he remains dead. There is no power in the preacher's voice. But when God speaks by the gospel, there is power, life-giving, resurrection power in the call that God issues (John 5:25; 1 Thessalonians 1:4, 5; Revelation 20:6).

We should also note the fact that this man was not made whole until he stretched forth his hand. When the Lord's command came, this poor man, believing Christ, stretched forth his hand. He did not raise questions. He did not quibble about whether or not he could do it, whether or not the Lord had ordained it, or whether or not he would be made whole by doing it. He simply stretched forth his hand. When he did, his hand was made whole.

A Dividing Saviour

"And they were filled with madness; and communed one with another what they might do to Jesus" (v. 11). The gospel of Christ and the wonders of his grace always divide people. Our Lord said, "I came not to send peace, but a sword." And whenever the gospel is preached, whenever God does his work of grace, a division is made because of Christ. The gospel separates men, families, churches and communities. It divides light from darkness. It separates the wheat from the chaff. It divides sheep from goats. It is a savour of life unto life to some, and a savour of death unto death to others (2 Corinthians 2:14-17). On this occasion the Pharisees were enraged, the man with the withered hand was made whole and the Lord's disciples were edified, instructed and encouraged.

"On Another Sabbath"

"And it came to pass in those days, that he went out into a mountain to pray, and continued all night in prayer to God. And when it was day, he called unto him his disciples: and of them he chose twelve, whom also he named apostles; Simon, (whom he also named Peter,) and Andrew his brother, James and John, Philip and Bartholomew, Matthew and Thomas, James the son of Alphaeus, and Simon called Zelotes, And Judas the brother of James, and Judas Iscariot, which also was the traitor. And he came down with them, and stood in the plain, and the company of his disciples, and a great multitude of people out of all Judaea and Jerusalem, and from the sea coast of Tyre and Sidon, which came to hear him, and to be healed of their diseases; And they that were vexed with unclean spirits: and they were healed. And the whole multitude sought to touch him: for there went virtue out of him, and healed them all" (Luke 6:12-19).

Chapter 32

Prayer, Preaching, Power

In the paragraph before us we have the Holy Spirit's description of our Lord's calling and ordination of his twelve apostles. Though the apostolic office ceased with the apostolic age, the calling of these men is still very instructive. This passage teaches us much concerning the blessed work of the gospel ministry.

First Ordination Service

These twelve men were the first men set apart by Christ in this gospel age and sent forth to proclaim the glad tidings of God's free grace in him. This was the beginning of what is often called "the Christian ministry". Without question, all the prophets of the Old Testament preached the same gospel these men preached. John the Baptist preached the same message, too. And God's servants today preach that same glorious gospel of the grace of God. The singular message of God's servants is Jesus Christ and him crucified. As Pastor Scott Richardson once said, "Any sermon that does not have Christ for its beginning, middle and end is a mistake in its conception and a crime in its execution."

This was the first ordination service of the New Testament era. Let it be observed that the ordination of a man to the work of the gospel is the work of the Lord God himself. If a man is called and sent of God to preach the gospel that is his ordination. Our public ordination services are only the public recognition of a man's gifts by the local church. We have no ability to make men preachers. All we do in ordaining a man to the ministry is publicly acknowledge our recognition of his gifts and publicly identify ourselves with him, commending him to men as God's messenger.

How far we have degenerated from the pattern of the New Testament in all things! This degeneration is seen most clearly in this first ordination of gospel preachers. What is called "ordination" today is similar only in name. When our Lord ordained twelve, the whole affair was simple and solemn.

As in all things relating to the Church and kingdom of God, everything concerning the work of the gospel ministry depends upon and is determined by Christ alone.

Prayer

When the Lord Jesus ordained these first twelve preachers, he did so after much prayer. "And it came to pass in those days, that he went out into a mountain to pray, and continued all night in prayer to God. And when it was day, he called unto him his disciples: and of them he chose twelve, whom also he named apostles" (vv. 12, 13).

This fact is here recorded to teach us the great place and importance of prayer in all aspects of divine service. It is particularly designed to show us that God's servants ought always to be the objects of his people's fervent prayers.

The most important thing for a congregation to do when seeking a pastor is pray. Pray for God to send a pastor after his own heart (Jeremiah 3:15). The most important thing for a man to do, before he takes up the work of the gospel ministry, is pray. Pray, like Moses did in Exodus 33:13-15, that God will direct him and show him plainly what his purpose is. "Show me now thy way ... If thy presence go not with us, carry us not up hence."

I will not attempt to say who is or who is not called of God to preach the gospel. That is God's work alone. But this I know: if God calls a man to this work he will be a man chosen of God for the work. "Of them he chose twelve." The Lord will give him the gifts sufficient for the work and a burden for the work. God's people will want to hear him; and God will put him in the work. If the Lord God puts a man into the ministry, he will give that man a love for the work; and he will give him success in the work.

An ego trip is not a call of God. Let no man run who has not been called and sent of God with the message of grace burning in his soul. Preachers who are not sent of God are a hindrance, not a help in the work of the gospel.

If you would help the cause of Christ, pray for his servants. "Brethren, pray for us."

"And we beseech you, brethren, to know them which labour among you, and are over you in the Lord, and admonish you; And to esteem them very highly in love for their work's sake. And be at peace among yourselves" (1 Thessalonians 5:12, 13).

"Finally, brethren, pray for us, that the word of the Lord may have free course, and be glorified, even as it is with you: And that we may be delivered from unreasonable and wicked men: for all men have not faith" (2 Thessalonians 3:1, 2).

If your pastor is to be useful in the hands of God, he needs your prayers. He must be faithful in prayer, in study, in the Word, in doctrine, and in behaviour. But you must be faithful in prayer for him. The work is heavy. He carries the burden of the Word of the Lord. The responsibilities are enormous. Your pastor, if he is a faithful man, carries the weight of speaking in God's name the message of life or of condemnation to eternity bound sinners! Yet, those men who preach the gospel know themselves to be insignificant, weak and sinful, nothing but worthless worms. The work of preaching the gospel requires wisdom, "knowledge and understanding;" but we are ignorant.

Preaching
"Who is sufficient for these things?" Gospel preaching is a work for which God alone can make a man sufficient. "Simon, (whom he also named Peter,) and Andrew his brother, James and John, Philip and Bartholomew, Matthew and Thomas, James the son of Alphaeus, and Simon called Zelotes, And Judas the brother of James, and Judas Iscariot, which also was the traitor" (vv. 14-16).

Look at these twelve men. Four of them were fishermen. One of them was a publican. They were, for the most part at least, Galileans. Not one of them was wealthy, politically connected, powerful, or influential. They were, obviously, in the world's esteem, "unlearned and ignorant men" (Acts 4:13). What are we to learn from these facts? Why were these things written?

The church and kingdom of God is entirely independent of the world. God's church is not built by might, nor by power, but by his Spirit (Zechariah 4:6; 1 Corinthians 1:26-31). The weapons of our warfare are not carnal, but spiritual (2 Corinthians 10:3-5; Romans 1:15-17).

I must not fail to call your attention to the fact that one of the first twelve preachers was Judas Iscariot, a devil and a betrayer. I have often wondered why the Lord Jesus put Judas among the twelve. Have you? The Master knew that Judas was a graceless man, that he was a deceiver and a hypocrite from the beginning. Yet, he put him among the apostles, preached with him and sat with him at the Lord's Table. Why? There are some things about this which ought to be obvious.

Our Lord would teach all preachers of the gospel the necessity of constant, personal self-examination. "Let him that thinketh he standeth take heed, lest he fall." God's servants must not be idolized. Esteem them highly.

Pray for them faithfully. Follow their faith, their doctrine and their example. But do not make an idol out of any man. "Let no man glory in men." No faithful man desires either adulation or blind allegiance (1 Corinthians 3:5-9; 2 Corinthians 4:1-7).

Yet, in the church of God, so long as we are in this world, we must expect to find the bad mixed with the good, tares among wheat, goats among sheep and unbelievers among faithful men. God will, in his time, separate the precious from the vile. We have no ability to do so. If a man's message is a false gospel, he clearly identifies himself as a false prophet. But we dare not assume that we can read the motives of a man's heart. So long as he preaches the gospel and lives uprightly, we must not attempt to judge whether he is or is not God's messenger.

Power

The great secret to the power and efficacy of gospel preaching is the presence of Christ. "And he came down with them, and stood in the plain, and the company of his disciples, and a great multitude of people out of all Judaea and Jerusalem, and from the sea coast of Tyre and Sidon, which came to hear him, and to be healed of their diseases; And they that were vexed with unclean spirits: and they were healed. And the whole multitude sought to touch him: for there went virtue out of him, and healed them all" (vv. 17-19).

The Lord Jesus Christ, the Son of God, came down. "He came down with them and stood in the company of his disciples." The people who came to hear the gospel came with great needs. They came to hear him. They came with great need desiring to be healed. And they sought to touch him. When they did, "Virtue went out of him and healed them all." May God the Holy Spirit ever show us and make us to know our great need of Christ. May he enable us, every time we gather with his saints to worship our God, to seek to hear our Saviour and seek to touch him and be touched by him, that virtue may come out of him to our souls!

"And he lifted up his eyes on his disciples, and said, Blessed be ye poor: for yours is the kingdom of God. Blessed are ye that hunger now: for ye shall be filled. Blessed are ye that weep now: for ye shall laugh. Blessed are ye, when men shall hate you, and when they shall separate you from their company, and shall reproach you, and cast out your name as evil, for the Son of man's sake. Rejoice ye in that day, and leap for joy: for, behold, your reward is great in heaven: for in the like manner did their fathers unto the prophets. But woe unto you that are rich! for ye have received your consolation. Woe unto you that are full! for ye shall hunger. Woe unto you that laugh now! for ye shall mourn and weep. Woe unto you, when all men shall speak well of you! for so did their fathers to the false prophets" (Luke 6:20-26).

Chapter 33

Four Great Contrasts

The things revealed in these few verses of Inspiration are the meat of the Word, upon which only the strong can feed. By comparison, the glorious gospel doctrines of divine sovereignty, eternal predestination, free election, particular, effectual redemption, irresistible grace and the everlasting security of God's elect in Christ are baby milk and baby food. Many who love to nurse upon the breasts of election and predestination choke on the things revealed in our Lord's doctrine here.

Here our Master proclaims some of the most important things taught in holy scripture. These are spiritual truths that are galling to our flesh. May God the Holy Spirit give us eyes to see, ears to hear and hearts to heed the things he inspired Luke to record in this place.

Obvious Differences

While the sermon which begins here and runs through the end of this chapter, in many ways resembles our Lord's Sermon on the Mount (recorded in Matthew 5-7), it must not be confused with it. I am aware that the vast majority of good commentators say they are the same; but a careful reading of the two makes it obvious that they are not. Though there are similarities, the differences are obvious.

For one thing, the sermon recorded by Matthew is properly called "The Sermon on the Mount", because it was a sermon delivered upon a mountain side. The sermon here was delivered in the plain (v. 17).

The Sermon on the Mount was delivered before our Lord had named his twelve apostles. This sermon was delivered immediately after he named them.

It is obvious that the two sermons are tremendously different in length. It might be thought that Luke was inspired to give a much more brief summary of the same message than Matthew was inspired to record, but there are some things found in this sermon which are not mentioned in the far more lengthy Sermon on the Mount. If this was just a shorter version of the same sermon, we would expect some things to be left out; but we would not expect things to be included here that were omitted from the more lengthy version.

In the passage before us the Master is speaking specifically to his disciples, to those who were truly his disciples and to those who were his disciples in name only. In these seven, short verses he lays the axe to the root of the tree and distinguishes clearly between true believers and mere lip service professors. He does so by making four great, glaring contrasts between true believers and false professors. First, he gives us four beatitudes, which characterize the true believer. Then he gives us four woes, which characterize the false professor.

Four Beatitudes
In verses 20-23 our Saviour gives four words of blessing, four beatitudes, four conditions of true blessedness and happiness, by which all true believers are characterized.

Who are those men and women whom the Son of God pronounces blessed? The list is both remarkable and shocking. It is totally contrary to the opinion of the world. Here, our Lord singles out those who are poor, hungry, sorrowful and hated, and calls them blessed. How can this be? Let us look at each beatitude and see what the Master here teaches us.

"Blessed are ye poor: for yours is the kingdom of God" (v. 21). He does not say, blessed are *the* poor, but blessed are *you* poor. In the Sermon on the Mount he said, "Blessed are the poor in spirit" (Matthew 5:1). Those who are poor in spirit are those men and women who have been taught of God the utter depravity, corruption and sinfulness of their hearts. They are men and women who are convinced of sin, righteousness and judgment by God the Holy Spirit. The poor in spirit confess their sins and find forgiveness in Christ, being washed in his blood and robed in his righteousness.

All who are blessed of God with grace, salvation and eternal life in Christ are poor in Spirit. But, here our Saviour speaks of something else.

Here, the Master says, "Blessed are ye poor". We must not imagine that the Lord is here making physical poverty a spiritual blessing and giving men a claim to heavenly glory upon the basis of earthly poverty. Here, our Lord is talking about physical, earthly, material poverty; but it is poverty accompanied by grace.

The Lord Jesus chose twelve apostles and sent them out to evangelize the world. He sent them out without any means visible of earthly support into a hostile world. When he did, he commanded them plainly not to provide for themselves and not to go begging for help from the world, and told them plainly that they would be hated, persecuted and driven out from the company of men.

Is it possible to conduct any kind of ministry in this way? Is it possible to evangelize the world this way? Not only is it possible, there is no other way! This is the only way God's servants and God's church can perform the work the Lord God has trusted to our hands.

Poverty itself is not virtuous and is not a blessing. In fact, poverty is often the result of divine judgment. In our text the Lord Jesus is talking about a willing, deliberate, self-imposed poverty. This is not the self-imposed poverty of hermits and monks, but the poverty men and women knowingly bring upon themselves by following Christ, obeying the will of God and serving the interests of his kingdom.

This is not the poverty which comes as the result of laziness, because a man pretends to be too spiritual to work. This is that poverty which comes when a man or woman counts the costs and forsakes all to follow Christ. In the early days of Christianity those who followed Christ literally gave up everything, often even life itself, because of their faith in and love for him.

Though our circumstances are somewhat different today, it is still true that those who follow Christ forsake all to follow him and love not their lives, even unto death. All true believers do exactly what our Lord required the rich young ruler to do. They sell all they have and follow him.

"Blessed are ye that hunger now: for ye shall be filled" (v. 21). In Matthew 5:6, in the Sermon on the Mount, our Lord said, "Blessed are they which do hunger and thirst after righteousness: for they shall be filled."

There our Lord declares that all who are born of God, hunger and thirst for the righteousness of God in Christ. They long to stand before God in the perfect righteousness of Christ, and long to be perfectly conformed to Christ in righteousness and true holiness (Philippians 3:7-15). All who do truly hunger and thirst after this righteousness shall have it. They shall be filled.

Here, our Lord is declaring that those who hunger for the gospel's sake shall be filled. Believers are people who willingly deprive themselves of that which they might otherwise lawfully enjoy for the gospel's sake. They are willing to get along on less, so that they can give more. They do not have to have the finer things. They do not have to lavish themselves in luxury, but rather prefer to do without so that they may have to give for the furtherance of the gospel. Believers know that things craved by the flesh are only temporal and can never satisfy. So they do not mind giving them up. We look for satisfaction, we look to be filled in another world.

These are matters which apply to and are seen in all true believers; and they are matters which must and do characterize gospel preachers. God's servants are men separated unto the gospel. They do not seek to enrich themselves by the gospel, but rather sacrifice the comforts and luxuries of life for the gospel. God's servants do not seek the possessions of men, but their souls.

"Blessed are ye that weep now: for ye shall laugh" (v. 21). Sorrow is not itself beneficial or sanctifying. Our Lord is here talking about those who weep for his sake. Believers, as long as we live in this world of woe, have countless nights of weeping and tears. Like all other people, we experience the sorrows of sickness, pain, bereavement, broken homes, wayward children and earthly trouble.

In addition to the sorrows of the world, those who know, trust, love and follow Christ carry other burdens which cause them to weep. We carry the heavy load of our corrupt nature and constant sin. We carry the load of care for the souls of men. And we carry the heavy load of care for the church, the kingdom and the glory of our God in this world. Yet, those who sow in tears will reap in joy. "Ye shall laugh"! "Weeping may endure for a night, but joy cometh in the morning." The time of laughter shall soon come. We shall, at last, be filled with consolation. We shall soon possess unending, uninterruptible, everlasting joy! The joy of perfect righteousness, perfect peace, perfect understanding and perfect satisfaction!

"Blessed are ye, when men shall hate you, and when they shall separate you from their company, and shall reproach you, and cast out your name as evil, for the Son of man's sake. Rejoice ye in that day, and leap for joy: for, behold, your reward is great in heaven: for in like manner did their fathers unto the prophets" (vv. 22, 23).

Our Lord is here talking about religious persecution, persecution brought upon us because of the gospel we preach. The words used here are used specifically with regard to ecclesiastical censure and discipline. Our Lord could not have used stronger words to picture the heaping of man's wrath upon his people for the gospel's sake.

Hatred, persecution, slander and reproach are the devices of Satan, not the tools of God's church and people. We ought not to allow Satan's rage, displayed in the wrath of men, to cause us too much pain. The tables will soon be turned.

Four Woes

"But woe unto you that are rich! for ye have received your consolation. Woe unto you that are full! for ye shall hunger. Woe unto you that laugh now! for ye shall mourn and weep. Woe unto you, when all men shall speak well of you! for so did their fathers to the false prophets" (vv. 24-26).

Stronger, more cutting, condemning statements than these cannot be found in the New Testament. But what do these words mean? We must not imagine that the mere possession of wealth is a curse. Job's great wealth was the token of God's favour toward him. We must not think that the mere display of laughter and joy is a sign of God's wrath. David was a man who often spoke of laughter and displayed it both in song and dance; and he was a man after God's own heart. We certainly must not imagine that the possession of a good name is an indication of a foul heart. Timothy was a man whose name was well spoken of by those outside the church as well as within it.

Who, then, are these men and women of whom the Master speaks, when he says, "Woe unto you"? They are those people who prefer the world to Christ, who prefer the riches of the world to the riches of his grace, who prefer the laughter of lusts to the happiness of holiness, who delight more in gain than in godliness, who love the praise of men more than the praise of God.

Our Lord knew, from the beginning, that there would be many in the professed church, many who claim to be his disciples in every age who, though convinced of the truth of the gospel and professing to love it, would yet live for the world in the lusts of their flesh. To all such men and women, the Son of God says, "Woe unto you"!

This is what our Lord declares. Let men think and say what they may. This is the doctrine of this passage. Those who are poor because they choose to follow Christ and serve him, rather than enrich themselves, are possessors of the kingdom of God. Those who choose and seek and get riches will perish with their moth eaten treasures. They have all here they will ever have, the consolation of thick clay. Those who prefer to be hungry in doing the will of God, to fullness in rebelling, shall be filled forever. Those who live to fill their bellies and their lusts shall be hungry forever in hell. Those who choose a path of sorrow for the glory of God, carrying the weight of weighty matters upon their hearts, shall be filled with the laughter of complete satisfaction in heaven. Those who live here for pleasure shall find nothing but sorrow forever in hell. Those who prefer the favour and praise of God to the favour and praise of men shall be numbered among the sons of God forever, in everlasting praise. Those who prefer the favour and praise of men to the favour and praise of God shall be the objects of everlasting contempt, from both God and men in hell forever!

"But I say unto you which hear, Love your enemies, do good to them which hate you, Bless them that curse you, and pray for them which despitefully use you. And unto him that smiteth thee on the one cheek offer also the other; and him that taketh away thy cloke forbid not to take thy coat also. Give to every man that asketh of thee; and of him that taketh away thy goods ask them not again. And as ye would that men should do to you, do ye also to them likewise. For if ye love them which love you, what thank have ye? for sinners also love those that love them. And if ye do good to them which do good to you, what thank have ye? for sinners also do even the same. And if ye lend to them of whom ye hope to receive, what thank have ye? for sinners also lend to sinners, to receive as much again. But love ye your enemies, and do good, and lend, hoping for nothing again; and your reward shall be great, and ye shall be the children of the Highest: for he is kind unto the unthankful and to the evil. Be ye therefore merciful, as your Father also is merciful. Judge not, and ye shall not be judged: condemn not, and ye shall not be condemned: forgive, and ye shall be forgiven: Give, and it shall be given unto you; good measure, pressed down, and shaken together, and running over, shall men give into your bosom. For with the same measure that ye mete withal it shall be measured to you again" (Luke 6:27-38).

Chapter 34

How Can I Live Among Men
For The Glory Of God?

How can I live among men for the glory of God? If you are a believer, I am sure that is a question you often ponder in the various situations you face day by day. How can I glorify God in this situation? How can I live among men for the honour of God my Saviour and the gospel of his grace? What would the Lord have me to do here? What is God's will in this place and at this time?

If we would live among men for the glory of God, we must love them. Love is always right. It is the will of God for us to love one another, to love our neighbours as ourselves; and our neighbours include family, friends, brethren in Christ, and even our most implacable enemies. That is our Saviour's doctrine in this passage. May he graciously apply his doctrine to our hearts by his Spirit.

The Lord Jesus here declares, that to all who profess to be his disciples, that those who follow him love people, not just that they love to be around people, but that they love people. Love is the great, identifying mark of true Christianity. Love is the sweet bond of peace. Love is the fulfilling of the law. Love is that without which we are nothing before God. Love is that sweet grace identified first as the fruit of the Spirit.

It will profit us greatly and may even make us profitable to others to carefully study and diligently practice that which is taught in these verses.

The Basis Of Appeal

I am calling for all who read these lines, professing to be followers of Christ, to live among the people of this world in exemplary love, to love your brothers and sisters in the kingdom of God and your neighbours for the glory of God. But before we can exemplify the love of Christ, we must know the love of Christ.

You cannot gather grapes among thorns, or figs among thistles. You cannot expect flowers where there are no roots, or fruit without trees. It is not possible to have the fruit of the Spirit unless you are united to Christ by faith, born of his Spirit and sanctified by his grace. Until you are born of God, it is not possible for you to exemplify the love of Christ.

So the basis of my appeal is this: if you have experienced the mercy, grace and love of God in Christ, show that same mercy, grace and love to others.

"And be ye kind one to another, tenderhearted, forgiving one another, even as God for Christ's sake hath forgiven you. Be ye therefore followers of God, as dear children; And walk in love, as Christ also hath loved us, and hath given himself for us an offering and a sacrifice to God for a sweetsmelling savour" (Ephesians 4:32-5:2).

It is not possible for anyone to possess the fruit of the Spirit who does not know the doctrine of the Spirit, the doctrine of Christ. There are hoards of people today who go to great pains to show other people how loving, self-denying and sacrificial they are, who utterly despise the gospel of Christ; but theirs is only the hypocritical pretence of love demonstrated by the Pharisees in John 8:1, 2 and in John 9.

"Once for all", wrote J. C. Ryle, "let us understand, that real, genuine, self-denying love, will never grow from any roots but faith in Christ's atonement, and a heart renewed by the Holy Ghost. We shall never make men love one another, unless we teach as Paul taught, 'Walk in love as Christ hath loved us.' Teaching love on any other principle is ... labour in vain."

Those who do not know the doctrine of Christ, who do not know the gospel of the grace of God, do not and cannot know the love of God. Those who do not have the love of God dwelling in them cannot walk in the love of Christ and exercise that love toward others.

Do you know the love of God? Have you experienced his grace? Are you born of his Spirit? Are you washed in the blood of the Lamb? Are you robed in the righteousness of God's dear Son? Are you a saved, justified, forgiven, heaven born soul? If you are, the basis of my appeal is the mercy, love and grace you have experienced. I am calling for saved sinners to act like their Saviour. Those who have experienced grace ought to be, and are, gracious.

230

Those who have experienced mercy ought to be, and are, merciful. Those who have been forgiven ought to be, and are, forgiving. Those who know the love of God in Christ ought to love others for Christ's sake, and do.

Love's Character

Our Lord Jesus plainly shows us the character of true love. The nature and character of true love is the nature and character of his love. How often have you said, or heard someone say, "They love in their own way."? Phooey on their way. If we love, we love God's way. There is no other way to love.

Who are we to love? The Lord Jesus Christ teaches us to love our neighbours. Religious Pharisees and hypocrites ask, "Who is my neighbour?" (Luke 10:29). Our Lord tells us exactly who we are to love.

"But I say unto you which hear, Love your enemies, do good to them which hate you, Bless them that curse you, and pray for them which despitefully use you" (vv. 27, 28).

Our love toward others is to be like our Redeemer's love toward us: unselfish, impartial, expecting no return of love from those we love. Our Lord Jesus loves us freely. So let us love others freely. He expects no return for his love, except wrath, unless he himself creates love for himself in the sinners he loves. So let us love, expecting nothing from the objects of our love. The Master says, "Love ye your enemies, and do good, and lend, expecting nothing in return" (v. 35).

How are we to love those who despise us? We would be wise to hear what the Son of God says about this, and ignore the psychologists, psychiatrists, marriage counsellors and social workers of this God-hating, self-loving society. How are we to love people? Read verses 29, 30, and you will see.

"And unto him that smiteth thee on the one cheek offer also the other; and him that taketh away thy cloak forbid not to take thy coat also. Give to every man that asketh of thee; and of him that taketh away thy goods ask them not again."

Our Lord is not here demanding utter passivity. He is not requiring that we allow those who would rob us, take our homes, or murder us to do as they wish. He is talking here about insignificant things. Oh, how I pray that God will give me grace to treat insignificant things as insignificant things!

Loves gives in. Love gives up much. Loves endures much. Love is kind. Love strives to avoid strife. Love sacrifices personal rights and desires for its object, and even submits to wrong for the sake of peace. Love, like the great Lover of our souls, is meek and lowly of heart, longsuffering, gentle and kind. This is what our Master teaches us concerning the character of love (Romans 12:9-21; 14:19; 1 Corinthians 13:1-13). May he give us grace to

231

exemplify it to one another in the house of God, in our homes, and to the world around us.

Essential To Godliness

Is your heart ruled, governed, and motivated by the love of Christ? Do you have within you the kind of love that Christ produces in his people! Do I? Love is absolutely essential to true godliness. Paul tells us that if we have all other things, and have not love, they shall profit us nothing. The absence of love is fatal. As you read such passages as I have cited in this study, do not think to yourself, "Love is a very great virtue, most commendable and useful; it would be a great thing if I could obtain it." Oh, no! We must have it! It is essential.

God the Holy Spirit tells us that this love is something which characterizes all who are born of God. We must have it, or else we are not born of God. If I do not have this love, no matter what else I may have, no matter what else I may do, if I do not have the love of Christ in my heart, I am a lost man; and the same is true of you. This love is not a condition to be met in order to get salvation; but it is one sure result of God's saving grace in Christ.

Christian love is greater than all other spiritual gifts and graces. Without love, all other gifts and graces are meaningless and useless (1 Corinthians 13:1-3). This one thing, love, is the fulfilling of the law of God (Matthew 22:36-40; Romans 13:8-10). And love is the one sure mark and evidence of a saving union with the Lord Jesus Christ. He said, "By this shall all men know that you are my disciples, if ye have love one to another" (John 13:35).

Where this love is absent, grace is absent. No man is born of God who does not have the love of Christ implanted in his heart as a ruling principle of life (1 John 2:9-11; 3:14, 23; 4:7, 8, 16, 20; 5:1).

The love of Christ, or the absence of it, is a thing easily identifiable. This is not some profound, mysterious point of theology. It is not some sweet-sounding, but useless, emotion. The love of Christ is a gift of divine grace, that is clearly demonstrated in the lives of God's elect (1 Corinthians 13:4-7). This love causes a person to be kind, patient, content, gentle, even tempered, humble, self-denying, generous, honest, truthful, forbearing and forgiving toward others, both in the church and out of it.

Love is preferable to all other gifts and greater than all other graces, because love is the only thing that will last forever (1 Corinthians 13:8-13). All other gifts will come to an end. All other graces will cease. But love will go on in heaven. Faith will be no more, when we see him whom we have believed. Hope will be no more, when we have that for which we have hoped. But love will continue and come to perfection, when we enter heaven. Love is the only thing we have in this world that we can carry with us into the world to come. Heaven is a world of love; perfect, unceasing, glorious, Christ-like love. No one will enter that city of peace and world of love, except those who have the love of Christ in their hearts.

Blessed Rule

Our dear Saviour, the Lord Jesus, gives us a very simple and blessed rule by which to live, the rule of love. "And as ye would that men should do to you, do ye also to them likewise" (v. 31). "Judge not, and ye shall not be judged: condemn not, and ye shall not be condemned: forgive, and ye shall be forgiven" (v. 37).

Our Lord knew that in this world the line between right and wrong, in dealing with neighbours and friends, family and foe, would often be very hazy. Personal feelings and private interests often dim our view of things and cloud our judgment. So the Lord Jesus gave us this guide. He tells us to treat others as we would have them treat us.

To do to others as they do to us, to return evil for evil, bite for bite, injury for injury, is beastly. To return good for evil is to walk in the steps of our Master. Let us always endeavour to put the best construction on the actions and words of others, judging them and their deeds as charitably as possible. Be very slow to condemn another and swift to forgive.

Let all error in dealing with other people be on the side of leniency, not on the side of severity. We do not have to form an opinion about everything, much less express an opinion about everything, everyone, or everyone's actions. Believers live by principles the world simply cannot understand. We live by the rule of Christ and walk by the the example of his love (John 13:15; 2 Corinthians 5:14).

"For if ye love them which love you, what thank have ye? for sinners also love those that love them. And if ye do good to them which do good to you, what thank have ye? for sinners also do even the same. And if ye lend to them of whom ye hope to receive, what thank have ye? for sinners also lend to sinners, to receive as much again. But love ye your enemies, and do good, and lend, hoping for nothing again; and your reward shall be great, and ye shall be the children of the Highest: for he is kind unto the unthankful and to the evil" (vv. 32-35).

As our heavenly Father is "kind to the unthankful and to the evil", so let us be. As he forgives, let us forgive. As his loving-kindness is unwearied, let ours be. As his mercy is unlimited, let ours be unlimited. As his compassions fail not, so let our compassion be unaltered by thanklessness, ingratitude and abuse from those upon whom compassion is bestowed.

Love's Reward

In verses 35-38 learn, if you have not yet learned, that love is its own reward.

"But love ye your enemies, and do good, and lend, hoping for nothing again; and your reward shall be great, and ye shall be the children of the Highest: for he is kind unto the unthankful and to the evil. Be ye therefore merciful, as your Father also is merciful. Judge not, and ye shall not be judged: condemn not, and ye shall not be condemned: forgive, and ye shall be forgiven: Give, and it shall be given unto you; good measure, pressed down, and shaken together, and running over, shall men give into your bosom. For with the same measure that ye mete withal it shall be measured to you again."

Our Lord Jesus does not here contradict the whole Bible. He is not here telling us that our love to other people earns God's grace, or earns us a place in heaven. Not at all! He is simply declaring that those who are born of God walk in love, and that those who walk in love are born of God. Those who do not are not. Walk in love, "hoping for nothing again, and your reward shall be great."

The God of all grace has gracious children. The God of all mercy has merciful sons and daughters. The God whose glory it is to forgive sin has a forgiving family. If you are lenient with men, men will be lenient with you. As you forgive men, you shall be forgiven of men. As you give, men will give to you. It is easy to be lenient with lenient people. It is very difficult to be unforgiving toward one who is ever forgiving others. And people are always quickest to give to those who are generous.

"Beloved, let us love one another: for love is of God; and every one that loveth is born of God, and knoweth God. He that loveth not knoweth not God; for God is love. In this was manifested the love of God toward us, because that God sent his only begotten Son into the world, that we might live through him. Herein is love, not that we loved God, but that he loved us, and sent his Son to be the propitiation for our sins. Beloved, if God so loved us, we ought also to love one another" (1 John 4:7-11).

234

How Can I Live Among Men For The Glory Of God?

"And he spake a parable unto them, Can the blind lead the blind? shall they not both fall into the ditch? The disciple is not above his master: but every one that is perfect shall be as his master. And why beholdest thou the mote that is in thy brother's eye, but perceivest not the beam that is in thine own eye? Either how canst thou say to thy brother, Brother, let me pull out the mote that is in thine eye, when thou thyself beholdest not the beam that is in thine own eye? Thou hypocrite, cast out first the beam out of thine own eye, and then shalt thou see clearly to pull out the mote that is in thy brother's eye. For a good tree bringeth not forth corrupt fruit; neither doth a corrupt tree bring forth good fruit. For every tree is known by his own fruit. For of thorns men do not gather figs, nor of a bramble bush gather they grapes. A good man out of the good treasure of his heart bringeth forth that which is good; and an evil man out of the evil treasure of his heart bringeth forth that which is evil: for of the abundance of the heart his mouth speaketh" (Luke 6:39-45).

Chapter 35

Three Great Dangers

In these seven verses our Lord Jesus Christ gives a very sobering, instructive parable, a parable by which he warns all who have ears to hear of three great dangers. Here are three great, spiritual dangers which we must strive to avoid, lest we perish forever.

The danger of following false prophets.
The danger of self-righteousness and hypocrisy.
The danger of a deceived heart.

By these three great snares, Satan has carried many to hell. Let us not be numbered among them.

Following False Prophets

First, the Son of God warns us of the great danger of following false prophets (vv. 39, 40).

"And he spake a parable unto them, Can the blind lead the blind? shall they not both fall into the ditch? The disciple is not above his master: but every one that is perfect shall be as his master" (vv. 39, 40).

These two verses are to be understood together. They cannot be separated. Our Lord is telling us plainly that those who follow false prophets shall perish with them in hell. If you follow a blind man, you cannot be walking in the light, and both of you will fall into hell. If you follow Christ, if he who is perfect is your Master, you shall at last be made perfect with him.

While he walked on the earth, our Lord warned us of the great danger of false prophets and false religion more frequently than anything else. The greatest dangers we face, the greatest dangers our children and grandchildren face in this world are not pimps, pushers and pornography (horrible as those things are). Oh, no. Our greatest dangers are false prophets and false religion. If the vices of the world have slain thousands, the pretended virtues of false religion have slain tens of thousands.

This is what our Lord teaches us in these two verses. If we hear and follow false prophets, we will go to hell with them. If your teacher is in error, you will be in error. If the man who leads you is blind, you are blind. If you follow your blind guide, when he falls into the ditch, so will you.

We constantly endeavour to avoid obvious facts. Pretending to be more kind, gracious and loving than God, we try to convince ourselves that men and women may worship at the altar of free will and still believe free grace, that they may follow blind guides, though they themselves see, that they may be involved in the practice of false religion and yet know the true God; but those things simply cannot be. Children of the Light walk in the light. Christ's sheep will not follow the voice of a stranger (Matthew 7:13-15; 2 Corinthians 11:2, 3; 1 Thessalonians 5:21, 22; 1 John 4:1-3).

Christ is the Door. Every other door is the door to destruction. Christ is the Way. Every other way is the way to hell. Christ is the Truth. Everything else is Satan's lie. Christ is the Life. Everything else is death. Christ is the Altar. Every other altar is idolatry. Christ is the Atonement. Every other attempt to make up with God is a denial of his atonement. Christ is Salvation (Wisdom, Righteousness, Sanctification and Redemption). Every thing added to him is damnation.

Beware of false prophets who would take you away from the simplicity that is in Christ. If you care for your soul, if you care for the souls of your sons and daughters, beware of following false prophets. If you do, you will follow them to hell (Revelation 18:4).

Self-Righteousness And Hypocrisy
Second, in verses 41 and 42 our Master warns us of the great danger of self-righteousness and hypocrisy.

"And why beholdest thou the mote that is in thy brother's eye, but perceivest not the beam that is in thine own eye? Either how canst thou say to thy brother, Brother, let me pull out the mote that is in thine eye, when thou thyself beholdest not the beam that is in thine own eye? Thou hypocrite, cast out first the beam out of thine own eye, and then shalt thou see clearly to pull out the mote that is in thy brother's eye."

Self-righteousness and hypocrisy always go together. It is impossible to have one without the other. Nothing is more natural to man or more obnoxious to God than self-righteousness and hypocrisy (Isaiah 65:3-5).

I would rather stand before God Almighty in the day of judgment charged with any crime than the crime of self-righteousness. Self-righteous people justify themselves and condemn others. Those who are made righteous in Christ condemn themselves and justify others. The self-righteous find splinters in the eyes of others and ignore the two-by-fours in their own eyes. Those who acknowledge and confess their sins before God struggle constantly with the two-by-fours in their own eyes and are not able to see the splinters in the eyes of others. Self-righteous hypocrites boast of their attainments. Believing sinners grieve over their failures. Self-righteous hypocrites think themselves strong and superior to others. God's saints know themselves weak and inferior to their brethren. Self-righteous people, hypocrites go about to establish righteousness. Believers look to Christ for righteousness (Romans 10:1-4).

A Deceived Heart
In verses 43-45 our Lord Jesus warns us of the great danger of a deceived heart.

"For a good tree bringeth not forth corrupt fruit; neither doth a corrupt tree bring forth good fruit. For every tree is known by his own fruit. For of thorns men do not gather figs, nor of a bramble bush gather they grapes. A good man out of the good treasure of his heart bringeth forth that which is good; and an evil man out of the evil treasure of his heart bringeth forth that which is evil: for of the abundance of the heart his mouth speaketh."

It does not matter how good your religion looks on the outside, "the Lord looketh on the heart." It does not matter how much you impress men, or yourself for that matter, with what you say and do, "the Lord looketh on the heart." It does not matter how sound your doctrine is, "the Lord looketh on the heart." It does not matter how precisely you keep the ordinances, "the Lord looketh on the heart." It does not matter how much money you give, how many chapters you read, how much scripture you memorize, how much you pray, or how often you attend church, "the Lord looketh on the heart."

God wants our hearts. God demands our hearts. The root of the matter is the heart. He says, "My son, give me thine heart." If the heart is right, the fruit is good, no matter how bad it looks to men. If the heart is evil, the fruit is evil, no matter how good it looks to men. Perhaps the best way for us to understand the meaning of our Lord's words here is to hear another parable.

"And he spake this parable unto certain which trusted in themselves that they were righteous, and despised others: Two men went up into the temple

239

to pray; the one a Pharisee, and the other a publican. The Pharisee stood and prayed thus with himself, God, I thank thee, that I am not as other men are, extortioners, unjust, adulterers, or even as this publican. I fast twice in the week, I give tithes of all that I possess. And the publican, standing afar off, would not lift up so much as his eyes unto heaven, but smote upon his breast, saying, God be merciful to me a sinner. I tell you, this man went down to his house justified rather than the other: for every one that exalteth himself shall be abased; and he that humbleth himself shall be exalted" (Luke 18:9-14).

Beware of following false prophets. Beware of self-righteousness and hypocrisy. Beware of a deceived heart. May the God of all grace save us from these three great dangers.

Three Great Dangers

"And why call ye me, Lord, Lord, and do not the things which I say? Whosoever cometh to me, and heareth my sayings, and doeth them, I will shew you to whom he is like: he is like a man which built an house, and digged deep, and laid the foundation on a rock: and when the flood arose, the stream beat vehemently upon that house, and could not shake it: for it was founded upon a rock. But he that heareth, and doeth not, is like a man that without a foundation built an house upon the earth; against which the stream did beat vehemently, and immediately it fell; and the ruin of that house was great" (Luke 6:46-49).

Chapter 36

What Is Your Foundation?

God saves sinners by free grace alone. We are not saved by what we will, or by what we do. Election is by grace. Redemption is the work of God's grace. Regeneration is the work of free grace alone. We are kept and preserved in grace by grace alone. The doctrine of holy scripture is crystal clear. From start to finish, "Salvation is of the Lord"! A spiritually dead sinner has no more to do with the work of the new birth than Lazarus did with his resurrection from the dead.

But that does not mean that sinners are passive in the experience of grace. God does not knock a man in the head and drag him to heaven, whether he wants to go or not. That is not the doctrine of Scripture. God makes his people willing in the day of his power, and graciously causes his chosen to come to Christ willingly (Psalms 65:4; 110:3).

In the passage now before us our Lord Jesus describes two groups of hearers, two kinds of religious people: Those who are saved and those who think they are saved, though they are lost.

True believers, those who have been made wise by grace, are people who do some things, people who, being quickened by his grace, called by his Spirit and drawn with the cords of love, have been made to want Christ and seek him with all their hearts. Therefore, they hear his Word gladly and do his bidding diligently. Digging deep, they have discovered the Foundation. They build upon the Foundation. And having built upon the Foundation, they stand.

The Lord Jesus also describes religious fools in this passage. The religious fool (Matthew 7:26) is one who does not take the things of God seriously. He hears the gospel, just like the wise man does; but everything with him is froth and folly. His religion is all on the surface, superficial and fake. With him, there is no digging, no building and no standing.

The religious fool is one who has made lies his refuge (Isaiah 28:14). They have a house of refuge; but it is a house with no solid foundation, a refuge of lies built upon the shifting sands of human effort, religious works and personal goodness. What is your foundation? Is your soul built upon a foundation of earth and sand, or are you built upon the Rock, Christ Jesus? Saved sinners are built upon and build upon the Foundation God has laid in Zion, Christ Jesus (Isaiah 28:16).

Christless Religion

Religion without Christ is a very common thing. The visible church has always been a mixed multitude. Tares grow wherever wheat is sown. Goats graze in the same field with sheep. Wherever you find gold, you are sure to find fool's gold. While he walked and preached in this world, the Son of God himself had many followers who were his disciples in word only, many who pretended to honour him by calling him Lord, but were yet rebels and refused to obey him.

This is the evil which our Lord exposes in verse 46. "And why call ye me, Lord, Lord, and do not the things which I say?" It has always been a painful fact, throughout the history of the church, that multitudes profess faith in Christ who do not know him. Multitudes wear his name and use it who do not follow him (Isaiah 29:13; Ezekiel 33:31; Matthew 15:8, 9; James 1:22).

Nothing is more soul numbing, nothing is more dangerous to your soul, nothing is more damning than religion without Christ. Nothing is more likely to keep you from Christ than deluding yourself into thinking you have him when you do not. Nothing in all the world is more treacherous to your soul than a mere form of godliness. Nothing is more likely to keep you from seeking refuge than a refuge of lies (Isaiah 28:14-20).

True Faith

True faith is an earnest heart pursuit of the Lord Jesus Christ. Those who are born of God know their need of Christ and seek him with all their hearts (Jeremiah 29:12, 13; Philippians 3:7-14). When a sinner knows his need of Christ, when he is fleeing from the wrath of God, when the gaping jaws of hell are before him, when God fixes it so that he is at his wits end and must either have Christ or die forever, he is in dead earnestness. There is nothing half-hearted, indifferent, or careless about him.

"Whosoever cometh to me, and heareth my sayings, and doeth them, I will show you to whom he is like" (v. 47). Believers are sinners who come to Christ as their Priest, their Saviour, trusting him alone for acceptance with God. They are people who hear Christ's words as their Prophet, as their

Teacher. And believers are people who obey Christ as their King, as their Lord and Master.

The Lord Jesus describes the believer as a wise man, who builds his house upon the rock. "He is like a man which built an house, and digged deep, and laid the foundation on a rock: and when the flood arose, the stream beat vehemently upon that house, and could not shake it: for it was founded upon a rock" (v. 48). He believes on the Rock. He digs deep, sparing nothing, refusing to build upon any foundation other than that foundation which God has laid, Christ Jesus (Isaiah 28:16; Romans 9:33; 10:11; 1 Peter 2:6).

> My hope is built on nothing less
> Than Jesus' blood and righteousness.
> I dare not trust the sweetest frame,
> But wholly lean on Jesus' name.
> Edward Mote

The house that is built upon the Rock, Christ Jesus, is stable and secure. Floods of heresies, streams of adversity, winds of troubles, temptations and trials beat vehemently upon the house, but cannot shake it! It stands firmly fixed upon the Rock, Christ Jesus.

"He only is my rock and my salvation: he is my defence; I shall not be moved. In God is my salvation and my glory: the rock of my strength, and my refuge, is in God. Trust in him at all times; ye people, pour out your heart before him: God is a refuge for us. Selah" (Psalm 62:6-8).

"He brought me up also out of an horrible pit, out of the miry clay, and set my feet upon a rock, and established my goings" (Psalm 40:2).

False Faith
False faith is shallow, superficial and unstable. "But he that heareth, and doeth not, is like a man that without a foundation built an house upon the earth; against which the stream did beat vehemently, and immediately it fell; and the ruin of that house was great" (v. 49). John Gill wrote …

"Such builders, and such a building cannot stand against the violent rain of Satan's temptations, the floods of the world's persecutions, the stream and rapid torrent of their own heart's lusts, nor the blowing winds of heresy and false doctrine, and much less the storms of divine wrath and vengeance. They are in a most dangerous condition; they cannot support themselves; they must fall, and great will be their fall; their destruction is inevitable, their ruin is irrecoverable."

The Lord Jesus here describes the religion of the one who merely professes, but does not have faith in him. His religion is a house built upon the shifting sands of the earth. His hope is built upon his poor emotions, his excited experience, his religious learning and knowledge, church tradition, his freewill decision, his self-righteous works or sentiments.

The false refuge house is a house quickly built. It may look very impressive, but when floods of heresies, streams of adversity and winds of troubles, trials and temptations beat upon the house, it falls. It falls because it has no foundation. Thus John Trapp could say:

"The unprofitable hearer is not cemented to Christ by faith, but laid loose, as it were, upon a sandy foundation, and so slips beside the ground work in foul weather. He is not set into the stock as a scion, but only stuck into the ground as a stake, and is therefore easily pulled up. Whereas the true Christian is knit fast to Christ the Rock by the ligament of a lively faith; and as a lively stone, is built up in a spiritual house (1 Peter 2:5), growing up in the mystical body with so much sweetness and evenness, as if the whole temple (like that of Solomon) were but one entire stone. 'He that is joined to the Lord is one spirit' (1 Corinthians 6:17)."

Christ is the Foundation God has laid. Will you stumble over him, or build upon him? God help you to build on him. May God the Holy Spirit join you to him and build you upon him (1 Corinthians 1:30, 31).

What Is Your Foundation?

"Now when he had ended all his sayings in the audience of the people, he entered into Capernaum. And a certain centurion's servant, who was dear unto him, was sick, and ready to die. And when he heard of Jesus, he sent unto him the elders of the Jews, beseeching him that he would come and heal his servant. And when they came to Jesus, they besought him instantly, saying, That he was worthy for whom he should do this: For he loveth our nation, and he hath built us a synagogue. Then Jesus went with them. And when he was now not far from the house, the centurion sent friends to him, saying unto him, Lord, trouble not thyself: for I am not worthy that thou shouldest enter under my roof: Wherefore neither thought I myself worthy to come unto thee: but say in a word, and my servant shall be healed. For I also am a man set under authority, having under me soldiers, and I say unto one, Go, and he goeth; and to another, Come, and he cometh; and to my servant, Do this, and he doeth it. When Jesus heard these things, he marvelled at him, and turned him about, and said unto the people that followed him, I say unto you, I have not found so great faith, no, not in Israel. And they that were sent, returning to the house, found the servant whole that had been sick" (Luke 7:1-10).

Chapter 37

A Certain Centurion

Here, the Holy Spirit gives us the account of a certain centurion, his remarkable character, his great faith, and the healing of his sick servant, by the mere will of the Lord Jesus Christ. This Roman soldier said to the Lord Jesus, "I am not worthy that thou shouldest enter under my roof ... Neither thought I myself worthy to come unto thee: but say in a word, and my servant shall be healed."

No Discrepancy

If you read Matthew's abbreviated account of this same great miracle, you will see that Matthew described the event as a conversation, which took place between the centurion and the Lord Jesus personally. Here, in Luke's narrative the Holy Spirit tells us plainly that the conversation was between the centurion's friends and the Master, not between the centurion and the Master.

There is no discrepancy, or contradiction between Matthew and Luke. Perhaps, Matthew simply makes the words of the centurion's representatives to be the centurion's own words, which is altogether appropriate (since a representative's words are really the words of the one he represents); or it may be that the centurion first sent messengers to the Master and, afterwards, came to the Lord Jesus himself. Whatever the case may be, both Matthew and Luke wrote their narratives as honest eye witnesses, exactly as God the Holy Spirit directed them.

The Centurion's Servant

"Now when he had ended all his sayings in the audience of the people, he entered into Capernaum" (v. 1). When Luke tells us the Lord had ended his sayings, he is referring to the sermon he had just finished preaching (Luke 6:20-49). In that sermon our Master's message had four main points. He taught us three great truths we will be wise to learn and remember.

Those who are privileged to suffer for the gospel's sake, those who suffer in this world for Christ's sake are blessed (Luke 6:20-26).

Faith in Christ causes men and women to walk in love, love that is kind, generous, and forgiving (Luke 6:27-38).

Nothing in all the world is so dangerous to our souls as false religion (Luke 6:39-49). If we follow blind men in spiritual matters, we will perish with them.

The primary concern in all things spiritual is the heart. If the tree is corrupt, the fruit is corrupt, no matter how good it may look to men. If the tree is good, the fruit is good, no matter how corrupt it may appear to men. Our souls must be built upon that Foundation which God himself has laid (the Lord Jesus Christ), or our house is sure to fall.

When our Lord had finished preaching this sermon, he entered into Capernaum. He had spoken with authority. Now, he comes to Capernaum to display the efficacy of his grace.

Capernaum was exalted, elevated, and blessed above all other places (Matthew 11:23), by virtue of the fact that the Lord Jesus performed more of his miraculous works in Capernaum than anywhere else. He had already healed the nobleman's son there (John 4). In all probability, the centurion had heard about that great work. Perhaps he had witnessed it.

"And a certain centurion's servant, who was dear unto him, was sick, and ready to die" (v. 2). Here is a centurion, a Roman soldier, who had the command of a hundred men under his authority. He was a Gentile. He was a soldier. And he was a believer. As John Bunyan put it, "A Roman soldier was the first fruit of the Gentile world." Here, the Holy Spirit tells us three things about this centurion's servant.

This servant was dear (held in great honour and precious) to his master. Blessed is the servant who has such a master! Words can never speak so powerfully as the experience of this centurion's servant does of the great advantage and blessed privilege of living in the home of one who believes God, walks with Christ, and seeks your soul's everlasting good.

This man's servant was sick, very sick. What multitudes there are in the same condition spiritually as this man was in physically. There is a plague, a death plague in the heart of man. There is a spiritual palsy in the soul (Isaiah 1:5, 6; 1 Kings 8:38).

The centurion's servant was "ready to die", at the very point of death. An immortal soul at the point of death, what a sobering sight! Each time we see one who is sick, or visit one who is dying we ought to be reminded of our own frailty, and ask God to give us the wisdom and grace to set our hearts upon Christ and eternity (Psalm 90:12-16; Colossians 3:1-3).

He Heard Of Jesus

"And when he heard of Jesus ... " (v. 3) We are not told how, but somehow this centurion "heard of Jesus"! Perhaps he had been present to hear the sermon recorded in chapter 6. Maybe he had heard the report of the gospel from someone else. How he heard is unimportant. What is important is this. "He heard of Jesus"!

God sent his Word to him. God the Holy Spirit had given him hearing ears, seeing eyes and a believing heart. We have no way of knowing how much knowledge the man had. That is altogether insignificant. The thing that is significant is who he knew. He knew the Lord Jesus Christ, and he knew the one true and living God in him (John 17:3).

In other words, he was born of God. The only way any sinner can ever have eternal life is by knowing God (John 17:3). The only way we can know God is in Christ (Matthew 11:27). And the only way any sinner can know Christ and believe on him unto life everlasting is by the preaching of the gospel (Romans 1:16; 10:17).

The Centurion

"And when he heard of Jesus, he sent unto him the elders of the Jews, beseeching him that he would come and heal his servant. And when they came to Jesus, they besought him instantly, saying, That he was worthy for whom he should do this: For he loveth our nation, and he hath built us a synagogue" (vv. 3-5).

This centurion was a man of remarkable character. He was a gracious, kind, generous man. His faith was that true faith which only God can give. It was "faith that worketh by love." He was a man of blameless reputation. He was a man of such magnanimous goodness in the eyes of men that the Jews did not hesitate to declare (though it betrayed their own ignorance) that he was worthy for the Son of God to give him what he asked.

He loved his servant. Many came to the Lord Jesus seeking mercy for others. One came for a son, another for a daughter, and once four for a friend; but we are told of none but this centurion who came to the Son of God seeking mercy for a servant. Not only did he love his servant, he loved his neighbours, too. "He loveth our nation." And this centurion was devoted to the worship and service of God. He built a synagogue, a house of worship at Capernaum. When these Jewish leaders said, "he hath built for us a synagogue", they were saying: this man has, at his own expense, by himself, built a church building and given us a place to worship the Lord our God! This man's faith was more than creeds, confessions, and rituals. He did not merely say he believed God. He lived as one who believed God. His love was not lip love, but deed love.

Kindness is something all people recognize and appreciate. Kindness adorns and commends the doctrine of God our Saviour. Kindness reflects the character of Christ. Kindness is one way to spread a little happiness in this world. Even these wretched Jewish elders (who would soon plot the murder of the Son of God) were moved by this man's kindness. Had his servant died of his sickness, he would have enjoyed the privilege of dying in the home and under the tender care of a kind friend. "Be ye kind one to another, tenderhearted, forgiving one another, even as God for Christ's sake hath forgiven you. Be ye therefore followers of God, as dear children; And walk in love, as Christ also hath loved us, and hath given himself for us an offering and a sacrifice to God for a sweetsmelling savour" (Ephesians 4:32-5:2).

"Then Jesus went with them. And when he was now not far from the house, the centurion sent friends to him, saying unto him, Lord, trouble not thyself: for I am not worthy that thou shouldest enter under my roof: Wherefore neither thought I myself worthy to come unto thee: but say in a word, and my servant shall be healed" (vv. 6, 7).

This centurion was a truly humble man. Humbled by grace, he sent messengers to the Lord Jesus, saying, "I am not worthy that thou shouldest enter under my roof"! All who are born of God, all true believers know their unworthiness before God and confess it. Others may look at the child of God and applaud him for his deeds; but he sees himself in another light.

Here is a remarkable expression of faith in the Lord Jesus Christ. "Say in a word, and my servant shall be healed"! He acknowledged what very few understood in his day and few understand in any day: that Jesus of Nazareth is himself God Almighty in human flesh. None but God himself can heal by the mere word of his power (Psalms 33:6, 9; 148:5). But there was much more to his faith than the bare acknowledgment of Christ's eternal deity.

"For I also am a man set under authority, having under me soldiers, and I say unto one, Go, and he goeth; and to another, Come, and he cometh; and to my servant, Do this, and he doeth it" (v. 8). This centurion asked for no sign or wonder. He simply believed God. He here declares his implicit confidence in Christ as God and confesses his faith in him as that One in whose hands all things are but clay, the mighty King of the universe, whose command rules in heaven, earth and hell, the Monarch of all things, before whom all things (including sickness and health, life and death) are but obedient servants. He confidently bowed to the Lord Jesus, confessing his omniscience, omnipresence and omnipotence as God. He believed that Man who stood on the sands of Capernaum to be the sovereign Lord of heaven and earth!

Jesus Marvelled

"When Jesus heard these things, he marvelled at him, and turned him about, and said unto the people that followed him, I say unto you, I have not found so great faith, no, not in Israel" (v. 9). Only twice do we see the Lord Jesus marvelling at something. In Mark 6:6 we are told that our Saviour marvelled at the unbelief of his kinsmen. Here, he marvels at the faith of a Roman centurion. What can be more marvellous than the fact that the Son of God marvelled?

In Mark 6:6 the word "marvelled" implies astonishing sorrow. Here, the same word implies great admiration. Let us learn to place admiration where our Lord did, not upon the gaieties of the world sought by men, but upon the grace of God in men. Our Lord Jesus was never impressed by a person's possessions, position or power, land, learning or living, fortune, fame or family. But he admired faith. What grace this shows in him! He gives faith, and then admires the man who exercises what he has given!

"And they that were sent, returning to the house, found the servant whole that had been sick" (v. 10). A greater miracle of healing than this is nowhere recorded in holy scripture. Without even seeing this centurion's servant, without so much as the touch of his hand or the look of his eye, our Lord restored the full vigour of health to a dying man! He willed it, and the disease departed!

May God give us grace, like this centurion, to believe him, to love others, to do them good, to seek the grace and mercy of God in Christ for their souls. May the Lord give us grace, like this centurion, to walk humbly before him, knowing and acknowledging to him our utter unworthiness of the very least of his favours.

"And it came to pass the day after, that he went into a city called Nain; and many of his disciples went with him, and much people. Now when he came nigh to the gate of the city, behold, there was a dead man carried out, the only son of his mother, and she was a widow: and much people of the city was with her. And when the Lord saw her, he had compassion on her, and said unto her, Weep not. And he came and touched the bier: and they that bare him stood still. And he said, Young man, I say unto thee, Arise. And he that was dead sat up, and began to speak. And he delivered him to his mother. And there came a fear on all: and they glorified God, saying, That a great prophet is risen up among us; and, That God hath visited his people. And this rumour of him went forth throughout all Judaea, and throughout all the region round about" (Luke 7:11-17).

Chapter 38

A Blessed Intrusion

On three separate occasions our Lord Jesus raised people from the dead, by his great omnipotence and grace. In John 11 he raised Lazarus from the dead, one who had been dead for four days. In the eighth chapter of Luke's gospel our Saviour raised the ruler's daughter to life. But the first display of our Saviour's power over death is found here in Luke 7:11-17.

We have before us a scene of great sorrow. As our Lord Jesus, his disciples, and the crowds following him came to the city of Nain, they ran into a funeral procession. A widow was taking her only son to the cemetery. When our Lord Jesus came upon this scene of woe, he stepped into the life of this widow at the time of her greatest sorrow. He intruded when no stranger ought to intrude. He stopped what no one ought to stop. He interrupted a funeral.

Oh, how I thank the Son of God for making such intrusions of grace as are portrayed in this passage! Multitudes are carried swiftly to their graves by the gaieties, glamour and glitter of the world, totally unaware of their lost and ruined condition, without feeling, without life, without hope, until the Lord Jesus Christ steps into their lives, stops their funeral processions and raises the dead by the power of his omnipotent grace! And whenever the Son of God intrudes into the lives of men and women in this world, those who experience his intrusion, bow before him in reverent fear and glorify God.

Without question, our Lord's miracles display the fact of his eternal Godhead and omnipotent power; but they are intended to do much more than that. They are all designed to be pictures of his grace and salvation freely bestowed upon and wrought in chosen sinners by his omnipotent grace. This story of the funeral in Nain is designed to display:

The Consequences Of Sin

First, the scene before us displays most vividly the consequences of our sin. "The wages of sin is death;" and everything preceding death in this world is but the forerunner of it. All funerals are sad; but here is a picture of sadness without any mixture of pleasure. Here is a widow, burying her young son, who is her only son. Everything in the picture, until the Lord Jesus steps in, is misery, sorrow, grief and woe.

That is exactly the case with us. The corruption, depravity and sin of race are evident because ours is a race of sick, dying, sorrowful men. We live in a world of sickness and sorrow, drudgery and death, wickedness and woe, misery and mortality, because we live in a world of sin. Sin is the root and fountain of all this sorrow. Were it not for sin, the world would be free of tears and cares. Were it not for sin, there would be no sickness, no doctors, no hospitals, no courts, no prisons, no broken homes, no shattered lives, no morticians, no funerals, no cemeteries. But all these woes portray the present state of things all over the world. What a thief, what a nuisance, what a great murderer sin is (Romans 5:12); but, blessed be God, things change when Christ comes! When the Lord Jesus steps into a sinner's world of woe, all that was misery before is seen to be mercy. And when he comes again, he will make all things new, and remove from his creation all the evil consequences of sin (Revelation 21:1-7).

The Compassion Of Our Saviour

Second, God the Spirit here gives us a beautiful display of our Saviour's compassion. "And when the Lord saw her, he had compassion on her, and said unto her, Weep not" (v. 13). Oh, how deep is the compassion of our Saviour's heart! None of us has yet begun to imagine how tender and compassionate our Lord Jesus is. He truly is "touched with the feelings of our infirmities". He who wept with Martha and Mary at their brother's tomb is still "touched with the feelings of our infirmities".

Here our Lord Jesus meets the mournful procession. As he observes what has happened and is happening, his heart is moved toward this poor woman. He does not wait for someone to ask for help. He just steps in, in sovereign mercy, and says to the woman, "Weep not"!

There is no friend or comforter to be compared with Christ. Perhaps those two words sounded strange to this woman, perhaps even cruel. Certainly, no one in the procession understood them; but, when the Lord Jesus says, "Weep not", he takes away the cause of weeping! In all our days of darkness he is our Light. He is yet the Sun of Righteousness. And the Son of God never changes (Hebrews 13:8). He cannot fail. He cannot disappoint. He cannot change.

Child of God, your dear Redeemer, who made the mourning widow's heart leap for joy, will yet turn your sorrow into laughter and your mourning into a song. He is a Friend who sticks closer than a brother. He lives to heal broken hearts, to mend broken lives, and wipe away all tears from our eyes; and he will do it.

The Character Of Our Sovereign

Third, this story sets before us the character of our Sovereign. Our Lord Jesus stepped in and took over. O blessed intrusion! There are those who say, "God is a gentleman. He never comes in uninvited." But those who talk such nonsense are as ignorant as they are blasphemous. Thank God, he never waits for permission to intervene. He never waits for an invitation to be gracious. When God comes to save, he comes in sovereign mercy. Our sovereign God always takes the initiative in salvation. He declares, "I was found of them that sought me not; I was made manifest unto them that asked not after me" (Romans 10:20; Ezekiel 16:6-8).

"And when I passed by thee, and saw thee polluted in thine own blood, I said unto thee when thou wast in thy blood, Live; yea, I said unto thee when thou wast in thy blood, Live. I have caused thee to multiply as the bud of the field, and thou hast increased and waxen great, and thou art come to excellent ornaments: thy breasts are fashioned, and thine hair is grown, whereas thou wast naked and bare. Now when I passed by thee, and looked upon thee, behold, thy time was the time of love; and I spread my skirt over thee, and covered thy nakedness: yea, I sware unto thee, and entered into a covenant with thee, saith the Lord GOD, and thou becamest mine" (Ezekiel 16:6-8).

The Conditions Of Salvation

Fourth, this event was brought to pass by God's wise, adorable and good providence specifically to show us the conditions of our salvation. The Word of God specifically identifies certain conditions that must be met before any sinner can enter into heavenly glory in everlasting salvation.

1. The Will of God: no sinner will ever be saved except God wills it. Man's will is totally insignificant. Only the will of God matters (John 1:11-13; Romans 9:11-18; John 5:21).

2. The Word of God has ordained the salvation of his elect by the preaching of the gospel. As this young man was made to live by the word of Christ, so "faith cometh by hearing and hearing by the word of God" (Romans 10:17; James 1:18; 1 Peter 1:23-25).

3. The Work of God: salvation is a supernatural, irresistible work of God's free and sovereign grace involving three mighty works of omnipotent,

effectual mercy, by which the complete redemption (deliverance) of God's elect is accomplished (1 Corinthians 1:30, 31).

All who obtain God's salvation must be ransomed from the curse of the law. That is what the Lord Jesus did for us by the sacrifice of himself at Calvary (Galatians 3:13, 14; 1 Peter 1:18-20). But blood atonement alone takes no one to heaven. Every ransomed sinner must be delivered from the prison and grave of sin by the power of God the Holy Spirit in regeneration (John 5:25). None will ever be saved except Christ be formed in them, except they be made new creatures in Christ, except they be born again (John 3:5-7). No one has any hope of glory until he is made a partaker of the divine nature. Yet, there is another work just as necessary as the ransom of our souls by the blood of Christ and just as necessary as the new birth. Every chosen, blood-bought, heaven-born soul must be transformed in resurrection glory into the very likeness of his Saviour (John 5:28, 29; 1 Corinthians 15:18-58; 1 Thessalonians 4:13-18).

A Blessed Intrusion

"And the disciples of John shewed him of all these things. And John calling unto him two of his disciples sent them to Jesus, saying, Art thou he that should come? or look we for another? When the men were come unto him, they said, John Baptist hath sent us unto thee, saying, Art thou he that should come? or look we for another? And in that same hour he cured many of their infirmities and plagues, and of evil spirits; and unto many that were blind he gave sight. Then Jesus answering said unto them, Go your way, and tell John what things ye have seen and heard; how that the blind see, the lame walk, the lepers are cleansed, the deaf hear, the dead are raised, to the poor the gospel is preached" (Luke 7:18-22).

Chapter 39

The Concern Of A Condemned Man

It is a terribly sad thing to see families divided. It is even sadder to see men and women who are brethren in Christ divided. With families, I suppose, divisions may be, in some circumstances, unavoidable, perhaps even justifiable. But there is absolutely no justification for strife, jealousy, and division among saved sinners. Yet, it is often the sad, shameful fact that men and women who are one in Christ are divided in this world.

There were some of whom Paul spoke when he was in prison at Rome, who, though they were his brethren, thought he was a fake, sought to add affliction to his bonds and were obviously motivated by envy and strife (Philippians 1:12-18). The church at Corinth was in a horrible state of strife and division when Paul wrote 1 Corinthians. In fact, the first three chapters of that book are taken up with the matter. Yet, they were brethren.

The same thing was true, even during the days of our Lord's earthly ministry. Our Lord's disciples were once divided about the matter of who would be greatest among them in heaven. And there was a sad, but obvious, jealousy between the disciples of John the Baptist and the disciples of our Lord.

We see this in the opening words of the passage before us. Our Lord had performed remarkable miracles; and his fame was immediate. In verse 16 we read, "There came a fear on all: and they glorified God, saying, That a great prophet is risen up among us; and that God hath visited his people." Then, in verse 18 we read, "And the disciples of John showed him all these things."

John's disciples were concerned that their beloved leader was losing fame and influence. They were a little put out by the increased fame of Jesus of Nazareth. But John the Baptist was a truly magnanimous man, faithful in all things to the glory of Christ and the souls of men. He is held before us here in his very last recorded act on this earth as an example for us to follow.

A Faithful Watchman

"And the disciples of John showed him of all these things. And John calling unto him two of his disciples sent them to Jesus, saying, Art thou he that should come? or look we for another? When the men were come unto him, they said, John Baptist hath sent us unto thee, saying, Art thou he that should come? or look we for another?" (vv. 18-20).

The message John sent to the Lord Jesus was not an indication of doubt or unbelief on his part. This is the man who had throughout his adult life pointed sinners to Christ and proclaimed him as the Lamb of God, that One whose shoes he was not worthy to untie, the man who was and is the eternal God. He was not now in doubt about those things. He had been taught of God.

The message John sent to the Master was intended to confirm his disciples in the faith and persuade them to follow Christ, whom he followed. It was to set the hearts of his disciples, those very disciples who seemed fearful that the Lord Jesus might be getting too much attention, on the Saviour.

John knew that he was a condemned man. Herod had thrown him into prison. His life was coming to an end. His opportunities of service in the cause of Christ were now ended. His day of labour was over. The prospects before him were obvious. Yet, even in the prospect of his violent death, John was a faithful man, faithful to his God, faithful to his Saviour, faithful to his charge as God's prophet and faithful to the souls committed to his trust. This faithful man sent his disciples to the Lord Jesus, that they might see for themselves who he was. This was the concern of his heart, even when he was himself a condemned man.

This was not just John's concern in the prospect of death. He was not trying, in his last days, to make up for past inconsistencies. Not at all. This was John's constant concern (John 1:19-29, 35-37; 3:22-36). It is ever the concern of faithful men to exalt Christ, point sinners to Christ, and urge those under their influence to believe and to follow Christ.

Like Paul after him, John the Baptist sought to unify God's people, by directing the hearts of those who heard him to Christ himself. With great wisdom and forethought, he sent his disciples directly to the Lord Jesus, asking, "Art thou he that should come? Or, look we for another?" he was keenly aware of the fact that his disciples might easily be led away by the petty strife that often divides men. He did what he could to head it off before he left his friends. Like his Master, he loved his disciples to the end.

What an instructive example John's action here gives us. Every pastor, every father, everyone who has influence over another ought to make it their business in life to direct those they influence to Christ. Let it be our hearts' concern to set the hearts of those we influence upon the Son of God (Romans 9:1-3; 10:1).

Spare no pains to instruct those trusted to your influence in the things of God. Press them into the Saviour's arms. Remind them often of their sins and his sacrifice, of their souls and his salvation, of their guilt and his grace, of their ruin and his redemption! Blessed are those men and women, mothers and fathers, pastors and elders who can on their dying beds look back upon the faces of those they leave behind, and say, "I've warned you of the wrath to come. I've told you, as best I could, who Christ is. I have not failed to show you the way of life and press you into it.

A Forceful Witness

"And in that same hour he cured many of their infirmities and plagues, and of evil spirits; and unto many that were blind he gave sight. Then Jesus answering said unto them, Go your way, and tell John what things ye have seen and heard; how that the blind see, the lame walk, the lepers are cleansed, the deaf hear, the dead are raised, to the poor the gospel is preached" (vv. 21, 22).

What a remarkable answer our Lord gave to these disciples of John. How would he convince them who he is? He offered no historic proof. He gave them no account of what other men had said about him. He simply pointed them to the facts. The works they saw and the doctrine they heard. That which they saw and heard convinced them that Jesus of Nazareth is the Christ promised by God's prophets (Isaiah 35:4-6).

Wherever Christ is, the blind are made to see, the lame walk, lepers are cleansed, the deaf hear, the dead are raised up and the poor (spiritually and materially) have the gospel preached to them.

We would be wise to hear the instruction of our Lord's example. By what standard are we to judge the ministry of any man, or any church? How are we to witness to men? How are we to convince others of the gospel we believe? Argument, debate and apologetics are useless. Creeds, confessions, and historic positions are meaningless. Just tell others what you have seen and heard, what you have experienced, observed, and learned for yourself (1 John 1:1-3).

263

Discovering Christ In The Gospel Of Luke

A Frank Warning

"And blessed is he, whosoever shall not be offended in me" (v. 23). John's disciples saw standing before them a man, to all outward appearance, as poor, unimpressive and needy as they were. His followers were a rag-tag band of fishermen. The only men of means among them were publicans, men of notorious ill-repute. It seemed incredible that this man could be the Christ, the Son of the living God. Multitudes have gone to hell because they found him an offence (1 Corinthians 1:18-31). Will you?

The offence of the cross has not ceased (Galatians 5:11). So long as the world stands, Christ and his gospel will be offensive to proud, self-righteous men. It is offensive to man's sense of self-worth to be told that he is a poor, lost, guilty, condemned sinner. It is offensive to our pride to be told that we are utterly helpless, incapable of saving ourselves or even contributing something to our salvation. It is offensive to self-righteous men to be told that they must be justified by the righteousness of another, washed in the blood of a Substitute and saved by free grace alone. It is offensive to our sense of dignity and superiority to be told that we must enter the kingdom of heaven side by side with publicans, harlots and sinners. It is offensive to our sense of personal intelligence to be told that salvation, the knowledge of Christ and of God, comes to men entirely by divine revelation. It is offensive to our sense of self-determination to be told that salvation is by God's will and not by our own. It is offensive to our rebel hearts to be told that we must bow to the rule and dominion of Christ as our rightful Sovereign, Lord, and King.

Untold thousands have heard the gospel and, being offended by it, have despised it. They would not stoop to "enter in at the strait gate". They would not bow to walk in "the narrow way". They despised God's terms of grace. Therefore, they are this hour in hell, tormented by the just wrath of the holy Lord God. They now know the meaning of these words "Blessed is he, whosoever shall not be offended in me."

The Concern Of A Condemned Man

"And when the messengers of John were departed, he began to speak unto the people concerning John, What went ye out into the wilderness for to see? A reed shaken with the wind? But what went ye out for to see? A man clothed in soft raiment? Behold, they which are gorgeously apparelled, and live delicately, are in kings' courts. But what went ye out for to see? A prophet? Yea, I say unto you, and much more than a prophet. This is he, of whom it is written, Behold, I send my messenger before thy face, which shall prepare thy way before thee. For I say unto you, Among those that are born of women there is not a greater prophet than John the Baptist: but he that is least in the kingdom of God is greater than he. And all the people that heard him, and the publicans, justified God, being baptized with the baptism of John. But the Pharisees and lawyers rejected the counsel of God against themselves, being not baptized of him" (Luke 7:24-30).

Chapter 40

Our Great Defender

Did you ever notice how often the scriptures portray the Lord our God as our Shield and Defence? Particularly in the psalms, we see our great God spoken of in this way. How often we see the man after God's own heart running to him for defence, hiding in him for refuge, seeking protection behind the mighty God of Jacob as his shield. David's son, Solomon, learned this valuable, soul cheering truth from his father (Psalms 119:114; 144:1, 2; Proverbs 18:10; 30:5). He who is our shield and hiding place is our Defender. The psalmist sang with joy, "God is my defence"! (Psalms 7:10; 31:2; 89:18; 94:22). The Lord Jesus Christ, our great God and Saviour, is the great Defender of our souls.

"Truly my soul waiteth upon God: from him cometh my salvation. He only is my rock and my salvation; he is my defence; I shall not be greatly moved. How long will ye imagine mischief against a man? ye shall be slain all of you: as a bowing wall shall ye be, and as a tottering fence. They only consult to cast him down from his excellency: they delight in lies: they bless with their mouth, but they curse inwardly. Selah. My soul, wait thou only upon God; for my expectation is from him. He only is my rock and my salvation: he is my defence; I shall not be moved. In God is my salvation and my glory: the rock of my strength, and my refuge, is in God. Trust in him at all times; ye people, pour out your heart before him: God is a refuge for us. Selah" (Psalm 62:1-8).

Christ Our Defender
In the passage before us God the Holy Spirit holds before us an instructive example of Christ our God defending one of his own. That is what we see in verses 24-28. Our Lord seems to have sensed that those who had heard his conversation with John's disciples might, as sinful men are prone to do, put a bad construction upon what they had heard. He seems to have read the

thoughts of their hearts, and what he read was not good. Perhaps the fact that John was imprisoned by Herod caused the multitudes to look upon him with suspicion. Perhaps the question he sent his disciples to ask caused those who heard it to look upon John as a weak, fluctuating, unsteady man, one whose faith had begun to fail. Whatever their thoughts were, they were obviously thoughts of unwarranted unkindness, harshness and evil regarding John the Baptist.

Whatever the reason was, our Lord Jesus immediately took up John's cause. Without a moment's hesitation, like a faithful friend, the Son of God takes upon himself the defence of his faithful servant. There is much to be learned here. Blessed are those who have Christ for their Friend; and blessed are those who follow his example as friends to others (Proverbs 17:17; 18:24).

The Lord Jesus pleaded John's cause earnestly, with the strong, firm, unquestionable language of a loyal, faithful friend. He took it upon himself to silence the suspicious thoughts and doubts in the minds of those around him about John. He said that John was no mere reed, shaken in the wind. He was not a man of unstable, wavering character, but a prophet, a great prophet. He asserted that John was not a man living in luxury, courting the favour of men, particularly of powerful men. He did not hang around the king's palace, grovelling for the king's smile. John was God's prophet; and he acted like God's prophet.

Indeed, John the Baptist was much more than a prophet. He was a prophet of whom the prophet Malachi wrote (Malachi 3:1), "Behold, I send my messenger before thy face, which shall prepare thy way before thee." John was that Elijah who came to prepare the way for the Christ, who came to turn the hearts of the fathers to the children by turning their hearts to Christ. Then, our Master said, "Among those born of women there is not a greater prophet than John the Baptist."

What a blessed picture we have before us! I find it sweet beyond expression, touching and instructive. Just a few years earlier, John was the best known, most popular, most highly esteemed preacher in the land. There was a time when all Jerusalem and Judea hung upon his words. They followed him from one place to another, walking for miles at a time, just to hear him preach. All men were baptized by him (Matthew 3:5). But now John the Baptist was a prisoner in Herod's hands, deserted by all, held in contempt by all but a few, friendless and alone. The only thing awaiting him was his execution. But he was not deserted by that One whose name is the Mighty God. John could say of him what all who ever knew him could, "This is my Beloved, and this is my Friend."

"Jesus! What a Friend for sinners! Jesus! Lover of my soul!
Friends may fail me, foes assail me, he my Saviour, makes me whole.
Jesus! What a Strength in weakness! Let me hide myself in Him;
Tempted, tried, and sometimes failing, He, my Strength, my victory wins.
Jesus! What a Help in sorrow! While the billows o'er me roll;
Even when my heart is breaking, He, my Comfort, helps my soul!
Jesus! What a Guide and Keeper! While the tempest still is high;
Storms about me, night o'ertakes me, He, my Pilot, hears my cry!
Jesus! I now flee unto him! More than all in him I find;
He has granted me forgiveness. I am his and he is mine!
Hallelujah! What a Saviour! Hallelujah! What a Friend!
Saving, helping, keeping, loving, he is with me to the end!"

J. Wilbur Chapman

John the Baptist had in the Son of God a Friend who never failed him and never forsook him. He is that Friend who says to all his Jacob's, "I am the Lord, I change not. I will never leave thee, nor forsake thee"

Let me show you what there is in all this for you. Do you know what it is to be held in suspicion? Do you know what it is to be slandered, falsely accused, to have your name evil spoken of, to have your character assaulted? There are few of God's children here who do not experience these things.

Noah's son Ham sought to mar his father's name among his own brothers. Moses was the object of much slander in Pharaoh's house; but the slander in the house of Israel was more bitter; and the suspicions of Miriam and Aaron were even worse. Joseph's brethren spoke evil of him. David was maligned by Saul, betrayed by Ahithophel, and cursed by Shimei. Jeremiah was falsely accused by those for whom he laboured, to whom he carried the burden of the Word of the Lord. John the Baptist was praised as a great prophet one day and accused of being possessed of the devil the next. Our Lord himself was slandered, maligned, falsely accused, betrayed and looked upon by the multitudes, those who would not hear him, as a vile, reprehensible man, a glutton, a drunk, and the constant companion of sinners. The women who anointed the Saviour had their motives suspected and were slandered, even by their fellow disciples. Paul was accused of being a self-serving false prophet, a promoter of licentiousness, and a wicked man.

These things are not easy to bear. In fact, there are few trials more difficult to endure. The fiend of hell is called "the accuser of the brethren" (at least in part), because false accusation is that which he most often uses as a weapon against our souls. Satan knows that a man's character is the point at which he is most easily, most painfully, and most permanently wounded. He knows that men and women who seek to honour God are most sensitive about maintaining an honourable name, seeking to live blamelessly before others. Therefore, he most often assaults us there.

J. C. Ryle wrote, "Slanders are easily called into existence, greedily received and propagated, and seldom entirely silenced." Lies and false accusations are the devil's chosen weapons, by which he tries to injure the Lord's people, seeks to destroy a person's usefulness and disturbs our peace.

Knowing these things, by bitter and painful experience, there is nothing more comforting and assuring than this: We have an Advocate in heaven who knows our sorrow and is touched by that which touches us. That same Advocate who took up the cause of John the Baptist before this Jewish crowd is our Advocate today. The Son of God will never desert his own. Our names may be cast in the mud and evil spoken of by wicked men. The world may frown upon us. But our Saviour never changes. He has undertaken our cause. He will protect and defend us in the best way. And, one day soon, he will plead our cause before the entire world (1 Corinthians 4:3-5).

Peculiar Blessedness

In verse 28 the Lord Jesus tells us that we live in an age of peculiar blessedness. "For I say unto you, Among those that are born of women there is not a greater prophet than John the Baptist: but he that is least in the kingdom of God is greater than he." The last phrase of this verse has been interpreted by faithful men in a variety of ways. "But he that is least in the kingdom of God is greater than he."

Without question, these words apply to our Lord himself. The Son of God became the least among men, the very least in the kingdom of God, though he is greater than all. "For ye know the grace of our Lord Jesus Christ, that, though he was rich, yet for your sakes he became poor, that ye through his poverty might be rich" (2 Corinthians 8:9; Philippians 2:5-11). He who is God over all and blessed forever became a man. He who created all things became the Servant of men. He who is our Lord and Master washed his disciples' feet. He who is holy, harmless, undefiled, and separate from sinners was made sin for us, that we might be made the righteousness of God in him. He who is life was made to die the painful, shameful, ignominious death of the cross, that we might have eternal life in him!

However, our Lord is here talking about his disciples in this gospel age. These words speak of the peculiar, distinctive privilege that is ours as the children of God in this gospel age. "He that is least in the kingdom of God is greater than he." Compared with the saints of the Old Testament era, believers in this gospel age enjoy a position of tremendous advantage and superiority. After describing and commending John's gifts and graces, the Saviour says, "but he that is least in the kingdom of God is greater than he."

He is not suggesting that believers in this age are superior to those of the Old Testament in gifts, in faith or in faithfulness. If we had no other passage than Hebrews 11 to convince us, Hebrews 11 is enough to convince us that our Lord is not suggesting that believers in this age are superior to those of the Old Testament in gifts, in faith or in faithfulness.

What he is saying is this: in this gospel age believers have superior light and revelation. We have the full, final, complete revelation of God in Christ inscripturated (Hebrews 1:1-3; 2 Timothy 3:16, 17; 2 Peter 1:19-21). Living on this side of the crucifixion and resurrection of Christ we live in a position of indescribably greater light than John the Baptist and those who lived in that age of types, pictures and prophecy.

I do not suggest that those believers of old did not know and believe the same gospel we do. They most certainly did. But they saw things as through a glass darkly. They were not given such a precise, exact and complete revelation of gospel truth as we now have in the full revelation of God. They saw the Fountain. We see the Fountain opened. They saw the veil. We see the veil rent in twain and the way to the holiest of all open. Priscilla and Aquila took Apollos home and instructed that great orator in the way of the Lord more perfectly.

This is exactly what God promised in the covenant. "They all shall know me ... A child shall lead them"! To put it in plain, simple terms, insofar as spiritual knowledge is concerned, the new born babe in this gospel age, knowing the wondrous doctrine of the cross, being taught of God, has greater spiritual knowledge than John the Baptist and those men and women of the Old Testament possessed. The Old Testament age was the church's age of infancy and childhood. This is the age of the church's maturity. The law was our schoolmaster unto Christ. But now that Christ has come we are no longer its pupils (Ephesians 3:1-11; Colossians 1:25-27; 1 Peter 1:10-17).

A Solemn Lesson

In verses 29 and 30 the Spirit of God sets before us a very solemn lesson. All who are privileged to hear the gospel either justify God or reject the counsel of God against themselves.

"And all the people that heard him, and the publicans, justified God, being baptized with the baptism of John. But the Pharisees and lawyers rejected the counsel of God against themselves, being not baptized of him."

To some the gospel is made of God to be the sweet savour of life and salvation. Being born of the Spirit, convinced of our guilt and sin, looking to Christ, all true believers justify God (Psalm 51:1-5). Self-righteous rebels reject, despise and cast off the counsel of God against themselves (Proverbs 1:23-33; Isaiah 65:1-5; 66:1, 2).

"And the Lord said, Whereunto then shall I liken the men of this generation? and to what are they like? They are like unto children sitting in the marketplace, and calling one to another, and saying, We have piped unto you, and ye have not danced; we have mourned to you, and ye have not wept. For John the Baptist came neither eating bread nor drinking wine; and ye say, he hath a devil. The Son of man is come eating and drinking; and ye say, Behold a gluttonous man, and a winebibber, a friend of publicans and sinners! But wisdom is justified of all her children" (Luke 7:31-35).

Chapter 41

"Wisdom Justified"

This Generation

First our Lord speaks about a group of people called, "this generation". At first glance, it looks as though he is using the word "generation" the way we commonly use it, to speak of that specific group of people living at the time. But that clearly is not the case. If you look through the scriptures, every time these words are used together, they are used to describe self-righteous religionists. They always refer to lost religious people, like the Pharisees, Sadducees and Herodians of our Lord's day. And those people called "this generation" are always hostile, persecuting people. They are the people of whom our Lord spoke specifically when he said, "In the world you shall have tribulation." The words "this generation" speak of the enemies of our God and of our souls in every age (Psalms 12:1-8; 71:12-18; Matthew 12:41, 42; 23:29-38).

In Luke 7:31-34 the Lord Jesus shows us that unbelieving religionists are always opposed to, find fault with, and are quick to slander God's servants and his people, because the carnal mind is enmity against God.

We ought to always take care not to offend the people of this world. We should always strive to be kind, gracious, thoughtful, and caring of those people among whom we live and with whom we work in this world. As much as possible, live peaceably with all men. Try to get along with people. Make sacrifices to do so. Endeavour to live blamelessly before your neighbours, for Christ's sake, for the honour of God, for the gospel's sake. Yet, we must not concern ourselves with the cavils of men. If men and women are determined to set themselves in opposition to us, as we endeavour to serve our God, they should not disturb us. We must not court the favour of men; and we must not fear the frowns of men. "This generation" is a hard, implacable, peevish, childish generation, which will never be made friends to the cause of Christ. The cross of Christ has always been an offence to them and always will be.

This is the lesson to be learned by our Lord's comparison describing "this generation" as children. If we would be saved, we must become as little children; meek, humble, inoffensive, trusting. Yet, lost religionists are also like little children, not adorable, sweet children, but peevish brats. Our Master compares "this generation" to perverse, rebellious children, who can never be pleased with anything. Nothing satisfies them. Nothing contents them. They find some fault with everything and everyone, but themselves.

John the Baptist came, leading a stern, austere, separated life of self-denial; and they said, "he hath a devil". After him, the Lord Jesus came adopting the habits of a more social man, a man who mixed with people; and the very same men of "this generation" said of him, he is "a glutton and a winebibber".

Their animosity was not really against either John or Jesus of Nazareth as men, or as preachers, but against the message they preached, the doctrine they taught, the God they represented. The men and women of "this generation" really do not care at all what kind of man the preacher really is. They know they can make their kind of preachers become whatever they want them to be.

John the Baptist and the Lord Jesus Christ preached exactly the same thing. Both preached repentance toward God and faith in Christ. But the men and women of "this generation" are determined not to hear God's Word, bow to his Son, confess their sin and seek salvation by free grace alone. The fact is, "the carnal mind is enmity against God". Nothing will ever change that, but grace itself.

The pretended objections of this generation to God's servants are only a smoke screen to cover their rebellion and hatred of God. Anyone who would hear God's message from the lips of the Master would also gladly hear it from John's lips. And any who would hear God's message from the lips of John the Baptist would gladly hear it from the lips of the Lord Jesus.

How often we see religious men and women who have a blind attachment to a preacher! They follow not the Shepherd's voice through the preacher, but the preacher's voice. Such people are always fickle and unstable. And rebels will always find an excuse for their rebellion. The carnal mind will always attempt to cover its hatred of God and justify its unbelief. For proud, self-righteous, self-willed religious men and women, no matter who the preacher is, free grace is too easy, faith in Christ is too simple, substitution is too dangerous.

Notice this, too. Most of those things which divide the unbelieving religious world are matters of complete insignificance and indifference. What was it that caused these people to talk? What was it that kept some from hearing John and others from hearing the Lord Jesus and all of them from hearing either? John the Baptist was a strict separatist, a Nazarite. The Lord Jesus was far more free in his conduct.

Let us not behave as such peevish, silly children. Rather, let us ever behave as mature men and women. We have no right to make indifferent matters of importance. Let us learn to be silent about all those things about which the Book of God is silent. We have no right to impose rules upon God's people that God never imposed. And we dare not make essential matters of indifference. The gospel of Christ, believer's immersion, the observance of the Lord's Supper are matters of primary importance. The doctrine of the gospel, (righteousness by the obedience of Christ, redemption by his effectual blood atonement, salvation by the irresistible gift and operation of grace) cannot be compromised; and these things are held forth perpetually in the symbolic ordinances of the gospel, when those ordinances are observed as our Lord gave them.

This generation is a wicked, perverse generation. But our Lord also speaks of something else.

Another Generation
There is another generation, called "his generation", "the generation of thy children", "the generation of the upright", and "a chosen generation". Look at verse 35. Here our Master draws a direct and distinct contrast between those of "this generation" and his own elect. "But wisdom is justified of all her children."

Certainly there is at least a reference here to the Lord Jesus Christ himself, who is our Wisdom (1 Corinthians 1:30). Christ is the wisdom of God. He is the Word, that One in whom and by whom we know God. He lived in wisdom here and shows us the way of wisdom. The Lord Jesus stood for us as our Wisdom in the council chambers of the Almighty in eternity. He fulfilled the wisdom of the covenant. He makes believing sinners wise unto salvation. And he gives us wisdom as we need it in the face of our numerous, subtle foes.

All God's elect justify him in all his person and work. "Wisdom is justified of ALL her children." All who are born of God, born of wisdom, repent before him and thereby justify God (Psalm 51:4). Repentance is taking sides with God against ourselves, coming into agreement with God, and justifying God in the way he saves sinners.

Yet, there is more. Believer's justify God's wisdom in all things and thereby prove themselves wise indeed. The scriptures make us wise unto salvation through faith in Christ (2 Timothy 3:15). And God the Holy Spirit is in his people the Spirit of Wisdom, Revelation and Grace. Thus, we are taught and enabled to see the justice and equity of our God in all his works and in all his ways (Psalms 36:6; 48:11; 97:8; 119:75; Isaiah 26:8, 9; Revelation 19:1-6).

A Great Saviour!

Even when he is spoken of in derision, our Lord Jesus Christ proves himself to be a great Saviour. His enemies constantly derided him, calling him "a friend of publicans and sinners." How I rejoice to declare that that is exactly who and what the Lord Jesus Christ is. In fact, he is the only friend of publicans and sinners, the only friend we have; and he is the Friend only of publicans and sinners (Matthew 9:12, 13; Mark 2:17; Luke 5:31, 32).

Oh, how willing God is to be gracious! Did you ever notice how often the Lord God refers to our sins as sicknesses, diseases and infirmities? One reason for that is this: our heavenly Father views the sins of his people as sicknesses calling for pity, not as crimes calling for punishment!

Come, ye sinners, poor and needy, weak and wounded, sick and sore.
Come, ye weary, heavy-laden, lost and ruined by the fall.
Come, ye sinners, come and welcome, God's free bounty glorify!
True belief and true repentance, every grace that brings us nigh!

Joseph Hart

"Wisdom Justified"

"And one of the Pharisees desired him that he would eat with him. And he went into the Pharisee's house, and sat down to meat. And, behold, a woman in the city, which was a sinner, when she knew that Jesus sat at meat in the Pharisee's house, brought an alabaster box of ointment, And stood at his feet behind him weeping, and began to wash his feet with tears, and did wipe them with the hairs of her head, and kissed his feet, and anointed them with the ointment. Now when the Pharisee which had bidden him saw it, he spake within himself, saying, This man, if he were a prophet, would have known who and what manner of woman this is that toucheth him: for she is a sinner. And Jesus answering said unto him, Simon, I have somewhat to say unto thee. And he saith, Master, say on. There was a certain creditor which had two debtors: the one owed five hundred pence, and the other fifty. And when they had nothing to pay, he frankly forgave them both. Tell me therefore, which of them will love him most? Simon answered and said, I suppose that he, to whom he forgave most. And he said unto him, Thou hast rightly judged. And he turned to the woman, and said unto Simon, Seest thou this woman? I entered into thine house, thou gavest me no water for my feet: but she hath washed my feet with tears, and wiped them with the hairs of her head. Thou gavest me no kiss: but this woman since the time I came in hath not ceased to kiss my feet. My head with oil thou didst not anoint: but this woman hath anointed my feet with ointment. Wherefore I say unto thee, Her sins, which are many, are forgiven; for she loved much: but to whom little is forgiven, the same loveth little. And he said unto her, Thy sins are forgiven. And they that sat at meat with him began to say within themselves, Who is this that forgiveth sins also? And he said to the woman, Thy faith hath saved thee; go in peace" (Luke 7:36-50).

Chapter 42

A Woman Who Was A Sinner

It would not be possible for us to conceive of two people more completely opposite to one another than Simon the Pharisee and this woman who was a sinner. Without question, there are many good, profitable lessons which may be gleaned from this passage of scripture. We would be wise to lay them to heart. May God the Holy Spirit, who caused these words to be written, write the lessons of this passage on our hearts.

A Form Of Godliness
Many, like this proud Pharisee, have a form of godliness, who know nothing of God's saving grace in Christ. Simon showed much outward respect for the Lord Jesus and his disciples. What could be more respectful? He had a large, extravagant dinner party in honour of our Saviour. Yet, he was utterly ignorant of Christ, his gospel and the grace of God. He had a form of godliness, but knew nothing of God's saving power and grace. His proud heart was repulsed by the sight of this unnamed woman, who was a notorious sinner, entering his house and being so readily and openly received by the Son of God. He, like most religious people, talked about grace and forgiveness, but never experienced it. This proud Pharisee could not stomach the idea that he must enter into the kingdom of heaven upon the same ground and side by side with this wretched sinner. He was religious, but lost. He knew his doctrine, but not God. He was respectable, but not gracious. Do not be satisfied with religion. We must have Christ!

Sin A Debt

Learn this, too. Sin has made us all debtors, owing a debt we can never pay. By reason of our sin, we are all head over heels in debt to the law and justice of God. The Lord Jesus Christ, the Son of God, our great Saviour, stepped in, paid our debt; and God, for Christ's sake, has freely and fully forgiven us our debt! The forgiveness of sins is an act of strict, unbending justice. Yet, in our experience of it, it is a matter of absolute freeness, an act of grace, pure, free grace. Christ paid our debt; and upon the ground of justice satisfied, we are freely forgiven all our sins.

Our Motivation

A third lesson that is obvious in this portion of scripture is the fact that the great mainspring and driving force of service to Christ is that love and gratitude which arises from a sense of great forgiveness.

How I wish I could drive this point home to the hearts of all who attempt to rouse men and women up to live for and serve Christ. The mainspring and driving force of true Christianity, the motive and inspiration for all devotion and service to Christ, that which compels and constrains believers to live in this world for the glory of God is grace experienced, forgiveness known and felt in the very soul of a man, and the deep gratitude to and love for Christ which arises from the experience of God's free, sovereign, saving grace in our Saviour. Believers are motivated by grace, gratitude and love, not by the threat of law, the promise of reward, or the hope of recognition (2 Corinthians 5:14, 15; 8:9).

Who Was This Woman?

This woman, who was a sinner, is here held before us in the Book of God as an example for all who would honour Christ to follow. Yet, wisely and graciously, the Holy Spirit tells us absolutely nothing about this woman except these things. She was a sinner. She was a sinner who trusted Christ. She was a forgiven sinner, forgiven of all her sins. She was a grateful sinner. She was a sinner who loved Christ much.

What Did This Woman Do?

"Behold, a woman in the city, which was a sinner, when she knew that Jesus sat at meat in the Pharisee's house, brought an alabaster box of ointment and stood at his feet behind him weeping, and began to wash his feet with tears, and did wipe them with the hairs of her head, and kissed his feet, and anointed them with the ointment" (vv. 37, 38).

This saved sinner made it her business to know where the Saviour was and came to him there. She brought with her an alabaster box of ointment.

She came with a sacrifice of faith, with which she sought to honour her Redeemer. She stood in humiliation at the Saviour's feet, behind him. She wept. She wept because she was full of sorrow, knowing that the Lord Jesus must suffer and die upon the cursed tree to put away her sin. She wept with loving gratitude because of his great love for her soul. She washed his feet with her tears and wiped them with her hair. She tenderly kissed the Saviour's feet, with lips of love, devotion and adoration. She anointed his feet in faith in anticipation of his death. In a word, as the Lord Jesus himself put it, she did what she could (Mark 14:3-9). Blessed are they to whom God the Holy Spirit gives such grace!

What Was Her Motive?

Why did this woman do what she did? How can such an act be explained? What would inspire a poor person to make such a great, extravagant (in the eyes of men) sacrifice? She had owed much. She had been forgiven much. And she loved much.

What Was The Result?

What was the result of this woman's love for Christ and her devotion and service to him?

She was scorned by Simon the Pharisee, ridiculed by Judas and misunderstood by her fellow disciples. Few there are who understand devotion, whole-hearted devotion to Christ. But she had not come to Simon's house to be honoured. She had come there to honour God her Saviour; and honouring him, she was honoured by him (1 Samuel 2:30).

This one who honoured her Lord was highly honoured by her Lord. When she was ridiculed and scorned, the Son of God came to her defence (v. 47). He said, "Let her alone; why trouble ye her? she hath wrought a good work on me" (Mark 14:6). The Master assured her, before her judges and slanderers, that he had forgiven her of all her sins. "Thy sins are forgiven" (v. 48). Then her Saviour assured her of her faith and spoke peace to her heart (v. 50).

The only way to inspire consecration and devotion to Christ is to preach Christ. The only way to promote good works is to preach free grace (Titus 3:4-9). The soul that has experienced redemption, forgiveness and saving grace is inspired by the knowledge of God's mercy, love and grace in Christ to love him and seek his glory. "We love him, because he first loved us" (1 John 4:19).

Let all who read this portion of holy scripture be reminded and tell sinners everywhere that the Lord Jesus Christ is a great Saviour, merciful, gracious, compassionate and able and ready to save the very chief of sinners.

281

"And it came to pass afterward, that he went throughout every city and village, preaching and showing the glad tidings of the kingdom of God: and the twelve were with him, And certain women, which had been healed of evil spirits and infirmities, Mary called Magdalene, out of whom went seven devils, And Joanna the wife of Chuza Herod's steward, and Susanna, and many others, which ministered unto him of their substance" (Luke 8:1-3).

Chapter 43

"The Glad Tidings Of The Kingdom"

"And it came to pass afterward." After our Lord had healed the centurion's servant at Capernaum, after he had had raised a widow's son from the dead in Nain, after he had shown John the Baptist's disciples who he was, after he had vindicated John in their presence and had sent them back to John and after he had, in the house of Simon the Pharisee, been honoured by the faith of a forgiven sinner and had honoured her, then we read that our Saviour "went throughout every city and village, preaching and showing the glad tidings of the kingdom of God."

Our Master

First, the Holy Spirit directs our attention to our Master, the Lord Jesus. "And it came to pass afterward, that he went throughout every city and village, preaching and showing the glad tidings of the kingdom of God." Here our Saviour sets before us a tremendous example of diligence and faithfulness as Jehovah's righteous Servant.

Let us never forget that our Lord's obedience to God as a man, his obedience unto death, even the death of the cross, was not only a substitutionary obedience, but also an exemplary obedience. Not only did he redeem us with his blood, our Lord Jesus Christ showed us how we ought to live in this world as the servants and children of God (John 13:13-15; 1 Peter 2:21-25).

Our Master was tireless in his labours, unwearied in doing good and constant in redeeming the time he had in this world. Man's unbelief did not stop him from preaching the glad tidings of the gospel. The slanders of his enemies, the reproaches heaped upon him, the scorn of the religious world and the laughter of his deriders did not in any way affect his labour. He always knew who he was, why he was here and what he was to do. He was always about his Father's business. His earthly ministry lasted only three short years. Yet, in those three years our Lord Jesus Christ did more, preached more and ministered more to the needs of others than any man before or since has done in a lifetime.

Let us follow his example. Without question, we will miss the mark and will be constantly aware that we are missing the mark. But let us follow his example and walk in his steps. "He that saith he abideth in him ought himself also so to walk, even as he walked" (1 John 2:6). We ought to try to leave our little corner of the world better than we found it. We ought to make it the business of our lives to do good to men and for men. May God give me grace to lay aside my own desires, pleasures and passions, my pride, self-serving and greed, and enable me to live to do good to those whose lives I touch.

Time is short; but much can be done in the short time we have. Let us arrange our affairs wisely and we will be amazed how much can be done in a short time. Few have any idea how much can be accomplished in eight, or ten, or twelve hours, if they simply stay at it and avoid idleness and frivolity. Let us "redeem the time" for Christ's sake.

Yes, time is short; but this is the only time we have to do the work God has given us to do in this world. Yes, we will serve him perfectly in the world to come; but in that world there will be no feet to wash. There will be none who are ignorant and need instruction, none who are hungry and need feeding, none who are sick and need visiting, none who are mourning and need comforting, none who are alone and need a friend, none in spiritual darkness who need enlightening, none who are fearful and need assurance, none who are in distress and need relief. Whatever work we do of this kind must be done on this side of the grave. Let us awake to a sense of our responsibility. Souls are perishing and time is flying. Let us resolve, by God's grace, to do something for God's glory before we die.

Luke tells us that our Lord Jesus "went throughout every city and village preaching and showing the glad tidings of the kingdom of God." There are many, many good and noble works to be done for men. We must never seek to hypocritically excuse ourselves from serving the physical needs of those around us, pretending that we have a higher service to their souls. Rather, while doing what we can to relieve men and women of physical, mental and emotional anguish, let us never forget that we do have a far higher, far more important service to perform for their souls. Like our Master, our primary business in life, our primary function as a local church and our primary purpose of existence is to preach the gospel everywhere, showing this generation "the glad tidings of the kingdom of God."

We have done men and women no good, but positive harm, if we teach them how to live, but do not show them the way of life! We do not serve men and women for good, if we comfort them without directing them to the consolation that is in Christ. We do not minister to our neighbours if we feed them, but do not teach them to eat of the Bread of Life and drink from the Fountain of the Water of Life.

We do not have to guess what Luke meant when he told us that our Master went everywhere preaching "the glad tidings of the kingdom". The context tells us. In the parable of the sower (vv. 5-18), in the calming of the sea (vv. 19-25), in the salvation of the Gadarene (vv. 26-40), in the healing of the woman with the issue of blood (vv. 41-49), and in the raising of Jairus' daughter (vv. 49-56), our Lord Jesus both displayed and proclaimed the glad tidings of the kingdom.

In the parable of the sower he shows us that faith is the gift of grace, that salvation comes by divine revelation, that the sinner must be given a new heart by grace to receive the word of grace. In the calming of the storm our Lord shows us that he is the Sovereign God, ruling all things absolutely. Not only is he the God who gives us grace and faith, he is the God who keeps us in grace and faith. In the healing of the Gadarene our Saviour marvellously displays the experience of salvation in the life of a man unfit for human society. In the healing of the woman with the issue of blood our Lord graciously shows us the desperation and confidence, as well as the power of God given faith. And in the raising of Jairus' daughter the Son of God shows us the glad tidings of the new birth. It is the work of God wrought in, for, and upon a dead sinner! That is how Luke was inspired to describe our Master.

His Disciples
Next, Luke was inspired by the Spirit of God to tell us something about the Lord's disciples. "And the twelve were with him." These men made it their business to be with him. They left all and followed him. For three and a half years, they were with him. They followed him everywhere. They attended him constantly. They watched him, listened to him and walked with him. Why? They saw him to be everything they wanted or needed. They loved him. They wanted to see him work. They wanted to learn of him. Therefore, "the twelve were with him." "These are they which follow the Lamb whithersoever he goeth. These were redeemed from among men, being the firstfruits unto God and to the Lamb" (Revelation 14:4).

Certain Women
Next, Luke was inspired to tell us about some women who had experienced the power and grace of God by Christ Jesus. "And certain women, which had been healed of evil spirits and infirmities, Mary called Magdalene, out of whom went seven devils, And Joanna the wife of Chuza Herod's steward,

and Susanna, and many others, which ministered unto him of their substance."

Who were these women? They were women who had experienced the power, mercy and grace of God in Christ. The Lord had healed them of evil spirits and great infirmities. They were women, like the one mentioned at the end of chapter seven, full of gratitude and love for Christ.

Can you imagine what peculiar hardships and trials these women endured for the Master? In those days women stayed at home, kept their mouths shut, and were seen in public only with their husbands, and when their husbands said it was permissible. Women seen in the company of another man in public, let alone in private, were looked upon not with suspicion, but as being, beyond doubt, women without character. Grateful for the mercy and grace they had received and experienced, these women gladly suffered whatever was heaped upon them that they might follow their Saviour. Strengthened by the power of his grace, they clave to him to the very end.

It was not a woman's kiss that betrayed him. It was not these women who forsook him in the Garden. It was not one of these women who denied him. These women stayed with the Saviour, weeping as he was led forth to be crucified. It was a few women, not men, who stood by the suffering Lamb of God unto the end. These women were the first at the tomb and the first to see the Lord of Glory on the resurrection morning.

Who were these women? Just three of them are named. The first one named is Mary Magdalene, out of whom the Lord Jesus had cast seven devils (Mark 16:9). The second is "Joana the wife of Chuza, Herod's steward."

When I read that description of Sister Joana, I have to ask, "Why did Luke write that?" This woman's husband was no ordinary Joe. When Luke tells us that he was "Herod's steward", the word "steward" does not mean "lackey". It means that this man Chuza was the man to whom Herod the Tetrarch entrusted the care of his entire house. Chuza was a wealthy, powerful, influential man. It is true, not many mighty, not many noble, not many wealthy are called, but some are. Not all of our Lord's followers were poor fishermen. Perhaps, in God's wise and good providence, it was for the salvation of God's elect, our sister Joana, that John the Baptist was put into prison.

The third of these sisters in grace is a woman named Susanna. Susanna is mentioned nowhere else in the Book of God, and nowhere else in history, so far as I can tell. We know only one thing about this dear lady's earthly life. She walked with Christ! What a grand, noble, ennobling biography!

What did these women do? Look at the last line of verse 3. They "ministered unto him of their substance". How condescending, how gracious, how merciful our Saviour is! He who owns the cattle on a thousand hills did not need these women to minister unto him, but he allowed them to! He who multiplied the loaves and fishes did not need to have someone feed him, but he let them! In doing so, our Lord graciously allowed those who loved him to prove the sincerity of their love (2 Corinthians 8:7-9).

These three dear ladies of grace ministered to (served) the Lord Jesus with their substance. They did not ask others for assistance. They took that which was their own, and out of that they ministered to the Saviour they loved. The text might be read, "They ministered unto them of their substance", suggesting that they used their means to provide for the company of the disciples. They counted it a service done to Christ to take of their substance and make provision for his disciples (Romans 16:1, 2).

God, grant me the grace to follow my Master's example of tireless devotion and service to the souls of men and the glory of my God. May God the Holy Spirit grant that I may, like the Lord's disciples, ever be found with him. I pray that God will graciously teach me to honour him with my substance, as these women did, and give me the will to do it for Christ's sake (Proverbs 3:5-10).

> Sinners Jesus will receive!
> Sound this word of grace to all,
> Who the heavenly pathway leave,
> All who linger all who fall!
>
> Come, and he will give you rest;
> Trust him, for his Word is plain;
> He will take the sinfulest;
> Christ receiveth sinful men.
>
> Now my heart condemns me not,
> Pure before the law I stand;
> He who cleansed me from all spot,
> Satisfied its last demand.
>
> Christ receiveth sinful men,
> Even me with all my sin;
> Purged from every spot and stain,
> Heaven with him I enter in.
>
> Erdmann Neumeister

"And when much people were gathered together, and were come to him out of every city, he spake by a parable: A sower went out to sow his seed: and as he sowed, some fell by the way side; and it was trodden down, and the fowls of the air devoured it. And some fell upon a rock; and as soon as it was sprung up, it withered away, because it lacked moisture. And some fell among thorns; and the thorns sprang up with it, and choked it. And other fell on good ground, and sprang up, and bare fruit an hundredfold. And when he had said these things, he cried, he that hath ears to hear, let him hear. And his disciples asked him, saying, What might this parable be? And he said, Unto you it is given to know the mysteries of the kingdom of God: but to others in parables; that seeing they might not see, and hearing they might not understand. Now the parable is this: The seed is the word of God. Those by the way side are they that hear; then cometh the devil, and taketh away the word out of their hearts, lest they should believe and be saved. They on the rock are they, which, when they hear, receive the word with joy; and these have no root, which for a while believe, and in time of temptation fall away. And that which fell among thorns are they, which, when they have heard, go forth, and are choked with cares and riches and pleasures of this life, and bring no fruit to perfection. But that on the good ground are they, which in an honest and good heart, having heard the word, keep it, and bring forth fruit with patience. No man, when he hath lighted a candle, covereth it with a vessel, or putteth it under a bed; but setteth it on a candlestick, that they which enter in may see the light. For nothing is secret, that shall not be made manifest; neither any thing hid, that shall not be known and come abroad. Take heed therefore how ye hear: for whosoever hath, to him shall be given; and whosoever hath not, from him shall be taken even that which he seemeth to have" (Luke 8:4-18).

Chapter 44

Take Heed How You Hear

The message of our Lord Jesus in this parable is searching and solemn. In this parable our Lord Jesus Christ teaches us plainly that the vast majority of those who hear the gospel of the grace of God preached, even the vast majority of those who profess faith in him after hearing the gospel, are unregenerate, lost and perish under the wrath of God. "He that hath ears to hear, let him hear" the parable of the sower.

The Sower
The sower is the man who preaches the gospel of the grace of God. Gospel preachers are like farmers sowing wheat. They broadcast the Word of God upon the ground, upon the hearts of eternity bound men and women. This is not a careless, thoughtless process. The preacher, if he is indeed a faithful, gospel preacher, has his heart in his work. He is not indifferent to those to whom he preaches, or indifferent to their response. Oh, no. God's servants care deeply for the souls of men. They sow in hope of harvest (Psalm 126:5; Ecclesiastes 11:1; 1 Corinthians 15:58). The sower is the servant of God, the gospel preacher who faithfully sows the seed of the gospel in hope of a great harvest.

The Seed
"Now the parable is this: The seed is the word of God" (v. 11). The seed sown is the Word of God, the gospel of the grace of God revealed in the

Word. We recognize, preach and rejoice in the glorious sovereignty of our God. I take a back seat to no one in preaching God's absolute sovereignty in all things, especially in the salvation of his elect. Yet, we recognize that God Almighty has chosen to use specific means for the accomplishment of his purposes. "It pleased God, by the foolishness of preaching, to save them that believe" (1 Corinthians 1:21). "Faith cometh by hearing, and hearing by the Word of God" (Romans 10:17).

That is Bible language. God declares that he saves sinners through the utility of the Word (James 1:18; 1 Peter 1:23-25). God saves chosen sinners only through, or by means of the faithful exposition of the scriptures. And the Word of God is faithfully expounded and preached only when the gospel of Christ is faithfully expounded and preached. Rolland Hill was exactly right when he said, "Any sermon that does not contain the 'Three R's' (Ruin by the Fall, Redemption by the Blood, and Regeneration by the Holy Spirit) ought never to have been preached." God's servants are not just preachers. They are gospel preachers. They do not just preach. They preach the gospel.

The sower is the gospel preacher. The seed sown is the Word of God, the gospel of Christ.

The Results

The results of gospel preaching are always exactly according to the purpose of God. We randomly preach the gospel to all who will hear us; but the results are not random. When God Almighty sends forth his Word, his Word always accomplishes his purpose. It either produces life and faith in Christ, or it produces judicial blindness and hardness of heart. Man's unbelief does not in any way, or to even the slightest degree alter the purpose of God. Rather, even the wilful unbelief of the reprobate fulfils God's sovereign purpose (Romans 3:3, 4; 2 Corinthians 2:14-16).

"And he said, Unto you it is given to know the mysteries of the kingdom of God: but to others in parables; that seeing they might not see, and hearing they might not understand" (v. 10). These words are taken from the Saviour's words to Isaiah, when the prophet of God saw the Lord Jesus in his glory, high and lifted up, sitting upon his throne (Isaiah 6:9, 10).

Faith in Christ is the gift of God. The seeing eye, the hearing ear, and the believing heart are from the Lord. Faith is not something men muster from within. Faith is the gift and operation of God's free grace in Christ. If you believe, it is because "unto you it is given in the behalf of Christ to believe on his name" (Philippians 1:29; Ephesians 2:8, 9; Colossians 2:12).

To those who will not believe, the Word of God is both blinding and binding. None are so blind as those who will not see; and none are so hardened as those who are gospel hardened. When men and women wilfully despise the gospel of the grace of God, when they resolutely harden themselves to the Word preached, the very Word which they despise becomes the instrument by which they are bound over to everlasting judgment, to eat the fruit of their own way (Proverbs 1:23-33).

Wayside Hearers

Some who hear the gospel receive it as seed sown by the wayside. "Those by the way side are they that hear; then cometh the devil, and taketh away the word out of their hearts, lest they should believe and be saved" (v. 12). Some hear with no concern for their souls, the glory of God, or eternity. They attend church because they have to, or because it is the respectable thing to do, or because they think it is their duty to do so. But they really have no interest in the things of God. They try their best not to hear a word the preacher speaks, or at least not to be bothered by what he says. They try to think about other things. And, unless God intervenes and does something for them, the gospel they hear will profit them nothing. Before they get out the door the old black crow of hell snatches away the seed from their hard hearts.

Stony Ground Hearers

Others are described as stony ground hearers. "They on the rock are they, which, when they hear, receive the word with joy; and these have no root, which for a while believe, and in time of temptation fall away" (v. 13). There are many stony ground hearers. The preaching of the gospel makes very quick, but only temporary impressions upon them. Their religion is all superficial, just a flash in the pan, nothing else. Like burning briars in a fire, they may crackle and pop, and make a lot of noise, but they produce nothing. They appear enthusiastic. They talk a good game. They are sometimes moved to tears. They may even speak about inward conflicts, hopes, desires, struggles and fears. But they lack one thing. They have no root. The root of the matter is not in them. Like seed sown in unprepared soil, the Word of God takes no root in them, because there is no work of the Holy Spirit in their hearts. Unconvinced, they have no Holy Spirit conviction. Unturned, they cannot and will not repent. Unbelieving, they have no faith!

These stony ground hearers endure for a while; but they will not last. Their religion is like Jonah's gourd. It springs up in a night and is gone in a night. They are like cut flowers. They look pretty and smell nice for a while, but soon wither and die. They have no root. Christ is not in them and they are not in Christ. A little trial, affliction, or temptation will be too great for the stony ground hearer to endure. Any persecution or opposition, because of the offence of the gospel, will destroy them.

Thorny Ground Hearers

Others are set before us in this parable as thorny ground hearers. "And that which fell among thorns are they, which, when they have heard, go forth, and are choked with cares and riches and pleasures of this life, and bring no fruit to perfection" (v. 14). The wayside hearer has no interest at all in the things of God. He could not care less who Christ is and what he did. The stony ground hearer is somewhat impressive. He makes a big splash, but does not last very long. The thorny ground hearer is something else.

The thorny ground hearer assents to the gospel, approves of it, and is moved by it. He appears to make a good start, and seems to go a long way in religion. He feels much, experiences much, and may even do much that appears to be truly spiritual; but he has a basic, fundamental, underlying problem. It is a problem that may lie under the surface, hidden from every eye but God's. It may even be hidden from his own eyes. But it will eventually destroy him. The problem is worldliness. The world still holds his heart. He loves the world.

Oh, beware of religion without Christ! You may think, "All is well with my soul. No one could ever feel what I feel and experience what I have experienced and yet be lost." You ought to think again! False faith is a strong delusion, a delusion by which, in this parable, one in four who profess faith in Christ are dragged down to hell! False faith may be greatly enlightened and knowledgeable of the gospel (Hebrews 6:4). False faith may greatly reform the outward life, like the Pharisees. False faith may speak very well of Christ, as the Jews did. False faith may confess personal sins, like Saul. False faith may humble itself in sackcloth and ashes with Ahab. False faith may repent in tears with Esau and Judas. False faith may diligently perform religious works with the Jews. False faith may be very generous and charitable, like Ananias and Sapphira. False faith may tremble under the Word with Felix. False faith may experience great things in religion (Hebrews 6:1-4). False faith may enjoy great religious privileges with Lot's wife. False faith may preach, perform miracles and cast out devils, like those mentioned by our Lord. False faith may attain high office in the church, like Diotrephes. False faith may walk with great preachers, like Demas. False faith may even be peaceful and carnally secure, like the five foolish virgins.

It is written, "If any man love the world, the love of the Father is not in him" (1 John 2:15). Sooner or later those who love the world will choose the world. The sad fact is that though they wilfully choose the world and turn from Christ, they are so thoroughly justified in their own minds that what they are doing is right that they never even realize they have done it, until they wake up in hell.

If you are one of these thorny ground hearers, the Lord Jesus plainly warns you that one of these three things will eventually destroy your soul: "the care of this world", "the deceitfulness of riches", "the pleasures of this life".

Good Ground Hearers

True believers are those who receive the gospel as seed sown in good ground. "But that on the good ground are they, which in an honest and good heart, having heard the word, keep it, and bring forth fruit with patience" (v. 15). The good ground is a regenerate heart, a heart prepared by God the Holy Spirit to receive the Word of grace. The fallow ground of the heart has been broken up by the deep cutting, sharp plough of the law. The hard clods have been broken by the heavy harrow of conviction, beaten to pieces by the thunderous rain of God's wrath, and at last softened by the sweet dew of heaven.

The Word of God sown in the regenerate heart, the heart prepared by the grace and power of God to receive it, brings forth fruit unto God. Some bear fruit more rapidly and more plentifully than others; but all bear fruit from God. The fruit they bear is the fruit of the Spirit (Galatians 5:22, 23).

Now, read these next three verses as they are given in this context, and hear the Master's warning.

"No man, when he hath lighted a candle, covereth it with a vessel, or putteth it under a bed; but setteth it on a candlestick, that they which enter in may see the light. For nothing is secret, that shall not be made manifest; neither any thing hid, that shall not be known and come abroad. Take heed therefore how ye hear: for whosoever hath, to him shall be given; and whosoever hath not, from him shall be taken even that which he seemeth to have" (Luke 8:16-18).

Take heed what you hear. Make certain that the message you hear is the gospel of God, not some false gospel of free will, works religion. Take heed that you hear. Make it your business to hear the gospel regularly. And take heed how you hear. Ask God the Holy Spirit to enable you to hear the gospel with a submissive, believing heart.

"No man, when he hath lighted a candle, covereth it with a vessel, or putteth it under a bed; but setteth it on a candlestick, that they which enter in may see the light. For nothing is secret, that shall not be made manifest; neither any thing hid, that shall not be known and come abroad. Take heed therefore how ye hear: for whosoever hath, to him shall be given; and whosoever hath not, from him shall be taken even that which he seemeth to have. Then came to him his mother and his brethren, and could not come at him for the press. And it was told him by certain which said, Thy mother and thy brethren stand without, desiring to see thee. And he answered and said unto them, My mother and my brethren are these which hear the word of God, and do it" (Luke 8:16-21).

Chapter 45

Everybody Ought To Know

When I attended Sunday School as a boy, the children often sang ...

> Everybody ought to know,
> Everybody ought to know,
> Everybody ought to know
> Who Jesus is!
> He's the Lily of the Valley!
> He's the Bright and Morning Star!
> He's the Fairest of ten thousand!
> Everybody ought to know!

That is exactly what our Saviour tells us in Luke 8:16-21. If we would interpret these verses properly we must keep them in their context. Our Lord has just given and explained the parable of the sower. Here he is making a very practical application of that parable to us. The things here written for our learning and admonition are intended to nail down and fix in our minds this mighty lesson. That which God teaches us by his grace we are to proclaim to others.

There are three great, weighty, important things taught in these short, simple verses of holy scripture. May God the Holy Spirit, whose Word we have before us, write these things upon our hearts by his grace.

Our Responsibility

First, our Master here teaches us that it is our responsibility to proclaim abroad the gospel we have learned by divine revelation.

"No man, when he hath lighted a candle, covereth it with a vessel, or putteth it under a bed; but setteth it on a candlestick, that they which enter in may see the light. For nothing is secret, that shall not be made manifest; neither any thing hid, that shall not be known and come abroad" (vv. 16, 17).

No one lights a candle to hide it. The reason for lighting the candle is that it may be held forth to diffuse its light. Whenever we read or hear these words from the lips of our Saviour, we ought first to think of ourselves. God has revealed the gospel to us for the saving of our souls. How we ought to rejoice in that and thank him for it! But he has also given us the gospel as a trust. He has put the light of divine truth into our hands so that we might carry it forth into this world of darkness for the salvation of other chosen, redeemed sinners. God did not give us the knowledge of his Son, his grace and his salvation, so that we might simply profess it, admire it and discuss it, but that we might proclaim it.

The gospel is a talent, a treasure, committed to our hands, with which we have been entrusted. That trust brings with it a great weight of responsibility. It is the responsibility of every believer, every local church and every gospel preacher to proclaim the gospel of Christ, to make Christ known in the generation in which they live (Matthew 28:18-20; 1 Corinthians 9:16; Ephesians 3:8).

When we hear or read these words (vv. 16, 17) falling from the lips of our dear Saviour, we ought to also think of others. We live in a world of darkness. The multitudes around us, in our homes, in our communities, around the nation and around the world, are perishing for want of knowledge. Behold the peoples of the world. Get them fixed in your heart. They are without God, without Christ, without hope!

Is there nothing we can do for them? Indeed there is something we can and must do for them. We must hold forth in this dark world the light of the gospel, with fervency, earnestness, and zeal (Romans 9:1-3; 10:1; 2 Corinthians 5:10-14). I fully agree with J. C. Ryle, who wrote, "The highest form of selfishness is that of a man who is content to go to heaven alone. The truest charity is to endeavour to share with others every spark of religious (gospel) light we possess ourselves, and so hold forth our own candle that it may give light to everyone around us." God never lights a candle that it may burn alone!

In verse 17 our Lord is declaring that the gospel must and shall be preached in all the world. Remember the context. Though in the Day of Judgment all things shall be brought to light, in the sense that God will cause all men to see clearly what he has done, this is not a declaration that God is going to show the world all our inmost secret thoughts. Our Lord is here telling his disciples that the things then hidden and spoken in parables would be openly proclaimed in this gospel day by them, by his church and by faithful gospel preachers in all succeeding ages (Matthew 24:14).

Hearing The Word
Second, our Lord teaches us in verse 18 that we must take heed how we hear the gospel. "Take heed therefore how ye hear: for whosoever hath, to him shall be given; and whosoever hath not, from him shall be taken even that which he seemeth to have." I dealt with this admonition extensively in the previous chapter, so I will not say much here. But we must not fail to heed this word of instruction. The degree to which we will benefit from the ministry of the Word depends greatly upon the way we hear it. Going to church and hearing sermons will do us no good, unless we hear right. If we would hear the Word of God right, we must lay to heart these four simple rules for hearing it.

Be sure that what you hear is the gospel. Like the noble Bereans, search the scriptures and see for yourself that the things you hear from the pulpit and the things written in the Book of God are the same. Hear the Word of God as the Word of God, with reverence. Be sure you hear the gospel with implicit faith, not as the word of man, but as the Word of God (Hebrews 4:1, 2). Hear the Word with prayer, praying for God to bless it to your own soul, making personal application of it to yourself.

God's Family
Third, in verses 19-21, we are taught that those, and those only, who hear and obey the gospel are the family of God.

"Then came to him his mother and his brethren, and could not come at him for the press. And it was told him by certain which said, Thy mother and thy brethren stand without, desiring to see thee. And he answered and said unto them, My mother and my brethren are these which hear the word of God, and do it."

What blessed privileges are ours in Christ! The person who hears the Word of God and does it is the sinner who hearing the gospel call comes to Christ. The Master says, "believe on me", and we believe. He says, "repent", and we repent. He says, "follow me", and we follow. Without question, to obey the gospel will bring a man or woman great trouble. To believe on the Lord Jesus Christ is to take up your cross and follow him. It is to enlist in an army, to engage in combat with the world, the flesh and the devil. But the privileges far outweigh, infinitely outweigh, the costs (Romans 8:17, 18; 2 Corinthians 4:16-5:1; 2 Timothy 2:11-13; 1 Peter 1:3-9).

Let us make it our business to do what we can in this our day for the furtherance of the gospel and the salvation of God's elect. Let us ever take heed how we hear the Word of God. And let us ever hold before our hearts and minds the great privileges that are ours in Christ Jesus our Lord.

"No man, when he hath lighted a candle, covereth it with a vessel, or putteth it under a bed; but setteth it on a candlestick, that they which enter in may see the light. For nothing is secret, that shall not be made manifest; neither any thing hid, that shall not be known and come abroad. Take heed therefore how ye hear: for whosoever hath, to him shall be given; and whosoever hath not, from him shall be taken even that which he seemeth to have" (Luke 8:16-18).

Chapter 46

Hearing The Word Of God

There is much need for some plain, simple, biblical instruction about hearing the Word of God, about how we ought to hear the preaching of the gospel.

"Keep thy foot when thou goest to the house of God, and be more ready to hear, than to give the sacrifice of fools: for they consider not that they do evil. Be not rash with thy mouth, and let not thine heart be hasty to utter any thing before God: for God is in heaven, and thou upon earth: therefore let thy words be few" (Ecclesiastes 5:1, 2).

"Every good gift and every perfect gift is from above, and cometh down from the Father of lights, with whom is no variableness, neither shadow of turning. Of his own will begat he us with the word of truth, that we should be a kind of firstfruits of his creatures. Wherefore, my beloved brethren, let every man be swift to hear, slow to speak, slow to wrath: For the wrath of man worketh not the righteousness of God. Wherefore lay apart all filthiness and superfluity of naughtiness, and receive with meekness the engrafted word, which is able to save your souls. But be ye doers of the word, and not hearers only, deceiving your own selves" (James 1:17-22).

In Luke 8:18 the Lord Jesus Christ is addressing his own disciples, both those who truly were his disciples and those who merely professed to be. Knowing that a great multitude of people were gathered together to hear him out of every city, and knowing (he is God, and knows all things) that most of them, would be hearers only, and not doers of the Word, our Lord spoke to them by a parable. He used the similitude of a farmer who went out to sow his seed (vv. 4-16). In that parable the Saviour plainly tells us that few there are, in any group of hearers, who receive any saving benefit from the preaching of the gospel. Three things are evident in the parable of the sower.

The preaching of the gospel is the sowing of the seed of life. Only those whose hearts are made good by the regenerating power and grace of God the Holy Spirit receive the Word to the saving of their souls. And, once we have received the good seed of the gospel into our hearts, we must take care that nothing chokes it out and destroys its influence. Then, in verse 18, the Lord Jesus says to all who hear the gospel preached, "Take heed, therefore, how ye hear." If we would profit from the ordinance of God, if we would profit spiritually and eternally from the preaching of the gospel, we must take heed how we hear it. Let us take heed what we hear, making certain that we hear no preaching but the preaching of God's free and sovereign grace in Christ. And let us take heed how we hear the gospel preached.

Seize Every Opportunity

Let it be clearly understood that we ought to seize every opportunity God gives us to hear the gospel. If you are wise, you will avail yourself of every opportunity God gives you to gather with his saints in public worship, to give him praise and hear his Word. I am not talking just about going to church. I urge all under my influence never to attend those religious circuses called churches. In those places, they hardly let people breathe, for fear of losing them. They keep people busy doing something every night of the week and most days. I do not suggest that we should simply go to church and entertain ourselves in the hearing of sermons and in the pursuit of religious activities. That will profit your soul nothing.

However, there is a trend today in many places that concerns me. The trend in many places, places where the gospel is preached, is to have less and less preaching, less and less public worship. I know of many places where the assembly meets only twice a week, others where they only have one service a week and others where they have even less. Many reasons are given for this. Perhaps there are situations in which it is justified. But I get hungry more often than that. Don't you? I need to be with my family more than that. I need to hear from God more often than that. Don't you? The Word of God does not tell us how often we should meet together. So we must set no rules in this regard; and we must never attempt to impose our practices upon others in areas where the scriptures are silent.

Still, I think there is something terribly dangerous and unhealthy about squeezing our time in the house of God down to as little as we can comfortably fit into our lives. Let us take care that nothing chokes out the influence of the gospel in our lives. Like Simeon and Anna, I want to be found in the house of God, beholding God's Salvation, speaking the praise of Christ and learning of him. Like Mephibosheth, I want to be found sitting at the King's table. Like Mary, I want to be found sitting at his feet.

The Gospel And Gospel Preaching

Make certain that in hearing, you hear the gospel. Do not ever delude yourself into thinking that religion is good. Only gospel religion is good. All other religion is deadly and damning. It is not going to church that profits our souls. It is not the hearing of sermons that profits us. It is not religious chatter that benefits us. It is the preaching of the gospel, the declaration of our great God, his greatness, his goodness, his glory and his wondrous works in the Lord Jesus Christ (Galatians 6:14).

It is from the house of God, the assembled body of Christ, that God commands the blessing upon his people (Psalm 133:3). No wonder David sang as he did about the blessedness of public worship (Psalms 122:1-9; 84:10). This matter of hearing the gospel is so important that our risen Saviour has specifically given the ministry of the gospel to his church as one of his chief ascension gifts (Psalm 68:18, 19; Ephesians 4:11, 12).

God has always gifted specific, chosen men for the work of the ministry, to serve the souls of men, men whom he has specifically called to that great work. Jude tells us, that "Enoch, the seventh from Adam, prophesied (or preached) concerning the Lord's coming with ten thousand of his saints to judgment." Peter tells us that Noah was "a preacher of righteousness", the righteousness of God in Christ. God never left himself without witness, even in those earliest times, but at sundry times, and after diverse manners, spoke to our fathers by the patriarchs and prophets.

After the giving of the law, the Lord God constantly separated to himself a certain order of men to preach to, as well as pray for, his people. Israel always had her prophets and her priests. Though the Jews were often carried away into captivity, and because of their sins scattered abroad among the nations, yet God faithfully and graciously kept up a remnant of prophets and preachers, like Ezekiel, Jeremiah, Daniel and others, to reprove, instruct and call men to repentance.

Great as those days were, we live in a better day with better provisions. When our Lord Jesus Christ, our great High-priest, had through the eternal Spirit offered himself, as a full, perfect, sufficient, effectual sacrifice and satisfaction for the sins of his people, and following his resurrection had all power committed to him, both in heaven and on earth, he gave commission to his Apostles, and in them to all succeeding gospel preachers, to "go into all the world and preach his gospel to every creature", promising "to be with us, (to guide, assist, strengthen, and comfort us always, even) unto the end of the world."

It is my responsibility, and that of God's servants everywhere, to preach the gospel (1 Corinthians 9:16), it is your responsibility to hear the message God sends his servant to deliver. God does not send a man to beat the air.

How insensible most people are of this unspeakable gift! They do despite to the Spirit of grace, crucify the Son of God afresh and put him to an open shame, by wilfully refusing to attend God's ordained means of grace! How terrible will the end of such men be? How tormenting it will be that light should come into the world, that the glad tidings of salvation should be so very frequently proclaimed in a place, only to be despised by many! The spiritual manna of the gospel, this angel's food, is despised as a worthless thing. Our Lord declares that it will be more tolerable for Tyre and Sidon, for Sodom and Gomorrah, than for those who despise the gospel (Matthew 11:20-24). Better that men had never heard of a Saviour being born, than after they have heard (or despised the opportunity to hear), not to give heed to the ministry of those who are employed as God's ambassadors, to declare the good news of free, saving grace in Christ! George Whitefield accurately interpreted our Saviour's doctrine when he said ...

"We may, though at a distance, without a spirit of prophesy, foretell the deplorable condition of such men; behold them cast into hell, lifting up their eyes, being in torment, and crying out, How often would our ministers have gathered us, as a hen gathereth her chickens under her wings? But we would not. O that we had known in that our day, the things that belonged to our everlasting peace! But now they are forever hid from our eyes. Thus wretched, thus inconceivably miserable, will such be as slight and make a mock at the public preaching of the gospel."

Suggestions For Hearing
Here are some suggestions that may, with the blessing of God the Holy Spirit, help you to hear the gospel with spiritual profit. Gospel preaching is the ordinance of God, the means appointed by Christ himself for saving of his people and the building of his kingdom among men. This is the method by which God the Holy Spirit does his work in the souls of men. Consider these facts, and you will gladly heed these four admonitions, though they may reprove you and though the reproof may be painful.

Never come to the house of God to gratify your religious curiosity. When we come to the house of God, let us come seeking to know Christ, to hear of Christ, to learn of Christ and to worship Christ. It is not an honourable thing, but a contemptible thing to sit around and discuss endless questions about nothing, ever learning but never coming to the knowledge of the truth (2 Timothy 3:5-7). Flee, flee religious curiosity, as you would flee the plague!

Come to the house of God with humility, ready to receive with meekness the engrafted Word, which is able to save your soul.

Listen carefully, attentively, to the message God sends his servant to deliver to your soul. Give earnest heed to the things that are spoken from the Word of God. Take great care to hear what God has to say to you. When the Lord God descended on Mount Sinai in terrible majesty, to give his law, the children of Israel sat up and paid attention to his servant Moses. If they were earnest to hear the thunderings, threatenings and terrors of the law, how gladly sinners ought to sit up and anxiously hear the preacher of the gospel, as he proclaims the glad tidings of free grace in Christ!

No gospel preacher is sent to deliver a dry, insipid lecture on moral philosophy, legal duty, religious history, or creedal accuracy. God Almighty sends his messengers to unfold before eternity bound sinners the great mystery of godliness and the mysteries of the kingdom of his grace: redemption, forgiveness, salvation, peace, pardon, free justification and eternal life in, by and with the Lord Jesus Christ! When a man opens the Word of God before men, he is not reading a dime store novel to you. He is proclaiming the Word of the eternal God.

Here is a third word of counsel we will all be wise to heed. Do not allow Satan, or any by whom he is served, to prejudice your mind against faithful men, sent of God to preach the gospel to you.

Take heed and beware of entertaining any dislike of those the Holy Ghost has made overseers over you. If a man faithfully preaches the gospel, receive him like the Galatians received Paul, before the Judaisers corrupted them, as an angel of God.

"And we beseech you, brethren, to know them which labour among you, and are over you in the Lord, and admonish you; And to esteem them very highly in love for their work's sake. And be at peace among yourselves" (1 Thessalonians 5:12, 13).

"Let a man so account of us, as of the ministers of Christ, and stewards of the mysteries of God" (1 Corinthians 4:1).

"For we are not as many, which corrupt the word of God: but as of sincerity, but as of God, in the sight of God speak we in Christ" (2 Corinthians 2:17).

"How beautiful upon the mountains are the feet of him that bringeth good tidings, that publisheth peace; that bringeth good tidings of good, that publisheth salvation; that saith unto Zion, Thy God reigneth" (Isaiah 52:7).

As you ought not to be prejudiced against God's servant, so you must be careful not to depend too much on a preacher, or think more highly of him than you ought to think.

God's servants are instruments in his hands, no more and no less, just instruments by which God works in his vineyard (1 Corinthians 3:5-9, 21-23). Their labours are made profitable to your soul only by the blessing of God. So pray for that man who is God's messenger to your soul. Pray that God will preserve him, give him a message for your soul and grace to deliver it; and pray that the Lord will graciously enable you to hear the message.

Always seek grace from God to personally apply the message to your own heart and life.

Always presume that the message was prepared with you in mind, and spoken to you alone. We are all terribly inclined to look across the room and behold a little splinter in our brother's eye, rather than deal with the plank in our own. Seek grace from God always to personally appropriate his message.

If you would receive a blessing from the Lord, when you hear his gospel preached, you should do something before the sermon, during the sermon and after the sermon.

Before the sermon, set things in order in your life so that you come to the house of God awake and alert. Pray for the preacher and for yourself; but do not neglect to pray for your brothers and sisters and for lost sinners, who hear the gospel with you.

During the sermon, listen attentively, constantly praying for God to speak to your heart, for Christ's sake, exposing and convincing you of your sin, correcting you, comforting your soul, reviving your heart, giving you a fresh view of the Lord Jesus. Again, seek the same for your brothers and sisters.

After the sermon, discuss the message with one another and with your family; and ask God to plant the seed sown in your own heart and in the hearts of others, for Christ's sake.

"Finally, brethren, pray for us, that the word of the Lord may have free course, and be glorified, even as it is with you" (2 Thessalonians 3:1).

"Praying always with all prayer and supplication in the Spirit, and watching thereunto with all perseverance and supplication for all saints; And for me, that utterance may be given unto me, that I may open my mouth boldly, to make known the mystery of the gospel" (Ephesians 6:18, 19).

If we would but take heed how we hear, we might yet, again see Satan cast out like lightning. We might yet see sinners converted. We might yet see God work in us, with us and in our midst! We might yet find the Word preached sharper than any two-edged sword and mighty, through God, to the pulling down of the devil's strong holds!

The Holy Spirit might yet fall upon our assemblies, as he did when Peter preached the gospel of Christ! The gospel of God might again run swiftly and run well, having free course in the hearts of men. God Almighty, our great God and Saviour, is he with whom nothing is impossible. He who added three thousand to the church on one day in one place, is perfectly capable of doing the same again today!

"Jesus Christ is the same yesterday, today, and for ever." He has promised to be with us always, even unto the end of the world. I am convinced that the reason we do not receive larger blessings from the presence of the Lord, is not because our all-powerful Redeemer's hand is shortened, but because we do not expect them (Psalm 81:13, 14; Isaiah 48:17-19).

Yes, sometimes, our God, to magnify his free grace in Christ Jesus, is found of them that sought him not. Notorious sinners are, sometimes, forcibly plucked as a firebrand out of the fire; but that is not God's ordinary way of acting. Normally, he visits those with the power of his Spirit who humbly take heed how they hear, seeking to know him, his will and his way, and sends the careless away not only empty, but hardened!

Take heed, therefore, how you hear. Remember, "we must all appear before the judgment seat of Christ." How will they stand at the bar of an angry, sin-avenging Judge, and see so many messages they have despised, so many preachers, who once longed and laboured for the salvation of their immortal souls, brought out as swift witnesses against them! But it shall not be so with you who with meekness receive the engrafted Word. You will be your pastor's joy, and crown of rejoicing in the day of our Lord Jesus: In that day, he will present you in a holy triumph, faultless, and unblameable, as a chaste virgin to Christ your common Redeemer, saying, "Behold I, O Lord, and the children which thou hast given me"!

"Now it came to pass on a certain day, that he went into a ship with his disciples: and he said unto them, Let us go over unto the other side of the lake. And they launched forth. But as they sailed he fell asleep: and there came down a storm of wind on the lake; and they were filled with water, and were in jeopardy. And they came to him, and awoke him, saying, Master, master, we perish. Then he arose, and rebuked the wind and the raging of the water: and they ceased, and there was a calm. And he said unto them, Where is your faith? And they being afraid wondered, saying one to another, What manner of man is this! for he commandeth even the winds and water, and they obey him" (Luke 8:22-25).

Chapter 47

"There Came Down A Storm"

I encourage you to read the accounts of this event in the lives of our Lord's disciples as they are recorded by Matthew and Mark (Matthew 8:23-27; Mark 4:35-41). This is an event of great importance. Both the story itself and the variations in each of these gospel narratives are preserved upon the pages of holy scripture by divine purpose and infallible inspiration. They are written and written as they are for our learning and instruction. May God the Holy Spirit now teach us what he would have us learn from this event.

As our Lord Jesus and his disciples were crossing the Sea of Galilee, "there came down a storm". The disciples, in the panic of their terror, were filled with unbelief. When they cried out, as Matthew records it, "Lord, Save us! We perish"! Mark reports their cry, "Master, carest thou not that we perish"! And Luke tells us that they cried, "Master, Master, We perish"! I suspect that with twelve terrified men in one small, storm tossed, little boat there were more cries than these three. But these three are recorded to show us the terror that filled the hearts of these poor men.

The Lord Jesus arose, calmly rebuked their unbelief, and, by the mere power of his word, calmed the sea and the storm.

Few, if any, of our Lord's miracles were so likely to leave his disciples with such an unforgettable, convincing demonstration of his divine omnipotence. At least four of these men were professional fishermen and skilled seamen. In all likelihood Peter, Andrew, James and John were very familiar with the Sea of Galilee. They had probably been exposed to its devastating and often fatal storms from their youth. Never, not even in the greatest of our Lord's other miracles, had they seen such power as he demonstrated here. By the mere word of his mouth, our Saviour stopped the storm!

Lessons

There are many important lessons taught in these verses. We would be wise to ask the Spirit of God to remind us of them frequently.

Faith in and obedience to Christ do not exempt God's saints from the storms that other people face. The fact that our Lord was weary and required sleep shows he was a real man. The fact that the wind and sea obeyed his word showed his complete deity. This Man is the omnipotent God! The wind and the sea knew the voice of their Creator! Only One who is both God and man could redeem us and save us from our sins. The greatest saints in this world are still sinners; and the strongest believers are sometimes filled with unbelief. Our Lord Jesus Christ is a tender, forgiving Saviour. He is kind, gentle, and gracious, even in the rebuke of his disciples. "Why are ye so fearful? How is it that ye have no faith?" Our Saviour's reason for everything he does is the salvation of his elect. He went to the other side of the sea because there was a wild, lost Gadarene for whom the fulness of time had come. All who are in the good ship Grace with Christ are perfectly safe as they pass through the stormy seas of this world.

Parable Of Life

The following seven lessons are lessons frequently taught in holy scripture. They should be frequently taught to God's people. They are lessons we all need to be reminded of. Yet, as I read these verses, I see a parable that portrays every believer's life as he makes his pilgrimage through this world.

When the Son of God enters the hearts of chosen sinners in his sovereign, saving power and grace, he brings us with himself into the church and kingdom of God; he brings us with himself into the ship of grace and salvation. As he does, he casts his eyes and ours across the waters of time to the other side of the sea of life, and says, as, he did to his disciples here, "Let us go over unto the other side". Read Psalm 107:23-31 and you will see a good, biblical basis for using this incident as a parable of our lives.

"They that go down to the sea in ships, that do business in great waters; These see the works of the LORD, and his wonders in the deep. For he commandeth, and raiseth the stormy wind, which lifteth up the waves thereof. They mount up to the heaven, they go down again to the depths: their soul is melted because of trouble. They reel to and fro, and stagger like a drunken man, and are at their wit's end. Then they cry unto the LORD in their trouble, and he bringeth them out of their distresses. He maketh the storm a calm, so that the waves thereof are still. Then are they glad because they be quiet; so he bringeth them unto their desired haven. Oh that men would praise the LORD for his goodness, and for his wonderful works to the children of men"!

A Voyage

First, every believer's life is a voyage. It is a voyage across a troubled sea to our "desired haven" on the other side. As we embark on this voyage, the Son of God takes us into the good ship Grace and says, "Let us go over unto the other side". Death is often spoken of poetically as a passing over, the crossing of a sea or a river. We sing,

> He will keep me 'til the river
> Rolls its waters at my feet,
> Then He'll bear me safely over,
> Where my Saviour I shall meet.
> Francis H. Rowley

However, this passing over the sea is not something we shall do someday. It is something we do every day. Living in this world, we are passing over the sea of time unto the other side. We are walking through the valley of the shadow of death.

The sea is a fit emblem for our lives and all the varied circumstances of our lives in this world. How quickly we pass across the sea. "What is your life? It is even a vapour, that appeareth for a little time, and then vanisheth away" (James 4:14). "My days are swifter than a weaver's shuttle, and are spent without hope" (Job 7:6). "Now my days are swifter than a post: they flee away, they see no good. They are passed away as the swift ships: as the eagle that hasteth to the prey" (Job 9:25, 26).

I have watched a lot of people die. As I look into the faces of eternity bound sinners day after day, as I am about to preach the gospel to them, I think to myself, "There go the ships, not painted ships upon a painted sea, but immortal souls, rising and falling upon the billows of time, disappearing one by one over the horizon of time into eternity." Soon, we must all pass over that horizon.

Perhaps, the horizon seems very far away to you. Do not be so foolish. Soon, you will pass from this changing world of time into the unchanging world of eternity. Here, all things are temporal and changing. There, all things are eternal and unchanging. How will it be for you in that day? How will it be for you in the swelling of the Jordan?

A Voyage Across A Stormy Sea

Second, life in this world is not only comparable to a voyage, but it is a voyage across a stormy sea. "But as they sailed he fell asleep: and there came down a storm of wind on the lake; and they were filled with water, and were in jeopardy" (v. 23). We must often sail into the tempests of sorrow, affliction, adversity, and grief; but Christ's presence assures us of safety no matter what the storm may be.

These disciples followed the Master into the ship at his command. It is important to note that fact, because we need to recognize that loyalty and obedience to Christ is often the surest course to trouble. The path of faithfulness is always right through the eye of the storm.

Though our storms are many and varied, basically, all our trials and troubles in this world arise from two sources: (1.) The contrary winds of our circumstances without, and (2.) the waves of sin and unbelief within (Romans 7:14-24; Psalm 73:1-3, 21-28).

A Voyage With Christ

Third, our life in this world is a voyage with Christ. A voyage, yes. A voyage through stormy seas, yes. But, blessed be God, it is a voyage in the company and constant presence, protection, and care of the Son of God, our Lord and Saviour.

The Lord Jesus does not say, "Go over to the other side and I will meet you there." He said, "Let us pass over unto the other side." And, though "there arose a great storm, and the waves beat into the ship, so that it was full", we read that the Lord Jesus "was in the hinder part of the ship". He was silent; but he was there. So it is with us. Our Lord may appear to be asleep. He may be silent. It may even appear at times to our feeble, sinful hearts that he does not care if we perish; but he is always with us!

How I pray that God will teach me and teach you to believe him. Did not our Saviour say, "Lo, I am with you alway"? Did he not promise, "I will never leave thee" (Hebrews 13:5)?

"Fear thou not; for I am with thee: be not dismayed; for I am thy God: I will strengthen thee; yea, I will help thee; yea, I will uphold thee with the right hand of my righteousness" (Isaiah 41:10).

"When thou passest through the waters, I will be with thee; and through the rivers, they shall not overflow thee: when thou walkest through the fire, thou shalt not be burned; neither shall the flame kindle upon thee" (Isaiah 43:2).

"Rejoice in the Lord alway: and again I say, Rejoice. Let your moderation be known unto all men. The Lord is at hand. Be careful for nothing; but in every thing by prayer and supplication with thanksgiving let your requests be made known unto God. And the peace of God, which passeth all understanding, shall keep your hearts and minds through Christ Jesus" (Philippians 4:4-7).

A Voyage Marked By Miracles

Fourth, ours is a voyage marked by miracles. "And he arose, and rebuked the wind, and said unto the sea, Peace, be still. And the wind ceased, and there was a great calm" (v. 39). The Charismatics talk about miracles. We experience them. They put on a show of sham tomfoolery; but God's saints are men and women whose biographies are histories of God's miraculous works. The redemption of our souls was accomplished by the miracle of God the Son assuming our nature, being made sin for us, dying in our place, and rising from the dead as our Surety. The new birth is a wonder of miraculous grace, accomplished by Christ himself invading our spiritually dead souls by his Spirit and taking up permanent residence in our hearts.

> It took a miracle to put the world in place.
> It took a miracle to hang the stars in space.
> But when God saved my soul,
> Cleansed and made me whole,
> It took a miracle of love and grace!
>
> John W. Peterson

And, soon, our blessed Saviour will perform another miracle, called the resurrection.

"Behold, I shew you a mystery; We shall not all sleep, but we shall all be changed, In a moment, in the twinkling of an eye, at the last trump: for the trumpet shall sound, and the dead shall be raised incorruptible, and we shall be changed. For this corruptible must put on incorruption, and this mortal must put on immortality. So when this corruptible shall have put on incorruption, and this mortal shall have put on immortality, then shall be brought to pass the saying that is written, Death is swallowed up in victory. O death, where is thy sting? O grave, where is thy victory? The sting of death is sin; and the strength of sin is the law. But thanks be to God, which giveth us the victory through our Lord Jesus Christ. Therefore, my beloved brethren, be ye stedfast, unmoveable, always abounding in the work of the Lord, forasmuch as ye know that your labour is not in vain in the Lord" (1 Corinthians 15:51-58).

Still, there is more, much more to consider. It is upon the dark background of our great troubles that our Lord most clearly displays his wondrous power and grace. It is in the fiery furnace of adversity that we know the preserving power of his presence. It is only in the lions' den that we see the Lord's dominion over the lions. The Lord God who is with us and for us is the God who is able to deliver us. He is God alone. He is God indeed!

311

A Voyage Free Of Fear

Fifth, our voyage with Christ across the stormy sea of life is a voyage that ought to be free of fear. The voyage we are on is a perfectly safe voyage. "And he said unto them, Where is your faith?" (v. 25) "Why are ye so fearful? How is it that ye have no faith?" (Mark 4:40).

The disciples' fear arose from their unbelief. Fear is the rank weed of nature that grows wild in the soil of unbelief. These poor disciples were so much like us. They should have been perfectly calm. They were on the Master's business. They were in the Master's presence. They had repeatedly seen and experienced the Master's power. They should have most reasonably looked to Christ; but they didn't. Instead of looking to the Lord God omnipotent, they looked at the terrible storm, their own weakness, and the apparent frailty of their ship.

Let us take the Lord's gentle rebuke personally. I try to apply it to myself. I hope God will enable you to do the same. Our greatest difficulties, our greatest temptations, our greatest falls are always the result of unbelief. Yet, unbelief on the part of one who has experienced the saving power and grace of God in Christ is the most absurd and unreasonable thing in the world.

"Where is your faith?" "Why are we so fearful? How is it that we have no faith?" Our Saviour is the sovereign God of providence, wise, good, and omnipotent. And he is in the boat with us. Yes, the Son of God is in the little boat of your heart and mine (Colossians 1:27; 1 John 4:4). The Lord Jesus Christ is in the boat of his Church (Deuteronomy 23:14; Psalm 46:5; Revelation 2:1). The Church of God, the true Church, is safe. She will pass over this sea. She will be brought to her desired haven. She will reach the other side. Not one passenger aboard the good ship Grace will be lost at sea.

A Voyage Well Charted

Sixth, our Lord Jesus Christ is in the boat of holy scripture. His Word is forever settled in heaven. It cannot be broken. All the shifting winds of pseudo-science and waves of unscholarly criticism will not sink the Vessel. We have no reason to fear the carping of reprobate men. The Word of God abides forever. When their laughter is turned to weeping and their criticisms burn as fire in their souls, the Word of God will still be forever settled in heaven!

The Captain Of The Voyage

Seventh, our Lord Jesus Christ is in the boat of Providence. Not only is he in the boat, he is at the helm. We do not trust providence, or worship providence (we are not Deists); but the Lord God Almighty, whom we do trust and worship, is the God of providence; and we rejoice to know it.

The Lord Jesus Christ, who is with us, has the whole world in his hands. All power in heaven and earth is given unto him. He holds the reins of universal dominion. This omnipotent God bids us cast our care upon him with these assuring words, "For he careth for you"! He says to us, "Be not afraid, only believe."

A Call To Faith

Are you yet without Christ? Has God brought you into deep waters and begun to cause you to reel to and fro like a drunken man by reason of your soul's trouble? Is the storm of God's wrath beating your little boat? May the Spirit of God make this parable a call to faith in your soul. Cry out from your soul to Christ, the Master. Appeal to his great compassion, "Carest thou not that I perish?" May the Son of God arise and speak peace to your troubled heart. If he will speak by his Spirit, his word of grace will bring great calm; and he will bring you to your desired haven.

Let us read again the words of Psalm 107. And pray that the Lord will bestow that spiritual wisdom by which we might observe the lovingkindness of the Saviour, Jesus Christ.

"They that go down to the sea in ships, that do business in great waters; These see the works of the LORD, and his wonders in the deep. For he commandeth, and raiseth the stormy wind, which lifteth up the waves thereof. They mount up to the heaven, they go down again to the depths: their soul is melted because of trouble. They reel to and fro, and stagger like a drunken man, and are at their wit's end. Then they cry unto the LORD in their trouble, and he bringeth them out of their distresses. He maketh the storm a calm, so that the waves thereof are still. Then are they glad because they be quiet; so he bringeth them unto their desired haven. Oh that men would praise the LORD for his goodness, and for his wonderful works to the children of men! ... The righteous shall see it, and rejoice: and all iniquity shall stop her mouth. Whoso is wise, and will observe these things, even they shall understand the lovingkindness of the LORD" (Psalm 107:23-31, 42, 43).

Believe him, only believe him, and you will see the glory of God (John 11:40).

"And they arrived at the country of the Gadarenes, which is over against Galilee. And when he went forth to land, there met him out of the city a certain man, which had devils long time, and ware no clothes, neither abode in any house, but in the tombs. When he saw Jesus, he cried out, and fell down before him, and with a loud voice said, What have I to do with thee, Jesus, thou Son of God most high? I beseech thee, torment me not. (For he had commanded the unclean spirit to come out of the man. For oftentimes it had caught him: and he was kept bound with chains and in fetters; and he brake the bands, and was driven of the devil into the wilderness.) And Jesus asked him, saying, What is thy name? And he said, Legion: because many devils were entered into him. And they besought him that he would not command them to go out into the deep. And there was there an herd of many swine feeding on the mountain: and they besought him that he would suffer them to enter into them. And he suffered them. Then went the devils out of the man, and entered into the swine: and the herd ran violently down a steep place into the lake, and were choked. When they that fed them saw what was done, they fled, and went and told it in the city and in the country. Then they went out to see what was done; and came to Jesus, and found the man, out of whom the devils were departed, sitting at the feet of Jesus, clothed, and in his right mind: and they were afraid. They also which saw it told them by what means he that was possessed of the devils was healed. Then the whole multitude of the country of the Gadarenes round about besought him to depart from them; for they were taken with great fear: and he went up into the ship, and returned back again. Now the man out of whom the devils were departed besought him that he might be with him: but Jesus sent him away, saying, Return to thine own house, and shew how great things God hath done unto thee. And he went his way, and published throughout the whole city how great things Jesus had done unto him" (Luke 8:26-39).

Chapter 48

Grace For The Gadarene

For every chosen, redeemed sinner there is an appointed time when he shall be called by God's almighty grace. That time is called "The Time of Life" and "The Time of Love". Though born children of wrath, even as others, God's elect were from eternity the objects of immutable mercy, love and grace. Though we ran hell-bent to destruction, the Lord God, from old eternity said, "Hitherto shalt thou go and no further." Though Satan roared against us, though the legions of hell sought to destroy us, though our hearts were in league with hell itself, at God's appointed time of love, the Lord Jesus Christ came to us, and, by the power of his omnipotent grace, saved us. For the poor maniac of Gadara, when the time of love came, the Lord Jesus came to him with the mighty operations of his saving grace.

It is a story that is told by Matthew, Mark and Luke. All three of these gospel writers were inspired of God the Holy Spirit to record this event in considerable detail. Mark gives us the most detailed account of what transpired that day in the land of the Gadarenes; but all three hold this story before us as a remarkable display both of our Lord's great grace to needy sinners and of his sovereign dominion even over the demons of hell. As the Lord Jesus Christ vanquished hell in the heart and life of this poor demoniac in Gadara two thousand years ago, so he vanquishes hell itself in the hearts of chosen redeemed sinners by the saving operations of his grace.

The Saviour Of Sinners
"And they arrived at the country of the Gadarenes, which is over against Galilee" (v. 26). The Lord Jesus had just come from the other side of the Sea

of Galilee to the shores of Gadara. When he set sail for Gadara, he knew that he was sailing directly into a storm. Yet, he set sail willingly. He was on an errand of mercy. He was going to Gadara to save one chosen sinner, for whom the time of love had come. The Lord Jesus came through the storm, across the sea, with willing heart to save the chosen sinner, when the fulness of time had come. When he had delivered the object of his grace, he returned to the other side of the sea, whence he came.

This is exactly what our Redeemer did for all his people. He left his lofty throne in heaven, came across the sea of time and mortality, suffered the horrible storm of God's wrath as our Substitute to save us, and, when he had done that mighty work by which his chosen must be saved (when he had satisfied the law and justice of God and put away our sins by the sacrifice of himself), he went back to the other side again (Matthew 1:21; Luke 19:10; 1 Timothy 1:15; Romans 5:8; 1 John 3:5; Hebrews 10:10-14).

He came to save the least likely of the Gadarenes, a wild man, a maniac, one who was entirely possessed of the devil. In fact, a legion of demons resided in his poor soul. However, as we shall see, this man would be the instrument of mercy by whom God would bring his grace and salvation to many others in days to come (1 Corinthians 1:26-29).

The Son of God came to Gadara to dispossess Satan of one of his captives, to bind the strong man, take his house, and spoil him of his goods; and he did not leave until he had done what he came to do. The Lord Jesus Christ, the Son of God, is the Saviour of sinners.

A Miserable Wretch
"And when he went forth to land, there met him out of the city a certain man, which had devils long time, and ware no clothes, neither abode in any house, but in the tombs. When he saw Jesus, he cried out, and fell down before him, and with a loud voice said, What have I to do with thee, Jesus, thou Son of God most high? I beseech thee, torment me not. (For he had commanded the unclean spirit to come out of the man. For oftentimes it had caught him: and he was kept bound with chains and in fetters; and he brake the bands, and was driven of the devil into the wilderness.) And Jesus asked him, saying, What is thy name? And he said, Legion: because many devils were entered into him" (vv. 27-30).

Matthew in his account tells us that there were two mad, demon possessed Gadarenes who met the Master on the shores of Gadara. Some point to that fact and say, "There, you see, the Bible is full of contradictions." I fail to see their brilliance. If there were two, there had to be one; and Luke was inspired of God to write about one, giving far more detail than Matthew did in his description of the two. Apparently, the man described by Luke was the more notoriously wicked of the two. Look at what the Holy Spirit tells us about this sinner. What a sad, sad picture it is.

This poor Gadarene was a miserable wretch. Though the picture falls far short of the thing portrayed by it, the distressing circumstances of the poor demoniac vividly portray the terrible consequences of the fall of our father Adam, and the utter ruin of our race in the fall. Every descendent of Adam is by nature under the full sway and influence of an unclean spirit. We are all by nature ruled by our own depraved, corrupt hearts and wills, and are taken captive by Satan at his will (Romans 3:10-19; 1 John 3:8; 2 Timothy 2:26). Robert Hawker rightly observed, "Were it not for restraining grace, of which the sinner is wholly unconscious, what tremendous evils, in ten thousand times ten thousand instances, would take place!" We are, because of the fall and Satan's conquest of our nature, in bondage to sin with all its dreadful consequences. The flesh with its lusts, the world with its deceits, and Satan with his devices rule the fallen sons of Adam with absolute sway.

In addition to all this, we are justly condemned by the law and justice of God threatening us with everlasting torment, and by the accusations of our own consciences. This is the state and condition of every fallen son and daughter of Adam, which causes all to live all their life time in the fear of death (Hebrews 2:14, 15).

An Unclean Spirit
Like this poor Gadarene, we all have an unclean spirit by nature. Yes, this man was possessed of the devil; but the devil could never have possessed him had he not been unclean by nature. Even so, the wicked, who opposing God oppose themselves, are this day "taken captive by Satan at his will" (2 Timothy 2:26). Isaiah declares that we are all as an unclean thing. Our hearts are deceitful above all things and desperately wicked. Out of our hearts come forth every abominable evil that exists in this world. Oh, if only we knew the evil of our hearts, the shocking horror of that wickedness that resides in us would prevent us from ever again saying, with regard of any vile act of a man, "How could a man do such a thing?"

Living Among The Dead
This poor, mad, depraved soul lived among the dead. Mark tells us that he was "dwelling among the tombs". Dead sinners, dead in trespasses and sins, live among dead sinners, like themselves. Is that the case with you? You who live without Christ live among the dead, for you are dead. This man was not dead physically, but he was dead spiritually. Therefore, he was most comfortable among the dead. That is where I was when the Lord found me; and that is where you are by nature (Ephesians 2:1-4).

Could Not Be Bound

This poor, wild man could not be bound with the fetters and chains that bind other men. The fetters of society, social acceptance, peer approval, social advantage, family pressure, reputation, and concern for the opinions of others, those things that bind most men and make them behave with an outward form of decency, simply have no effect on some. The law of God has no influence upon most. They refuse to acknowledge its power, and cannot be bound by it. Night and day they run to destruction in a life of mad behaviour that will inevitably bring them to hell, except the grace of God intervene.

I say it to my shame, but that was my condition. Like the maniac of Gadara, social fetters could not bind me; and the fetters and chains of religion were no more effectual. I knew something of the terror of God's law. The wrath of God, the terrors of judgment, hell, and endless death tormented my soul, sometimes for months on end. Those terrors would sometimes appear effectual; but those fetters were also easily cast off. The fear of hell never changes a sinner's heart.

Could Not Be Tamed

No man could tame this madman. When society sees that chains and fetters cannot bind a man and make him better, it tries by refinement, education, reward, and gentle persuasion to tame him into moral respectability. The Lord Jesus does not bind or tame. He renews, regenerates, and breaks! And when he gets done, the broken sinner rejoices to be broken.

This poor maniac, like me, like some who read these lines, was hell bent to the destruction of his own soul. He was "always, night and day, in the mountains, and in the tombs, crying, and cutting himself with stones." Imagine the terror that this man wreaked upon others as they passed by this place, especially at night. Imagine yourself living near such a man. You would put iron bars around your windows and doors, and sleep with a gun under your bed every night. Whenever you saw him coming down the street, you would nod politely to keep from incurring his fury; but you would hurry away and try every way possible to protect your family from the influence of his madness.

But, can you imagine what misery such a person is in himself. His wickedness is his own doing; and it is inexcusable. But I also know the misery of his soul. I have been there among the tombs, moaning, groaning, crying, and cutting myself, always playing with death, yet always terrified of dying, despising loneliness and isolation, yet always doing that which of necessity brought me into greater loneliness and isolation.

318

Are you like this poor wretch? Were you once like him? If you are now in Christ, saved by his omnipotent mercy and infinite grace, you know that you were once unconscious of such mercy and grace. If you are yet without Christ, you are in the bondage of sin, Satan, and death, though you are completely unconscious of your lost and ruined condition.

A Worshipping Devil

"When he saw Jesus, he cried out, and fell down before him, and with a loud voice said, What have I to do with thee, Jesus, thou Son of God most high? I beseech thee, torment me not" (v. 28). Here is the confession of a demon spirit. I do not know much about demons and demonology, and I do not want to know much. But I do know this: Demons are real! You will be wise to stay as far away from the occult, spiritism, witchcraft and Satanism as you can.

Here the devil pretends to be a worshipper of Christ. He does not hesitate to assume the character of an angel of light, when it serves his purpose. I have seen him at work often. He makes people religious and think they have become worshippers of God, though there is no worship in their hearts. What a cunning, crafty adversary Satan is! Many serve the devil best when they pretend to be worshippers of Christ! Worship from the teeth outward is not worship, but blasphemy! Many there are on the road to hell who have nothing but the faith of devils. They know that the Lord God is the most high God, and that Jesus Christ is the Son of God, but there is no commitment of heart to him as God. John Owen once wrote ...

"Of all the poison which at this day is diffused in the minds of men, corrupting them from the mystery of the gospel, there is no part that is more pernicious than this one perverse imagination, that to 'believe in Christ' is nothing at all but to 'believe the doctrine of the gospel'."

Run To Christ

Yet, Matthew, Mark and Luke show us in this Gadarene a picture of a poor, lost sinner coming to Christ. I cannot pass this without pointing out the fact that our great Saviour sovereignly and graciously used the very devils who would destroy the Gadarene to bring him to him for mercy!

Look at this man. He was "afar off"! That is our place by nature. He was afar off from Christ, and the Lord Jesus was afar off from him. In character he was afar off. This man and the God-man had nothing in common. In knowledge he was afar off. The demoniac knew who Christ was, but did not know him. In possessions he was afar off. This man had nothing to offer Christ, no good feelings, no repentance, no good thoughts, no holy desires.

He cried, "What have I to do with thee?" The poor demoniac was utterly helpless and hopeless.

If you are yet without Christ, no words can paint the picture of your desperate need. You are so far off from God that you cannot and will not, of your own accord and by your own ability, return to him.

But notice this, though he was afar off, the Lord Jesus came to him, and he saw him coming! How he knew, I do not know; but this poor sinner knew some things about the One coming to him. I suspect he knew, because whenever Christ comes to a sinner in saving mercy, he makes himself known as the God of mercy and the Saviour through whom mercy comes. He saw that the Lord our God is God Almighty, the most high God. He saw that the man Christ Jesus is God the Son. He saw that this great Saviour has total, sovereign power over all things, even the devils who possessed him. And he saw that if he would, he could deliver him from the devils and from himself.

"He ran and worshipped him." The poor soul was in a terrible mess. He was torn by powerful influences. Here is the Son of God who has come to save him. Yet, there is within him a legion of devils bent on destroying him. He loves the evil that is destroying him; yet, he has grown to hate it, because it is destroying him. He did the only thing he could do. In utter despair he ran to the only One who could help him, prostrated himself before his sovereign majesty, and worshipped him. C. H. Spurgeon said ...

"A needle will move towards a magnet when once a magnet has moved near to it. Our heart manifests a sweet willingness towards salvation and holiness when the great and glorious good will of the Lord operates upon it. It is ours to run to Jesus as if all the runnings were ours; but the secret truth is that our Lord runs towards us, and this is the very heart of the business."

Do you need the mercy and grace of God? Run to Christ! With nothing but sin within you, with time fleeing from you, with eternity pressing upon you, with hell gaping beneath you, with heaven above you, O sinner, run, run to Christ! If you would have forgiveness, peace, pardon, and eternal life, run to Christ! This I know, if you do, you will find God your Father running to you in saving mercy, love and grace! When sinners need mercy, they run to get it and God runs to give it!

What a blessed picture we are given of this in Luke 15:20. When the poor prodigal came to himself, as he was coming to his father, with overwhelming shame, we are told that, "when he was yet a great way off, his father saw him, and had compassion, and ran, and fell on his neck, and kissed him." What a picture that is! The only time in the Bible we have any indication of the eternal God ever being in a hurry, it is here, hurrying to welcome his darling, chosen prodigal home! In a sermon preached almost 400 years ago

Tobias Crisp made the following comments on Luke 15:20. The quote is lengthy, but too precious and needful to be omitted or edited.

"His father sees him first. He spies him afar off. He stands ready to welcome a sinner, so soon as his heart looks but towards him. He that will draw nigh to them that are afar off will certainly draw nigh to them that draw near to him (Jeremiah 31:18). Nay, the father had compassion on him. His bowels yearn towards him, whilst he is afar off. Nay, he runs to meet him. He prevents a sinner with speed; mercy comes not on a foot-pace, but runs; it comes upon wings, as David speaks, 'he rides on the cherubs, he did fly; yea, he did fly on the wings of the wind' (Psalm 18:9, 10) ... The son's pace is slow.

He arose and came. The father's is swift. He ran. Though the son had most need to run, bowels moving with mercy out-pace bowels pinched with want. God makes more haste to shew mercy, than we to receive. Whilst misery walks, mercy flies; nay, he falls on his son's neck, hugging and embracing him.

Oh! The depth of grace! Who would not have loathed such a person to touch or come near him, whilst he smells of the swine he kept? Could a man come near him without stopping his nose? Would it not make a man almost rid his stomach, to smell his nastiness? Yet, behold, the Father of sinners falls upon the neck of such filthy wretches! Mercy and grace are not squeamish. The prodigal comes like a rogue. Yet the father clips him like a bride. He falls a kissing of him, even those lips that had lately been lapping in the hog trough and had kissed baggage harlots. A man would have thought he should rather have kicked him than kissed him. Yet this token of reconciliation and grace he gives him, with this seal he confirms his compassion. Nay, he calls for the best robe, and kills the fatted calf for him. The son's ambition was to be but as a hired servant, and lo, he is feasted in the best robes. God will do far better for a sinner than he can imagine, above all he is able either to ask or think.

How then do poverty, nakedness, emptiness pinch thee, because of thy riot? Canst thou see enough in thy father's house, and therefore begin to pant in heart after him? Wouldest thou then have admittance? The Father of mercy is ready to deal thus with thee. Therefore object not unworthiness; for who more unworthy than such a son?"

I say, again, run to Christ for mercy; and you will find the God of heaven running to you with mercy, infinite, overwhelming, saving mercy. Oh! That every poor sinner God the Father has given to his Son, whose redemption Christ has purchased with his own precious blood, may be led by God the Holy Spirit to flee to Christ, as this Gadarene demoniac was for deliverance.

321

"And they besought him that he would not command them to go out into the deep. And there was there an herd of many swine feeding on the mountain: and they besought him that he would suffer them to enter into them. And he suffered them. Then went the devils out of the man, and entered into the swine: and the herd ran violently down a steep place into the lake, and were choked. When they that fed them saw what was done, they fled, and went and told it in the city and in the country. Then they went out to see what was done; and came to Jesus, and found the man, out of whom the devils were departed, sitting at the feet of Jesus, clothed, and in his right mind: and they were afraid. They also which saw it told them by what means he that was possessed of the devils was healed. Then the whole multitude of the country of the Gadarenes round about besought him to depart from them; for they were taken with great fear: and he went up into the ship, and returned back again. Now the man out of whom the devils were departed besought him that he might be with him: but Jesus sent him away, saying, Return to thine own house, and shew how great things God hath done unto thee. And he went his way, and published throughout the whole city how great things Jesus had done unto him. And it came to pass, that, when Jesus was returned, the people gladly received him: for they were all waiting for him" (Luke 8:31-40).

Chapter 49

"They Besought Him"

I do not pretend to know much about prayer, though I very much want to know how to pray. But this I do know: prayer has something to do with worship. Prayer has something to do with gratitude, praise and thanksgiving. Prayer is primarily a work of the heart. Prayer has something to do with seeking and bowing to the will of God. It has something to do with the glory of God, the welfare of the kingdom of God and faith in Christ.

I know, beyond a doubt, that most of what men and women imagine is prayer and call prayer has nothing whatever to do with prayer. To all who think that prayer is simply asking God to give us what we want and receiving it, I say, "Read Luke chapter 8." To those multitudes who vainly imagine that answered prayer is evidence of saving grace, I say, "Read Luke chapter 8."

Here is a legion of demons praying to the Lord Jesus Christ, a legion of demons whose request the Lord immediately granted. Here is an entire city pleading with the Son of God to depart from their coasts, a city whose request the Lord Jesus granted on the spot. Here is a saved sinner, one whose heart burned with love and gratitude to Christ, who prayed that the Lord would graciously allow him to stay in his company, the prayer of an earnest soul, whose request the Lord Jesus denied.

What are we to learn from these things? Why are they here recorded in the Book of God? May God the Holy Spirit who caused theses words to be written now teach us their meaning.

Praying Devils

First, in verses 31-33, we see devils praying; and the Lord Jesus Christ immediately grants the request of a legion of demons. The Lord Jesus answered their prayer, doing exactly what they requested

"And they besought him that he would not command them to go out into the deep. And there was there an herd of many swine feeding on the mountain: and they besought him that he would suffer them to enter into them. And he suffered them. Then went the devils out of the man, and entered into the swine: and the herd ran violently down a steep place into the lake, and were choked."

Even the demons of hell when terrified by the impending wrath and judgment of God pray; but such prayer is not prayer at all. The very demons of hell are under the command of the Son of God, totally controlled by him, and they both know it and acknowledge it; but such an acknowledgement is not true worship.

As the herd of swine was plunged into destruction by the influence of those demons, the demons who possessed the poor Gadarene, so the influence of hell that possesses unbelieving men and women will destroy their souls, unless the Son of God intervenes.

Praying Reprobate

Second, in verse 37, we see an entire city of lost, reprobate sinners pleading with the Son of God to leave them, and he did. The Lord Jesus answered their prayer, doing exactly what they requested, just as he answered the prayer of the demons who possessed the Gadarene.

"Then the whole multitude of the country of the Gadarenes round about besought him to depart from them; for they were taken with great fear: and he went up into the ship, and returned back again."

What an awesome, frightful sight this is! At the request of these men, the Son of God, the Lord of Glory, the Saviour of the world, "went up into the ship and returned back"!

What possessed these men to make such a request? They knew exactly what the Lord had done. They knew his power. They saw the evidence of his goodness, grace and saving majesty sitting before them. Yet, they prayed not for him to work among them, for them, in them and with them, but for him to depart from them! Why?

These men prayed for the Holy Lamb of God to leave their city. They begged the Dispossessor of demons to depart from them. They wanted the Healer of men's souls to leave them, their wives and their children. They asked the King of Glory to depart from their town. They prayed for the Saviour of the world to leave them alone. Why?

Why did these men beg such a man to depart from their coasts? Would the Gadarenes prefer to have a wild, demon possessed man roaming their streets than the Son of God? Obviously they did; but why? I will give you the answer in one short sentence: They loved the world and refused to give it up. These men were convinced in their own consciences that they would lose much if the Son of God stayed among them. Therefore, counting the cost, they said, "Give us the world! Give us the demons of hell, if you must; but give us the world and leave us alone"! And that is exactly what he did!

Nothing has changed. All men by nature are exactly like these Gadarenes. We all prefer the raging, unbridled, uncontrolled lusts of our hearts, the horrid dominion of Satan, the dark influence of hell, the pursuits and follies of the world to the sweet dominion of the Son of God and the mercy, love and grace of God he brings. John Trapp observed, "Take up your cross is a hard saying. Therefore Christ must be prayed to be gone, lest all our pigs be drowned."

There is a day of grace, a time of visitation from the Lord, which if despised will become a day of wrath, vengeance and eternal ruin. Light despised will be turned into darkness. Mercy spurned will bring eternal misery. Let us take heed that we do not sin the sin of the Gadarenes (Job 21:14; Hosea 4:17; Proverbs 1:23-33; 29:1). Let it rather be our constant prayer, "O Lord God, do not leave us to ourselves"!

Yet, even in this, I am reminded of God's great mercy to our souls. Aren't you? There was a time, not long ago, when we, too, besought the Son of God that he would depart from us. Did we not? Thank God, he refused to grant us our hearts' desire. He refused to leave us alone. He refused to leave us to ourselves. He refused to give us up. He cried for us, "How shall I give thee up?"

Nothing less than a miracle of grace, nothing less than the intervention of sovereign mercy, nothing short of omnipotent love stepping into our lives could cause us to turn and seek the Lord our God, whom we most vehemently despised all our lives.

A Believer's Request Denied

Third, in verses 38 and 39 the Holy Spirit gives us another highly instructive picture. Here is a saved sinner praying for permission to ever abide in the Lord's presence, whose request the Lord Jesus graciously denied.

"Now the man out of whom the devils were departed besought him that he might be with him: but Jesus sent him away, saying, Return to thine own house, and show how great things God hath done unto thee. And he went his way, and published throughout the whole city how great things Jesus had done unto him."

Without question, the man before us is a true believer. He is a heaven born soul. Not only had the demons been cast out of him, the Son of God had established his throne in him. Can you picture him? There he is sitting at the Saviour's feet, beaming with gratitude. He is clothed in the garments of salvation, filled with praise. He is, for the first time in his life, in his right mind. This newly regenerate, heaven-born soul was full of love, gratitude, joy and zeal.

Did you ever notice how striking the differences are in the ways our Master dealt with men? To this man he refused permission to forsake his family and homeland. He commanded the rich young ruler to forsake all and follow him. The healed leper was strictly charged to tell no man what the Master had done for him. Another was not even allowed to go home and bury his father. Our Saviour knew what was in the hearts of all. He knew precisely what each case before him required, and he dealt with each according to the needs of their situation.

Why did the Lord Jesus refuse this man's earnest request? It was, without question, the prayer of an earnest, loving, grateful, adoring heart. There was nothing selfish or self-serving in it. But the Master would not allow this man to go with him for good reasons. Our Master knows, far better than we the best place for us. This was an act of great mercy to the Gadarenes. This was a marvellous display of goodness to this man's family. In a word, the Lord Jesus refused to grant the request of this man's lips, so that he might give him the request of his heart (Romans 8:26; Matthew 6:9-13).

By refusing to allow this saved sinner to go with him, the Lord Jesus secured his best place and circumstances in which to glorify God. The Son of God graciously ordered his steps to walk in the will of God (Proverbs 3:5, 6). The Master graciously used him to build up the kingdom of God. The Lord Jesus graciously led him not into temptation but delivered him from evil.

This young convert wanted to go immediately with Christ and become a preacher; but the Lord would not allow it. How many there are who have mistaken a desire to be a preacher for a call to the ministry. It is not. The Lord Jesus sent him home to his family and friends with a message to deliver to them.

The Master would not allow him to go where he wanted to go or do what he wanted to do; but he was given something far better, far more useful to do. God made him a witness to his own community. Now, that's a preacher! The Lord told him exactly what to tell those of whom he would be a witness. He was sent to tell his family and friends what great things the Lord had done for him and how he had compassion on him.

And this sinner, saved by the grace of God, did what the Lord told him to do. "And he departed, and began to publish in Decapolis how great things Jesus had done for him: and all men did marvel." Notice the language here. He was told to publish what great things the Lord had done. So he told everyone what great things Jesus had done. He knew that Jesus is Lord. He learned it by experience from the Lord himself.

The Lord Jesus graciously used this man in Decapolis for the good of many. The next time the Saviour came into the region, he was readily received. Many came to him. Many were healed by him. Multitudes were fed by his hand (Mark 7:31- 8:1). Mercy came to many, because one sinner saved by grace faithfully told other sinners what great things the Lord had done for him!

What a wonderful change grace had wrought in the Gadarene! He who was a madman, possessed of the devil, was immediately so transformed by the saving grace of Christ that he desired never to leave his Lord's side. Is this not the case with every child of God, when delivered from the power of darkness and translated from the cruel bondage of sin and death in to the kingdom of God's dear Son? Once we have tasted that the Lord is gracious, we cannot but long to be "absent from the body, and present with the Lord." But this must not immediately be the case. "To abide in the flesh is more needful." Saved sinners are to go home to their lost families and friends, and proclaim "the praises of him who hath called us out of darkness into his marvellous light."

Christ has, by his saving grace, made us members of his church upon earth. In this capacity we are to serve him and the souls of eternity bound sinners, until the time he has appointed comes to take us home. None of us will live here beyond that appointed time. And that appointed time cannot be too long, if God our Saviour will be pleased to employ us for the welfare of his chosen. Mr. Hawker wrote, "Let this make us happy in waiting 'all the days of our appointed time, until our change come'." Until then, may God give us grace to make it our lives' business to tell our family and friends, and all who will hear us, "what great things the Lord hath done for us, and hath had compassion on us."

"And, behold, there came a man named Jairus, and he was a ruler of the synagogue: and he fell down at Jesus' feet, and besought him that he would come into his house: For he had one only daughter, about twelve years of age, and she lay a dying. But as he went the people thronged him. And a woman having an issue of blood twelve years, which had spent all her living upon physicians, neither could be healed of any, Came behind him, and touched the border of his garment: and immediately her issue of blood stanched. And Jesus said, Who touched me? When all denied, Peter and they that were with him said, Master, the multitude throng thee and press thee, and sayest thou, Who touched me? And Jesus said, Somebody hath touched me: for I perceive that virtue is gone out of me. And when the woman saw that she was not hid, she came trembling, and falling down before him, she declared unto him before all the people for what cause she had touched him, and how she was healed immediately. And he said unto her, Daughter, be of good comfort: thy faith hath made thee whole; go in peace" (Luke 8:41-48).

Chapter 50

"Who Touched Me?"

Our Lord Jesus was on his way to Jairus' house to perform a miracle of mercy upon his daughter, who was at the point of death. No doubt, word had gotten around in a hurry about what the Saviour had done in Gadara. Therefore, Jairus ran to the Master, fell down at his feet, and begged him to come to his house and heal his daughter. As they went along, the crowds began to gather. You can imagine the commotion.

"And, behold, there came a man named Jairus, and he was a ruler of the synagogue: and he fell down at Jesus' feet, and besought him that he would come into his house: For he had one only daughter, about twelve years of age, and she lay a dying. But as he went the people thronged him" (Luke 8:41, 42).

Excitement filled the air. Here was a man, who claimed to be God's Messiah, the Christ, God incarnate. Everyone knew his claim; but he had begun to back it up and substantiate it by doing things that no one else could possibly do. In Gadara the devils themselves were constrained to publicly acknowledge him as the Lord their God, who had absolute power over them. Now, he is going to heal a young girl, whose father was a very prominent citizen in the community. This little girl was at the point of death. Everybody wanted to see the miracle. They followed the Lord as closely as possible, pressing him as he walked along. Everyone was excited. Everyone was curious. Everyone was filled with anticipation.

As they moved along, a poor, stooped, anaemic woman, a woman who had been plagued with an issue of blood for twelve, long, tormenting years, made her way through the crowd. I can almost see her. She must not let herself be seen. She is unclean. She has no right by law to even be in the streets; but she is dying. She has heard about the Lord Jesus. No one else could help her. She had tried everything imaginable. Yet, she believed that Jesus of Nazareth was indeed the Christ, the Son of God. She said, "If I could just touch the hem of his garment, I am sure, he would make me whole." So she crawled through the thronging crowds, until she got close. Then, weak and trembling, she stretched out her hand in faith and touched the Lord Jesus.

As soon as she touched him, the Lord Jesus stopped dead in his tracks. He felt virtue, power and efficacy go out of him. Therefore, he turned around and said, "Who touched me?" The disciples said, "You've got to be kidding. With all these people around, you are asking, 'Who touched me?'" Then, the Master said, "Somebody touched me."

Just as this poor woman was immediately healed of her plague when she touched the Lord Jesus, so sinners are healed of the plague of their hearts, freed from the curse of the law and the guilt of sin as soon as they touch the Lord Jesus Christ by faith.

Because Mark gives us a more detailed account of this event, we will pick up some of the details recorded by him in Mark 5.

The Curse

"And a woman having an issue of blood twelve years, which had spent all her living upon physicians, neither could be healed of any" (v. 43).

"And a certain woman, which had an issue of blood twelve years, And had suffered many things of many physicians, and had spent all that she had, and was nothing bettered, but rather grew worse" (Mark 5:25, 26).

There is no greater evidence of the total depravity of all human beings by nature than the fact that we all incur disease, get sick and die. All sickness, disease and death are the result of sin and the curse of God upon the human race because of sin.

This woman's sickness was a specific example of sin and the curse of God's law upon us all by nature. Her sickness, her unceasing issue of blood was something that made her ceremonially unclean. So it is with us all by nature. We are plagued with sin. The plague of sin makes us unclean. Being unclean, we are cursed and barred from the holy Lord God. Look at what the Holy Spirit tells us about this woman.

She "had an issue of blood twelve years." She was ceremonially unclean (Leviticus 15:25), because of a disabling sickness that was killing her. This poor soul "had suffered many things of many physicians." She had been to every doctor in town, including the quacks, the charlatans, the snake oil herbalists and the faith healers. There are countless "physicians of no value" (Job 13:4) to the souls of men. Dr Decision tells sinners that they can be saved if they will simply make their decision for Jesus. Dr B. Good exhorts the sinner to reform his life. Dr Free Will admonishes the sinner to will himself into life. Dr Ceremony urges the poor soul to observe religious ordinances and sacraments to get the grace he needs. Dr Right Church tells poor souls that they can be made whole if they get into the right church. Dr Excitement urges the sin-sick soul to seek a miracle, speak in tongues, pray through and wrestle with God until he gets God to save him. Dr Emotion prescribes introspection, urging dead sinners to look within themselves for feelings of repentance and sorrow, or longings for Christ, by which they may know they are fit to be saved.

Next, we are told that the poor, dying woman "spent all that she had". Like those described in Isaiah 46:6 lavishing out everything for the help of idols, though she spent everything she had seeking help from "physicians of no value", she "was nothing bettered, but rather grew worse". Religion without Christ is of no value to lost sinners. It never helps. Rather, it only makes the sinner's condition worse. The practice of religion without Christ is but eating and drinking damnation (1 Corinthians 11:29). Oh, that sinners crippled with sin, instead of looking to "physicians of no value" in tears and attempted reforms in their own strength, might, like this woman, be brought to Christ!

The Crowd

"And Jesus said, Who touched me? When all denied, Peter and they that were with him said, Master, the multitude throng thee and press thee, and sayest thou, Who touched me?" (v. 45)

"And Jesus went with him; and much people followed him, and thronged him. And a certain woman, which had an issue of blood twelve years, And had suffered many things of many physicians, and had spent all that she had, and was nothing bettered, but rather grew worse, When she had heard of Jesus, came in the press behind, and touched his garment" (Mark 5:24-27).

Like the crowds that pressed the Lord Jesus, people come to church, profess faith and claim to follow him for many reasons. Some come being stirred by religious excitement, following the crowd. Some take up a profession because of peer pressure. Many do so because they fear going to hell. The crowds of people thronged our Lord; but only one person gained any benefit. Only one person came from behind and touched him. Only one person in this great crowd needed him. Only one person believed the Lord Jesus could actually cure her of her plague. Believing him, she touched him. Be wise and follow her example.

The Cure

"And Jesus said, Who touched me? When all denied, Peter and they that were with him said, Master, the multitude throng thee and press thee, and sayest thou, Who touched me? And Jesus said, Somebody hath touched me: for I perceive that virtue is gone out of me" (vv. 45, 46).

331

Again she, "When she had heard of Jesus, came in the press behind, and touched his garment. For she said, If I may touch but his clothes, I shall be whole. And straightway the fountain of her blood was dried up; and she felt in her body that she was healed of that plague. And Jesus, immediately knowing in himself that virtue had gone out of him, turned him about in the press, and said, Who touched my clothes? ... And he said unto her, Daughter, thy faith hath made thee whole; go in peace, and be whole of thy plague" (Mark 5:27-30, 34).

There are several things here, which ought to catch our attention. Many reading this story miss the most important aspects of it. They put all the emphasis upon the woman. Inspiration puts the emphasis on the woman only as the recipient of mercy and benefactor of grace. But, insofar as the act of mercy and the work of grace are concerned, the emphasis must be placed upon the Saviour. This woman was made whole in exactly the same way every sinner saved by the grace of God is made whole. She was made whole by a fivefold work of God Almighty.

A Work Of Providence

Her sickness was not an accident, but a work of God for her soul to bring her to Christ. That which was the destruction and death of others was for her the instrument of mercy. By his wise, gracious and good providence, the God of all grace brought the chosen sinner and the appointed Saviour together at the time of love.

A Work Of The Word

She came to Christ in faith "when she had heard of Jesus" (Mark 5:27), not before. No one is ever saved apart from the hearing of Christ, the hearing of the gospel (Romans 10:17; James 1:18; 1 Peter 1:23-25). God never bypasses the appointed means of grace. There is no need for him to do so.

A Work Of Grace

The grace of God is not verbally mentioned in the text; but it is written all over it. Grace had chosen "a certain woman". Grace brought the Lord Jesus to pass her way. Grace caused her to hear about him. And grace gave her faith and wrought faith in her (Ephesians 1:19; 2:8; Philippians 1:29; Colossians 2:12).

A Work Of Faith

This woman's faith, like all true faith, was the gift of God. Yet, it was her faith. She chose to come to Christ. She chose to believe on the Son of God.

She was made willing in the day of his power; but she was willing. She was caused to come by the sweet constraint of grace; but she did come.

A Work Of Omnipotence
The arm of God's omnipotent, almighty, irresistible power brought this thing to pass exactly according to his everlasting purpose of love and grace toward this chosen sinner. The virtue that went out of the Saviour to this woman was his own omnipotent grace.

The Confession
"And when the woman saw that she was not hid, she came trembling, and falling down before him, she declared unto him before all the people for what cause she had touched him, and how she was healed immediately" (v. 47).

"And Jesus, immediately knowing in himself that virtue had gone out of him, turned him about in the press, and said, Who touched my clothes? And his disciples said unto him, Thou seest the multitude thronging thee, and sayest thou, Who touched me? And he looked round about to see her that had done this thing. But the woman fearing and trembling, knowing what was done in her, came and fell down before him, and told him all the truth" (Mark 5:30-33).

Our Saviour did not ask, "Who touched me?" because he needed to learn who had done this, but because we need to learn the necessity of confessing Christ before men. "With the mouth confession is made unto salvation." This woman came and told the Saviour publicly, "all the truth". She told the Lord Jesus all about her plague, the power of his grace she experienced within, and the cure his omnipotent mercy had wrought.

"In the greatest throng, as well as in the secret place", Robert Hawker wrote, "Jesus sees all, knows all, and both appoints and will sanctify all ... We never can sufficiently admire the abundant tenderness the Lord Jesus manifested upon this occasion, to this poor woman. She wished the cure to be in secret: but no! Jesus will have her faith in him made public. His grace to poor sinners shall be proclaimed thereby; and, her trust in him shall make her history illustrious through endless generations."

It is not needful for us to blow the trumpet in the streets and force others to hear us when they choose not to listen. However, it is required that we identify ourselves with Christ and his gospel publicly. We must not be ashamed to confess Christ before men, both in believer's baptism and as his witnesses.

This woman's confession did not cause her to be healed any more than the believer's confession of Christ causes him to be saved. Our confession of faith in Christ is not a confession made that we might be saved, but a confession made of salvation granted. With our mouths we make confession with reference to the salvation Christ has bestowed.

The Commendation
"And he said unto her, Daughter, be of good comfort: thy faith hath made thee whole; go in peace" (v. 48). Here, our Lord Jesus declares the source of comfort. It is faith in him. He also commends faith, that great work of grace of which he is himself both the Object and the Author. Nothing brings such glory to Christ as that faith which looks to Christ for everything. Nothing is so useful to our souls as faith in Christ. The believer's life is a life of faith in Christ. We begin in faith, live by faith, stand in faith, walk by faith, have peace with God by faith, see the glory of God by faith, and die in faith. Nothing is so important as this "Dost thou believe on the Son of God?"

Yet, the primary object of this miracle is not the woman's great faith, but our blessed Saviour's great grace. Though at the time unknown to her, the faith she had in him was faith he had given her and had wrought in her by his Spirit (Colossians 2:12). Obviously, the poor soul thought she had escaped the notice of all; as soon as she touched him, the Master let her know that he both knew her need and performed her cure.

Let this be a point of personal self-examination for each of us. Is my faith real? Do I really believe on the Lord Jesus Christ? Is this gift of God mine?

"Who Touched Me?"

"And, behold, there came a man named Jairus, and he was a ruler of the synagogue: and he fell down at Jesus' feet, and besought him that he would come into his house: For he had one only daughter, about twelve years of age, and she lay a dying. But as he went the people thronged him.

And a woman having an issue of blood twelve years, which had spent all her living upon physicians, neither could be healed of any, Came behind him, and touched the border of his garment: and immediately her issue of blood stanched. And Jesus said, Who touched me? When all denied, Peter and they that were with him said, Master, the multitude throng thee and press thee, and sayest thou, Who touched me? And Jesus said, Somebody hath touched me: for I perceive that virtue is gone out of me. And when the woman saw that she was not hid, she came trembling, and falling down before him, she declared unto him before all the people for what cause she had touched him, and how she was healed immediately. And he said unto her, Daughter, be of good comfort: thy faith hath made thee whole; go in peace.

While he yet spake, there cometh one from the ruler of the synagogue's house, saying to him, Thy daughter is dead; trouble not the Master. But when Jesus heard it, he answered him, saying, Fear not: believe only, and she shall be made whole. And when he came into the house, he suffered no man to go in, save Peter, and James, and John, and the father and the mother of the maiden. And all wept, and bewailed her: but he said, Weep not; she is not dead, but sleepeth. And they laughed him to scorn, knowing that she was dead. And he put them all out, and took her by the hand, and called, saying, Maid, arise. And her spirit came again, and she arose straightway: and he commanded to give her meat. And her parents were astonished: but he charged them that they should tell no man what was done" (Luke 8:41-54).

Chapter 51

"Maid, Arise"

The two miracles described in this passage are deliberately blended together by the Spirit of God for our learning and consolation. Who can imagine what a great trial it must have been to Jairus' faith to see the Lord Jesus stopped by the woman? What fears must have risen in his heart! His need was urgent. His daughter was dying. He must have been completely distraught. Yet, the Lord Jesus stopped to heal a poor woman before going to heal his dying child. Often, that is exactly what the Lord Jesus does with us. He seldom answers our prayers immediately or in the way we expect. He requires us to trust him to do what is best. Jairus did just that. What compassion he showed! What patience he exercised! What self-denial he exemplified! What faith he practised!

I do not doubt that all the time the events recorded in verses 43-48 were going on, Jairus was thinking about his dying child. Yet, he said nothing. He just waited patiently before the Lord Jesus, trusting that he who had moved toward his daughter would heal his daughter in his time. Then, while the Lord Jesus was still talking to the woman, "there cometh one from the ruler of the synagogue's house, saying to him, Thy daughter is dead; trouble not the Master."

Yet, Jairus continued to look to the Lord Jesus. What a great miracle of mercy, love, and grace the Master performed for this needy soul who believed him! His dead daughter was raised to life by the power of the Saviour's word. Death is called, "The King of Terrors". But here is One who is mightier than the king of terrors. The Son of God, our Lord Jesus Christ is he who has the keys of death and hell in his hands. He who is the Resurrection and the Life vanquished death by his death and rose again as our Substitute. Soon, he will "swallow up death in victory" (Isaiah 25:8); and, just as he raised this young girl from death to life, he will raise all the hosts of God's elect from death and the grave to everlasting life in resurrection glory.

Vanity

The first thing demonstrated most clearly in this passage is the utter vanity of all earthly, material things. "Vanity of vanities, all is vanity! saith the preacher." Those are not the words of a frustrated, grumpy old man, but the words of the wisest, mere mortal ever to walk the face of God's earth. When Solomon considered all the things a man can possess and enjoy in this world of time and space, in this present state of things, he said, all earthly, material things are utterly vain and meaningless.

Jairus was, in all likelihood, a man of political power and influence, and of considerable wealth. He was "a ruler of the synagogue". Yet, his daughter, his only daughter lay dying. The apple of his eye, the darling of his heart was dying; and she was only twelve years old. Go ask Jairus, "How important is money? How useful is power, influence and fame? If the world were yours for the asking, what would you want now?" He would tell you, I want only one thing. I want the Son of God. I want him to come under my roof, to visit my family, to have mercy upon my only dear, dying daughter. Nothing else matters.

I wonder if we will ever learn that nothing here is really of any value, significance, or importance. "The things which are seen are temporal"! Everything here is temporal. Be wise. "Set your affection on things above, not on things on the earth." Let us ever beware of the "cares of this world, the deceitfulness of riches and the lusts of other things"! Let us value nothing in this world more highly now than we will value it when we stand before God.

Death

This passage also demonstrates the certainty and universality of sorrow, sickness and death. Jairus' daughter was only twelve years old. Yet, she became ill and died. Sickness, sorrow and death are common things that believers must suffer, just as all other people do. Jairus was a believer, yet, his young, darling daughter was dying when he left home to seek the Lord's help; and she died while he was seeking that help that Christ alone could give.

Like Jairus' daughter, each of us must soon die. We will all die at the time appointed, by the means appointed, in the place appointed. For believers, death is a blessed rest. Our Lord said, concerning Jairus' daughter, "Weep not; she is not dead, but sleepeth" (v. 52). That is the same thing he said regarding Lazarus. In reality God's elect never die. Did not the Son of God say, "Whosoever liveth and believeth in me shall never die" (John 11:26)? Those who die in the Lord sleep in the arms of Jesus. Their bodies sleep in the earth; but they have entered into heavenly rest. Yet, for the unbeliever, death is the beginning of sorrow and woe everlasting.

Prayer

"Behold, there came a man named Jairus, and he was a ruler of the synagogue: and he fell down at Jesus' feet, and besought him that he would come into his house" (v. 41). Wherever there is true prayer in the heart of a man or woman before God, it has these five characteristics.

Prayer arises from a knowledge of the Lord Jesus Christ. Mark tells us that Jairus "saw him". Prayer bows to and worships Christ. Jairus "fell at his feet". True prayer is importunate. We read that Jairus "besought him greatly"! True prayer is always persevering, because it arises from a heartfelt, desperate need. "My little daughter lieth at the point of death." True prayer arises from a heart of faith in the Son of God. "I pray thee, come and lay thy hands on her, that she may be healed; and she shall live."

None of us knows, "what we should pray for as we ought" (Romans 8:26). We never know what is best. None of us knows what is best for the glory of God, the good of our own souls, or the accomplishment of God's purpose of grace in Christ. Because we do not know what is best, we do not know how to pray for anything as we ought.

Prayer is not for the gratification of our carnal lusts. It is not the means by which we obtain what we want from the Lord. Prayer, true prayer, involves submission to the will of God. It is the cry of the believer's heart to his heavenly Father to do what is right and best. If I am God's child, if truly I know him and trust him, I want what he has purposed. I bow to him, surrendering my will to his will, my desires to his purpose, my pleasure to his glory, knowing that his will is best. Therefore, when we pray (in our ignorance), the Holy Spirit cleans up our prayers and presents to the Father the true groanings of our hearts (Romans 8:26).

Jairus demonstrates this spirit and attitude in this passage. He had come to the Lord Jesus seeking that his daughter might not die. When he heard that she had died, he continued trusting the Saviour, bowing to his will.

God's Requirement

Verses 49 and 50 show us what our God requires of us. The one thing that God requires and demands of us is faith. I am fully aware that faith is the gift of God and the operation of his grace in us. Yet, faith is what he requires of us. He requires that we "only believe".

"While he yet spake, there cometh one from the ruler of the synagogue's house, saying to him, Thy daughter is dead; trouble not the Master. But when Jesus heard it, he answered him, saying, Fear not: believe only, and she shall be made whole."

If we would be saved, the Lord Jesus says, "only believe". If we would honour God, his command is "only believe". If we would see the Lord God work, he says, "only believe". If we would see the glory of God, we must "only believe". In John 11:40 we read, "If thou wouldest believe, thou shouldest see the glory of God."

In all our exercises of faith, if the Lord seems to give no gracious answer to prayer, if he brings us into trials, when our hearts appear cold and dead and our spirits languish, let us remember Jairus, and look still to our blessed Saviour. It is one thing to trust the Son of God when things appear hopeful; but it is something else to trust him when everything appears hopeless.

With regard to our own selves, when we most feel and know our own impotence before God, the depravity of our hearts, and the corruption of our souls, when we feel utterly dead before him, it is a good thing to have "the sentence of death in ourselves, that we should not trust in ourselves, but in God which raiseth the dead" (1 Corinthians 1:9). In such times let us rejoice to trust him who says to our souls, "I am the resurrection, and the life: he that believeth in me, though he were dead, yet shall he live: And whosoever liveth and believeth in me shall never die" (John 11:25, 26).

Omnipotent Christ

Surely the Holy Spirit inspired Luke to record this to remind us our Lord is the omnipotent God to whom alone "belong the issues from death" (Psalm 68:20). "And he put them all out, and took her by the hand, and called, saying, Maid, arise. And her spirit came again, and she arose straightway: and he commanded to give her meat. And her parents were astonished: but he charged them that they should tell no man what was done" (vv. 54-56).

In this glorious miracle we are once more shown what Christ can do for dead sinners and how he does it. When God our Saviour saves a sinner, when he calls a sinner from spiritual death to life and faith by the power of his omnipotent grace, he secretly, sovereignly touches the dead soul by the hand of his irresistible mercy. He calls the chosen sinner by the power of his Spirit through his Word. The dead, being called by omnipotence, arises and comes to Christ. And everyone who sees it is astonished. The living sinner is astonished. The observant saints are astonished. And the confused religionists are astonished.

340

Christ's Provision
In verse 43 the Lord Jesus "commanded to give her meat". He said to those who stood by, "give her something to eat". Our blessed Saviour has provided and continually provides food for the souls of his children in this world, by which he sustains us in life and causes us to grow in his grace. To this end he has given his church pastors according to his own heart, called and gifted by his Spirit, to feed his people by the preaching of the gospel with knowledge and understanding (Jeremiah 3:15; Ephesians 4:8-16).

Resurrection
The resurrection of Jairus' daughter stands before us in the Book of God as a remarkable pledge of our own resurrection in the last day. As our Lord Jesus came to Jairus' house and raised his daughter from death to life, soon he shall come again to this earth and raise us up to glory (1 Corinthians 15:51-58; 1 Thessalonians 4:13-18).

"Then he called his twelve disciples together, and gave them power and authority over all devils, and to cure diseases. And he sent them to preach the kingdom of God, and to heal the sick. And he said unto them, Take nothing for your journey, neither staves, nor scrip, neither bread, neither money; neither have two coats apiece. And whatsoever house ye enter into, there abide, and thence depart. And whosoever will not receive you, when ye go out of that city, shake off the very dust from your feet for a testimony against them. And they departed, and went through the towns, preaching the gospel, and healing every where" (Luke 9:1-6).

Chapter 52

Are There Any Like These?

Here in Luke 9:1-6 the Lord Jesus Christ sent out his twelve disciples, the twelve apostles, as God's messengers to eternity bound men and women, to do the work of prophets. He sent them forth to preach the gospel. These twelve men were the first men to be sent forth in this gospel age as God's messengers to men. The instructions our Lord gave to these men tell us plainly what the work of the ministry is and what is expected of any man God puts into the work. In these six verses the Son of God tells those men he sends forth what men who speak to men in God's stead must be and do.

Divine Authority

Men who are sent of God to preach the gospel are men who possess a God given authority to do their work. "Then he called his twelve disciples together, and gave them power and authority over all devils, and to cure diseases" (v. 1). The power and authority with which God's messengers are endued is not trumped up authority and power, demagoguery or religious showmanship. Our Lord gives his messengers power and authority, power and authority by which they prevail over Satan, the influence of hell and the havoc of sin in the lives of men. What is this power and authority? The Word of God gives us, very clear answers to that question.

The power and authority Christ gives his servants is the power and authority of the gospel we preach (1 Thessalonians 1:2-5; Romans 1:15, 16; Hebrews 4:12; John 12:32).

It is the power and authority of the anointing and unction of God the Holy Spirit upon the man by whom he speaks (1 Corinthians 2:1-5).

The power and authority by which God's servants preach is the power and authority that arises from confident faith (Galatians 1:11, 12; 2 Timothy 1:9-12).

This power and authority, which only God himself can give to a man, is the power and authority of true meekness (2 Timothy 2:25).

The meekness which gives God's servants the power and authority to do the work to which they are called is not the pretence of meekness that men display and pretend to admire, but the meekness of Noah in his generation, the meekness of Moses before Pharaoh, the meekness of Elijah on Mount Carmel, the meekness of John the Baptist before Herod, the meekness of Peter before the Sanhedrim, and the meekness of Paul at Jerusalem. Meekness is not an outward show of weakness and humility, but a humbling awareness that we are God's, that we belong to and serve the living God, a humbling awareness that we have a mandate from God himself. That gives a man power and authority. It is something only God can give.

Minister's Work

God's ministers are men who know their work and stick to it. "And he sent them to preach the kingdom of God, and to heal the sick" (v. 2). I am a preacher, nothing else, just a preacher. I do not pretend to know anything at all about any other man's work. I do not make any claim or pretence of being a man of learning, a theologian or historian. But I do know exactly what God has called me to do. I know exactly what my work and responsibilities are as a pastor and preacher. "The glorious gospel of the blessed God has been committed to my trust" (1 Timothy 1:11). It is a trust for which I am responsible. Therefore, I am determined, for the glory of God and the sake of the gospel, to let nothing and no one turn me aside from this great work. It is all-consuming. Basically, it is a work that demands three things.

Study. Incessant study! A man cannot preach who does not study. Let every man who calls himself a preacher addict himself to the study of holy scripture, ever seeking the message of God for his people.

Prayer. Fervent prayer! Preachers, true preachers, are men of prayer. They do not talk much about prayer, because they are ashamed of themselves in this area. While others talk piously about their "prayer lives", men of prayer ever beg the Lord to teach them to pray. Yet, they live in unceasing awareness of their utter dependence upon God, seeking grace to honour him, honour his Word and serve his people.

Preaching. Gospel preaching! Preachers preach. I know this will offend, but it must be said: God called men are preachers, not social workers, not counsellors, not promoters, not entertainers, but preachers! Sadly, many who pretend to be preachers really want to be priests. So they spend the bulk of their time visiting and counselling. Their offices are large confession booths in which they hear confessions of sin and prescribe deeds of penance. That is what people call "pastoral work". Not so! Pastoral work is study, prayer and preaching. The very reason the Lord gave his church deacons (Acts 16) to take care of routine affairs was that the preachers might give themselves relentlessly to study, prayer and preaching.

Pastoral Care
Those men who are called and sent of God to the great work of preaching the gospel are men who care for men. These twelve men went about serving and ministering to both the bodies and the souls of men, preaching the gospel to them and healing them. They made the needs of others their own. They hurt for those who hurt. They wept for those who wept. They carried in their hearts the burdens of those to whom they preached. If I am God's servant, if I am God's messenger to the souls of men, I do and I will care for them, their families and their needs, both spiritual needs and carnal needs (Romans 9:1-3; 10:1; 16:1-27).

Live By The Gospel
Men who are called, gifted, and sent of God to preach the gospel must live for the gospel and live by the gospel. "And he said unto them, Take nothing for your journey, neither staves, nor scrip, neither bread, neither money; neither have two coats apiece" (v. 3). Our Lord here specifically forbids his servants to provide a living for themselves (1 Corinthians 9:7-14). There is no scarcity of material in the Book of God regarding the financial support of the gospel ministry. It is a subject which appears again and again throughout the Bible. This is the universal doctrine of Scripture.

Under the Mosaic economy of the Old Testament those who ministered about the holy things of divine service lived upon the things of the temple. Those who served the altar were partakers of the altar (1 Corinthians 9:13). God prescribed by law that the priesthood, the children of Levi, should receive a tenth of all the possessions of the children of Israel, a tenth of their money, property, crops and herds, for their service in the tabernacle of the congregation. The Jews were required to pay a tithe to be used exclusively for the financial support of the ministry of the Levitical priesthood (Numbers 18:21). Failure to do so, for any reason, was regarded as robbing God himself (Malachi 3:8, 9).

However, we are not under the law today. God's people are no more required to pay a tithe in this gospel age than we are required to keep the sabbath day or observe the Passover (Colossians 2:16-23). We are free from the law. A. D. Muse, the late pastor of Hearts Harbor Tabernacle in Louisville, Kentucky, used to say, "If you tithe, you're under the law; and if you don't tithe you're an outlaw." In other words, the person who just pays his tithe is a mere legalist; and anyone who does not do that much is an

345

antinomian. Anyone who uses his freedom from the law as an excuse for being a niggardly miser and selfishly refuses to give of his means for the support of the gospel of Christ is, I fear, without grace. God's people give. They give generously; and they give cheerfully.

The instructions given in the New Testament regarding the financial support of the gospel ministry are unmistakably clear. Those men and women who believe the gospel of the grace of God are expected to support generously those who preach it. Not only is this expected, among God's saints it is practised. God's children are not miserly, self-centred worldlings. They are stewards who use what God has put in their hands for the cause of Christ. They need only to be instructed from the Word of God, and they gladly submit to it.

Our Lord Jesus Christ tells us plainly and repeatedly that those who preach the gospel are to live by the gospel (Matthew 10:9, 10; Luke 10:4-7; 1 Timothy 5:17, 18). Those men who faithfully preach the gospel of God's free and sovereign grace in Christ are to be supported and maintained by the people to whom and for whom they labour in the Word. Faithful missionaries should be as fully and generously supported by the churches that send them out as the pastors of those local churches.

There were times when Paul and his companions were required to make tents to support themselves in the work of the gospel. It was an honourable thing for them to do so. Paul tells us that his goal was not to enrich himself, but to avoid being a burden to young churches (1 Thessalonians 2:9), and to avoid causing an offence to young, weak believers (1 Corinthians 9:15-19). But the fact that God's messenger had to spend his time and efforts making tents was a shameful reproach upon the churches. Those churches that were established in the gospel should have assumed the responsibility of supplying Paul's needs and the needs of his companions, as they travelled from place to place preaching the gospel. The New Testament clearly makes it the responsibility of every local church to provide for the financial, material support of those who preach the gospel of Christ.

Separated To God
God's messengers are men who care not for the world. They are separated unto God and separated unto the gospel. "And whatsoever house ye enter into, there abide, and thence depart" (v. 4). They are separated unto the gospel. They seek nothing for themselves: They seek neither their place of service, nor personal property, nor positions of prominence, nor recognition and fame. God's servants seek neither the approval of the world, nor the riches of the world. A minister of the gospel is content to serve God wherever God sends him. He is content to live and labour without recognition. A

preacher is content to live in this world as a stranger and pilgrim, passing through for only a brief time (Philippians 4:12, 13).

Undaunted Men
God's sent men are men undaunted by men. "And whosoever will not receive you, when ye go out of that city, shake off the very dust from your feet for a testimony against them" (v. 5). They seek to please God, not men. If their work appears to be in vain, they go on, knowing that their labour is not in vain in the Lord (1 Corinthians 15:58). They go on sowing the good seed, planting and watering as God enables them, knowing that it is God alone who gives the increase. They cast their bread upon the waters, knowing that it will return in due season. They preach the gospel faithfully, knowing that God's Word will not return to him void (Isaiah 55:11).

Used Of God
There are really only two kinds of preachers: those who use and those who are used. False prophets are preachers who use men for their own advantage. True prophets are preachers who are used of God for the benefit of his elect. "And they departed, and went through the towns, preaching the gospel, and healing every where" (v. 6). The Lord Jesus sent these men to preach the gospel; and they preached it everywhere. The Master sent them out to heal the sick; and they healed them. The Son of God sent these twelve men out to be a blessing to the world; and what a blessing they have been! May the Lord God give such men to his church again, for Christ's sake (2 Corinthians 4:1-7).

"Now Herod the tetrarch heard of all that was done by him: and he was perplexed, because that it was said of some, that John was risen from the dead; And of some, that Elias had appeared; and of others, that one of the old prophets was risen again. And Herod said, John have I beheaded: but who is this, of whom I hear such things? And he desired to see him. And the apostles, when they were returned, told him all that they had done. And he took them, and went aside privately into a desert place belonging to the city called Bethsaida. And the people, when they knew it, followed him: and he received them, and spake unto them of the kingdom of God, and healed them that had need of healing" (Luke 9:7-11).

Chapter 53

"Who Is This?"

When he had heard of the great works Christ had done, Herod asked, "Who is this, of whom I hear such things?" All believers rest the hopes of their immortal souls upon the fact that Jesus of Nazareth is the Christ. We believe that Jesus is the Christ (1 John 5:1). He is the Foundation upon which we have built our hopes of eternal life. We believe that Jesus of Nazareth is the Christ, the Messiah, promised by God in all the Old Testament prophets.

Peter's confession, "Thou art the Christ, the Son of the living God" (Matthew 16:16), is the foundation of the entire Christian world, the church of God, and the gospel of God. If Jesus of Nazareth is not the Christ, the Messiah promised in the Old Testament scriptures, he is not the Son of God. If Jesus of Nazareth is not the Christ, his obedience to God is of no benefit to us. If Jesus of Nazareth is not the Christ, his death upon the cross has no saving virtue and we are yet in our sins. If Jesus of Nazareth is not the Christ, if he is not the Messiah, if he is not God incarnate, he was the slickest, most devious charlatan who ever lived.

Our faith says, "We believe and are sure that thou art the Christ, the Son of the living God" (John 6:69). But are you really sure? There have been many others who claimed to be Christ, the Messiah, the Son of God, the Saviour of the world. Perhaps it would be good for us to ask of Jesus what John the Baptist asked of him "Art thou he that should come, or do we look for another?" (Matthew 11:3). Herod asked, "Who is this?"

Suppose you were witnessing to a Jew and he said to you, "Show me from the Old Testament scriptures that the Jesus you worship is the Messiah." Could you do it? I want to show you from the Old Testament scriptures that Jesus of Nazareth, the son of Joseph and Mary, who was crucified at Jerusalem more than two thousand years ago, is indeed the Christ, the Son of the living God.

To answer Herod's question, look first at Psalm 40:6-8. "Sacrifice and offering thou didst not desire; mine ears hast thou opened: burnt offering and sin offering hast thou not required. Then said I, Lo, I come: in the volume of the book it is written of me, I delight to do thy will, O my God: yea, thy law is within my heart." It is impossible to honestly apply these words to anyone but the Messiah. Indeed, the Jewish commentators from ancient times have said that this Psalm is a messianic prophecy. And, of course, the Apostle declares in the Book of Hebrews (10:5-10) that this prophecy is fulfilled in the Person and work of Jesus of Nazareth. In these three verses the Prophet David tells us four things which will identify the true Messiah of Israel. These four things find their fulfilment only in Jesus Christ our Lord. Here David tells us that when the Christ, the Messiah comes ...

(1.) The sacrifices and ceremonies of legal worship will cease. (2.) He will be Jehovah's voluntary Servant. (3.) The body of scripture prophecy will be fulfilled. (4.) He will perfectly accomplish the will of God.

Search the scriptures and see for yourself that the types, promise, and prophecies of the Old Testament scriptures weave a garment that is tailor made to fit only one man. That man is the Messiah, the Christ, the Son of God. And that man is our Saviour, the Lord Jesus.

The End Of The Law
First, David tells us that when the Messiah has come all the sacrifices and ceremonies of legal worship would cease. "Sacrifice and offering thou didst not desire." The sacrifices, ceremonies and laws of the Mosaic economy were never intended to be a means of salvation. God never had pleasure and satisfaction in them. They could not remove sin, satisfy justice or make men righteous before God (Hebrews 10:1-10). The sacrifices and ceremonies of the law were only useful as types and shadows of Christ to show the nature and necessity of his redemptive work. Once they were fulfilled they must cease to be, because they have no other service.

The law given by Moses was designed by God to identify and expose sin, to deter men from deeds of iniquity, and to show the necessity of a Substitute. Once the law had served its purpose, since it has been fulfilled by Christ, it has no other use and has ceased to have power over men (Romans 10:4).

The Old Testament scriptures constantly reminded the Jews that God had no regard for their sacrifices and ceremonies except as they typified Christ and were observed by faith in him.

"And Samuel said, Hath the LORD as great delight in burnt offerings and sacrifices, as in obeying the voice of the LORD? Behold, to obey is better than sacrifice, and to hearken than the fat of rams" (1 Samuel 15:22).

"Hear, O my people, and I will speak; O Israel, and I will testify against thee: I am God, even thy God. I will not reprove thee for thy sacrifices or thy burnt offerings, to have been continually before me. I will take no bullock out of thy house, nor he goats out of thy folds. For every beast of the forest is mine, and the cattle upon a thousand hills. I know all the fowls of the mountains: and the wild beasts of the field are mine. If I were hungry, I would not tell thee: for the world is mine, and the fulness thereof. Will I eat the flesh of bulls, or drink the blood of goats?" (Psalm 50:7-13).

"For thou desirest not sacrifice; else would I give it: thou delightest not in burnt offering. The sacrifices of God are a broken spirit: a broken and a contrite heart, O God, thou wilt not despise" (Psalm 51:16, 17).

"To what purpose is the multitude of your sacrifices unto me? saith the LORD: I am full of the burnt offerings of rams, and the fat of fed beasts; and I delight not in the blood of bullocks, or of lambs, or of he goats. When ye come to appear before me, who hath required this at your hand, to tread my courts? Bring no more vain oblations; incense is an abomination unto me; the new moons and sabbaths, the calling of assemblies, I cannot away with; it is iniquity, even the solemn meeting. Your new moons and your appointed feasts my soul hateth: they are a trouble unto me; I am weary to bear them" (Isaiah 1:11-14).

"And he shall confirm the covenant with many for one week: and in the midst of the week he shall cause the sacrifice and the oblation to cease, and for the overspreading of abominations he shall make it desolate, even until the consummation, and that determined shall be poured upon the desolate" (Daniel 9:27).

These five passages from the Old Testament scriptures, read without comment, demonstrate clearly that the sacrifices and ceremonies of legal worship were never intended to be perpetual. They were only temporary pictures of Christ. Even the Mosaic covenant, as set forth in what we commonly call "The Ten Commandments", was only designed to be a temporary covenant (Jeremiah 31:31-34; cf. Hebrews 8:7-13). The law of God as a covenant, a rule of life and the revelation of God's righteous requirements from men was designed to lead us to Christ, by whom it is fulfilled (Galatians 3:24, 25). And when Christ came, the sacrifices and ceremonies of the Old Testament did cease to be observed.

David, at least a thousand years before Christ came, intimated that when he came, he would accomplish that which no sacrifice, ceremony, or law could accomplish (redemption, justification, righteousness and forgiveness). The laws, sacrifices, and ceremonies of Israel were only scaffolding, temporarily necessary for the building of his kingdom, but now removed. All the Jewish sacrifices and ceremonies ceased to have significance when Christ died. And all ceased to exist when God destroyed both Jerusalem and Judaism in 70 A.D. The priesthood ceased. The temple ceased. The sacrifices ceased. The nation ceased!

Here is the first evidence that Jesus of Nazareth is the Christ, the Messiah. When he finished his work, the sacrifices and ceremonies of legal worship ceased. To demonstrate it, the veil of the temple was ripped apart. "And, behold, the veil of the temple was rent in twain from the top to the bottom; and the earth did quake, and the rocks rent" (Matthew 27:51). Though the Jews look for a future Messiah and deny that Jesus is the Christ, their hopes are as foolish as they are vain. How could this prophecy be fulfilled again?

Jehovah's Servant

Second, David shows us that the Messiah, the Christ, must be a man who is Jehovah's voluntary Servant (Exodus 21:1-6). The Lord Jesus Christ came into this world and performed his work as the voluntary Servant of his Father (Isaiah 42:1-4; 50:5-7; Hebrews 10:5-7; John 10:16-18; Luke 12:50).

He who is Jehovah's voluntary Servant is Jehovah's equal! All angels, men, creatures, devils and events must serve God, because he is the Creator of all things. All rational beings are morally obligated to serve God, because we live upon his bounty. But Christ came to serve the Father voluntarily. He owed nothing and had nothing to gain, for he is himself Jehovah. That Man who is the Christ is himself God (Psalm 45:6, 7).

Jehovah's Servant came into the world with a specific mission to accomplish (Matthew 1:21). Throughout the Old Testament scriptures, Messiah was promised, looked for and trusted as that One who would come to restore his fallen people to the everlasting favour of God, by putting away their sins (Isaiah 61:1-3; Luke 4:18). Either Jesus of Nazareth has effectually redeemed and saved God's elect, or he is not the Christ. The Christ of Arminian, freewill religion is a false christ. We know he is, because Messiah's eternal glory and exaltation is dependent and conditioned upon the success of his redemptive, saving work (Psalms 2:7, 8; 65:4; 110:3). The Lord God declares of his righteous Servant, whom he chose to be our Saviour, "he shall not fail"! (Isaiah 42:4). And fail he will not (John 6:37-40; 10:16; Hebrews 10:10).

352

Prophecy Fulfilled

Third, the Prophet David assured us that when the Christ, the Messiah, has come, the volume of scripture prophecy would be fulfilled. "Then said I, Lo, I come: in the volume of the book it is written of me." These words, "the volume of the book", may refer to the book of God's secret, eternal decrees (Revelation 5:1; 10:2); but they certainly refer to the written revelation of God contained in the Old Testament scriptures.

The writings of the Old Testament prophets abound in predictions of the Messiah, the Christ. God promised Abraham, "In thy seed shall all the nations of the earth be blessed." When Jacob blessed the tribe of Judah, he spoke of Shiloh to whom the gathering of the people would be. Moses spoke of that Prophet whom the Lord God would raise up, whom the people of God would hear. In the Psalms and the prophets Messiah is given a variety of titles: "The Anointed of the Lord", "The King", "David's Lord", "The Child Born", "The Son Given", "The Mighty God", "The Everlasting Father", "The Prince of Peace", "God's Servant Whom He Upholds", "Messiah the Prince", "God's Elect In Whom He Delights", "The Branch", "The Lord Our Righteousness", "The Messenger Of The Covenant".

All these names and titles belong to the Messiah. But are they all fulfilled in Jesus of Nazareth? If they are, then he is the Christ. If they are not, we must look for another. The prophecies of the Old Testament give us eight specific things which must characterize the Messiah. By these eight things, the Christ is identified. And these eight things can be, with honesty, applied to no man in history, past or future, except Jesus of Nazareth, who is indeed the Christ, the Son of the living God.

1. The time of Messiah's coming was clearly marked out in prophecy. God told no one the day and hour when Christ would come. But he did identify the time in history. Those looking forward to the coming of Christ could not predict it. But those looking back cannot mistake it. Christ has come! The coming of Messiah must fit into a very specific time frame. It had to be before the destruction of civil government in Judah (Genesis 49:10), but while the temple was still standing in Jerusalem (Haggai 2:6-9). Messiah had to appear about the middle of Daniel's 70th week (Daniel 9:24-27), which would be 453-457 years after the rebuilding of the Temple at Jerusalem began (33 A.D.), the year that Christ died (Daniel 9:24-27). Thirty-seven years later (70 A.D.) Jerusalem was destroyed. The Messiah had to come into the world during the time that Jesus of Nazareth lived upon the earth. He could not have come at any other time.

2. The place where Messiah would be born was plainly foretold. "But thou, Bethlehem Ephratah, (not Zebulon, but Ephratah!) though thou be little among the thousands of Judah, yet out of thee shall he come forth unto me

that is to be ruler in Israel; whose goings forth have been from of old, from everlasting" (Micah 5:2).

3. The family from which Messiah must come was the house of David (Psalm 132:11; Isaiah 11:1). The Jews debated about many things. But they never questioned the genealogy of the Lord Jesus.

4. Furthermore, all the miracles performed by the Lord Jesus declare him to be the Messiah, the Christ, the Son of David (Isaiah 29:18; 35:5, 6; 42:6, 7; Matthew 11:2-4).

5. The Messiah must be one who comes as a King distinguished by his humiliation, meekness and lowliness (Zechariah 9:9; Matthew 21:1-9).

6. It was prophesied that the Messiah must suffer and die by the hands of wicked men. "Messiah shall be cut off, but not for himself" (Daniel 9:26; Isaiah 53:1-12). Our Lord's tormenters used the very words and performed the very deeds he had predicted by his prophets (see Psalm 22). Those words which describe the betrayal, shame, crucifixion and death of the Christ could find fulfilment only in the death of Jesus of Nazareth.

7. The scriptures declared plainly that Messiah would rise from the dead before his body had begun to decay (Psalm 16:9-11; Isaiah 53:10-12).

8. And the prophets plainly asserted that Messiah, the Christ, would set up his kingdom among the Gentiles by the outpouring of his Spirit upon them (Isaiah 49:5, 6; Joel 2:28-32; Galatians 3:13, 14).

Here are the prophecies given by David and fulfilled by Jesus of Nazareth, by which we know and are sure that Jesus is the Christ, the Son of the living God: he put an end to the sacrifices and ceremonies of legal worship by fulfilling them. He came into the world as Jehovah's voluntary Servant. He fulfilled the volume of Old Testament prophecy to the letter.

God's Will Performed

But I have saved the best until the last. Here is the greatest, most blessed assurance we have. By this, above all else, we know that Jesus our Saviour is the Christ. David tells us that the Christ, the Messiah, whoever he is, will perfectly accomplish the will of God. "I delight to do thy will, O my God: yea, thy law is within my heart."

When the Lord Jesus came into this world, he came with delight to do his Father's will. He delighted in that of which God approves. He delighted in that which God had appointed. And the law of God was in his heart, so that both inwardly and outwardly, he was perfectly holy, harmless, undefiled and separate from sin. He knew no sin!

We know that Jesus is Christ, the Son of the living God, because he perfectly performed all the precepts of God's revealed will in the law. He brought in an everlasting righteousness. He freely yielded himself to all the performances of God's providential will. His life showed his heart's desire and determination, which he spoke in Gethsemane, "Not my will, thy will be done"! Our Lord Jesus made complete satisfaction and propitiation to God's justice, satisfying the penalty of the law. And in doing these things he accomplished the complete salvation of God's elect (Hebrews 10:5-14).

Christ came to do the Father's will. He came to save his people. And he has done it. We know that Jesus is the Christ, because God accepted his work (Romans 1:9, 10; 8:32-34; 1 John 5:1).

"Who is this?" Jesus is the Christ. We know he is because he has fulfilled all that God said the Messiah would do. He put an end to legal sacrifices and ceremonies. He came as a voluntary Saviour. He accomplished all the prophecies. He performed all the will of God. We who believe know that Jesus is the Christ, because he has been revealed in us by the power of his Spirit in saving grace; and his blood, applied to our hearts, has purged our consciences of guilt before God. We prove his Divinity, Messiahship, and Saving Power by faith. We trust him. "We believe and are sure that thou art that Christ, the Son of the living God" (John 6:69).

"Now Herod the tetrarch heard of all that was done by him: and he was perplexed, because that it was said of some, that John was risen from the dead; And of some, that Elias had appeared; and of others, that one of the old prophets was risen again. And Herod said, John have I beheaded: but who is this, of whom I hear such things? And he desired to see him. And the apostles, when they were returned, told him all that they had done. And he took them, and went aside privately into a desert place belonging to the city called Bethsaida. And the people, when they knew it, followed him: and he received them, and spake unto them of the kingdom of God, and healed them that had need of healing" (Luke 9:7-11).

Chapter 54

Healing For All Who Need It

A Guilty Conscience

"Now Herod the tetrarch heard of all that was done by him: and he was perplexed, because that it was said of some, that John was risen from the dead" (v. 7). It is hard to live with a guilty conscience. The wise man tells us, "The way of the transgressor is hard" (Proverbs 13:15). Nothing on earth is more persistently tormenting to a man than a guilty conscience. This is what Herod discovered.

Herod was a powerful, wealthy, influential man; but the news of our Lord's ministry and the great power of God he demonstrated caused that "great" man to tremble like a child. His guilty conscience caused him to imagine things that terrified him. His numerous guards and fortified palace could not secure him from the fears stirred in his soul by a tormenting conscience.

Though he was surrounded by everything the world thinks will make life easy and enjoyable, Herod was a miserable man. The report of a preacher of righteousness reminded him of that great Prophet's forerunner and filled him with terror. The remembrance of his sin in murdering John the Baptist was a burning fire in his soul that he could not quench. He saw the Baptist's head on a charger day and night; and he could not get it out of his sight. He could not put it out of his mind.

Herod's sin found him out. The prison and the sword had silenced the Baptist's tongue; but they could not silence his voice. It kept ringing in Herod's ears, reverberating through his soul and screaming in his conscience. At this very hour, in hell Herod is still tormented by the memory of that preacher of righteousness whom he refused to hear, whom he beheaded. Here are three mighty, instructive lessons to be learned from this single verse of holy scripture.

God's truth can never be bound or silenced. The preaching of the gospel will either bring forth fruit unto life eternal in your soul, or it will be the fire of hell in your soul forever. It will be to you either a savour of life unto life or of death unto death; but you will not silence God's Word (2 Corinthians 2:14-16).

Your conscience is the undying echo of God's holy law in your soul. Mock and laugh if you dare; but you know that is the truth. You may never acknowledge it this side of eternity; but you do not even question that fact. You know it is so. Your conscience is the undying echo of God's holy law in your soul. Conscience is the most powerful part of our constitution as moral creatures. Conscience cannot save us. Conscience can never bring anyone to Christ. Every man's conscience is, by reason of sin, blind, ignorant and misdirected. Yet, the conscience raises a loud testimony and protest in the soul against sin. It makes the guilty soul uneasy. It causes the transgressor to tremble. It is the consciousness of guilt and sin that causes all men to fear death, judgment and eternity.

Untold millions will testify in the last day that Herod's experience is their own. Their consciences will call their old sins out of their graves, parade them around in their hearts, and cause them to burn as unquenchable fire in their souls and gnaw as undying death worms upon their hearts!

There is only one cure for a guilty conscience: the blood of Christ! Nothing can satisfy my conscience except that which satisfies the law and justice of God. Nothing can quieten my screaming conscience but the perfect righteousness and blood atonement of the Lord Jesus Christ. But, blessed be God, his blood satisfies and silences the screams of my guilty conscience. Indeed, his blood compels my conscience to declare me justified (Hebrews 9:11-14).

"And of some, that Elias had appeared; and of others, that one of the old prophets was risen again" (v. 8). Elijah, Isaiah, Jeremiah and Malachi had all been dead for hundreds of years; but they being dead continued to speak. Their voices could not be silenced. Though Herod was a pagan, though the Jews did not believe them, though the Gentiles held them in utter contempt, those prophets still troubled those who lived as rebels against God.

That old heathen, Herod, when his guard was down, acknowledged as matters of fact that he could not deny the resurrection of the dead and the everlasting immortality of his soul. Eternal life and eternal death are things inscribed upon every soul. You may pretend it is all fiction; but when guilt rises in your soul and your conscience screams at the prospect of death, try as you may, you will never convince yourself that eternity is a myth.

"And Herod said, John have I beheaded: but who is this, of whom I hear such things? And he desired to see him" (v. 9). He whom John the Baptist had declared to be the Lamb of God, the Messiah, the Christ, the King of Israel, now began to make himself known as the incarnate God, of whom all the prophets spoke; and Herod was terrified. The Lord Jesus verified John's ministry so plainly that Herod trembled when he heard of Christ's doctrine, his miracles and his divine authority.

An Accounting

"And the apostles, when they were returned, told him all that they had done" (v. 10). The Master had sent these men out to preach the gospel. When their work was done, they returned to him and gave an account of all that they had done in his name: the doctrine they preached, the methods they employed, the people who received their word and those who received them not. Soon, we shall do the same. The hour is coming when we shall return to him who sent us out to serve in his kingdom and give an account.

"And he took them, and went aside privately into a desert place belonging to the city called Bethsaida" (v. 10). Let us learn what is set before us here. Those who labour for the glory of Christ, the interests of his kingdom, the furtherance of his gospel and the souls of men must be careful that they make time to be alone with God themselves. This is essential to our spiritual health and well being. If we neglect our own souls, we will soon be compelled to weep with bitter sorrow, "They made me keeper of the vineyards, but my own vineyard have I not kept" (Song of Solomon 1:6).

Laziness is an abominable thing. It is utterly reprehensible for men and women to spend their lives in idleness and leisure. Gospel preachers, particularly, ought to devote themselves to the work of the ministry, to study, to prayer, to preaching, to the furtherance of the gospel. But, we must not neglect our own souls; and we must be careful not to neglect God's appointed means of grace: public worship, the preaching of the gospel, personal reading and study of the scriptures, private meditation, prayer and communion with our God

At times, I find it necessary to put my books and my pen down, push back from my desk, perhaps go for a drive, take a walk, or even get away from things for a day or two, to make earnest inquiries of my heart. "Where are you?" "What are you doing?" "Why are you doing this?" Blessed are those Christ Jesus takes "privately into a desert place", that he might minister to their souls' needs.

The Kingdom Of God

"And the people, when they knew it, followed him: and he received them, and spake unto them of the kingdom of God, and healed them that had need of healing" (v. 11). What a tender, gracious man our Saviour was as he walked on this earth. He was tired. He had laboured feverishly. He had now come aside with his disciples for some much needed rest. Yet, when the people followed him, pouring out their hearts' needs, waiting to hear his word, "he received them". May God give me grace to imitate my Master!

"He spake unto them of the kingdom of God." If you read through the four gospels again and read them with care, you cannot fail to see that this was always the subject of our Lord's ministry in public and in private. He spoke of the spiritual nature of the kingdom of God. He proclaimed the gospel of the kingdom of God. He declared salvation to be nothing less than the establishment of God's rule in our hearts. Faith in Christ is nothing less than the voluntary surrender of ourselves to his dominion as our Lord and King. It is the willing surrender of our lives to him (Luke 9:24).

Healing For All Who Need Healing
Next we read that the Son of God graciously "healed them that had need of healing". It is true, he will neither break the bruised reed, nor quench the smoking flax. But this text says more. Our Saviour "healed them that had need of healing". I take that to mean this: the Son of God is gracious to all who need grace, heals all who need healing and saves all who need saving.

On this occasion, there was not a single soul in the presence of Christ who needed that healing which he alone could give who was not healed by him. The extremity of the cases did not baffle him. The multitude of needs did not diminish his supply of grace. The weakness and inabilities of the multitude to assist in their healing did not prevent them from being healed. Be sure you understand the meaning of this: there is still healing for all who need it in Christ!

Our Saviour's name is Jehovah-Rapha "The LORD that healeth thee"! There is no lack of saving power and grace in him. There is no want of ability with the Almighty. Do you need healing in your soul? Many like you have been healed by the Lord Jesus. Somewhere in the Word of God you will find another just like you who was healed by the Son of God. Are you full of great, horrible wickedness? Did not the Lord Jesus cast seven devils out of Mary Magdalene? Perhaps your wickedness seems to be greater than even seven devils. Did he not drive a whole legion of devils out of the demoniac of the Gadarene? You may find that you cannot pray, but he healed one possessed of a dumb devil. Are you hardened and insensible? He cast out a deaf devil. Maybe you think you cannot believe. I assure you that you cannot. Neither could that man with the withered arm stretch out his arm, but he did it when the Son of God said, "Stretch forth thy hand." He can give you faith. Though you are dead in sin, the Lord Jesus can heal still. He raises the dead! Your case is no match for his grace. The Lord Jesus has conquered the like before many times. I know that the Lord Jesus can heal you, because in all the history of the world there is no record of a solitary soul who came to him for healing who was not healed. His promise is sure. "Him that cometh to me, I will in no wise cast out."

There is no question that he can heal you, for this Man is himself God Almighty. He is God come to save. He came here specifically to bind up the broken hearted. Pause and consider all that he has done for the healing of sinners. He earned the authority to exercise almighty grace by his Mediatoral accomplishments (John 17:2).

I know that the Lord Jesus can heal you. I have no question about that, because he has healed and is healing me. The only question to be answered is this: do you need healing? If you do, if you need healing, he will heal you. If you need grace, he will give it. If you need mercy, he will bestow it. If you need saving, he will save you.

The Lord Jesus still heals all that need healing. If you believe on the Lord Jesus Christ, your faith in him is the gift of his grace to you and in you. He has healed you of your soul's disease. You are born of God. You cannot perish.

I once read the story of a man who had been condemned to die by a Spanish court. In the first week of September in 1869 he stood before a firing squad. All appeals on his behalf had been denied. The United States government declared that the Spanish courts had no power to try him, much less execute him. But the Spanish were determined to carry out their sentence. On the day he was to die, the Ambassador of the United States walked out onto the field between the condemned man and his executioners. He wrapped the condemned man in an American flag and defiantly said to the marksmen, "Fire if you dare. If you defy the nation represented by that flag, you will bring all the fury and power of the United States of America upon you." There stood the man. Before him were the executioners of death. A single shot would have been his death. But wrapped in the stars and stripes, he was as completely invulnerable as if he had been wrapped in a coat of steel.

It is thus with every believer. The Lord Jesus Christ has wrapped us in the blood red flag of Calvary, and before God's holy law can pierce that flag, it must declare the blood of Christ null and void; and that shall never be! There is healing for all who need it in Christ Jesus, our Lord.

"And when the day began to wear away, then came the twelve, and said unto him, Send the multitude away, that they may go into the towns and country round about, and lodge, and get victuals: for we are here in a desert place. But he said unto them, Give ye them to eat. And they said, We have no more but five loaves and two fishes; except we should go and buy meat for all this people. For they were about five thousand men. And he said to his disciples, Make them sit down by fifties in a company. And they did so, and made them all sit down. Then he took the five loaves and the two fishes, and looking up to heaven, he blessed them, and brake, and gave to the disciples to set before the multitude. And they did eat, and were all filled: and there was taken up of fragments that remained to them twelve baskets" (Luke 9:12-17).

Chapter 55

Two Fish, Five Loaves
And Five Thousand To Dine

This passage gives us Luke's inspired account of our Lord's great miracle of feeding five thousand men with five pieces of bread and two small fish. This miracle is recorded more frequently and more fully than any of our Lord's other miracles. Matthew, Mark, Luke, and John were all inspired to record it. Evidently, the Holy Spirit intends for us to give it special attention.

The Holy Spirit inspired all the gospel writers to record these stories of our Lord's dealings with men upon the earth so that we might read them often, study them carefully, and learn from them continually. His miracles have not yet been fathomed. His words and his ways have not yet been comprehended. Like the cloud that Elijah's servant saw (1 Kings 18:44), these gospel stories seem to get bigger and bigger every time we look at them. Like the widow's barrel of meal, there is an inexhaustible fullness of spiritual instruction in this holy Book. I read a lot of books. Most of them can be comprehended with one or two careful readings. But the more I read the Word of God, the more I am lost in the richness, fullness, and freshness of it.

I have said all that because I want you to realize that when I have finished this study, there will be much more that needs to be said. I will have only scratched the surface of this deep, deep mine. Having scratched around the surface of this rich mine, I have found five, choice nuggets of gold that I want to show you.

Nothing Impossible

First, this passage gives us a display of the fact that with God our Saviour nothing is impossible. Oh, how I wish I could learn this, really learn it. With God nothing is impossible. Our Lord Jesus Christ, he who is God our Saviour is God omnipotent! By the mere exercise of his will, he fed 5000 men with five pieces of bread and two small fish.

This is not a fable, or even a parable, or an allegory. This great miracle was performed in public before thousands. That same divine power that created all things out of nothing in the beginning, here made food where there was none.

This was not the trickery of some snake oil huckster, nor the work of some make believe miracle worker. Nothing except the fact that Jesus Christ is God can explain this great deed. Five thousand hungry men would not have said they were full had they still been hungry. Twelve baskets of fragments would not have been left over had any of the men remained hungry. The very same hand that sent quails in the wilderness, rained manna from heaven and caused water to gush forth out of the rock here multiplied five small loaves and two small fish to feed five thousand men.

He who is God our Saviour, the Lord Jesus Christ, is King over creation, King over providence and the King of grace. He "calleth those things which be not as though they were" (Romans 4:17). With Christ our God, nothing is impossible! When he wills something, it is done. When he commands a thing, it is performed. He creates light out of darkness, makes order out of chaos and brings strength out of weakness. He turns sorrow into laughter, weeping into singing, and mourning into gladness of heart. And he brings food out of nothing!

With regard to the work we are set upon, we might well despair were we not the servants of him who is God mighty to save! When I see the corruption of men's lives and know the depravity of their hearts, when their obstinate hardness of heart is repeatedly manifest, when unbelief appears so firmly and wilfully established in the hearts of men, I would be in utter despair were it not for this one thing: he who is our God and Saviour is God the Almighty! He is God mighty to save! His power is unlimited. His grace is unconstrained. His arm is mighty. Well might the prophet ask, "Can these bones live?" If God says, "live", they can! Can that poor soul over there be saved? If God saves him, he can! Can this rebel son be converted? If God turns him, he can! Can this profligate daughter be won? If God is set to win her, she can!

It is written of our great Saviour, "Thou hast given him power over all flesh, that he should give eternal life to as many as thou hast given him" (John 17:2). We have before us an undeniable proof of our Saviour's omnipotence as the mighty God. It was promised by Isaiah that the Messiah would be both a man born of a woman (Isaiah 7:14) and "the Mighty God" (Isaiah 9:6). Here is a display of his omnipotence as the mighty God. With five loaves and two small fish, the Lord Jesus fed 5,000 men, beside women and children. The task was manifestly impossible for anyone other than God himself, who alone has creative power, who alone "giveth food to all flesh" (Psalm 136:5).

Let every believer treasure up in his heart these blessed facts. Our Saviour, who is full of compassion toward us, is himself "the Mighty God", the Creator and Sustainer of all things, and nothing is too hard for him!

Faith

Second, this miracle is intended to give us a lesson about faith. The disciples wanted to "send the multitude away". They were ready to limit the Holy One. By their actions they were saying, like Israel of old, "Can God prepare a table in the wilderness?" They measured the Lord Jesus' ability by their own ability, or inability. They looked upon the Son of God as Naaman did the Jordan River, with Syrian eyes! Let us learn from their mistake and be warned. When we think of God, we must put down Hagar and raise up Sarah, silence human reason and act according to God-given faith. Faith believes without evidence, and even contrary to evidence, that "things which are impossible with men are possible with God." Two sentences in these verses are bursting with spiritual instruction. Hear these two words from the lips of the Son of God, and ask for grace to trust him.

"He said unto them, Give ye them to eat." Matthew tells us that he preceded that command with this sweet assurance, "They need not depart" (Matthew 14:16). What a blessed word of grace and assurance! If there was no necessity for these hungry souls to depart from Christ for food, there can never be a reason for you and me to depart from him. There is no need for the bride of Christ to wander from beneath his banner of love. Mary may sit at Jesus' feet always!

"They need not depart." That means that there is never an excuse for compromising the gospel. There is never a reason for disobedience to Christ. There is never a cause for neglecting Christ, his worship and his service. Whatever we need, our Saviour is ready to give to us or do for us (Hebrews 4:16; Proverbs 3:5, 6).

"Then he took the five loaves and two fishes, and blessed them" (v. 16). Bring all that you are and all that you have to Christ. He will remove the curse, add his blessing, and make our paltry loaves and fishes instruments of great usefulness and spiritual benefit to chosen sinners in his kingdom. Little is much in the Master's hands! It has always been God's delight and glory to use that which men consider useless. He used a baby's cry to move the heart of Pharaoh's daughter. He used a shepherd's crook to work miracles in Egypt. He used a boy and a slingshot to bring down Goliath. He used a poverty-stricken widow to feed his prophet. He used a little girl to lead Naaman to Elisha. He used Balaam's ass to teach him obedience. He used the jawbone of an ass to slay a thousand Philistines. He used a little child to teach his disciples humility. He used a boy's lunch to feed thousands. And he uses men, who are in themselves useless sinners, to call out his own elect (1 Corinthians 1:26-29; 2 Corinthians 4:7).

The Gospel
Third, this miracle serves as a beautiful and clear allegory of the gospel of God's grace. We must never attempt to make allegories where the Holy Spirit does not make them. We must never try to make the scriptures say what they obviously do not say. But just as Paul used Sarah and Hagar as an allegory to teach the distinction between law and grace (Galatians 4), so the Holy Spirit has given us these recorded miracles of Christ to teach us spiritual, gospel truths.

This hungry multitude in a desert place is a good representation of lost mankind in this world. All the sons of Adam are an assembly of perishing souls, lost, helpless, starving, and upon the verge of eternal ruin, without the gospel of Christ. There is but a breath between them and everlasting ruin. Their only hope of salvation is the gospel of Christ (Romans 1:15, 16).

The loaves and fishes, so readily despised as being inadequate to meet the needs of so many, might well be looked upon as representing the preaching of the gospel, Jesus Christ and him crucified, which God has ordained for the saving of his elect (1 Corinthians 1:21-23; John 6:33). Like the loaves and fish in this passage, the preaching of the cross of Christ meets all the spiritual needs of sinners in this world.

Human Instrumentality
Fourth, the Lord our God graciously condescends to use human instruments to accomplish his work in this world. No, a thousand times no, God does not need us. He who fed this multitude could easily have done so without the use of his poor, weak, unbelieving disciples; but that was not his purpose. He commanded his disciples to do what they could not do. "Give ye them to eat." Then he put bread and fish in their hands and those empty handed men fed five thousand souls! This entire event seems expressly arranged to give us a picture parable of the kingdom of God.

The hungry multitude is a vivid emblem of mankind. Sinners in this great wilderness, this "desert place", are a company of empty souls in the midst of empty souls, starving for lack of bread, sheep without a shepherd, hungry souls with no bread. But our blessed Lord Jesus Christ is a great, compassionate Saviour. Mark and Luke both tell us that our Lord "had compassion" when he saw the multitude before him. And he has given us that which will meet all the needs of men's souls in the gospel. The gospel of the grace of God is the bread of heaven. It is the power of God unto salvation.

These disciples, who had the great privilege of distributing the loaves and fish, are representatives of all God's preachers in this world. We have no bread; but he does! And he has given it to us to give to men. Our work is simple. The Master says, "Give ye them to eat"! Yet, it is vital. Had they not received the bread and fish from the hands of his disciples, this crowd would have gone away hungry. And those who will not submit to being fed by faithful pastors will remain without bread (Romans 10:17; Hebrews 13:7, 17). The preaching of the gospel is vital to the welfare of your soul (Ephesians 4:8-12). See that you do not neglect it.

All Filled

Fifth, we read in verse 17 that all who ate were filled. The satisfaction of all the crowd and the basketsful leftover appear to me to be a beautiful representation of the fullness of grace to be found in the Lord Jesus Christ. You will never go away from his table hungry. Those whom he feeds he fills. When Christ gives, he always gives enough. All who are fed by the Lord Jesus Christ are filled. There is enough in him for all and enough in him for each one. He freely gives all to all who trust him. All who come to him have all they want and need. Finding all in him, we find satisfaction for our souls. Drinking the water that he gives, we never thirst again. Yet, the storehouse of grace is never diminished. He replenishes every hungry soul, abundantly satisfies it with the goodness of his house. There were twelve baskets of fragments taken up, assuring us that in our Father's house there is "bread enough and to spare" (Psalms 34:7-10; 37:23-26; 107:9; 23:1-6).

Our Saviour's name is Jehovah-Jireh. He is the Lord who will provide all our needs. Those who serve him will never lack anything because of their service to him (Luke 22:35). And he always supplies our needs to serve him (Philippians 4:19). Our great God and Saviour can cause the empty barrel of meal to overflow and the cruise of oil to be constantly flowing. As we use what he puts in our hands for his glory, he graciously supplies us with more to use for his glory. The old proverb is, "Little is much when God is in it." The blessing of Christ will make very little go a long way. It is written, "The little that the righteous man has is better than the riches of many wicked, a dinner of herbs better than a stalled ox."

"And it came to pass, as he was alone praying, his disciples were with him: and he asked them, saying, Whom say the people that I am? They answering said, John the Baptist; but some say, Elias; and others say, that one of the old prophets is risen again. He said unto them, But whom say ye that I am? Peter answering said, The Christ of God. And he straitly charged them, and commanded them to tell no man that thing; Saying, The Son of man must suffer many things, and be rejected of the elders and chief priests and scribes, and be slain, and be raised the third day" (Luke 9:18-22).

Chapter 56

Peter's Confession

At first glance, the careless reader might pass over these words, thinking there is nothing extraordinary in them; but such thoughts arise from great ignorance. Peter's confession here is truly remarkable. The more I study it, the more remarkable and blessed it appears. Consider it carefully.

This confession put Peter at odds with the rest of the world. Few were with Christ in those days. Many were against him. But Peter confessed him. When the rulers of his own nation and all the religious people he knew, the scribes, the Pharisees, the Sadducees, the priests and the people, all opposed Christ, Peter confessed him. Many would gladly acknowledge him to be a prophet, even a great prophet, even a resurrected prophet. But Peter confessed him to be "The Christ of God".

This confession of faith came from a man of tremendous faith, character, commitment and zeal. Say what you will about Peter. He had his faults, I know. But do not underrate this man. His heart was under the rule of Christ. Grace is evident in him. Peter was a true-hearted, fervent, faithful servant of our God.

Matthew gives a more complete record of Peter's confession. Looking in the face of the Son of man, Peter said to that man, "Thou art the Christ, the Son of the living God" (Matthew 16:16). Peter confessed that the man Jesus is both the Christ of God and God the Son in our nature. He confessed that the despised Nazarene is the Christ, the promised Messiah, the One of whom all the prophets spoke. In a word, he confessed that the Man, Jesus, is God come to save his people from their sins (Matthew 1:21). I do not know what all Peter knew or did not know. But he knew Christ and confessed him. Do you?

Alone Praying

The first obvious lesson set before us is the fact that those who undertake great work for God must spend time alone with God in prayer. "And it came to pass, as he was alone praying, his disciples were with him: and he asked them, saying, Whom say the people that I am (v.18)?" Never was there a man who worked so feverishly as our Lord. Never was there a preacher who was so constantly engaged in ministering to the souls of men as our Saviour. Remember, this man was and is himself God. Yet, there was never a man so much engaged in private prayer to God. How frequently we read in Matthew, Mark, Luke and John that our Lord Jesus Christ was alone, or alone with a few of his brethren, praying.

The pioneer missionary, William Carey, once said, "Expect great things from God. Attempt great things for God." Carey would not object to me adding this: if we would attempt great things for God and expect great things from God, we must spend time alone with God praying. In all spiritual endeavours prayer is the secret to usefulness. Let us follow our Master's example. Pray. Pray for grace to pray as we ought. Pray for one another. Pray for God's guidance and his blessing upon our labours. Pray for the power and grace of God to attend the ministry of the Word.

Religious Chatter

Second, read verse 19 and learn that talk and speculation about Christ, his gospel, and the things of God are snares by which Satan destroys multitudes. "They answering said, John the Baptist; but some say, Elias; and others say, that one of the old prophets is risen again." Many a man attempts to cover his ignorance by endless chatter, speculation and debate, speaking when he ought to listen, attempting to teach when he needs to learn and offering dogmatic opinions about things of which he has no knowledge.

During the days of our Lord's earthly ministry, if you stopped any man or woman on the street and mentioned Jesus of Nazareth, you would be sure to hear that person's opinion about him. A multitude of opinions could be heard in any district. Some were dead sure John the Baptist had been raised from the dead. Others were equally certain that Elijah had come back to the earth. Others were absolutely positive that Jeremiah or one of the prophets had been reincarnated!

One thing is obvious. All were agreed that our Lord was not at all like the other preachers and religious leaders around. No one ever mistook him for a scribe, a Pharisee, or a Sadducee! His doctrine distinguished him from all others. Read through the gospel narratives (Matthew, Mark, Luke and John) again. You will find that the masses, religious and otherwise, never denied or even challenged our Lord's miracles, his doctrine, or even his Divine authority. They did not refuse to acknowledge him as a "Christ", (an anointed man), or a Saviour. That which disturbed men in our Lord's day and disturbs men in this day was the exclusiveness of his message. Our Lord declared himself to be, and his apostles declared him and him alone to be "the Christ", "the Way", "the Truth", "the Life", "the Door", "the Saviour", "the Good Shepherd", "the King", "the Redeemer", "the Son of the Living God".

We should never be surprised or at all confused by the fact that men and women everywhere have very strong, outspoken opinions about Christ and his gospel, opinions as foreign to holy scripture as hell is to heaven.

The fact is God's truth disturbs people. No one can sit under the ministry of the gospel and not be affected by it. If the gospel is plainly preached in unmistakable terms, it will cause people to think. If they refuse to bow to the Revelation of God, they will conjure up reasons for their rebellion and unbelief, invent doctrinal theories of their own, speculate about what they judge to be right and seek to persuade others.

Multitudes spend their lives this way, ever learning and never able to come to the knowledge of the truth. I meet them everywhere I go. They are always anxious to hear some new thing. They get hold of it, whirl it around, and run everywhere with it, as excited as a child with a ten cent sparkler, until it fizzles out. Then they go find another sparkler.

Multitudes know nothing more about the things of God than what they think they have learned by religious gossip. They content themselves with examining and criticizing everything they hear or read. "Bro. Mahan is getting a little weak." "Bro. Nibert is too strong." "Bro. Bell is too emotional." "Bro. Fortner is too dogmatic." "Bro. Harding is beginning to compromise." They approve of this and disapprove of that. They say this man is sound, or that man is unsound.

They cannot make up their own mind what is true and what is not, what is right and what is wrong. So they run from one place to another in the name of truth, wreaking havoc wherever they go, never contributing anything anywhere but confusion.

Year rolls after year, and they are in the same state, just as confused as ever and just as dogmatic; talking, criticizing, finding fault, speculating and tearing down, but never contributing. They hover like the moth around the things of God, but never settle down like the bee to feed upon them. They never lay hold on Christ. They never set their faces toward heaven. They never take up the cross. They never become followers of Christ. We will be wise to read and heed the warnings given in holy scripture about such people (1 Timothy 6:3-5, 11, 12, 20, 21; 2 Timothy 2:16-18, 21-23; 3:1-9; Titus 3:9).

God's salvation is personally experienced, personally embraced, personally felt, personally known, personally possessed and personally cherished. It is not something bantered about over coffee and doughnuts like politics. It is more, much more than speculation and theory. It is life everlasting in Christ. Our Lord said, "If any man will do God's will, he shall know the doctrine whether it be of God" (John 7:17). God's will is that we believe on his Son (1 John 3:23); and believing Christ, we are taught and learn of God. God given faith then walks before God with confident, assured knowledge regarding the things of God, for we who believe "have the mind of Christ."

Faith's Confession
Third, true, saving faith knows and confesses that the man Jesus of Nazareth is the Christ of God. "He said unto them, But whom say ye that I am? Peter answering said, The Christ of God" (v. 20). Peter was, at times, erring and unstable, in some matters ignorant and unbelieving, far too proud and far too quick to action. But when all is said and done, Peter was a remarkable man. In the midst of unbelieving religionists, when the overwhelming tide of religious opinion was rushing the other way, Peter was confident, loyal, willing to stand alone and bold because he believed and loved his Saviour.

When he declared that the man standing before him was "The Christ of God", he was asserting plainly that that man was and is the Incarnate God, the woman's Seed, Abraham's Seed, David's Son and David's Lord, the Saviour, that One of whom the scriptures speak.

A Time For Silence
Fourth, in verse 21 we are taught that there is a time to be silent as well as a time to speak. "And he straitly charged them, and commanded them to tell no man that thing." Many imagine that they must buttonhole everyone they see, shove a tract into their hand, tell them they are going to hell, and in doing so content themselves with being clear of their blood. But there is a time to be quiet as well as a time to speak. May God give us wisdom and grace to know when to speak and when to be silent.

"And he straitly charged them, and commanded them to tell no man that thing." For the present time our Lord was pleased to make himself known to a few and to conceal himself from the multitudes. Contrary to popular opinion, it is still his purpose to make himself known to some and to hide himself from others. He sends the gospel to some and refuses to send it to others. He calls some, but not others, exactly as it pleases him to do so.

There is a lesson here for us all. There is a time for us to speak to men about the things of God and a time for us to be silent. As you endeavour to be faithful witnesses remember this. Ever be ready and willing to speak for Christ regardless of cost or consequence. But seek to be led of God. If he would have you speak a word for him, you will not have to force it. He will open the way and make it obvious. Let our words be words in season and fitly spoken.

Determined To Die

Fifth, we see our great Saviour's loving determination to suffer and die under the wrath of God as our sin-atoning Substitute. "The Son of man must suffer many things, and be rejected of the elders and chief priests and scribes, and be slain, and be raised the third day" (v. 22). I am sure there is much, much more in this verse than I have yet grasped. But these two things are both obvious and vital.

Our Lord Jesus Christ died as a voluntary Surety. He died for us because he wanted to die, because he loved us. He died by his own free, voluntary will. He did not die as the helpless victim of circumstances beyond his control, but by the determination of his own heart's love for us. The Son of God loved me and gave himself for me! Imagine that!

There was a necessity for our Saviour's death. He "must" die. The Old Testament scriptures must be fulfilled. The purpose of God must be accomplished. His covenant engagements must be finished. The justice of God must be satisfied. And the salvation of his people must be obtained. Therefore, our all-glorious Redeemer declared, "The Son of man must suffer many things, and be rejected of the elders and chief priests and scribes, and be slain, and be raised the third day"!

"And he said to them all, If any man will come after me, let him deny himself, and take up his cross daily, and follow me. For whosoever will save his life shall lose it: but whosoever will lose his life for my sake, the same shall save it. For what is a man advantaged, if he gain the whole world, and lose himself, or be cast away? For whosoever shall be ashamed of me and of my words, of him shall the Son of man be ashamed, when he shall come in his own glory, and in his Father's, and of the holy angels. But I tell you of a truth, there be some standing here, which shall not taste of death, till they see the kingdom of God" (Luke 9:23-27).

Chapter 57

What Is Christianity?

The words of our Lord Jesus Christ in these five verses of scripture are solemn and weighty words. They separate the precious from the vile. They are a winnowing fan in the Master's hand, by which he distinguishes wheat from the chaff. These are words which ought to be read often, prayed over much, and mediated upon continually. These few words define true Christianity more distinctly than all the volumes of theology and apologetics written by men. Robert Hawker observed ...

"A single soul is of more value than the whole world; and for this plain reason: The time is coming, when the whole world and all that is in it will be destroyed; but the soul of every individual must live, either in happiness or misery, forever. Reader, pause over the subject, and calculate, if possible, the value of a single soul. The creation of it called forth the council of the whole persons of the Godhead. The redemption of it cost Christ his blood. The regeneration of it was the work of God the Holy Ghost. The everlasting happiness of it engageth the services of angels and of men continually. Angels rejoice in heaven in the recovery of every sinner. Hell rageth in the event of their salvation. The soul hath a capability of grace here, and glory forever. And therefore what a loss, incalculably great, must it be, that a being of such qualities, and so formed, should be exposed to everlasting destruction."

Coming To Christ
Throughout the scriptures faith is portrayed as a matter of coming to Christ. To believe on the Son of God is to come to him. To come to him is to believe on him. We come to him by following after him, as disciples follow after

their Master. Our all glorious Christ says, "If any man will come after me, let him deny himself" (v. 23).

Coming to Christ is the result of a deliberate, purposeful choice. It is an act of the will. Our Master says, "If any man will". Let us never alter his Word. I know that faith is a gift of God. I know that none will ever come to Christ unless God the Holy Spirit graciously, effectually causes them to come. Yet, it is certain that any who come to him, come to him because they want him and choose him. God does not save sinners by knocking them in the head and dragging them to Christ. He saves sinners by causing them to want Christ more than life itself.

Faith in Christ is not a matter of conscription, but a voluntary act. The soldiers in Christ's army are not drafted, forced soldiers, but volunteers. It is written, "Thy people shall be willing in the day of thy power" (Psalm 110:3). "Blessed is the man whom thou choosest, and causest to approach unto thee, that he may dwell in thy courts" (Psalm 65:4).

Coming to Christ is an act of the heart, a spiritual, not a carnal thing. No one has ever come to Christ by walking a church aisle, kneeling at an altar, saying a prayer someone taught him to repeat, or signing a decision card. If you would come to Christ, you must do so without moving a muscle. You must come to him in your heart. Faith is a heart work (Romans 10:8-10). True faith is the wilful, deliberate, voluntary confidence of my heart in the power and grace of the Lord Jesus Christ. It is trusting the merits of his blood and righteousness as my only acceptance before God. Faith in Christ involves the willing surrender of my heart to him as my Lord. It is the bowing and submission of my heart to him as my Lord (Luke 14:25-33).

Coming to Christ is a continual thing. Our Saviour does not speak of coming to him as a one time thing, as a single act, but as a constant, continual, lifelong thing. Faith in Christ is not an event in life, but a way of life. "If so be ye have tasted that the Lord is gracious. To whom coming, as unto a living stone, disallowed indeed of men, but chosen of God, and precious" (1 Peter 2:3, 4).

Not only are sinners bidden to come to Christ, we are commanded to come (1 John 3:23). The warrant of faith is not my feeling, my emotion, my meeting certain prescribed conditions, but God's Word. If the Son of God says for me to come to him, then I may come to him!

Any sinner in all the world who will come to Christ may come to Christ. Our Master uses that blessed world of universal application and uses it frequently "Whosoever". I am so thankful he said, "If any man will", rather than, "if Don Fortner will". Had he said that, I would have concluded he must have meant some other Don Fortner. But I cannot doubt that "any man" includes me!

"Come unto me, all ye that labour and are heavy laden, and I will give you rest. Take my yoke upon you, and learn of me; for I am meek and lowly in heart: and ye shall find rest unto your souls. For my yoke is easy, and my burden is light" (Matthew 11:28-30).

"He that believeth on the Son hath everlasting life: and he that believeth not the Son shall not see life; but the wrath of God abideth on him" (John 3:36).

"And the Spirit and the bride say, Come. And let him that heareth say, Come. And let him that is athirst come. And whosoever will, let him take the water of life freely" (Revelation 22:17).

Carrying The Cross Of Christ
The first aspect of faith is coming to Christ. The second is carrying his cross. This is not an optional thing. Here, and throughout the Word of God, our Master tells us plainly that if we would follow him, if we would be his disciples, if we would be saved, self-denial is an absolute necessity. "And he said to them all, If any man will come after me, let him deny himself, and take up his cross daily, and follow me" (v. 23).

Again, this is a matter of personal, deliberate choice. Carrying your cross for Christ is not enduring providential hardships with patience, but deliberately choosing a course that is sure to bring trouble upon you, because trouble lies in the path of following Christ.

Salvation is by grace alone, through faith alone, in Christ alone. We are not saved by what we do, but by what God does and has done. We are saved by grace alone (Ephesians 2:8-10). Yet, if we are saved by the grace of God, we must through much tribulation enter into the kingdom of God; and we must deny self. J. C. Ryle was correct when he wrote, "A religion which costs nothing is worth nothing. It will do us no good in the life that now is. It will lead to no salvation in the life to come." If I am saved by the grace of God, I take up my cross and follow my Master. I must take up the cross of his doctrine, the cross of his will and the cross of his honour. Our Saviour's words here are as plain as the noonday sun. If I choose not to bear his cross on this earth, I shall never wear his crown in heaven.

Our Master teaches us that true, saving faith involves deliberate and persevering self-denial and consecration. Matthew Henry wrote, "The first lesson in Christ's school is self-denial." Those who deny themselves here for Christ shall enjoy themselves in Christ forever. Grace is free; but it is not cheap. Faith in Christ involves the total surrender of myself to him, to his dominion as my Lord and Saviour, my Priest and King. That is what it is to take up your cross and follow Christ.

Christianity, true Christianity, true saving faith involves a total surrender to Christ the Lord. Either you will be a servant under the dominion of King Jesus, voluntarily giving up all to his claims, or you will go to hell. You may not have to give up anything in actuality. But surrender to Christ must be just as real and complete in your heart as if you had actually given up everything, even down to life itself. Our Lord Jesus Christ requires total and unreserved surrender to himself. Christ will be Lord of all, or he will not be Lord at all. Is Jesus Christ, the Son of God, your Lord? Is he truly your Lord?

But we must never imagine that this is a matter dealt with only in the initial experience of grace and in the initial act of faith. Here our Lord Jesus addresses these words to men who had been his faithful disciples for a long time. How graciously he warns us and teaches us to guard against the terrible tendency of our sinful flesh to rebel against his rule and his will. How much evil we bring upon ourselves by our carnal misapprehensions! We are all, like Peter (v. 33; Mark 8:33), inclined to judge things by our emotions, personal desires and carnal reason. We must not do so. Rather, we must seek grace to know and bow to the will of God our Saviour in all things. Oh, for grace to savour the things which are of God, and not those which are of men!

Consecration To Christ.

"For whosoever will save his life shall lose it: but whosoever will lose his life for my sake, the same shall save it. For what is a man advantaged, if he gain the whole world, and lose himself, or be cast away?" (vv. 24, 25)

Faith is coming to Christ, carrying the cross of Christ and consecration to Christ. If I would save my life, I must lose it to Christ. I repeat myself deliberately. Salvation is neither more nor less than surrender to the rule and reign of Jesus Christ as my Lord and King.

"And there went great multitudes with him: and he turned, and said unto them, If any man come to me, and hate not his father, and mother, and wife, and children, and brethren, and sisters, yea, and his own life also, he cannot be my disciple. And whosoever doth not bear his cross, and come after me, cannot be my disciple. For which of you, intending to build a tower, sitteth not down first, and counteth the cost, whether he have sufficient to finish it? Lest haply, after he hath laid the foundation, and is not able to finish it, all that behold it begin to mock him, Saying, This man began to build, and was not able to finish. Or what king, going to make war against another king, sitteth not down first, and consulteth whether he be able with ten thousand to meet him that cometh against him with twenty thousand? Or else, while the other is yet a great way off, he sendeth an ambassage, and desireth conditions of peace. So likewise, whosoever he be of you that forsaketh not all that he hath, he cannot be my disciple" (Luke 14:25-33).

Faith in Christ is giving over the rule of your life to Christ; but that is no great sacrifice at all. "For what is a man advantaged, if he gain the whole world, and lose himself, or be cast away?" That question is so well known and so often repeated that I fear few take it to heart. It ought to sound in our ears like a trumpet whenever we are tempted to neglect our eternal interests. Each of us has an immortal soul, a soul that will live forever, either in the bliss of eternal life or in the torments of eternal death. There is nothing the world can offer, nothing money can buy, nothing a man can give, nothing to be named in comparison to our souls. We live in a world where everything is temporal. We are going to a world where everything is eternal. Let us count nothing here more valuable than we shall when we have to leave it behind!

It is a very easy thing for you to lose your soul. You can murder it, by loving and clinging to the world. You can poison it with the deadly wine of false, freewill works religion. You can starve it, by neglecting God's ordained means of grace, the preaching of the gospel, by keeping from it the Bread of Life, by the neglect of prayer, the neglect of worship and the neglect of God's Word. There are many ways to hell. Which way you choose is a matter for which you alone are responsible (Proverbs 16:25). There is only one way to life eternal. Christ is that Way.

Confessing Christ
Faith in Christ involves coming to Christ, carrying the cross of Christ, consecration to Christ, and confessing Christ. "For whosoever shall be ashamed of me and of my words, of him shall the Son of man be ashamed, when he shall come in his own glory, and in his Father's, and in the holy angels. But I tell you of a truth, there be some standing here, which shall not taste of death, till they see the kingdom of God" (vv. 26, 27).

Who is capable of being ashamed of Christ and his words? None among the sons of men can be compared to him. We do not have to guess what it is to be ashamed of Christ. It is to refuse to confess him, to refuse to identify ourselves with him. All show themselves ashamed of him and his gospel who refuse to seek salvation in his name, trusting him as Saviour and Lord. All who seek to add their own works to his righteousness and his precious blood for acceptance with God prove themselves ashamed of him. To refuse to trust the Lord Jesus Christ is to deny him. That is what it is to be ashamed of him.

If you are ashamed of Christ's doctrine, you are ashamed of him (Romans 1:16, 17). If you are ashamed of Christ's ordinances, you are ashamed of him. If you are ashamed of Christ's people, ashamed to identify yourself with them, you are ashamed of him. If you are ashamed of Christ in this adulterous and sinful generation, he will be ashamed of you when he comes in the glory of his Father with his holy angels to judge the world.

"And it came to pass about an eight days after these sayings, he took Peter and John and James, and went up into a mountain to pray. And as he prayed, the fashion of his countenance was altered, and his raiment was white and glistering. And, behold, there talked with him two men, which were Moses and Elias: Who appeared in glory, and spake of his decease which he should accomplish at Jerusalem. But Peter and they that were with him were heavy with sleep: and when they were awake, they saw his glory, and the two men that stood with him. And it came to pass, as they departed from him, Peter said unto Jesus, Master, it is good for us to be here: and let us make three tabernacles; one for thee, and one for Moses, and one for Elias: not knowing what he said. While he thus spake, there came a cloud, and overshadowed them: and they feared as they entered into the cloud. And there came a voice out of the cloud, saying, This is my beloved Son: hear him. And when the voice was past, Jesus was found alone. And they kept it close, and told no man in those days any of those things which they had seen" (Luke 9:28-36).

Chapter 58

The Transfiguration: A Glimpse Of Glory

We commonly refer to that which is described in these verses as "the transfiguration." It is one of the most remarkable events in the history of our Lord's earthly ministry. Here the Holy Spirit lifts the corner of the veil which yet hangs over the world to come and gives us a glimpse of the glory which awaits us.

When the angel appeared to John he said, "Come up hither". He was about to see and enter into things he had never seen or experienced before. The holy Lord God was about to bring him experimentally near to himself, about to make such great manifestations of himself, his glory, his grace and his purpose in his Son as John had never known before. John saw a door open in heaven and was bidden, as it were, to enter into heaven itself for a while, though he was yet on the earth.

That is the position we are in as we come to the Mount of Transfiguration. Standing before this awesome, majestic passage of Scripture, we hear the Spirit of God saying, "Come up hither" leave your worldly thoughts; and, for a little while, forget the earth. May God the Spirit graciously enable us to ascend "the holy mount", as Peter calls it, and see, and learn, and experience what those chosen disciples did on that day. Let us, as it were, go up on Pisgah's mount, and take a view of the Promised Land awaiting us.

It is true, indeed, eye has not seen, ear has not heard, neither has it entered into the heart of any man to conceive the great and good things which God has prepared for his people even here on earth, much less, those infinitely greater and more gloriously good things that he has laid up for us in the world to come. Yet, God has been pleased to leave upon record this magnificent event that we may form some faint idea of that glory that awaits us in his kingdom above.

The Connection

When we observe the fact that there is a clear, intended connection between verses 27 and 28, it is obvious that this event is recorded to give us a glimpse of heavenly glory. In verse 27 the Lord Jesus declared, "I tell you of a truth, there be some standing here, which shall not taste of death, till they see the kingdom of God." Then, in verse 28 we read, "And it came to pass about an eight days after these sayings, he took Peter and John and James, and went up into a mountain to pray."

That which came to pass in verse 28 is that which our Lord had spoken of about eight days earlier in verse 27. This was obviously what our Lord had in mind when he promised that some standing before him at that time would see the kingdom of God before they tasted death. He had been speaking about the glory of his coming and of his kingdom. Knowing that in their weakness his disciples might think, "This is too good to be true", the Master promised that he would give some of those very disciples, (Peter, James and John), a glimpse of that glory.

The Chosen Three

All three of the accounts given of this great event tell us that the Lord Jesus took Peter, James and John with him into the mount to see his transfiguration. Why do you suppose he did not take more of the disciples with him? Why just three? Why these three? The Master was pleased to take three and no more to show us his sovereignty. Our God always keeps before us the fact that he is absolutely sovereign in all things. He is sovereign in the election of some to salvation (Ephesians 1:3-6), sovereign in the redemption of his elect by Christ (Isaiah 53:4-10), sovereign in calling of his elect by the irresistible grace of his Spirit (Psalms 63:5; 110:3), sovereign in the revelation of his grace (Galatians 1:15, 16), sovereign in the bestowment of the blessings and gifts of his grace (1 Corinthians 4:7), and sovereign in his sweet visitations of mercy (Romans 9:16).

Our Lord took three rather than one, because three were sufficient to verify the truthfulness of this event. "In the mouth of two or three witnesses every word shall be established." He took no more than three, because these three were enough. And he took these three, Peter, James and John in particular, because they would be the same three who were later to see him agonizing in the garden, sweating great drops of blood falling unto the ground. Seeing him in his glory helped to prepare them for that day when they would see him in his humiliation and agony of heart.

The God-man In Prayer

Our Lord Jesus took Peter, James and John "up into a mountain to pray". He had no corruption to acknowledge or sins to confess. Yet, our Master was a man of prayer. Often, he rose to pray, went aside to pray, and at least once spent an entire night in prayer. What an example he left for us to follow! "In the days of his flesh, when he had offered up prayers and supplications with strong crying and tears unto him that was able to save him from death, our great Saviour was heard in that he feared" (Hebrews 5:7). If we would serve our God, seek his glory, do his will, and serve the souls of men, we must learn something about prayer, seeking the honour and glory of God, the will of God, and the interests of the kingdom of God.

Our Saviour began, it seems, every work he undertook for the glory of God in prayer. When he came to be baptized by John the Baptist, at his baptism, he was engaged in prayer. When he went into the wilderness to meet Satan in his great temptation, he fasted and prayed. When he was transfigured, as a pledge of his exaltation and glory, he prayed. When he was about to go to Calvary to die as our Substitute, he prayed. On both occasions when God the Father spoke from heaven and declared, "This is my beloved Son", our Master was engaged in prayer.

"And as he prayed, the fashion of his countenance was altered, and his raiment was white and glistering" (v. 29). Here we see the result of our Lord's praying. There is an obvious emphasis here upon the fact that our Lord was transfigured as he was praying. You will recall that when Moses went up to the mount of God and God spoke to him face to face, as he came down from the mount Moses' face shined so brightly that he had to put a veil over his face. The shining of his face was a proof to the people that he had been talking with God. After that, Moses told the people that the Lord would raise up unto them a prophet like unto him, whom the people were to hear (Deuteronomy 18:15-18). Christ is that Prophet! God the Father, in order to give his Son confirmation as that prophet, not only caused his face to glitter or shine, but, also, to show that he was a prophet far greater than Moses, made his very garment white and glittering, and "his countenance did shine as the sun". What a thing to see! What a change!

Moses, Elijah And The Saviour

"And, behold, there talked with him two men, which were Moses and Elias: Who appeared in glory, and spake of his decease which he should accomplish at Jerusalem" (vv. 30, 31). What a sight that must have been! Peter, James and John must have been utterly astounded! I am sure there is much, much more in these two verses than I have yet understood; but the things the Holy Spirit intends for us to learn from them appear to me to be obvious. He seems particularly to call our attention to three things.

1. Their descent: "there talked with him two men, which were Moses and Elijah." Moses and Elijah descended from heaven and spoke to the Lord Jesus in the hearing of Peter, James and John. Moses had been dead for 1500 years. Elijah was taken up to heaven in a whirlwind, in a chariot of fire, 900 years earlier. Yet, both stood upon the mount with the Lord Jesus, Peter, James and John. The very fact that these two men stood physically with our Lord on the mount and spoke audibly to him is instructive.

First, it tells us that our departed brethren are, indeed, alive and well. Second, Moses and Elijah are specific representatives of all the law and the prophets. Both acknowledged our Saviour as the Christ of God, of whom all the law and prophets speak. "To him give all the prophets witness." Third, Moses and Elijah are representative of the saints who will appear with Christ in his glory at his second advent. Moses represents all God's elect whose bodies are in the grave. Elijah represents those who are found alive upon the earth at the Lord's coming, who shall be "caught up to meet the Lord in the air" (1 Thessalonians 4:17).

Blessed be God, there is a world above. All is not over when we have drawn our last breath here. We will live beyond the grave. There is a resurrection day coming. Until that day, our departed friends are safe with the Saviour! They are in good keeping. Christ is taking care of them. They are in good company. They are with him! They are not lost, but have gone before us; and the Lord Jesus will bring them with him when he comes again.

Fourth, the fact that Moses and Elijah were immediately recognized by these three disciples, though they had never seen either of them, makes it obvious that God's saints shall know one another in glory, intuitively and by special revelation. How dim our present vision is of things to come! Fifth, the fact that Moses and Elijah spoke with the Lord Jesus about "his decease which he should accomplish at Jerusalem" tells us that God's saints in heaven are very much aware of and interested in that which God's saints are doing on the earth. They are that "great cloud of witnesses" spoken of in the Book of Hebrews.

2. Their dress: they "appeared in glory". Moses and Elijah seem to have appeared in the very same glory as that in which the Lord Jesus appeared. While that may or may not have been the case, this much is certain: When the Lord God has at last brought us into glory at the last day, the glory which Christ now enjoys as our God-man Mediator shall be ours (John 17:5 and 20; Romans 8:28, 29). In glory all God's saints shall possess the same glory!

3. Their discourse: "they spake of his decease which he should accomplish at Jerusalem." What language that is! Moses and Elijah spoke of our Lord's death at Jerusalem as "his decease" (his exodus) "which he should accomplish". Never was any other man's death spoken of as a thing that he accomplished. The word really means "fulfil". Our Lord's death was something he accomplished by which he fulfilled God's law and justice, all the types and prophecies of the Old Testament, his mission as our Substitute and Surety, and the everlasting redemption of his elect.

The saints in glory speak much about that decease which our Lord Jesus accomplished at Jerusalem (Revelation 5, 7 and 14). They know its meaning. They know what depended upon it. They know what was accomplished by it. They know that they are there because of it, only because of it. The saints in glory see such magnificent beauty in the death of God's darling Son that they must talk much about it; how much more should saved sinners upon the earth be utterly consumed with it. This is our only hope. This is our only peace. This is our only message to poor, lost sinners. Redemption is accomplished, finished by the Lord Jesus Christ!

The Disciples
The appearance of Moses and Elijah with Christ in glory, the transfiguration they observed, and the conversation they heard had an overwhelming effect upon our Lord's disciples. "But Peter and they that were with him were heavy with sleep: and when they were awake, they saw his glory, and the two men that stood with him" (v. 32). Peter, James and John have been unjustly accused of being bored in prayer, even as the Lord Jesus was transfigured before them, and Moses and Elijah spoke to him of his death at Jerusalem. But that was not the case at all. The sleep spoken of here was not that kind of sleep. Rather, it was a sleep of an almost unconscious state of one utterly overwhelmed, shocked, dumbfounded by something before him. If you will look at the cross reference in the margin of your Bible, you will see that this is exactly what happened to Daniel when Gabriel appeared to him and when Christ himself appeared to him in the form of a man (Daniel 8:18; 10:9).

Peter, James and John were overcome by the sight of the glory of Christ's garments, the glittering of his body, the glory in which Moses and Elias appeared, and the things they heard. Like the Queen of Sheba, when she saw Solomon's glory, they had no life in them. But they quickly recovered. "When they were awake", that is, when they had recovered their strength, when God had put renewed strength into them, as the angel put strength into Daniel, "they saw his glory, and the two men that stood with him".

"And it came to pass, as they departed from him, Peter said unto Jesus, Master, it is good for us to be here: and let us make three tabernacles; one for thee, and one for Moses, and one for Elias: not knowing what he said" (v. 33). Peter, who was always the first to speak, when he had drank a little of Christ's new wine, spoke like a person intoxicated. He was overpowered with the brightness of the manifestation. "Let us make three tabernacles, one for thee, and one for Moses, and one for Elias". It is well added, "not knowing what he said." That he should cry out, "Master, it is good for us to be here", in such good company and in so glorious a condition, is no surprise. Which of us would not have done the same? But to talk of building tabernacles, one for Christ, one for Moses and one for Elias, was saying something for which Peter himself must stand reproved. He was so high on the mountain that his head was spinning.

Still, as always with Peter, there was something in this that revealed the manly honesty and integrity of his heart. Peter knew that the glory of the Lord filled the tabernacle and the temple of old. Now that the Lord Jesus is transfigured, and Moses and Elias appeared with him in glory, he thought it only proper that new tabernacles should be erected for them. George Whitefield said, concerning this incident:

"Such a mixture of nature and grace, of short-sightedness and infirmity, is there in the most ardent and well-meant zeal of the very best of men, when nearest the throne of grace, or even upon the mount with God. Perfection in any grace must be looked for, or expected, only among the spirits of just men made perfect in heaven. Those who talk of any such thing on earth, like Peter, they know not what they say."

No doubt, there is much to be blamed in Peter's outburst; but there is much to be admired. When Peter saw the Lord Jesus in his glory, surrounded by such companions, knowing that he had said he was going to Jerusalem to suffer and die, when he had but a glimpse of glory, he said, "It is good for us to be here." Oh, how indescribably good it will be for us to be there, with Christ and all who are his in heavenly glory!

"While he thus spake, there came a cloud, and overshadowed them: and they feared as they entered into the cloud" (v. 34). Matthew tells us it was a bright cloud, not dark like that on Mount Sinai, but bright, because the gospel opens to us a far brighter dispensation than that of the law. This cloud was like the veil thrown on the face of Moses, and prepared them for the voice which they were soon to hear coming out of it.

Both Matthew and Luke tell us that they feared as they entered into the cloud. Mark says, "they were sore afraid". Since the fall of our father Adam, there is such a consciousness in us all of guilt and deserved wrath that we cannot help fearing when we enter into a cloud, though Jesus Christ himself be in the midst of it. How quickly those fears were dispelled. How soon is the tumult of their minds hushed and calmed, with that soul-reviving voice that came from the excellent glory.

A Voice From Heaven

"And there came a voice out of the cloud, saying, This is my beloved Son: hear him" (v. 35). Matthew adds, "in whom I am well pleased". God the Father hereby gives Moses and Elias a solemn discharge, as though they were sent from heaven on purpose to give up their commission to their rightful Lord, and like the morning star, disappear when the Sun of Righteousness himself arises to bring in the gospel Day. "This is my beloved Son, hear him." Understand what the God of heaven declared in those words: This Man is "my beloved Son". He is God incarnate! This Representative Man, this Surety, this Mediator is the One "in whom (alone) I am well pleased"! The Triune God is well-pleased with the Lord Jesus Christ as the Representative of his elect; and he is well-pleased with all his elect in his Son! "Hear him"! "Hear ye him." Believe on, love, serve and obey him. "Hear him." Hear what he says, for he comes with a commission from above. Hear his doctrine. Obey his word. Follow his example. Christ alone is our Master. Christ alone we must hear!

We are repeatedly told that the Lord God declared himself well pleased in Christ our Redeemer (Matthew 3:17; 12:18; 17:5; Mark 1:11; Luke 3:22; 2 Peter 1:17). The Lord God intends for us to hear and understand this wondrous declaration of mercy. God the Father speaks from heaven to Peter, James and John, and by them to us, declaring that he is well pleased with his dear Son, and only with his Son. Moses was there; but God was not pleased with him. Elijah was there; but God was not pleased with him. Peter was there; but God was not pleased with him. James was there; but God was not pleased with him. And John was there; but God was not pleased with him. God never has been and never can be pleased with any sinful man. But God always has been and always must be well pleased with his dear Son, the God-man.

It goes without saying that God the Father is essentially well pleased with his Son as his Son. But here we are told that God the Father is well pleased with his Son as the God-man Mediator. God was well pleased with his Son eternally as our Surety and Mediatorial Representative in the covenant of grace (Isaiah 42:21). He is well pleased, honoured by, and delights in the representative life of his Son, by which he brought in everlasting righteousness for us (Matthew 3:13-17). God is well pleased with the substitutionary, sin atoning death of his Son, by which he both satisfied divine justice and put away the sins of his people (Isaiah 53:10; Psalm 85:9-11). He is well pleased with the heavenly intercession of his Son as our

Advocate and great High Priest (1 John 2:1, 2). God is well pleased with the providential rule of his Son as the sovereign King of the universe (Isaiah 42:1-4). As our Saviour said of his earthly life, he might say of his heavenly rule, "I do always those things that please him" (John 8:29). And God shall be well pleased with the results of his Son's covenant engagements and mediatorial rule (1 Corinthians 15:24-28). Christ, as the Mediator, as the God-man, shall present his kingdom to the eternal Father, that God the Father, the Son, and the Holy Spirit may be forever glorified (Revelation 19:1-7).

But the voice that was heard from heaven did not say, "This is my beloved Son with whom I am well pleased", but "This is my beloved Son in whom I am well pleased." God is well pleased with his people in his Son. Imagine that! The holy, righteous, just, and true God, Lord of heaven and earth, is honoured by, delights in, and is well pleased with us in his Son! In our natural condition we are all displeasing to God. This is our miserable state by nature. But our God is well pleased with us for Christ's sake, because he is so in Christ. He was well pleased with us in Christ eternally (Ephesians 1:6). He is well pleased with all that we offer to him and do for him in Christ (1 Peter 2:5). And he is always, immutably well pleased with us in Christ (Jeremiah 23:6; 33:16).

"And when the voice was past, Jesus was found alone. And they kept it close, and told no man in those days any of those things which they had seen" (v. 36). Let me call your attention to just two things here.

First, the fact that Moses and Elijah were gone and the Lord Jesus stood before these disciples alone was a vivid declaration that he is the end of the law and the fulfilment of the prophets, and the message of both the law and the prophets. When Peter, James and John awoke, when they saw clearly and distinctly, they saw "no man, save Jesus only"! Blessed, indeed, are those chosen, redeemed, called men and women who see no man's hand in the whole affair of salvation, except the hand of Christ.

Second, the disciples told this to no one until after the resurrection. If we compare verse 36 with the records of Matthew and Mark, we see that this was done by Christ's order: Peter, James and John would otherwise have gone down and told the whole world that they had seen the Lord Christ upon the mount of transfiguration; but our Lord ordered them to keep it silent. Why? If they had gone down from the mount and told it to the other disciples, it might have stirred jealousy and strife among the believers. Besides, the Lord had declared that he would give no signs to that generation. They must believe him and his word, or they must perish. And, had they told others about this before the resurrection, Peter, James and John would have appeared utterly foolish in the eyes of any who did not believe their testimony. By keeping it secret until after his resurrection, until he had broken the gates of death, the things they witnessed upon the mount were credible in the eyes of others. There is a time to speak and a time to be silent. Our Lord would not have us cast our pearls before swine.

Eternity

As there is life beyond the grave for the righteous, so there is death beyond the grave for the wicked. As the righteous shall know one another in glory, so the damned shall know one another in hell. As our knowing one another in heaven will make heaven more blessed, so the wicked knowing one another in hell will make hell more horrible and tormenting.

We have a glimpse of glory before us in the transfiguration. When Christ comes to gather us home, we shall be like him upon the mount of transfiguration. Wonderfully changed! Wonderfully owned! Wonderfully approved!

"And it came to pass, that on the next day, when they were come down from the hill, much people met him. And, behold, a man of the company cried out, saying, Master, I beseech thee, look upon my son: for he is mine only child. And, lo, a spirit taketh him, and he suddenly crieth out; and it teareth him that he foameth again, and bruising him hardly departeth from him. And I besought thy disciples to cast him out; and they could not. And Jesus answering said, O faithless and perverse generation, how long shall I be with you, and suffer you? Bring thy son hither. And as he was yet a coming, the devil threw him down, and tare him. And Jesus rebuked the unclean spirit, and healed the child, and delivered him again to his father. And they were all amazed at the mighty power of God. But while they wondered every one at all things which Jesus did, he said unto his disciples, Let these sayings sink down into your ears: for the Son of man shall be delivered into the hands of men. But they understood not this saying, and it was hid from them, that they perceived it not: and they feared to ask him of that saying" (Luke 9:37-45).

Chapter 59

When They Came Down

When our Lord Jesus came down from the Mount of Transfiguration, he found his disciples being harassed by the scribes, apparently because they were not able to perform the miracle of casting out the demon which possessed a young man who was brought to them. When the Lord Jesus saw what was going on, he immediately stepped in to defend the nine disciples who were baffled by their inability to perform this miracle and baffled by the learned scribes who were disputing with them. He asked the scribes why they were disputing with (questioning) his disciples. But, before the scribes said anything, before any of the disciples said anything, a man butted into the conversation (Mark 9:14-29). Normally, in polite society, such an intrusion is looked upon as rudeness and is disdained. However, this man's intrusion was most welcome, because it was the intrusion of a desperate, loving father for his demon possessed son.

This poor man cared nothing for the dispute between the scribes and our Master's disciples. His son was possessed of the devil! His son was pining away under satanic influence. His son was perishing and he was helpless! Therefore, he came directly, as soon as he had opportunity, to the only One who could help. He brought his son to the Son of God, seeking mercy, grace and life for his son by the power of our great and glorious Saviour.

Mountains And Valleys
The first thing I see in this passage is the fact that mountain top experiences seldom last very long. The contrast between this paragraph and the one preceding it is very striking and must not be overlooked. We move from the

Mount of Transfiguration to the valley of sorrow, from the vision of Christ's glory to a sad, sad history of Satan's power and influence in the life of one young man.

Peter, James and John had been in the blessed company of Moses and Elijah. They had just heard God the Father speak from heaven. They had just seen the Son of God transfigured before their eyes. Now they come into the scene of conflict, pain, weakness and misery. Here is a boy in agony, tormented by the devil. Here is a father with a broken heart, in deep distress. Here is a band of weak disciples, baffled by Satan's power and unable to help.

That is a fairly vivid picture of every Christian's life in this world. Mountain top experiences are delightful, blessed times; but we must not expect them too often or expect too many of them. Most of the believer's life is spent in conflict with the world, the flesh and the devil. Our blessed visions of glory, those sweet foretastes of heaven, those seasons spent on the holy mount with the Lord are to be seized and enjoyed when God gives them. But that is the exception, not the norm.

When we are in the valley, let us try always to remember that the Lord Jesus comes to his disciples in the valley, just as he does in the mountain. He always comes, manifesting himself to us at precisely the right time. The sorrows and conflicts of our valleys are as much by divine arrangement as the joys of our mountain tops.

Utterly Dependent

We are also reminded by this story that we are utterly and entirely dependent upon our Lord Jesus Christ. Like Moses, when he came down from Mount Sinai, our Lord Jesus found his disciples in a state of complete confusion. They were under the assault of a malicious group of scribes (Mark 9:14-16). The occasion of this was the fact that the disciples had attempted to cast the demon out of this man's son without success. These are the same men who had, just a short time earlier, done many miracles and cast out many devils. Yet, before this man and his son, they were utterly helpless.

These disciples learned by humble experience a very needful lesson. It is a lesson we must learn, a lesson that must be burned into our hearts. You will find it in the words of our Lord Jesus Christ to his chosen disciples in John 15:5. "I am the vine, ye are the branches: he that abideth in me, and I in him, the same bringeth forth much fruit: for without me ye can do nothing." Without him, without his grace, without his strength, without his wisdom, we can do nothing. This is a lesson contrary and bitter to our flesh. However, it is a lesson demonstrated over and over again in Scripture. We must not forget it. If the Lord leaves us to ourselves, we have no strength to do anything or in any way resist the devil.

May God the Holy Spirit teach us daily that we are weak; weakness itself, and utterly helpless without the wisdom, presence, power and grace of Christ, which he alone can give us.

Satanic Power

This story is also recorded upon the pages of holy scripture to teach us and warn us of the horror of satanic power. Let none imagine that Satan is a fictional force of evil. Let none be so foolish as to laugh, and think that Satan is just a religious boogie man conjured up by crotchety old men to scare little children. If we read the gospel narratives together, we find that this father described the power and influence of Satan over his son in five ways.

(1) He called this satanic spirit a foul spirit. Every foul, unclean thing proceeding out of the heart of man is promoted and encouraged by satanic influence. Those things that are contrary to nature, the moral perversities of homosexuality, are the result of God giving men and women over to the influence of hell (Romans 1:24-27).

(2) The satanic spirit possessing the father's child was a destructive spirit, tearing the boy apart from within, causing him to foam at the mouth like a mad dog, gnash his teeth and pine away. It is satanic influence that causes people to run to destruction.

(3) The spirit possessing this young man made him both deaf and dumb. The evil spirit from Satan kept the boy from hearing any who might help him and from crying out for help to any. So it is with poor, lost sinners. Satan blinds the eyes, stops the ears, and ties the tongues of men. He endeavours to keep sinners from seeing the glory of God in the face of Christ. He seeks to prevent any from hearing the gospel. And he tries to keep the needy soul from crying to the God of all grace for help. But, blessed be his name, the Friend of sinners is God's Mighty One, by whom the prince of darkness is cast out!

(4) The satanic spirit possessing this man's son made the boy "a lunatic". John Gill described his condition as "a form of epilepsy which causes fainting and dumbness, καρδιακος, a disorder of the heart." He was, as Paul tells us, taken captive by Satan at his will (2 Timothy 2:26). What a sad picture! Yet, this is the picture of all sinners without Christ. Wicked men and women perform horrid atrocities in a seizure of wickedness, because sinners have no ability to resist the wicked one, until Christ comes to dwell within by the saving operations of his grace.

(5) This demon took possession of this young man as a mere child. This is a matter of deepest importance. We must labour to do good to our children

and to serve the interests of their souls, even from their earliest years. If Satan begins early to destroy them, we must begin early to save them. We must, to the best of our ability, control those who have influence over them, guide them in choosing their friends and companions, instruct them in the scriptures and the blessed doctrine of the gospel, and pray for them.

Dual Natures

We also see in this passage another of the numerous examples given in scripture of the dual natures of every believer. This is brought out clearly by Mark (Mark 9:23, 24).

"Jesus said unto him, If thou canst believe, all things are possible to him that believeth. And straightway the father of the child cried out, and said with tears, Lord, I believe; help thou mine unbelief."

Who can read those words and fail to see that faith and unbelief, righteousness and sin are found in the same person? The father of this child said, "Lord, I believe, help thou mine unbelief." He believed. Yet, he had some doubts. He brought his child with hope. Yet, he was fearful. He seems to have expressed this honestly in Mark 9:22. He said to the Lord Jesus, "If thou canst do anything, have compassion on us and help us."

You may think, "That's not much faith." You would be right in your thinking if you did. But it was enough. He took his son home completely freed of the demon's power. He had faith as a grain of mustard seed; but it was true, God-given faith. The fact is: none of God's people in this world are perfect, not even in a single area. It is not our faith, neither its strength, nor its quality, nor its quantity that matters, but Christ, the Object of our faith. Luke 9:43-45 shows us this fact: not only is true faith very often weak faith, true believers are often terribly ignorant of many very important things. Yes, all who are taught of God know the gospel. They all know all that they need to know to exercise true faith in Christ. All true believers know Christ. But it is a very dangerous thing for us to start trying to determine how much a person must know to be saved. It is not what we know that saves us, but WHO!

"And they were all amazed at the mighty power of God. But while they wondered every one at all things which Jesus did, he said unto his disciples, Let these sayings sink down into your ears: for the Son of man shall be delivered into the hands of men. But they understood not this saying, and it was hid from them, that they perceived it not: and they feared to ask him of that saying" (Luke 9:43-45).

Christ's Dominion

We are taught here, by vivid example, the totality of Christ's dominion. There are many who foolishly imagine that Satan and the demons of hell are rivals to God, that they are somehow out of control. Nothing could be further from the truth. The devil is God's devil. He is under God's control. God uses him to accomplish his own purposes. And when he gets done with him, he will destroy him.

Do you see this? Our Lord Jesus Christ exercises total dominion over Satan and his agents at all times. He speaks with almighty, sovereign authority, and Satan and his demons immediately, implicitly, totally obey his voice. Satan is strong, malicious and busy. We are no match for the fiend of hell. But the Lord Jesus Christ is yet able to save to the uttermost all who come unto God by him. He will save his elect from Satan's power. Satan can never snatch us from our Saviour's almighty, omnipotent hands. Soon, the God of peace will bruise Satan under our heels (Romans 16:20).

Believing Parents

I must not fail to call your attention to the fact that this story is recorded upon the pages of Inspiration to remind us again of the privileges and responsibilities of believing parents. We cannot save our children. We cannot change their nature. We cannot give them life and faith in Christ. Many believing men and women have raised houses full of rebels. Let none of us arrogantly and ignorantly imagine that because children are wicked something must be amiss with the parents. Such talk betrays pride and self-righteousness!

Still, there are some things we can and must do for our children. We can do for our sons and daughters what this man did for his son. He brought his son to the Saviour, to the place where Christ was to be found; and we can bring our children to the house of God to hear the gospel. He brought the Saviour to his Son by fervent prayer; and we can seek the Lord's mercy for our children. He acknowledged his son's condition to the Lord Jesus. This poor father acknowledged that his only child was possessed of the devil, deaf and dumb, a lunatic, wicked to the core, and dying. Then, he acknowledged that he had always been that way.

Mark shows us that his son's desperate need was his need. His prayer to the Saviour was, "Have compassion on us, and help us"! And he believed God for his son. He could not believe instead of his son as a proxy. There is no such thing as proxy faith. But he did believe for his son. This man understood that foolishness is bound in the heart of every child. The rod of correction must be used to drive it from him; but only the grace of God can effectually deliver a sinner from the foolishness that is in him and from the power of Satan that rules him.

Operations Of Grace

There is in this passage of scripture an instructive, beautiful picture of God's mighty operations of grace. Whenever God saves a sinner, there are certain things you can expect to see, and certain things you can expect to happen. I do not suggest by any means that all who are saved have the same experiences; but every believer's experience is similar. Death is death. Life is life. Grace is grace. And salvation is salvation. This is how God performs it. This is how the Lord God performs his mighty operations of grace in us.

First, when God saves a sinner, there is a Divine call. "Bring thy son hither" (v. 41). The Lord God of all grace orders providence to bring the chosen, redeemed sinner under the sound of the gospel and sends forth his Spirit to call his chosen to himself, by irresistible, effectual grace (Psalms 65:4; 110:3).

Second, whenever the Lord Jesus calls sinners to himself, as they are coming to him, there is usually a satanic throw (v. 42). Satan is now in a rage because he knows his time is short (Revelation 7:12). So he unleashes upon the sinner God is about to save, all his hellish power.

Third, when the Lord comes to give eternal life, there is a hopeful slaughter. God always brings us down, before he lifts us up. He always wounds, before he heals. He always strips, before he clothes. He always empties, before he fills. And God always kills, before he makes alive (Mark 9:25, 26).

"When Jesus saw that the people came running together, he rebuked the foul spirit, saying unto him, Thou dumb and deaf spirit, I charge thee, come out of him, and enter no more into him. And the spirit cried, and rent him sore, and came out of him: and he was as one dead; insomuch that many said, he is dead."

Then, blessed be his name, when the Lord Jesus comes in saving power, there is a resurrection from the dead (Ephesians 2:1-4). "But Jesus took him by the hand, and lifted him up; and he arose" (Mark 9:27).

When They Came Down

"Then there arose a reasoning among them, which of them should be greatest. And Jesus, perceiving the thought of their heart, took a child, and set him by him, And said unto them, Whosoever shall receive this child in my name receiveth me: and whosoever shall receive me receiveth him that sent me: for he that is least among you all, the same shall be great. And John answered and said, Master, we saw one casting out devils in thy name; and we forbad him, because he followeth not with us. And Jesus said unto him, Forbid him not: for he that is not against us is for us" (Luke 9:46-50).

Chapter 60

Two Things We Must Avoid

Let us be sure we read this paragraph in its context. The Lord's disciples were not able to cast out the demonic spirit possessing the young man brought to them (vv. 37-40). They ran across a man they did not know who was preaching the gospel, who cast out devils in the name of Christ, and told him to quit. Then, as they walked along, congratulating themselves on their great works, they started arguing about which of them would be the greatest in the kingdom of heaven!

In verses 46-50 our Lord Jesus Christ gives us two very important warnings. These are warnings needed in every age, warnings needed in every congregation, warnings needed by every believer. Here our Master tells us plainly that there are two things we must ever strive to avoid. We must strive to avoid these two terrible evils, because they are evils to which we are all prone and evils we seldom recognize in ourselves. We are very quick to spot them in others, but very slow to see them in ourselves. May God the Holy Spirit graciously cause us to hear his Word to us in this brief paragraph. Here our Master warns us that we must ever guard against and seek to avoid the horrible evils of pride and censorship.

Dispensational Premillenialism

"Then there arose a reasoning among them, which of them should be greatest" (v. 46). As the Lord's disciples were walking from Caesarea Philippi to Capernaum (Mark 9:33), they began to engage in an argument about which of them would be greatest in the kingdom of heaven (Matthew 18:1). I am only guessing, but the argument probably got pretty heated.

The dispute was not about degrees in glory, or in grace, or who should be the greatest apostle and preacher of the gospel. The dispute was bad enough, but not that bad. You see, these men still thought the Lord Jesus had come here to establish a carnal, earthly, Jewish empire, a literal rather than a spiritual kingdom, an earthly kingdom rather than a heavenly kingdom. Their argument was about who should be prime minister to the Messiah, to the Lord Jesus in his kingdom.

Prophecy is not and should not be a matter of great concern in the church of God. We rejoice to know that Christ is coming again (Revelation 1:7). When he comes, he will raise the dead, make all things new and sit in judgment over all his enemies (1 Thessalonians 4:13-18, 2 Thessalonians 1:7-10; 1 Corinthians 15:51-58; 2 Peter 3:10-14; Revelation 20:11-15). When the Lord Jesus comes again, our salvation will be complete. We are not in the least concerned about looking for signs and trying to figure out when the end shall be. It is absolutely evil to do so. Our business is serving and honouring our Redeemer until he comes.

Yet, the notion of dispensational, premillenialism is horribly evil. As it is with many today, it was the idea of the Jews, of the Pharisees in particular, and of these poor disciples that Christ, the Messiah, would establish a carnal, earthly, Jewish kingdom. And with that carnal doctrine, of necessity comes many carnal ideas, such as those expressed here. Be sure you understand these things ...

Our Lord Jesus Christ is the King now, seated upon the throne of David, as David's Son in heaven (Acts 2:22-36).

Our Lord's kingdom is his Church, the Israel of God, Abraham's spiritual seed, God's elect whom he redeemed with his own precious blood. "The kingdom of God is in you." "The kingdom of God is not in meat and in drink, but in righteousness, and peace, and joy in the Holy Ghost" (Romans 14:17).

We are born into the kingdom of heaven by the new birth (John 3:5-7; Revelation 20:1-6). Faith in Christ is neither more nor less than bowing to the Son of God as your rightful Lord and King.

There is no such thing as a secret rapture, a seven year tribulation period, or a literal 1000 year millennial reign. It matters nothing to me what you believe or do not believe about prophetic systems, as long as you are not deluded by such baseless nonsense as that. The reason these things concern me is that they are not only without foundation in Scripture, they promote pride, divisiveness and carnal lusts after material things in the name of Christianity. Carnal religion promotes carnal hope; and carnal hope promotes carnal desires.

Deity Manifest

"And Jesus, perceiving the thought of their heart, took a child, and set him by him" (v. 47). Here is another of those almost casual declarations of our Saviour's deity. He who is the omniscient God perceives the thoughts of men's hearts. None but God can perceive the thoughts of another's heart. And he who is God perceives the thoughts of all. Nothing is hidden from him. All things are naked and open to him with whom we have to do (Hebrews 4:13).

When our Master perceived the thoughts of the disciples' hearts, when he would reprove them for their carnal strife, he picked up a child and set it beside himself in the presence of them all.

Matthew tells us that he sat this child in the midst of them all (Matthew 18:1). He wanted them all to see the child. Seeing this child, had he said nothing at all, they should have perceived his purpose. The Lord Jesus wanted them to see that he who is but a child, the most humble and least in his own eyes, is the greatest in the Church and Kingdom of God. Putting this child beside himself, pointing to him, perhaps putting his arm around his shoulders, the Lord Jesus said, "Whosoever shall receive this child in my name receiveth me: and whosoever shall receive me receiveth him that sent me: for he that is least among you all, the same shall be great" (v. 48).

We must be careful not to make anything more of this than is intended, and not to make anything less of it than is intended. There is nothing taught or implied here about children, about the baptism of children, or the conversion of children. Nothing! Certainly, there is nothing here to indicate that children are innocent and without sin before God until they reach an imaginary age of accountability!

Christianity

The lesson is about Christianity. Our Lord is here teaching us that as a child is simple, humble, dependent, trusting and unconcerned about worldly fame, power and wealth, so we ought to walk before God. As a child, knowing its weakness, depends upon its father, so we ought, as men and women conscious of our weakness, to depend upon Christ (2 Corinthians 12:10). As a little child realizes that he is ignorant and helpless, and therefore depends upon others to teach him, guide him, hold his hand and protect him, so we ought to look to Christ for everything. As children are quickly pacified when injured by others, so we ought to be quick in forgiving those who injure and offend us. As children naturally embrace other children, so we ought to embrace others, avoiding and putting aside those things that divide men and women from one another.

"Whosoever shall receive this child", one like this child, not in age, but in meekness and humility, one that is not proud and haughty, ambitious of worldly honour and envious of others, whoever receives such a one into his house and heart (specifically, our Lord is talking about gospel preachers and the gospel we preach.) "In my name" because he belongs to me, because he is sent by me, because he represents me, because he delivers my message "Receiveth me" his Lord and Master, his Saviour and King.

Let us receive one another as Christ himself, in his name. Receive your brother because he belongs to Christ, because is one of his, bears his image, is a partaker of his grace, is loved of God, chosen, redeemed, accepted and an heir of God, joint heir with Christ and with us, one with Christ and one with us in the family of God! Such is Christ's great regard to his people that he takes anything done for one of his elect as if it had been done to him.

"And whosoever shall receive me, receiveth him that sent me." In exactly the same way as all who receive Christ receive the Father, so all who receive one of Christ's disciples receive him. And all who mistreat one of his disciples mistreat him.

"For he that is least among you all", in his own opinion, the one who truly considers himself the least, "the same shall be great", highly honoured, greatly used of God.

"And John answered and said, Master, we saw one casting out devils in thy name; and we forbad him, because he followeth not with us" (v. 49). Again, be sure to read this statement in its context. John was not here suddenly seeking to change the subject. Just the opposite: The Master's words pricked his heart. The Word of God brought to light the evil of something he and his brethren had recently done. Tender-hearted John was immediately broken hearted because he knew what they had done was totally contrary to the spirit of Christ.

In essence, he was saying, "Oh, how terribly proud and haughty we have been! Master, I have something to confess. We saw a man the other day who was casting out devils in Your name, and we rebuked him, because he was not one of us."

"And Jesus said unto him, Forbid him not: for he that is not against us is for us" (v. 50). The Master plainly rebuked that censorious spirit. He said, "Do not ever take it upon yourself to rebuke, cut yourself off from, condemn, or even speak evil of any man (in public or in private) who is doing the same work you are doing, preaching the same gospel you are preaching, labouring in my name against the prince of darkness and for the souls of men, just because he is not one of your little group."

Pride

Pride is horribly evil and always divisive. We must ever guard against and strive to avoid that sinful, shameful pride that causes us to seek to promote, elevate, and exalt ourselves. Here is a little band of insignificant nobodies, publicans and fishermen, whom the Lord Jesus had chosen, sought out, called by his grace and made to be his disciples, (sinners forgiven! rebels conquered! prodigals recovered!), arguing about who should be the greatest! And each one thought he was more deserving of high honour than any of the others!

Such is the depravity of our hearts still! There is no sin, no evil to which we are more naturally and wickedly inclined than pride. May God give us grace ever to realize this and ever be aware of this monster in our hearts that we may watch and pray. No sin is more deeply rooted in our depraved hearts. It clings to us like glue. It is as much a part of us as darkness is a part of night. It never dies, until these bodies cease to breathe. It does not even weaken.

There is no evil of our hearts so hypocritical and deceitful as pride. It wears the robe of humility. It pretends to be meek. It wants desperately to appear self-abasing. Pride is found in the ignorant and the brilliant, the poor and the rich, the most useless and the most gifted.

Yet, there is absolutely nothing about us, any of us that should make, or even allow us to be proud. What can be more absurd than a proud man? Of all creatures, we who are the sons and daughters of Adam have the least reason to be proud. Of all men, we who are made to be the objects and recipients of God's free grace in Christ have the least excuse for pride. Of all believers, sinners called and gifted of God to preach the gospel of Christ have the least reason to be proud! Nothing in this world is more contrary to the grace of God than our pride (1 Corinthians 4:7; Ephesians 3:8).

Nothing in the world is more contrary to the example our Lord Jesus left for us to follow than pride. Nothing is more contrary to our Saviour's character than our pride (John 13:1-5, 12-15; Philippians 2:1-8; 3:10).

Censorship

We must also constantly guard ourselves against and avoid our arrogant, proud tendency to censorship of our brethren. We should studiously avoid sitting in judgment over, criticizing, condemning, or in any way seeking to undermine the ministries of others who serve Christ, but are not aligned with us. That is precisely the meaning of our Lord's words in verse 50. "And Jesus said unto him, Forbid him not: for he that is not against us is for us."

One of the most shameful, God dishonouring, gospel crippling deeds of Church history is the fact that throughout the history of God's Church there have been many who equate serving Christ and defending the faith with dividing brethren. And this evil has never been more pervasive than it is today.

Be sure you understand my meaning. Our Lord is not here telling us that we are to be indifferent to sound doctrine, or that we are to compromise the gospel for the sake of getting along with others. Heresy is to be and must be exposed, identified and condemned. But there are many who serve the cause of Christ, who preach the gospel of God's free and sovereign grace in Christ, who are not a part of our "little group", our denomination, or our small circle of fellowship.

Let others, if they must, speak ill of us, separate themselves from us, censure us, and condemn us. We must not engage in such evil. For Christ's sake, for the gospel's sake, let us do what we can to promote unity in God's Kingdom, among God's people, and promote those who preach the gospel of God's free grace in Christ. As in the days of Elijah, God still has his seven thousand (though, perhaps, unknown to us), who have not bowed the knee to Baal. We are all too prone to think like those of whom Job spoke, "We are the men, and wisdom shall die with us" (Job 12:2). If others choose not to identify themselves with Don Fortner and think and speak evil of Don Fortner, that is no big deal. If they preach the gospel of Christ, if God is using them, I rejoice and thank God for them (Numbers 11:27-29; Philippians 1:12-18).

May God give us grace to cease from strife and contention. May God the Holy Spirit teach us to rejoice in the labours, usefulness and success of others who serve his cause by the gospel, pulling down the strong holds of Satan and building the kingdom of our God. "Forbid him not: for he that is not against us is for us." Let us give our time, efforts, and energies to the preaching of the gospel, aiming at the glory of God and the salvation of sinners on the brink of everlasting ruin. Let us preach Christ, not controversy, seek God's glory, not personal greatness, seek to build up, not to tear down, hold up the cross, not a creed and seek the good of men's souls, not the smile of their approval. Like John the Baptist, let us point needy sinners to Christ, the Lamb of God, and say, "Follow him", not us. Christ is not divided. Let us not be (Romans 14:4; 1 Corinthians 1:10; 3:9, 10, 16, 17; 10:15-17; Colossians 3:12-15).

Two Things We Must Avoid

"And it came to pass, when the time was come that he should be received up, he stedfastly set his face to go to Jerusalem, And sent messengers before his face: and they went, and entered into a village of the Samaritans, to make ready for him. And they did not receive him, because his face was as though he would go to Jerusalem. And when his disciples James and John saw this, they said, Lord, wilt thou that we command fire to come down from heaven, and consume them, even as Elias did? But he turned, and rebuked them, and said, Ye know not what manner of spirit ye are of. For the Son of man is not come to destroy men's lives, but to save them. And they went to another village" (Luke 9:51-56).

Chapter 61

"When The Time Was Come"

From old eternity the Son of God determined to save his people by the sacrifice of himself; and nothing could keep him from the accomplishment of his determined purpose. Having pledged himself as our Surety in the covenant of grace, he never went back on his word, or even thought about doing so (Proverbs 8:23-32). Though we fell in the garden through the sin and fall of our father Adam, our Lord's purpose never changed. At last the appointed time came; and the Son of God assumed our nature that he might die in our stead upon the cursed tree (Romans 5:6-8; Galatians 4:4-6). He had a baptism to be baptized with. He had a cup to drink. With ardent desire, he longed to eat the last passover supper with his disciples. Now, his hour had come. Now, in due time, when the fulness of time was come, Luke tells us "It came to pass, when the time was come that he should be received up, he stedfastly set his face to go to Jerusalem"

He had set his face like a flint upon the accomplishment of the great work he had undertaken for us and refused to be hindered. With the Son of God, there was no turning back. Though there were none to help and many who tried to hinder him, he would not be deterred from his great work.

A Ready Substitute
Because of his great love for us, the Son of God went to Calvary to die as our Substitute willingly (v. 51). Our great Saviour, the Lord Jesus Christ came into this world resolutely determined to fulfil his covenant engagements as our Surety. Never once did he flinch. When his hour came, "he stedfastly set his face to go to Jerusalem."

There was a time fixed in the purpose of God from eternity for the sufferings and death of our Redeemer. He knew the hour appointed. He knew his time was at hand. He never paused, never hesitated, never flinched from his purpose. He never thought about hiding from his enemies or saving himself. He had come to save others. Himself he could not and would not save.

When he saw the hour approaching, he looked through his death and sufferings and looked beyond them, to the glory that should follow. The Lord Jesus knew what his reward would be. He knew that soon he would be received up into glory (1 Timothy 3:16), received up into the highest heavens, to be enthroned as Zion's King. Moses and Elias spoke of his death as his departure out of this world, as the decease he would accomplish at Jerusalem. The Master himself looked upon it as a thing to be desired. Why? By his death, he would save his people. By his death, he would glorify his Father. And by his death, he would be translated into a better world, a better life, in better company.

May God give us grace to look upon death as a desirable thing, not a thing to be dreaded and feared. If we are Christ's, death should be looked upon as a welcome friend. Soon we shall be "received up", to be with Christ where he is (John 14:1-3; 2 Corinthians 5:1-9; Philippians 1:21-23).

Knowing that the hour had come, anticipating the joy set before him, the Lord Jesus stedfastly set his face to go to Jerusalem the place where he was to suffer and die. He was fully determined to go, and would not be dissuaded. He went directly to Jerusalem, because there his business lay. There he must lay down his life for his sheep. Courageously and cheerfully, he went to Jerusalem to die for us.

Yes, he knew all that would befall him there. But he had a mission to accomplish. He did not fail; neither was he discouraged; but set his face as a flint, knowing that he should be not only justified, but glorified too by the redemption he would accomplish there as our Substitute (Isaiah 50:7).

How should this shame us for, and shame us out of, our reluctance and backwardness to do anything for him, suffer anything for his sake, or bear any reproach for him! How can we draw back and turn from him and his service who stedfastly set his face against all opposition, to go through and finish the great work of obtaining eternal redemption for us by the sacrifice of himself at Jerusalem?

Let us ever give thanks to God our Saviour for his willingness to suffer for us and save us! The Lord Jesus knew full well all that awaited him at Jerusalem; the betrayal, the mock trial, the mockery, the crown of thorns, the spit, the spear, the agony. Yet, he never flinched! His heart, set upon us from eternity, drove him as it were, to the torment of divine wrath and judgment.

His love for us caused him to hasten to his torment, that he might redeem us from the wrath of God. It was the desire of his soul to die in our place at Jerusalem!

In the light of these things, who could ever question the willingness of God to save sinners? Jesus Christ is an able, ready, willing Saviour! He who was ready to suffer at Jerusalem is ready to save today! Nowhere is it written that he is unwilling. Everywhere it is written that he is willing to save!

May God give us grace to follow our Lord's example. Like my Master, I pray that God will give me grace to spend my life for him who spent his life for me. Let me be ready and willing to go anywhere for Christ, do anything for Christ, endure anything for Christ. When his will is known, my duty is clear. Let my face be set stedfastly, for the glory of God.

The Samaritans' Great Loss

There was a village of Samaritans who allowed racial prejudice to rob them of eternal blessedness (vv. 52, 53). If you want to see the origins of the racial strife between the Samaritans and the Jews, you can read about it in 2 Kings 17 and Ezra 4. But whatever the origin, racial prejudice is a horrible evil and often is the cause of even greater evil. These unnamed Samaritans would not receive the Lord Jesus because he was evidently determined to go to Jerusalem, and the Jews had no dealings with the Samaritans.

What a sad picture this is of man's obstinate unbelief! The Lord Jesus sends his messengers. By the gospel we preach, we make ready for him, preparing the way of the Lord. Yet, multitudes, the vast majority, like these Samaritans, find a reason not to receive him.

Angry Apostles

James and John were enraged by the behaviour of these Samaritans who so ill-treated the Master. "And when his disciples James and John saw this, they said, Lord, wilt thou that we command fire to come down from heaven, and consume them, even as Elias did?" (v. 54) They were in a tizzy! They said, "Lord, give us leave to do so and we will command fire to come down from heaven and burn them to ashes. We will make them like Sodom!"

Much could and should be said about this. James and John were zealous, but wrong. They used the Scripture, but did so rashly. They cited the prophets, but cited them in an manner never intended. Let me just say this: zeal without knowledge is a dangerous thing. It is an army without a general, a ship without a rudder. Multitudes have done great harm in the kingdom of God with zeal for the honour of Christ, but zeal that refused direction. Be warned!

The Lord Jesus sternly rebuked James and John for their suggestion and thereby sternly rebukes the spirit of persecution. "But he turned, and rebuked them, and said, Ye know not what manner of spirit ye are of" (v. 55). The reproof he gave to James and John for their fiery, furious zeal is highly instructive. Human religion often seeks to establish itself by the sword or by legislation. The church and kingdom of God has other weapon (2 Corinthians 10:4). The only weapons God's church ever uses or seeks to use, the only weapons by which God is honoured, in opposing evil and in overthrowing false religion is prayer and preaching. Godliness cannot be legislated, faith cannot be forced and righteousness cannot be established by the laws of men, by political might, or by the sword of war.

Our Master's Mission
"For the Son of man is not come to destroy men's lives, but to save them. And they went to another village" (v. 56). The Lord Jesus came to save his people from their sins (Matthew 1:21; John 3:16, 17; 1 Timothy 1:15). Everything revealed in holy scripture about the Lord Jesus Christ proclaims with loud voice, "Jesus saves! Jesus saves"! His sovereign purpose in predestination is his purpose of grace. His covenant is the covenant of grace. His incarnation is the incarnation of God in human flesh, God come to save! His miracles of mercy were but pictures of mercy flowing from his heart to needy souls. His doctrine is the doctrine of grace. Grace was poured into his lips from eternity as the sinner's Surety; and grace pours from his lips to everlasting!

> We have heard the joyful sound:
> "Jesus saves! Jesus saves!"
> Spread the tiding all around,
> "Jesus saves! Jesus saves!"
> Priscilla Jane Owens

He says to needy sinners, "Look unto me, and be ye saved, all the ends of the earth: for I am God, and there is none else." He calls poor, lost, helpless, ruined, doomed, damned sinners to himself with the promise of mercy, grace, salvation and eternal life to all who come to him!

410

"When The Time Was Come"

"And it came to pass, that, as they went in the way, a certain man said unto him, Lord, I will follow thee whithersoever thou goest. And Jesus said unto him, Foxes have holes, and birds of the air have nests; but the Son of man hath not where to lay his head. And he said unto another, Follow me. But he said, Lord, suffer me first to go and bury my father. Jesus said unto him, Let the dead bury their dead: but go thou and preach the kingdom of God. And another also said, Lord, I will follow thee; but let me first go bid them farewell, which are at home at my house. And Jesus said unto him, No man, having put his hand to the plough, and looking back, is fit for the kingdom of God" (Luke 9:57-62).

Chapter 62

A Fake Disciple And Two Misguided Preachers

The first two of these men are mentioned by Matthew as well (Matthew 8:19-21). The third is mentioned by Luke alone. The fact that Luke was inspired to give us these three men and our Lord's conversations with them in this particular place, and the fact that the three are lumped together is not accidental. The Holy Spirit has given us these three, brief conversations; and he has given them to us in this particular context for specific reasons, to teach us specific lessons.

If we would understand the lessons taught in this short paragraph, we must not fail to see the context in which it is given and keep it in mind. The Lord Jesus had just finished instructing his disciples about serving him (Luke 9:43-50, 55). Then we are told that he set his face stedfastly to go up to Jerusalem to die as our Substitute (Luke 9:51). The Lord Jesus had just announced his mission in this world, saying, "The Son of man is not come to destroy men's lives, but to save them" (Luke 9:56). And he was about to send out seventy of his disciples to preach the gospel (Luke 10:1). But just before he sends out the seventy to proclaim the gospel of his grace, Luke tells us about the Master's conversation with these three men. His purpose in doing so is obvious: If we would follow Christ, if we would serve him, we must do so wholeheartedly, with singleness of mind and clarity of purpose.

A Fake Disciple
Here is a man who volunteers to become one of Christ's disciples (vv. 57, 58). Matthew gives us just a little bit more information about him than Luke. Matthew tells us that this man was a scribe (Matthew 8:19, 20).

He was a very religious man, a scribe, a man who spent his life in the scriptures; but he was a lost man. Judging purely from the Lord's reply to his bold, confident declaration, this man had the idea in his head that it would be to his advantage to be numbered among the Lord's disciples. He seems to have thought to himself, "If this man is the Christ, if he is going to Jerusalem to establish his kingdom, I don't want to be left out and miss the great opportunity of being a part of his royal court."

He made a big, presumptuous promise. "And it came to pass, that, as they went in the way", going up to Jerusalem, where it was commonly thought the Messiah would first appear in his glory, "a certain man said unto him, Lord, I will follow thee whithersoever thou goest."

At first glance, this would seem to be a very good thing. After all, this is what all believers must do. All who are Christ's are people who follow the Lamb wherever he goes (Revelation 14:4). They willingly follow him. Whether through rain or fire, whether into prison or into death, they follow him. They are resolutely determined to do so.

The poor man, blinded by his religion, as well as by his own depraved heart, had no idea what is involved in following Christ. He did not ask. He did not care. He was not concerned about what it means to be a follower of Christ. He was only concerned about what he could gain by following him. Besides, he was quite confident that he was up to the task, whatever it might be.

Frequently, we meet with men and women just like this scribe. They are very quick to declare, "I will". They will make their declaration publicly and confidently, just like this scribe. "I will follow Christ, no matter what." But like this scribe, they speak rashly, without consideration, and speak amiss. They stand up and say, "I now give my heart to the Lord."

How often we hear preachers urging people to give their hearts to Christ. Indeed, we must give our hearts to him; but salvation does not come by us giving our hearts to him. Salvation comes by him giving grace to us, by which we are constrained to give our hearts to him. Salvation comes by Christ giving you something, not by you giving him something.

This poor scribe, like all men are naturally, was a will worshipper. He thought salvation could be his by the mere exercise of his will. He thought his decision to follow Jesus would make him part of the Kingdom of God. He thought his decision would open the door of heaven. He made a big promise. He was very confident that he could keep his promise. But he was totally ignorant of the things of God. Like Nicodemus, he could neither see, nor enter into the Kingdom of God, because he had not been born again.

The fact that this man was a fake disciple is obvious, because those things that are both essential to and vital parts of faith in Christ were missing.

It is a fact, plainly revealed in scripture, that no one can come to Christ until Christ first comes to him (John 6:44). This man came to the Lord physically, but not spiritually. He came in word, but not in heart. He came outwardly, but not inwardly. I will make no attempt to say whether he was sincere or purely hypocritical. The fact is, he could not come and did not come to Christ in saving faith. He had no divine call. He was not taught of God. There is no indication that he had experienced any conviction of sin, righteousness and judgment. He made no confession of sin, no cry for mercy, no plea for grace, and expressed no need of Christ.

This scribe simply decided he would join the "Jesus' club", become a "promise keeper", and get in on a good thing. He did not need grace. He was very confident he could follow Christ anywhere, through anything. After all, he had made his decision! But his decision could not change his heart (Romans 9:16).

Look at our Lord's answer to this scribe and learn the lesson taught in it. The path of faith in Christ is the costly, painful path of self-denial. "And Jesus said unto him, Foxes have holes, and birds of the air have nests; but the Son of man hath not where to lay his head" (v. 58).

Foxes have holes in which to bear their young, and birds have nests in which to lay and hatch their eggs; but the Lord Jesus had not even a place in which to lay his head. Though he is Lord of all, in order to save us, the Lord Jesus Christ sacrificed his very life, laid down everything (2 Corinthians 8:9; Philippians 2:5-8). If we would follow him, we must count the cost; and, counting the cost, we must willingly lay down our lives, lose our lives to him (Luke 14:25-33).

Misguided Loyalty

"And he said unto another, Follow me. But he said, Lord, suffer me first to go and bury my father. Jesus said unto him, Let the dead bury their dead: but go thou and preach the kingdom of God" (vv. 59, 60). Here is a preacher with misguided loyalty. If we only had Luke's account, we could not be certain about the fact that this man was already one of the Lord's disciples; but Matthew tells us plainly that this man was already a disciple (Matthew 8:21).

The man had been called. He was one of those like Matthew, Peter, James and John to whom the Lord Jesus had come, to whom he had said, "Follow me." Being called, he was a believer. He was a true disciple. He was, in fact, one of those whom the Lord Jesus was about to send out as a gospel preacher. It seems that he was willing to go, and wanted to go; but he desired deferment for a while, because he had another, more pressing, more important responsibility. Before he could go out preaching, he must first take care of his family's needs. He said, "Lord, suffer me first to go and bury my father."

415

Perhaps he was, as many think, saying, "Lord, let me first take care of my aging father until he dies. Then I will go." Perhaps, as our version suggests, he was saying, "Lord, my father has just died. Let me go home and bury him, and I will go." Either way, his request seems very honourable. After all, a man is responsible to honour his parents. Funerals are important. It is always proper to show respect for others. It is always proper to take care of personal responsibilities.

Why, then, did the Lord Jesus respond to this man's request the way he did? "Let the dead bury their dead: but go thou and preach the kingdom of God."

The Lord was simply saying this: There are others who can and will take care of that matter. You have more important things to do. There are other people to bury your father. I have called you and sent you to preach the gospel.

Many good men, men who know, believe, and preach the gospel spend far too much time and energy burying the dead instead of preaching the gospel. Without question, there are lots of dead people who need burying; but there are plenty of dead people to bury them. Those who have been called of God to preach the gospel must never be turned aside from their calling. Family, friends and neighbours may not (almost certainly will not) understand such devotion to Christ and his cause. But those who are called and sent of God to preach the gospel must not allow concern for the welfare of their families to interfere with obedience to God. If I am God's servant, serving the interests of his Kingdom and his glory, he will take care of those things that concern me concerning my family and its welfare.

No man can serve God on his terms. Sadly, there are many who attempt to do so, and pretend to do so; but the fact remains: no man can serve God on his terms! There are many who attempt to serve Christ with divided loyalties, like the man in our text, attempting to be part-time preachers, attempting to both follow Christ and pursue the cares of the world. They are willing to be preachers. They are willing to serve Christ. But they put off their service to Christ, dividing their time and energy between Christ and other matters of concern and responsibility. They fail to understand, or refuse to obey the scriptures. Those who are called of God to preach the gospel must give themselves entirely to the work of the gospel ministry: to prayer, to study and to preaching (1 Timothy 4:12-16).

If the Lord God has called me to preach the gospel, if Christ has sent me to serve his Kingdom, he will take care of my affairs. He is honour bound to do so (Exodus 34:23, 24; Luke 22:35). Matthew Henry wrote, "The way of duty is the way of safety. If we serve God, he will preserve us; and those that venture for him shall never lose by him. While we are employed in God's work, and are attending upon him, we are taken under special protection, as noblemen and members of parliament are privileged from arrests." If I feed God's family, he will feed mine. If I serve his house, he will serve mine. If I protect his children, he will protect mine. If I provide for his, he will provide for mine (2 Timothy 2:4).

Looking Back

"And another also said, Lord, I will follow thee; but let me first go bid them farewell, which are at home at my house. And Jesus said unto him, No man, having put his hand to the plough, and looking back, is fit for the kingdom of God" (vv. 61, 62). Here is a preacher who put his hand to the plough and looked back.

This man's conduct stands here as a warning to all to whom God has given the privilege of preaching the gospel. Because of the context in which this is found, I am confident this man, like the one before him and those following in chapter 10, was a man sent out by the Lord Jesus to preach the gospel. The lesson taught in these two verses is to be applied in its strictest sense to all who are sent of God to this blessed work. The lesson is clear: We cannot serve Christ with divided hearts!

This man appears to have had a divided heart. He wanted both the ease and joy of other men and the nobility of preaching the gospel. He seems to have looked upon the work of the ministry as a sacrifice rather than a privilege. He seems to have been willing to expose himself to the strongest temptation possible to turn him aside from the work to which he had been called.

This man's conduct stands as a warning to all who follow Christ. We cannot serve Christ with divided hearts! Those who look back to the world, like Lot's wife looked back to Sodom, betray something in themselves that wants to go back! Be warned. Christ will not share his throne with anyone, not even with our dearest relatives. He requires our hearts. He must be first. Abraham had to leave his father and his father's house, for Christ's sake. When he tried to both follow Christ and stay with his father, God killed his father. Moses had to forsake the woman who raised him as her own son, for Christ's sake. God forced him to choose between pleasing his wife, or obeying him (Exodus 4:24-26; Proverbs 4:20-23; 23:17, 18, 23, 26). We cannot serve Christ with divided hearts!

"After these things the Lord appointed other seventy also, and sent them two and two before his face into every city and place, whither he himself would come. Therefore said he unto them, The harvest truly is great, but the labourers are few: pray ye therefore the Lord of the harvest, that he would send forth labourers into his harvest. Go your ways: behold, I send you forth as lambs among wolves. Carry neither purse, nor scrip, nor shoes: and salute no man by the way. And into whatsoever house ye enter, first say, Peace be to this house. And if the son of peace be there, your peace shall rest upon it: if not, it shall turn to you again. And in the same house remain, eating and drinking such things as they give: for the labourer is worthy of his hire. Go not from house to house" (Luke 10:1-7).

Chapter 63

"Whither He Himself Would Come"

"After these things", after the Lord Jesus had told his disciples plainly that he must go to Jerusalem and be delivered into the hands of wicked men (9:44), after he had stedfastly set his face to go up to Jerusalem to die as our Substitute (9:51), after the Master corrected some of the errors of his disciples and showed them what was required of those who follow him (9:43-62), after exposing their pride and ambition and teaching them the necessity of childlike humility (9:47, 48), after correcting their censorious spirit (9:49, 50), after he rebuked them for wanting to call down fire from heaven upon the Samaritans (9:52-55), after the Lord Jesus again declared his mission as the Son of man (9:56), after the Master had demonstrated the necessity of whole-hearted consecration and devotion to him (9:57-62), "After these things" the Lord Jesus sent out seventy men in pairs of two to preach the gospel.

Luke here records for our learning an incident that is not mentioned by the other gospel writers. He here describes our Lord's commission of the seventy to go before his face preaching the gospel in every city and place to which he himself would come. We do not know who these men were. Their names are nowhere given. The subsequent history of their labours is not revealed. But the information set before us in these seven verses of Inspiration is very instructive and sets before us lessons that demand our careful attention.

God's Servants

The things revealed in these verses are matters which primarily concern gospel preachers. Some of the statements in this passage cannot be strictly applied to any except these seventy men. However, it is a serious mistake to think that because these things were spoken to these men specifically, or because they are specifically instructions for preachers, they therefore have no meaningful relevance to other believers. Nothing could be further from the truth.

Pastors, elders, missionaries and teachers of the gospel ought in all things to be exemplary standards for all believers to follow. But faithful gospel preachers are, first and foremost, believers; sinners saved by the grace of God, just like all God's saints. Gospel preachers, like you, are Christ's disciples, people who follow the Lamb whithersoever he goeth, and, like other believers, the servants of God. What our Lord here tells us is required of all who preach the gospel. He also requires of all who follow him.

Are you a believer? Are you one of Christ's disciples? Are you redeemed by his blood, forgiven, justified, accepted in the Beloved? Are you born of God, an heir of eternal life, a possessor of God's great salvation? If you are, the instructions here given are instructions for you. The lessons of this passage are lessons for you and me to learn, lay to heart, and follow all the days of our lives. May God the Holy Spirit teach us the lessons here revealed and give us grace to govern our lives by them for the glory of God.

Divinely Appointed

"After these things the Lord appointed other seventy also, and sent them two and two before his face into every city and place, whither he himself would come" (v. 1). These seventy men were appointed by the Lord Jesus himself to preach the gospel. The word translated "appointed" is a word that is used in only one other place in the New Testament (Acts 1:24). It means to "show" or "demonstrate". It has the idea of marking out distinctly, appointing to an office or work, by an obvious sign. A very similar derivative of the word is found back in Luke 1:80, where Luke describes the showing of John the Baptist to Israel. As John the Baptist was distinctly and manifestly appointed as God's prophet, so every God called, gospel preacher is made manifest as a man called of God by the gifts God gives him to preach the gospel.

These men appointed by Christ to preach the gospel were sent by him in pairs, two by two. They were sent in pairs because two are better than one. If the one falls, the other will pick him up. The lesson here should be obvious. Believers need one another. We cannot serve Christ alone. And preachers need the aide, encouragement and strength of other faithful men.

Our Lord did not merely send these men out like we might send a child outside to play. The words "sent forth" in verse two are very forceful. They mean "to send forth with force".

Why does Luke use that particular expression? He did so because, though every proud heart loves attention and wants to be in the spotlight (lots of men want to stand in the pulpit and preach and wear the title of a pastor or a preacher!), nothing will ever cause a man to give himself to the work of the gospel, nothing will ever cause a man to go forth as a labourer in God's vineyard, except the constraint of God's omnipotent grace and irresistible call. Bible colleges, seminaries and personal ambition put multitudes of men in pulpits. But only God can make a preacher. Only God can send forth labourers into his vineyard. Many run who are not sent; but they run in vain. Those who are sent forth by God never run in vain or never labour in vain (Isaiah 55:11; 1 Corinthians 15:58).

Before His Face

Those men sent forth by Christ into his vineyard are sent forth "before his face"! I cannot imagine a more awesome, more sobering, more weighty thought. We labour not before the faces of men, but before the face of God! All that we do, we do before his face!

Be sure you do not miss the last line of verse one. "After these things the Lord appointed other seventy also, and sent them two and two before his face into every city and place, whither he himself would come." Forceful as our English translation is, the original language is even more forceful. Luke is quite literally saying that our Lord sent these men into every city and place into which he himself was about to come.

Wherever the Son of God sends a gospel preacher, he himself comes! This is how the Lord God comes to men and women by his Spirit. He comes in by and through the preaching of the gospel (Romans 10:14-17; Titus 1:1-3; 2 Timothy 1:9, 10; 1 Peter 1:23-25; Hebrews 4:12, 13). Look at Luke 10:16 and get some idea of the seriousness with which the gospel is to be heard. If the Lord Jesus is pleased to speak to you by the gospel, you dare not receive the grace of God in vain. "He that heareth you heareth me; and he that despiseth you despiseth me; and he that despiseth me despiseth him that sent me."

Men Of Prayer

"Therefore said he unto them, The harvest truly is great, but the labourers are few: pray ye therefore the Lord of the harvest, that he would send forth labourers into his harvest" (v. 2). If we would serve Christ, honour God and serve the souls of men while we live in this world, we must be men of prayer (v. 2). This is the leading thought with which our Lord sends these men out to preach the gospel. Before he tells them what is required of them, before he tells them of the dangers they must face, before he bids them go, he says, "pray"! Prayer is the most powerful weapon we have in this world, with which and by which to serve our God (James 5:16). Prayer is the one thing in which all believers can engage. Children of God, pray for one another. Pray for God's servants. Pray for the success of the gospel. Pray that the Lord of the harvest would send forth labourers into his vineyard.

Men In Peril

"Go your ways: behold, I send you forth as lambs among wolves" (v. 3). If we would follow Christ, serve his cause and proclaim the gospel of his grace, we must be prepared, as we go through this world, to live as men in peril (v. 3). Like those earliest disciples, we live in perilous times. If we would follow Christ, if we would serve the souls of men, if we would live for the glory of God, if we would serve the interests of his kingdom, if we would make known to men the gospel of the grace of God, we must not expect to be treated any different than our Lord and his disciples were treated (1 Peter 3:18; 2 Timothy 3:12; 1 John 3:13).

The plain fact is, the offence of the cross has not ceased, and will not cease while the world stands (Galatians 5:11). As Cain hated Abel because of Abel's faith in Christ, so the children of Cain will hate and persecute the sons of Abel until the end of the world. As Martin Luther put it, "Cain will murder Abel, if he can, to the very end of the world."

Men Of Purpose

"Carry neither purse, nor scrip, nor shoes: and salute no man by the way. And into whatsoever house ye enter, first say, Peace be to this house. And if the son of peace be there, your peace shall rest upon it: if not, it shall turn to you again" (vv. 4-6).

If we would serve our God and the souls of eternity bound men and women, we must be men of purpose. Like David, we must know the cause we serve is God's cause, the cause of his Kingdom and the cause of his glory; and serve it with determination.

Those who preach the gospel are not to provide for themselves. Money and material matters must not be matters of concern to us (Nehemiah 6:3). God's servants are to provide nothing for themselves. Those who preach the gospel are to live by the gospel, by the generosity of God's people.

And God's servants must not court men. If we would follow Christ, we must be thoroughly devoted to him. Gospel preachers, in particular, must behave as men who have no time to waste on trivial matters. Let all who serve God give honour to whom honour is due. Let us ever be thoughtful, kind and courteous. But God's servants must not court men. Though we live

422

by the free generosity of faithful men and women, we must never court the favour of any.

God's servants are to be messengers of peace. Our message is the gospel of peace. We are servants of the Prince of Peace. We show men and women the path of peace. We guide people with the counsel of peace. We promote peace. And wherever Christ, the Son of Peace is, God's people and God's servants are received.

Men Of Plainness

If we would live in this world for the glory of God and lead others to do so, we must be men of plainness. "And in the same house remain, eating and drinking such things as they give: for the labourer is worthy of his hire. Go not from house to house" (v. 7).

We must strive to live as, indeed, we must strive to be, men and women whose first thoughts are about Christ, his glory, heaven, eternity, our own souls and the souls of others. These are matters of first, primary importance.

This admonition is especially applicable to all who seek to set before men and women the weighty matters of eternity. If ever a preacher becomes thought of as a man who seeks wealth, luxury and earthly pleasure, his usefulness as a preacher is at an end. It does not matter how vehemently I urge eternity bound men and women to seek the unseen world of eternity (Colossians 3:1-7; 2 Corinthians 4:15-18), if by my actions I lead them to seek those things that are seen.

The Master commands his servants to be content with the place where he sends them and with the provision he gives them, eating what is set before them. Assuring us that the labourer is worthy of his hire, he tells his servants never to go from house to house begging. The King of Glory provides well for his own. Begging, grovelling, discontent preachers are a reproach to themselves, a reproach to the gospel, a reproach to God's people and a reproach to the King!

423

"And into whatsoever city ye enter, and they receive you, eat such things as are set before you: And heal the sick that are therein, and say unto them, The kingdom of God is come nigh unto you. But into whatsoever city ye enter, and they receive you not, go your ways out into the streets of the same, and say, Even the very dust of your city, which cleaveth on us, we do wipe off against you: notwithstanding be ye sure of this, that the kingdom of God is come nigh unto you. But I say unto you, that it shall be more tolerable in that day for Sodom, than for that city. Woe unto thee, Chorazin! woe unto thee, Bethsaida! for if the mighty works had been done in Tyre and Sidon, which have been done in you, they had a great while ago repented, sitting in sackcloth and ashes. But it shall be more tolerable for Tyre and Sidon at the judgment, than for you. And thou, Capernaum, which art exalted to heaven, shalt be thrust down to hell. He that heareth you heareth me; and he that despiseth you despiseth me; and he that despiseth me despiseth him that sent me" (Luke 10:8-16).

Chapter 64

"Be Sure Of This"

Luke alone was inspired by God the Holy Spirit to record the event describe in the first part of this chapter. He tells us of the Lord Jesus sending out seventy unnamed men into the cities into which he was about to come. These men were sent with the message of his grace, sent to preach the gospel, because he was about to come to these places himself (v. 1).

You can mark this down: whenever and wherever, to whomsoever the Lord Jesus Christ is about to come in saving power, mercy and grace, he will first send a man to that place and to that person preaching the gospel. This is God's chosen, ordained method of grace; and he does not depart from it.

"Therefore said he unto them, The harvest truly is great, but the labourers are few: pray ye therefore the Lord of the harvest, that he would send forth labourers into his harvest. Go your ways: behold, I send you forth as lambs among wolves. Carry neither purse, nor scrip, nor shoes: and salute no man by the way. And into whatsoever house ye enter, first say, Peace be to this house. And if the son of peace be there, your peace shall rest upon it: if not, it shall turn to you again. And in the same house remain, eating and drinking such things as they give: for the labourer is worthy of his hire. Go not from house to house" (vv. 2-7).

Let us pick up the narrative at verse 8. These nine verses (vv. 8-16) contain lessons we need to lay to heart and remember, as we seek to serve Christ and the souls of men in this world.

Simplicity
The first thing to be learned from these verses is a lesson commonly ignored, despised, and neglected in the religious world. We have before us in verses 8-11 a very clear display of the simplicity of the gospel.

How I wish men understood this, especially those men who are preachers! The gospel of God's free, sovereign, saving grace in Christ is the most profound thing in the universe. It is a mystery of such depth and wisdom that the angels of God desire to look into it. It is such a wonder that we shall spend eternity learning its wonders (1 Corinthians 15:1-3). The gospel is a mystery of infinite proportions; but the preaching of the gospel and the faith of the gospel, believing Christ is a matter of utter simplicity (2 Corinthians 11:2-4).

When our Master sent out these seventy men, he gave them a very plain, simple, singular task. They were sent out to serve the souls of men, not to be served by men. "And into whatsoever city ye enter, and they receive you, eat such things as are set before you. And heal the sick that are therein" (vv. 8, 9). He taught his servants to live modestly, be easily satisfied, and to heal the sick. It is the responsibility of all who are sent of God to preach the gospel to heed these instructions. Preachers who seek wealth and luxury are repugnant. God's servants live upon the generosity of God's people, and rightfully so; but God's servants refuse to enrich themselves, even when given the opportunity to do so. Gospel preachers serve the souls of men. They do not seek to be served by men. Faithful men seek to heal the needs of those they serve. They do not seek to be "well heeled" by men.

Next, the Master says, "And say unto them, The kingdom of God is come nigh unto you." These men were sent out to proclaim a very plain, singular, vital message to eternity bound sinners. "The kingdom of God is come nigh unto you." They were required to preach with great simplicity and plainness of speech, to preach with boldness and confidence, urgently pressing upon their hearers the claims of Christ, the sovereign Lord. Gospel preaching is always confrontational. It always demands the surrender of rebels to Christ the Lord (Luke 14:26-33).

Rolfe Barnard used to say, "Preach for a verdict." He meant by that that preaching should always press those who hear us to do something (Come to Christ. Repent. Devote oneself more completely to the Saviour, etc.). As my old Homiletics'/Pastoral Theology professor used to tell us at the opening of almost every class, "Where there is no summons, there is no sermon." Preaching is not feeding people religious, doctrinal facts, but setting before needy souls the riches and glory of Christ, demanding faith in and surrender to him. What is preaching? It is expounding the scriptures, testifying of our experience of grace in the kingdom of God and persuading sinners to believe on the Lord Jesus Christ (Acts 28:23).

Would to God preachers would quit trying to reason men and women into faith. Sinners cannot be reasoned into faith. They can be reasoned into religion, but not into Christ. The weapons of our warfare are not carnal, but spiritual. If we would do good for the souls of men, we must preach the gospel of Christ with simplicity and boldness.

We must not be discouraged, or turned aside from our great work because some refuse to believe. See what the Lord's instructions are in this regard in verses 10, 11. "But into whatsoever city ye enter, and they receive you not, go your ways out into the streets of the same, and say", Even the very dust of your city, which cleaveth on us, we do wipe off against you: notwithstanding be ye sure of this, that the kingdom of God is come nigh unto you" (Read Romans 3:3, 4). The first lesson is this: the preaching of the gospel is a matter of singularity. We have but one message, the gospel of the Kingdom of God. The message is to be preached with deliberate simplicity. And it is to be preached with sincerity, earnestly seeking the salvation of God's elect.

Sovereignty

Second, in verses 12-15 our Lord Jesus gives us a tremendous display of divine sovereignty.

"But I say unto you, that it shall be more tolerable in that day for Sodom, than for that city. Woe unto thee, Chorazin! woe unto thee, Bethsaida! for if the mighty works had been done in Tyre and Sidon, which have been done in you, they had a great while ago repented, sitting in sackcloth and ashes. But it shall be more tolerable for Tyre and Sidon at the judgment, than for you. And thou, Capernaum, which art exalted to heaven, shalt be thrust down to hell."

Here our Saviour shows us that the Lord God Almighty, in his wisdom and sovereignty, hides the gospel from some and reveals it to others, as he will. In other words, he has mercy on whom he will have mercy; and whom he will he hardens. I know this is the meaning of our Lord's words here because he tells us so in a similar passage in Matthew 11:20-27.

"Then began he to upbraid the cities wherein most of his mighty works were done, because they repented not: Woe unto thee, Chorazin! woe unto thee, Bethsaida! for if the mighty works, which were done in you, had been done in Tyre and Sidon, they would have repented long ago in sackcloth and ashes. But I say unto you, It shall be more tolerable for Tyre and Sidon at the day of judgment, than for you. And thou, Capernaum, which art exalted unto heaven, shalt be brought down to hell: for if the mighty works, which have been done in thee, had been done in Sodom, it would have remained until this day. But I say unto you, That it shall be more tolerable for the land of Sodom in the day of judgment, than for thee. At that time Jesus answered and said, I thank thee, O Father, Lord of heaven and earth, because thou hast hid these things from the wise and prudent, and hast revealed them unto babes. Even so, Father: for so it seemed good in thy sight. All things are delivered unto me of my Father: and no man knoweth the Son, but the Father; neither knoweth any man the Father, save the Son, and he to whomsoever the Son will reveal him."

Does this mean that man has no responsibility for his own soul? Certainly not! Read Matthew 11:28-30.

"Come unto me, all ye that labour and are heavy laden, and I will give you rest. Take my yoke upon you, and learn of me; for I am meek and lowly in heart: and ye shall find rest unto your souls. For my yoke is easy, and my burden is light."

Responsibility

The third lessons taught in theses verses is this: if you go to hell, it will be altogether your own fault, your own doing. Many foolishly imagine that any talk of man's responsibility implies some ability in depraved, spiritually dead sinners; but that is not the case. It is the responsibility of all who hear the gospel to believe the gospel. If that declaration does not fit your theological system, you should scrap your system, not the Word of God (Proverbs 1:23-33; John 3:18; 16:9; 1 John 5:10).

The wages of sin is death. There is not a soul in hell that raises his proud head and declares to the Almighty, "I am damned because I wanted to trust you, I wanted to believe on Christ, but you would not give me grace, you would not give me faith, you would not save me." Rather, the damned are everlastingly tormented by the fact that they are justly damned because of their wilful unbelief.

Without question, the most abominable evil in this world is unbelief. Unbelief declares that God himself is a liar (1 John 5:10). That means that if you go to hell, you will have no one to blame but yourself! You are responsible for, and you shall be held accountable for every gospel sermon you ever heard, or could have heard, for every ray of light you have despised, and for every witness of truth you have spurned.

God's Ambassadors

Here is a fourth lesson. It is found in verse 16. Faithful gospel preachers are God's ambassadors to your soul. The Lord Jesus declares, "he that heareth you heareth me; and he that despiseth you despiseth me; and he that despiseth me despiseth him that sent me." That is exactly what the Apostle Paul asserts in 2 Corinthians 5:20-6:1. Faithful gospel preachers, men sent of God to declare his gospel are God's ambassadors, God's representatives, by whom God speaks to your soul. They are to be heard, received and treated as God's ambassadors (Isaiah 52:7; 1 Thessalonians 5:12, 13; Hebrews 13:7, 17).

"Be Sure Of This"

"And the seventy returned again with joy, saying, Lord, even the devils are subject unto us through thy name. And he said unto them, I beheld Satan as lightning fall from heaven. Behold, I give unto you power to tread on serpents and scorpions, and over all the power of the enemy: and nothing shall by any means hurt you. Notwithstanding in this rejoice not, that the spirits are subject unto you; but rather rejoice, because your names are written in heaven" (Luke 10:17-20).

Chapter 65

Joy Checked And Joy Encouraged

The Lord our God would ever have us rejoice in him and in his goodness. Indeed, true believers are described as a people who "rejoice in Christ Jesus, and have no confidence in the flesh." We are commanded to "rejoice in the Lord alway." This joy, true, spiritual joy, "joy in believing", is joy that is in the Lord and arises from the knowledge of his grace. We should always rejoice; but that admonition is tempered with "in the Lord".

Luke 10:17-20 gives us an example of our Saviour teaching his disciples to rejoice in him, his grace, and his providence; but not in other things. The Lord Jesus had sent seventy of his disciples out preaching the gospel. Here they have returned with exuberant joy. I want us to learn four things from these verses. May God the Holy Spirit inscribe these four lessons upon our hearts. They will serve us well as we seek to serve our Master in this world.

Pride
First, we are all too easily puffed up with pride. We must not blame these disciples too severely for their excitement and joy. Who would not be elated by such experiences? Yet, the report these men made, and the Master's response to it seems to suggest that their joy on this occasion needed to be tempered with more grace than they displayed. There was apparently much false fire mingled with their joy. There was too much of self in it.

"And the seventy returned again with joy, saying, Lord, even the devils are subject unto us through thy name. And he said unto them, I beheld Satan as lightning fall from heaven" (vv. 17, 18).

Young soldiers, with their first taste of victory, are often lifted up with far too much self-confidence and self-congratulation. The Lord Jesus seems to have read this evil in their hearts. Therefore, he seems to say to them, "Calm down a little. What you have seen and experienced is not your doing, but mine." "I beheld Satan as lightning fall from heaven" long before you were born (Revelation 12:3, 4; Isaiah 14:12-17). He foresaw and promised Satan's fall through the preaching of the gospel (Matthew 16:18). He had come specifically to topple Satan's throne in the hearts of men (Ezekiel 28). He had come to bind the old serpent.

Yet, as I said, we must not be too severe with these men. Every faithful gospel preacher wants success. We all want to see the Word of God run swiftly and run well. We long to see Satan fall, sinners converted, and Christ triumphant over the hearts of men. Such desires are right and good. But, when the Lord condescends to grant us a little usefulness in this great work, we tend to forget that we are only instruments by which he works (1 Corinthians 3:5-7). We can do nothing! Our hearts are easily depressed when we see no success, and easily elated when we taste success. There are few who can, like Samson, kill a lion without telling of their feat (Judges 14:6).

Paul's warning to Timothy is well-founded and should be constantly heeded (1 Timothy 3:6). It is the gospel we preach, not the ability we possess to preach it, that is the power of God unto salvation (1 Corinthians 1:18-24).

Satan

Second, Satan is an enemy under the complete dominion and control of our great Saviour. He who saw Satan fall is the one who felled him! He cast Satan out by his death on the cross, binding the Deceiver by his almighty power as Lord over all, lest he continue to deceive the nations (Revelation 20:1-3). He causes Satan to fall every time he saves a sinner by his omnipotent grace (Matthew 12:29; John 12:28-32).

While it is exciting and joyous to see Satan's power broken, we ought rather to expect it than be surprised by it (Ezekiel 28:11-19). Satan does not and cannot move without our Master's permission. Yes, he walks about as a roaring lion seeking whom he may devour; but he is a chained lion, without power, a lion with neither fangs nor claws to harm God's elect. He is God's devil, not God's rival!

Things We Fear

Third, I pray that our God will graciously teach us that nothing can ever hurt us. Our Saviour's promise is as clear as it is great: "Behold, I give unto you power to tread on serpents and scorpions, and over all the power of the enemy: and nothing shall by any means hurt you" (v. 19).

Without question, God's servants during this apostolic era were given special powers, gifts which no man has possessed since that day. So the words of this verse are to be taken literally, insofar as those men were concerned (Mark 16:18; Acts 28:3-5).[11]

---

[11] The Lord's disciples were not crazed snake handlers! He did not promise them (or us) security against idiocy! He promised them (and us) protection as they went about serving his interests, preaching the gospel.

Yet, this 19th verse is our Saviour's promise to us as well. Understand the serpents and scorpions as figurative representations of the power of the enemy. The Lord Jesus here promises us that satanic power will never harm God's elect (2 Timothy 3:1-14). Neither the poison of sin, nor the sting of the scorpion, nor the bite of the serpent shall hurt God's elect. Neither the poison of false doctrine, nor the sting of persecution, nor the serpent of hell shall harm one of God's own (Romans 16:20). Indeed, "Nothing shall by any means hurt you" (Psalm 91:9-13; Proverbs 12:21; Isaiah 3:10; 11:8, 9; Hosea 2:18; Romans 8:35-39). No enemy can hurt us. Satan cannot hurt us. Sickness shall not hurt us. Trials shall not hurt us. Wicked men shall not hurt us. All our sorrows and woes shall never hurt us. Death shall not hurt us. Yes, at last, even sin itself shall not hurt us (Revelation 21:4).

Electing Love And Saving Grace
Fourth, in all things and above all things, we ought always to rejoice in God's electing love. Here is a cause for true joy! "Notwithstanding in this rejoice not, that the spirits are subject unto you; but rather rejoice, because your names are written in heaven" (v. 20). There is a book called the Lamb's Book of Life (Revelation 13:8; 17:8). In that blessed book all the names of God's elect were written before the world began. Eternally, immutably, forever written in heaven!

God's election is our security. Yes, we are secured by the blood of Christ, by the seal of the Spirit, and by the gift of grace. But all these things are the result of and flow from God's electing love (Jeremiah 31:3). And that electing love ought to give us constant joy before our God. As it caused David to dance before the ark (2 Samuel 6:12-21), our election to eternal life ought to make our hearts dance with joy before our God. It was his election by the grace of God that comforted David on his death bed (2 Samuel 23:1-5); and it is election that comforts God's saints in all ages as they leave this world.

Is your name written in heaven? There is only one way anyone on earth can ever know whether his name is written in this book. The only way a sinner can know that his name is written there is by faith in Christ. I know that my name is there because I believe on the Son of God, and God has declared, "he that believeth on the Son of God hath everlasting life." "And whosoever was not found written in the book of life was cast into the lake of fire" (Revelation 20:15).

"In that hour Jesus rejoiced in spirit, and said, I thank thee, O Father, Lord of heaven and earth, that thou hast hid these things from the wise and prudent, and hast revealed them unto babes: even so, Father; for so it seemed good in thy sight. All things are delivered to me of my Father: and no man knoweth who the Son is, but the Father; and who the Father is, but the Son, and he to whom the Son will reveal him. And he turned him unto his disciples, and said privately, Blessed are the eyes which see the things that ye see: For I tell you, that many prophets and kings have desired to see those things which ye see, and have not seen them; and to hear those things which ye hear, and have not heard them" (Luke 10:21-24).

Chapter 66

Our Saviour's Only Joy

There are five tremendous lessons revealed in these verses which deserve our careful attention. May God the Holy Spirit inscribe them upon our hearts.

Our Saviour's Joy
First, we learn from these verses that which is the joy of God our Saviour. The only thing revealed in the Book of God that gives joy to the Lord Jesus Christ is the salvation of his people.

This is the only place on record in the four gospels of our Saviour rejoicing. We read that in that hour "Jesus rejoiced in spirit". Three times we are told that our Lord Jesus Christ wept (Luke 19:41; John 11:35; Hebrews 5:7). Once only we are told that he rejoiced. And what was the cause of our Saviour's joy? It was the conversion of lost souls, the salvation of poor, needy sinners. It was the reception of the gospel by the weak and lowly, the poor and despised, the downtrodden and outcasts, when the "wise and prudent" on every side rejected it.

Our blessed Lord no doubt saw much in this world to grieve him. He saw the obstinate blindness and unbelief of the multitudes and wept. But when he saw a few poor men and women receiving the glad tidings of salvation, his holy heart was refreshed. He saw it and was glad. The only thing I find in the Book of God that causes him joy is the salvation of his people. Yet, of this one thing we are assured repeatedly (Micah 7:18-20; Zephaniah 3:14-17; Hebrews 12:1, 2).

This fact ought to encourage sinners to seek God's mercy and grace in Christ. If he delights in mercy, if he rejoices in the salvation of sinners, if the conversion of lost souls makes the Son of God rejoice, why should any sinner doubt that he will be gracious to him?

Our Saviour's example in this ought to inspire us to seek such a heart of compassion and mercy toward needy souls. Spirit of God, stamp my Master's image on my heart! Give me the grace to follow his example! Did the Son of

God weep over the lost? Shall we care nothing? Did he have compassion upon the rich young ruler who walked away from him? Shall we harden our hearts against such? Did he rejoice in the salvation of sinners? Shall we not rejoice in the same?

I fear we find joy in the very things that ought to grieve us most and grieve over things that are really of no consequence. The multitudes around us are walking in the broad way that leads to destruction; careless, hardened, and unbelieving. Few, precious few, believe to the saving of their souls! How we ought to rejoice in the conversion of sinners! How we ought to labour for it! "Brethren, if any of you do err from the truth, and one convert him; Let him know, that he which converteth the sinner from the error of his way shall save a soul from death, and shall hide a multitude of sins" (James 5:19, 20).

How can we be so indifferent in our attitude regarding the salvation of eternity bound sinners? Do we not realize that sinners around us are in immediate danger of eternal torment, perishing without Christ? We fail, I fear, to look upon the conversion of lost sinners as a miracle of grace, a miracle as great as the raising of Lazarus from the dead. Perhaps we find so little relish and joy in our souls over the salvation of sinners because we have begun to look upon the grace of God, the blood of Christ, and covenant mercy as common, ordinary things. God save us from such thoughts!

Divine Sovereignty

Second, we see in this passage a lesson about Divine sovereignty. Let us always recognize and bow to this fact. The Lord God Almighty is absolutely sovereign in the exercise of his saving mercy. "In that hour Jesus rejoiced in spirit, and said, I thank thee, O Father, Lord of heaven and earth, that thou hast hid these things from the wise and prudent, and hast revealed them unto babes: even so, Father; for so it seemed good in thy sight" (v. 21).

Yes, our Saviour rejoiced in the exercise of sovereignty by the Holy Lord God; but he rejoiced in the exercise of sovereignty to the salvation of perishing souls. It is not merely the concept of sovereignty that gives us hope, joy and peace, but the gracious exercise of it!

The meaning of these words has been twisted. Be sure you understand what the Master's words here mean. They do not express joy at the fact that multitudes perish, but at the fact that some are saved. When the Master said, "I thank thee, O Father, Lord of heaven and earth, that thou hast hid these things from the wise and prudent, and revealed them unto babes", he was saying, "Father, I thank you that you have in your infinite goodness revealed these things to these chosen babes, though you have in just judgment hidden them from those who, being wise and prudent in their own eyes, will not repent." Similar expressions are found in Isaiah 12:1 and Romans 6:17.

Having said that, be sure you understand this. The God of the Bible, the only true and living God is absolutely sovereign and always exercises his sovereign right over men, especially in the exercise of his saving mercy, love and grace in Christ. This fact is as plainly revealed in holy scripture as the fact that God is! It is not a deep, complicated, indiscernible mystery, but a plainly revealed truth of the Bible. It is so plainly revealed that it cannot be denied or misunderstood except by those who refuse to bow to Divine Revelation. Yes, it is as high as heaven and as deep as hell. Yet, it is as plain as the noonday sun.

Why are some converted and others remain dead in sins? Why does God send the gospel to one land and leave another groping about in the darkness and superstition of idolatry? Why do some believe while others believe not? No answer can or should be given to these question by any mortal other than this: "Even so, Father, for so it seemed good in thy sight" (John 10:25-27; Romans 9:13-16).

Yet, the fact of God's sovereignty does not in any way destroy or even contradict the fact that every man is responsible for his own soul. The fact is, if we are saved, it is all God's work, God's gift, and God's operation. But if we are lost, if we perish, if we go to hell, it will be our own fault alone, our own work alone, our own blame alone.

Wherever the gospel is hidden, wherever eyes are blinded, there is a just and right cause (Proverbs 1:23-33; Matthew 15:38). Israel was cut off because of their unbelief (Romans 10:20). Wherever grace is given, wherever Christ is revealed, wherever salvation comes, there is no cause except in God himself. "For the wages of sin is death; but the gift of God is eternal life through Jesus Christ our Lord" (Romans 6:23). God's sovereignty does not nullify our responsibility. That same God who does all things according to the counsel of his own will; always addresses sinners as responsible and accountable creatures, whose blood shall be on their own heads if they are lost (Proverbs 29:1; Matthew 23:37, 38).

Objects Of Grace
Third, we learn something here about the objects of God's saving grace. The Lord God commonly hides the gospel from the wise and prudent and reveals it unto babes. Our Saviour said, "Thou hast hid these things from the wise and prudent and hast revealed them unto babes."

Those words do not imply that some are naturally more deserving of God's grace and salvation than others. We are all alike sinners, and merit nothing but wrath and condemnation. Rather, our Lord is here simply stating a fact. The wisdom of this world often makes people proud, and increases their natural enmity to Christ and the gospel. The man who has no pride of knowledge, or fancied morality to fall back on often has the fewest difficulties to get over in coming to the knowledge of the truth. The publicans and sinners are often the first to enter the kingdom of God, while the Scribes and Pharisees stand outside.

Beware of self-righteousness! Nothing so blinds the eyes of our souls to the beauty of the gospel as the vain, delusive idea that we are not so ignorant and wicked as others, and that we have a character that will bear God's inspection. Blessed is that person who has learned that he is "wretched, and miserable, and poor, and blind, and naked" (Revelation 3:17). To see that we are vile is the first step towards being made righteous. To know that we are ignorant is the beginning of all saving knowledge. God's grace commonly comes to the most unlikely, most unexpected, and most despised (1 Corinthians 1:18-31).

Christ's Pre-eminence
Fourth, this passage shows us the pre-eminence of our Lord Jesus Christ. The sinner's only Saviour and Friend has all power put into his hands. "All things are delivered to me of my Father: and no man knoweth who the Son is, but the Father; and who the Father is, but the Son, and he to whom the Son will reveal him" (v. 22).

These words are intended to set before us a sense of the majesty and dignity of our Lord Jesus Christ as that One to whom the Father has given all pre-eminence and glory. No man but the God-man ever used words like these. They reveal to our wondering eyes a glimpse of the great mystery of our Lord's nature and person. He is the only God-man Mediator, by whom we must be saved. He is the Head over all things, and King of kings. Our Lord Jesus Christ is God the Son, one with the Father, yet distinct from the Father (1 John 5:7).

Our Master here declares that he alone is the Revealer of God to the sons of men, as the God who pardons iniquity, and loves sinners for his Son's sake: "No man knoweth who the Father is but he to whom the Son will reveal him." Robert Hawker rightly observed,

"Nothing can be more plain, than that it became impossible for the creation of God to know anything of Jehovah, in his three-fold character of persons, but by the immediate act of the Son, begotten into his mediatorial character, God-Man in one person, thereby to reveal him. By this voluntary act of the Son of God, and by this humbling himself, in order to make this revelation through the medium of the manhood, he hath done that, which, without this union of nature, never could have been done. And by this act, he hath brought in a new glory to the Godhead, in that his creatures have now a knowledge of the Father, Son, and Spirit; and which opens to the felicity of God's intelligent creation to all eternity."

This great, glorious, exalted, sovereign God-man, this great Saviour is exactly the Saviour we need. Let us confidently rest our souls, yea our lives, yea all things upon him. He is one who is "mighty to save." Many and weighty as our sins are, Christ can bear them all. Difficult as the work of our salvation is, Christ is able to perform it. If Christ was not God as well as man, we might indeed despair. But with such a Saviour as this, we may begin boldly, and press on hopefully, and await death and judgment without fear. Our help is laid on one that is mighty (Psalm 89:19). Christ over all, God blessed forever will not fail any who trust him.

Our Great Blessedness

Fifth, we are reminded of the great blessedness that is ours. There is no greater privilege afforded sinners on this earth than the privilege of hearing the gospel of God's free, sovereign, saving grace in Christ. "And he turned him unto his disciples, and said privately, Blessed are the eyes which see the things that ye see: For I tell you, that many prophets and kings have desired to see those things which ye see, and have not seen them; and to hear those things which ye hear, and have not heard them" (vv. 23, 24).

I am sure none of us will ever comprehend on this earth the full significance of those words. I am sure we have no idea how blessed we are to live in this gospel age. The difference between the knowledge of believers in the Old Testament and those of this age, we simply cannot conceive.

The saints in the Old Testament trusted Christ by faith. They believed the gospel. They believed in the resurrection and a life to come. But the coming of Christ and the accomplishment of redemption by his death, his resurrection and exaltation unlocked hundreds of scriptures which before were closed, and cleared up scores of doubtful points which before had never been solved. As Paul puts it, "the way into the holiest was not made manifest, while the first tabernacle was standing" (Hebrews 9:8).

Our Lord would have us aware that the privilege of hearing the gospel, the privilege of having a place of worship, a regularly established, faithful gospel ministry, and the blessed fellowship of his people is the greatest privilege God can give to any sinner in this world. The greatest curse would be for him to take from us this great privilege! What a deep sense of our own debt to God we ought to have! What a great sense we ought to have of our responsibility to make the gospel known to immortal souls! Let us strive to make good use of our many privileges. Having the privilege and benefit of the gospel, let us take care that we do not neglect it. "To whomsoever much is given, of them will much be required" (Luke 12:48).

"And, behold, a certain lawyer stood up, and tempted him, saying, Master, what shall I do to inherit eternal life? He said unto him, What is written in the law? How readest thou? And he answering said, Thou shalt love the Lord thy God with all thy heart, and with all thy soul, and with all thy strength, and with all thy mind; and thy neighbour as thyself. And he said unto him, Thou hast answered right: this do, and thou shalt live. But he, willing to justify himself, said unto Jesus, And who is my neighbour? And Jesus answering said, A certain man went down from Jerusalem to Jericho, and fell among thieves, which stripped him of his raiment, and wounded him, and departed, leaving him half dead. And by chance there came down a certain priest that way: and when he saw him, he passed by on the other side. And likewise a Levite, when he was at the place, came and looked on him, and passed by on the other side. But a certain Samaritan, as he journeyed, came where he was: and when he saw him, he had compassion on him, And went to him, and bound up his wounds, pouring in oil and wine, and set him on his own beast, and brought him to an inn, and took care of him. And on the morrow when he departed, he took out two pence, and gave them to the host, and said unto him, Take care of him; and whatsoever thou spendest more, when I come again, I will repay thee. Which now of these three, thinkest thou, was neighbour unto him that fell among the thieves? And he said, he that shewed mercy on him. Then said Jesus unto him, Go, and do thou likewise" (Luke 10:25-37).

Chapter 67

The Good Samaritan

We are not told whether this is a narrative of fact or merely a story, a parable, our Lord used to illustrate the gospel, because that is really unimportant. The story here given by our Saviour, like all those he so masterfully wove into his preaching, was intended to teach spiritual, eternal truths of the gospel.

Parable's Purpose
Our Master's purpose in giving us this story was to show us the utter impossibility of salvation by the works of the law, and his own glorious, sweet blessedness and efficacy as the sinner's only Friend.

That this is the intent of the narrative before us is obvious. The story was given in response to the question raised by a lost, self-righteous religionist, a man who hoped to justify himself before God and in his own conscience by his religious devotion. That proud worm, by his pretence of sincerity, "tempted" (tried to confuse) the Lord Jesus. His only intent was to catch the Lord Jesus in his snare; but the Saviour seized the opportunity to teach the gospel, causing the wrath of man to praise him (Psalm 76:10).

You will observe that the Lord Jesus sent this proud lawyer to the law to show him his evil, to convince him of his sin, to silence him. That is the purpose of the law.

"Now we know that what things soever the law saith, it saith to them who are under the law: that every mouth may be stopped, and all the world may become guilty before God. Therefore by the deeds of the law there shall no flesh be justified in his sight: for by the law is the knowledge of sin" (Romans 3:19, 20).

When blessed of God to the sinner's heart, the law is our schoolmaster, pointing us to Christ and always bringing us to Christ, that we might be justified by faith in him (Galatians 3:24). It is never made a yoke of bondage to God's saints. We who trust Christ are dead to the law; and the law is dead to us (Romans 7:4; Galatians 2:19). We are not under the law, but under grace. We are assured of this blessed fact so often and in so many ways that error concerning the believer's freedom from the law is inexcusable (Romans 6:14, 15; 10:4; Galatians 5:1-4, 18). The law was made, not for a righteous (justified) man; but for the unrighteous (1 Timothy 1:5-11). Therefore, when this proud lawyer sought to trap our Lord Jesus, the Master sent him to the law to condemn him in his own conscience.

A Lawyer And The Law
"And, behold, a certain lawyer stood up, and tempted him, saying, Master, what shall I do to inherit eternal life? He said unto him, What is written in the law? How readest thou? And he answering said, Thou shalt love the Lord thy God with all thy heart, and with all thy soul, and with all thy strength, and with all thy mind; and thy neighbour as thyself" (vv. 26, 27).

The word "lawyer" here does not refer to the kind of lawyer we think of when we use that term. This lawyer was a lawyer of the absolute worst kind. He was worse than an ambulance chaser or one of those "Call Me, Let's Sue" men you see in television ads. This man was a religious lawyer, a scribe. He was one of those men who was absolutely devoted to religion, religious works, and religious activity. He was a man who thoroughly believed he could make himself worthy of God's acceptance, if he just put his mind to it. He is called a "lawyer" because he was a scribe, a promoter of law religion.

As I said before, his purpose in raising his learned and pious question was to tempt the Son of God. He was trying to get him to say something against the law. He was trying to catch him in a slip up, and thereby demonstrate the Master's ignorance of holy scripture. He wanted to discredit the Lord of Glory and discredit the gospel of God's free, sovereign, saving grace in him. So he asked a very sincere sounding question. "Master, what shall I do to inherit eternal life?" You will remember that this was the same question raised by the rich young ruler in Mark 10:17. They were both cut from the same bolt of cloth. Both sought eternal life by the works of the law, by the doing of their own hands.

The Master answered him with a question of his own. "What is written in the law? How readest thou?" The man came seeking to justify himself by the law, so the Master sends him to the law, because those who seek righteousness by the law simply do not understand the law (Galatians 2:19-21; 3:10; 4:21).

When the Lord Jesus asked him what the law required, this fine specimen of religion answered him without the least hesitation. "Thou shalt love the Lord thy God with all thy heart, and with all thy soul, and with all thy strength, and with all thy mind; and thy neighbour as thyself." He had a bad case of "versitus". Like most religious people, he had a verse for everything. This was one of those scriptures the Pharisees carried in their phylacteries. They recited it morning and evening, like a papist rubs his rosary beads, for good luck. This poor, deluded soul, this empty-hearted, empty-headed religionist, like the Jews at Sinai, was perfectly confident that he had done this and would continue to do it in a manner completely acceptable to God.

This Do
Then, in verse 28 the Lord Jesus "said unto him, Thou hast answered right: this do, and thou shalt live." This man understood the letter of the law, but nothing of the spirit. Our Lord here declares what this poor man did not understand, and, indeed, few men understand: Eternal life is not to be had without a complete and perfect obedience to all that is required in the law. If you would be saved (justified, sanctified, assured of acceptance, made righteous in any way or to any degree) by keeping the law, you have got to keep it! You must love God perfectly. You must love your neighbour (your worst, most implacable enemy) perfectly. In other words, it is impossible to obtain eternal life by obedience to the law for one very obvious reason: no sinful man can obey God's law!

The Master's declaration is this: righteousness cannot be obtained by law obedience, by anything a man can do. Like most people, this man ignored the Lord's word and, rather than acknowledging his failure and sin, attempted to justify himself. Embarrassed he had to cover himself. "But he, willing to justify himself, said unto Jesus, And who is my neighbour?" (v. 29).

If only he could make the law say and require less than it does, he might have been able to find comfort in it, or at least make people think he found comfort in it. Therefore, ignoring what he had just quoted about loving God with all his heart, he says, "And who is my neighbour?" The indication seems to have been. I have loved my neighbour and do. Perhaps he was saying, "I love my family, my relatives, my kinsmen, my friends, and my nation." That is easy. They're yours. But your neighbour, those God requires us to love, and love as ourselves, are not our family and friends, but our worst enemies.

The whole purpose of this story of the good Samaritan is to show us that the law of God requires that we do what no man can do; and that Christ Jesus, the God-man our Mediator, has done for his elect precisely what the law requires. The Lord Jesus Christ came down here to fulfil the law for us, loving God with all his heart and his neighbour as himself. This is what the story of the good Samaritan declares (Romans 5:6-8).

A Certain Man

"And Jesus answering said, A certain man went down from Jerusalem to Jericho, and fell among thieves, which stripped him of his raiment, and wounded him, and departed, leaving him half dead" (v. 30).

Remember, our Lord's purpose here is to answer this religious legalist who desired to justify himself. He is not giving out a lesson on brotherly love. He does that elsewhere. To do so here would be like saying to this self-righteous legalist, "You're on the right course. See that you follow through and you will be just fine." Our Lord's purpose here was to expose this man's sin, show him the utter folly of his hope, and tear down his refuge of lies. Our Lord's purpose was to show this man, and us, the utter necessity of salvation by a Substitute.

This "certain man who went down from Jerusalem to Jericho" is our father Adam [12] who went down from his original state, fell among thieves, who stripped him, wounded him, and left him half dead.

This describes the sin and fall of our race in that certain representative man Adam. As this man went down from Jerusalem, which stood on high ground, to Jericho, which was in a low place, so our father Adam and all the human race in him went down. How far down we went, how far we fell, when Adam sinned in the Garden, when we sinned against God in him, no mortal can know, let alone declare! "Lo, this only have I found, that God hath made man upright; but they have sought out many inventions" (Ecclesiastes 7:29).

Adam fell from a state of happiness into misery, from a state of uprightness into a state of grovelling baseness, and from a state of righteousness into a state of sin. Our father Adam fell from a state of acceptance and communion with God into a state of separation and woe, from a state of blessedness into a state of cursedness, and from a state of peace (Jerusalem) into a state of condemnation (Jericho). He fell from a state of unity with God into a state of enmity against God, from a state of worship into a state of sensuality, and from a state of knowledge and prosperity into a state of ignorance and poverty.

---

[12] There are only two "certain" men mentioned in the text. The thieves, the priest, and the Levite were utterly insignificant. So there are but two men with whom God works, two men by whom God deals with all men: The First Adam and The Last Adam (A Certain Man and a Certain Samaritan) (Romans 5:12-20).

This man, in his journey from Jerusalem to Jericho, fell among thieves. So did we! When we forsook our Creator, when we rebelled against God, our race fell into the hands of two thieves, sin and Satan. How they have robbed us! They robbed us of great honour, the image of God in which we were created. They robbed us of great nobility, living for the glory of God! These thieves left us in a state of utter depravity and spiritual deprivation. They have stripped us of righteousness, leaving us naked. Fallen man is a naked creature, has nothing with which to cover himself, and stands exposed to the law, justice, and wrath of God. We are a people totally destitute of righteousness, with no ability to perform righteousness, justify ourselves, and bring ourselves back into Divine favour!

As they have stripped us and robbed us, sin and Satan have wounded us and left the entire human race half dead. This does not suggest anything to deny the total depravity and spiritual death of our race. Rather it is an accurate picture of it. We are alive physically, but dead spiritually. We are under the sentence of eternal death; but it is a sentence that is not yet executed. Like the nation described in Isaiah 1, we are a people wounded with an incurable wound, and but for the balm of sovereign grace, covered from head to toe with wounds and bruises, and putrefying sores. The plague of our race is a heart plague that none can heal but the Son of God.

A Priest And A Levite

"And by chance there came down a certain priest that way: and when he saw him, he passed by on the other side. And likewise a Levite, when he was at the place, came and looked on him, and passed by on the other side" (vv. 31, 32).

These two men represent the whole law of God, moral and ceremonial, and show us the utter inability of the law to save, or even to help fallen man. As such, they represent the whole of works religion. They declare in loud, clear, thunderous words, "By the deeds of the law shall no flesh be justified" (Romans 8:1-4; Hebrews 10:1-9).

Look at the picture drawn by our Lord in Luke 10:31, 32. When this priest saw this poor wretch, he passed by on the other side. When he saw the poor soul, naked and in such a bloody condition, he crossed the road, lest he be defiled by coming into contact with such a corrupt, vile thing. Nothing so hardens the hearts of men as self-righteous, legalistic religion. Nothing on earth makes a man more useless to men than legalism! Nothing is more cruel than religion without Christ; and nothing makes men more cruel to one another!

"Likewise, a Levite, when he was at the place, came and looked on him, and passed by on the other side." Can you picture the scene? This fine Levite comes over, takes a look at the poor creature laying in the gutter, wallowing in his blood, and shakes his head. I can almost hear him as he crosses the street: he shakes his head and says in very humble, teary tones, "There, but for the grace of God, go I." But he still crossed the street without any effort to help, comfort, or assist the man.

The priest and the Levite both passed by without the slightest movement of heart toward this poor soul. They did not help. They could not help. They did not and could not fetch any help. And they did not even point the poor man in the direction of help. They left him exactly as they found him. He was not one wit better off because they passed his way! O Heavenly Father, do not allow me to come into contact with any needy soul and leave him no better off than he was before!

Still, the thing our Lord is showing us here is the utter inability of the law to help fallen man. It was never the purpose of the law to do so. Be sure you hear and understand what God says about this. The law is unbending. There is no mercy in the law.

The law will not and cannot abate its demands. The law makes no allowance for the weakness of our condition. The law gives no consideration to age, position, knowledge, environment, or circumstance. The law simply demands perfection or death. The law leaves us where it finds us. The law is no milder in this gospel age than it was at Mount Sinai. It will not and cannot accept an imperfect, though very sincere, obedience. It demands perfect holiness, inward and outward, without a flaw.

The law is deaf to the cries of sorrow, repentance, and fear. It demands perfection. It offers no relief, no hope, no cure to anyone. The law can do nothing except show us our nakedness, our wretchedness, our helplessness, our guilt, and our doom. It can do nothing else. All the law does is condemn and kill. It cannot give life. It is a ministration of death, nothing else. It terrifies, but never comforts. It condemns, but never gives hope. It brings despair, but never peace. It wounds, but never heals. The law cannot come down to us. The law cannot touch us. All the law can do is condemn and kill.

The gospel does not teach men and women to live by or obey the law. The gospel teaches us to seek to honour God in all things; but it never threatens condemnation or punishment. It never inspires or motivates by law. God's elect are "free from the law". Yet, the law demands satisfaction. The law must be fulfilled.

Help must be had from another. We need someone to come to us in our low, fallen, depraved, helpless ruin, someone who will be a true friend, a friend to meet our need, without looking to us for anything. Thanks be unto God, the Lord Jesus Christ is just such a Friend! Look at Luke 10:33-35.

A Certain Samaritan

"But a certain Samaritan, as he journeyed, came where he was: and when he saw him, he had compassion on him, And went to him, and bound up his wounds, pouring in oil and wine, and set him on his own beast, and brought him to an inn, and took care of him. And on the morrow when he departed, he took out two pence, and gave them to the host, and said unto him, Take care of him; and whatsoever thou spendest more, when I come again, I will repay thee."

This Good Samaritan is the Son of God, our Lord Jesus Christ. No, our Saviour was not a Samaritan, but a Jew, a son of Abraham. But the Jews called him a Samaritan (John 8:48) and treated him as such, as one who was utterly hated and despised by them. Our Lord takes the title. He came here to love his neighbour, to do good to his neighbour, to help his fallen neighbour, to save those who are his sworn enemies (Romans 5:6-8).

Look at these three verses in Luke 10, and learn how the Son of God saves poor, needy sinners by his almighty grace. He took a journey. That represents our Saviour's incarnation and sojourn in this world (2 Corinthians 8:9). He came to where we were. Not only did the Lord of Glory take into union with himself our nature and come into this world, in his substitutionary, sin-atoning death our blessed Saviour came to where we were. He was made to be what we are by nature, made sin for us, that we might be made the righteousness of God in him (2 Corinthians 5:21). He was made a curse for us, his cursed people, that we might receive the gift of life by his Spirit (Galatians 3:13, 14).

When he saw us, he had compassion on us. He saw us, loved us, and delighted in us as his chosen bride and companion from everlasting (Psalms 21:1, 2; 45:13, 14; Proverbs 8:22, 30, 31; Jeremiah 31:3). His love and compassion remains the same, unchanged and perfect, through all the ages of time and in all the circumstances of our lives!

At the appointed time of love, he came to us! First, the Samaritan came to where this man was. Then, "he went to him." When we could not and would not come to him, he came to us in sovereign, saving mercy. He did not come to offer help. He came to help! He bound up all our wounds: heart wounds and conscience wounds. He healed our wounds by pouring in the oil of his Spirit (grace) and the wine of his blood.

Then, he set us on his own beast. I cannot say with certainty what this beast refers to; but it may refer either to the red horse of his holy humanity (Zechariah 1:8), or to the white horse of his gospel, upon which he rides triumphantly through the ages of time.

Next, he brought us into his Inn, the Church and House of God, where he sees to our constant care. The host of the inn is a faithful pastor, a gospel preacher, one who feeds the Lord's people with knowledge and understanding (Jeremiah 3:15). The two pence is the price of redemption under the law an half shekel (Exodus 30:11-16). Two things are required for the redemption of our souls: his blood and his righteousness. The Lord Jesus has charged his servants to take care of his people; and he promises his servants that whatever it costs to care for his people, he will repay when he comes again.

An Impossible Command
Now, look at verses 36, 37. Here, our Lord shuts us up to the free grace of God in him. He does so by issuing an impossible command.

"Which now of these three, thinkest thou, was neighbour unto him that fell among the thieves? And he said, he that showed mercy on him. Then said Jesus unto him, Go, and do thou likewise."

If you would justify yourself, this is all you have to do. Be a neighbour, be a good Samaritan. Love your most implacable enemies, all of them, just like you love yourself. Pay all their debt to God. Lift them from the dead. Deliver them from the curse. Bring them to Glory. If you would justify yourself, all you have to do is meet all the demands of God's holy law perfectly, without a flaw. The only way a sinner can ever be saved, the only way we can ever be justified with God is by Christ, by faith in the Son of God (Romans 3:19-26, 31; 5:12-21).

The Good Samaritan

"Now it came to pass, as they went, that he entered into a certain village: and a certain woman named Martha received him into her house. And she had a sister called Mary, which also sat at Jesus' feet, and heard his word. But Martha was cumbered about much serving, and came to him, and said, Lord, dost thou not care that my sister hath left me to serve alone? bid her therefore that she help me. And Jesus answered and said unto her, Martha, Martha, thou art careful and troubled about many things: But one thing is needful: and Mary hath chosen that good part, which shall not be taken away from her" (Luke 10:38-42).

Chapter 68

"One Thing Is Needful"

In these five short verses we have one of the most instructive bits of history recorded in holy scripture. It describes an event in Bethany, at the home of Martha and Mary, and their brother, Lazarus.

Bethany was a little town on the east side of the Mount of Olives, about two miles east of Jerusalem. Today it is called El-'Azariyeh, perhaps because it was there where Lazarus lived, died, and was raised from the grave by the Word of the Lord Jesus.

When the Lord Jesus and his disciples came to Bethany, Martha, Mary, and Lazarus, being true disciples themselves, opened their home to the Lord Jesus and his servants, and received them with warmth and hospitality (Hebrews 13:1, 2). Apparently, our Saviour frequently visited in the home of this beloved family. But this particular visit is recorded by Luke, because there are lessons to be learned from this story involving Martha, Mary, and the Lord Jesus, which the Holy Spirit intends never to be forgotten. When we connect this event with the things recorded in John 11 and 12, it gives us a very instructive picture of the inner life of a family who loved Christ and was loved of Christ.

No Exemption From Trouble

First, let us be reminded that faith in Christ is no exemption from trouble. Believing families have troubles just like other families. We realize, of course, that grace does not run in bloodlines. The fact is we seldom see whole families walking with God and worshipping him. No one is saved because he is related to someone who is saved (John 1:11-13). Salvation comes to sinners who are chosen of God (Romans 9:16), redeemed by Christ (Galatians 3:13, 14), and born of the Spirit (Psalm 65:4).

Martha, Mary, and Lazarus were an exception. Here are three siblings living under one roof. And all three of them worshipped God. What a blessing! Yet, this godly household at Bethany was not exempt from trouble. Grace is no exemption from trouble. Faith in Christ is no exemption from heartache. Salvation is no exemption from adversity.

They had trouble with sin because they were yet sinners. Martha appears to have lost her temper. She said things she wished she had not said, and did things she wished she had not done. They had trouble with sickness, bereavement, and death because they lived in a sin-cursed world, just like we do, where such things are common. We sometimes ask, "Why me? Why mine?" We might better ask, "Why not me? Why not mine?" And they had trouble with persecution because they were devoted to Christ. When Mary anointed the Saviour with her precious ointment, Judas mocked her (John 12:3-5). When Lazarus was at the table with the Lord Jesus, the Pharisees sought to kill him (John 12:10). Martha, Mary, and Lazarus had experienced the power of his grace. They believed him. They walked in sweet communion with him, served him, and sought to make him known to others. Because they loved Christ and followed him, they were despised and persecuted of men.

Grace does not exempt us from trouble; and true godliness is not perfection. God has fixed it so that his people in this world can never have any grounds for boasting, self-confidence, and self-righteousness. We must ever look to Christ.

Individuals
Second, we see in this beloved family a clear example of the fact that God's saints are individuals. Genuine believers are often people of different temperaments and personalities. How very different Martha and Mary were! Both were faithful disciples of Christ. Both were believers. Both were born of God, converted by grace, and justified. Both honoured Christ, when few gave him honour. Both loved the Saviour. And both were loved by the Saviour. Yet, they were obviously of different temperaments and personalities.

Martha was an active, impulsive, strong-willed, hard-working woman. She felt things strongly and spoke her mind openly. She was a woman truly devoted to Christ. She was cumbered with much serving, but she was serving! Mary was a quiet, contemplative woman, more easy-going than Martha, but not less firm in her convictions. She felt things deeply, but said far less than she felt. She was a woman genuinely devoted to Christ!

Martha, when the Lord Jesus came to her house, was delighted to see him and immediately began to make preparations for his entertainment in the most lavish manner she could. Mary also rejoiced to see the Lord coming into their home, but her first thought was to sit at his feet and hear his word.

Grace reigned through righteousness in them both. But each of those ladies showed the effect of grace in different ways and at different times. We need to remember these things. We must never imagine that this person or that is not converted simply because he or she does not have our temperament and personality. (What foolish pride!) God's sheep all have their own peculiarities. The trees of the Lord's garden are not all exactly the same. All are trees of righteousness. All are cedars. But they all come in different shapes.

All true believers are alike in principle things. All confess their sins. All trust the Lord Jesus alone as their Saviour, finding in him alone all wisdom, righteousness, sanctification, and redemption (1 Corinthians 1:30). Yet, in many, many ways believers are different. In the church and kingdom of God we have both Marthas and Marys. I thank God for both!

Influence Of Carnal Care
Third, I am certain the Holy Spirit inspired Luke to record this event at Bethany to remind us of the fact that carnal cares have a way of choking out the influence of God's Word in our lives. The cares of this world that legitimately demand our attention may become a snare to our souls, if we allow them to come between us and the worship and service of our Redeemer. Nothing is so dangerous to our souls as the care of this world.

Verse 40 says, "Martha was cumbered about much serving." Her anxiety to provide the best entertainment possible for her honoured guests put her under tremendous pressure. (She had 15 or 16 or more unexpected guests drop in for dinner!) Her excessive zeal concerning temporal things caused her, for a brief period, to forget far more important spiritual things. She got carried away in herself. After a while her conscience began to torment her. She knew her thoughts were terribly selfish and sinful. But when she found herself serving tables, waiting on everyone, cleaning up the spills all by herself, while Mary sat leisurely hearing the Saviour's word, she got a little ruffled. There was a warfare going on in her soul.

Warfare Within
Martha's biting conscience and the pressure of her labour combined, and the old man Adam broke out into an open complaint, "Lord, dost thou not care that my sister hath left me to serve alone?"

How sad! Martha, for a moment, forgot who she was and to whom she was speaking. She brought upon herself a solemn rebuke and an embarrassing word of reproof that must have made a lasting impression. "How great a matter a little fire kindleth"! All of this happened because Martha allowed the innocent, household affairs of preparing dinner to come between her and her Lord. Her anger with her sister degenerated into something far worse, anger with her God!

Martha's fault should be a perpetual warning to us all. Let us ever beware of the cares of this world (Matthew 13:22). She was doing things that needed to be done and was doing them for the Lord Jesus; but she was overdoing them. She was consumed by them. They were important, but she made them too important. When the cares of this world interfere with the worship of Christ, they bring leanness to our souls.

It is not open sin and the flagrant breach of God's law alone that leads souls to eternal ruin. More often than not, it is an excessive attention given to things that are perfectly legitimate in themselves. We must ever hold the things of this world with a very loose hand and never allow anything to have first place in our hearts but Christ (Matthew 6:33, Colossians 3:1-3). All temporal things need to be labelled in our minds with a skull and cross bones, as poison. Used in moderation, they are blessings. Excessively cherished, they are a positive curse. That which we purchase by giving up worship and communion with Christ, we purchase at a very high price! "Beware of covetousness"! J. C. Ryle rightly observed, "A little earth upon the fire within us will soon make that fire burn low."

You and I must learn to leave God's servants and God's people to God's care (Romans 14:4). God's people are God's people. They are not yours; and they are not mine. They are his. God's servants are God's servants. They are not yours; and they are not mine. They are his. I sure wish we could learn that. They are not to be judged by us. They are not to be controlled by us. Their lives are not to be run by us. In the New Testament every time anyone came to our Lord and complained to him about what someone else was doing, was not doing, might do, or might not do, he rebuked them sharply (Luke 9:49, 50; John 21:21, 22).

It is absolutely none of your business, or mine, how someone else serves Christ. It is none of your business, or mine, what someone else does for his Master, or does not do. It is none of your business, or mine, what someone else gives, or does not give. The Lord God Almighty is perfectly capable of taking care of his own. Most of us have a full time job, with plenty of overtime, taking care of ourselves.

Though Martha greatly erred, she was a genuine believer. Three things demonstrate the indisputable genuineness of her faith in and love for Christ. (1) She took his rebuke with humility as being an act of love. (2) Two of the greatest confessions of faith to be found in the Bible fell from Martha's heart and lips (John 11:21, 22 and 27). And, (3) she continued to serve the Lord in the same capacity, but with a better spirit (John 12:1, 2). Do not judge someone an unbeliever because of an evil act; and do not judge yourself to be a lost soul because of an evil act (1 John 2:1, 2).

One Thing Needful
Fourth, our Saviour here teaches us that among all the many things in this world that clamour for our attention only "One thing is needful." Oh, may

God teach me that! The only thing that is needful is Christ, having Christ, knowing Christ, worshipping Christ, serving Christ, and hearing his Word! Health and prosperity, property and power, rank and honour may all be good things in their place; but they are not needful. Multitudes of God's elect never attain those things in this world. Yet, they live happily, die peacefully, and enter into glory at last. The many things for which men and women struggle and fight in this world, will in the Day of Judgment, prove to be things not needful, but rather a great weight dragging them down into hell.

Only Christ is needful! If you have Christ you have all and abound. Only grace is needful. If you have all the riches of God's grace in Christ, you have riches that shall enrich your soul forever. Only salvation is needful. If I am saved, nothing else much matters. If you are lost, nothing else should matter. Nothing else can do you any good.

At His Feet

Let us be wise and join Mary at the Saviour's feet. This is the place of mercy, grace, and salvation (Mark 5:22; 7:25; Luke 8:35). At his feet is the place of reverence, adoration, and worship (Esther 8:3; Revelation 1:17). This is the place of gratitude, thanksgiving, and praise (2 Kings 4:37; Luke 17:16; Mark 14:3). At the Saviour's feet is the place we should choose, for this is the place of faith, hope, and prayer (1 Samuel 25:24; John 11:32). At his feet is the place to be chosen, because this is the place of instruction, learning, and discipleship (Acts 22:3). Here alone we learn his Word, his will, and his way. This is the place of humility, surrender, and submission (Ruth 3:8-14), consecration, devotion, and love (Luke 7:36-50).

A Choice To Be Made

If we would have, enjoy, and benefit from this one thing needful, a choice must be made. Read verse 42 again. "One thing is needful: and Mary hath chosen that good part, which shall not be taken away from her." Our Lord's words are intended to make us wholehearted and single eyed. They are designed to inspire us to follow the Lord fully and walk closely with our God, making our souls' business our first business, and to think comparatively little of the things of this world (2 Corinthians 4:18-5:11).

Christ is the one thing needful. He is the believer's portion (Lamentations 3:25). Christ is a portion that shall never be taken from us (Psalm 89:28; John 10:28; Romans 8:38, 39). Christ is the portion that must be chosen. He is the one Pearl of Great Price. Sell all, and buy this Pearl without money and without price!

"And it came to pass, that, as he was praying in a certain place, when he ceased, one of his disciples said unto him, Lord, teach us to pray, as John also taught his disciples. And he said unto them, When ye pray, say, Our Father which art in heaven, Hallowed be thy name. Thy kingdom come. Thy will be done, as in heaven, so in earth. Give us day by day our daily bread. And forgive us our sins; for we also forgive every one that is indebted to us. And lead us not into temptation; but deliver us from evil" (Luke 11:1-4).

Chapter 69

"Teach Us To Pray"

Without question, every heaven born soul prays. Prayer is the cry of our hearts to our Father, the breath of the new born child, the panting of the believer's heart after God, the constant dependence of faith upon the God of all grace. Yet, I have no doubt, every child of God often cries out to the Lord Jesus Christ in his soul, like that unnamed disciple of whom Luke speaks in our text, "Lord, teach us to pray." That is, unless I am utterly deceived, the cry of my heart. "Lord, teach me to pray"!

Few passages of scripture are so often quoted and about which men and women are so commonly ignorant as this. Almost any child can recite what is called by most, "The Lord's Prayer." The words are memorized early and recited often. Sometimes, the words are even sung. Yet, I do not doubt, there are very few who have any idea what is here taught.

The Son of God only on two occasions verbally taught us how to pray, here and in Matthew 6. Luke is not simply repeating what Matthew said. These were two distinct occasions. The instruction in Matthew 6 is part of our Lord's Sermon on the Mount in Galilee. Here our Lord was with his disciples in Judea. There, the instruction was part of his sermon. Here his instruction is in response to the request of one of his disciples, after the Saviour himself had been engaged in prayer.

"One of his disciples" said, "Lord, teach us to pray, as John also taught his disciples." Verses 2-13 give us our Saviour's answer to that request. In this study, we will focus of attention on our Lord's instructions in verses 2-4, line by line. If we can grasp just a portion of what is written in theses three verses, it will be profitable to our souls forever.

These brief, simple lines are a mine of spiritual treasure. To expound them fully is impossible. Volumes have been written on just these brief lines. Yet, there are treasures in this deep mine that have not yet been brought to the surface. I make no pretence of being able to bring out the richest diamonds or largest nuggets. When I am done there will be much, much more left unsaid than is said. But I want, by the Spirit of God, to show you what I know to be the most prominent and most important things here taught by our Saviour. I want to show you how the Lord Jesus taught his disciples to pray.

"And it came to pass, that, as he was praying in a certain place, when he ceased, one of his disciples said unto him, Lord, teach us to pray, as John also taught his disciples. And he said unto them, When ye pray, say, Our Father which art in heaven, Hallowed be thy name. Thy kingdom come. Thy will be done, as in heaven, so in earth. Give us day by day our daily bread. And forgive us our sins; for we also forgive every one that is indebted to us. And lead us not into temptation; but deliver us from evil."

This Is Not The Lord's Prayer

This is not "The Lord's Prayer", but "The Disciples' Prayer". The Lord's prayer is found in John 17. Our Lord Jesus did not, should not have, and could not have prayed for divine forgiveness! He had not yet been made sin for us. He had no sin to be forgiven.

This is not a prayer to be memorized and recited, but a model and representation of how we are to pray and for what. Here our Lord, knowing that we do not know what to pray for as we ought, helps our infirmities. Here he teaches us what we are to pray for and how to do it.

Never do we find the disciples reciting these words as a prayer. In fact, the only other reference made to them is in Matthew 6. And here our Lord Jesus deliberately avoided giving us an exact replica of what he said in Matthew 6. The first three petitions are the same. The rest is worded very differently, though the meaning is the same. And the doxology found in Matthew 6 is here omitted altogether.

In these few, short statements, our Lord Jesus teaches us all the vital aspects of prayer. Our prayers should be simple, sincere, spiritual, and short, avoiding everything like pretence, formality, and show. In prayer we simply spread before God, our heavenly Father, the great desires and needs of our hearts, trusting him to fulfil those desires and meet those needs by his grace for the glory of his name.

What are the great desires of the believer's heart? What are the great needs we have, which cause us to wait in utter helplessness before God? Let us look at these few verses, by which our Lord teaches us how to pray, line by line.

"Our Father, Which Art In Heaven"

We do not pray to saints or angels, but to God our Father, the God and Father of our Lord Jesus Christ, the God of glory, who is in heaven. Our God and Father is the Father of all men as our Creator (Acts 17:28). Because he is the God and Father of all men by creation, it is proper for all men to praise him and pray to him. We must never forbid any to pray, or even discourage prayer by anyone!

But, God is the Father of his elect in a very distinct and very special sense (Colossians 1:20-22). We are the children of God by adoption, by election, by regeneration, and by faith. Do you trust the Lord Jesus Christ? If you do, it is right for you to call God Almighty your Father, and to come to him as such in prayer (Hebrews 4:16). We have the right, the privilege, the bold freedom and confidence of faith to pray to God Almighty in heaven, as our Father.

When we pray privately, in our closets or with our families, and when we pray collectively in the house of God, we pray as the children of God, being taught and led by God the Holy Spirit to lift our hearts to heaven and call the God of Glory "our Father"! Nothing unites hearts like mutual prayer, collectively worshipping and praying to God "our Father"!

"Hallowed Be Thy Name"

The name of God represents all his attributes by which he reveals himself to us. His name represents his Being, all that he is. When we say, "Hallowed be thy name", we are simply praying, like the Lord Jesus did, "Father, glorify thy name" (John 12:28).

God created the universe for his glory (Revelation 4:11; Proverbs 16:4). All providence works for his glory (Romans 11:36). God's object in saving sinners is his glory (Psalm 106:8). The object of Christ in his death was, above all else, the glory of God (John 12:28). It is the heart desire of every believer, above all else, that God's name be honoured, magnified, and glorified (Psalms 35:27; 40:16; 70:4; 1 Corinthians 10:31; 1 Peter 4:11). Therefore our Lord Jesus teaches us to pray, "Our Father which art in heaven, Hallowed be thy name."

"Thy Kingdom Come"

Our first concern is and must be the glory of God himself. Our second concern is for the kingdom of God. We seek, in all our prayers, that the Lord God will be pleased to establish and enlarge his church and kingdom in this world. (Psalm 122:6, 7). To pray "thy kingdom come" is simply to pray,

"Lord, save your people, establish your kingdom in this world." We pray for the kingdom of grace to be filled (Romans 11:26). And we pray for the kingdom of glory to be established (2 Peter 3:13). If our hearts' concern is for the kingdom of God, his sheep, his people, his elect, his church, let us ever pray, "Thy kingdom come".

"Thy Will Be Done, As In Heaven, So In Earth"
Prayer is not us trying to get God to do our will. Rather it is a voluntary leaving of our will to his will. "Our truest happiness", wrote J. C. Ryle, "is perfect submission to God's will." We want to obey God's revealed will. We want men and women everywhere to surrender to and obey God's revealed will. But here, our Lord is teaching us to sincerely and heartily surrender everything to and earnestly desire that God's will be done in this world exactly as it is in heaven, knowing that it always is (Ephesians 1:11).

The fact is, we simply don't know what to pray for as we ought (Romans 8:26). Most of our prayers, I fear, are accurately described by James in James 4:3. "Ye ask, and receive not, because ye ask amiss, that ye may consume it upon your lusts." Let us give thanks to our ever gracious God that, even in our prayers, he overrules the evil that is in us and done by us for our good and his glory (Romans 8:26).

In all that we have seen thus far, the concern of true prayer is altogether spiritual. Our Lord Jesus teaches us to pray for the glory of God, the people of God, and the will of God. He teaches us to submit all other matters to those greater, far more important matters.

"Give Us Day By Day Our Daily Bread"
What an instructive word this is! We are to seek God's providential supplies for ourselves and our brethren. "Give us." We seek our daily food as a gift from God, knowing that if we have bread to eat we are fed by the hand of God.

Here we are taught to seek no more than is needful for us, "bread", not gold, just bread. And we are taught to seek no more than our "daily" provision of bread. "Give us day by day", or as our Lord told us in the Sermon on the Mount, "this day our daily bread".

As we look to our God, our heavenly Father, to provide the needs of our souls, we must also look to him to give us daily bread for our bodies. We acknowledge our entire dependence upon God for life, and breath, and all things. We ask him to take charge of us, and provide for us in all that concerns this world. Our prayer ought ever to be, "Feed me with food convenient for me" (Proverbs 30:8).

"And Forgive Us Our Sins"

We must especially remember this. Our Lord here teaches us to constantly acknowledge our sinfulness and constantly seek forgiveness through his blood. We are to confess our sins continually, not in the ear of an earthly priest, but in the ear of our Father in heaven, seeking forgiveness by the merit of our great High Priest who is in heaven, the Lord Jesus Christ (1 John 1:9).

Our sins are here compared to debts, which we have incurred. They have made us debtors to God, who demands of us both righteousness and satisfaction. The Lord Jesus Christ fully paid our debt. He brought in righteousness for his elect by his obedience as our Representative. And he satisfied justice by his death. By the sacrifice of himself, our blessed Saviour obtained eternal redemption with his own blood for his chosen.

Christ is our atonement! The Triune Jehovah freely forgives our debts through the merits of Christ our Lord.

Yet, though the work was finished in the purpose of God from the foundation of the world (Hebrews 4:3) and finished in the execution of that purpose at Calvary (John 19:30), we constantly need forgiveness because we constantly sin; and we constantly have it through the infinite, perpetual merit and efficacy of Christ's blood (1 John 2:1, 2).

Without question, every child of God is fully justified and forgiven of all sin before God. But it is the life of true faith to apply daily for fresh supplies of all our grace. Though full forgiveness is ours in Christ, we want it constantly, and our Father delights to hear us cry for it, constantly, confessing and acknowledging both our sin and our faith in his dear Son for the forgiveness of our sins. Though washed, we need daily to wash our feet. (John 13:10). We make no excuse for ourselves. We plead nothing in our own behalf. We simply ask for the free, full, grace and mercy of our Father in Christ Jesus.

We must never forget the next line of this sentence. "Forgive us our sins; for we forgive everyone that is indebted to us." This is the only line in this passage that our Lord expands and explains. He does so because this is the part we are most apt to overlook (Matthew 6:14, 15). Our Lord here teaches us that if we are unforgiving, we are yet unforgiven. If we are not gracious, it is because we have not yet experienced grace. He is not suggesting that the forgiveness of sin is conditioned upon sinners forgiving one another! He is simply declaring that grace experienced in the soul makes saved sinners gracious to one another.

There is one great blessing in being wronged by others. Injuries done by others give us opportunities to imitate our great and gracious God in forgiving those who wrong us. "And be ye kind one to another, tenderhearted, forgiving one another, even as God for Christ's sake hath

461

forgiven you. Be ye therefore followers of God, as dear children; And walk in love, as Christ also hath loved us, and hath given himself for us an offering and a sacrifice to God for a sweetsmelling savour" (Ephesians 4:32-5:2). Without this brotherly love our prayers are nothing but noise, the hollow echoes of empty hearts. If we cannot forgive, we have not been forgiven.

"And Lead Us Not Into Temptation"

As long as we are in this world we are liable to temptation. As long as we are in this body of flesh, we may be drawn away of our own lust, enticed by our own nature, tempted and overcome by the snare of Satan. Here our Saviour says, "You need to be constantly aware of your weakness and Satan's strength. You need to be constantly aware of your helplessness, so that you will constantly look to me for help." Prayer, in its essence, is the conscious spreading out of my helplessness before God! Wise people seek to avoid danger. And we ask God who rules all things to keep us from the danger of temptation. May he who orders our steps order them away from temptation!

"But Deliver Us From Evil"

J. C. Ryle wrote, "We include under the word evil, everything that can hurt us, either in body or soul, and especially every weapon of that great author of evil, the devil. We confess that ever since the fall the world 'lieth in the wicked one' (1 John 5:19.) We confess that evil is in us, and about us, and near us, and on every side, and that we have no power to deliver ourselves from it. We apply to the strong for strength. We cast ourselves on him for protection. In short, we ask what our Saviour himself asked for us, when he said, 'I pray not that thou shouldest take them out of the world, but that thou shouldest keep them from the evil' (John 17:15)."

Let us ever pray that God our Father may, by his unceasing, abundant grace, "Deliver us from evil", from the evil that is in the world, the evil that is in our hearts, the evil one who seeks to destroy us, from all the evil that is the result of sin!

Blessed be his name, our God will deliver us from all evil! (Jude 24, 25). He will deliver us from evil while we live in this evil world (1 Corinthians 10:13). When he takes us out of the world in death, he will be delivering us from evil (John 14:1-3; Isaiah 57:1, 2). And in the great and glorious resurrection day, our great God will completely deliver us from all evil in resurrection glory, when he presents us before himself in the spotless perfection and beauty of Christ (Ephesians 5:25-27; Jude 24, 25).

"Teach Us To Pray"

"And he said unto them, Which of you shall have a friend, and shall go unto him at midnight, and say unto him, Friend, lend me three loaves; For a friend of mine in his journey is come to me, and I have nothing to set before him? And he from within shall answer and say, Trouble me not: the door is now shut, and my children are with me in bed; I cannot rise and give thee. I say unto you, Though he will not rise and give him, because he is his friend, yet because of his importunity he will rise and give him as many as he needeth. And I say unto you, Ask, and it shall be given you; seek, and ye shall find; knock, and it shall be opened unto you. For every one that asketh receiveth; and he that seeketh findeth; and to him that knocketh it shall be opened. If a son shall ask bread of any of you that is a father, will he give him a stone? or if he ask a fish, will he for a fish give him a serpent? Or if he shall ask an egg, will he offer him a scorpion? If ye then, being evil, know how to give good gifts unto your children: how much more shall your heavenly Father give the Holy Spirit to them that ask him?" (Luke 11:5-13).

Chapter 70

Shameless Desperation

It is very, very late. Midnight. All the lights are out. You're in bed. All your children are sound asleep. Suddenly someone rings the doorbell and starts knocking at the door. "Friend! Could you help me? I need some bread! A friend of mine has come unexpectedly, and I have nothing in the house to feed him"! You try to ignore the unwelcome, shameless intruder. But he knocks again. "Friend! I need some help. I need bread"! Still, you ignore him. Then, he knocks again. "Friend, friend! I must have some bread"! Finally, you go to the door, trying not to wake the family. Without opening the door, you say in a rather angry, unsympathetic voice, "Go away. Leave me alone. Can't you tell we are all asleep? I can't help you."

That silences the man, for a while. He stands on the stoop. Then, he turns to go home. But he cannot go home. He dare not go home. He still doesn't have any bread to set before his friend who has dropped in on him. So, he comes back. He knocks on the door again, louder than before. "Friend! Friend! Friend"! He cries, till the dogs begin barking and the neighbours start opening their doors to see what's happening. He puts his ear to the door. He knows you're there. Finally, he hears you moving. Then, he sees a light come on inside. At last, the door opens and you hand him all the bread he can possibly use. All you want to do is get rid of him and go back to bed. All he wanted was some bread to satisfy his friend. That is the story set before us in Luke 11:5-13.

Context

Be sure you read this parable in its context. Is our Lord here teaching us that if we want something bad enough all we have to do is badger God into giving it to us, like a spoiled child badgers his parents into getting what he wants, or a nagging wife gets her husband to do what he does not want to do just to stop the nagging? No. Is the Master here teaching us that if we really pray hard enough and believe strongly enough we can get anything we want from God, if we really want it, if we just refuse to give up? No.

Many faithful men and women, having pleaded with God to spare a dying loved one, as David prayed for his dying son, soon buried the one for whom they had so earnestly prayed. Many parents have prayed for their rebel children, whose children perished still in unbelief. Many of God's saints have prayed for God to relieve them of some heart wrenching trouble, as Paul prayed for God to remove his thorn in the flesh, who found that God would not grant them their request. You have experienced this, and I have too.

Our prayers never alter God's purpose or change his will. Prayer is not the art of twisting the arm of omnipotence, getting God to do what we want him to do. Prayer has something to do with our compliance with God's will. Our prayers are effectual when our prayers are in accordance with the will and purpose of God.

This parable is part of our Lord's answer to his disciple's request, "Teach us to pray." In verses 2-4 he teaches us what we should pray for and how.

"And he said unto them, When ye pray, say, Our Father which art in heaven, Hallowed be thy name. Thy kingdom come. Thy will be done, as in heaven, so in earth. Give us day by day our daily bread. And forgive us our sins; for we also forgive every one that is indebted to us. And lead us not into temptation; but deliver us from evil."

Our Lord's instruction about prayer here is not the same as that which was given in his Sermon on the Mount. Here, our Lord ends his words of instruction by telling us to seek from God the forgiveness of sin and deliverance from all evil. Then, he illustrates his doctrine by giving us the parable of the man who knocked at midnight in verses 5-13. That is the connection; and that is the secret to interpreting this parable.

In this parable our Saviour is telling us how to obtain God's salvation, the forgiveness of sins and deliverance from all evil.

Midnight

Did you ever notice how many things in the Bible took place at midnight? It was at midnight that the Lord God passed through Egypt, killed all the firstborn, and brought Israel out of the land of bondage with his mighty hand

and stretched out arm (Exodus 11:4; 12:29). That was a picture of redemption by the blood of Christ and by the power of his grace.

It was at midnight that Samson (Judges 16:3) took the gates of the city of Gaza, and the two posts, bar and all, put them on his broad shoulders, and carried them away up to the top of a high hill before Hebron. That was a picture of reconciliation by Christ's death.

It was at midnight that Ruth came into the threshing floor and laid herself at Boaz's feet (Ruth 3:8). That portrayed a needy sinner seeking God's saving grace in Christ.

It was at midnight the woman in 1 Kings 2:20 found her son gone, a dead one laid in his place. It was a picture of life destroyed by sin and life restored by the wisdom of God our Saviour in the exercise of his saving mercy.

Elihu said to Job's three miserable friends, "the mighty shall be taken away without hand" at midnight (Job 34:20). That portrayed the withering work of God the Holy Spirit in conviction.

When taught to understand God's righteous judgments, the Psalmist David said, "At midnight I will rise to give thanks unto thee because of thy righteous judgments" (Psalm 119:62). That speaks of our gratitude to the just God, our Saviour, by whom we are granted free justification.

At midnight the cry is made, "The Bridegroom cometh; go ye out to meet him" (Matthew 25:6), because Christ Jesus our Lord is coming for his bride in grace and at the second advent.

It was at midnight that the Lord God shook the earth and broke open the prison doors at Philippi that held the Philippian Jailor (Acts 16:25).

And it was at midnight that Paul and those who travelled with him across the stormy sea drew near some country hoping for safety (Acts 27:27).

Every reference to midnight in the Word of God is connected with an event that clearly pictures God's wondrous works of redemption and grace in Christ. It is no accident that our Lord in this parable speaks of a needy man coming to his friend at midnight. The parable is a word of instruction, telling us how sinners obtain God's grace in Christ.

When the time of love has come, when the appointed time of mercy has arrived, when the time has come for God to save a chosen sinner, he graciously brings the object of his love into utter desperation. He creates midnight in the soul.

Is that the case with you? Are you a poor, needy sinner sitting in darkness? Once you thought you had light. Once everything was fine. Once you thought you had everything you needed. Once you presumed that you knew everything. Now, you are utterly engulfed in thick darkness. The darkness in your soul is so thick it hurts. Is that your condition? If so, this parable is especially for you.

The Lord Jesus Christ

Our Saviour was often like this importunate poor man, out at midnight, knocking for bread. Often, after a long day of labour for the souls of men, struggles with his adversaries, warfare with Satan, and heartfelt trouble, our Master went at midnight to the gate of heaven and knocked again and again, until he got as much as he needed. These things are recorded by divine inspiration in the gospel narratives, written without emotion or exclamation. They are things at which our hearts stand still, when we suddenly come upon them. "He went up into a mountain to pray: and when the morning was come he was there alone." Again, "he departed into a mountain himself alone." And again, "It came to pass in those days that he went out into a mountain to pray, and continued all night in prayer to God."

He continued all night. Do you see Him? Do you hear Him? Can you make out what he is asking? He stands up. He kneels down. He falls on his face. He knocks in the thick darkness that lays heavy on his holy soul. All night he prays, and refuses to faint, till the sun rises, and he goes down to his disciples like a strong man to run a race.

Yonder, in Gethsemane as he anticipated being made sin for us, the Lord Jesus knocked, and knocked, and knocked again, until his sweat was as it were great drops of blood falling to the ground! Indeed, we have not an high priest who cannot be touched with the feeling of our infirmities. Rather, our Lord Jesus Christ, our great High Priest in heaven, is One, "Who in the days of his flesh, when he had offered up prayers and supplications with strong crying and tears, and was heard in that he feared." Like us, he "learned obedience through the things that he suffered." "And being made perfect, he became the author of eternal salvation unto all them that obey him."

Conversion

However, in this passage the clear, primary thing set before us is the experience of grace in conversion. A friend of ours (God's holy law) comes to us in his journey; and we have nothing to set before him. Oh, yes, the law of God is our true friend. It is a schoolmaster unto Christ. It is our friend, because it shuts us up to and forces us to flee to him, who is our souls' Friend, the Lord Jesus Christ.

God's law comes and says to us, "Be ye holy." "The soul that sinneth, it shall die." It demands of us perfect righteousness and complete satisfaction. We are all death and sin; but the law comes, and demands life and righteousness. Immediately, we set out to do what we are told from God to do; but we find that we have nothing to set before it. The law says, "This do, and thou shalt live" (Luke 10:25-37). But we cannot do what the law requires. We cannot make ourselves clean (Isaiah 1:16-18).

And then, in our famine of life, and peace, and strength, we think of God in Christ. How unwelcome is the thought! He has all that we need. If we ask it of him, he will give us all we need! There is no question about that fact. Yet, if we could make any other shift we would make it.

The holy Lord God might very well and very rightly say to us, "I do not know you. Get some of your own friends to help you." Indeed, we expect far worse from him. How we dread the thought of seeing him, worse yet, of him seeing us!

We turn back. We simply cannot go to God. But the intolerable pangs of hell are in our souls. Darkness is in our hearts. The fire of hell burns in our consciences. Famine in our souls has us bent to the ground in weakness. We have nothing. We must go on to God. No one else can help.

This horrid sinking goes on until hell itself is at the door. Then, we say like the four lepers at the entering in of the gate of Samaria: "Why sit we here until we die? Now, therefore, come and let us fall unto the host of the Syrians: if they save us alive, we shall live: and if they kill us, we shall but die."

> I can but perish if I go,
> I am resolved to try;
> For if I stay away, I know,
> I must forever die.

I grant this is not the best frame of mind in which to come to God. We ought to come to him full of confidence, full of assurance, doubting nothing. But I never knew a sinner in my life who did.

This is not a very becoming frame of mind in which to arise and go to our Father. But every father knows that a father does not stand upon points with his son who was dead, and is alive again, who was lost, and is found.

Is there midnight in your soul? Has the law of God come demanding what you know you must give, but what you cannot give? Come, then, come now to the throne of grace.

"For he satisfieth the longing soul, and filleth the hungry soul with goodness. Such as sit in darkness and in the shadow of death, being bound in affliction and iron; Because they rebelled against the words of God, and contemned the counsel of the most High: Therefore he brought down their heart with labour; they fell down, and there was none to help. Then they cried unto the LORD in their trouble, and he saved them out of their distresses. He brought them out of darkness and the shadow of death, and brake their bands in sunder. Oh that men would praise the LORD for his goodness, and for his wonderful works to the children of men"! (Psalm 107:9-15).

If today your friend, God's holy law, has come to you, and you have nothing to set before him. If, in our Saviour's words, you have come to yourself today. If it is midnight in your soul. If you are now weighed in the balances and found wanting, amid fear, or want, or whatever form your awakening may take, hear a word of grace and promise: "Ask, and it shall be given you: seek, and ye shall find: knock, and it shall be opened unto you."

Do it, as if the books were to be opened before sunrise tomorrow. Do it, as if already the thief were at your window. Go through this parable. Go through it on your knees, if not on your face. Read it, see it. This is instruction given by the Son of God himself to sinners. He is telling us how to obtain forgiveness, how to be delivered from all evil.

See the man at midnight. Imitate that man. Act out the parable in your soul's lone midnight. Leave nothing out. Look at this poor soul in his straits. Hear his knocks sounding in the silence of the night. Hear his loud cry, and cry it after him. He needed three loaves. Do you not need three vital loaves? Do you not need life from Christ? Do you not need atonement by Christ? Do you not need the righteousness of Christ? Go to the throne of grace and tell the God of all grace what you need. "If we confess our sins, he is faithful and just to forgive us our sins, and to cleanse us from all unrighteousness."

Lifelong
But conversion is not a one time thing. It is a lifelong turning to God, a lifelong coming to Christ, a lifelong struggle of soul. I have repented. I am repenting. And I shall repent. I have come to Christ. I am coming to Christ. And I shall come to Christ (1 Peter 2:1-4).

This midnight intruder represents God's elect throughout the days of their lives in this world. So long as we live in this body of flesh, we will need to be just like this poor soul: ever knocking at heaven's door, ever asking, ever seeking, because we are always in great need of grace.

Let Zion's watchmen give him no rest, until he establishes his kingdom in its fulness and makes Jerusalem a praise in the earth (Isaiah 62:6, 7). Let us ever put God in remembrance of his covenant and plead for his grace (Isaiah 43:25, 26).

Shameless Desperation
Our great, gracious God would have us come to him in shameless desperation. We have nothing to bring!

How often we feel ashamed to come to the throne of grace. How embarrassed we are that we seem only to seek him when we are in utter desperation. Yet, in this parable our Saviour teaches us to come in just that condition. If we did not need grace, we would not need to seek it. So he tells us plainly to come in our desperation, to come shamelessly, that we may obtain mercy and find grace to help in time of need.

"I say unto you, Though he will not rise and give him, because he is his friend, yet because of his importunity he will rise and give him as many as he needeth. And I say unto you, Ask, and it shall be given you; seek, and ye shall find; knock, and it shall be opened unto you. For every one that asketh receiveth; and he that seeketh findeth; and to him that knocketh it shall be opened" (Luke 11:8-10).

The word "importunity" does not adequately express our Lord's intent. In fact, the word ought to be translated, "shamelessness"! This was what our Lord really said: "I say unto you", he said, "though he will not rise and give him because he is his friend, yet because of his shamelessness he will rise and give him as many as he needeth."

"What shamelessness!" the man cried out, who was in bed, with his door shut. "What shamelessness!" the disturbed neighbours cried out. "What shamelessness!" the late passers-by said. "Hold your peace", they said, "and let honest men's doors alone at this time of night."

"Never mind", says our Lord on the other hand. "Never mind them. They have bread enough at home. It is easy for them to cry shame to a starving man. Never mind them. Knock on. Knock on. The man must rise if you go on knocking. Give him no rest. Well done! Knock again!"

Yes, shamelessness! "What a shameless wretch I am!" you will say about yourself, "to ask such things, to have to ask such things at my age, to knock so loud after the way I have rebelled against God, despised his grace, and trampled under my feet the blood of his dear Son!"

"At my age!" You now number your days and will blush with shame. "At my age, and only beginning to pray in any earnest! How many nights have I had no time to give to God! And, now, to expect that when I lift up my finger, and go down five minutes on my carpeted knees, God Almighty is to hasten and set everything aside to hear me!"

Yes. Repentance requires shameless humiliation, the very shamelessness with which Ruth went to Boaz at midnight on the threshing floor. As Christ says here, it takes "shamelessness" in us for proud rebels like you and me to come to the throne of grace in our souls' midnight and sue for mercy. There is much to aggravate our shamelessness.

The shameful things we have to ask for: pardon, atonement, grace. The incredibly shameful things we have to admit and confess. The lives we have lived. The way we have spent our days and nights. The result of our wasted lives!

It kills us to have to say such things even with our doors shut. But it is infinitely better to say all these things in closets than have them all proclaimed from the housetops in the Day of Judgment!

Knock, man! Knock! For the love of your soul, knock! Knock as Noah's neighbours knocked once the door was shut and the rains began to fall! Knock as they knock to get into heaven after the door is shut! Knock, as they knock to get out of hell! For Christ's sake, knock! Knock until the door opens and you have obtained the blessing. Like Jacob, cry out to the Son of God, "I will not let thee go except thou bless me!"

The Blessing Sought

The thing we need, the thing we must have, the thing God alone can give is the blessed gift of eternal life, grace and salvation by his Holy Spirit.

"If a son shall ask bread of any of you that is a father, will he give him a stone? or if he ask a fish, will he for a fish give him a serpent? Or if he shall ask an egg, will he offer him a scorpion? If ye then, being evil, know how to give good gifts unto your children: how much more shall your heavenly Father give the Holy Spirit to them that ask him?" (Luke 11:11-13).

This gift of the Spirit includes the whole experience of God's salvation, all the blessedness of God's covenant promised to his elect before the world began, flowing to every redeemed sinner by the merit, power, and efficacy of Christ's atoning blood (Galatians 3:13, 14).

Just before he ends his sermon on prayer, our Lord in one word gets to the heart of his doctrine. This shameless desperation in prayer is for the Holy Spirit. It is for God's salvation. It is no longer a prayer for bread, or for a fish, or for an egg. It is not a prayer for long life, or for riches, or for good health. It is not what shall we eat? or what shall we drink? or wherewithal shall we be clothed?

This is shameless importunity for life, eternal life! Our Lord would hear us saying at the end of his sermon: "One thing do I desire, and that will I seek after." We have wrestled at midnight when we saw Esau coming to meet us with his armed men. We have made our couches swim with tears when our sin found us out. We have fallen on our faces when death approached. But this one thing we must have. We must have Christ. We must have God's salvation. We must have the Holy Spirit.

It is God the Holy Spirit who weds the soul to Christ. It is God the Holy Spirit who gives dead sinners life. It is God the Holy Spirit who gives us faith. It is God the Holy Spirit who sprinkles our hearts with the blood of the Lamb. It is God the Holy Spirit who speaks peace and pardon to our souls. It is God the Holy Spirit who puts on us the garments of salvation.

The Blessing Obtained

Our Lord here promises that all who do, in the shameless desperation of faith, look to God for grace, salvation and eternal life shall obtain the blessing they seek. "And I say unto you, Ask, and it shall be given you; seek, and ye shall find; knock, and it shall be opened unto you ... If ye then, being evil, know how to give good gifts unto your children: how much more shall your heavenly Father give the Holy Spirit to them that ask him?" (vv. 9, 13; Hebrews 11:6; Jeremiah 29:10-15). When your midnight is no longer, when the Holy Spirit has finished his midnight work in you, then, (Oh blessed blessedness!) after grace, he will give glory, too!

"After this I beheld, and, lo, a great multitude, which no man could number, of all nations, and kindreds, and people, and tongues, stood before the throne, and before the Lamb, clothed with white robes, and palms in their hands; And cried with a loud voice, saying, Salvation to our God which sitteth upon the throne, and unto the Lamb. And all the angels stood round about the throne, and about the elders and the four beasts, and fell before the throne on their faces, and worshipped God, Saying, Amen: Blessing, and glory, and wisdom, and thanksgiving, and honour, and power, and might, be unto our God for ever and ever. Amen. And one of the elders answered, saying unto me, What are these which are arrayed in white robes? and whence came they? And I said unto him, Sir, thou knowest. And he said to me, These are they which came out of great tribulation, and have washed their robes, and made them white in the blood of the Lamb. Therefore are they before the throne of God, and serve him day and night in his temple: and he that sitteth on the throne shall dwell among them. They shall hunger no more, neither thirst any more; neither shall the sun light on them, nor any heat. For the Lamb which is in the midst of the throne shall feed them, and shall lead them unto living fountains of waters: and God shall wipe away all tears from their eyes" (Revelation 7:9-17).

"And he was casting out a devil, and it was dumb. And it came to pass, when the devil was gone out, the dumb spake; and the people wondered. But some of them said, he casteth out devils through Beelzebub the chief of the devils. And others, tempting him, sought of him a sign from heaven. But he, knowing their thoughts, said unto them, Every kingdom divided against itself is brought to desolation; and a house divided against a house falleth. If Satan also be divided against himself, how shall his kingdom stand? because ye say that I cast out devils through Beelzebub. And if I by Beelzebub cast out devils, by whom do your sons cast them out? therefore shall they be your judges. But if I with the finger of God cast out devils, no doubt the kingdom of God is come upon you" (Luke 11:14-20).

Chapter 71

"The Kingdom Of God Is Come Upon You"

The claims of Christ are the claims of the sovereign King. If you do not bow to him as your King, you have not received him as your Saviour. Whether you bow to him or not, he is still your King. We are all his subjects, some willingly, others unwillingly, some loyal, some rebel; but we are all his subjects. And, sooner or later, we will all bow to him. Bow to him now, and life eternal is yours. If you refuse to bow to him now, you will bow in the Day of Judgment; but eternal death will be your portion. May God give you grace now to bow. O "kiss the Son, lest he be angry when his wrath is kindled"!

The Kingdom of God is not something yet to come. It is here. It is present. The Kingdom of God is not carnal, but spiritual. It is among you. The Kingdom of God is not a temporary kingdom, but an eternal, everlasting kingdom.

Remember Context
In interpreting holy scripture, it is of utmost importance that we interpret every passage in its context. In this case, the context is strikingly instructive. Our Lord Jesus has just told us how sinners obtain God's salvation in him. He said, "Ask, and it shall be given you." That is the promise of God held before sinners throughout the Book (Romans 10:13; Mark 16:16; Acts 16:31; Isaiah 45:22). The fact is, all who are lost, all who are without Christ, all who perish under the wrath of God do so because they stubbornly refuse to seek mercy through the merits of Christ, the sinner's Substitute. "There is none that seeketh after God"! If you are yet without Christ, it is because you refuse to trust Christ.

Hope

Yet, there is hope for you. I have hope for lost sinners, because I know that though our Saviour waits to be gracious, his grace does not wait on the sinner. All lost sinners are like the man in our text, possessed of the devil and dumb, so dumb that they cannot and will not call upon the name of the Lord, except the Lord himself come, cast out the devil, set up his kingdom in them, loosen their tongues and cause them to call upon him by his sweet, omnipotent, irresistible grace (Psalm 65:4).

The great miracle recorded in Luke 11:14-20 is intended to show us how lost sinners are compelled by almighty grace to call upon Christ in faith. He who promises that if we ask it shall be given unto us is he who destroys the power of Satan in us and causes us to call upon him for mercy.

> He breaks the power of cancelled sin,
> He sits the captive free,
> He makes the lame to walk again,
> And causes the blind to see.
>
> Hear him, ye deaf! His praise, ye dumb!
> Your loosened tongues employ!
> Ye blind, behold your Saviour come,
> And leap, ye lame for joy!

Satan's Devices

Satan's devices by which he seeks to destroy our souls are legion. We read here of a man possessed of a devil that was dumb. In other places, we see Satan's imps described as unclean spirits. Sometimes they are violent. In other places they come as blind spirits, in other places as deaf spirits. Whatever the appearance, Satan's devices are many; and they are always designed for destruction.

Do not imagine that because demonic possession is not so glaringly obvious and common today as it once was that the fiend of hell is less active or his designs less destructive. That is not the case. Men and women are still taken captive by Satan at his will. No doubt, some who read these lines are possessed of a dumb spirit, just like this poor soul. Are you like this man, possessed of a dumb spirit? Though you speak much, do you ever speak to God? Though you call upon many for many things, do you call upon the name of the Lord? If so, you do not call upon him because you have neither the will nor the ability to do so. You are spiritually deaf and spiritually dumb.

Thanks, eternal thanks be unto God, the Lord Jesus Christ still makes the dumb to speak. He who cast this demon out is still in the business of casting Satan out of the hearts of men! When the time of love has come for chosen, redeemed sinners, though Satan rules in the hearts of lost, dead sinners, the Lord Jesus binds the strong man, casts him out, spoils his house, takes all his armour, and establishes the dominion of grace in their hearts by the power and grace of his Spirit for the glory of God. Only Christ can raise the dead. Only Christ can give eyes to see the glory of God shining in his face. Only Christ can open the sinner's ears to hear the glorious sound of his grace. Only Christ can give the tongue of supplication. But, blessed be his name, he can! Jesus Christ our Lord is mighty to save (John 12:32; Hebrews 7:25).

Wilful Unbelief

I want you to see that unbelief is a wilful, deliberate act. Unbelief is not something about which sinners are passive, for which they have no responsibility. Unbelief is the deliberate, wilful defiance of the rebel heart. Every rebel sinner is just exactly like the people described in this passage of holy scripture.

It could not be denied that the Lord Jesus had cast out a devil, that he had loosened the tongue of a man who could not speak before. Those who were present could not dispute the miracle. The work of grace was as glaring and obvious as the noonday sun. Still, they would not believe.

Some wondered and marvelled; but they would not believe! How many there are like them today! Many there are who marvel at electing love, stand in awe at divine predestination, wonder at the display of God's saving grace, and are astonished by substitutionary redemption, who yet believe not!

Others sought to discredit the Lord Jesus, saying he cast out the devil by the devil. They could not deny the work. So they tried to discredit the Son of God.

Still others said, "Show us a sign from heaven." Is that not amazing? Yet, it is ever the betrayal of rank unbelief in the hearts of men that demands a sign. "Show us a sign" is the cry of hell. The Jews require a sign. The Greeks seek after wisdom. But we preach Christ crucified, the power of God and the wisdom of God.

The fact is all unbelief is inexcusable. It is not adultery that will take a sinner to hell, but unbelief! It is not theft that will take the lost to hell, but unbelief! It is not drunkenness that takes people to hell, but unbelief! Unbelief is blameable. It is wilful. It is deliberate. Those who believe not believe not because they choose to believe not. If you read these lines and continue to believe not, you will forever die under the wrath of God (John 3:14-19, 36; 1 John 5:1, 6-10).

Christ's Divinity

There are several incidental, but divinely inspired, displays of our Saviour's eternal divinity in this passage. We trust him who is both God and man in one glorious person. That man who died for us at Calvary is himself God the eternal Son. Because he is God, his obedience is of infinite worth. Because he is God, his death is of infinite merit. Because he is God, his grace is of infinite efficacy. Here are three great manifestations of our Saviour's eternal divinity: his dominion over hell; devils obey him! His omniscience; he knew their thoughts! His marvellous grace; he made the dumb speak!

Family Strife

Our Lord Jesus here declares in a parable a word of warning that needs frequent repetition. It is a warning against needless strife.

"But he, knowing their thoughts, said unto them, Every kingdom divided against itself[13] is brought to desolation; and a house divided against a house falleth. If Satan also be divided against himself, how shall his kingdom stand? because ye say that I cast out devils through Beelzebub. And if I by Beelzebub cast out devils, by whom do your sons cast them out? therefore shall they be your judges" (vv. 17-19).

Without question, our Master is here telling these rank, ridiculous rebels that their blasphemous assertions were as absurd as they were blasphemous. If Satan casts out Satan, his kingdom would soon fall. But there is a much needed lesson here for us. It is a lesson we are mournfully and sinfully slow to learn. Strife between brethren is both shameful and destructive. Civil strife destroys a nation. Domestic strife destroys families. And strife between brethren destroys local churches. Strife breaks the house at the foundation; and any house broken at the foundation will soon fall.

We cannot and must not compromise the gospel of the grace and glory of God in Christ. With regard to the gospel, all God's people and all God's servants see eye to eye (1 Corinthians 16:22; Galatians 1:6-9; 5:12; Philippians 3:18, 19; 2 John 1:9-11). But when it comes to matters that do not involve the gospel of Christ and the glory of God in Christ, in all matters of indifference we must cease from strife. There is no place in the house of God for petty quarrels and proud strife. The only remedy for this horrid evil is grace. O, may God teach us to be gracious! Let everyone who names the name of Christ be slow to anger, quick to forgive, anxious to serve, ready to make concessions, and hard to offend (Ephesians 4:17-5:2).

---

[13] Broken at the foundation.

A Confrontation

Our text ends with a confrontation. "But if I with the finger of God cast out devils, no doubt the kingdom of God is come upon you" (v. 20). The Lord Jesus Christ has, by the finger of God, cast out devils, both at Calvary by the power of his blood, crushing the serpent's head, and in the saving operations of his omnipotent grace (Colossians 2:11-15). When King Jesus establishes his throne and his kingdom in the hearts of chosen, redeemed sinners, he makes saved sinners kings and priests unto God (Exodus 19:6; 1 Peter 2:5, 9; Revelation 1:6; 5:10; 20:6; 22:5). Thus, the Kingdom of God has come and is now coming to sinners upon the earth.

"When a strong man armed keepeth his palace, his goods are in peace: But when a stronger than he shall come upon him, and overcome him, he taketh from him all his armour wherein he trusted, and divideth his spoils. He that is not with me is against me: and he that gathereth not with me scattereth. When the unclean spirit is gone out of a man, he walketh through dry places, seeking rest; and finding none, he saith, I will return unto my house whence I came out. And when he cometh, he findeth it swept and garnished. Then goeth he, and taketh to him seven other spirits more wicked than himself; and they enter in, and dwell there: and the last state of that man is worse than the first" (Luke 11:21-26).

Chapter 72

The Strong Man Armed Bound And Cast Out

From the beginning of time the prince of darkness has been at war with the Son of God, and the Son of God has been at war with him (Genesis 3; Isaiah 14; Revelation 12). It is a mutual conflict, a mutual enmity. It is ever the purpose of that fiend of hell and the myriads of demons ruled by him to topple the throne of God, usurp his authority, and destroy the souls of men. His principle weapon of warfare is religious self-righteousness and will-worship (2 Corinthians 11; Galatians 1:6-9).

But the fiend of hell, that old serpent, the devil shall accomplish nothing. He is God's devil. He is by the omnipotent power of Christ forced into servitude. And soon he shall be cast into hell, crushed beneath our Saviour's feet and ours. Yes, he shall be crushed beneath the feet of us, poor, weak mortals whom he seeks to destroy (Romans 16:20).

Because he knows he has but a short time, he is in a rage (Revelation 12:12) and goes about as a roaring lion, seeking whom he may devour. But, blessed be God, our all-glorious, omnipotent Saviour has everything in control. This lion can do nothing but roar! He cannot hurt anything or anyone in God's holy mountain, Zion! The warfare is real but victory is sure!

Beyond these things, we know nothing. Let us be wise, and leave these matters alone. Do not investigate witchcraft, demonism, and the occult. Playing with these things is indescribably more dangerous than playing with arsenic. It is enough for us to know only what God has revealed.

In Luke 11:21-26 our Lord Jesus lifts the corner of the veil and allows us to have and instructive peek at the warfare that takes place in the spirit world for the souls of men. The Lord's instruction here is not instruction about demonology and exorcism. It is instruction about the wonders of God's almighty, saving grace in Christ.

A Great Destroyer

In verse 21 Satan is described as a strong man armed, keeping his palace. The palace he keeps is the heart of a man. This is a picture of fallen man in his natural state and condition. We have before us a picture of all fallen men, deceived and being deceived by the prince of darkness. "When a strong man armed keepeth his palace, his goods are in peace" (v. 21).

Our hearts ought to be the throne of God, but they have become the palace of Satan. When our father Adam was the obedient servant of the Most High, his body was a temple for God's love. No more! Now, through the fall, we have become the servants of sin, and our bodies have become the workshops of Satan, "the spirit that now worketh in the children of disobedience" (Ephesians 2:1-4).

Satan is here called "a strong man". Who can stand against him? The monster of darkness, the red dragon of hell is well named Abaddon and Apollyon Destroyer! He has been at the business of soul destruction for thousands of years. No mortal has ever been a match for him. Adam, in all his created perfection, could not stand before the great destroyer. Samson, with all his might, was no match for the prince of darkness. Solomon, with all his wisdom, was weak as water before the fiend of hell. Satan is so strong that if all men should combine against him, he would laugh at us as Leviathan laughs at the grappling hook.

Satan is strong, not simply as one possessing force, but in the sense of intense, fiendish cunning. He knows how to adapt his temptations to our besetting sins. He knows the best time to assail us. He understands that there is a time when kings go forth to battle, and he is ever ready for the fray. He is a good swordsman. He is a supreme marksman. He knows our weak places. He sees every chink in our armour. Therefore, unsuspecting men are taken captive by him at his will.

He is a strong man with a vengeance, full of fury and full of envy (Hebrews 2:9-14). We should ever bless and praise our God that there is One stronger than this fiend of hell. Satan would crush us to eternal ruin if it were not that the omnipotent Christ comes in to rescue chosen, redeemed sinners by almighty grace.

This strong man, the Destroyer, we are told here, is armed. He is armed with the most cunning deception, the most appealing temptations, and the most alluring charms. He finds in our own hearts his willing accomplices: Our inward lusts. our stubborn pride, our wilful compliance, our hardness of heart! And he is armed with the lie of freewill, works religion.

The Prince of Darkness always keeps his palace; and his goods are in peace. Satan is never caught sleeping off guard. Whenever the Son of God comes, whenever the Holy Spirit begins to work, he will do everything he can to keep his palace. And the best way to keep his palace in the City of Mansoul is to keep his goods in peace.

While we sleep he sows tares. He never sleeps. He is always the busiest one around. We may neglect our souls; but Satan never does. He is always making visitations and going from place to place upon his evil business to watch after his black sheep. The sinner's heart must be carried away by storm, if it be ever taken, for there is no hope of taking the Evil Spirit by surprise. "He keepeth his palace. His goods are in peace"!

Kept in peace, the unbelieving soul has no fear of God before his eyes. He has no great sense of guilt before God, no uneasiness, no tormenting conscience. He is at peace. He has all the peace of one dead!

Yet, all his strength is withered muscle, all his armour is melting plastic, all his palace is unfortified, all his goods are vulnerable before that One who is stronger than he. Thank God, there is One stronger than he! And that One who is stronger than he is the Son of God, the sinners' Friend, and he is ...

A Great Deliverer

The Lord Jesus Christ, when he comes in the saving operations of omnipotent grace, comes upon and assails the Prince of Darkness in his palace, and spoils his goods (Luke 11:22; Matthew 12:29; Isaiah 49:24, 25; 53:10-12; Colossians 2:15). He comes upon the fiend of hell, binds him, overcomes him, takes away his armour, and divides his spoils.

There is an obvious reference here to Isaiah 53:12. The Lord Jesus comes and takes possession of those very goods once used by the fiend of hell for evil and makes them instruments of good in the palace of his grace!

The fact that Satan sets up and maintains an empire of sin in every human heart is a fact too obvious to be questioned by any rational person. The terrible effects of it are too well known to be denied. Here we have that fact plainly stated. "It was", as Robert Hawker wrote, "the setting up this kingdom against God and his Christ, for which the devil and his angels are said to have been cast out of heaven and to have left their own habitation (Revelation 12:7-12; Jude 6)." It was by Satan's seduction of Eve that Adam was brought down, and by Adam's transgression that the whole human race was made a fallen, corrupt, sinful race (Romans 5:12). It is Satan who works in all the children of disobedience continually (Ephesians 2:2-4).

Because Satan's kingdom of darkness, deception, and sin takes in the entire human race, he is called "the prince of this world" (John 16:11). Because he seeks to destroy our souls and seeks to destroy the church and kingdom of God, he is called "a roaring lion" (1 Peter 5:8) and "the dragon" (Revelation 12:7), "the devil" and "Satan". Here he is called "the strong man

483

armed". So powerful is his influence over the unregenerate, that men are taken captive by him at his will (2 Timothy 2:26).

How happy and thankful we ought to be to read in the Book of God that "the Son of God was manifested that he might destroy the works of the devil" (1 John 3:8). One great purpose and design of the gospel is the overthrow of Satan and his kingdom and the restoration of perfect order in God's creation. Let us rejoice! The Son of God came into this world to "save his people from their sins" and "that he might destroy the works of the devil" and that which he came to accomplish shall be accomplished! The Word of God reveals a threefold binding of Satan.

First, by his death upon the cross, in the accomplishment of our redemption, and by his resurrection from the grave our Saviour bound Satan and broke the power of his usurped dominion over the nations of the world of Satan (John 12:31-33; Colossians 2:13-15; Hebrews 2:14, 15; Revelation 20:1-6).

Then, in regeneration and conversion, by the power of his grace, through the operations of his Holy Spirit in the new birth, the Son of God binds Satan in the hearts of chosen, redeemed sinners and takes possession of his house.

That is what is described in Luke 11:21-26. Our Saviour is the man stronger than the strong man armed. He comes by omnipotent mercy into the hearts of chosen sinners, binds Satan, casts him out, and spoils him of all. This is what happens every time he saves a sinner. He does not stand knocking at the door of the lost sinner's heart, hoping that the sinner might choose to let him enter. He knocks the door down, bolt and bar, enters the house of the ransomed soul, and sets up his throne in the heart, bringing his welcome with him. Thus it is that we have been "translated from the kingdom of darkness into the kingdom of God's dear Son" (Isaiah 49:24; Mark 3:27; Luke 11:21, 22; John 12:31; 14:30; 16:7-11; Ephesians 2:1-4).

Finally, when he comes again to make all things new, the Lord Jesus will cast Satan out of this world into the lake of fire, where he shall have no more power (Revelation 20:10).

There is a day coming when Christ will come again in his glory, when the total and everlasting destruction of Satan's kingdom will take place. In that day we who are one with Christ will triumph over the prince of darkness in complete victory (Romans 16:20). There is no such thing as "a devil's hell". Hell belongs to God. It is his torture chamber in which he will forever torment the devil and all who have followed him to destruction.

Now, look at verse 23, and observe this fact. There is among men in this world ...

A Great Division

Those who are not with Christ are against him. There is no middle ground. "He that is not with me is against me: and he that gathereth not with me scattereth." The Lord Jesus here shows us the impossibility of neutrality with regard to him, his gospel, and his kingdom. Multitudes try to straddle the fence, halting between two opinions, not wishing to deny Christ altogether, and not wishing to serve him altogether, not wanting to engage in open rebellion to the Son of God, but not wanting to engage in the cause of Christ. Such neutrality is impossible.

There are, with regard to spiritual things, only two camps; there are only two sides. Either we are with Christ, committed to him and his cause, or we are against Christ, committed to the world, the flesh, and the devil. We cannot serve both God and mammon. If we do not serve Christ, we oppose him. There is no middle ground. In a word, the gospel of Christ demands decisiveness (Joshua 24:15). John Gill wrote:

"Since there is such an open war proclaimed and carried on between Christ and the devil, none ought to be neutral; whoever is not on the side of Christ, is reckoned as an enemy; and whoever is not concerned by prayer or preaching, or other means to gather souls to his word and ordinances, and to his church, and to himself, is deemed by him a scatterer of them."

Next, in verses 24-26 our Lord gives us a warning concerning spurious conversions.

A Great Deception

That which is Satan's greatest weapon of defence against Christ and the gospel of his grace, that by which he most securely keeps his palace is a refuge of lies.

"When the unclean spirit is gone out of a man, he walketh through dry places, seeking rest; and finding none, he saith, I will return unto my house whence I came out. And when he cometh, he findeth it swept and garnished. Then goeth he, and taketh to him seven other spirits more wicked than himself; and they enter in, and dwell there: and the last state of that man is worse than the first."

The unclean spirit goes out of his own free will. He is not cast out, but goes out. He walks through dry, desert places seeking rest, but finds none. He returns to his house from which he came out. When he returns, he finds his house in wonderful condition. It was swept, not washed, but swept. It was garnished, not made new, but garnished. When he returns, he brings seven spirits more wicked than himself. Then the last state of that man is worse than the first. When the sinner takes for himself a refuge of lies, seeks to hide from God in false religion, he is worse off than a person with no religion

485

(Isaiah 28:14-20). But even here, the soul is not beyond the reach of omnipotent grace (Isaiah 28:16, 20; Hosea 4:17; 11:8, 9; 13:4, 9, 12, 14).

O Lord Jesus, Great Deliverer, O Blessed Son of God, Almighty Saviour, if you are passing by, travelling in the greatness of your strength, come and show your mighty prowess. Turn aside, O Heavenly Samson, and rend the lion in this vineyard. If you have dipped your robes in the blood of your foes, come dye them all again with the blood of my cruel sins! If you have trodden the winepress of Jehovah's wrath, and crushed your enemies, here is another of the accursed crew. Come drag him out and crush him! Here is an Agag in my heart, come and hew him in pieces! Here is a Dagon in my soul, break, O break, his head and set me free from my old state of sin! Deliver me from my fierce enemy, and unto you alone shall be the praise, forever and ever. Amen.

The Strong Man Armed Bound And Cast Out

"And it came to pass, as he spake these things, a certain woman of the company lifted up her voice, and said unto him, Blessed is the womb that bare thee, and the paps which thou hast sucked. But he said, Yea rather, blessed are they that hear the word of God, and keep it. And when the people were gathered thick together, he began to say, This is an evil generation: they seek a sign; and there shall no sign be given it, but the sign of Jonas the prophet. For as Jonas was a sign unto the Ninevites, so shall also the Son of man be to this generation. The queen of the south shall rise up in the judgment with the men of this generation, and condemn them: for she came from the utmost parts of the earth to hear the wisdom of Solomon; and, behold, a greater than Solomon is here. The men of Nineve shall rise up in the judgment with this generation, and shall condemn it: for they repented at the preaching of Jonas; and, behold, a greater than Jonas is here" (Luke 11:27-32).

Chapter 73

Looking For A Sign

Are you looking for a sign? Are you waiting for the Lord to show you a sign? We live in an age of such religious deception and perversity that men and women are taught from the pulpits to do so. Such a generation is described by the Son of God in this passage of holy scripture as a wicked, perverse and adulterous generation.

Any faith that is based upon a sign, the observation of a miracle, the proof of logic, a feeling of something spiritual, an experience, or anything else other than the revelation of God in holy scripture is a false faith. True, God-given, saving faith has for its foundation the Word of God alone.

That is the message of the text before us. "Faith comes by hearing, and hearing by the Word of God." May God give us grace to believe him, not our experiences! him, not our feelings! him, not our reason! him, not signs and wonders!

The Blessedness Of Faith

The greatest blessing God can bestow upon anyone in this world is the gift of faith in Christ. "And it came to pass, as he spake these things, a certain woman of the company lifted up her voice, and said unto him, Blessed is the womb that bare thee, and the paps which thou hast sucked. But he said, Yea rather, blessed are they that hear the word of God, and keep it" (vv. 27, 28).

The Lord Jesus had just cast out a devil, by the power of his omnipotent grace, causing a dumb man to speak. After performing this great miracle, he was accused by the "religious right", the "moral majority", of performing his work by the power of Satan, of being in league with the devil, maybe of even being the devil himself.

Then, the Son of God explained publicly who he is (the King of Glory), by what power he works (the Finger of God), the result of his work (Satan cast out) and, at the same time, exposed the hypocrisy of those whited sepulchres who were indeed the servants of Satan.

Hearing these things, observing the power of his grace, perhaps rejoicing in the embarrassment of the Pharisees, perhaps remembering what the Son of God had done for her by his grace, there was a woman in the crowd whose adoration of Christ, because of her remembrance of his mercy, caused her to break the rules of politeness. She cried out, "Blessed is the womb that bare thee, and the paps which thou hast sucked"!

These words were not a pronouncement of praise and veneration of Mary. It is sad that such a statement as that must be made; but the Mariolatry of Rome is so profuse that often the mother of Jesus is elevated in the minds of people above other women to a position of kinship to divinity. It is utter idolatry to pray to Mary! Mary is not God; and she certainly is not, as the papists chant, "the mother of God"!

This was not a word of praise to Mary. Rather it was a figure of speech, by which this woman expressed adulation and praise for the Lord Jesus Christ. We do not use the same words, but we often praise someone in the same way. "That child is an honour to his parents." "That child speaks well of his parents." "That child must make his parents very proud."

Mary was indeed a blessed woman. Both the angel Gabriel and Elizabeth, the mother of John the Baptist, spoke of her blessedness (Luke 1:28, 42). I do not doubt for a moment that sister Mary was a woman of remarkable character, exemplary faith and behaviour, and stedfast virtue. I am certain that she was such a woman.

However, Mary's blessedness was the blessedness of a sinner saved by grace, nothing less, and nothing more. Her blessedness did not arise so much from the fact that the Son of God was in her womb, but from the fact that he was in her heart. Mary was highly favoured of God as the object of his grace; chosen, redeemed, called, sanctified and accepted in Christ, just like us. She worshipped the baby in her belly as God her Saviour in her heart. After she had given birth to the Lord Jesus, to our Saviour's humanity, she came to the temple with the sacrifice of the law, because of her uncleanness, because she was a sinner who needed the blood atonement of Christ just like us (Luke 2:24; Leviticus 12:6-8).

When the Saviour heard this woman's praise, he immediately knew what horrid blasphemy would soon come to be attached to those words by the deceivers in Rome. So he immediately gives us a word of instruction, declaring, "Yea rather, blessed are they that hear the word of God, and keep it."

True blessedness is the blessedness of grace bestowed upon all who are born of God. How great are the privileges of grace bestowed upon sinners in this world who hear the Word of God and keep it! It is a great privilege indeed to hear the Word of God faithfully preached. But our Saviour is not talking about the mere outward hearing of the gospel. That will prove an everlasting curse, unless there is, with the hearing of the Word, the accompaniment of saving grace causing us to hear the Word and keep it. We must hear it with faith and understanding; guard it, prize it and keep it as the Word of God. All to whom God grants the gift of faith in his Son are truly blessed of God. Blessed with all the blessings of grace (Ephesians 1:3). Blessed with all the blessings of providence (Romans 8:28). Blessed with all the blessings of heavenly glory (Ephesians 1:11).

The Demand Of Unbelief

Unbelief always demands something more than the Word of God. "And when the people were gathered thick together, he began to say, This is an evil generation: they seek a sign; and there shall no sign be given it, but the sign of Jonas the prophet." Matthew tells us that our Lord Jesus also declared, "An evil and adulterous generation seeketh after a sign" (Matthew 12:39).

Without question, our Lord was speaking specifically of the generation in which he then walked in this world. It was a distinctly evil and adulterous generation, a generation much like our own. Like the day in which we live, those were days of indescribable, horrid evil. Philosophical, political, moral and spiritual evil was seen everywhere (Romans 1:18-32).

But the emphasis, both here and in Matthew's account, appears to be upon the evil of those who seek after a sign as a basis for believing God. The people gathered in thick crowds to hear the Son of God preach. But they were a people who demanded a sign, something they could see, something they could feel, something they could understand, something they could prove, as the basis of faith. They professed that they would believe God, if the Lord God would simply prove himself in the court of carnal reason and experience. They wanted evidences for faith. But faith that is based upon evidence is not faith.

The God of glory will never bow to you and me. We must bow to him. He condescends in great grace to save sinners. But he will never stoop to be judged by us! If we would be saved, we must bow to him, believing him (1 Corinthians 1:17-31).

The Sign Of Jonah

The only sign upon which faith can rest is the accomplishment of redemption proclaimed and revealed in the gospel. "For as Jonas was a sign unto the Ninevites, so shall also the Son of man be to this generation" (v. 30). The sign of Jonah was both a declaration of grace and a prophecy of redemption accomplished. Jonah declared, "Salvation is of the LORD"! Jonah's being raised to life again after three days in the belly of the whale was a prophetic picture of our redemption by Christ's death and resurrection as our Substitute.

As Jonah was cast into the sea and swallowed by the whale to appease the storm of judgment, another man, the God-man, Christ Jesus, was swallowed up in the wrath of God. When wrath was turned away, that man, our Substitute, arose from the belly of hell, after three days in the heart of the earth. And as Jonah went and preached to the men of Nineveh, that risen man, Christ the Lord, proclaimed grace to sinners deserving the wrath of God.

The Judgment Of God

Be sure you understand our Lord's doctrine in verses 31, 32. Divine justice will make everything that should have been a means of blessedness and salvation here an instrument of torment in hell.

"The queen of the south shall rise up in the judgment with the men of this generation, and condemn them: for she came from the utmost parts of the earth to hear the wisdom of Solomon; and, behold, a greater than Solomon is here. The men of Nineveh shall rise up in the judgment with this generation, and shall condemn it: for they repented at the preaching of Jonas; and, behold, a greater than Jonas is here" (vv. 31, 32).

The Queen of Sheba, when she heard report of Solomon's riches, greatness, wisdom and glory, travelled many miles at great expense to meet that great man, on the basis of nothing but the word of men. And Solomon was only a sinful man. "Behold, a greater than Solomon is here"! The men of Nineveh, when they heard the message of God by the lips of Jonah, a prophet who was at best less than desirable, repented. "Behold, a greater than Jonah is here"! You have heard and read the Word of God, the gospel of his grace. Will that be to you a blessing, or a curse? If the Lord God gives you faith in his dear Son, the Word that you have heard and read will be an everlasting blessing of God's grace to you. But if you refuse to trust Christ, that same word shall rise up in judgment against you and forever torment your soul in hell (2 Corinthians 2:14-16; 1 John 5:1-14).

Looking For A Sign

"No man, when he hath lighted a candle, putteth it in a secret place, neither under a bushel, but on a candlestick, that they which come in may see the light. The light of the body is the eye: therefore when thine eye is single, thy whole body also is full of light; but when thine eye is evil, thy body also is full of darkness. Take heed therefore that the light which is in thee be not darkness. If thy whole body therefore be full of light, having no part dark, the whole shall be full of light, as when the bright shining of a candle doth give thee light" (Luke 11:33-36).

Chapter 74

Light Or Darkness?

Our Master used the symbolism of light (a candle on a candlestick) for various purposes (Matthew 5:15; Mark 4:21; Luke 8:16). His intention here is clearly revealed by the context. He is talking about himself. He is declaring that he (the Light of the World) had stood before these men as a bright, shining light. His works, his claims, his ministry were open, public and unmistakably clear. "These things were not done in a corner."

He who is greater, a greater light and witness, than both Jonah and Solomon is the Light which no man lighted. He is indeed the Light! Our Lord is here declaring that man's unbelief and rebellion is inexcusable. He is continuing with the same line of thought and doctrine as he gave in verses 29-32. The doctrine of our text is plain. Light has come into the world, but because men love darkness rather than light, they despise light and choose darkness.

"And this is the condemnation, that light is come into the world, and men loved darkness rather than light, because their deeds were evil. For every one that doeth evil hateth the light, neither cometh to the light, lest his deeds should be reproved. But he that doeth truth cometh to the light, that his deeds may be made manifest, that they are wrought in God" (John 3:19-21).

Christ is the Light. Some, seeing the Light, are dazzled by it. One, seeing something of our Lord's brightness, cried, "Blessed is the womb that bare thee, and the paps which thou hast sucked." The malicious Pharisees and religionists saw nothing of the Light. They blatantly imputed the Master's works of mercy to the devil. Many profess to see some light in him, but see so little that they ask for a sign from heaven to make the light more clear!

Our Lord's constant answer in his day was the same as it is in ours. The Light just keeps on shining, unaffected by the darkness that cannot see. Brilliantly that Light shined in Palestine; it shines more brilliantly today. The Light is meant to be seen. Therefore the Lord God has put the Light of the World upon a lamp stand and lifted him up. The Light was lifted up by John the Baptist. The Light was lifted up upon the Cross. The Light was lifted up in the Lord's resurrection. The Light has been lifted up in our Saviour's ascension and exaltation as Lord and King. And the Light is lifted up in the preaching of the gospel.

In the Old Testament, under the types and shadows of the law, the Light was, as it were, hidden under a bushel and not yet lit. Today, the Light shines in all the world, to men and women of every race, kindred, tribe and tongue. The Light now shines. If you do not see, it is no fault of the Light, but of your own blindness (2 Corinthians 4:3-6).

Light is essential to spiritual life. Ignorance is not the mother of faith, but of superstition. Faith is the gift of God; but it is a gift given by the light and knowledge of the gospel. If the Light of God does not shine in our soul, the life of God is not there. We must have light, or we have no life. If the Sun of Righteousness does not shine to illuminate our dark hearts, darkness and death yet prevail. We must have light within us, or the Light shining outside us will be of no benefit to our souls (Ephesians 1:15-20).

The Entrance Of Light

"The light of the body is the eye." Light enters the body through the eye. But how does light enter the soul? If we have no eyes to see, we cannot see, no matter how brightly the sun shines around us.

Our problem is not that there is no light. Our problem is that we have no eyes. The natural man is totally blind spiritually. Therefore, he cannot see. But his condition is far worse even than that. He does not want to see the Light. By nature, we all love darkness rather than light. "The light of the body is the eye: therefore when thine eye is single, thy whole body also is full of light; but when thine eye is evil, thy body also is full of darkness" (v. 34).

The eye of the soul is the mind, the understanding, the conscience, the heart. When the eye is clear, single, unclouded, then the whole body is full of light. When the eyes of our souls are opened and enlightened by the Spirit of God to the truths of the gospel, when there is nothing clouding our vision of the glory of Christ in the gospel, the whole soul is filled with light, joy, comfort and peace.

But when the eye is evil, the whole body is full of darkness. When a person has cataracts covering his eyes, he cannot see. If he has glaucoma, once it is full blown, he is engulfed in darkness. Spiritually, when the understanding is darkened through the blindness and ignorance there is in all men, with respect to the gospel, all the powers and faculties of the soul are engulfed in darkness, and man gropes about in gross darkness.

The eyes of men are blinded by many things. The darkness of our fallen, depraved nature blinds every man. The cataracts, the blinding scales of religious tradition and heresy, blind people. The glaucoma, the haziness, of self-righteousness blinds multitudes. The myopia, the short-sightedness, of materialism and worldliness repays its worshippers with blindness.

Self-seeking, in every form, obscures the light of the soul. The glitter of gold blinds the eye. How could Judas see the beauty and glory of Christ when he saw greater value in the thirty pieces of silver? How can a man set his heart upon heaven and eternity when his eye is fixed on material things?

Of all antichrists, self is the hardest to kill. Pride, ambition, the desire for honour and respect, the craving of man's approval and applause blind the eye to the light of heaven. Oh, how we crave the approval of men! I am convinced that nothing makes a man more resistant to the gospel doctrine of Christ than the fear that others will not approve. This proud antichrist, self, is never so strong, so vigorous, so unconquerable as in the proud desire human flesh has for the glory of salvation that belongs to God alone. Man, whose god is his belly, is blinded by his god!

A single eye, a clear understanding is God's gift! A single eye comes from having your eye fixed upon a single Object, Christ (2 Corinthians 11:2, 3). If you see Christ, if you see the glory of God in the face of the Lord Jesus Christ, then "blessed are your eyes for they see"! Then your whole body is full of light.

Light Made Darkness

Our Lord says, "When thine eye is single, thy whole body also is full of light; but when thine eye is evil, thy body also is full of darkness." The evil eye here is not talking about the evil eye of witchcraft, but the understanding that is perverted, so perverted that light is turned into darkness. In the natural world light can never become darkness; but in spiritual matters it often does. "When thine eye is evil, thy body also is full of darkness. Take heed therefore that the light which is in thee be not darkness."

Take heed to the gospel and the ministry of the gospel, take heed, lest you despise the light and it become darkness to your soul. Light despised will become darkness; and there is no blindness like judicial blindness. From such there is no recovery. Perhaps you are thinking, "How can the light that is in a person become darkness?" Let me show you. Men turn light into darkness when ...

> They turn the grace of God into lasciviousness.
> They pervert the ordinances of the gospel into sacraments.
> They make God's holy law a means of holiness.
> They make freedom from the law a license to sin.
> They make the graces of the Spirit conditions of grace.
> They make the doctrine of Christ salvation.
> They make divine sovereignty an excuse for irresponsibility.
> They make character and conduct meaningless.
> They make character and conduct a basis of hope and assurance.

"Take heed therefore that the light which is in thee be not darkness"!

Light Shines

What does light do? I cannot think of anything light does except this: Light shines. That is what we see in verse 36. "If thy whole body therefore be full of light, having no part dark, the whole shall be full of light, as when the bright shining of a candle doth give thee light."

When light comes, it shines. If the eye is right, if it is single and clear, there is no great work for it to do that it may get light. The light is shining. All the eye does is see it. When the sun is shining, if you want light, just open your eyes. You don't need to rub your eyes. Just open them. You don't need to exercise your eyes. Just open them. You don't need to discipline your eyes. Just open them. You don't need to get your eyes into the proper position to see. Just open them! You don't need to adorn your eyes. Just open them!

When the eye is sound, it takes in light and takes pleasure in the light. It conveys the image of things external to the mind within. If the Lord, in his great grace, has made your eye single, so that you desire only to know the truth, then, without toil or labour, you shall know the truth. The light enters when the window is open. And when the Light comes in, you know it. It is not possible to pass from darkness into light without knowing it, because the shining light dispels darkness, exposing all that is in us. That same shining light reveals that which is outside us. God's salvation in Christ! And the light shining in us shines out of us to others. The darker the night the more radiant the light (1 John 1:5-7).

Light Or Darkness?

"And as he spake, a certain Pharisee besought him to dine with him: and he went in, and sat down to meat. And when the Pharisee saw it, he marvelled that he had not first washed before dinner. And the Lord said unto him, Now do ye Pharisees make clean the outside of the cup and the platter; but your inward part is full of ravening and wickedness. Ye fools, did not he that made that which is without make that which is within also? But rather give alms of such things as ye have; and, behold, all things are clean unto you. But woe unto you, Pharisees! for ye tithe mint and rue and all manner of herbs, and pass over judgment and the love of God: these ought ye to have done, and not to leave the other undone. Woe unto you, Pharisees! for ye love the uppermost seats in the synagogues, and greetings in the markets. Woe unto you, scribes and Pharisees, hypocrites! for ye are as graves which appear not, and the men that walk over them are not aware of them. Then answered one of the lawyers, and said unto him, Master, thus saying thou reproachest us also. And he said, Woe unto you also, ye lawyers! for ye lade men with burdens grievous to be borne, and ye yourselves touch not the burdens with one of your fingers. Woe unto you! for ye build the sepulchres of the prophets, and your fathers killed them. Truly ye bear witness that ye allow the deeds of your fathers: for they indeed killed them, and ye build their sepulchres. Therefore also said the wisdom of God, I will send them prophets and apostles, and some of them they shall slay and persecute: That the blood of all the prophets, which was shed from the foundation of the world, may be required of this generation; From the blood of Abel unto the blood of Zacharias, which perished between the altar and the temple: verily I say unto you, It shall be required of this generation. Woe unto you, lawyers! for ye have taken away the key of knowledge: ye entered not in yourselves, and them that were entering in ye hindered. And as he said these things unto them, the scribes and the Pharisees began to urge him vehemently, and to provoke him to speak of many things: Laying wait for him, and seeking to catch something out of his mouth, that they might accuse him" (Luke 11:37-54).

Chapter 74

Self-righteousness

I would rather stand before God guilty of any crime than stand before him in the Day of Judgment guilty of self-righteousness. Self-righteousness is man's foolish, ignorant attempt to make himself righteous. It is the hypocritical claim of men and women that they are good, righteous and holy. It is that great noise of religion and piety, by which people try to silence the inward torments of a guilty conscience. Self-righteousness is the religion of fools.

"Ye fools"! (v. 41) is exactly what our Lord called the Pharisees and Scribes of his day; and that is exactly what I call them today. It takes a little intelligence to be selfish; but it takes total ignorance to be self-righteous! The word our Lord uses for "fools" here is not the same word used in the Sermon on the Mount (Matthew 5:22). This is the word Paul used to describe those who denied the gospel in Corinth (1 Corinthians 15:36). It means "people without mind or understanding"! Truly, all who pretend to be righteous of themselves are totally without mind or understanding!

There is nothing in all the world so contemptible, so obnoxious, so hateful to our God as self-righteousness (Isaiah 65:2-5). "For who maketh thee to differ from another? and what hast thou that thou didst not receive? now if thou didst receive it, why dost thou glory, as if thou hadst not received it?" (1 Corinthians 4:7). Yet, there is nothing more natural to us!

Our Lord Jesus was invited to have dinner with a Pharisee; and he accepted the invitation. While he was there, the Pharisees, the scribes and the lawyers, those who pretended to be righteous, gave him exactly the background upon which to show the character and folly of self-righteousness. That is the picture set before us in Luke 11:37-54.

Traditions Or The Word
Self-righteousness is always more concerned about the traditions of men than the Word of God. "The Pharisee marvelled that he had not first washed before dinner" (v. 38). These Pharisees of Christ's day not only held the traditions of the elders about hand-washing, but in their superstitious zeal also bathed (washed, baptized) their bodies before eating a meal (Mark 7:3, 4). Yes, the law of God required the ceremonial purification to which their tradition pointed; but by adding their traditions to the Word of God, they nullified the commandment of God.

Multitudes today follow this evil example of the Pharisees, setting religious traditions over the Word of God. Throughout the history of Christianity, men have held traditions superior to the scriptures, even as they have pretended to be defending and protecting the scriptures. Churches around the world have man written creeds and confessions, by which they determine what is to be believed and practised, setting traditions above the Word of God. Denominational customs are rigidly followed, while the Book of God is ignored. Historical theology is made the basis of faith, rather than the revelation of God. Church covenants are made the rule by which church members are to be governed, rather than the scriptures. Religious taboos are imposed upon people from one generation to another, taboos nowhere found in holy scripture, by which churches and preachers seek to control the lives of God's saints. The creed of all Pharisees, the creed of self-righteous religion is "touch not, taste not, handle not" (Colossians 2:21).

In the heavenly truthful dignity of his character, our Master purposefully ignored the Pharisees' traditions. We ought to follow his example. The sons of God are not to be in bondage to the traditions and customs of men! Those who are made free by Christ are free indeed!

Here is the Son of God, the embodiment of truth and holiness, standing before this Pharisee. Yet, this self-righteous hypocrite despised the Lord of Glory and judged him to be a sinner, because he did not conform to the petty custom of washing his hands at a public dinner!

Outward Or Inward
Self-righteous religionists are always more concerned about the outward form of godliness than heart faith and worship. "They make clean the outside of

the cup, but the inward is full of ravening and wickedness" (v. 39). They live for the approval and applause of men, not for the acceptance of God. Their religion is a religion men can see and measure. All hypocrites are men pleasers. They will make their hands clean, though their hearts are full of wickedness. They look upon the things which are seen. They profess to know God; but in works they deny him (Titus 1:16). They deny that "out of the heart proceed evil thoughts", that these are the things which defile a man (Matthew 15:19, 20). They make a great show of godliness, but have no concern for God or man. Their only object is themselves. They have a form of godliness, but deny the power of it. That is to say, though they practise religion and dutifully perform religious duties, they deny the gospel of Christ, which is "the power of God unto salvation". They say their prayers, but know nothing of prayer. They go to church, but know nothing of worship. They pay their tithes, but know nothing of giving.

True religion, true godliness does not ignore or despise public worship and the observance of gospel ordinances. True believers delight in those things. But our religion is not an outward show. It is primarily inward and spiritual. It is primarily a heart matter.

Spiritual Ignorance
Self-righteousness is always totally ignorant of all things spiritual. "Ye fools"! When it comes to spiritual matters, they have neither mind nor understanding.

I do not say they are not smart. They may be brilliant. I do not even say they are not orthodox. They may be thoroughly so. But they do not understand anything about themselves, God, Christ, sin, righteousness, or salvation. They know neither the law of God nor the gospel of God. All they know is religious words, customs, traditions and facts. Being ignorant of their own hearts they vainly imagine they are good. Being ignorant of God's righteousness they go about to establish their own righteousness (Romans 9:30-10:4). The self-righteous religionist foolishly convinces himself that God will look on his outward behaviour and thereby be blinded to his heart!

Fallen man has no righteousness of his own. And he is totally ignorant of God's righteousness. He is ignorant of God's character of righteousness, God's requirement of righteousness, and God's accomplishment of righteousness in Christ. Being ignorant of both the righteousness of God and his own sinfulness, fallen man ever goes about to establish his own righteousness. Fallen man made an apron of fig leaves, by which he hoped to meet with God's approval. His firstborn son followed the example and nature he had received from his fallen father. Cain offered God a bloodless sacrifice, which he had produced by the works of his own hands. But God despised it.

No one will ever trust Christ until he sees that he has no righteousness of his own and that it is utterly impossible for him to produce any righteous work acceptable to God. Yet, fallen, ignorant, sinful men and women continue the vain, futile work of trying to establish their own righteousness. They take bricks from the kiln of their corrupt hearts and slime of their defiled hands for mortar, and try to build a tower of Babel that will bring them to heaven. By works of legal obedience, moral reformation, personal sacrifice, self-denial, devotion, sacramentalism, penitence and religious zeal, foolish man hopes to establish righteousness for himself. But when he has done the very best he can do and offers it up to God, giving God his righteousness is like throwing a vile, discarded, loathsome menstruous cloth in the face of the triune God (Isaiah 64:6)!

God will not have it. God requires perfect obedience. He cannot and will not accept anything less than perfection, both inward and outward (Galatians 3:10). Fallen man cannot produce righteousness, because his heart is evil (Matthew 15:19). A corrupt fountain cannot bring forth pure water. Everything man does is defiled, because his motives are defiled. No man can make atonement for his sin (Hebrews 10:11). Even if man could cleanse his heart and begin to do righteousness, he could never be accepted with God on that basis, because he still bears the guilt of sin and must be punished.

The Lord Jesus declares, "Except your righteousness shall exceed the righteousness of the scribes and Pharisees, ye shall in no case enter into the kingdom of heaven" (Matthew 5:20). We must have perfect righteousness, even the righteousness of God that is in Christ Jesus. That righteousness was obtained for chosen sinners by the faith of Jesus Christ, and is bestowed freely upon all who believe on the Son of God (Romans 3:22). It cannot be earned, merited, or gained by the works of men.

Trifles Cherished

Self-righteous religionists are always sticklers for trifles, and neglect that which is indispensable. Self-righteous men and women attempt to make atonement for their sins, mistakes, faults and errors by doing good works that men applaud.

"Ye fools, did not he that made that which is without make that which is within also? But rather give alms of such things as ye have; and, behold, all things are clean unto you. But woe unto you, Pharisees! for ye tithe mint and rue and all manner of herbs, and pass over judgment and the love of God: these ought ye to have done, and not to leave the other undone" (vv. 40-42).

They give alms and feel very good about their great philanthropy. Verse 41 is not a commendation, but an accusation. Our Lord is saying, "You fools! You wash your cups and platters, fill them by devouring widows' houses, and

504

then give alms of such things as you have, and ignorantly imagine that you are holy and clean before God"!

They pay tithes (on the gross, not the net!) while ignoring both the justice of God and the love of God. The self-righteous do not understand that God truly is just and he will only deal with men upon the grounds of justice. The self-righteous love themselves and hate both God and their neighbours, while pretending to love them. In religious matters they are scrupulously orthodox and equally malicious! They will argue vehemently for the rules of church order and discipline and ignore the gospel! They will split hairs about polity and pass over the law of the spirit of life which is in Christ Jesus! They will split churches and start new denominations over the singing of psalms or hymns, and never give a thought about brotherly love! After hearing a sermon on Christ's getting a Bride from among sinners, they want to discuss where Cain got his bride!

Recognition And Praise

Self-righteousness loves the recognition and praise of men. "Woe unto you, Pharisees! for ye love the uppermost seats in the synagogues, and greetings in the markets" (v. 43). The hypocrite is religious, but only so far as it will help to honour himself and minister to his vanity. He has no thought of adorning the doctrine of God our Saviour; but he seeks to be adorned by the doctrine. If he holds office in the church, it is that it may add to his dignity. He may seldom be out of his place in the house of prayer, but his god is his belly. He will be very zealous in religion if he can gain the flattery of others.

Someone said, "The hypocrite is like a glow-worm; it seems to have both light and heat, but when you touch it, it has neither."

Covering For Corruption

Self-righteousness is always but hypocritical. It is nothing but a covering for inward corruption. Self-righteousness is really a manifestation of self-contempt. The loud noise of self-righteousness is designed to silence the turmoil in a man's guilty soul. "Woe unto you, scribes and Pharisees, hypocrites! for ye are as graves which appear not, and the men that walk over them are not aware of them" (v. 44).

We seldom think of the foulness and rottenness inside the graves and tombs when we walk through a cemetery; but those graves and tombs are "within, full of dead men's bones and of all uncleanness." A sow that is washed is still only a washed sow. A hypocrite may manage by his white-washing to give no offence to his fellow-man; but God looks on the heart (1 Samuel 16:7). Be not deceived, God is not mocked; the hidden man of the heart is naked and bare before the eyes of the Lord (Psalm 7:9). The hypocrite lives for that which is "highly esteemed among men", but that which is highly esteemed among men is "an abomination in the sight of God" (Luke 16:15).

Offended By Christ
Self-righteousness is always offended by Christ. Then answered one of the lawyers, and said unto him, Master, thus saying thou reproachest us also" (v. 45). The cross is always an offence to self-righteous men, because Christ is always an offence to them. The self-righteous are offended by everything our Master taught. Everything revealed in the gospel reproaches them (divine sovereignty, total depravity, unconditional election, limited atonement, irresistible grace, perseverance of the saints, faith in a substitute, free justification, imputed righteousness, knowledge by revelation).

Imposed Laws
Self-righteousness always imposes upon others laws and rules that it excuses in itself. "And he said, Woe unto you also, ye lawyers! for ye lade men with burdens grievous to be borne, and ye yourselves touch not the burdens with one of your fingers" (v. 46). Self-righteous work-mongers raise a great ruckus about sabbath keeping, throw people out of church for going to a restaurant on Sunday, or watching a football game on Sunday. Yet, not one of those who pretend to live by Old Testament, Jewish law observes the very things they impose on others. They only pretend to keep the law.

Persecution
Self-righteousness is the mother of persecution. Self-righteous religionists build monuments to dead prophets, while honouring the men who killed them and are themselves persecutors of living prophets.

"Woe unto you! for ye build the sepulchres of the prophets, and your fathers killed them. Truly ye bear witness that ye allow the deeds of your fathers: for they indeed killed them, and ye build their sepulchres. Therefore also said the wisdom of God, I will send them prophets and apostles, and some of them they shall slay and persecute: That the blood of all the prophets, which was shed from the foundation of the world, may be required of this generation; From the blood of Abel unto the blood of Zacharias, which perished between the altar and the temple: verily I say unto you, It shall be required of this generation" (vv. 47-51).

Hinders Faith
Self-righteousness keeps sinners from entering the kingdom of God. "Woe unto you, lawyers! for ye have taken away the key of knowledge: ye entered

not in yourselves, and them that were entering in ye hindered" (v. 52). While practising religion, observing religious customs, defending creeds and establishing churches, mission boards, denominations, Bible Colleges and Seminaries, the religious hypocrites of this world take away Christ, the key of knowledge. They refuse to enter the Strait Gate, Christ Jesus. And they stand in the way, blocking the Door, lest others enter in into life everlasting.

Always Deceitful
Self-righteousness is always deceitful, conniving, and underhanded; never open and above board. "And as he said these things unto them, the scribes and the Pharisees began to urge him vehemently, and to provoke him to speak of many things: Laying wait for him, and seeking to catch something out of his mouth, that they might accuse him" (vv. 53, 54).

Once, while preaching near Anchorage, Alaska, I saw a large sign hanging over the entrance to a bar. When I read it, I thought to myself, that ought to be hung over the doorway of every church building in the world. So that both upon entering and leaving, all would be compelled to read it. The sign read, "If you wear your halo too tight, you give the rest of us a headache."

"In the mean time, when there were gathered together an innumerable multitude of people, insomuch that they trode one upon another, he began to say unto his disciples first of all, Beware ye of the leaven of the Pharisees, which is hypocrisy. For there is nothing covered, that shall not be revealed; neither hid, that shall not be known. Therefore whatsoever ye have spoken in darkness shall be heard in the light; and that which ye have spoken in the ear in closets shall be proclaimed upon the housetops. And I say unto you my friends, Be not afraid of them that kill the body, and after that have no more that they can do. But I will forewarn you whom ye shall fear: Fear him, which after he hath killed hath power to cast into hell; yea, I say unto you, Fear him. Are not five sparrows sold for two farthings, and not one of them is forgotten before God? But even the very hairs of your head are all numbered. Fear not therefore: ye are of more value than many sparrows" (Luke 12:1-7).

Chapter 75

A Message For The Master's Friends

We have in this portion of Luke's Gospel a message to the Master's friends. While the scribes and Pharisees were laying wait for him, seeking some pretentious ground for hurling vile accusations at him (11:54), as literally thousands of people crowded to hear him, the Lord Jesus turned to his disciples, those men and women who followed him, and particularly to those men whom he had chosen and sent out to preach the gospel, and gave them the message contained in these verses. The message is simple, clear and forthright. I will give it to you in seven statements.

The Lord Jesus Christ Was An Exemplary Preacher

This first lesson I take not from our Master's words so much as from his behaviour. "In the mean time, when there were gathered together an innumerable multitude of people, insomuch that they trode one upon another, he began to say unto his disciples first of all, Beware ye of the leaven of the Pharisees, which is hypocrisy" (v. 1).

Our Lord Jesus was constantly concerned for the welfare of his people. While the scribes and Pharisees were seeking his ruin, his heart and mind were occupied with his chosen. His every thought was focused on his disciples. He did nothing to defend or protect himself. He was concerned for his people.

What an example he is. I pray that he will make me such a preacher, a preacher and a pastor fully devoted to the welfare of God's people, serving the souls of men, with no thought of self-interest!

Now, watch the Master. There were, as I said, literally thousands of people gathered around him. What would he say? How would he speak? Here is God who is love incarnate, the only man who ever loved men perfectly. How will he speak? Surely every preacher will be wise to emulate him.

Our Lord began his message with a severe, public denunciation of the most powerful, influential religious leaders and the religion they represented. Unsparingly, unflinchingly, without partiality, he denounced the scribes and Pharisees as utter hypocrites. How different things might be today if gospel preachers everywhere would follow his example! Our Master was more concerned for the glory of God than the approval of men. He was more concerned for the welfare of men's souls than their applause. He was more concerned for his people than for his own reputation, safety and comfort. Here's the second lesson:

We Must Constantly Guard Against Hypocrisy

"He began to say unto his disciples first of all", notice that the Lord Jesus directed his message not to the Pharisees, nor to the multitude, but to his disciples. These were the men he had chosen to be the preachers of his gospel. It was, therefore, needful that they (and we) be made aware of the pretentious devices and arts of the scribes and Pharisees. He knew that we need to be warned and prepared for the devices of Satan and his messengers who come as wolves in sheep's clothing.

"Before all things, beware of the leaven of the Pharisees, which is hypocrisy." This warning, he says, is to stand before us above all cautions, above all beacons, before all things. Ever beware of this leaven, which will ultimately ruin everything: HYPOCRISY!

In doctrine and in conduct, the whole of the Pharisees' religion was nothing but an outward show of piety. The whole of their religion is outward, designed and practised for man's approval. It is all appearance only.

Our Lord compares it to leaven. Though, perhaps, very small at first, it gradually increases and spreads itself. Like leaven, it lies hidden and covered, and is not easily discerned. Its agenda and influence and effects are not open and above board. But given time, it infects and corrupts the whole of men's principles and practices. Religion without Christ puffs and swells men with pride like nothing else. Beware of every doctrine and religious practice that is obviously intended for show. Beware of everything that seems pretentious. Beware, above all else, of your own tendency to such things!

If we would avoid the danger of hypocrisy, the deadly plague of pretence, we must ever seek to be simple, sincere and open, honest with God, especially about ourselves (2 Corinthians 11:2, 3).

Someday All Things Shall Be Revealed And Made Known

"For there is nothing covered, that shall not be revealed; neither hid, that shall not be known." Our Lord repeated this fact so often that all who heard him must have thought it was a matter he intended for us to lay to heart (Matthew 10:26; Mark 4:22; Luke 8:17). "There is nothing covered, that shall not be revealed; neither hid, that shall not be known." What a warning this is for hypocrites! What a consolation it is for true believers! Both Job and the Apostle Paul considered it a matter of great joy that all things will be made manifest in that great day (Job 16:19; 1 Corinthians 4:3, 4).

That which the Lord God has been pleased to reveal to us we must proclaim to the world (v. 3).

"Therefore whatsoever ye have spoken in darkness shall be heard in the light; and that which ye have spoken in the ear in closets shall be proclaimed upon the housetops." Has the Lord God revealed to us the gospel of his grace? Then let us proclaim it from the housetop.

"So, as much as in me is, I am ready to preach the gospel to you that are at Rome also. For I am not ashamed of the gospel of Christ: for it is the power of God unto salvation to every one that believeth; to the Jew first, and also to the Greek. For therein is the righteousness of God revealed from faith to faith: as it is written, The just shall live by faith" (Romans 1:15-17).

There Are People Whom The Son Of God Has Made To Be His Friends

Look at the opening line of verse 4. "And I say unto you my friends." Isn't that remarkable? Christ Jesus makes sinners his friends! He is the Friend of publicans and sinners. Rejoice! He is the Friend that sticketh closer than a brother. Give thanks! But here is something else. He has made us his friends.

"Ye are my friends, if ye do whatsoever I command you. Henceforth I call you not servants; for the servant knoweth not what his lord doeth: but I have called you friends; for all things that I have heard of my Father I have made known unto you" (John 15:14, 15).

Nothing Is So Destructive To Usefulness As Fear Of Man

"And I say unto you my friends, Be not afraid of them that kill the body, and after that have no more that they can do. But I will forewarn you whom ye shall fear: Fear him, which after he hath killed hath power to cast into hell; yea, I say unto you, Fear him."

The fear of man is bondage. The only cure there is for the fear of man is the fear of God. If we fear God, there is no reason to fear anyone else. Life and death are in his hands alone; and none can harm us, except by the will and consent of our heavenly Father.

Learn this, too. Hell and everlasting judgment and wrath are real.

God's Elect Have Nothing To Fear

"Are not five sparrows sold for two farthings, and not one of them is forgotten before God? But even the very hairs of your head are all numbered. Fear not therefore: ye are of more value than many sparrows."

Nothing whatever, whether great or small, can happen to one of God's elect, without God's decree and direction.

The providential government of our great God over everything in this world is a truth which is clearly revealed and constantly taught in the Word of God. Just as the telescope and microscope show us that there is order and design in all the works of God's hand, from the greatest star down to the least insect, so the Book of God teaches us that there is an infinite wisdom, divine order, and gracious design in all the events of our daily lives. There is no such thing as "chance", "luck", or "accident" in God's creation or in our journey through this world. All is arranged and appointed by God, our heavenly Father. And all things "work together" for our good (Romans 8:28; 11:33-36).

Let us seek to have an abiding sense of God's hand in all our affairs. Our Father's hand measures out our daily portion. All our steps are ordered by him who loves us with an everlasting love. Confidence in God's wise and good providence is a mighty antidote against murmuring and discontent. In the day of trial and disappointment, as in the day of joy and happiness, all is right and all is well done. When we are laid on the bed of sickness, there is a "needs be" for it. Else, it would not come to pass. Because it comes to pass, the very fact that it comes to pass should assure us that it is for our souls' advantage. Let us bow and be still, and bear all things patiently. Ours is "an everlasting covenant ordered in all things and sure" (2 Samuel 23:5). That which pleases our God ought to please us. Truly, "he hath done all things well"! And he will yet do all things well.

"Also I say unto you, Whosoever shall confess me before men, him shall the Son of man also confess before the angels of God: But he that denieth me before men shall be denied before the angels of God. And whosoever shall speak a word against the Son of man, it shall be forgiven him: but unto him that blasphemeth against the Holy Ghost it shall not be forgiven. And when they bring you unto the synagogues, and unto magistrates, and powers, take ye no thought how or what thing ye shall answer, or what ye shall say: For the Holy Ghost shall teach you in the same hour what ye ought to say" (Luke 12:8-12).

Chapter 76

Two Warnings And A Promise

The passage we have read contains some "things hard to be understood". The principle thing that is dealt with in this text is "the blasphemy against the Holy Ghost". This is a subject about which it must be acknowledged little is known. The best and fullest explanations of it are, in my opinion, far from being exhaustive and satisfactory. And I have no delusions about being able to fathom the depths of this subject. I will say no more about it than I am confident of as a matter of divine revelation and no less.

We must never be surprised to find things in the Bible that are simply beyond the reach of our minds. If it had no deep places here and there, which no man is capable of understanding, much less explaining, it would not be the Word of the infinite God. However, rather than stumbling and falling over the things we cannot understand, we ought to give thanks to God for those revelations of wisdom and grace, which even the simplest minds are able to grasp. When we find things written in the Word of God that we do not understand, or that appear to our puny brains to be inconsistent with matters of clear revelation, let us reverently bow to the scriptures, knowing that God is true, praying and waiting for clearer understanding that only God the Holy Spirit can give. Let us never speculate about divine truth, or offer opinions about things beyond our comprehension.

Confessing Christ And Denying Him

In verses 8 and 9 our Lord warns us about denying him, teaching us that true faith confesses him before men and will not deny him.

"Also I say unto you, Whosoever shall confess me before men, him shall the Son of man also confess before the angels of God: But he that denieth me before men shall be denied before the angels of God."

If you would be saved, you must come to Christ (Matthew 11:28-30). There is no salvation without coming to the Lord Jesus. I am often asked, "How do I come to Christ?" Come to Christ any way you can, but come. This coming to Christ is an act of faith. If you come to Christ in saving faith, you must do so personally. I wish that I could believe God for my family; but a father cannot trust Christ for his children. Each must trust the Son of God personally. Unless a person in his own heart believes on the Lord Jesus Christ, he will perish.

If you come to Christ, you must come sincerely. You must not only be persuaded that Christ is the Way, but in your heart you must lovingly and sincerely agree with God's terms of salvation. He says, "My son, give me thine heart" (Proverbs 23:26). It is the heart or nothing in this heavenly marriage.

This matter of faith in Christ, coming to Christ, is a rational, reasonable thing. All who come to Christ do so rationally, in knowledge and understanding. Faith is not a leap in the dark, but a reasonable, rational, knowledgeable trust. I know what Christ saved me from. He has saved me from sin's curse and condemnation. I know who saved me. The Lord Jesus Christ, the God-man saved me. I know how he saved me. He saved me by grace alone, through the merits of his perfect obedience and precious blood. And I know why he saved me. He did so "according to the good pleasure of his own will" (grace, grace, and more grace).

I know this, too: If you come to Christ, you will never quit coming to him. Believers are sinners who are ever coming to Christ, seeking him, trusting him, and worshipping him (1 Peter 2:1-4; Colossians 2:6). The gift of faith is a permanent gift of grace; and those who come to Christ come permanently, with no intention of ever leaving him; and, by his grace, with no possibility of ever being forsaken by him.

Having come to Christ, we confess him (Romans 10:9-13). We confess our Saviour before God, the Church, and the world in believer's baptism (Romans 6:1-6); and we confess him before men in daily conversation, bearing witness to others of his marvellous, free, saving grace. If we deny Christ before men in this world, he will deny us before the angels of God in the world to come.

When our Saviour said, "he that denieth me before men shall be denied before the angels of God", was not talking about an act of denying him, as Peter did. Such a horrid thing a true believer may do. Our Lord is here talking about a person who denies Christ and goes on denying him, a person who persists in denying him (2 Timothy 2:12; 1 John 2:23).

Let us ever take care that we confess Christ before men. I am not talking about button-holing people, making a lot of religious noise, or obnoxiously badgering people with our religion. However, as God gives you opportunity, or in his providence constrains it, do not allow anyone or anything to make you ashamed of Christ. Confess him.

I do not go around talking to people about my wife everywhere I go; but I never miss an opportunity to talk about her. It is not a forced thing, but very natural. I love her; and it is very natural to talk about someone you love. Should I ever be in a place where someone speaks ill of her, I would be ashamed if I did not speak boldly of her honour. If I failed to do so, she and all who observed such silence would have every reason to be suspicious of my professed love for her.

Ever confess Christ before men. Never be ashamed of him, the gospel of his grace, and the goodness and mercy you experience at his hands. If we deny him, he will deny us. In the world to come we will reap the consequences of such cowardice and hypocrisy. In the Day of Judgment he will refuse to own us; he will refuse to plead for us; and he will refuse to be an Advocate for us.

The Unpardonable Sin

In verse 10 our Lord warns us of that sin which shall not be forgiven, neither in this world nor in the world to come. "And whosoever shall speak a word against the Son of man, it shall be forgiven him: but unto him that blasphemeth against the Holy Ghost it shall not be forgiven."

I will say no more about this than is obvious; but I will say no less. There is such a thing as the unpardonable sin. Many who spoke against the Son of man while he was upon the earth, not knowing who he is, were later converted and forgiven; but those who blaspheme against the Holy Ghost are forever damned (Matthew 12:31, 32; Mark 3:28; 1 John 5:16).

We must not make more of this warning than our Lord does. What is this unpardonable sin, this blasphemy against the Holy Spirit that shall never be forgiven? It is not difficult to show from the scriptures what this sin is not. The difficulty is showing clearly what it is.

Our Saviour clearly declares the free, full, absolute, and everlasting forgiveness of all sin to all believers. "All manner of sin and blasphemy shall be forgiven unto men." "If we confess our sins", no matter what they are, no matter how vile they are, no matter how many they are, no matter how old or how new they are, the Lord God "is faithful and just to forgive us our sins", all of them, completely, and forever, "and to cleanse us from all unrighteousness" (1 John 1:9). "The blood of Jesus Christ, God's Son, cleanseth us from all sin" (1 John 1:7).

Yet, the Son of God does speak about one particular sin that is unpardonable. It is called "the blasphemy against the Holy Ghost". What is "the blasphemy against the Holy Ghost?" "The blasphemy against the Holy Ghost" does not involve sins of ignorance. The distinction drawn between "speaking against the Son of man" and "speaking against (blaspheming) the Holy Ghost" must not be overlooked. The sin against Christ as the Son of man was committed out of ignorance by those who did not know that he is the Messiah. Therefore, they did not receive him, believe him, and obey him, but opposed, persecuted, and even crucified him. But they did it ignorantly (1 Corinthians 2:8), as Saul of Tarsus did (1 Timothy 1:13).

This sin and blasphemy against the Holy Spirit, which our Saviour declares is unpardonable, is committed by men and women who wilfully persist in unbelief and obstinate impenitence, deliberately rejecting the counsel of God against themselves, and are therefore given up to a reprobate mind. J.C. Ryle accurately describes it as, "The union of the clearest head-knowledge of the gospel with deliberate rejection of it, and deliberate choice of sin and the world."

John Gill wrote, "It is a despiteful usage of the Spirit of grace, an opposing, contradicting, and denying of the operations wrought, or the doctrines revealed by him, against a man's own light and conscience, out of a wilful and obstinate malice, on purpose to lessen the glory of God, and gratify his own lusts. Such was the sin of the Scribes and Pharisees; who, though they knew the miracles of Christ were wrought by the Spirit of God, yet maliciously and obstinately imputed them to the devil, with a view to obscure the glory of Christ, and indulge their own wicked passions."

This unpardonable sin is the wilful, deliberate rejection of Christ by one who is fully convinced that he is the Son of God and the only Saviour of sinners. It is a deliberate refusal to bow to him as Lord. It is choosing to save your life, rather than lose it to the dominion of the Son of God. It is nothing less than running over the top of the Son of God to get to hell!

Those who are troubled with the fear that they may have committed this unpardonable sin, most assuredly have not done so! The one thing that always characterizes those people described in the scriptures as reprobate is a callousness and hardness that is the result of a seared conscience. When God gives a man up in reprobation, that man is no longer concerned for the glory of God, the knowledge of Christ, and the things of God.

Lot's wife, Pharaoh, King Saul, Ahab, and Judas Iscariot stand out as beacons to warn all. Each of them had crystal clear knowledge. Yet, each of them deliberately rejected Christ. They had light in their heads, but darkness in their hearts. Each of them today is in hell, suffering the wrath of God. Beware of despising the light God has given you. Do you know the truth? Then walk in the truth. Walk in the light God has given you. That is the only safeguard against the unpardonable sin.

In the context in which this and our Lord's other warnings about it are given, this blasphemy against the Holy Spirit appears to be that which was the preeminent crime of the Pharisees. It is the wilful, persistent rejection of the gospel, the wilful, persistent hardening of the heart against the claims of Christ in the gospel (2 Corinthians 2:14-16; Proverbs 1:23-33; 29:1).

No doubt, some who read these lines will ask themselves, with terror in their souls, "Have I committed this unpardonable sin? Have I committed this blasphemy against the Holy Ghost?" To you, I say again, the sin here described is a sin accompanied by utter deadness, hardness, and insensibility of heart. The person whose sin shall never be forgiven him is precisely the person who will not seek to have his sins forgiven. That is the very essence of his condemnation. God has left him alone! He is "twice dead"! Sin hardened and gospel hardened, his conscience is seared as with a hot iron (1 Timothy 4:2). Do not be so foolish as to trifle with such things. Come to Christ now. Trust him now. Today, if you will hear his voice, harden not your heart!

God's Promise

In verses 11 and 12 our Lord Jesus promises grace to help in time of need.

"And when they bring you unto the synagogues, and unto magistrates, and powers, take ye no thought how or what thing ye shall answer, or what ye shall say: For the Holy Ghost shall teach you in the same hour what ye ought to say."

Whatever your trial may be, my brother, whatever your difficulty, my sister, as surely as God is on his throne, he who brings you into the trial will bring you through the trial; and he will do it in such a way that it will be obvious that he did it. He will give you what you need, when you need it, enabling you to persevere, enabling you to serve him, enabling you to honour him. "There hath no temptation taken you but such as is common to man: but God is faithful, who will not suffer you to be tempted above that ye are able; but will with the temptation also make a way to escape, that ye may be able to bear it."

"And one of the company said unto him, Master, speak to my brother, that he divide the inheritance with me. And he said unto him, Man, who made me a judge or a divider over you? And he said unto them, Take heed, and beware of covetousness: for a man's life consisteth not in the abundance of the things which he possesseth. And he spake a parable unto them, saying, The ground of a certain rich man brought forth plentifully: And he thought within himself, saying, What shall I do, because I have no room where to bestow my fruits? And he said, This will I do: I will pull down my barns, and build greater; and there will I bestow all my fruits and my goods. And I will say to my soul, Soul, thou hast much goods laid up for many years; take thine ease, eat, drink, and be merry. But God said unto him, Thou fool, this night thy soul shall be required of thee: then whose shall those things be, which thou hast provided? So is he that layeth up treasure for himself, and is not rich toward God" (Luke 12:13-21).

Chapter 77

The Parable Of The Rich Fool

We have before us the parable of the rich fool. It sets before us a striking example of man's readiness to mix wealth and godliness, as though the two were inseparable. We are told that a certain hearer of our Lord asked him to assist him about his temporal affairs.

Here is a man who wanted what God had given to his brother (v. 13). "Master", he said, "speak to my brother, that he divide the inheritance with me." How little this man knew of the Lord Jesus, or of his business in this world! He probably had some vague idea that the Lord Jesus was going to set up a kingdom in this world, and would reign upon earth as a mere earthly monarch. He certainly regarded him as a rabbi, a respected religious teacher. Therefore, he sought the Master's help in securing an earthly inheritance. He tried to get the Son of God to cater to his covetousness. He should have set his heart on the world to come; but his heart was consumed with greed for this present perishing world and its wealth. When David envied the prosperity of the wicked, his very soul was horrified by his covetousness (Psalm 73).

How many there are just like this man! Multitudes incessantly plan and scheme about the things of time, even under the very sound of things eternal! The natural heart of man is always the same. Even the preaching of Christ did not arrest the attention of all his hearers. Those who preach the gospel of Christ in the present day must never be surprised to see those for whose souls they labour consumed with worldliness, just as this poor man was

Here is a man who tried to get Jehovah's righteousness Servant involved in the affairs of state (v. 14). "And he said unto him, Man, who made me a judge or a divider over you?" It would be a good thing if every gospel preacher would imitate our Master's conduct in this. Let us walk in his steps. The less preachers have to do with secular things, the better. That applies most particularly to political and civil matters. The gospel preacher has no business involving himself in such drivel! When the preacher of the gospel undertakes any work except the preaching of the gospel, it is the work of the gospel that suffers. God's servants must be men of one thing! Let us confine ourselves exclusively to that one thing! "Give thyself wholly to these things"! Like Paul, let us be "separated unto the gospel"!

Here is a man who was very covetous. He looked upon all he possessed as his own. He thought upon his treasure. It was the consuming thought of his heart. He looked upon his wealth as the fruit of his labour. He bestowed his goods to his barns, a hole in the ground!

"And he said unto them, Take heed, and beware of covetousness: for a man's life consisteth not in the abundance of the things which he possesseth. And he spake a parable unto them, saying, The ground of a certain rich man brought forth plentifully: And he thought within himself, saying, What shall I do, because I have no room where to bestow my fruits? And he said, This will I do: I will pull down my barns, and build greater; and there will I bestow all my fruits and my goods" (vv. 15-18).

In response to this man's request, the Lord Jesus pronounced a very solemn warning against covetousness. "He said unto them, take heed and beware of covetousness." I am sure I am safe in saying that there is no evil to which our hearts are more prone than covetousness. It was covetousness that led God to cast down the angels who fell. They were not content with their first estate. They coveted something better. It was covetousness that drove Adam and Eve out of the garden and brought death into the world. Our first parents were not satisfied with the things God gave them in Eden. They coveted, and so they fell. It is covetousness that, ever since the fall, has been the cause of misery and unhappiness in this world. Wars, quarrels, strifes, divisions, envyings, disputes, jealousies, hatreds of all sorts, both public and private, may nearly all be traced to this foul fountain.

Let us hear the Master's warning. Let us seek wisdom and grace to be content with such things as we have. Strive to learn the lesson that Paul learned, when he wrote, "I have learned in whatever state I am therewith to be content" (Philippians 4:11). Pray for a thorough confidence in God's wise and good providence over all our earthly affairs, trusting his perfect wisdom in all his arrangements concerning us. If we have little, it would be not good for us to have much.

If that which we have is taken away, there is a needs be. Happy is the man or woman who is persuaded that whatever is is best, and has ceased from vainly wishing for more. That person and that person alone is "content with such things as he has" (Hebrews 13:5).

Idolatry comes in many packages and wears many names, but none is more deceitful, dangerous, and destructive than covetousness. How often the Word of God warns us to "beware of covetousness" (Colossians 3:2-5; Ephesians 5:5; 1 Timothy 6:10, 11).

Covetousness is an ardent desire for the things of this world, an undue affection for and attachment to the riches, pleasures, and comforts of this world. Some covet the world's money, others its applause. Some covet the world's fame, others its comforts. Some covet the world's honour, others its pleasures. But all covetousness is idolatry.

What fools they are who love and seek this world! We cannot be warned sufficiently of the danger of worldliness, that is of loving, seeking, and living for this world! "The fashion of this world passeth away"! Trying to hold to this world is like gripping sand. The tighter you grip it, the faster it slips away. If you love and seek the things of this world, you cannot love and serve the Lord God (Matthew 6:24; James 4:4; 1 John 2:15-17).

Nothing is more likely to ruin our souls than "covetousness, which is idolatry"! Nothing will more effectually keep a person from faith in Christ than "covetousness, which is idolatry" (Luke 18:18-26). Nothing is more likely to turn the hearts of men away from Christ and the gospel than "covetousness, which is idolatry"! "The care of this world and the deceitfulness of riches choke the word" (Matthew 13:22). May the Spirit of God inscribe these words upon our hearts: "Take heed, and beware of covetousness: for a man's life consisteth not in the abundance of things which he possesseth"!

If we would avoid this snare of Satan, we must set our affection on things above and get our priorities in order. Seek grace to honour God in the use of those things with which you have been trusted. Use what God has given you for hospitality and the thoughtful care of others. Be generous. Out of our abundance, let us ever minister to those who are in need and generously provide for the preaching of the gospel around the world.

Our Lord Jesus clearly displays the folly of worldliness. He gave this parable a rich man who was a fool[14]. His heart and mind were set on earthly things. He schemed and planned for his wealth, and ways to secure it. He

---

[14] The rich man talks of "my" barns, "my" fruits, "my" goods, with all the self-sufficiency and petty importance of one who knows no will but his own. and no master but his own selfishness. It should remind us of Nabal's language in 1 Samuel 25:11. Of him, too, it is written, *"Fool is his name, and folly is with him"* (1 Samuel 25:25).

acted as if he was master of his life, as if had but to say, "I will do a thing", and it would be done.

Then the picture changes. God required the worldling's soul, and asked, "Whose shall those things be which thou hast provided?" "Folly", nothing less than "folly", is the right word by which to describe the conduct of the man who thinks of nothing but his money. The man who "lays up treasure for himself, and is not rich towards God", is the man whom God declares to be a "fool".

The character our Lord brings before us in this parable is very common. Multitudes in every age of the world have lived continually doing the very things that are here condemned. Multitudes are doing them at this very day. They are laying up treasure upon earth, and thinking of nothing but how to increase their riches. They continually add to their riches, as if they were to enjoy them forever, as if there was no death, no judgment, and no world to come.

These are the men who are called clever, and prudent, and wise! These are the men who are commended, and flattered, and held up to admiration! Truly, "the Lord seeth not as man seeth"! The Lord declares that the rich man who lives only for this world is a "fool"!

Nothing is more dangerous to the souls of men than riches. "It is easier for a camel to go through the eye of a needle than for a rich man to enter the kingdom of heaven." He who is given wealth is in great danger. A very eminent, wealthy man, said on his deathbed, "Heaven is a place to which few kings and rich men come."

Even those wealthy men and women who are converted by the grace of God carry a great weight and run the race to heaven under great disadvantages. The possession of money has a hardening effect upon the conscience. We never know what we may do when we become rich. "The love of money is the root of all evil. While some have coveted after it, they have erred from the faith and pierced themselves through with many sorrows" (1 Timothy 6:10). Poverty has many disadvantages; but riches are dangerous.

Here is a man who speaks to his soul. "And I will say to my soul, Soul, thou hast much goods laid up for many years; take thine ease, eat, drink, and be merry" (v. 19). Oh, how sad it is to read of a man speaking to his soul in such a way! Someone said, "If this man had only had the sense of a hog, what other thing could he have said?"

In spiritual matters, multitudes think themselves rich before God, rich in righteous deeds, rich in knowledge, and rich in grace, and say to themselves, "All is well", when nothing is well. Those who know God and experience his free grace in Christ know that they are poor and seek riches in heaven, seeking Christ and his righteousness. "Blessed are the poor in spirit: for theirs is the kingdom of heaven ... Blessed are they which do hunger and thirst after righteousness: for they shall be filled" (Matthew 5:3, 6).

Here is a question for my soul and yours: Are we rich toward God?

"But God said unto him, Thou fool, this night thy soul shall be required of thee: then whose shall those things be, which thou hast provided? So is he that layeth up treasure for himself, and is not rich toward God" (vv. 20, 21).

Blessed are they who are rich toward God! O soul, Seek to be rich toward God! This is true wisdom. This is truly providing for time to come. This is genuine prudence. The wise man is he who does not think only of earthly treasure, but of treasure in heaven (Matthew 6:31-33; Colossians 3:1-3).

When can it be said of a man, that he is rich towards God? Never, until he is rich in grace, and rich in faith. Never, until he has come to Christ, and bought of him gold tried in the fire (Revelation 3:18). Never, until he has a house not made with hands, eternal in the heavens! Never, until, by believing on the Lord Jesus Christ, he reads his name inscribed in the book of life, and is made an heir of God and a joint heir with Christ!

He that is rich toward God, acknowledges that he receives all his riches from God. He gives all into the hands of God. He depends upon the providence of God. He seeks to use all he has for the honour and glory, the furtherance of the gospel, and the good of men's souls. He who is rich toward God is principally concerned for the riches of God's grace and glory in Christ. He who is rich toward God has Christ! Such a man is truly rich! Rich with grace (Ephesians 1:3), rich in grace (Galatians 5:22, 23), rich with forgiveness, rich in righteousness, rich in glory.

Such a man, I say, is truly rich! His treasure is incorruptible. His bank never breaks. His inheritance fades not away. Man cannot deprive him of it. Death cannot snatch it out of his hands. All things are his already: life, death, things present, and things to come (1 Corinthians 3:23). Best of all, what he has now is nothing to what he will have hereafter.

The eternal riches of God's free grace in Christ are within reach of every sinner who comes to Christ. Never rest until they are yours, until the Son of God says to you, "Thou art rich" (Revelation 2:9; 1 John 2:15-17; 1 Timothy 6:6-11, 17-19; Proverbs 21:26; Ecclesiastes 5:10; Job 21:7-15; Proverbs 8:18-21).

"The life is more than meat, and the body is more than raiment. Consider the ravens: for they neither sow nor reap; which neither have storehouse nor barn; and God feedeth them: how much more are ye better than the fowls? And which of you with taking thought can add to his stature one cubit? If ye then be not able to do that thing which is least, why take ye thought for the rest? Consider the lilies how they grow: they toil not, they spin not; and yet I say unto you, that Solomon in all his glory was not arrayed like one of these. If then God so clothe the grass, which is to day in the field, and to morrow is cast into the oven; how much more will he clothe you, O ye of little faith? And seek not ye what ye shall eat, or what ye shall drink, neither be ye of doubtful mind. For all these things do the nations of the world seek after: and your Father knoweth that ye have need of these things. But rather seek ye the kingdom of God; and all these things shall be added unto you" (Luke 12:23-31).

Chapter 78

"Neither Be Ye Of Doubtful Mind"

In this passage, our Saviour bids us care for our souls and the eternal interests of our immortal souls. Our chief concern regarding ourselves ought to be our hearts, specifically our hearts' relationship to God. Solomon said, "Keep thy heart with all diligence; for out of it are the issues of life." Most people take great care in adorning their bodies, but give little thought to the ornaments of the soul. The feeding of the body involves much care, but the supply of spiritual food is neglected. But our bodies are only the abode in which we dwell for a time. We are living souls! The soul is immortal. The body will soon become food for worms. How I wish we could grasp this fact! "For what shall it profit a man, if he shall gain the whole world, and lose his own soul? Or what shall a man give in exchange for his soul?" (Mark 8:36, 37).

Trust God's Providence
The Son of God calls our attention to the higher and nobler part of our beings, and bids us see to it that our souls are in a right state. He here teaches us, his true disciples, to seek God's grace, to trust him as our Lord and Saviour, and to make certain that all is well with our souls. But our Lord's instruction in this passage is principally about trusting his wise and good providence in the everyday affairs of our lives.

No doubt there are some people who are in easier circumstances than others, some who are in positions where they enjoy many comforts, while others are in places where they suffer many hardships. But our circumstances have little to do with our lives in reality. Our circumstances are temporary and change quickly.

Happiness, contentment, peace of mind are not found in circumstances, but in our inner beings, in our soundness of heart, in our minds. The inner man has far more to do with one's joy or sorrow than anything outside us.

There have been some who have been perfectly free in a prison, while others have been in absolute bondage with wide estates to roam over. I have known some, whose spirits have triumphed when all around has tended to depress them. I have seen others, who were wretched and despondent when they had, apparently, all that heart could wish.

It is the heart, the mind, the soul, that is the main thing. Your inner self is that which brings you daylight or midnight, wealth or poverty, peace or war. If we spent half the time, energy, and care on our souls that we spend in trying to better our circumstances we would be in a far better condition. We would all be wise to concentrate on fitting circumstances to our hearts rather than trying to fit our hearts to our circumstances.

Try as you may, you cannot alter the world in which your lot is cast, and you cannot alter God's providential arrangements. Would it not be better to alter yourself to God's providence and be resigned to his will? Of course it would!

Indoor Work

Did you ever notice how often, in the Book of God, the inspired writers of holy scripture busied themselves with what one old writer called "indoor work" the work that has to be done within one's own heart?

"Bless the Lord, O my soul", says David, in the 103rd Psalm; "and all that is within me, bless his holy name." This indoor work always pays best; and our Lord Jesus, in his exhortations, constantly urges us to attend to it. He said to his disciples, "Let not your heart be troubled." A little later, he said, "In the world ye shall have tribulation." He says the same to his disciples in every age. We cannot avoid tribulation. Yet, our Master says, "Let not your heart be troubled." All the water in the sea will not hurt your ship so long as you keep it outside. The danger starts when it gets inside the ship. It matters little what is outside you, if all is right within. So long as the Dove of heaven in our hearts enables us to sing sweetly of the love of God and causes the flower "heart's-ease" to bloom in our souls, we can and will be at peace; content, and joyful in the wilderness of trouble, the desert of care, and the raging sea of tribulation.

As C. H. Spurgeon put it, "A hurricane of afflictions may beat about you, yet you shall be a blessed man, for all the elements of blessedness are within your own heart. God has given them to you, and the devil himself cannot take them away."

Doubtful Mind

This is God's message to you and me: "Seek not ye what ye shall eat, or what ye shall drink, neither be ye of doubtful mind" (v. 29). The language used by our Lord in this verse is very unusual. The word translated "doubtful" is not used anywhere else in the New Testament. It means "mid-air." It appears to have something to do with meteors, so that the passage might be rendered, "Neither be ye of meteoric mind." Even more literally, we might read it, "Neither have your mind in the clouds", or "Do not have a cloudy mind."

Our Lord's word here is an imperative command. He is saying, "Stop seeking what you shall eat or what you shall drink, and stop living in suspense." He is telling us to quit living like birds in the air, flighty and unsettled. He is saying, "Do not let your mind be tossed about like clouds in the air by every wind of circumstance."

The word "doubtful" is so pregnant with meaning that I have no hope of expounding it. Rather, I will simply give you some of the things suggested by it. "Neither be ye of doubtful mind."

Stop Being Anxious

The first thing our Lord requires of us here is this: Child of God, stop being anxious. Stop worrying. Stop being tossed up and down by your outward circumstances. If God prospers you, do not allow that to make you soar. If he empties you, do not allow that to make you sink. If God sends you a little pleasure, do not allow that to put your head in the clouds. If he sends you heaviness and sorrow, do not allow that to put your head in the dust. Stop being so greatly affected by external things. Stop worrying! Do not allow your heart to fret. Cease from your anxious care about your circumstances.

"Rejoice in the Lord alway: and again I say, Rejoice. Let your moderation be known unto all men. The Lord is at hand. Be careful for nothing; but in every thing by prayer and supplication with thanksgiving let your requests be made known unto God. And the peace of God, which passeth all understanding, shall keep your hearts and minds through Christ Jesus. Finally, brethren, whatsoever things are true, whatsoever things are honest, whatsoever things are just, whatsoever things are pure, whatsoever things are lovely, whatsoever things are of good report; if there be any virtue, and if there be any praise, think on these things. Those things, which ye have both learned, and received, and heard, and seen in me, do: and the God of peace shall be with you" (Philippians 4:4-9).

"If ye then be risen with Christ, seek those things which are above, where Christ sitteth on the right hand of God. Set your affection on things above, not on things on the earth. For ye are dead, and your life is hid with Christ in God" (Colossians 3:1-3).

Our Saviour's injunction in Luke 12:29 means, "Do not be anxious about your temporal affairs." Be prudent. We have no right to spend the money of other people, nor even our own, in wastefulness. We are to be careful and discreet. Every believer should constantly remember that he is only a steward, and that he is accountable to his Master for whatever he has, and the use he makes of it. But when we have done our best with what God has trusted to our hands, do not worry because you cannot make more of it. And when you have done your best to meet your expenses, do not sit down, and wring your hands because you cannot make them less.

I cannot turn a dime into a dollar. If I must sometimes live from hand to mouth, that is God's purpose. He commonly feeds his children with daily manna. Seldom does he give bread to his own for weeks and months and years, but daily. Why, then, should we be staggered, much less astonished by such experiences?

It is irresponsible for anyone to live greedily and bring hardship upon himself and his family because he can never have enough toys. But it is insane to fret about things over which you have absolutely no control. All the worrying in the world will not alter what is, has been, or shall be.

Have you ever made any profit by biting your nails and pacing the floor? Have you ever gained anything by worrying? I have never seen anyone get comfort from the blanket of worry. I have never seen anyone fetch grist to the mill by fretting, or any meal to the barrel.

Perhaps you are thinking, "I know that is right, but I cannot help fretting and worrying." I beg your pardon. Are you a believer? The Lord Jesus says to you, "Stop worrying." "Stop being of a doubtful mind." That means stop. And he would not tell us to stop, if we could not stop. Would he? No. The fact is, our worrying is a matter of disobedience and unbelief.

More than that, we only make matters worse by worrying. Have you not always found that to be the case? It is not our difficulty that makes us unfit for anything, but our unbelief that makes us unfit for our difficulties. In all the troubles of our lives, we would be wise to heed the often repeated words of Moses to the children of Israel before the Red Sea: "Stand still and see the salvation of the Lord"! "The battle is not yours, but the Lord's."

"Fear thou not; for I am with thee: be not dismayed; for I am thy God: I will strengthen thee; yea, I will help thee; yea, I will uphold thee with the right hand of my righteousness. Behold, all they that were incensed against thee shall be ashamed and confounded: they shall be as nothing; and they that strive with thee shall perish. Thou shalt seek them, and shalt not find them, even them that contended with thee: they that war against thee shall be as nothing, and as a thing of nought. For I the LORD thy God will hold thy right hand, saying unto thee, Fear not; I will help thee. Fear not, thou worm Jacob, and ye men of Israel; I will help thee, saith the LORD, and thy redeemer, the Holy One of Israel" (Isaiah 41:10-14).

"He sits a Sovereign on his throne
And ruleth all things well"?

Our Saviour demands that we stop worrying, and cast all our care upon him, because he truly does care for us.

Stop Being Ambitious
Worry has far more to do with proud, personal ambition than any of us want to acknowledge. So, I cannot fail to show you second, that another meaning of our Lord's admonition is "Stop being ambitious." God's word to Baruch is God's word to us all. "Seekest thou great things for thyself? Seek them not. Behold, that which I have built will I break down, and that which I have planted will I pluck up" (Jeremiah 45:4, 5).

Most of us are too much like meteors in the sky, soaring high with great thoughts about ourselves, but sporadic and unstable. That ought not be. May God give us grace to seek wisdom not wealth, faith not fame, and patience not praise. We all need to have the wings of our proud ambition clipped. We ought not soar so high as we do in ambition for ourselves. We ought to strive to be great, and stop striving for greatness. We ought to be ambitious for goodness, not for glory. We ought to seek acceptance with God, not the applause of men. We ought to be ambitious for favour with God, not fame among men.

Stop Being Unstable
A third meaning of the Saviour's exhortation is this: "Stop being unstable in your mind." We ought to be men and women of resolute, decisive, stable character. If you look at the context, you will see that this meaning fits very well. Many there are who are time-servers. Their thoughts are consumed with what they shall eat, or what they shall drink, or how they shall be clothed. They are always watching to see which is the best way to go to get what they want. As the old proverb has it, "they know on which side their bread is buttered." They wait to see which way the wind blows, and then are moved with great passion in the same direction.

God's people are cut from different cloth. Grace makes people resolute, decisive, and stable. "God hath not given us the spirit of fear, but of power and of love and of a sound mind." Like Jephthah of old, having lifted their hands to the Lord, they cannot and will not go back. Like Joshua, they are determined, no matter which way the tide runs, "As for me and my house, we will serve the Lord."

Our Lord says, to you and me, "Neither be ye of doubtful mind." The long and short of it is this, in any circumstance, at any time, tell me what is right, and you have told me what I must do. If I give consideration to anything else, I will not do what I know is right. Show me God's will, and you have shown me my path. If I give consideration to anyone else's will I will not do God's will. If we would walk with God, we must not confer with flesh and blood (Galatians 1:16).

Stop Doubting God

Fourth, our Lord Jesus here says to his believing people, "Stop being of a doubtful mind with regard to God's goodness, grace and mercy. Neither be ye of doubtful mind regarding your soul's salvation."

There are many who are not saved who are very confident that they are. There are many, who know nothing of the grace of God who sing, and sing with great liveliness,

> Blessed assurance! Jesus is mine,
> O what a foretaste of glory divine!

Such presumption is deadly. But, then, there are those who make doubt a vital point of godliness. That too is horrible. Our Lord says to you who trust him, and to me, no matter what our circumstances, no matter what our feelings, no matter what our failings may be, no matter how great, "Neither be ye of doubtful mind"! Our salvation is a matter of faith, not of feeling. Child of God, hear and heed the word of your Saviour, "Neither be ye of doubtful mind"!

We have entirely too many fears for a people to whom the Lord God has said, "Fear thou not; for I am with thee: be not dismayed; for I am thy God: I will strengthen thee; yea, I will help thee; yea, I will uphold thee with the right hand of my righteousness" (Isaiah 41:10).

Why can't we believe God? Has he not proved his great faithfulness to us? David heard God's promise and believed him. His faith in God gave quietness to his heart. God's promises quietened his fears. Did they not? "Yea, though I walk through the valley of the shadow of death, I will fear no evil: for thou art with me; thy rod and thy staff they comfort me" (Psalm 23:4). "I will both lay me down in peace, and sleep: for thou, LORD, only makest me dwell in safety" (Psalm 4:8). "When my father and my mother forsake me, then the LORD will take me up" (Psalm 27:10).

We have far too much anxiety and worry about earthly, material things for a people to whom the Son of God has said, "Why take ye thought for raiment? Consider the lilies of the field, how they grow; they toil not, neither do they spin: And yet I say unto you, That even Solomon in all his glory was not arrayed like one of these. Wherefore, if God so clothe the grass of the field, which to day is, and to morrow is cast into the oven, shall he not much more clothe you, O ye of little faith?" (Matthew 6:28-30).

It is written in the scriptures, "But my God shall supply all your need according to his riches in glory by Christ Jesus" (Philippians 4:19). Why should I worry, fret and pace the floor by day and by night, when God my Saviour has promised that my Father will for his sake provide me with everything I need in this world? Why should I concern myself about that which God, who cannot lie, has promised?

"Therefore take no thought, saying, What shall we eat? or, What shall we drink? or, Wherewithal shall we be clothed? (For after all these things do the Gentiles seek:) for your heavenly Father knoweth that ye have need of all these things. But seek ye first the kingdom of God, and his righteousness; and all these things shall be added unto you. Take therefore no thought for the morrow: for the morrow shall take thought for the things of itself. Sufficient unto the day is the evil thereof" (Matthew 6:31-34).

We have far too many doubts concerning God's mercy, love and grace for a people to whom the Lord Jesus Christ has said, "All that the Father giveth me shall come to me; and him that cometh to me I will in no wise cast out" (John 6:37). Our shameful, sinful, baseless doubts are inexcusable. "And I give unto them eternal life; and they shall never perish, neither shall any man pluck them out of my hand" (John 10:28).

Upon what grounds dare we call into question the mercy, love and grace of God? We have absolutely no reason to entertain any doubt concerning him! Did he promise; and shall he not fulfil it? Perish the thought! The scripture says, "he that believeth on the Son of God hath everlasting life." I believe the Son of God. I have life! Why should we question that, ever? Paul was a sinner, just like us, saved by grace, just like us. He did not question God's promise (2 Timothy 1:12; 4:6-8; Romans 8:33-39).

I am not going to doubt God's love because of something I have thought, or said, or done. His love is unconditional and free! I am not going to question his grace because of my sin. His grace superabounds where sin is found! I am not going to be suspicious of his mercy because I do not deserve his mercy. His mercy is for the undeserving! I am not going to doubt his faithfulness because of my unfaithfulness. His faithfulness stands forever! "If we believe not, yet he abideth faithful: he cannot deny himself" (2 Timothy 2:13). "Nevertheless the foundation of God standeth sure, having this seal,

The Lord knoweth them that are his. And, Let every one that nameth the name of Christ depart from iniquity" (2 Timothy 2:19).

We spend entirely too much time grumbling and complaining about our trials and troubles for a people to whom the Lord Jesus has said. "These things I have spoken unto you, that in me ye might have peace. In the world ye shall have tribulation: but be of good cheer; I have overcome the world" (John 16:33).

We ought not be surprised when troubles come our way. We ought to be surprised when they don't come! As long as we live in this world, we are going to have trials, troubles, temptations and sorrows.

> God in Israel sows the seeds
> Of affliction, pain and toil.
> These spring up and choke the weeds
> That would else o'erspread the soil.

Every ounce of gold that has ever been perfected and made valuable has been refined by fire. And if God puts the gold of his grace in us, he will also make us pass through the fire. "Behold, I have refined thee, but not with silver; I have chosen thee in the furnace of affliction" (Isaiah 48:10). "Beloved, think it not strange concerning the fiery trial which is to try you, as though some strange thing happened unto you" (1 Peter 4:12).

Trouble is not a strange thing. For the believer, the absence of trouble is a strange thing. Yet, when we meet with some great difficulty, some heavy trial, some heart-breaking sorrow, though we may not say it, our first shameful, wicked thought is usually, "Why me?" Our first thought really ought to be, "Why not me?"

> Shall I be carried to the skies
> On flowery beds of ease,
> While others fought to win the prize
> And sailed through bloody seas?

Our trials are nothing compared to what others have had to endure before us. Our sorrows are nothing compared to the sorrows our Master endured to have us. Our grief is nothing compared to the glory that shall be revealed in us!

We have entirely too much attachment to this world and to this present life, for a people who are looking for a city whose Builder and Maker is God

(Hebrews 11:8-10; 2 Corinthians 5:1). We know that "to be absent from the body is to be present with the Lord." We have a desire to depart and be with Christ, which is far better. Believers are a people who long to be with Christ. Yet, it is so difficult for us to be torn loose from this present existence called "life".

The only way for us to be delivered from these carnal principles, the only way we will ever be delivered from the cares of this world, the only way we will ever be saved from our fears, concerns, doubts, grumblings, and attachments to this world is to find something better. Our religious works will be dropped like a hot potato, if we ever see and get hold of Christ's finished work. Our boasted good deeds will be of no value, if we are allowed and made to see what Christ has done for sinners. Our righteousnesses will appear to us as they really are, as filthy rags, if ever we behold the righteousness of God in Christ. Our goodliness will wither and die like mown grass in a furnace, if we ever see the goodness and glory of God in Christ (Isaiah 6:1-6). If ever we see Christ there will be no more, argument about our goodness, debate about our worth, or fuss about our will.

Even so, our fears, our doubts, our grumblings, our complaints against our little trials, our complaints against our God's providence and purpose will disappear in proportion to the faith we have in his promises (Isaiah 43:1-5; 46:4; Romans 8:28-35). The more fully I believe his "I WILL", the less I will fear. The less I believe his "I WILL", the more I will fear.

"And he said unto his disciples, Therefore I say unto you, Take no thought for your life, what ye shall eat; neither for the body, what ye shall put on. The life is more than meat, and the body is more than raiment. Consider the ravens: for they neither sow nor reap; which neither have storehouse nor barn; and God feedeth them: how much more are ye better than the fowls? And which of you with taking thought can add to his stature one cubit? If ye then be not able to do that thing which is least, why take ye thought for the rest? Consider the lilies how they grow: they toil not, they spin not; and yet I say unto you, that Solomon in all his glory was not arrayed like one of these. If then God so clothe the grass, which is to day in the field, and to morrow is cast into the oven; how much more will he clothe you, O ye of little faith? And seek not ye what ye shall eat, or what ye shall drink, neither be ye of doubtful mind. For all these things do the nations of the world seek after: and your Father knoweth that ye have need of these things. But rather seek ye the kingdom of God; and all these things shall be added unto you" (Luke 12:22-31).

Chapter 79

First Things First

When our daughter was a child, my wife and I tried to teach her to look beyond the end of her nose. Even as a small child, we tried to get her to focus her attention on things that really mattered. That did not mean that she was not allowed to play games, have fun, and enjoy the various stages of her childhood. Not at all. But we did work at not allowing her to live for games and fun and frivolity.

Why? Because a child that grows up without learning responsibility is likely to live that way for the rest of his/her life. Such a child grows up to be a miserable, useless, self-centred, whining adult. We did not want that for our daughter, any more than you want that for your children. So we constantly pressed her to keep her priorities in order and to keep her mind focused on things that really matter.

Why was it necessary for us to constantly remind her of the importance of these things? The sad fact is, unless we are continually reminded that some things are unimportant, other things slightly important, other things very important, and a few things most important, we will all spend our lives pursuing, worrying about, and crying over things that are utterly insignificant, while neglecting those things that are truly important.

In the passage before us the Lord Jesus tells us to get our priorities focused. Remember the context. Our Lord has just given us the parable of the rich fool, telling us that those who live for this world, neglecting their immortal souls, are fools. Then, he gives us the rich, instructive words found in Luke 12:22-31.

We will have that upon which we set our hearts. So, "set your affection on things above, not on things on the earth" (Colossians 3:2).

A Fact To Remember
"And he said unto his disciples, Therefore I say unto you, Take no thought for your life, what ye shall eat; neither for the body, what ye shall put on. The life is more than meat, and the body is more than raiment" (vv. 22, 23).

Here is a fact to remember. There is more to life than the gratification of animal cravings and the adornment of the body. Yet, these are the things about which all men and women most naturally devote most of their thoughts and energy. This is the very thing Paul is talking about when he says, "Having food and raiment, let us therewith be content" (1 Timothy 4:8).

We only live in these bodies. Life is what is inside the body. Life is not that which is sustained by meat; but that which is sustained by grace. Beauty is not something you can buy in a clothing store, or in a plastic surgeon's office. Beauty is the hidden man of the heart, Christ Jesus, "Christ in you, the hope of glory" (Colossians 1:27; 1 Peter 3:1-6).

Some Things To Consider
Here are some things to consider. Our Saviour is calling us away from the care of the world and calling us to faith, calling us to honour God by believing him. He does so by pointing out some things that ought to be obvious to every kindergarten child. They may seem to be simple, insignificant, almost trivial lessons to carnal minds; but the things mentioned in this passage are matters of deepest importance. The more I ponder them, the weightier they become. The more I study them, the more profound they appear.

Consider the ravens. "Consider the ravens: for they neither sow nor reap; which neither have storehouse nor barn; and God feedeth them: how much more are ye better than the fowls?" (v. 24). If God Almighty condescends to provide for the needs of a bird, a raven at that, if he orders the affairs of providence to give the ravens their daily food, is it reasonable for us to ever imagine that he might fail to provide for us?

Consider yourself. "And which of you with taking thought can add to his stature one cubit?" (v. 25). The word here translated "stature" should probably be translated "life", or "age", as it is in John 9:21 and 23 and Hebrews 11:11. What our Lord is saying here is that none of us can, by any means, add one thing to the height of our physical frames, or to our age, or to the days of our lives.

Our days are "as an handbreadth" (Psalm 39:5). Considerably less than one cubit! If we are not able to add anything to the number of our days on this earth, it is utterly absurd to spend our time and energy fretting about how we can do so! "If ye then be not able to do that thing which is least, why take ye thought for the rest?" (v. 26). Far better it is for us to say with David, "My times are in thy hands", and rejoice to know that it is so.

Consider the lilies. "Consider the lilies how they grow: they toil not, they spin not; and yet I say unto you, that Solomon in all his glory was not arrayed like one of these. If then God so clothe the grass, which is to day in the field, and to morrow is cast into the oven; how much more will he clothe you, O ye of little faith?" (v. 27, 28). If the Lord God every year provides the lilies with fresh foliage and fresh blooms, how absurd it is for us to imagine that he might fail to clothe us today, or tomorrow.

Consider the heathen. "For all these things do the nations of the world seek after: and your Father knoweth that ye have need of these things" (v. 30). What a shame it is for God's people to grovel like the heathen of this world after the things of the world. If God is my Father and Christ my Saviour and the Holy Spirit my Comforter, if heaven is my home and eternity is the span of my life, I ought not find it difficult to live above the cares of and anxieties of the heathen. Faith in Christ ought to make my heart light. The light of eternity ought to make the things of earth grow dim. Heavenly glory ought to make the baubles of earth utterly insignificant to me.

Consider your Father. "Your Father knoweth that ye have need of these things" (v. 30). This fact alone ought to make us perfectly content. All our needs in this world are perfectly known to our Father, the Lord of heaven and earth. He can relieve our needs whenever he sees fit; and he will relieve our needs whenever it is best for us that they be relieved. He who spared not his own Son, but delivered him up to death to ransom our souls, he who gave us his darling Son will not fail to give us everything we need.

Let us consider these facts. May God the Holy Spirit write them upon the tables of our hearts and cause them to bring forth fruit in our lives. Nothing is more common to men than worrying about things over which they have no control. Nothing is more contradictory to our professed faith in the living God than worrying about the things of this world and our lives in it. And nothing so honours our God as confidently trusting him.

"The LORD is my shepherd; I shall not want. He maketh me to lie down in green pastures: he leadeth me beside the still waters. He restoreth my soul: he leadeth me in the paths of righteousness for his name's sake. Yea, though I walk through the valley of the shadow of death, I will fear no evil: for thou art with me; thy rod and thy staff they comfort me. Thou preparest a table before me in the presence of mine enemies: thou anointest my head with oil; my cup runneth over. Surely goodness and mercy shall follow me all the days of my life: and I will dwell in the house of the LORD for ever" (Psalm 23:1-6).

A Call To Faith
Here is a call to faith in our God. "If then God so clothe the grass, which is to day in the field, and to morrow is cast into the oven; how much more will he clothe you, O ye of little faith? And seek not ye what ye shall eat, or what ye shall drink, neither be ye of doubtful mind. For all these things do the nations of the world seek after: and your Father knoweth that ye have need of these things" (vv. 28-30). Oh, may God the Holy Spirit create and sustain in our souls confident faith in God our Saviour, teaching us day by day to trust his infinite wisdom, goodness, grace, love, power, promises, faithfulness, and mercy, teaching us day by day to rest in his providence!

A Kingdom To Seek
In verse 31 our Lord directs our hearts heavenward and tells us of a kingdom to seek. "But rather seek ye the kingdom of God; and all these things shall be added unto you." We all know that our first priority in life ought to be the kingdom and glory of our God. We must not give our hearts to this world. Let us not live as though we were animals, without immortal souls. May God give us grace to live as men and women who are constantly aware that our lives in this world are but a very brief prelude to another world, as men and women with immortal souls to be saved or lost. You and I have a death to die, a God to meet, a judgment to face, and an eternity awaiting us!

Those things need to be ever before our hearts and minds. But when can it be said that a person is seeking the kingdom of God? Am I seeking the kingdom of God? Are you? I know this: The kingdom of God is the only thing worth seeking! And I know this: A person is seeking the kingdom of God when he is living in the pursuit of Christ. "Follow peace with all men, and holiness, without which no man shall see the Lord" (Hebrews 12:14; Philippians 3:3-14).

A Promise From Christ
Here is a promise from Christ to content our hearts. "All these things shall be added unto you" (v. 31). That person who sets his heart upon Christ and eternity shall never lack anything in this world that he needs. He shall always have exactly enough of everything (Psalms 37:25; 84:11; Isaiah 3:10; 33:16; Romans 8:28-35; Psalm 23:1-6).

First Things First

"Fear not, little flock; for it is your Father's good pleasure to give you the kingdom. Sell that ye have, and give alms; provide yourselves bags which wax not old, a treasure in the heavens that faileth not, where no thief approacheth, neither moth corrupteth. For where your treasure is, there will your heart be also. Let your loins be girded about, and your lights burning; And ye yourselves like unto men that wait for their lord, when he will return from the wedding; that when he cometh and knocketh, they may open unto him immediately. Blessed are those servants, whom the lord when he cometh shall find watching: verily I say unto you, that he shall gird himself, and make them to sit down to meat, and will come forth and serve them. And if he shall come in the second watch, or come in the third watch, and find them so, blessed are those servants. And this know, that if the goodman of the house had known what hour the thief would come, he would have watched, and not have suffered his house to be broken through. Be ye therefore ready also: for the Son of man cometh at an hour when ye think not" (Luke 12:32-40).

Chapter 80

"Your Father's Good Pleasure"

What tremendous words of consolation, instruction, and hope we have before us in this passage. How well our Master knows our hearts! How quick he is to condescend to our low estate and meet our needs!

A Soul-cheering Assurance

The first thing I see in our text is a soul-cheering assurance. "Fear not, little flock; for it is your Father's good pleasure to give you the kingdom" (v. 32). Our Lord Jesus knew that these disciples were filled with many fears, and that we would often be tossed about with the same. They were few in number. Their adversaries were many and great. They had to face great difficulties. They were but weak, sinful men. They had a great work to do. And they knew themselves unworthy and altogether insufficient for the work. Being aware of all these fears that these disciples faced, all the fears that we must face, our ever gracious Redeemer speaks this word of grace: "Fear not, little flock; for it is your Father's good pleasure to give you the kingdom." In that one, golden sentence, he gives us great assurances to comfort our hearts and cheer our souls.

God's church in this world is a "little flock". The word might be better translated "very little flock". The fact is, God's people in this world are now, always have been, and always shall be but a very little flock. There are multitudes who wear the name of Christ, multitudes who meet regularly in houses of worship, multitudes who have a profession of faith; but true believers are always but a very little flock in this world. We ought never to be surprised by this fact. It is vain to expect it to be otherwise, "Because strait is the gate, and narrow is the way, which leadeth unto life, and few there be that find it" (Matthew 7:14).

There shall always be a remnant according to the election of grace; but God's elect shall always be but a remnant, until our Lord comes again. Yes, God's people are but a very little flock; but we are his little flock! Christ is our Shepherd. He chose us to be his sheep. He bought us with his blood. He sought us out and found us. He is carrying us home. He will never let us go. We are constantly under his tender care.

This passage also assures us that we have a great and gracious Father. You and I are tenderly loved by God the Father, who has made himself our Father. What a privilege! The God of Glory is our heavenly Father. He adopted us as his dear children. He rejoices over us as the objects of his love. He sees no spot in us. He delights in us as he delights in Christ. He receives us graciously. He is well-pleased with us in Christ, even as he is well-pleased with Christ.

Even now, when the holy Lord God looks down upon us from heaven, with all our fears and infirmities, he sees us in Christ and smiles with approval, just as fully as he shall when he presents us before his glory and welcomes us into his kingdom (Jude 24, 25). Because our heavenly Father is well-pleased with his chosen in Christ, as one with Christ, it is our Father's good pleasure to give us his kingdom. "Fear not, little flock; for it is your Father's good pleasure to give you the kingdom."

There is a glorious, eternal kingdom awaiting us, a kingdom of our Father's pleasure which he delights to give us. Here we are troubled, tried, and tempted. We are mocked, ridiculed, and despised. We are counted the off-scouring of the earth. But that will not be the case for long (Romans 8:18; Colossians 3:4; Revelation 19:1-9). It is our Father's good pleasure to give us his kingdom, all of it; and that which God is pleased to do, God will do.

Are you a part of God's little flock? If we are a part of this flock, we have nothing to fear. Our God has given us exceeding great and precious promises (2 Peter 1:4), and they are all yea and amen in Christ Jesus. God is ours. Christ is ours. Eternity is ours. All things are ours. The world, the flesh and the devil may oppose us; but God is for us. And, "if God be for us, who can be against us?"

A Heart-searching Fact

Next, in verses 33 and 34 I see a heart searching fact. "Where your treasure is, there will your heart be also." Our Saviour's exhortations are plain and demanding, but plain and unmistakable. "Sell that ye have." He says, "Give alms." His requirement is, "provide yourselves bags which wax not old, a treasure in the heavens that faileth not, where no thief approacheth, neither moth corrupteth." Then, he adds this heart-searching fact: "Where your treasure is, there will your heart be also."

We are to sell what we have. Without question this is a figurative thing, not to be taken literally. There is nothing in the New Testament that suggests that a person is to impoverish himself, or sell off his property to be a follower of Christ. On the contrary, we are required to faithfully and diligently provide for our families (1 Timothy 5:8).

What, then, is the meaning of this exhortation? It is just this: We are to sell, or give up anything and everything that stands between us and Christ. This is an exhortation to self-denial. Faith in Christ involves the giving of our lives, of all that we are and have to the dominion and disposal of our Lord.

Next, the Lord Jesus teaches us that we are to give. The giving of alms speaks of charity and kindness to those in need. We are to be more ready to use what God has trusted to our hands for the benefit of others, particularly for the benefit of his kingdom and the furtherance of the gospel, than to hoard it up for ourselves and to gratify our carnal lust for earthly things.

The New Testament teaches nothing about tithing; but it teaches us much about giving. All of 1 Corinthians 9, 2 Corinthians 8, and 2 Corinthians 9 are taken up with this subject. But there are no commands to the people of God anywhere in the New Testament about how much we are to give, when we are to give, or where we are to give. Tithing and all systems like it are things altogether foreign to the New Testament. Like all other acts of worship, giving is an act of grace. It must be free and voluntary. Yet, there are some plain, simple guidelines laid down in the New Testament for us to follow.

Christian giving must be motivated by love and gratitude for Christ (2 Corinthians 8:8, 9). Love needs no law. It is a law unto itself. It is the most powerful and most generous of all motives.

Our gifts must arise from willing hearts (2 Corinthians 8:12). If that which we give arises from a willing heart, if it is given freely and cheerfully, it is accepted of God. The Lord is not concerned with the amount of our gift, be it great or small. He looks to the motive behind it.

We should give to the work of the gospel in proportion to our blessings from the Lord (1 Corinthians 16:2). We are expected to give generously in accordance with our own ability.

All of God's people should give; "everyone" (1 Corinthians 16:2); "every man" (2 Corinthians 9:7). Men and women, rich and poor, old and young, all who are saved by the grace of God are expected to give for the support of God's church and kingdom.

We should be both liberal and sacrificial in our giving (2 Corinthians 9:5, 6). We have not really given anything until we have taken that which we need, want and have use for and given it to the Lord (Mark 12:41-44). Our gifts must be voluntary (2 Corinthians 9:7).

We are to give as unto the Lord (Matthew 6:1-5). We give, not to be seen of men, but for the honour of Christ, hoping for nothing in return. This kind of giving is well-pleasing to God (Philippians 4:18; Hebrews 13:16).

Then our Lord here tells us to provide ourselves treasure in the heavens. That is to say, we are to make our calling and election sure, to lay hold of eternal life, to make certain that Christ is ours. This is true wisdom. This is true prudence. As J. C. Ryle put it ...

"The man who does well for himself is the man who gives up everything for Christ's sake. He makes the best of bargains. He carries the cross for a few years in this world, and in the world to come has everlasting life. He obtains the best of possessions. He carries his riches with him beyond the grave. He is rich in grace here and rich in glory hereafter. And, best of all, what he obtains by faith in Christ he never loses. It is that good part which is never taken away."

"Where your treasure is, there will your heart be also." Where is your treasure? If we will be honest, that question will be easily answered. What do we love? What occupies our hearts and minds? Upon what is our affection set? It matters nothing what we say, what we profess to believe, how orthodox our creed is, or how highly respected we are by others. Where is our treasure? That is where our heart is. If our treasure is here, our hearts are here. If our treasure is in heaven, our hearts are in heaven.

A Readiness For Christ
Third, our Lord shows us what it is to be ready for his glorious second advent.

"Let your loins be girded about, and your lights burning; And ye yourselves like unto men that wait for their lord, when he will return from the wedding; that when he cometh and knocketh, they may open unto him immediately. Blessed are those servants, whom the lord when he cometh shall find watching: verily I say unto you, that he shall gird himself, and make them to sit down to meat, and will come forth and serve them. And if he shall come in the second watch, or come in the third watch, and find them so, blessed are those servants. And this know, that if the goodman of the house had known what hour the thief would come, he would have watched, and not have suffered his house to be broken through. Be ye therefore ready also: for the Son of man cometh at an hour when ye think not" (vv 35-40).

We have here a picture of what we ought to be at all times. We ought to be a people watching for Christ's return, always living upon the tiptoe of faith and expectation (Titus 2:11-14). If we would live in the relentless anticipation of Christ's return, we must gird up our loins, ready always to do our Master's bidding. We must ever have our lights burning, watching for and welcoming our Lord.

Luke 12:37 is one of the most remarkable passages to be found in all the volume of holy scripture. "Blessed are those servants, whom the lord when he cometh shall find watching: verily I say unto you, that he shall gird himself, and make them to sit down to meat, and will come forth and serve them." Christ is coming again. He is coming now (Revelation 1:7). When he comes, he will gird himself, make us sit down at his table, and serve us! What can that mean?

We have a hint of this in Luke 22:18. "For I say unto you, I will not drink of the fruit of the vine, until the kingdom of God shall come." There is reference to this back in Isaiah 25:6. "And in this mountain shall the LORD of hosts make unto all people a feast of fat things, a feast of wines on the lees, of fat things full of marrow, of wines on the lees well refined." The meaning of this promise is indescribably beyond the scope of my comprehension; but of this I am sure: there is no degree of honour, glory, happiness, and bliss that the Lord Jesus Christ will withhold from those who love his appearing (John 14:1-3; Revelation 1:7; 1 Thessalonians 4:13-18; 2 Timothy 4:8). "Fear not, little flock; for it is your Father's good pleasure to give you the kingdom"!

Fear not, O little flock, the foe
Who madly seeks your overthrow;
Dread not his rage and power;
What though your courage sometimes faints,
His seeming triumph o'er God's saints
Lasts but a little hour.

Be of good cheer; your cause belongs
To Him who can avenge your wrongs;
Leave it to Him our Lord.
Though hidden yet from all our eyes,
He sees the Gideon who shall rise;
To save us, and His word.

As true as God's own word is true,
Not earth nor hell with all their crew
Against us shall prevail.
A jest and by-word are they grown;
God is with us, we are His own,
Our victory cannot fail.

Amen, Lord Jesus, grant our prayer!
Great Captain, now Thine arm make bare;
Fight for us once again.
So shall thy saints and martyrs raise
A mighty chorus to Thy praise,
World without end.

Jacob Fabricius

"Your Father's Good Pleasure"

"Then Peter said unto him, Lord, speakest thou this parable unto us, or even to all? And the Lord said, Who then is that faithful and wise steward, whom his lord shall make ruler over his household, to give them their portion of meat in due season? Blessed is that servant, whom his lord when he cometh shall find so doing. Of a truth I say unto you, that he will make him ruler over all that he hath. But and if that servant say in his heart, My lord delayeth his coming; and shall begin to beat the menservants and maidens, and to eat and drink, and to be drunken; The lord of that servant will come in a day when he looketh not for him, and at an hour when he is not aware, and will cut him in sunder, and will appoint him his portion with the unbelievers. And that servant, which knew his lord's will, and prepared not himself, neither did according to his will, shall be beaten with many stripes. But he that knew not, and did commit things worthy of stripes, shall be beaten with few stripes. For unto whomsoever much is given, of him shall be much required: and to whom men have committed much, of him they will ask the more" (Luke 12:41-48).

Chapter 81

God's Servants: The Faithful And The Evil

Poor Peter, it appears that he always had his foot in his mouth. But how many of us, like him, have heard a message, maybe a little biting, and thought to ourselves, if we did not openly ask, "Was he talking to me?" Peter just blurted it out. He said, "Lord, were you talking to us or to everybody?" The Lord Jesus seems to have just ignored the question; but he really didn't. He gave the same instruction again in more detail.

In these verses our Saviour again gives us a parable in which he describes two servants, one faithful, the other evil. Notice that both the faithful and the evil are the Lord's servants. The fact is, all things serve the gracious purposes of God toward his elect (Proverbs 16:4; 21:1; Psalm 76:10). Satan is as much the servant of God, though unwillingly, as Gabriel is willingly. The fallen angels, the very demons of hell, are as fully the servants of God, though they despise him, as are the angels of heaven who adore him. Every human being is the servant of God, too.

Some of us rejoice in that fact. What a privilege is ours to serve the living God! Others despise the thought of God's dominion; but they are nonetheless under God's dominion and serve his purposes (Romans 8:28; 11:36; Ephesians 1:11). Our God rules everywhere, everything, and everyone, totally and absolutely!

Even those evil men who are false prophets and messengers of Satan, deceiving the souls of men with their perverse doctrine, are the servants of our God, sovereignly used by him to accomplish his purpose (1 Corinthians

11:19). This parable is a word of instruction, inspiration, and warning to those men who stand in the house of God as his servants.

God's Faithful Servants

In verses 42-44 our Lord gives us a description of God's faithful servants. Without question, the instruction of the parable may be applied to every believer in his particular calling in life. We who believe on the Lord Jesus Christ gladly bow to his dominion as our Lord. We are his servants. Our lives are spent in his service. Whatever your particular gifts are, whatever your station in life may be, that is the place of your calling and service in the kingdom of God where you are to use your gifts for the glory of Christ and the good of his people. Be God's faithful servant where you are.

Those men who are gifted of God to be preachers and teachers in his church and are not called and gifted as pastors, are also his servants. They ought to be highly regarded as such. God gifts some local churches with more than one man, sometimes with many men who are clearly gifted of God as preachers and teachers of the Word, though only one is gifted and called to pastor the assembly. Those men are to be heard and treated with the respect that their gifts demand, as the servants of God. But in this passage our Lord is talking about that specific group of men who are trusted of God with the care of his household as pastors of local churches (v. 42). What a great trust (2 Corinthians 4:7; Ephesians 3:7, 8).

You may never be a pastor; but you will, as long as you are in this world, need the services of a faithful pastor. You will be wise to know what to expect from God's servant, how to pray for him, and how best to assist him in the work God has trusted to his hands. And you need to know how to recognize and distinguish between a faithful and an evil servant. You will be wise to ask God the Holy Spirit to teach you the things here taught by the Son of God.

In these verses our Lord Jesus Christ describes his faithful servant, a faithful gospel preacher, a faithful pastor by four things in which he is distinguished from a self-serving false prophet. These four things describe and are characteristic of God's true servants in every age of the church and in every place where gospel churches are found.

His Position

God's servant is here described as one "whom his lord hath made ruler over his household."

The church of God is his household, the household of faith, and the household of his Son, the Lord Jesus Christ. It is God's family and God's church, not mine, not yours, not this or that denomination's, but the Lord's! It is God's house and God's temple (1 Corinthians 3:16, 17; Ephesians 3:15; 1 Timothy 3:15).

In the family of God there are some fathers, some young men, and some children. There are some who are strong and some who are weak. There are some who are very independent and need little attention, and some who need a good bit of attention. Each one has been placed in his house and family exactly according to the Master's will.

God ordained pastors have been placed by him as rulers over his household. They are not tyrants, dictators, or lords over God's household, but rulers placed over the house to govern it as stewards under Christ (Acts 20:28; 1 Timothy 3:4, 5; Hebrews 13:7, 17).

Most preachers these days are Junebug preachers. The church, the deacon board, the board of elders, or the denomination has a string tied to his leg and controls everything he does, like a little boy ties a string around a Junebug's leg. Not God's servants. God's servants serve his people; but they are not controlled by them.

Where in the word of God can you find a prophet, or a preacher who was ruled, governed, or even influenced by the will of the people to whom he was sent to preach? The only preacher like that you can find in the Book of God is a hireling prophet. God's servants are responsible under God to rule his house by his Word, according to his revealed will (2 Timothy 3:16).

A faithful steward rules his Master's house exactly according to his Master's will. As he does, all in the house are expected to honour and obey the steward in charge of the house. And that household is most honourable and most happy that is well-governed, with each member of the family knowing his place, working together with every other member in love for the welfare of the whole family.

His Work

The pastor's work is "to give them their portion of meat in due season."

How I wish I could make this generation understand that it is the work, the calling, and the responsibility of gospel preachers to feed the church of God with knowledge and understanding, with gospel truth (Jeremiah 3:15; Acts 20:28). It is not the pastor's work to be a good socialiser, an analyst, a therapist, a counsellor, a priest, or a community door knocker. God's servants are preachers! They feed the house of God by preaching the gospel, by opening the bread of life and dispensing it to the family. If a pastor does that, he has to spend his time in his study, not running the roads and chasing ambulances (2 Timothy 2:15).

It is the work of the pastor "to give", not to take (Ezekiel 34:7, 8). That which is to be given is "meat". It is not our business to enact laws, but to give meat. It is not our business to regulate the lives of men, but to feed their souls. And that with which God's servants feed his children is the sweet meat of the gospel, not the husks of intellectualism, the mists of mysticism, the stones of useless doctrinal speculation, or the poison of heresy. God's servants come with the meat of saving grace in the knowledge of Christ, declaring ruin by the fall, redemption by the blood, and regeneration by the Holy Spirit!

We are to feed the saints of God with "meat in due season". The Word of God must be rightly divided; and each member of the family must be fed with the meat that is suitable for him at the time: grace for the guilty, pardon for the fallen, redemption for the ruined, righteousness for the wicked, cleansing for the defiled, reproof for the wayward, comfort for the troubled, strength for the weak, Christ for all!

His Character

Our Lord describes his servants as men with these two traits of character: "faithful and wise".

God's servants are faithful men (1 Corinthians 4:2). They are stewards of the mysteries of God, of the manifold grace of God, and of the unsearchable riches of Christ (1 Corinthians 4:1; 1 Peter 4:10; Ephesians 3:8). John Gill wrote ...

"They are faithful to the trust reposed in them. They preach the pure gospel of Christ, and the whole of it; conceal no part, nor keep anything of it; seek not to please men, but God; neither seek their own things, their ease, honour, and profit, but the glory of God, the honour of Christ, and the good of souls; and abide by the truths, cause, and interest of the Redeemer at all costs."

A faithful minister of Jesus Christ is one that sincerely seeks his Master's honour, not his own. He preaches Christ crucified in all the counsel of God, not his own thoughts and whims. He follows Christ's doctrine and adheres to his ordinances exactly as the Master gave them. And he exercises the work of the ministry, caring for the souls of men, without respect of persons.

As they are faithful, God's servants are wise. They are neither faithful nor wise by nature; but God makes them faithful and wise by grace and by his gifts upon them, making them fit and able ministers of the gospel. They are well-instructed in the things of God, given a clear understanding in the doctrine of the gospel, and wisely exercise their talents and gifts for the glory of God.

They constantly seek to improve their knowledge and understanding of the scriptures, making the best use of their time in prayer and study, labouring in the word and doctrine of Christ. They arrange and manage the affairs of their lives to best serve Christ and his people. God graciously gives his servants wisdom to guide and direct his people and to care for them, as a father guides and cares for his family.

The faithful and wise pastor is a man who is doing what God called him to do. "Blessed is that servant, whom his lord when he cometh shall find so doing" (v. 43). God's servant always has something to do. And he is always found doing what he has been sent and called of God to do. He is not found dreaming, or loitering, or talking, but doing his Master's will and work, feeding his sheep. God's servant is constant in his labour and perseveres in the work God has put into his hands. Someone once asked John Calvin, "What do you want the Lord to find when he comes?" Calvin answered, "I want him to find me not idle when he comes?"

His Reward
"Blessed is that servant, whom his lord when he cometh shall find so doing. Of a truth I say unto you, that he will make him ruler over all that he hath" (vv. 43, 44).

The scriptures nowhere teach, or even imply that there shall be degrees of reward in heaven. That is contrary to everything taught in the gospel (Romans 8:17). Certainly, our Lord does not exalt one servant in his kingdom above another. But God does reward faithfulness, both in this world and in the world to come. Those who are faithful over a few things shall be made Lord over many things (Luke 19:17). Frequently, God honours faithful service by giving greater service to perform. God's servants shall find immensely great reward in seeing those for whom they have laboured around the throne of Christ in glory (1 Thessalonians 2:19). And God's faithful and wise servants shall themselves inherit all things with Christ in glory (John 17:5, 22). "He will make him lord over all that he hath."

"How beautiful upon the mountains are the feet of him that bringeth good tidings, that publisheth peace; that bringeth good tidings of good, that publisheth salvation; that saith unto Zion, Thy God reigneth! Thy watchmen shall lift up the voice; with the voice together shall they sing: for they shall see eye to eye, when the LORD shall bring again Zion" (Isaiah 52:7, 8).

"I have set watchmen upon thy walls, O Jerusalem, which shall never hold their peace day nor night: ye that make mention of the LORD, keep not silence. And give him no rest, till he establish, and till he make Jerusalem a praise in the earth" (Isaiah 62:6, 7).

"And we beseech you, brethren, to know them which labour among you, and are over you in the Lord, and admonish you; And to esteem them very highly in love for their work's sake. And be at peace among yourselves" (1 Thessalonians 5:12, 13).

God's Evil Servants

"But and if that servant say in his heart, My lord delayeth his coming; and shall begin to beat the menservants and maidens, and to eat and drink, and to be drunken; The lord of that servant will come in a day when he looketh not for him, and at an hour when he is not aware, and will cut him in sunder, and will appoint him his portion with the unbelievers. And that servant, which knew his lord's will, and prepared not himself, neither did according to his will, shall be beaten with many stripes. But he that knew not, and did commit things worthy of stripes, shall be beaten with few stripes. For unto whomsoever much is given, of him shall be much required: and to whom men have committed much, of him they will ask the more" (vv. 45-48).

Here our Lord Jesus describes those men who are evil servants in the house of God. Here again, our Lord gives us four things which are descriptive of that man who is a false prophet, an evil servant in the house of God. I will not say much about him. But you will see immediately what such a man is.

His Character

Unbelief (v. 45) "My lord delayeth his coming."

His Conduct

"But and if that servant say in his heart, My lord delayeth his coming; and shall begin to beat the menservants and maidens, and to eat and drink, and to be drunken" (v. 45). In other words, he is legalistic, judgmental, and self-serving.

His Astonishment

"The lord of that servant will come in a day when he looketh not for him, and at an hour when he is not aware, and will cut him in sunder, and will appoint him his portion with the unbelievers" (v. 46).

"His watchmen are blind: they are all ignorant, they are all dumb dogs, they cannot bark; sleeping, lying down, loving to slumber. Yea, they are greedy dogs which can never have enough, and they are shepherds that cannot understand: they all look to their own way, every one for his gain, from his quarter" (Isaiah 56:10, 11).

His Doom (v. 46-48)

In every age, both the faithful and the evil are sovereignly controlled, ruled, overruled, and absolutely under the dominion of our great God. Used by him to accomplish all his will in all the earth. Blessed be the name of the Lord!

"I am come to send fire on the earth; and what will I, if it be already kindled? But I have a baptism to be baptized with; and how am I straitened till it be accomplished! Suppose ye that I am come to give peace on earth? I tell you, Nay; but rather division: For from henceforth there shall be five in one house divided, three against two, and two against three. The father shall be divided against the son, and the son against the father; the mother against the daughter, and the daughter against the mother; the mother in law against her daughter in law, and the daughter in law against her mother in law" (Luke 12:49-53).

Chapter 82

"I Am Come To Send Fire On The Earth"

In Luke 12:49 the Lord Jesus Christ makes a statement that must be shocking to many as they read it. "I am come to send fire on the earth; and what will I, if it be already kindled?" What does that mean? I do not pretend to know all that is contained in this passage of Scripture, but there is much here to cheer the hearts of God's elect, inspiring us with devotion, zeal in the cause of Christ, and joyful assurance and hope with regard to everlasting glory. And there is much here to strike terror in the hearts of rebels against the King of Glory and those who merely pretend to serve him in this world.

The Lord Jesus Christ is our Master and Lord, yet he washed his disciples' feet. But that is not all. If we are his, if when he comes again he finds us watching for him and serving him, our Master and Lord declares that in that day, in all his robes of glory, he shall gird himself and serve us (Luke 12:35-37). What a remarkable declaration of grace!

Rebels Warned

Then, in verses 38-40 our Saviour issues a warning to all who yet believe not. Believers are people who live in the anticipation, hope, and expectation of the Lord's return. We are watching for him. Only the unbelieving imagine that he delays his coming. Suppose the Son of God were to appear in his glory as you read the words on this page. Where would you be? Have you lived all your life as if you were your own master? Do you refuse to bow to Christ, refuse to be his servant? Where will you be when the Lord Jesus returns in his glory? Read verses 41-44 if you dare.

"Then Peter said unto him, Lord, speakest thou this parable unto us, or even to all? And the Lord said, Who then is that faithful and wise steward, whom his lord shall make ruler over his household, to give them their portion of meat in due season? Blessed is that servant, whom his lord when he cometh shall find so doing. Of a truth I say unto you, that he will make him ruler over all that he hath."

What rewards Christ has in store for his own people eye has not yet seen, ear has not yet heard, and heart has not yet conceived. We cannot begin to imagine the glory that awaits us in heaven! If we are Christ's servants and the servants of our brethren in this world, he will make us rulers over all that he has in the world to come. I have no idea what that means; but it's got to be good. It is a matter of absolute certainty. We shall reign with Christ forever! But that is not true of all.

"But and if that servant say in his heart, My lord delayeth his coming; and shall begin to beat the menservants and maidens, and to eat and drink, and to be drunken; The lord of that servant will come in a day when he looketh not for him, and at an hour when he is not aware, and will cut him in sunder, and will appoint him his portion with the unbelievers" (Luke 12:45, 46).

Hell's Horrors

I have no idea what the horrors of hell are; but horrors they are! What horror, what terror, what everlasting torment shall be the punishment of every unfaithful steward! The preacher who is untrue to his professed calling! The professed believer, who says that he is a child of God, and a servant of Christ, and yet is unfaithful to his Master and Lord! The evil servant is pictured here as that man or woman who is religious, but self-serving, self-righteous, judgmental of others and cruel.

Read the Lord's words again, and tremble. We are often accused of exaggerating about hell and the wrath of God in the world to come. But, the fact is, these things have not yet been spoken of adequately by any mortal. Read the Book of God. You will find in the holy scriptures expressions about hell, the wrath of God, and the torments of the damned that are unparalleled in the writings of men. Hell is a bottomless pit, a place of unquenchable fire, gnawing worms that never die, blackness, darkness, abandonment, everlasting hopelessness, fire and brimstone, torment, and death, an everlasting dying under an everlasting curse!

No, we do not overstate the matter. These are the words of him who loved as never a man loved, of him who is the most tender, gracious, compassionate spirit in the universe. "The lord of that servant will come in a day when he looketh not for him, and at an hour when he is not aware, and will cut him in sunder, and will appoint him his portion with the unbelievers." Added to everything else, those who find themselves in hell will forever be tormented by the fact that it is their just due!

"And that servant, which knew his lord's will, and prepared not himself, neither did according to his will, shall be beaten with many stripes. But he that knew not, and did commit things worthy of stripes, shall be beaten with few stripes. For unto whomsoever much is given, of him shall be much required: and to whom men have committed much, of him they will ask the more" (Luke 12:47, 48).

Let each judge for himself or herself what talents, abilities, and opportunities the Lord God has put in your trust. We must never be content to have done this or that. We are responsible to serve our Master, our Lord, our God in proportion with the talents, abilities, and opportunities he has given us. Who among us is not humbled, broken, and ashamed before God when he thinks of this?

But this passage speaks distinctly of those who serve themselves and not God who made them. Great talents, gifts, abilities, and opportunities are great responsibilities. They are to be feared rather than coveted. Those who seek great things for themselves seek great damnation for their souls.

Gospel Fire

"I am come to send fire on the earth; and what will I if it be already kindled?" (v. 49). The Son of God did not come to send peace on the earth but a sword. Nothing in all the world is more unifying than the gospel of the grace of God; but nothing is more divisive. It is our Lord's intention that it should be. The language of this passage in the original is very, very strong. John Trapp very accurately paraphrased it: "I am come to send fire on the earth. Let the fire kindle as soon as it will. I am contented. I know much good will come of it."

The gospel of Christ is not a creed enshrined in a temple, but a fire burning in the soul. The gospel is not a theological system entombed in the brain, but a fire erupting in the heart. The gospel is not an icy system of ceremonies and rituals, but a fire burning in the earth.

Our Saviour here tells us that the gospel is an ardent, fervent, flaming thing a subject that stirs enthusiasm a theme that rouses intense devotion something that excites men's souls stirs them in the depths of their beings. The gospel does this both in those who love it and in those who hate it.

Men may be and often are indifferent about religion; but no one is indifferent about the gospel. It is a fire, the fire that our Lord Jesus came to send on the earth, the fire he was anxious to light by his death, resurrection, and exaltation, and by the out pouring of his Spirit upon all flesh.

But I have a baptism to be baptized with; and how am I straitened till it be accomplished" (v. 50). How anxious our Lord was to suffer and die for us! How anxious he was to glorify the Father by his sacrifice as our Substitute! How anxious he was to redeem and save his people! How anxious he still is to bring us to glory. And as the direct result of his work at Calvary, there is a division among men. The gospel we preach is a fire in the earth, a dividing fire. Read verses 51-53.

"Suppose ye that I am come to give peace on earth? I tell you, Nay; but rather division: For from henceforth there shall be five in one house divided, three against two, and two against three. The father shall be divided against the son, and the son against the father; the mother against the daughter, and the daughter against the mother; the mother in law against her daughter in law, and the daughter in law against her mother in law."

This is exactly what Paul tells us in Galatians 5:11. The cross of Christ is an offence to men. It always has been and always will be. The clear, simple preaching of the gospel, the message of the cross, the doctrine of the crucified Christ is an offence. It divides men. It divides friends. It divides families. It divides churches. Why? What is there in the gospel that causes such offence? The offence of the gospel is the fact that it is a declaration of salvation by grace alone, without works. It offends man's dignity, because it addresses all men as sinners. It offends man's wisdom, because it asserts that salvation comes only by divine revelation. Christ cannot be known by anyone, except he reveal himself to you and in you. It offends man's pride, because it declares that the only way of salvation is substitution, particular and effectual redemption, and imputed righteousness. It offends man's love of self, because it demands surrender to Christ as Lord. It offends man's sense of self worth, because it declares that salvation is by grace alone, distinguishing, free, sovereign, irresistible, effectual grace.

This gospel by which we are saved, this gospel which is always so divisive is the good news of heaven. It is "how that Christ died for our sins according to the scriptures", not the mere fact that Christ died, but "*how* that Christ died for our sins according to the scriptures" (1 Corinthians 15:1-3). He died as our voluntary Surety, our justice-satisfying Substitute, our effectual, sin-atoning Sacrifice. The gospel of Christ is the revelation of God as a just God and a Saviour, the revelation of the righteousness of God in the exercise of saving grace (Isaiah 45:21; Romans 3:24-26).

The Comparison

The Master says, "I am come to send fire on the earth." "Is not my Word like a fire? Saith the Lord; and like a hammer that breaketh the rock in pieces?" (Jeremiah 23:29). How can the gospel be compared to fire. If you read the

Book of God, you cannot avoid being struck with the extraordinary doctrine of the gospel revealed in its sacred pages. If ever the Lord God applies it to your heart, it will cease to be matters of curiosity, philosophy, and religious theory and debate. It will grab your soul, pierce your heart, and radically and forever change your life.

Perhaps that which first overwhelms the heart of a sinner in the experience of grace is the wondrous revelation of the love, mercy, and grace of God in Christ. What sweet, golden words these are: "God so loved the world, that he gave his only-begotten Son, that whosoever believeth in him should not perish, but have everlasting life" (John 3:16; 1 John 3:1, 16; 4:9, 10). Pause, O my soul, and think about the love of God! Eternal, electing love! Undeserved, free, and unconditional Love! Redeeming, sin-atoning love! Everlasting, unquenchable love! The Son of God loved me, and gave himself for me. Imagine that!

This is the wondrous revelation of the gospel: The love of God is revealed and known only in connection with the most astonishing display of justice, wrath, and severity imaginable The sacrifice of God's own dear Son! If ever you come to know God, if ever God reveals his Son in you, if ever you learn the gospel, it will come to you like fire and ignite a fire in your soul. That is what Isaiah tells us he experienced (Isaiah 6:1-7)

The gospel of the grace of God is the sword of the Lord. And it is fire. It cannot sleep. The truths of the gospel: blood atonement, free justification, complete forgiveness, salvation by grace, are not just words and religious slogans. They are living principles. Like the breath in our lungs, they cannot be contained. They must break out. And when they do, they break out like fire in the earth. As soon as you confess the gospel of Christ in the ears of men, you will see the meaning of our Lord's words, "I am come to send fire on the earth ... and (with the fire) division."

But in Luke 12 our Lord Jesus is primarily talking about the preaching of the gospel. He who makes his ministers a flame of fire, puts fire in them. The fire in the preacher who is sent of God is not merely the fire of emotionalism, or the fire of brilliant intellect, or the fire of passionate oratory. It is something far greater. It is the power and influence of God the Holy Spirit upon his servants. The Holy Ghost sent down from heaven anoints all true evangelists, and is the true power and fire of every true gospel ministry. I will leave it to others to explain or debate that fact; but that is the fact.

God Almighty makes his ministers a flame of fire; and when they preach the gospel, the effect is always the same. It causes a division. Some believe and some believe not. And those who believe not always turn upon those who believe in a mad rage of fury, just as Cain did upon Abel.

The gospel, like fire, is wondrously pure. There is no mixture of impurity, error, or unrighteousness in it. It is free from every alloy of earth. And it is altogether spiritual. Christ, our Altar, is a spiritual altar, not a carnal one. Our sacrifices to our God are spiritual sacrifices, offered from spiritual motives. We worship God in the Spirit.

The gospel, like fire, gives light. It gives the light of the knowledge of the glory of God in the face of Jesus Christ. It sheds light upon our hearts and teaches us about ourselves, exposing our sin. The gospel gives us the light of God's salvation, light about the world and time, and light about judgment and eternity.

The gospel, like fire, has a great testing quality. Nothing tests earthly things like fire. And nothing tests spiritual and heavenly things like the gospel (1 Corinthians 3:13). By that which is written in the Book of God, and by that alone we test and prove every doctrine, every ordinance, every religious practice, and every religious trend.

The gospel, like fire, is cheering and comforting. Those who have experienced it find that the cold of this world no longer pinches as it once did. We may be poor, but the gospel's fire takes away the chilliness of poverty. We may be sick, but the gospel gives our souls joy even in the body's decay. We may be slandered and neglected, but the gospel honours us in the sight of God. The gospel, wherever it is experienced in the heart, becomes a divine source of matchless consolation.

Fire is tremendously aggressive. So is the gospel of Christ. Take a few live coals, put them down in a pile of dry straw, and tell the fire, "I have given you a pile of straw to burn. Now burn, burn away to your heart's content. That straw is yours. But you can go no further. You must burn only this pile of straw. Give off no sparks or flames. Ignite nothing else." While you are talking so foolishly, you will soon find your barn in a heap of ashes. Fire is aggressive. It is never naturally contained. So it is with the gospel. It spreads as naturally as fire and licks up everything in its path, wherever the Wind of Heaven blows it.

As fire ultimately prevails, so the gospel of Christ shall prevail. It is clearly revealed in scripture that as the world was once destroyed by water, it will a second time be destroyed by fire. It is predestined that earth and all the works that are therein shall be burnt up, and the elements shall melt with fervent heat. Fire will win the day. The oceans roll and roar, as it were, in great pride, and laugh at fire; but fire will lick up the waters of the sea with its tongues of flame. All the cities, and nations, and elements of the earth shall soon be consumed with fire.

So it is with the gospel. The seas of iniquity shall ultimate dissolve before our God and his Christ. The day shall soon come when the fire of the gospel shall make the whole world to be a burnt-offering unto the Lord God Most High.

One more comparison: Like fire, the gospel consumes (Psalm 39:4, 10, 11). When the Lord God, by the application of the gospel, makes a man to know his end, the measure of his days, and how frail he is, he is consumed by the revelation. Blessed Saviour, send your fire, and consume my unbelief, my pride and self-righteousness, consume my apathy and indifference, my love of the world, consume my heart, consume my life!

> "Now, for the love I bear his name,
> What was my gain I count my loss;
> My former pride I call my shame,
> And nail my glory to his cross.
> Yes, and I must and will esteem
> All things but loss for Jesus' sake:
> O may my soul be found in him,
> And of his righteousness partake."

"And he said also to the people, When ye see a cloud rise out of the west, straightway ye say, There cometh a shower; and so it is. And when ye see the south wind blow, ye say, There will be heat; and it cometh to pass. Ye hypocrites, ye can discern the face of the sky and of the earth; but how is it that ye do not discern this time? Yea, and why even of yourselves judge ye not what is right? When thou goest with thine adversary to the magistrate, as thou art in the way, give diligence that thou mayest be delivered from him; lest he hale thee to the judge, and the judge deliver thee to the officer, and the officer cast thee into prison. I tell thee, thou shalt not depart thence, till thou hast paid the very last mite" (Luke 12:54-59).

Chapter 83

Discerning The Time

In these verses our Lord Jesus spoke specifically to the common people, the people who heard his doctrine and saw his miracles, those men and women who claimed to believe God, who claimed to be the people of God. Yet, he denounces them in exactly the same way as he had denounced the scribes, the Sadducees and the Pharisees, as hypocrites. Their teachers and preachers were blind men, but wilfully blind as well. Both the religious leaders and the people who followed them, our Lord here denounces and rebukes as hypocrites.

Our Responsibility
First, we must understand that it is our responsibility in this day, the day in which we live, to judge what is right by discerning the time in which we live (vv. 54-57). Our Master is not here suggesting that natural men have spiritual discernment. The scriptures universally declare that the natural man is totally blind to all things spiritual and ignorant (1 Corinthians 2). What he does tell us is that his claims as the Christ, the Messiah, the Saviour of the world were so evidently true that the only reason the men and women of his generation did not acknowledge him as such, the only reason they did not judge what was right was the fact that they were not honest. They were hypocrites. The sceptre of civil government had departed from Judah. Daniel's seventieth week had been fulfilled. Elijah (John the Baptist) had come. And our Lord's miracles clearly attested his Messiahship.

Yet, the men and women of his day refused to acknowledge that which was manifestly true and right. Why? They chose their religious customs and refused to give them up. They preferred the approval and acceptance of men to the approval and acceptance of God. They loved the praise of men more than the praise of God. They loved religion, but hated God. They were unwilling to be separated from family and friend for the truth and glory of God.

We read in 1 Chronicles 12:32 that "the children of Issachar, which were men that had understanding of the times, to know what Israel ought to do." Oh, how desperately we need such men today! Israel was passing through some troublesome, unsettling times. Critical issues had to be faced and dealt with. At a time when the cause and kingdom of God was under assault, the men of Issachar understood the times and stepped forward. They knew what had to be done, and they did it. I repeat, we desperately need such men today.

Let us judge, discern, and seek to understand the times in which we live. I ask only that we read the Book of God. In the light of the plain statements of holy scripture, I assert that we are living in perilous times of Apostasy, divine judgment, and spiritual darkness, such as the world has never seen before (Romans 1:18-32; 2 Thessalonians 2:1-16; 1 Timothy 4:1-3; 2 Timothy 3:1-5; Revelation 20:1-8).

These are days of horrid apostasy. These are times of unparalleled evil, moral degeneracy, political corruption, and spiritual darkness. These are times of horrible indifference and spiritual lukewarmness. These are times of universal compromise. These are times of ambiguity and tolerance toward everything abominable and evil, and times of utter intolerance for the truth and glory of God.

What does this day require of us? What do these present, perilous times demand of you and me? Times like these demand of God's people a bold, uncompromising, unflinching adherence to the singular authority of holy scripture, a distinct and decided, untiring declaration of gospel doctrine, and faithfulness, dedication and sacrifice for the cause of Christ. Times like these demand of us a clear recognition of our most important priorities and our most weighty responsibilities, and a diligent watchfulness over our own souls.

This day is God's day and these times are God's times. Let there be no mistake about that fact. This is the day God has made for us. What a great day in which to serve him! I would rather live in this day than any other. Never was there a day that provided the church of God with greater needs, greater opportunities, and greater means of usefulness than we have at our fingertips.

Day Of Grace

Now, I want you to look at verses 58 and 59 and learn that this is the day of grace and salvation. If you are wise, you will make it your business to be delivered from your adversary before you meet your Judge. Today is the day of salvation. Tomorrow will be too late. The Lord Jesus here compares us to a man on his way to meet the magistrate, the judge, with an adversary. You and I are on our way to meet the God of Glory on his great white throne judgment seat. The adversary walking with us is God's holy, condemning law. If we are not delivered from the claims of this adversary before we meet God in judgment, we must forever be cast into hell.

The only way we can ever appease this adversary is by a mighty Advocate, who has a payment, a sacrifice by which he is and must be satisfied. That Advocate and Sacrifice is the Lord Jesus Christ (2 Corinthians 5:17-6:2; 1 John 2:1, 2; 4:9, 10; Romans 8:1; Galatians 3:13, 14; Colossians 2:12-15; 1 Peter 3:18). Believe on the Lord Jesus Christ and be reconciled to God. The time is short. Judgment is at hand. "We pray you in Christ's stead, be ye reconciled to God."

Index Of Bible Verses

Psalms cont'd

33:6, 9	252
34:7-10	367
35:27	459
36:6	276
37:23-26	367
37:25	540
39:4, 10, 11	565
39:5	539
40:2	245
40:6	54
40:6-8	350
40:16	459
45:6, 7	352
45:13, 14	447
46:5	312
48:11	276
50:7-13	351
50:16-23	137
51:4	275
51:1-5	271
51:16, 17	351
62:1-8	267
62:6-8	245
63:5	382
65:4	160, 186, 212, 243, 352, 376, 396, 451, 476
68	121
68:17-20	121
68:18, 19	301
68:20	340
70:4	459
71:12-18	273
72:17	96
73	521
73:1-3, 21-28	310
76:10	85, 441, 551
81:13	305
84:10	301
84:11	540
85:9-11	387
85:10	194
89:1	69
89:18	267
89:19	439
89:28	455
90:12-16	251
91	153
91:9-13	433
91:11	153
94:22	267
96:3	42
97:8	276
103	528
103:1	79
105:3-7	42
106:8	92, 459
107	178, 313
107:9	367
107:9-15	470
107:23-31	308
107:23- 43	313
107:31	68
107:42, 43	69
110:3	160, 186, 243, 352, 376, 382, 396
115:1	79
115:3	160
119:62	467
119:75	276
119:114	267
122:1-9	301
122:6, 7	459
126:5	289
132:11	354
133:3	301
135:6	160
136:5	365
144:1, 2	267
148:5	252

Revelation cont'd

19:1-6	93, 276
19:1-7	388
19:1-9	544
20:1-3	148, 432
20:1-6	400, 484
20:1-8	568
20:6	213, 479
20:10	484
20:11-15	400
20:15	433
21:4	433
21:1-7	256
22:5	479
22:17	377

Index Of Bible Verses

www.ingramcontent.com/pod-product-compliance
Lightning Source LLC
Chambersburg PA
CBHW030941150426
42812CB00062B/2688